CW01064301

TEMPTING
ALL THE GODS

TEMPTING ALL THE GODS

JOSEPH P. KENNEDY
AMBASSADOR TO GREAT BRITAIN, 1938–1940

JANE KAROLINE VIETH

Michigan State University Press | *East Lansing*

Copyright © 2021 by Jane Karoline Vieth

♾ The paper used in this publication meets the minimum requirements
of ANSI/NISO Z39.48-1992 (R 1997) (Permanence of Paper).

Michigan State University Press
East Lansing, Michigan 48823-5245

LIBRARY OF CONGRESS CATALOGING-IN-PUBLICATION DATA
Names: Vieth, Jane Karoline, author. | Rock, William R., writer of foreword.
Title: Tempting all the gods : Joseph P. Kennedy, ambassador to Great Britain, 1938–1940
/ Jane Karoline Vieth.
Other titles: Joseph P. Kennedy, ambassador to Great Britain, 1938–1940
Description: East Lansing : Michigan State University Press, [2021]
| Includes bibliographical references and index.
Identifiers: LCCN 2020020842 | ISBN 978-1-61186-390-1 (cloth)
| ISBN 978-1-60917-664-8 (pdf) | ISBN 978-1-62895-423-4 (ePub) | ISBN 978-1-62896-424-0 (Kindle)
Subjects: LCSH: Kennedy, Joseph P. (Joseph Patrick), 1888–1969.
| Ambassadors—United States—Biography. | United States—Foreign relations—Great Britain.
| Great Britain—Foreign relations—United States. | United States—Foreign relations—1933–1945.
| Great Britain—Foreign relations—1936–1945. | World War, 1939–1945—Diplomatic history.
| Munich Four-Power Agreement (1938)
Classification: LCC E748.K376 V54 2021 | DDC 973.9092 [B]—dc23
LC record available at https://lccn.loc.gov/2020020842

Book design by Charlie Sharp, Sharp Des!gns, East Lansing, MI
Cover design by Erin Kirk
Cover art: Joseph P. Kennedy Sr. (1888–1969, *second from right*), the new U.S. Ambassador to
the United Kingdom, leaves the US Embassy to present his credentials to the King George VI at
Buckingham Palace, London, March 8, 1938. He is accompanied by Sir Sidney Clive (1874–1959, *third
from right*), Marshal of the Diplomatic Corps. (Photo by Becker/Fox Photos/Hulton Archive/Getty
Images).

Michigan State University Press is a member of the Green Press Initiative and is
committed to developing and encouraging ecologically responsible publishing
practices. For more information about the Green Press Initiative and the use of
recycled paper in book publishing, please visit *www.greenpressinitiative.org*.

Visit Michigan State University Press at *www.msupress.org*

Contents

vii   FOREWORD, *by William R. Rock*

xi   PREFACE

xv   ACKNOWLEDGMENTS

1   CHAPTER 1. The Irish Prince

39   CHAPTER 2. The Lion's Mouth

81   CHAPTER 3. Shirt-Sleeve Diplomacy: Trade, Treaties, Troubles

115   CHAPTER 4. Peace for Our Time

143   CHAPTER 5. Into an Abyss

173   CHAPTER 6. Peace at Any Price

211   CHAPTER 7. It's the End of the World . . . The End of Everything . . .

243   CHAPTER 8. This Is Not Our Fight

267   CHAPTER 9. England at Bay

297   CHAPTER 10. Very Well, Alone

347   CHAPTER 11. To Be *and* Not to Be

391   CONCLUSION

403   NOTES

536   BIBLIOGRAPHY

548   INDEX

Foreword

William R. Rock

Tritely put, "when to hold and when to fold" is a decision-making dilemma inherent in every aspect of human relationships, ranging from intense personal problems to the highest level of international issues. This certainly characterized the situation in European international affairs in the latter 1930s, as the fascist nations of central Europe, particularly Germany under the leadership of Hitler and the Nazi Party, which prevailed from 1933 onward, lunged increasingly toward aggressive behavior relative to the peace settlement that ended the First World War (Versailles Treaty) and began to exhibit intentions not only to destroy the peace settlement but to rearrange territorial control ever more broadly in Europe, perhaps even in broader areas of the world.

With the United States caught up in a deep sentiment of isolation, emerging from the disillusionment of costly participation in the First World War and the deep economic depression of the 1930s, and failing to participate in the League of Nations established by Versailles as the international arena in which to process and resolve disputes that might arise among member states, it fell primarily to Great Britain and France, as the major remaining victors of World War I, to assume leadership in settling, by open discussion and negotiation, problems in international relationships that might emerge. But the League had never assumed the stature or power early envisioned for it, and at length some other approach to looming conflicts of interest seemed necessary.

By the time Neville Chamberlain assumed the prime-ministership of Great Britain in May 1937, signs of serious trouble had already arisen. Germany had already remilitarized the Rhineland, prohibited by the Versailles Treaty, and had also undertaken, in violation of the treaty, an extensive program of rearmament. The League had failed to respond to these actions in any effective way (only verbal condemnation), and they seemed to initiate a series of aggressive moves that had to be confronted in another way. Thus it was that Chamberlain devised a policy of appeasement, largely personally, but also with the French premier,

Daladier, tagging along in a rather docile way, content to let Chamberlain take the lead. This policy was intended to open discussion with the dissatisfied powers, listen to their grievances, and attempt to appease their dissatisfactions by making substantial agreed-upon revisions to the peace settlement of 1919—all this to be done by calm, peaceful negotiation and agreeable rearrangements in the interest of preserving peace and tranquility.

But this did not seem greatly to interest Adolf Hitler, Führer of Germany since 1933, who clearly envisioned destroying Versailles, reestablishing a much larger and greater Germany, and was not disposed to a slow, methodical process. He had risen to office on the idea of reasserting German strength, expanding her territorial borders, and asserting the European—and perhaps world—leadership of the superior Teutonic people. Having risen to power on the basis of such a crusade, he was temperamentally ill-disposed to be patient, understanding, and open to reason.

Chamberlain initially had strong support from the ruling Conservative Party, but faced a small but growing (with the passing of time) group of dissident Conservatives, including Winston Churchill and, later on, Anthony Eden, who resigned as foreign secretary in February 1938, in strong disagreement over Chamberlain's deal with Mussolini recognizing the earlier Italian conquest of Abyssinia. The Labour Party was constantly in opposition, hoping fervently but less than confidently that the League of Nations could be sufficiently resuscitated to be of use, whereas most Liberals and others were divided on various issues.

The German remilitarization of the Rhineland and the undertaking of rearmament had initiated a slowly, but almost methodically developing series of aggressive Nazi moves that seemed to aim systematically at revising the Versailles Treaty by force. The year 1937 saw increasing Nazi influence and interference in Austria, resulting in the Anschluss (March 1938), the German takeover of Austria by military force. Shortly thereafter, the Germans initiated a vitriolic campaign against Czechoslovakia, aimed at first at returning "home" the three million Sudeten Germans surrounding the outside areas of the nation. It was this issue that prompted Chamberlain to undertake three separate September flights to Germany to talk with Hitler (who, according to existing accounts, treated him abominably), the Munich Agreement providing for the immediate transfer of the Sudetenland to Germany—against strong Czech opposition—and Chamberlain's enthusiastic, emotional "Peace for Our Time" speech from the Buckingham Palace balcony upon his arrival home. But the British euphoria over Munich and the avoidance of war swiftly dissipated, and before many months had passed, Germany was executing the military takeover of rump Czechoslovakia in mid-March 1939. Thereupon, after two weeks of intense soul-searching debate and anguish, the British, with French concurrence, extended an unconditional guarantee of her territorial integrity to Poland, Hitler's next obvious victim. It was the German attack on Poland in early September, then, that launched the Second World War in Europe—although not before a cadre of Chamberlain's cabinet colleagues had beaten down a hint from the prime minister that he might be prepared to negotiate with Hitler once again.

It was into this developing set of circumstances that Joseph Kennedy was appointed United States ambassador to Great Britain in February 1938. In many ways it was a curious appointment, consisting of a mixed bag of conflicting and questionable motivations ranging from Roosevelt's desire to reward Kennedy's earlier political and financial support of the Democratic Party and Roosevelt's election, to the president's desire to get a potential trouble-maker out of Washington to a place where his penchant for unwelcome interference would be reduced. The author covers them all, including the irony of sending an Irish-American Catholic to the Court of St. James's. While the news of the appointment was greeted with widely divergent reactions, there was substantial expressed public concern that Kennedy was simply a misfit for the appointment, his inexperience in foreign relations and lack of understanding of them being only one of many issues fully delineated herein. Several recognizable public voices flatly predicted failure.

By the time Kennedy arrived in London, increased division within the British government—and public—had begun to appear over the validity of appeasement, spawned particularly by Anthony Eden's resignation as foreign minister over Chamberlain's concessions to Mussolini over Abyssinia. Thus Kennedy was immediately engulfed in what would eventually become a firestorm of controversy within both the British government and wider public over appeasement and what the role of the United States might be in helping to resist the rising tide of aggressive fascist behavior. Kennedy's posture on all this can only be mentioned here in a very general way, but Professor Vieth, who clearly knows and understands all this in intricate detail, does a masterful job of describing the shifting attitudes and outlooks adopted by the ambassador as circumstances changed and the requirements of the position overwhelmed him.

Fundamentally, Kennedy tended to be an ardent appeaser, but it's not as simple as that. Other studies of Kennedy have generally depicted him as quixotic and unpredictable, with his overwhelming concerns being his business interests, the welfare/promotion of his family, and keeping America out of war. The same personal characteristics appear in this study, particularly of course in relation to how he looked at major developments in European affairs. Sometimes his postures on certain issues—taken together over time—appear inconsistent, as for example his great desire to keep America out of entanglements in Europe and certainly free from participation in a pending world war, while later on supporting the U.S. destroyer contribution to Britain's effort early in World War II as well as the vitally necessary Lend-Lease program. But these postures no doubt sprang from his motive to keep the United States entirely free of direct entanglement in the conflict. If so, this is a good illustration—and there are many more—of how he seemed unable to "connect" things appropriately in the realm of international relations, and lends substantial credence to the view that he simply was "out of his element" and not the appropriate person for the important post that he occupied during 1938–40.

As the policy of appeasement gradually became untenable to a strongly growing majority of Englishmen (Parliament, press, and public) during 1939, there was little obvious change in Kennedy's outlook. Even the onset of war changed him little, and his puzzling postures led to a kind of ostracization insofar as British officials were concerned. Chamberlain had gradually come to ignore him, and ranking members in the Foreign Office increasingly made him the butt of jokes and critical observations on various dispatches that passed among them. The highly respected Robert Vansittart observed that "Mr. Kennedy is a very foul specimen of double-crosser and defeatist. He thinks of nothing but his own pocket. I hope that this war will at least see the elimination of his type." William Bullitt, U.S. ambassador in Paris, reported a conversation with Kennedy in which he predicted that Germany would win the war, Britain could "go to hell," and that his one interest was in saving money for his children. And an exasperated President Roosevelt told Henry Morgenthau that "Joe Kennedy . . . will always be an appeaser; he's just a pain in the neck to me."

Those who know of Joseph Kennedy in a broader sense know that he was a complex person, very ambitious insofar as his own career was concerned, exceedingly ambitious for his family, and strict with his children in ways that would no doubt have spawned a real sense of rebellion in the filial relationships of many other families. His commitment to the superiority of his own ability and judgment was a hallmark of his persona, and the possibility that his judgment might sometimes be more than a little bit wrong seldom, if ever, seemed to enter his mind. Possessed of a sense of defeatism relative to combating the Nazis and fascists in Europe, he seems to have doubted the resilience of democratic institutions and believed that to fight fascism, the United States might have to adopt some of its unsavory features. This did not sit well in London or Washington.

Jane Vieth probably knows more about the record of the United States ambassador Joseph Kennedy in London during 1938–1940 than any other person. She has spent a large portion of more than forty years, intermittently, pursuing the research presented in this volume. And she has tested her scholarly findings in numerous conference presentations to academic scholars pursuing knowledge about subjects closely related to her own—in my particular case, the British policy of appeasement and the effort at its implementation. Kennedy's performance as ambassador to Britain can be variously interpreted according to the assessor's personal perspective and predilections, but the strong historical record presented here, and the interpretations that emerge therefrom, will certainly stand the test of time insofar as scholarship is concerned. All the ingredients are here for making an informed assessment, even to the point, perhaps, of causing a few readers to falter under the very substantial amount of detailed information presented. In that case, readers will find a very effective concluding chapter that summarizes the nature of the man and his conflicted ambassadorship (including his relationship with President Roosevelt and a range of important British officials), and has all the earmarks of historical accuracy and sound professional judgment.

Preface

Joseph Patrick Kennedy is remembered not for his public service as a supporter of Franklin D. Roosevelt's presidential campaigns in 1932, 1936, and 1940, nor for his able chairmanship of the Securities and Exchange Commission in 1934 and the Maritime Commission in 1936, nor even for his disastrous ambassadorship at the Court of St. James's from 1938 to 1940. Instead he is remembered for his private achievements, for his Midas-like talent for making money, and for siring a dynasty to immortalize his name and attain the political power he could barely grasp at and never rise to. If one of his sons had not become the president of the United States and been elevated by his assassination to near-mythic proportions as the embodiment of grace and youth, Joseph Kennedy would be unremembered as a public figure except by a handful of scholars interested in Franklin Roosevelt's New Deal or his foreign policy on the eve of America's entry into World War II.

Although Kennedy played only a minor role in the public life of the nation, he dominated the lives of his nine children—his "nine hostages to fortune" he called them[1]—especially the lives of his four sons. When a friend asked what he was doing, Kennedy's reply was "My work is my boys."[2] A modern-day Daedalus, Kennedy sculpted them to fulfill his soaring political ambitions by training them in public service and by expecting them to reflect and enhance his glory. Throughout his life, Kennedy's preoccupations were to safeguard and promote his family's welfare, particularly his sons', and to avenge the snubs the Boston Brahmins heaped on him as an Irish-Catholic saloon-keeper's son from Boston's East End. His concerns also explain why he so desperately wanted to be the ambassador to the Court of St. James's, the most prestigious diplomatic post, traditionally reserved for Boston Brahmins of old Yankee-Protestant stock.

As the American ambassador in a sensitive capital like London, Joseph Kennedy had a tremendous opportunity to influence the president's views. He was nominally under the authority of the Department of State, yet Roosevelt's personal appointees were allowed to report directly to Roosevelt himself. Thus Kennedy's friendly relationship with Roosevelt gave Kennedy a large degree of freedom and an unusual opportunity to influence foreign policy.

An examination of Kennedy's attitudes toward American foreign policy before and after the outbreak of World War II, the reasons for these views, and their impact on Anglo-American relations is essential to an evaluation of his controversial performance as ambassador. An analysis of the diplomatic background against which he worked, the political philosophies and personalities of the statesmen with whom he dealt, and his relations with them, particularly Roosevelt and Britain's prime ministers Neville Chamberlain and Winston Churchill, will assist in an assessment of Kennedy's diplomacy.

His appointment by Roosevelt was the pinnacle of his career; it ended in self-inflicted public disgrace, embarrassment, and failure. Kennedy failed because, like Daedalus, he suffered from hubris, a tragic and fatal flaw that blinded him to the limits of his abilities. He thought he could do anything. But the ambassadorship was a job for the expert, not the amateur. Standing at the height of his powers with supreme confidence in his abilities, inspired by his considerable success in moneymaking and in public service, Kennedy's political and social ambitions and intense Irish pride made him incapable of refusing a position he lacked the temperament, education, and experience for. His egocentrism, his devotion to his family, his parochial vision, and his penchant for risk-taking kept him from seeing the folly and unwisdom of equating his ambitions and fears for his family with those of his nation. And when his ambassadorship was over, the name Kennedy had become synonymous with isolationism, pro-appeasement, pro-Nazism, anti-Semitism, defeatism, and flagrant indiscretion. He even had the unfortunate distinction of being singled out by Hermann Göring, Hitler's Reichsmarschall, as "the best and fairest Ambassador in Europe," or so Kennedy bragged to Rose in 1940.[3]

Kennedy's professional failure was coupled with personal tragedy brought by the war he fought so hard to prevent, as one by one his hostages to fortune were taken from him. On August 12, 1944, his favorite son and namesake, Joe Jr., the heir to the family's immense political ambitions and a lieutenant in the United States Navy, was killed in a plane crash. His father's son, Joe Jr. had a reputation for risk-taking. He volunteered to fly a secret, near-suicidal mission. In his last letter to his father and mother, dated August 4, 1944, he told them that he was "working on something different. It is terribly interesting, . . . but . . . quite secret. . . . Don't get worried about it, as there is practically no danger."[4] His plane, a B-24 Liberator bomber loaded with 22,000 pounds of high explosives and heading for Hitler's rocket-launching site in Calais, exploded in midair over the English Channel near Dover.[5] No trace of him was ever found. He was posthumously awarded the Navy Cross "for extraordinary heroism and courage," the Distinguished Flying Cross, the Air Medal, the Purple Heart, and several other decorations.[6] He was twenty-nine.

In the fall of 1945 the navy launched Destroyer 850 and named it the USS *Joseph P. Kennedy, Jr.* His nineteen-year-old brother, Robert, without his family's permission, went to Washington to ask Secretary of the Navy James Forrestal to reassign him from the Naval Reserve Officer's Training Corps to the destroyer named for his brother.[7] In Joe Jr.'s honor the family established the Joseph P. Kennedy Jr. Foundation, which, on Rosemary's behalf, focuses on mental retardation.[8] The father was inconsolable and sank into gloom at the loss not just of his son but of his own future, interwoven as it was with his ambitions for his firstborn. "The pain was inextinguishable. . . . The wound never healed," wrote Arthur Schlesinger Jr., a close family friend.[9] Nothing had meaning anymore.[10]

A further tragedy was the death of the ambassador's son-in-law, William Cavendish, the ninth Marquess of Hartington, who had married Kennedy's favorite daughter, Kathleen. Ambitious, passionate, and rebellious like her father, Kathleen—"Kick"—dared to spurn convention and the Catholic Church. She defied her mother's wishes when she married Billy Hartington outside the Church and became Kathleen Kennedy Cavendish, Marchioness of Hartington. Hartington, a Protestant and pillar of the English aristocracy, heir to the Dukedom of Devonshire, was a major in the Coldstream Guards. He was killed by a German sniper as he led his men into the Belgian town of Heppen on September 9, 1944. He was twenty-seven years old. In 1948 Kick herself died in a plane crash on the mountains in the Ardèche, on her way to meet her father in Paris and to introduce him to the man she planned to marry, Lord Peter Fitzwilliam. Kennedy, grief-stricken, identified his beloved daughter's mangled body. It had been brought down from the mountain in a peasant's cart.[11] Kennedy gave his blessing to the Devonshire proposal to bury Kick in the family plot near Chatsworth. Her mother-in-law, Lady Mary Alice Gascoyne-Cecil, the Duchess of Devonshire, suggested Kick's epitaph: "JOY SHE GAVE/JOY SHE HAS FOUND."[12] Kick was twenty-eight.

After the war ended, tragedy continued to stalk Kennedy's sons. His second son, John Fitzgerald Kennedy, became president of the United States and was assassinated in Dallas on November 22, 1963. He was forty-six. The third son, Robert Francis Kennedy, was his brother's attorney general from 1961 until Jack's death in 1963. Robert then was Lyndon Johnson's attorney general until 1964, a senator from New York from 1965 to 1968, and a candidate for the presidency of the United States in 1968. On June 5, 1968, while campaigning in Los Angeles, Robert Kennedy was shot and killed. He was forty-two. In 1962, the fourth son, Edward Moore (Ted) Kennedy, then thirty years old, was elected to his brother John's old seat in the Senate and represented Massachusetts from then until his death on August 25, 2009. Of the sons only he outlived his father; but he was never free of the aura of tragedy. He was nearly killed in a plane crash in 1964, and he was the driver of a car in which Mary Jo Kopechne drowned on July 18, 1969, on Chappaquiddick Island, when the car fell off a bridge into the water. She was twenty-eight. He pleaded guilty to leaving the scene of an accident and received a suspended sentence of two months. He gave a television speech asking for the public's support for his fall campaign. The voters of Massachusetts reelected him. His father's son, to whom everything came easily, Edward Kennedy gave the impression of entitlement, that a Kennedy owed no explanation for his behavior. But "nothing any critic ever said or wrote, nothing any enemy ever did, was as damaging to Edward Kennedy and his family as the self-inflicted wounds of that episode." Just as Joe Kennedy outlived so many of his children, so he outlived the Kennedy legend. With the accident on Chappaquiddick Island, the Kennedys began their slow descent into "mere celebrity."[13]

Acknowledgments

I n 1962, I spent most of the summer in Hyannis Port with a group of my Delta Delta Delta sorority sisters and other sorority and fraternity friends from Ohio State University. My sorority sisters and I worked as waitresses in Bruce's and as chambermaids in restaurants and hotels; the fraternity men were milkmen. We were quite aware that the president of the United States had a home in Hyannis Port. Some of us used to stroll by the Kennedy Compound, flirt with the guards, and visit the church Rose Kennedy often went to Mass at. For some of us and for the country, it seemed to be a time of youthful, carefree exuberance and innocence, one that would not come again. As I walked barefoot through the sand on the beach, a junior in college, wondering what my future held, I never dreamed that I would one day be working on a book on the patriarch of the family, the "founding father," as Joe Kennedy has been called.

The research for this project has been conducted at a host of institutions. In the United States, I have examined the papers relating to Kennedy's ambassadorship in the John F. Kennedy Library in Columbia Point, Boston, particularly Joseph Kennedy's diary, diplomatic memoir, and public and personal correspondence, all essential to an understanding of Kennedy's diplomacy. Of particular importance has been a draft of Kennedy's memoir about his ambassadorship in the James Landis Papers in the Library of Congress. A more polished version of this memoir is at the Kennedy Library in Massachusetts. I have also read documents relating to Kennedy's ambassadorship in the Franklin D. Roosevelt Library in Hyde Park, in the Oral History Research Office at Columbia University, as well as in the Library of Congress and the National Archives in Washington, in the Archdiocese Archives in Detroit, and in the Northwestern University Archives in Evanston.

In Britain, I have consulted documents in the Public Record Office in Kew Gardens, the Neville Chamberlain Papers in Birmingham, the Beaverbrook Papers in London, the papers of Lord and Lady Astor in Reading, collections at the libraries of the universities of Cambridge and Oxford and Newcastle, the Borthwick Institute for Archives at the University of York, the Kent Archives Office at Maidstone, and the National Maritime Museum at Greenwich. I also examined collections in Edinburgh at the National Library of Scotland and the National Records of Scotland, formerly the National Archives of Scotland, and documents in private collections. I am indebted to the staff at these institutions for their kindness and efficiency and to the curators of the private collections.

In 2001 Amanda Smith published *Hostage to Fortune: The Letters of Joseph P. Kennedy*, an edition of her grandfather's letters. The book contains correspondence with political figures, journalists, and businessmen, among others, some of it duplicated elsewhere, as well as correspondence with friends and family, and parts of Kennedy's diplomatic memoir and diary. After the publication of Amanda Smith's book, the Kennedy family opened the ambassador's papers to the scholarly community. These sources, along with Kennedy's dispatches previously published in the *Foreign Relations of the United States* book series, now allow a definitive assessment of his ambassadorship.

Doris Kearns Goodwin's conversations with Rose Kennedy have also been helpful, particularly in the first chapter of this book. They yield insights into Joe Kennedy's character and his attitudes about World War I, and forecast his position on World War II. The records of the interviews between Goodwin and Rose Kennedy remain closed to scholars. I have relied upon Goodwin's conversations with Rose cited in *The Fitzgeralds and the Kennedys*. Goodwin's writing has been a source of inspiration for me and has influenced my own.

The John F. Kennedy Library gave me several grants to complete my research, and Mark Kornbluh provided me with grants from the Sesquicentennial Fund from Michigan State University. Marietta Baba, Walter Hawthorne, and Lisa Fine of Michigan State University have been unfailing in their kindness and generosity to me and in their financial and moral support of this project.

Over the many years that it took me to complete this book, a number of colleagues and friends have been helpful, and in many ways. Clayton Roberts at The Ohio State University shepherded me through graduate school, and Philip Poirier, my dissertation adviser, suggested the topic of Kennedy's ambassadorship. Robert Cole at Utah State University and colleagues at Michigan State University—John Coogan, F. DeWitt Platt, Roy Matthews, and Gordon Stewart—have given me much encouragement. Conversations with David Dilks from the University of Leeds, the late Donald Cameron Watt at the London School of Economics, and the late Sir Martin Gilbert of Merton College, Oxford, Churchill's official biographer, helped me shape my interpretations of Kennedy as ambassador and my understanding of the diplomatic world in which he operated.

Others have read various versions of my manuscript. Their sound and generous advice has greatly improved it. They include Donald Lammers and the late Henry Silverman of the Department of History at Michigan State University, and the late Bentley Gilbert at the University of Illinois at Chicago. I am indebted to them all.

The directors of the Michigan State University Press have steadily demonstrated an interest in publishing this project over the many years it took me to finish it. Richard Chapin, Fred Bohm, and Gabriel Dotto all gave me a long leash and much encouragement to pursue Kennedy's ambassadorship wherever the journey took me. They must be as relieved as I to see its completion. I am very pleased to work with Julie Loehr, my editor at the press. I've always admired her professionalism, her extensive editorial experience, and her respect for the English language. I appreciate her infinite patience with me. Kristine Blakeslee and other staff at the press have also been extremely helpful and a joy to work with.

My thanks to my long-suffering editor, Katherine McCracken, who has a sense of English equaled by few, and a mastery of grammar and syntax that would make H. W. Fowler proud, not to mention Strunk and White. She can say in one word what it takes me three words to say. "Kat" has helped me revise virtually everything I have written for professional presentation and publication, and she has often saved me from myself, except where I wouldn't let her. Her patience and dedication to this project is extraordinary. Ours is a long, long collaboration.

Martha Bates, a former acquisitions editor at the MSU Press, has been my research assistant for four years. She has checked and rechecked quotations and notes and saw to it that everything is in accordance with the *Chicago Manual.* We make a good team.

Rebecca Koerselman, my ever-cheerful, prompt, and extremely capable research assistant while a doctoral candidate in history, and now a PhD and associate professor herself, patiently added note after note, looked up quotation after quotation to ensure their accuracy, and somehow managed to decipher two species of illegible handwriting, mine and Kat's. I am much indebted to "Reb" too.

Several of my undergraduate students have helped me with the manuscript. Gregory Radcliff, Madeline Nash, and Aubrey Catrone were all stellar students and stellar research assistants. They helped check sources, carted books from the library, read and commented on various chapters of the manuscript, and gathered information from the presidential and public libraries. I appreciate the scholarly contributions of these Spartans to this work.

My deep gratitude also goes to Carol Cole, who first introduced me to the computer over my strenuous protests, and to Joann Silsby, my indispensable computer guru. They both have been extraordinarily kind and have the patience of Job.

I am also profoundly grateful to my colleague, mentor, confidante, and friend, my fairy godmother, Pauline Adams. She has always provided me with keen analysis and advice and with wisdom and unwavering support about every aspect of my professional and sometimes my personal life. She has cheered me on in everything I have undertaken, especially the manuscript.

Alan Suits, my late husband, raised by his mother to be a feminist son, to respect and support women, was the perfect partner for a professor. He was my rock. He always encouraged me to be all that my talents, training, and ambition make me. Whenever I felt discouraged, or scared, or doubted my ability to do something, he'd say: "You know who you are." He endured endless complaints from me about what a pain writing is, left parties and concerts and plays early so that I could work another hour on the manuscript or grade papers or review a class assignment. He listened as I rehearsed lectures and presentations. And he did the cooking.

Most of all I am indebted to my mother, Caroline Shaw Vieth, for her faith in me, her unwavering support, and her inspiration to me in all ways. She never finished her own doctorate at Ohio State, but she always believed I would finish mine. She received her BA, BS, and MA from OSU and was a doctoral candidate there in the 1940s while my father was in China in the army. Despite taking virtually every course in the history department and being an excellent student, she suffered from gender discrimination: she was a woman, married, and a mother. No one could fathom why she was working on her doctorate! Her graduate school experience made me a second-generation feminist. This book is a labor not of love but for love, and it is dedicated to my mother.

And I? I kept her faith.

CHAPTER 1

The Irish Prince

Joseph Patrick Kennedy, born on September 6, 1888, was the eldest of four children and the adored and only surviving son of Patrick Joseph Kennedy and Mary Augusta Hickey. His father was a sensible, conservative soft touch, a Robin Hood politician from Boston's East End who eventually prospered enough to buy a stately brick four-story mansion on elegant Webster Avenue at number 165, a mile and a quarter from where Joe had been born. His mother had been a catch: the Hickeys were a cut above the Kennedys. Her father had been a prominent businessman, and her three brothers were all distinguished members of the Irish-Catholic community—a police lieutenant, a doctor who had graduated from Harvard Medical School, and an undertaker. Joe, his mother's favorite, inherited her mischievous and whimsical nature and an ability to laugh at himself. She doted on him, especially after her younger son, Francis, died of diphtheria when he was two. His father doted on Joe, too, and always had time for his son; the pair were inseparable—young Joe went with him everywhere.

The family's favoritism toward their thin, wiry, charming, red-haired, freckle-faced, blue-eyed Irish prince with a captivating smile, whom they had bred to conquer, was accepted, apparently without resentment, by Joe's two adoring younger sisters, Loretta and Margaret. Throughout their lives they each proudly referred to him as "my Joe."

Joe expected things to go his way; they always had. This expectation was reinforced at school.[1] Both at Boston Latin School and at Harvard, Joe's friendliness and likability enabled him to cross the boundaries of class, money, and status and won him stature. He was the colonel of a drill team, directed backyard dramas, organized and turned a profit on his church's baseball team, of which he was captain, and was elected class president of Boston Latin. From 1908 to 1912 Joe was at Harvard, where his pattern of success persisted. He took "four years of economics and government; three years of German, English, and history; two half-year courses in comparative literature; a year of Latin; and half-year courses in education, social ethics, and public speaking" and he got good-enough grades.[2] He won his "H" by making the winning baseball play against Yale and defied tradition by not giving the game ball to the team captain.[3] He made the grade socially and emerged as a class leader by helping to run the smokers and dances and the student council.[4] He was elected in his sophomore year, itself an honor, to the Institute of 1770, to the Hasty Pudding Club, and to ΔKE, or the Dickey, thus making himself eligible for membership in one of Harvard's exclusive final clubs.

Nothing in his experience had prepared him for the stinging rejection he felt when he was excluded from all seven of Harvard's final clubs. Clubs like the Porcellian or the AD epitomized the summit of social acceptance at Harvard and were dominated by the Gold Coast crowd, the scions of Boston Brahmins, and other social elites. Selection by them meant admittance into their counterparts in Boston's business community and perhaps even into one of the prestigious brokerage houses. It guaranteed lifelong associates and friendships united by class, money, and background, a world from which Irish Catholics were barred.[5]

Speaking more than fifty years later, Joe's wife, Rose Fitzgerald Kennedy, gave the family's biographer, Doris Kearns Goodwin, her views about the rejection of her husband:

> It's a curious thing but I am now convinced that being selected for the Dickey was the worst thing that could have happened to Joe, for it spawned in his heart the illusory hope that it qualified him as a good bet for membership in one of the exclusive final clubs. To be sure, he understood that even with the ΔKE designation the odds of making a final club were tremendously against him. Still, he somehow believed he would. It would have hurt him less, I believe, if he had accepted the social divisions at Harvard from the very start, just as I accepted them in Boston, as elementary facts of life not worth worrying about.[6]

Joe was forced to accept that there were some boundaries that even his gregariousness and charm would not allow him to cross and some social distinctions he could not acquire. Harvard's rejection, Goodwin wrote, "ripped something out of him . . . ; never again would he experience loyalty to any institution, any place or any organization. And in the place of that loyalty, resentment had crystallized out hard as rock; whether he knew it or not, his siege against the world had already begun."[7]

Rejection left an indelible mark on him, as it may well have done on Franklin Roosevelt, also excluded by the Porcellian. Yet unlike Kennedy, Roosevelt came from the right family, the right background, the right church, the right schools. His rejection could not be dismissed as a result of his bloodline. Roosevelt took little pleasure in his final selection by the Fly Club. His wife, Eleanor, believed that rejection by the Porc "gave him something of an inferiority complex." "It was the bitterest moment of his life," said another relative.[8] It may also have explained his hostility toward the Morgans and the Whitneys, pillars of the banking establishment who lived the life of modern-day Medicis surrounded by servants, tutors, and nannies, with magnificent mansions and manicured lawns, incomparable art collections, and yachts hundreds of feet long. They monopolized power and exuded prestige, privilege, and position.[9]

Harvard's social stratification, symbolized by its clubs, mirrored Boston's in the early years of the century. In her memoir, *Times to Remember*, Rose Fitzgerald Kennedy, the shrewd, sensible daughter of Boston's mayor John Francis Fitzgerald ("Honey Fitz") gave her perceptive view:

> Actually there were two societies in Boston. One of them was almost entirely Protestant and was mainly of English descent . . . all descended from colonial or early American settlers, blended into the general breed called Yankee or . . . 'proper Bostonians.' Their main citadel and symbol was the region known as Back Bay where wealthy and distinguished families such as the Cabots and Lodges lived serenely. . . . With the advantages of inherited wealth and status and close-knit interfamily ties, they controlled . . . almost all the usual routes to success, and thus were a self-perpetuating aristocracy. They had many admirable qualities. But they were a closed society.
>
> The other predominant group consisted of Irish Catholics, descendants of those impoverished hordes who had fled from the great famines of the 1840s and 1860s. Through hard effort and much ingenuity, often by way of politics . . . , large numbers of second- and third-generation offspring had achieved prosperity, and many had achieved a cultural level fully equal to that of the Back Bay Brahmins. Between the two groups feelings were, at best, suspicious, and in general amounted to a state of chronic, mutual antagonism.[10]

Kennedy's world was one in which "No Irish Need Apply" was less often seen in the "Help Wanted" ads and on signs in windows than in his father's day.[11] By the early twentieth century direct conflict had disappeared, but the social gulf remained, separating the two Bostons. Each group merely tolerated the other in a display of quiet contempt.

Kennedy graduated from Harvard in the class of 1912 and decided to enter banking, a world dominated almost exclusively by the most distinguished Brahmin families. They "sat on their fortunes like broody hens on fertile eggs," recalled Rose, and met "intrusions into their hen houses . . . with resentful cluckings."[12] But Joe's ambition refused to be thwarted by these clucking Bostonians. "I saw, even in my limited dealings, that sooner or later, the source of business was traced to the banks," he later said. "'Banking was the basic business profession' which 'could lead a man anywhere, as it played an important part in every business,'" and Kennedy liked being at the center of action.[13]

With his father's influence, he became a clerk in the Columbia Trust Company, a small bank in East Boston, and passed the civil service examination in 1912 to become a bank examiner. His new job allowed him to study the financial structure of banking as an industry. In 1914 he was elected president of the Columbia Trust Company. "He was then twenty-five years old: the youngest bank president in the United States, probably the youngest one in the world," Rose wrote in her autobiography many years later.[14]

On August 20, 1914, Kennedy made a $2,000 payment on what Rose called "a small home"—a nine-room house (with two maids' rooms on the top floor) at 83 Beals Street in predominantly Protestant Brookline.[15] On October 7, 1914, Joseph Patrick Kennedy married Rose Elizabeth Fitzgerald, and they started his family. On July 25, 1915, Rose gave birth to a ten-pound, rugged little boy with dimpled cheeks, blue eyes, and fair skin. Joe Kennedy wanted his eldest son to be his namesake and an extension of himself. The child, the first of their nine children, was called Joseph Patrick Kennedy, Junior.

"From the very beginning," Rose Kennedy later said, "'home' was the center of her husband's world and the only place that really, finally, counted in his plans. . . . Moreover, . . . he had a strong need for privacy, for independence, for being able to choose the people he wanted to be with in close association."[16] Having endured Harvard's snubs, he left it with an Irishman's contempt for the rules of the Establishment and was determined to play by his rules, to do what he wanted, and to win. "What is it you really want?" a friend asked him. Kennedy looked steadily at him and paused a moment. "Everything," he said.[17]

A perceptive historian and Kennedy family friend, Arthur Schlesinger Jr., later described him:

> His character was formed by his Irish cultural inheritance—the pessimism, the romantic defiance, the political instinct, the irony, the sexual chauvinism, the Catholicism, the sense that the world was a mess and not likely to improve very much—though he fused these traits with a strictly American passion for competition, achievement and victory. Still, powerful as this passion was, it was conditioned by the Irish tradition; above all by his supreme belief in the family—in *his* family.[18]

"The measure of a man's success in life," Kennedy often said, "is not the money he's made. It's the kind of a family he has raised."[19] Beyond his family and a few close friends, mostly Irish, he cared for no one and nothing.[20] Toward them his love, loyalty, and generosity were limitless and fully returned; others, however, felt his coldness, brutality, and duplicity. He could be charming and caring or treacherous and cruel, whichever suited his purposes. Let his enemies call him a scoundrel so long as his family and friends believed him to be a prince.[21] People were often pawns in his game, subordinated to his relentless ambition, his calculating mind, and his conquering will. The way to achieve the independence and freedom that would enable him and his family to thumb their noses at the Establishment was to acquire power, and Kennedy saw that the basis of power was wealth. With an unerring instinct he used money to make more money.[22]

He particularly desired "the freedom which money provides," Rose later commented, "the freedom to come and go where he pleased, when he pleased and how he pleased."[23] He set out to become a millionaire by the age of thirty-five and succeeded several times over. His fortune allowed him to construct a fortress around himself, his family, and his friends. Try as he did, however, he could not make it impenetrable or shut out the events in Europe.

By the time of Kennedy's wedding in early October 1914, the Great War had been raging in Europe for two months. Absorbed in his own ambitions for his career and his family, he refused to be swayed by anything as vague and sentimental as patriotism. Tough, ambitious, and calculating at twenty-six, he expected no sacrifice from anyone on his account, nor would he make any for anyone or anything. His cynical attitude, honed against the background of Yankee snubs, made him see no honor in bloodshed or glory in sacrifice for the nation.[24] "Through all the early years of the First World War," Rose remembered, "Joe could never accept the idea that war had a nobility of its own. He could never understand how anyone could really believe that all that killing and bloodshed could ever settle anything. As he saw it," she explained to Doris Kearns Goodwin, "the essence of war was waste and destruction—the destruction of wealth, the destruction of order, the destruction of property and the destruction of lives. And nothing, he believed, could ever be worth all that destruction."[25] These sentiments he would utter again with remarkable consistency more than twenty years later at the Court of St. James's in another time, in another place, about another war.

Sixty years later, Rose Kennedy could still recount an incident that vividly and poignantly illustrated her husband's attitude toward that war. She and Joe had invited three bachelor friends from Joe's Harvard days to his parents' home for the long Fourth of July celebration in 1916, the same weekend the great Allied offensive, the Battle of the Somme, was taking place in France. The newspapers were filled with glamorous and detailed accounts of the battle, and conversation at the Kennedy home revolved around a discussion of the beauty of sacrifice and the glory of war. At first Joe Kennedy just listened quietly to his three friends. He sadly shook his head; their enthusiasm was incomprehensible to him, his wife recalled. Then he responded vigorously: "Thousands of young men [are] dying out there on that bloody field, cut off from the world of their parents and their memories, cut off from their dreams of the future," Kennedy finally said. "All those men [cannot be going] to their deaths singing and laughing, fearlessly charging ahead into a torrent of bullets. . . . Dying out there on that scarred land [has] to be intolerably painful and horribly lonely." Reporters' descriptions of the tremendous numbers in battle struck him as "barbaric and monstrous." "No amount of recaptured territory could ever atone for the lives of hundreds of thousands of dead young men." Further, Kennedy chided his friends, "by accepting the idea of the grandeur of the struggle, they themselves [are] contributing to the momentum of a senseless war, certain to ruin the victors as well as the vanquished."[26] These views he would repeat in the late 1930s as ambassador to the Court of St. James's.

Joe's vigorous outburst during that long, rainy weekend strained the group's comradery and made Rose welcome the weekend's end. "I can still remember how quiet the house seemed after Joe's friends had gone," she recalled. "When I went upstairs, I could hear only the even breathing of our baby in his crib. Just then, Joe too came into the bedroom and looked down at our sleeping child. 'This is the only happiness that lasts,' he said softly, and then he walked away."[27]

Kennedy was right; the battle was barbaric and monstrous, a daily contest for little forests and littler hamlets along a twenty-five-mile front.[28] The great Somme offensive of July 1, 1916, was the most destructive day in Britain's military history, more devastating than Kennedy ever dreamed even in his most melancholy moments.[29] A quarter of a million shells were fired at the Germans in slightly more than sixty minutes, about 3,500 a minute. The noise was so loud that it could be heard on Hampstead Heath, in the north of London.[30] Out of 110,000 British soldiers, 60,000 had died or been wounded, and perhaps 20,000 of that number killed the first hour or the first minute of the first day. One thing was clear by the day's sunset: the only victor had been War. "The War had won, and would go on winning," wrote Edmund Blunden.[31] By the fall rains, which made further action impossible, the line of advance had only been pushed to Les Boeufs, seven miles from where it began on July 1.[32] The German effort had cost the Germans some 600,000 killed and wounded, and the Allies about the same number. French casualties were 194,451; the British, an unbelievable 419,654.[33] The Somme killed an entire generation of those holding the greatest promise and wiped out the male line in families that had prospered for centuries. "It [had been] a time of intense, almost mystical patriotism,"[34] "a time of sublime faith and unthinking confidence, a time of innocent love that would never come to England again."[35]

When in April 1917 the United States entered the war to make the world "safe for democracy," Kennedy watched as his closest friends at Harvard enlisted. "Wasted effort and wasted lives," he said to Rose of his friends' joining up. Kennedy quickly became "a stranger in his own circle," she recalled.[36] Nor had he any illusions about the nobility of America's sacrifice for the independence of small European countries an ocean away. America's involvement would only bring misery to all combatants. No doubt he had a tinge of the Irishman's cynicism about Britain's stirring support for Belgium's neutrality, particularly given Britain's refusal to grant Ireland's independence.[37]

Although he believed he was right in refusing to be swayed by patriotic feelings and for refraining from enlisting in the military, Joe was distressed. His wife said that he felt a "sameness to his life" and a "feeling of sadness." A "sense of regret" overcame him. The bank routine bored him; Kennedy wanted action. Since the United States was at war, perhaps he should accept the situation and work to win the war, he said to Rose.[38]

Kennedy decided to support the war effort without subjecting himself to the hazards of war. After winding up his affairs at Columbia Trust most satisfactorily by having his father succeed him as president of the bank, he entered the shipping business as an assistant general manager at the Fore River plant of Bethlehem Steel in October 1917 at a salary of $15,000 a year.[39] Joseph Powell, one of Bethlehem's top executives and Kennedy's new shipping boss, had urged him to do his "patriotic duty . . . in an undertaking of such national importance" as shipbuilding.[40] Kennedy also felt that he "was doing something worth while [*sic*]" for his country—so worthwhile, he thought, that it would earn him a deferment from military service.[41] Although he had a wife, two small children, and a third child on the way, criteria that normally would exempt him from military service, and Bethlehem's certification that his job was indispensable to them and to the war, the local draft board rejected his application for a deferment. Perhaps it did so because Kennedy admitted he had "absolutely no technical knowledge of shipbuilding."[42] He then appealed to the district level, asking for the overturn of the local board's decision. The board refused. Kennedy's Class I status made him instantly eligible for active service. Thereupon his boss, Joseph Powell, appealed to Washington—successfully—to get this service deferred. Kennedy remained at his desk at Bethlehem for the rest of the war, out of harm's way, and advanced rapidly in the shipping world. "He always knew," Rose said, that "but for the grace of God and the powers of Washington," he too could have been one of the hundreds of thousands of doughboys sent to the bloody battlegrounds in France.

In later accounts of his life, Kennedy moved the date of his employment at Bethlehem back to 1916, before America entered the war. Such a stretch may indicate that he felt guilty about avoiding the draft and wanted to negate the charge that he used his employment at Fore River to escape military service.[43] Kennedy's decision to stay at Bethlehem, though perhaps costly to his self-esteem and reputation, illustrated his basic life principle: Let nothing or no one stand in the way of his self-interest and his family's advancement—no sentiment, no ideology, no organization, no place, no nation. In contrast to the depth of his ambitions for himself and his family, Kennedy's patriotism was simply too shallow to allow him to make sacrifices he considered unnecessary, a stance that would shape his attitude about America's role during World War II.

But he met his match in Franklin D. Roosevelt, one man even Kennedy could not outwit. As undersecretary of the navy from 1913 to 1920, Roosevelt had traveled extensively, dealt with foreign problems, and loyally served the interests of the navy. Raised in the big-navy tradition of Admiral Alfred T. Mahan and Theodore Roosevelt, Franklin Roosevelt campaigned vigorously for the expansion of the navy, which he had kept in an aggressive state of preparedness. He developed considerable skill as an administrator and cultivated personal contacts in labor circles, especially in the volatile shipbuilding industry, Kennedy's old bailiwick.[44]

Kennedy's relationship with Franklin Roosevelt began, as it would end, as a stormy one. A harried Roosevelt in his mid-thirties first met and fought with Kennedy, a harried executive from Bethlehem Steel still in his twenties. About his earliest encounter with Roosevelt as assistant secretary of the navy, Kennedy wrote, "We never got along then. He would laugh and smile and give me the needle, but I could not help but admire the man. We had great confidence in him . . . and we made millions of dollars' worth of supplies for the government with no more authority than a telephone call from him."[45]

The two got into a squabble over the delivery of warships ordered by the financially troubled Argentine government from Bethlehem's Fore River Shipyards in Massachusetts. Kennedy's boss, Charles M. Schwab, refused to deliver the ships unless they were paid for. "Don't worry about this matter," Roosevelt curtly told Kennedy. "The State Department will collect the money for you." "Sorry, Mr. Secretary, but Mr. Schwab refuses to let the ships go until they are paid for." "Absurd," said Roosevelt. "Not at all absurd, sir," said Kennedy. "Positively no ship will be delivered until it is paid for." Roosevelt escorted Kennedy to the door, his arm around Kennedy's shoulder. He had been pleased to meet him, he said, and hoped he would stop by to see him again sometime. But, Roosevelt promised, unless the Bethlehem executives changed their minds and delivered the ships by two o'clock that afternoon, he would send a fleet of tugboats to Fore River Shipyards to pick up the vessels. Over Kennedy's protest, he called out: "Hope to see you very soon again." Roosevelt was a "smiling four-flusher," Kennedy concluded. Schwab agreed. They decided to call "this youngster's bluff," and the battleships stayed in the yard. To the surprise and dismay of the workers, four navy tugboats chugged up, manned by Marines armed with bayonets. The Marines climbed onto the dock, confiscated the ships, cast off their lines, and towed the ships into the harbor to an Argentine crew waiting nearby.[46] "Roosevelt was the hardest trader I'd ever run up against," Kennedy recalled years later. Reminiscing about a particularly severe arm-twisting session, he remembered: "When I left his office I was so disappointed and angry that I broke down and cried."[47] It had been rumored that Roosevelt was indecisive; "I certainly never have seen anything indecisive about him," Kennedy said.[48]

The Great War finally ended when the official German delegation met the Allied delegation in a railway car in the Forest of Compiègne and there, on the eleventh hour of the eleventh day of the eleventh month of 1918, signed an armistice ending four years of the most foolhardy and ferocious fighting known to man. But American participation in the Great War had not brought the just and lasting peace prophesied by Woodrow Wilson, but only a Carthaginian treaty and a sullen truce. Many Americans held that the United States had been tricked into war by Allied propaganda and the plots of munition manufacturers. So, in the 1920s Americans abandoned their brief and bitter moment of internationalism and turned inward. Safe and smug "behind their broad ocean moats,"[49] they came to regard foreign affairs with bemused detachment and wariness. They demanded that American foreign policy guarantee their political isolation from international squabbles and rejected membership in the League of Nations and the World Court. Americans' insularity was further reflected in their advocacy of economic nationalism and immigration restriction. They insisted on higher protective tariffs and repayment of war debts owed by European nations. Their resentment of foreigners led to the Immigration Act of 1924, which reversed the country's traditional liberal immigration policy by establishing severely restricted quotas.

Just seven months after the signing of the armistice, Kennedy left Bethlehem Steel, as he and Roosevelt drifted into different worlds. The end of war production brought an abrupt halt to Kennedy's career at Fore River. In June 1919 he became the manager of the Boston branch of the prestigious brokerage house of Hayden, Stone and Company. He spent the new decade amassing a fortune on Wall Street, in land speculation, and as a movie mogul dubbed the "Financial Wizard of Hollywood."[50] He entered Hollywood in 1926 worth little more than a million and left it four years later many times a millionaire. He had engineered several extremely profitable mergers and ultimately created Pathé-RKO.[51] He built up a large number of useful and influential acquaintances in a variety of fields.

Yet he had not successfully stormed the insular citadel of the Bostonian establishment. Kennedy's humiliating rejection by the Porcellian was replicated when he was blackballed by the Cohasset Golf Club in 1922.[52] "Greenbloods," sneered the Brahmins at people like the Kennedys, and turned their backs on them. Years later the rejection still smarted: "Those narrow-minded bigoted sons of bitches barred me because I was an Irish Catholic and son of a barkeep. You can go to Harvard and it doesn't mean a damned thing. The only thing these people understand is money," he said.[53] It was clear, even to Kennedy, that no matter what he accomplished, no matter how much money he made, he would not find the social acceptance he thirsted for among the Anglo-Saxon Bostonians. He would always be the Irish-Catholic barkeep's son, and Rose, looked down on by the women of Cohasset, would only be the daughter of Boston's flamboyant and controversial Democratic mayor. "When do you think the nice people of Boston will accept us socially?" Rose once asked Blair Clark, a Harvard student and friend of her son Jack's, who she mistakenly assumed was a scion of a Brahmin family.[54]

In 1926 Joe Kennedy's festering wounds and resentment of Brahmin snubs made him move his family from the city where Kennedys and Fitzgeralds had lived for three generations to the more cosmopolitan and sophisticated world of New York City, a world in which he could command the unqualified social respect due a man of his financial status.[55] The move to New York made him more determined to live by his own code and more disdainful of conventions and loyalties. He bent or broke the traditional rules to suit his own purposes and relished being the lone wolf, unencumbered by loyalties to anyone or anything except his family and a few friends.

Years later, he told Joe McCarthy, a reporter and author of a campaign piece on John Kennedy, that he had moved to New York because he had wanted his children to grow up in a more congenial and open social environment than that dominated by the blatantly anti-Irish and anti-Catholic prejudices of the Bostonian Yankees. "They wouldn't have asked my daughters to join their debutante clubs," he said. "Not that our girls would have joined anyway—they never gave two cents for that society stuff. But the point is they wouldn't have been asked in Boston."[56] The only society that really mattered was the family. The Kennedys developed a tribal quality, intensely loyal; they closed in upon themselves, virtually impenetrable, fortress-like, ruled over by an indomitable paterfamilias who lived for and through his children and expected to be obeyed in all things. "The Kennedys," Rose smiled, in an interview with *Reader's Digest*, "are a self-contained unit. If any of us wants to sail or play golf or go walking or just talk, there's always a Kennedy eager to join in."[57]

Writing in 1935, Rose recalled an incident aboard the *Normandie* that demonstrated the intense family loyalty Kennedy expected. He, Rose, Jack, and Kick were sailing for Europe when, on deck, he met Lawrence Fisher, a member of the famous Fisher family of General Motors. Kennedy immediately sent for Jack, who arrived all askew because he had been playing deck tennis. His father introduced him to Fisher and told his son: "Jack, I sent for you because . . . I wanted you to see what success brothers have who stick together."[58]

Meanwhile, FDR, Kennedy's former adversary, had become the Democratic Party's 1920 vice-presidential nominee on a slate headed by Ohio's James Cox. Continuing in the Wilsonian tradition of international cooperation and collective security, Cox and Roosevelt defended the "internationalist" party platform and campaigned for America's entry into the League of Nations. But the mood of Americans had begun to change, and Cox and Roosevelt were defeated in a landslide by another Ohioan, Warren G. Harding. His victory ushered in "a period of materialism and conservatism," Roosevelt wrote. "People tire quickly of ideals."[59]

After his defeat, FDR withdrew from the political arena for nearly a decade. From 10:30 in the morning until 1:30 in the afternoon he worked for the surety bonding section of the Fidelity and Deposit Company, and in the afternoon he would listlessly return to the sedate law office of Emmet, Marvin and Roosevelt. He pursued numerous business adventures, many unsuccessfully, and nursed his polio-stricken legs. And yet he never really left politics; he worked tirelessly to keep his name before the public through a variety of good causes. He became the Party's spokesman during the years of Republican ascendancy; twice nominated Al Smith, the "Happy Warrior," for the Democratic ticket; and in 1928 finally won the governorship of New York by a hairsbreadth. Poised and watchful, he waited for a chance to jump into national office. Foreign affairs dictated patience and prudence.[60]

Widespread popular and congressional acceptance of isolationism forced even a staunch internationalist and big-navy man like Franklin Roosevelt to trim sail. Even he found it expedient publicly to reverse his earlier internationalism and Wilsonian past and to advocate an isolationist approach to foreign affairs by calling for disarmament, world peace, and Europe's repayment of its war debts. The future explained his apparent change of heart: the presidential election of 1932 lurked on the horizon.[61]

Long before the spring of 1932, Joseph Kennedy had jumped on Roosevelt's bandwagon, but not because of his views on foreign policy. Kennedy had made a killing during the stock market crash of 1929 and feared a violent social revolution that could take his entire fortune and destroy his family's financial security. A few years later he wrote, "In those days I felt and said I would be willing to part with half of what I had if I could be sure of keeping, under law and order, the other half. Then it seemed that I should be able to hold nothing for the protection of my family."[62]

Kennedy's cool analysis of the economic crisis led him to conclude that President Herbert Hoover, whom he liked personally, was not "temperamentally" suited to leading the country during this emergency.[63] Both he and the business community were ill equipped and unprepared to provide the powerful leadership necessary to break out of the fear of social disorder and of increasing economic paralysis that gripped the country. Their solution was to urge patience, hoping that recovery was just around the corner. Kennedy, however, instinctively grasped that the times required a decisive, forceful leader who could restore confidence and optimism and unite a divided nation through bold national action.

He found one at the governor's mansion in Albany, New York, in 1930. Kennedy accepted the invitation of FDR's close personal friend and loyal Democrat, Henry J. Morgenthau Jr., to lunch with Roosevelt at the mansion and to renew his association with his old adversary. Roosevelt could not have been more gracious, charming, and attentive. After a long afternoon Kennedy left with his mind made up: Roosevelt could "save the country."[64] Kennedy pledged himself not only to campaign strenuously on FDR's behalf but also to contribute financially to his election. "I was the first man with more than $12 in the bank" who was for Roosevelt.[65]

Joe Kennedy's motives in supporting Roosevelt were a mixture of admiration, fear, and opportunism. "Roosevelt was a man of action. He had the capacity to get things done," said Kennedy. "I had seen him in action. I knew what he could do and how he did it."[66] Recalling his licking in 1917, Kennedy later mused, "I remember what a fighter he was in the Navy Department. He cut more red tape and accomplished more than anybody else could have. He is the only man in sight with the imagination and guts to get us out of this mess."[67]

Later, Joe Kennedy described his own fears after the crash of the stock market to his friend Joe McCarthy, a reporter, freelance writer, and author of *The Remarkable Kennedys*, a campaign book about John Kennedy.

> I was really worried. I knew that big, drastic changes had to be made in our economic system and I felt that Roosevelt was the one who could make those changes. I wanted him in the White House for my own security, and for the security of our kids, and I was ready to do anything to help elect him.[68]

Finally, being Joe Kennedy, he wanted to be in the thick of things and in the winner's circle. He was certain Roosevelt was a winner.[69] Kennedy hoped that his own new interest in politics would keep him at the center of the action. Just as he had recognized that business was the source of power in the 1920s, he now realized that political affairs would dominate the country in the 1930s; as before, so again he wanted to be involved with the great issues of the day.[70] Although his opportunism made the sickly, jealous, hollow-eyed Louis Howe, Roosevelt's devoted adviser and longtime secretary, suspect him, his strong support of Roosevelt may have worked to Kennedy's personal advantage.[71] Congress began a public investigation into Wall Street's activities in April 1932. Kennedy was not among those asked to testify. He may have been as responsible as many other businessmen for the economic chaos; but as a vigorous Roosevelt supporter, he was an unlikely example of a Wall Street businessman.[72]

Kennedy also contributed handsomely to Roosevelt's campaign. He gave Roosevelt $25,000, and he lent the Democratic Party $50,000 more.[73] Having the Wall Street millionaire in their corner often helped Roosevelt's workers tap new sources of support. It would eventually convert formidable critics like Kennedy's old Hollywood friend William Randolph Hearst, the fervent isolationist publisher whose life the film *Citizen Kane* was based upon. Hearst greatly respected Kennedy's financial acumen but was wary of his pro-Roosevelt political views.

FDR's internationalism made him suspect and kept Hearst, one of the kingmakers at the 1932 Democratic National Convention, undecided about whom to support for the presidential nomination. The two Democratic frontrunners were Roosevelt and Al Smith, the 1928 Democratic candidate for the presidency. Hearst, himself a frustrated office seeker, relished cracking the whip over Roosevelt and Smith. In 1931, two days after Hearst announced his support for John Nance Garner, Roosevelt bowed to Hearst's demand and disavowed his Wilsonian past. He announced that he now opposed American entry into the League of Nations.

Still unplaced, Hearst, in a signed editorial, "A Plague O' Both Your Houses," appearing in *The American* in the spring of 1932, labeled Roosevelt and Smith equally obnoxious internationalists and explained the rivalry between them as a "natural rivalry—based on past performances—as to which one could lead the Democratic Party to the greater disaster in the Presidential year of 1932." Hearst let Roosevelt know that while he accepted his "repudiation" of America's participation in the League of Nations as "sincere or perhaps opportune," it had struck him as odd that the man who had made his political career on the basis of internationalism could "suddenly adopt the principles of George Washington . . . on the eve of a Presidential election." He further warned against any attempt at "projecting the United States into foreign entanglements by the back door of the League Court."[74]

In the spring of 1932, with no nod still from Hearst and in need of a further act of atonement, Roosevelt sent Kennedy on a "business trip" to win Hearst's support. Kennedy, every bit as staunch an isolationist as Hearst, repeatedly assured him of Roosevelt's sincerity. Upon his return, Kennedy visited Roosevelt in Warm Springs on May 8, 1932. The *New York Times* reported their meeting and expressed "considerable curiosity" about their conversations. Would the Garner forces retain their independence as the Roosevelt supporters predicted, or would they join with Smith in a "stop-Roosevelt" drive?[75] Shortly before the Democratic convention, Kennedy met the governor in Albany and promised: "I will keep my contact with W. R. [Hearst] on a day-and-night basis."[76]

At the convention in Chicago, however, Hearst held out despite Kennedy's efforts. Pledged to the politically hapless John Nance Garner from Texas and allied with California's William

G. McAdoo, Hearst controlled forty-two Texas delegates and forty-four Californians. But there was another political hopeful in Chicago. A name frequently heard in the hotel lobbies and corridors was that of Newton D. Baker, Wilson's former secretary of war, who was on Hearst's blacklist. In the *New York American* in February 1932, Hearst had written that "Newton D. Baker's new pair of 'spring heel' League of Nations gum shoes, that he now wears for 1932 campaign purposes, do not conceal the cloven hooves of his internationalism."[77] By convention time Hearst was still appalled at the possibility that Baker, an ardent internationalist and defender of the League, might get the nomination.

On the fourth day in Chicago, Roosevelt's workers were desperate. They had sat miserably through three drawn-out ballotings and feared that the prediction of a deadlocked convention and a dark-horse winner would come true. Roosevelt was stalled, only eighty votes short of the two-thirds necessary for victory. His men turned the pressure on California and sat for hours waiting to get a connection to the California delegates through the jammed switchboard. Finally, Kennedy did get a call through to Hearst. Arthur Krock of the *New York Times* overheard Kennedy demanding: "W. R., do you want Baker?" "No," Hearst said. Then, Kennedy informed him, "if you don't want Baker, you'd better take Roosevelt, because if you don't take Roosevelt, you're going to have Baker." Was there was a chance, Hearst asked, for another dark horse, like Maryland's governor Albert Ritchie? "No, I don't think so," Kennedy said. "I think if Roosevelt cracks on the next ballot, it'll be Baker." "All right," Hearst must have said, "I'll take Roosevelt."[78] Kennedy's persuasiveness may well have helped convince Hearst to throw his delegations behind Roosevelt.

Pandemonium broke out that evening as delegation after delegation swung over to FDR, who became the party standard-bearer on the fourth ballot, and the convention rocked to his theme song, "Happy Days Are Here Again." Roosevelt broke with tradition and flew from Albany to Chicago to deliver personally what Kennedy described as "a very bullish" acceptance speech.[79] As he sat in the Chicago Coliseum, he heard Roosevelt promise the hushed audience, "I pledge you, I pledge myself, to a new deal for the American people."[80]

Roosevelt's campaign advisers were a mixed bag. They spoke from every point of view—left, right, center, and nowhere. They included idealistic university professors, cynical party chieftains, old Harvard friends, old Wilsonians, old Bryanites, high-tariff men, low-tariff men, and Joe Kennedy. The *East Boston Leader*, proud of their local boy who had made good, described Kennedy as a "personal advisor and confidential companion of the Democratic nominee."[81] Newsmen dubbed him one of Roosevelt's "silent" six Brain Trusters[82] with constant access to the governor,[83] and described him as a "fiery Boston and New York financier" so argumentative and passionate in conferences that he temporarily arouses enmity among the advisers.[84]

An appreciative Roosevelt asked Kennedy to serve on his campaign's executive committee, but Kennedy declined the honor because of the friction between himself and the ever-vigilant and irksome Louis Howe.[85] Kennedy was also offered a berth in one of the staterooms aboard a forty-foot yawl that Roosevelt used for a week's vacation after the campaign. Once again Kennedy declined and gave up his berth to Eddie Moore, his devoted personal secretary. Moore remained on board no doubt to keep his boss informed and regaled his cabinmate with his silly story that one of Kennedy's sons would one day be the first Irish-Catholic president of the United States.[86]

Even so, Kennedy remained influential. He continued to buttonhole wealthy Democrats for campaign contributions—for instance, W. R. himself, who contributed $25,000 for the Democratic national campaign fund for the radio program. That Hearst gave the check to Kennedy to forward to the national campaign meant that he had "delivered Hearst" to the convention, as W. R. intended and Roosevelt understood.[87] Kennedy's ability to tap Hearst increased his stature in the candidate's eyes. "I realize that this check coming to the Committee through me helps a great deal in having consideration paid to any suggestions that I might want to make," Kennedy wrote Hearst and promised in his thank-you note that he would always lobby for Hearst's interests with Roosevelt.[88]

Kennedy also contributed suggestions on economic reform to Raymond Moley, Roosevelt's speechwriter. One Moley effort, delivered by FDR in Columbus, Ohio, became a blueprint for the Securities and Exchange Commission, one of the most progressive New Deal measures.[89] As Kennedy casually contributed his ideas, he could hardly have guessed that one day the chairmanship of this commission would go to him as a reward for his efforts.

In the fall of 1932, Roosevelt invited Kennedy to accompany him on his whistle-stop campaign train, the "Roosevelt Special,"[90] and to ride in the compartment just in front of the private car of the candidate, giving Kennedy constant access to him.[91] During the first leg of its thirteen-thousand-mile trip, Kennedy often withdrew from the official party to sell Roosevelt to local businessmen, to run down rumors, and to spread a few of his own. He lunched in a cafeteria and spoke to the barber or the pharmacist "just to find out what people are talking about."[92]

Kennedy himself usually operated as a loner, staying quietly behind the scenes and acting as Roosevelt's eyes and ears. Even in his hometown of Boston, he stayed in the background, living up to his reputation as "a man of mystery"—so much so that his father-in-law, John F. Fitzgerald, hardly saw him. Fitzgerald told the press that he believed that Kennedy "keeps tabs on things independently of the official party."[93]

Kennedy was also given the extremely delicate task of keeping the immensely popular, radio-ranting, anti-Semitic priest from Detroit, Father Charles E. Coughlin, on friendly terms with Roosevelt.[94] Coughlin, a Roosevelt admirer in 1932 whose slogan was "Roosevelt or ruin," preached a blend of progressive Catholic doctrine and *argumenta ad hominem*. He captivated a weekly audience of thirty million with his tremendous charm and persuasive, melodic baritone voice on his CBS radio broadcast, "The Golden Hour of the Little Flower," from the Shrine of the Little Flower in Royal Oak, Michigan.[95] He also published *Social Justice*, a Coughlin rather than Catholic magazine that provided a platform for his brand of social Catholicism shared by the sympathetic bishop of Detroit, Michael Gallagher. It established Coughlin as a supporter of the working man and provided a podium for his virulent anti-Semitic ranting in the 1930s and 1940s.[96] It also worried Church officials for its "well-known lack of dignified restraint," particularly in its criticism of the president.[97] Despite the flamboyant priest's interpretation of Catholic doctrine and his opinion that "the power of *coining* and *regulating* money held in the hands of a few"—which could certainly include Kennedy but was more probably a veiled attack on Jewish bankers—"is the source of all social evils," the two men became good friends.[98] However, Kennedy found him troubling and "a very dangerous proposition" throughout the entire country.[99] Coughlin's supporters included people as diverse and wide-ranging as Babe Ruth, "Joseph Kennedy, Clare Boothe Luce, Eddie Rickenbacker, Douglas MacArthur, and Bing Crosby."[100] Once, to bring Hearst around, Kennedy had touted his own isolationism. Now, to keep Coughlin in line, he presented himself as a notable Catholic layman sympathetic to social causes. The many facets of Kennedy's character and his ready access to a variety of worlds proved to be one of his most valuable contributions to Roosevelt; no wonder he liked Kennedy. The wily candidate found Kennedy's versatility useful.

Staging a lavish two-story party at New York's Waldorf Astoria, Kennedy celebrated Roosevelt's triumph as though it were his own personal victory. The familiar tune "Happy Days Are Here Again," repeatedly played that evening, perfectly expressed his mood of exuberance and expectation. He accepted Roosevelt's invitation to continue the festivities in Florida and to join him on Vincent Astor's yacht for a post-election cruise. On shore, Kennedy's in-laws, "Honey Fitz" and the regal Mrs. Fitzgerald, went to a victory party. Dancing, Mrs. Fitzgerald looked up and reportedly exclaimed to her partner, actor-producer Eddie Dowling: "Isn't it wonderful! My son-in-law Joe Kennedy has made Franklin D. Roosevelt President!"[101]

Almost everyone who had played a role in Roosevelt's victory received a reward—except Joe Kennedy. The press touted him as a natural for a high governmental post, especially for that of secretary of the treasury, a position he wanted.[102] He was bitterly disappointed when Roosevelt selected his old reliable friend, the dreary and dependable William H. Woodin, who kept it for a year and then resigned. He was succeeded by Henry Morgenthau Jr. Thus Kennedy's hopes for the Treasury post were twice smashed. Howe objected to Kennedy's being appointed, and so Kennedy was snubbed.[103] He did, however, keep in touch with the Washington scene by living like a potentate and lavishly entertaining at Marwood, his thirty-three-room Maryland estate. Rose Kennedy wrote in her autobiography that he was offered several positions, including that of minister to Uruguay and of ambassador to Ireland,[104] but declined them all. Kennedy had very specific requirements: a position had to help Roosevelt and enhance the Kennedy family's prestige.[105]

Not welcomed by the New Dealers and never fully accepted by them, Kennedy returned to Wall Street, bitter and hurt at not being included in the new administration. He kept up a barrage of private criticism of Roosevelt and railed against his performance. He cultivated a friendship with James Roosevelt, the president's eldest son, who described Kennedy as his "foster-father"[106] and looked upon him as "a rather fabulous figure."[107] Kennedy, on the other hand, regarded his role as "nursemaid to Jimmie,"[108] whom he entertained lavishly at Palm Beach. Kennedy also helped him land lucrative clients in the insurance business in Boston. Joe and Jimmie and their wives vacationed in Britain in September 1933, whereby Joe acquired the franchises for Haig and Haig, Dewar's Scotch, and Gordon's Gin from the status-conscious British impressed with anyone accompanied by the president's son. Thus when Prohibition officially ended in 1933, Joe Kennedy's warehouses were overflowing with scotch and gin, enabling him to make a killing on repeal.[109]

The prize was worth the agonizing two years' wait. The chairmanship of the newly created Securities and Exchange Commission was finally bestowed upon Kennedy in 1934.[110] The bill, which had been passed in June, was designed to establish federal regulation of trading practices, registration of securities, and strict limits on how much money speculators could borrow. FDR asked Ray Moley, a New Deal "insider," to suggest nominees for the commission. At the top of his list was Kennedy's name. Moley admired Kennedy's administrative skills. Furthermore, as an extremely wealthy man, Kennedy, Moley reasoned, would not need to use to his own advantage the inside information he would hear. Moreover, FDR owed him. Political reality required that he handsomely repay Kennedy for his loyalty and substantial support and particularly for helping him get the party nomination.[111] Appointing him to the chairmanship of the commission would also help restore Wall Street's confidence. Besides, no one could pull anything on Kennedy—he knew every move. "OK," said FDR, won over despite Louis Howe's objections, and convinced that it would take a thief to catch a thief, "get Joe here."[112]

As news leaked out about Kennedy's likely appointment as chairman, criticism mounted. Some felt he was too much an "insider" and too "professional" to enforce the rules fairly. There were other candidates: Ferdinand Pecora wanted to be chairman;[113] so did James Landis.[114] Kennedy vowed, "unless it was the chairmanship for me, I was not at all interested."[115] To resolve the issue, the president invited him to the White House on Saturday, June 30, 1934, a hot, muggy Washington night, the start of a heat wave. "Nuts!" Kennedy responded when Moley passed on Roosevelt's invitation. But he came anyhow.[116]

When Kennedy arrived, his old friend Bernard Baruch was there. As the conversation revolved around the membership of the commission and the chairmanship, Baruch pointed to Kennedy and demanded, "What's the matter with that redhead over there?"[117] The president held up a sheet of paper with names on it in order. Kennedy's headed the list. "This is the list I made up two weeks ago, and I see no reason to change it," FDR replied, as he rambled on for fifteen minutes without indicating who his final choice was, no doubt enjoying his game of cat and mouse with Kennedy. Finally Roosevelt said to Kennedy in a jocular tone, "I think you can be a great liberal on that, and I think you would do a great job running it."[118] Kennedy rose to his feet and said, "Mr. President, I appreciate this honor more than I can tell you, but before I accept it, I'd like to tell you what my observations are, and the dangers to you in offering me this position."[119] Moley, knowing the president's intentions, responded: "Joe,

I know darned well you want this job. But if anything in your career in business could injure the President, this is the time to spill it. Let's forget the general criticism that you've made money on Wall Street."[120] Predictably, Moley recalled, Kennedy sprinkled his remarks with liberal doses of profanity as he lectured the president and his advisers for fifteen minutes. Kennedy pointed out the opposition of Roy Howard of the Scripps-Howard newspapers, who had called the appointment of Kennedy "ridiculous" and promised to attack it vigorously. Kennedy also told the president that, having been involved with Wall Street for twenty-five years, he had done many things that people would take exception to.

He defied anyone to question his devotion to the public interest or to point to a single shady act in his whole life. The president did not need to worry about that, he said. What was more, he would give his critics—and here again the profanity flowed freely—an administration of the SEC that would be a credit to the country, the president, himself, and his family—clear down to the ninth child.[121]

Roosevelt listened and then offered his hand to Kennedy: "If you are happy, it is perfectly satisfactory to me."[122] The conversation then switched to more general topics that kept Kennedy, Moley, and Baruch with the president until the wee hours.

The president knew his man. Realizing that Kennedy had made his fortune, FDR understood that he now wanted to add luster and prestige to his name, through public service, for the sake of his family. Just before FDR left for a Caribbean cruise the next day, he announced Kennedy's nomination. The celebrated Wall Street speculator was now to become its watchdog: the chief poacher made gamekeeper. When Kennedy's unanimous election by the five new commissioners as chairman was announced to the press on July 2, he responded good-naturedly to their bantering: "Boys, I've got nine kids. The only thing I can leave them that will mean anything is my good name and reputation. I intend to do that and when you think I'm not doing so, you sound off."[123]

"You know, when I took this job I told the boss that I didn't want to tie myself down or take on work that would be more than temporary," Kennedy said after serving on the SEC for about a year, "but I must admit I do get a kick out of it. . . . There is always something interesting turning up."[124] In late July, Kennedy was elected to another term as chairman of the SEC. He remained there until early September, resigning soon after Labor Day. He had told FDR he would remain only long enough to get the commission on its feet. Routine bored Kennedy, and he disliked being tied down by any job for too long. It was time to move on. He wrote the president, "At the time of my appointment to the Securities and Exchange Commission in 1934 . . . I indicated to you the probability that I could not remain in office much longer than a year. For personal reasons it is now necessary for me to ask you to relieve me."[125]

Roosevelt made Kennedy's resignation public, releasing to the press his thank-you letter. "Of course, I am very sorry to let you go," he had written Kennedy, but the agreement had been "that your private affairs would not permit you to stay beyond a year. . . . In the future, as in the past, I shall freely turn to you for support and counsel." He also praised Kennedy for his "skill, resourcefulness, good sense, and devotion to the public interest."[126] The praise was much deserved: Kennedy's accomplishments had indeed been impressive.[127] Businessmen generally regarded the SEC as being the most successful of the New Deal reforms. Its meticulously written requirements made the SEC the most likely to withstand a legal challenge.[128]

Not only was Roosevelt pleased by Kennedy's performance at the SEC, but he also valued Kennedy's easy access to Wall Street and his financial expertise, along with his frankness, his fun-loving nature, and his irreverent sense of humor. In fact, one of Kennedy's greatest assets was his "faculty for expressing opinions in short and easily understood words not hampered by the fact that he was addressing the President of the United States," commented one *New York Times* special correspondent.[129]

Arthur Krock, the Washington-based newsman for the *New York Times*, observed that Kennedy was a particular favorite of Roosevelt's because of his "agreeable personality, his ready laugh, his loyalty, his high ability and his Celtic pugnacity." Krock wrote: "The two argue constantly over acts and policies, and the President hears more objections than assents from the chairman of the SEC." Still, FDR "consults Mr. Kennedy on everything, and, when the argument is over, President and adviser relax like two school boys."[130] Even Eleanor Roosevelt once said to Kennedy: "Go right on telling Franklin exactly what you think."[131]

Their relationship deepened as FDR began to respect Kennedy's judgment more and more and to consult him on a variety of subjects. Kennedy became a frequent guest at the White House, there as often as three or four evenings a week. He also served as a troubleshooter and skillfully wooed potential critics. He carried soothing messages back and forth between Roosevelt and Wall Street critics and let the president use his rented French Renaissance chateau, Marwood—complete with movie theater, recreation rooms, big swimming pool, and newly installed elevator—as a spot for private meetings with businessmen.[132]

FDR encouraged everyone, as he did Kennedy, to overestimate FDR's dependency on him, a habit that sometimes backfired. "The trouble with Kennedy is you always have to hold his hand," the president complained to Morgenthau.[133] Yet neither viewed the other uncritically. By mimicking and ridiculing Kennedy behind his back and playing practical jokes on him, Roosevelt pointedly reminded him that he served at the president's pleasure.[134] And Kennedy knew that his vitriolic attacks on the president, which would continue even when he was ambassador, were sure to be reported to the White House. Their relationship seemed to have all the necessary elements for friendship except personal loyalty and mutual trust.

Another Kennedy habit was his careful crafting of his public image as a devoted family man with a Midas touch in business, and as a reluctant public servant who sacrificed his private interests when the president beckoned. Of all the early New Dealers, he had perhaps the best news coverage. His ongoing friendship with Hearst had been advantageous for Roosevelt in the 1932 election. And Kennedy's close friendship with Krock, who often sent up trial balloons for him in his column, proved extremely valuable too.[135] Henry R. Luce authorized two cover stories on Kennedy in *Time* and *Fortune* and even allowed him to see the drafts before publishing the stories. Kennedy took exception to the *Fortune* article and described it as "permeated with distrust of my character, dislike of my occupations and social prejudice against my origin."[136] Luce allowed him to amend it before it was published.[137]

Kennedy also courted Eugene Meyer of the *Washington Post* and was on good terms with muckraker Drew Pearson.[138] Kennedy even dared to criticize the powerful isolationist publisher of the *Chicago Tribune*, Colonel Robert McCormick, and objected to the *Tribune*'s editorial of January 18, 1936. It referred to Kennedy as a "stock market manipulator" and hinted that he was guilty of "political fixing, market manipulation and abuse of public office."[139] Kennedy protested that the editorial's characterization of him was "wholly false and most unfair." He cherished his reputation and record as a public servant and would not allow it to be besmirched. His performance at the SEC had been "a praiseworthy job," Kennedy told McCormick in no uncertain terms. As chairman he had altogether refrained from negotiating lucrative transactions and thereby suffered heavy losses, making a "great financial sacrifice." He also defended his activities as adviser to the Radio Corporation of America as "ethical" and said that he had not compromised any of his ideals or sought to influence SEC or other government rulings.[140] Kennedy's success in cultivating a favorable press by his sometimes outrageous candor, exuberant praise, and lavish gifts to those who were useful contributed to his contemptuous attitude toward them and fed his hubris.[141]

Besides becoming a national figure who had earned Roosevelt's goodwill and gratitude with a record of impressive accomplishments, and a shrewd manipulator of his public image, Kennedy had acquired a string of memberships in country clubs and other exclusive clubs. As a partner in the presidential political family, his social stock had jumped. He had joined the Burning Tree Golf Club, recommended by the president's secretary, Colonel Marvin McIntyre, as well as several other swanky clubs in Washington, New York, Bronxville, Hyannis Port, and Palm Beach. His list of memberships must have reduced the sting of Brahmin rejection. And yet they too were not enough to heal his wounded pride.[142]

In the little more than two years since the president's election and the beginning of 1935, only a handful of Americans had maintained any interest in foreign policy. Those who did were largely businessmen and bankers concerned with trade, debts, and monetary policy, or else idealists worried about the rise of fascism in Japan, Italy, and Germany and its threat to Europe's fragile peace. By early 1935 the possibility of a European war provoked an isolationist response in international affairs, symbolized by the Senate's rejection of America's entrance into the World Court on January 29, 1935. The Court fight aroused a powerful isolationist opposition led by Coughlin and Hearst that hamstrung Roosevelt's conduct of foreign affairs throughout the decade and ushered in a period of noncooperation. People were "jumpy and very ready to run after strange gods," FDR observed after his Court defeat. "This is so in every other country as well as our own."[143]

Roosevelt asked his former SEC chairman to serve as his informal adviser and secret emissary during his upcoming European tour. "When I lie awake at nights, as I often do, I worry about the condition of Europe. . . . I wish you would do a trouble-shooting job and find out for me just what the threat to peace amounts to," he wrote Kennedy.[144] Roosevelt had good reason to worry: The League of Nations, now moribund, had failed to provide collective security to the victims of aggression and to settle the conflicts between Bolivia and Paraguay, Italy and Corfu, or Japan and Manchuria. In early 1935 Europe was unhappily awaiting Benito Mussolini's promised invasion of Ethiopia, launched on October 3, 1935, soon after Kennedy arrived in Europe; but once again collective security failed to protect the victim of aggression and to punish the aggressor. And Hitler, hungrily eyeing the Rhineland, would in 1936 take advantage of Italy's breach with the Western democracies over its invasion of Ethiopia to violate the Treaty of Versailles in 1919 and the Treaty of Locarno (the Locarno Agreement) in 1925, both of which provided for the permanent demilitarization of the Rhineland.

In September 1935, Kennedy and his family sailed for Europe aboard the *Normandie* for a six-week tour, with letters of introduction from Roosevelt to prominent political figures and heads of state in Britain, France, the Netherlands, Switzerland, and Italy. FDR's friend and sometime adviser Bernard Baruch suggested to Winston Churchill, politically isolated and labeled an office-seeking Cassandra, that he see Kennedy. "He is important and good relationship between you two might have far reaching results," Baruch cabled Churchill.[145]

So, the Kennedys lunched at Chartwell, Churchill's estate, in October 1935 and were given a tour of Churchill's paint shop and the brick wall surrounding the house—bricks that he himself had laid—an odd hobby for a cultivated aristocrat, Rose Kennedy wrote in her diary. The style-conscious Mrs. Kennedy noted that both Churchills were clad in tweeds; this, along with Churchill's "puckish face," made him look "more like a country squire than an English statesman."[146]

The crowning event of their visit was to sit and listen to Churchill—"one of the great men of the generation," Rose believed—deliver, with "ease and facility and satisfaction," an oration on the importance of Anglo-American relations. The future prime minister "talked expansively, narrating, explaining and trying to convince us of the wisdom of his points." Prophetically, Churchill argued that the combined navies of the United States and England could police the world and subdue the Nazis. He acknowledged, however, that it would be hard to "sell" Americans on this idea. Too many were isolationists, "too many [were] Irish haters of England, too many people . . . would prefer to remain outside England's sphere."[147]

Kennedy cabled Roosevelt that he was meeting "everybody" in London: the governor of the Bank of England, Montagu Norman, and the chancellor of the exchequer and Baldwin's likely successor, Neville Chamberlain—men with whom he, as ambassador, would one day work closely.[148] Kennedy marveled at the president's personal popularity with the British; it was simply "amazing," he told FDR.[149] If the businessmen and journalists in the United States give you even 10 percent of the support you enjoy here, you could be elected to anything, and could be "President for the rest of your life."[150]

When Kennedy returned to the United States in mid-November 1935, he stayed overnight at the White House. The European scene was "unsettled and confused."[151] It had a "top-sy-turvy" look to it, Kennedy reported; any diplomatic move had "an Alice-in-Wonderland quality."[152] He noted the failure of collective security by the League of Nations to resist the Italian invasion of Ethiopia, and the irony that the sanctions imposed by the League deprived Italy only of materials it did not need, but not of oil or copper, essential for Italy's war. Further, Europe's economic recovery was lagging, slowed by increased spending on arms. As each European nation followed its own tangled path, "I was glad we had our new neutrality laws, to keep us from getting involved in the war that would probably come . . . over the Polish Corridor," Kennedy predicted to Roosevelt.[153]

Kennedy filled up the years out of government service by agreeing to work temporarily as a consultant for RCA and Paramount Pictures. Actually, he was eagerly awaiting another assignment from the president. He promoted his own candidacy by writing to FDR's secretary, "Missy" LeHand: "I am fairly free now of any business activities, and so if [Roosevelt] thinks I can be of any service to him, please let me know. I am going to take up the 'bum's life' again . . . but shall be available if there is anything he wants me to do."[154]

By the summer and fall of 1935, Kennedy had in fact become one of the most vigorous campaigners for Roosevelt's reelection. Kennedy proved to be particularly valuable once again as an emissary to the disenchanted business community. To get backing from business, he, with the help of Arthur Krock, and Roosevelt's unequivocal blessing,[155] wrote a little campaign book, *I'm for Roosevelt*, published by Reynal and Hitchcock in the early fall. "Conceived in righteous indignation and born of strict determination to take a crack at the people who should be down on their knees thanking Roosevelt instead of abusing him," Kennedy told columnist Robert Allen,[156] its purpose was to present in one-syllable words "a business man's argument for the re-election of Roosevelt" by showing business that it had never had it better.[157] "I have no political ambitions for myself or for my children," Kennedy disingenuously wrote; "I put down these few thoughts about our President, conscious only of my concern as a father for the future of his family and my anxiety as a citizen that the facts about the President's philosophy be not lost in a fog of unworthy emotion."[158]

Most of the campaign piece was "an enthusiastic and amazingly sweeping endorsement" of the New Deal and a defense of the national debt incurred under Roosevelt.[159] Not only was the national debt's increase a sensible form of borrowing, Kennedy argued, but it had cooled a potentially revolutionary situation. It was also justified from a business perspective because it had produced increased earnings. Kennedy's major argument was that Roosevelt had saved capitalism, not through socialism, but by his middle-of-the-road liberalism. Kennedy wrote:

> An organized functioning society requires a planned economy. The more complex the society the greater the demand for planning. Otherwise there results a haphazard and inefficient method of social control, and in the absence of planning the law of the jungle prevails.[160]

The New Deal's approach to economic planning would end the cycle of depression and periodic unemployment, he predicted. But the return of the "Old Dealers" to power, the "rugged individualists," as Kennedy called them, would probably undo all of Roosevelt's good work.

As a piece of campaign literature, *I'm for Roosevelt* was impressive. It presented some well-conceived and interesting arguments, it cost only a dollar, it sold well, and it was generally well received. It is also valuable today for the insights it gives into the New Deal philosophy. But it was hardly a sound analysis of New Deal economic theory, which it embraced uncritically. Kennedy disregarded such questions as the unconstitutionality of the National Recovery Act and the more controversial New Deal experiments like Social Security. He ignored any broader explanations of economic improvement, attributing all to the New Deal instead, and remained silent about any limits on governmental planning.

The book's "lasting significance," predicted the *Saturday Review*, was "Kennedy's enthusiastic support" for more governmental authority.[161] Critics hurled charges of "un-American" and "communism" at the New Deal and questioned the soundness of Kennedy's argument for more "regulation" of the individual.[162] But the president was apparently pleased. "Dear Joe," Roosevelt's thank-you note began, "I'M FOR KENNEDY. The book is grand. I am delighted with it."[163] "I thought the manuscript splendid and that it will be of real service, not only from a campaign point of view but also as a distinct step in sane education of the country."[164] In two years the collaborator, Krock, would repudiate the book's main thesis because of Roosevelt's attack on business, and within five years the book's title and Roosevelt's thank-you note would mock their authors.[165]

As the tempo of the election picked up during the summer, so did business criticism of "That Man in the White House." The businessman's hatred of the New Deal obviously annoyed Kennedy, as he revealed to an interviewer at Hyannis Port. "Some of my friends in the business and financial world have told me that I might as well make up my mind I have had my last job from anyone in the business world once the book is published." He continued:

> I'm afraid some people are laying up bad trouble for themselves the way they are acting. The time when they could sit tight and write their own ticket is gone. You can't tell the public to go to Hell any more. Fifty men have run America. . . . The rest of America is demanding a share in the game and they'll get it. These fellows talk against the New Deal . . . but all their stock

prices and the indices of their own business operations show that they don't act on their talk. They don't mean what they say or they don't know what they mean.[166]

He proceeded to lecture the business community and to laud Roosevelt: "The total debt of the country is less today than when the New Deal started.... I regard Mr. Roosevelt definitely as the type of person who possesses the background and sympathies as well as the ability to perpetuate the things which have made this country great."[167]

In a spate of magazine articles and speeches, Kennedy put his case for Roosevelt's reelection before a hostile business community. The Democratic National Committee presented "A Businessman's Estimate of the New Deal," which Kennedy had written and published in the *Review of Reviews*. Kennedy described his feelings about the New Deal as ones of "gratitude for preserving our American system" and for creating a "perfectly amazing" economic recovery.[168] In another article, "The Administration and Business," published in the *New York Times Magazine*, Kennedy showed his campaign strategy. He was trying to drive a wedge between the established Wall Street executives who represented big business and those who presided over smaller and newer companies and were more inclined to support FDR. He condemned the former as "Economic Royalists," as the *few*—the "irresponsible wealthy who have no heed for the social obligations of money and power."[169]

The president's son James gave an insightful analysis of Kennedy's motive. He believed that his friend's willingness to criticize the Wall Street titans grew from his failure to be fully accepted by them. In fact, J. P. Morgan once told Kennedy that he was too busy to see him. Roosevelt thought that snubs like this explained Kennedy's ambition to be secretary of the treasury: If he could not be accepted by Wall Street businessmen, he would go around them.[170] No doubt this also explains why the Court of St. James's later appealed to Kennedy: It was one of the most prestigious and desirable positions in government service and traditionally the preserve of Brahmins.

New Dealer businessman Kennedy also took to the airwaves on behalf of the president and delivered three speeches in October, again written with the able assistance of columnist Arthur Krock. Receiving White House approval for his ideas, Kennedy cautioned small businessmen not to be "jockeyed into a position of antagonism to the rest of the nation because a few stuffed shirts have lost their silk hats." Kennedy declared:

> The most fundamental dogma of Americanism was that to become rich was not only a worthy aim in itself but the fulfillment of a beneficent duty towards the community.... Mr. Roosevelt has repeatedly inferred that if a man had attained financial success it did not necessarily follow that this man was either a better man or a more useful citizen.

This widespread transition in values has "debunked the millionaire as a hero," Kennedy declared.[171]

Upon Roosevelt's urging, Kennedy agreed to organize a series of banquets for businessmen on the president's behalf. This was an arduous task since the invitations were unwelcome or unappreciated and many businessmen declined, often on the silliest of pretexts. The dinners were held in cities throughout the country in October. Their high point was Roosevelt's dinner speech by telephone from Washington. Another indication of the low esteem in which business held Roosevelt was the short list of names of potential contributors to his reelection. The list had been prepared for Kennedy's use by Daniel Roper, the secretary of commerce, and comprised only some fifty names.[172]

Although Kennedy was a success as emissary to the business community, his usefulness to Roosevelt as a prominent Catholic layman was seriously called into question when he once again accepted the nearly impossible task of placating Father Charles Coughlin, and the even harder one of reconciling priest and president. Kennedy, in his Rolls Royce, picked Coughlin up at the railway station early in the morning on September 10, 1935, and drove him to Hyde Park for "a social visit" with FDR. After "the Padre" made breakfast for the trio, they had a seven-hour conversation that rambled from the recent assassination of Huey Long to Coughlin's scheme to abolish the Federal Reserve System and to his charge that the Democrats were soft on communism. But the stalemate between the two old adversaries, priest and president, continued.[173] Coughlin's request to name his own candidate to a federal judgeship in Detroit, forwarded by Kennedy, was ignored by the president.[174]

Coughlin intrigued Kennedy. He was fascinated by Coughlin's demagoguery on the radio and by his use of power.[175] Though they frequently disagreed on politics, they had a liking for each other. Early in the 1936 campaign, the priest interrupted one of his blistering attacks on "Franklin Double-Crossing Roosevelt," "liar," "betrayer," and "scab,"[176] to praise Kennedy as "a shining star among the dim 'knights' of the present administration's activities."[177]

Kennedy was troubled by Coughlin's wild tirades against the president. They stirred up the fear of communism among Catholics and damaged Roosevelt's political position, especially in states necessary for a Democratic victory in the 1936 election. "There is nothing new in the situation," Kennedy told Robert Bingham, ambassador to the Court of St. James's; "it's the same old stuff."[178] Kennedy's credentials as a distinguished Roman Catholic enabled him to lead an effective counterattack against Coughlin's vicious attacks against Roosevelt during the campaign in the fall. Addressing members of the Boston business community, Kennedy jabbed at the priest's National Union for Social Justice by describing the president as "a God-fearing ruler who has given his people an increased measure of social justice." "I resent the efforts made for low, political purposes to confuse a Christian program of social justice with a Godless program of communism," Kennedy said against an unnamed enemy. Kennedy countered Coughlin's charge of "dictatorship" by arguing that in 1933 "we could have had a dictatorship in the twinkling of an eye—President Roosevelt's eye." But that threat had passed. If there had been any kind of a dictatorship, "the words 'liar' and 'dictator' would have been uttered only once." Kennedy's vigorous defense of the president ended his collaboration with Coughlin.

On November 5, 1936, two days after the election in which Roosevelt had carried every state except Maine and Vermont, the Kennedys went to Hyde Park, accompanied by Eugenio Cardinal Pacelli, the papal secretary of state who would one day be Pope Pius XII.[179] Those speculating on the nature of the trip believed that Father Coughlin would be a principal topic of conversation. Though the discussion between president and cardinal has not been made public, Coughlin later said that he believed that they had made an agreement: In return for his shutting up, the United States would establish a special presidential emissary in Rome.[180]

Two days later, on November 7, 1936, Coughlin announced to his audience that because of Roosevelt's landslide in the election and the decisive defeat of his own political organization, the National Union for Social Justice (NUSJ), formed in 1934, he was withdrawing from any further radio programs. A "very wise" decision, Kennedy thought.[181] Henceforth Coughlin's NUSJ would maintain a "policy of silence" with respect to Roosevelt's administration, a most unusual position.[182] Coughlin ceased his radio broadcasts in 1936 but resumed them two years later; they ended for good in 1940. In 1942, his weekly paper, *Social Justice*, was closed down when a special grand jury was established to investigate charges of sedition and Coughlin was silenced, much to the relief of Bishop Gallagher's successor, Archbishop Edward Mooney, Coughlin's dogged ecclesiastical superior who had been desperately trying to muzzle him.[183] In December 1939 President Roosevelt appointed Myron C. Taylor "Personal Representative of the President to His Holiness Pope Pius XII."[184]

Kennedy hoped his extensive campaign efforts would win him a Cabinet post in Roosevelt's second administration, and he still dreamed of occupying the Treasury. But FDR "wouldn't have it." He told Jim Farley: "I couldn't put Joe Kennedy in [Morgenthau's] place . . . because Joe would want to run the Treasury in his own way, contrary to my plans and views."[185] Furthermore, the Roosevelts and the Morgenthaus were close friends and Dutchess County neighbors. To request the secretary's resignation would have been unthinkable. Instead, Kennedy received an SOS from the president in February 1937 asking him to accept the "dirty" job of chairing the new Maritime Commission and trying to revive the reputation and prestige of the Merchant Marine. "Such is the penalty," wrote Arthur Krock, "of having once performed a miracle."[186]

"I am very anxious to have the U.S. Maritime Commission appointed and functioning at the earliest possible date," Roosevelt wrote to Kennedy on February 26, 1937:

> I am naturally anxious that in its organizing stage the commission shall have the advice and help of the most outstanding person available. My thoughts have turned to you and although I know that you are not anxious to return to public service, I am writing to ask your favorable consideration of my desire to appoint you as Chairman of the Commission.[187]

"I accept the appointment," Kennedy wrote back a few days later (March 2, 1937). It was made official on April 16, 1937.[188] Rose Kennedy attributed Roosevelt's decision to appoint her husband to a "long skein of circumstances," from their first meeting in 1916 when the president was the assistant secretary of the navy and Kennedy was the Fore River shipyard manager. Their prior association "made Joe the President's first and logical choice."[189]

Although Kennedy feigned hesitation before accepting the assignment, the old Roosevelt charm and his personal appeal proved to be as potent as ever. For two weeks running, FDR arranged to have a limousine pick Kennedy up at the Washington airport and whisk him off to the White House. There he was coaxed and cajoled.[190] Kennedy was won over, delighted to be back in public life. In a note to John Boettinger, Roosevelt's son-in-law, Kennedy jokingly complained: "I give up my business, give up my leisure to take up the most unworkable bill I ever read in my life, but you know that man's winning ways. It is pretty good when you can give up a perfectly good reputation and throw it into the ash can when you can be of service."[191]

Kennedy agreed to stay just long enough to put the commission together and to carry out Roosevelt's orders. They were to revamp the entire system and write a report for Congress that would allow it to pass legislation outlawing the current abuses and to draft policy to control the commission's future growth.[192] "For the first time, America's merchant marine problems are in the hands of a two-fisted, fighting, sandy-gray-haired Irishman with blue eyes, Joseph P. Kennedy, who made a rip-snorting success out of a previous job every one said was impossible," Boake Carter wrote in his column for the *Daily Mirror*.[193] Carter predicted that Kennedy would gain another success.

"This is the toughest job I ever handled in my life, without any reservations whatever," the new commissioner said.[194] "As head of the new National Maritime Commission, Mr. Kennedy has a job that makes other government chiefs in Washington shudder." They should, the *New Republic* wrote.[195] Congress had created the National Maritime Commission in the Maritime Act of 1936, legislation without equal in its looseness, unintelligible standards, and lack of safeguards, as the *New Republic* described it. The purpose of the agency was to rescue American shipping from its habitual malaise, something it badly needed. "The brutal truth is that the American Merchant Marine has been living off its fat for the past 15 years," the commissioner declared.[196]

Kennedy's new job thrust him into the bloody battleground between management and labor and the various unions struggling to control American shipping. At one point Kennedy was put in an anti-union position by arresting and prosecuting fourteen striking crewmen of the S.S. *Algic* who refused to work with scab labor in the port of Montevideo. Joseph Curran, the president of the militant National Maritime Union, threatened to "get Kennedy's scalp."[197] In response to Roosevelt's attempt to moderate Kennedy's stance, he informed the president that if Kennedy accepted FDR's compromise, "'We'll land in the _____' [At which mention of the ignoble but functional edifice to which Kennedy was wont to refer, came a delighted roar . . . from the other end of the wire]," wrote Arthur Krock, who overheard their spirited conversation.[198] The arrest of the crewmen led to a Senate investigation into "communistic influences" in the maritime industry and the union's demand to get Kennedy "summary [*sic*] dismissed."[199]

Carter's prediction that Kennedy would be successful was right. Kennedy's contribution to the Maritime Commission was significant. Although he stayed at the commission for less than a year, resigning to take the ambassadorship, it was enough time for him to transform it, to revise the subsidy list completely, and to create better working conditions. In his 40,000-word, hard-boiled, blunt report to Congress in November 1937, Kennedy called for schools to train American seamen and for the compulsory mediation of grievances. The *New York Times* called it "one of the finest reports of its kind."[200] It provided the foundation for the commission's policy for several years. With his administration and organizational talent, Kennedy had breathed new life into American shipping. It henceforth would be conducted on a more businesslike and profitable basis despite its ongoing problems with instability in the labor force and increasing shipbuilding costs, which he warned about in his letter of resignation to the president.[201] His colleague Rear Admiral Emory Scott Land regarded him as "an outstanding administrator, executive and financier."[202] Kennedy therefore completed "another hectic stretch of government service," he wrote in his memoirs, and was no doubt relieved to move on.[203]

"I want to . . . express my appreciation, so generally shared, for the fine work you have done," the president wrote to him. "You have maintained your justly earned reputation of being a two-fisted, hard-bitting [*sic*] executive."[204] The magazines and newspapers were also laudatory. The *Boston Herald* called Kennedy "Roosevelt's trouble shooter," "who dares to say no to the President" and is often consulted by him.[205] *Time* called Kennedy FDR's "most effective and trusted extra-Cabinet friend."[206] The *New York Journal* called Kennedy the "ace trouble shooter of the Roosevelt administration" and praised him for creating a "renaissance" in the American Merchant Marine.[207]

During his months at the commission, Kennedy kept giving broad hints about the long-sought-after Treasury position. When they evoked no response from FDR, he began to cast about for something else.[208] "To continue where I am is certainly a waste of whatever talents I possess because, with the five-man commission and the outline that we have made for the future, it is silly for me to sit around there and waste my time," he wrote to Jimmy Byrnes.[209]

As a shrewd Wall Street businessman, Kennedy was also more and more disturbed by the economic climate in 1937 and by the "Roosevelt recession." "We're going to have another crash!" Kennedy predicted to James Roosevelt.[210] With the advice of Kennedy and Morgenthau, the president had balanced the budget by trimming federal expenditures. But he also raised taxes, thereby, it was argued, preventing business from compensating for reduced federal spending. Kennedy publicly opposed the tax policy and apparently felt it was responsible for the recession. Yet he also told the New York Economic Club to "'stop bellyaching,' stop saying Roosevelt and the administration were 'no good.' . . . Whether they liked it or not, Mr.

Roosevelt was going to be in office for three more years." Businessmen should cooperate with the president in his efforts to improve the economic situation. As for himself, Kennedy said, he was "more of a New Dealer than ever."[211] His speech made many of his conservative friends question his sincerity, particularly those to whom he had "bellyached" privately about various aspects of the New Deal. "Joe wins the 1937 China Egg diamond belt prize for this one," wrote columnist Frank Kent, a Kennedy intimate, to Barnard Baruch, implying that Kennedy had been trying to curry favor with Roosevelt.[212] Kent knew about the imminent vacancy at the Court of St. James's in London and of Kennedy's ambition to fill it.

For months it had been rumored that the ambassador there, Robert Worth Bingham, had taken a medical leave to return to the United States in the spring of 1937. By late fall he had been hospitalized again. The Kennedys knew that Bingham, whom Rose described as "a most competent and respected man," was gravely ill and on the verge of resigning. Rose loyally supported her husband's ambition. "I felt that Joe deserved something better, something really special, . . . and I told him so," she wrote in her memoirs. The Kennedys discussed the situation with administration confidants and with trusted newsmen like Arthur Krock. They ruled out other Cabinet posts as uninteresting. A high-level ambassadorship to a non-English-speaking country was impossible, given Kennedy's tin ear; that left only London. "Thus the suitable possibilities really were reduced to only one post, that of being ambassador to Great Britain," Rose recalled. So it was settled within the Kennedy family; all eyes turned to London, the most prestigious of all diplomatic posts. The next task was to convince Roosevelt.

When Kennedy returned to Cape Cod on the weekends to escape Washington's heat and the commissioner's job, Mrs. Kennedy would ask, "What has the President said?" "Couldn't you tell him what you want?" Joe would say, "Well, I can't just walk into the office of the President of the United States and say 'I want to be ambassador to England.'"[213] Rose Kennedy believed that a deal had been struck behind the scenes. If Kennedy "did his usual excellent job at the Maritime Commission the next step beyond would be the ambassadorship," she wrote in her memoirs. So sure was Kennedy of the appointment that by the fall of 1937 he had not only confided it to his wife but to his two eldest college-age sons, so that they could make plans. At last, Kennedy would have his revenge for the Porcellian, for Cohasset, and for all the other putdowns he had endured.

The ambassadorship to the Court of St. James's was the most important diplomatic post, to whom the most distinguished and respected men had been sent, including five who were to become American presidents: John Adams, the first ambassador to the Court of St. James's; his son, John Quincy Adams; James Monroe; Martin Van Buren; and James Buchanan.[214] London was the best European "listening post," in part because it drew the most able diplomats from every country. It was particularly significant for Americans, because their cultural kinship with the British made contacts and the exchange of information easy.[215] The ambassadorship was also the monopoly of the Brahmins and represented the summit of their social ambition. That was reason enough for Kennedy; he was determined to have it. Thenceforward, he and his family would be able to return the snubs. Speaking as one Irishman about another, presidential assistant Tom Corcoran explained Kennedy's determination to a perplexed Secretary of the Interior Harold Ickes: "You don't understand the Irish. London has always been a closed door to [Kennedy]. As Ambassador of the United States, [he] will have all doors open to him."[216]

Throughout the spring and into the fall of 1937, Kennedy campaigned fiercely for the job. He made his wishes known to FDR directly and indirectly through Jimmy Roosevelt and James Farley. He also lobbied friends in Congress, in the White House, and in the press. "Everybody seems to be for me but the White House," he told a senator from Virginia. "Poor old felt-minded Joe," said Frank Kent. "What a sucker he is going to look if he does not get this appointment."[217]

Roosevelt realized that Kennedy was disgruntled. James Roosevelt recalled his father's telling him: "We've got to do something for old Joe, but I don't know what. He wants what he can't have, but there must be something we can give him he'll be happy with. Why don't you go see him and feel him out and see what you can come up with?"[218]

When Kennedy told James Roosevelt what he wanted, even James was taken aback. "I really liked Joe, but he was a crusty old cuss and I couldn't picture him as an ambassador, especially to England." "Oh, c'mon, Joe, you don't want that," the president's son said. "Oh yes I do," Kennedy replied. "I've been thinking about it and I'm intrigued by the thought of being the first Irishman to be ambassador from the United States to the Court of St. James's." James Roosevelt dutifully promised to relay the message to the president. "Sure enough," he recalled, "when I passed it on to father, he laughed so hard he almost toppled from his wheelchair." London was out of the question, FDR replied, when he had caught his breath. But before James Roosevelt could give Kennedy the bad news, the president became "intrigued" with the precedent-shattering idea. It would be a great way "of twisting the lion's tail," he decided.[219] When Mrs. Roosevelt lamented FDR's intention of appointing "that awful Joe Kennedy" to the Court of St. James's, a buoyant president threw his head back and laughed. Kennedy's appointment would be "a great joke, the greatest joke in the world."[220]

Few things could be more likely to confound His Majesty's Government than the appointment of an Irish American Catholic to the Court of St. James's. But Roosevelt relished the dramatic and the unexpected. He had other reasons, besides, for making such a precedent-shattering appointment. Kennedy's untraditional background was a political asset for FDR's administration. As an outsider, Kennedy could be counted on to view Britain as a nation of shopkeepers, not literary gentlemen, and would presumably be more immune to British charms than American ambassadors traditionally known for their thoroughgoing Anglophilia. Roosevelt also believed that he could use him as a disinterested critic of appeasement, an eavesdropper, a candid reporter, a spokesman—Roosevelt's eyes and ears.[221] Furthermore, if war were to break out in Europe, Kennedy's presence in London could help overcome the isolationism and anti-British sentiment of the northeastern Irish-Catholic Democrats, who were important to Roosevelt's political coalition. Besides, the president valued the big-happy-family image the Kennedys and their nine handsome children presented. Moreover, Kennedy was rich, a prerequisite for any ambassador, and he had cultivated many of the leading British economic and political officials he had met on his 1935 tour. And certainly Kennedy deserved a handsome reward for his service as a campaigner and contributor to the Party, for his political fence-mending and eager brainstorming, for his willingness to serve as an emissary to the business and Irish American communities.

Another likely factor in Kennedy's appointment was his being something of an obstacle should FDR decide to run for an unprecedented third term. Washington gossips claimed that Kennedy wanted to be the first Catholic president of the United States. *Liberty Magazine* ran a lead story in 1938: "Will Kennedy Run for President?"[222] But it seems unlikely that Roosevelt viewed Kennedy as so great a political rival that he decided to "exile" him. Certainly the astute president knew that the road to political power in the twentieth century was not through an ambassadorship: An ambassadorship could assuage a man's ego, but not a man's lust for power. It is more likely that he feared Kennedy as a critic of the faltering New Deal, especially among the president's opponents on Wall Street. Furthermore, the president warily regarded him as unpredictable and a little frightening. "No one can tell what an Irishman will do," he once remarked to Morgenthau.[223]

Thus it was decided. Kennedy would get London, but at the cost of putting up with the president's ribbing. "Joe, would you mind taking your pants down?" FDR asked as Kennedy was ushered into the Oval Office in the fall of 1937. Had he heard the president right? He had indeed, the president told him. Kennedy let down his pants. "Joe, just look at your legs. You are just about the most bowlegged man I have ever seen," Roosevelt teased. "Don't you know that the ambassador to the Court of St. James's has to go through an induction ceremony in which he wears knee britches and silk stockings? Can you imagine how you'll look? When photos of our new ambassador appear . . . we'll be a laughingstock. You're just not right for the job, Joe."

Kennedy asked for two weeks to get a special letter from the British government excusing him from the time-honored tradition. FDR gave his permission. "Joe pulled up his pants and his dignity and went on his way, leaving father chuckling contentedly," James Roosevelt recalled."[224] Kennedy had called Roosevelt's bluff, and Roosevelt agreed to name him ambassador at a yearly salary of $17,500.[225]

The playful president conferred on Kennedy the provisional degree of Doctor of Oratory and the accolade of "The Silver Tongue" from the "J. Russell Young School of Expression," as a twentieth-century embodiment of the tradition of Demosthenes and Daniel Webster. The diploma was signed by the president himself, class of 1936. It would cease to be "provisional" once Kennedy demonstrated that he still "speaks our mother tongue in its full American purity free from all foreign entanglements."[226]

"I haven't any idea how well I will get along abroad, either from the point of view of doing much for the country, or doing a job of which my friends will feel proud, but if I don't get the results that I feel are necessary, I would get out at once," Kennedy wrote to Jimmy Byrnes. "I will stick along with this Administration as long as I can do any good or as long as I have the confidence of the leaders, regardless of the inconveniences that accrue to me."[227]

Worried that the Foreign Office would object to Kennedy's Catholicism, Roosevelt had second thoughts.[228] He sent his son to Marwood to see whether Kennedy could be talked out of the ambassadorship. Would he take Commerce instead of London? "Well, I'm not going to," Kennedy replied. "FDR promised me London, and I told Jimmy to tell his father that's the job, and the only one, I'll accept."[229]

Roosevelt, too, had second thoughts about the wisdom of the appointment in general. "He considered Kennedy a very dangerous man [he told Morgenthau] . . . and he was going to send him to England as Ambassador with the distinct understanding that the appointment was only good for six months and that, furthermore, by giving him this appointment, any obligation that he had to Kennedy was paid for."[230] When Morgenthau reminded him of the sensitivity of the British post and of Kennedy's indiscreet criticism of Roosevelt's administration, FDR replied, "I have made arrangements to have Joe Kennedy watched hourly—and the first time he opens his mouth and criticizes me, I will fire him."[231] "If a policy disagreement ever arose between them," FDR's son later said, "he would simply shift Kennedy to another job."[232]

The ever-faithful Krock wrote to Kennedy on December 8, 1937, the day before the story on Kennedy's appointment broke on the front page of the *New York Times*, and told him that he had received Jimmy Roosevelt's permission for an exclusive scoop, on the understanding that Kennedy not be cited as its source. Jimmy also promised to bear full responsibility with his father if any questions arose about it.[233] The publication of the story embarrassed Roosevelt's administration because it was reported in the press before Bingham had officially resigned. Apparently Jimmy Roosevelt had failed to get the president's permission before telling Krock.

FDR was livid. "You know, I've been annoyed by stories that I appointed Joe before Robert Bingham resigned," he complained to Farley. "Actually the late Ambassador had said he wanted to resign. He telephoned from abroad saying he wanted to come home for a physical examination and would resign, but wanted to defer his resignation until the check-up. He wanted to go back to close his affairs at the embassy. The story by Arthur Krock in the *New York Times* was annoying to me and to Bingham in the hospital where he died."[234] Roosevelt even accused the journalist of hastening Bingham's death.[235]

Among American officials and public figures, the reaction to Kennedy's appointment was generally favorable. Bingham himself said he was pleased, although State Department officials greeted the news with shrugs of disbelief and some Bostonians sniffed in disdain. Senator Key Pittman congratulated Kennedy on his appointment and told him that he would have the pleasure of presenting his nomination to the Senate for confirmation.[236] Senator Jimmy Byrnes had mixed feelings about Kennedy's selection. He thought that the appointment was "unwise." "I do not believe you can promote peace on earth by sending an Irishman to

London," he told Arthur Krock, who had anticipated criticism over the appointment. And, Byrnes warned, "you know what kind of language that fellow speaks." Kennedy will have to clean up his language, which will make our lives much less joyful, although it may qualify him for the Holy Name Society, he added. Nevertheless he did promise Krock that he would withdraw his statement objecting to Kennedy's confirmation, and remarked that he intended to give him a copy of Emily Post's latest book of etiquette.[237] Krock, too, could hardly wait to see the effect of Kennedy's vocabulary on Britain's more proper folk and shuddered to think what use he would make of Mrs. Post's book.[238]

"Joe Kennedy will interest you very much," the American ambassador in Rome, William Phillips, wrote to Sir Arthur Murray, an old Roosevelt friend from his days as assistant British military attaché in Washington during World War I. Kennedy "has a striking personality and is typical of that dynamic quality which all Americans are supposed to have."[239] Eleanor Roosevelt was gracious. She congratulated Kennedy on the appointment, and she warned him: "I know that it will not be an easy job and I feel sure that this is why the President is sending you, but I do think it will be interesting and there will be many things which you will enjoy."[240] Kennedy agreed that the job would not be an easy one, but promised the First Lady: "I shall do my best with it and endeavor to justify the confidence which the President has placed in me."[241]

The American press reaction to Kennedy's appointment was overwhelmingly favorable. The *Boston Globe* chortled: "The little clique of high hats in Secretary Hull's department will have to accustom themselves to dealing with a red-blooded ambassador. Joe Kennedy will not have to be warned not to let the Britishers pull the wool over his eyes."[242]

New York Times correspondent Arthur Krock reported an incredible charge made by the president's conservative critics: Kennedy's appointment to London was part of a diabolical plot by Roosevelt to establish a dictatorship by removing Kennedy's restraining hand on the president. Kennedy scoffed at this allegation. Krock regretted that "so wise, practical and influential a Presidential counselor" would have little chance in London to keep the president personally informed of his business views. He concluded, true to form, that Kennedy's appointment was a blessing because "close Anglo-American cooperation in many fields may be achieved in part by his efforts and such a consummation would be of far more importance than anything he could do by staying here."[243]

The *Washington Times* wrote a most glowing endorsement of Kennedy, which it would later repudiate. He will "make a great ambassador," because the British will like his "honesty, his passion for fairness and his thoughtfulness for the most insignificant person around him." Further, the editorial claimed, Kennedy was appointed for several "behind-the-scenes reasons." These included the administration's policy of countering the growth of dictatorships in Europe, the Far East, and South America and moving closer to the Western democracies by stabilizing the dollar, renewing the negotiations over war debt, and establishing a trade treaty.[244]

The British reaction among public officials and journalists was mixed. Colonel Josiah Wedgwood, a Liberal member of Parliament, completely disapproved of Roosevelt's decision. He gave his sage and prophetic views to Harold Ickes, who shared much of his liberal philosophy. "At a time when we should be sending the best that we have to Great Britain, we have not done so," Ickes wrote, recalling Wedgwood's views. "We have sent a rich man, untrained in diplomacy, unlearned in history and politics . . . a great publicity seeker and . . . apparently ambitious to be the first Catholic President of the United States."[245] Yet Sir Ronald Lindsay, the British ambassador to the United States, informed his government that even those in the United States who disapproved of Kennedy's appointment "regret his departure . . . because they regard him as the sole surviving counsellor of moderation to President Roosevelt." They predicted dire consequences "now that Mr. Roosevelt is left without any such controlling influences."[246]

But in Britain, the more judicious *Times* greeted Kennedy's appointment as ushering in "a new era in the history of the American Embassy in London." It emphasized that he was one of the president's closest business advisers and dismissed his lack of experience as a bar to success. It also predicted that Kennedy would be a "peculiarly authoritative envoy" during the upcoming Anglo-American trade negotiations.[247] *The Economist* had greeted the announcement of Kennedy's appointment as holding out "the greatest hope that the recent substantial improvements in the relations between the two Governments may be not merely maintained but further extended."[248]

But the *Daily News* saw it quite differently. "Irish-Catholic Joseph Patrick Kennedy, hard-boiled, sophisticated, trouble-shooter of the New Deal, emerged tonight as the Crown Prince of the Roosevelt regime—FDR's personal selection as his successor to White House honors in 1940." The president was "trying out his 1940 Presidential candidates in heats."[249]

In contrast to all the praise, the new appointee designate received a thoughtful, prophetic letter from Boake Carter, a reporter who knew Kennedy well.

The job of U.S. Ambassador to the Court of St. James [*sic*] is not merely a business job. . . . It is a surgeon's job. It is a job where the most delicate surgery is needed, where a man who had been trained in surgery should operate. . . .

You are a sincere man, Joe. You are a man of courage. You possess that great faith that so many Irishmen have—the faith that no matter what he tackles, he can't be licked. You are an honest man. But the job of Ambassador to London needs not only honesty, sincerity, faith and an abounding courage—it needs skill brought by years of training. And that, Joe, you simply don't possess.

Do not think me unkind in saying that. On the contrary, I'm trying to save you some heart aches. I don't condemn the trolley car driver because he cannot pilot a plane off the ground. . . . I do not condemn Kennedy, the organizer, the businessman, because he is not a trained diplomatic surgeon.

But, I say this to you in all sincerity from the bottom of my heart—it takes a mighty big man to know when a job is to [*sic*] big for him—or let us say, when there is a job before him which he knows is not his type of job.

You've got enough horse sense to know that with the experience you've had, and the experience that this sort of job demands, in view of the fact that the probable welfare of 130,000,000 lives may hang on the results of the conduct of that post, you tempt all the Gods of the World in diving into the Court of St. James [*sic*] as an expert. Joe, in so complicated a job, there is no place for amateurs. . . . For if you don't realize that soon enough, you're going to be hurt as you were never hurt in your life.[250]

But Kennedy did lack the "horse sense" to see that he had neither the temperament nor the training for the job and to realize that it was "too big for him." His remarkable record of achievements by the age of only forty-nine, his utter confidence in his seemingly limitless ability to do anything and to create even grander accomplishments, his festering resentment at snubs and his desire for revenge, and his overweening ambition for himself and his family led him to "tempt all the Gods of the world" by accepting the ambassadorship. Had he followed Carter's advice and said no, the history of his dynasty and perhaps even the history of his country would have been quite different. Had he said no, there was no reason to assume that he would not have had another prestigious government position in domestic affairs. But his mercurial temperament; his habit of equating his country's welfare with his own and his family's; his tendency to personalize events and to interpret them in terms of personalities, not principles; his inability to recognize his limitations and to grasp that the ambassadorship was not a job for the amateur—all contributed to his eventual public humiliation and to the diplomatic embarrassment that was to destroy his career in public service. He would be brought down by his own fatal flaw. It was simply not in Joseph Kennedy's character to say no to the honor of being the first Irish American and first Roman Catholic to be appointed ambassador to the Court of St. James's.[251]

Kennedy considered the new post a challenge and hoped that if he performed admirably in London, he might still be appointed secretary of the treasury.[252] He relished breaking precedent and enjoyed the prestige of his new position. For the rest of his life he would be referred to as "the ambassador." Writing in his "Diplomatic Memoir," Kennedy noted that the Americans accepted the widespread assumption of British social superiority as an article of faith and doubted that their own diplomats could be trusted to remain American. He believed that the United States, as the "younger and more impressionable" member of the alliance, was "too easily persuaded by the British" to follow the leadership of Mother Britain—a well-founded attitude, Kennedy observed, inherent in the Anglo-American diplomatic tradition and illustrated both before and during World War II. He obviously assumed that he would have no difficulty confounding this tradition and proudly noted that his Irish and Catholic heritage and his "outspoken vocabulary" would inoculate him against British charm.[253]

"I want to say now," Kennedy wrote to FDR, "that I don't know what kind of a diplomat I shall be, probably rotten, but I promise to get done for you those things that you want done. Rose and I are deeply grateful."[254] Indeed she was; she had an opportunity for revenge on "the nice people of Boston." Her new position as the ambassador's wife elevated her social status well beyond being the mayor's daughter. Never missing a beat when it came to sizing up the political and social implications of events, Rose wrote to Roosevelt: "I do want to thank you for the wonderful appointment you have given to Joe. The children and I feel deeply honored, delighted and thrilled, and we want you to know that we do appreciate the fact that you have made possible this great rejoicing."[255] Kennedy revealed his motives to a friend in an oft-repeated statement: "I've got nine kids and the only thing I can leave them that will mean anything is my good name and reputation."[256] That legacy seemed safe enough as he sailed for London.

Whatever his political debts to Kennedy, FDR's levity in appointing him to such an important post during such unstable international times illustrated rashness and a certain irresponsibility. Although he was distrustful and resentful of Kennedy, whose views on foreign policy were ill defined and a repetition of the isolationist sentiment of men like Hearst and Coughlin, Roosevelt apparently expected that his new emissary would support his foreign policy with the same loyal fervor as he had the New Deal. He also assumed that his more sweeping and encompassing view of the country's welfare could contain Kennedy's smaller and more parochial vision of his and his family's own interest. Roosevelt, ever famous for his shrewdness, would be shown by events how poorly he had judged his new ambassador. Jimmy Roosevelt recalled: "Father never dreamed that Joe might put ideology above loyalty."[257] But Roosevelt should have.

Kennedy was to be an unusual envoy. Soon after appointing him, Roosevelt arranged a White House meeting between the new diplomat and his titular boss, courtly Cordell Hull. As Hull sat there sizing him up, Kennedy mentioned that he had had a conversation over lunch with Arthur Krock. The two were discussing the revelation that Roosevelt's new Supreme Court justice, Hugo Black, had been a member of the Alabama Ku Klux Klan. Krock expressed shock and dismay that Black would fail to disclose such a fact to the president. Roosevelt leaned back in his chair as Kennedy was talking and asked, "Joe, when Krock said that, what did you say to Krock?" "I said to him," Kennedy responded, "if Marlene Dietrich asked you to make love to her, would you tell her you weren't much good at making love?" Roosevelt howled in laughter. Hull's mouth fell open as he just sat there, stunned and silent. Ever willing to spit at conventional ways and delighting in shocking people, Kennedy later gleefully described the scene. "Hull must have been saying to himself, 'My God, is this the kind of a guy we're going to send to the Court of St. James [*sic*]?'"[258]

On February 18, 1938, Roosevelt's ambassador took the oath of office from Justice Stanley Reed in the Oval Room of the White House. FDR was there, along with a band of photographers. A few days after the swearing-in ceremony, on February 22, Kennedy visited the president at Hyde Park for a lengthy farewell luncheon accompanied by the usual good-natured gossip and cheerful teasing over knee breeches. "Flit lightly" over the subject, FDR admonished, if his tradition-minded mother should ask him whether he planned to abolish the custom of wearing them. She just might refuse to serve them lunch if she did not like Kennedy's answer, the president teased. After lunch, Kennedy and Roosevelt retired to the quiet of the president's study to discuss the uneasy situation in Europe and to speak "generally" about foreign affairs to his new ambassador.[259]

During the two months before he left to take up his post in London, the events on the international scene had changed dramatically, the new ambassador wrote in his "Diplomatic Memoir." The dictators had grown increasingly menacing on the Continent and deeply disturbing to Roosevelt, who wanted to restore peace and order in Europe and throughout the world. Japan had expanded into the Far East and continued to persecute and oppress Americans in China despite promises to safeguard their rights.[260] Spain was in the throes of a vicious civil war as the fascist General Francisco Franco's Nationalist forces, aided by the Germans and Italians, were gaining victories over the democratically elected Republican forces. Austria's independence was compromised when Germany's chancellor Adolf Hitler demanded that the Austrian chancellor Kurt von Schuschnigg appoint Nazi leader Arthur Seyss-Inquart to the post of minister of security, giving him control over the country's police force. On February 20, 1938, Hitler announced that he had assumed the role of protector of the ten million Germans outside of Germany, an ominous statement for Austria and Czechoslovakia, and troubling to both Roosevelt and his new ambassador. And on that same day, just before Kennedy left for England, Britain's young foreign secretary, Anthony Eden, resigned his position. Kennedy noticed that FDR had considerable affection for him and seemed deeply disappointed by his resignation.[261] It looked to Kennedy that Benito Mussolini and his son-in-law, Count Dino Grandi, the Italian ambassador to London, had forced Eden to resign, and that this illustrated the growing influence of the dictators in international affairs. But Kennedy also knew that Eden had serious disagreements with Prime Minister Neville Chamberlain over his conduct of foreign policy regarding the United States and Italy, differences not made public at that time.

Eden's resignation on February 22, 1938, led Roosevelt to tell Kennedy of his proposal to convene a meeting of diplomats on Armistice Day in 1937 to urge a "return to the fundamental rules of international conduct."[262] He wanted to host a conference to devise the means by which countries would adhere to traditional principles of international diplomacy, to reduce armaments, to promote the economic welfare of all by removing economic barriers to trade, and to develop the world's resources. Roosevelt also informed Kennedy that he had sounded out Chamberlain on the feasibility of his plan in early January 1938 and told him that he wanted to establish "a policy of active, though unacknowledged, 'cooperation'" through parallel action with Britain and its appeasement policy.[263] The president, who still seemed to favor this scheme, Kennedy noted, had been forced to abandon it because of the nearly hysterical opposition of the State Department. In addition, Roosevelt had initially had a cold response from the prime minister, who feared that FDR's proposal would encourage Germany and Italy to delay a review of the issues that Chamberlain had been urging with Britain and France. His opposition further alienated him from Eden, who favored Roosevelt's proposal.[264]

"Joe, I still have not lost heart," FDR told him, seemingly without resentfulness at the prime minister. "If Chamberlain succeeds in pacifying the Dictators the time may soon come when my plan can be put into effect. The United States . . . cannot participate in any political settlements but it can, and I believe it will be able to, lead the world out of the economic morass in which it is floundering." Roosevelt blamed the worldwide economic crisis for creating other problems, a position with which his new ambassador was in complete agreement. "We shall have to mark time until we see whether or not Chamberlain accomplishes anything," the president told Kennedy.[265] But "be careful about one thing, Joe." "Don't forget that this country is determined to be neutral in the event of any war." We must not show favoritism to any country. "The United States must be kept out of any and all involvements abroad." Kennedy wrote in his diary: "The president's emphasis on neutrality had my fullest concurrence and I told him so."[266] Thus the views of the new ambassador and his president were in complete harmony with each other in the early stages of Kennedy's ambassadorship; their great divergence and bitter disagreement would come later.

At the news conference that day in his cramped office with Kennedy by his side, the president refused to speak off the record and gave a succinct "no comment" to reporters' questions about the effect on American foreign policy of the resignation of Anthony Eden and of Hitler's latest Reichstag address. Even Kennedy, normally so unreserved and outspoken, remained silent about the recent events in Europe and told inquiring reporters that he preferred to study the situation before commenting publicly.[267] Roosevelt's bon voyage gift was a photograph of himself, inscribed "To my old friend and new ambassador." The president granted him "every wish in the world" as he left to prepare to sail for England aboard the *Manhattan* along with the American ambassador to Poland, Anthony J. Drexel Biddle Jr. "I was on my way," Kennedy wrote.[268]

CHAPTER 2

The Lion's Mouth

O n February 23, 1938, five minutes before sailing, Kennedy held a brief press conference in his crowded stateroom aboard the *Manhattan*, surrounded by friends and well-wishers like Jimmy Roosevelt and Mrs. Kennedy and eight of the Kennedy children who had come to see him off. Also present were old Boston Irish friends of the family, rounded up by Loretta, Joe's sister, who had come to celebrate one of their own in his prestigious role.[1] The new ambassador told newsmen that he had not received "any instructions" from the president. "I'm just a babe, being thrown into . . . ," he began. "The lion's mouth?" someone supplied. Kennedy gave a cautious grin.[2] Gossips who had been speculating that Kennedy's appointment would last no longer than a year and that he would be dealing primarily with England's war debt and the proposed Anglo-American Trade Agreement must have been disappointed with his discreet silence.[3]

Kennedy's quip at his shipboard press conference may have been prophetic. He had been sent to England to represent a virtually policyless nation during a time of considerable international tension. Roosevelt had been repeatedly thwarted by isolationist public sentiment and congressional opposition in his attempts to seek a politically acceptable way to deal with the international crisis in Europe and the Far East. He had withdrawn from making diplomatic overtures after Chamberlain rejected his mid-January 1938 proposal.[4] The president also faced a suspicious and rebellious Congress leery of attempts to revise the neutrality laws to allow him to distinguish between victim and aggressor, with the right to provide arms to the former.[5] Domestic problems like the seven-month recession that had produced four million unemployed were far more compelling than events overseas. FDR was hence politically immobilized and distracted and unable to exert more control over foreign policy in the winter and spring of 1938. Thus the country's foreign policy remained makeshift and ill-defined, characterized by dissembling and acquiescence to the popular national preference for a passive policy.

Now the diplomatic novice was set adrift, apparently without specific instructions, in the international confusion prevailing in Europe in 1938, as he was well aware.[6] In his "Diplomatic Memoir," Kennedy noted that his assignment was of a "necessarily unspecified nature," coming when American foreign policy had "no clear statement," and essentially had to be "somewhat general and scanty."[7] Nor were there any detailed instructions from the secretary of state except about topics already under negotiation between Britain and the United States, such as a treaty on trade; revision of the naval treaty and its escalation clause; differences over the mutual control of Canton and Enderbury, two islands in the Pacific useful in the air traffic; and the Treasury's stabilization agreement between Britain, France, and the United States.

International events were of less than compelling interest for Kennedy throughout the early and mid-1930s. So preoccupied was he with making a name for himself in public service and working ably in Roosevelt's campaigns that he took little opportunity to educate himself in the complicated issues or to understand the unstable alliances governing the international order. Nothing in his previous positions had prepared him for the art of diplomacy. His lack of training and interest in foreign affairs made it hard for him to grasp their significance, a bad omen for a new ambassador. His views on American foreign policy, such as they were, appeared to be undigested scraps of isolationist sentiment reminiscent of Hearst or Coughlin and reflected the fears of foreign-policy commitments and overseas adventures shared by many Americans. Kennedy's dominant concern in foreign affairs as in domestic policy would continue to be protecting his family. The events in London, Paris, Rome, or Berlin that occupied governments throughout the early and mid-1930s must have seemed far removed from the happy Kennedy family at Hyannis Port, Brookline, or Palm Beach.

There was a slight drizzle on that cold and dark day, March 1, 1938, when Kennedy's ship docked in Plymouth. Although he had left most of his family behind for the moment, the ambassador was accompanied by Harold Hinton, a young journalist from the *New York Times* and a colleague of Arthur Krock's. Hinton was to write Kennedy's speeches, serve as his liaison with the press, and act as his personal public relations man, an uncommon and controversial employee for an American ambassador.[8] Harvey Klemmer, whom Kennedy met at the Maritime Commission, also traveled with him. "We're going to London," his boss had told him, but "only to get the family in the *Social Register*. When that's done, we come on back and go out to Hollywood to make some movies and some money." Klemmer remembered that Kennedy was in high spirits throughout the voyage except when the two discussed the possibility of war. "Oh, Christ, Harvey, drop that war business," the new ambassador insisted. "You're just a pessimist." But Klemmer persisted. "No, its [sic] coming," he insisted. "There'll be war, and before its over, your sons are going to go out there and do and die like everyone else." Kennedy looked alarmed and changed the subject, Klemmer recalled.[9] "I'd hate to think how much money I would give up rather than sacrifice Joe and Jack in a war," he once said to their grandfather after becoming ambassador.[10]

When the party of reporters who greeted Kennedy in Plymouth asked the usual "fairly innocuous"[11] questions about Eden's resignation, the proposed Anglo-American Trade Agreement, and the British war debt, Kennedy's stock reply was "I will have to wait until I see what the situation is."[12] Although the weather conditions—the high winds and high waves—made him seem uncharacteristically nervous,[13] he made a good impression on the journalists, who liked his hearty good humor and noted that he had his president's "respect and confidence."[14]

Beneath Kennedy's gay exterior lurked a thoroughgoing streak of Irish pessimism. He told American newsmen in an off-the-record luncheon interview a few days after his arrival that he had the president's confidence only "temporarily" and that in their columns they could "make or break" him as a diplomat. England was the "bad boy" of foreign affairs, because "England will expect America to pull her chestnuts out of the fire." "I hope" he said, and foretold the future, "all you boys will be down to see me when I am recalled."[15] He wrote in the same vein to his old crony Jimmy Roosevelt:

> Well, old boy, I may not last long over here, but it is going to be fast and furious while it's on. My love to Missy and tell her the minute I get any scandal, I'll start a social column for her, and tell the boss that, leaving aside the Kennedy family, there are two things I am for—the U.S.A. and F.D.R. and you can put this last paragraph on the letter I write when I leave here.[16]

Kennedy settled into the palatial six-story, thirty-six-room American embassy. It had been given by J. P. Morgan and was just off Hyde Park in Grosvenor Square, at 14 Princes Gate. It was just barely big enough to accommodate all eleven Kennedys. It had only eight bedrooms—two single and six double. Rose Kennedy made room for everybody by taking over some of the thirteen bedrooms in the servants' quarters for the children and for guests.[17] Newsmen noted delightedly that the owner of the apartment building next door put up a sign that read, "Large Family Flats."[18] Kennedy's office, spacious and light, mortified him and filled him with a combination of horror and amusement. He gave Jimmy Roosevelt his impressions of his "beautiful blue silk room." "All I need to make it perfect is a Mother Hubbard dress and a wreath to make me Queen of the May. If a fairy didn't design this room, I never saw one in my life." He also deplored the building's design. "If there was ever a badly laid out building for which the United States government has to pay regular money, this tops it all."[19]

One problem Rose Kennedy was not able to overcome was the six-month quarantine of the family dogs—an Airedale and a poodle. The British enforced the quarantine, an embassy official explained, against "high and low" without class distinction or exception. Rose Kennedy's request to waive the quarantine "got turned down cold."[20]

On Kennedy's first days in London, he jotted down his firsthand impressions of the British, received well-wishers, made the expected courtesy calls on other ambassadors and dignitaries, and presented his credentials.[21] He decided to establish the practice of writing letters twice a week to a group of friends in a variety of professions. This had two purposes, he wrote in his memoir: One was to inform them of his candid reactions to people and events, and the other was for him to be kept informed of events in the United States.[22] No doubt there were other motives, such as ensuring a favorable press and keeping his name in the limelight.

Kennedy wrote to Krock the first in a series of many letters to him to thank him for "urging me to come here" and for "holding my hand during those uncertain days."[23] Kennedy also gave Jimmy Roosevelt a shrewd assessment of Britain's gloomy economic situation. "Being reasonably an expert in economic matters, I can tell you after forty-eight hours in this place, that England is faced with an economic problem that makes ours look like a tea party," Kennedy told him. "England has used up practically all of its aces." Only the armament program "is keeping the wolf from the door." Underneath, Britain is in a situation as dangerous as America's in 1929, he said, noting the huge debts, the high taxes, and the tariffs. "And boy, when [armament spending] stops they're in for it."[24]

The ambassador informed the State Department about his initial impressions and his informal chats with Halifax and Chamberlain. Kennedy described Eden's successor, Lord Halifax, the new foreign secretary, as a "tall, spare, ascetic-looking man."[25] In his impeccably tailored clothes, he bore the distinct look of the patrician with an "Olympian manner."[26] Kennedy would see much of this "efficient saint,"[27] with the patience of Job during his ambassadorial tenure,[28] "a sort of Jesus in long boots,"[29] appropriately nicknamed the "Holy Fox,"[30] a subtle play on his name.

At their first meeting on March 2, 1938, they discussed Eden's resignation and the disagreement between Eden and Chamberlain. Chamberlain, Halifax told Kennedy, believed that there really existed a serious opportunity for achieving a practical understanding with Germany and Italy and that they should be immediately approached; Eden had disagreed vehemently. Kennedy told Halifax that he inferred that Chamberlain's rejection of Roosevelt's proposal for a worldwide economic conference was an issue of contention as well. "No doubt that was hard for Eden to take," Halifax replied, "but the basic difference concerned the wisdom of attempting to make settlements with the dictator countries."[31]

Kennedy had his first meeting with Chamberlain three days later and left quite impressed by his "quiet and incisive" manner and, for a man of seventy, youthful appearance. He has "a strong character; one that could easily dominate a situation." And he possesses a "realistic practical mind."[32] As Chamberlain discussed his general policy, it was clear to the new ambassador that the prime minister assumed it was his responsibility to make concessions to Germany and Italy, "enduring adjustments," as the only way to avert a war. Chamberlain was disdainful of talk about collective security; it had little practical application. Countries threatened by Germany would not appeal for aid to the League of Nations but to France and England. "Therefore, what is the sense of talking about collective security?"[33] Although Chamberlain did express sympathy and support for Roosevelt's mid-January 1938 proposal "for a world-wide conference," he told Kennedy that he wanted political issues to take precedence over economic ones. The prime minister added that he did not expect anything from the United States. Chamberlain's attitude toward Americans was consistent. On December 17, 1937, he wrote to his sister Hilda: "It is always best & safest to count on *nothing* from the Americans except words."[34] Chamberlain realized that America's neutrality legislation and the mood of isolation throughout the country profoundly influenced much of what Roosevelt could and could not do in foreign policy. This fact made Chamberlain wary of America's intentions. "The Americans have a long way to go yet before they become helpful partners in world affairs," he told Hilda on August 29, 1937.[35] And even after Roosevelt's "quarantine" speech on October 5, 1937, Chamberlain thought that "after a lot of ballyhoo the Americans will somehow fade out & leave us to carry all the blame & the odium" and may make the Germans and the Italians draw closer to the Japanese.[36] Nevertheless, he was still willing to try "to educate American opinion to act more & more with us," he wrote on November 21, 1937.[37]

For his part, Kennedy, speaking candidly, said that Roosevelt and Secretary of State Hull were anxious to see a reduction in political tensions, but the American people were totally opposed to war and reluctant to engage in any foreign-policy commitments, particularly with Britain, their most likely ally in the event of war. The ambassador also pointed out that the trade treaty was now even more important for Britain than ever, given the weak economic conditions that Great Britain and the United States both faced; it would illustrate the best proof of the "concreteness" of Anglo-American friendship. Their interview ended pleasantly, Kennedy told Washington, and Chamberlain promised to meet with him and to keep him as well informed as practicable, an offer the ambassador quickly took up.[38] "I think I am now on a fairly understandable basis with both Halifax and the prime minister," Kennedy cabled Hull. "I have not sung any hopeful songs on Anglo-American relationship." He did, however, urge Chamberlain and Halifax to keep him well versed so that he could advise Washington of their actions. "Some helpful suggestions might be made from there," Kennedy explained.[39]

The ambassador was also swept up in a flurry of other courtesy calls, which he was surprised to enjoy.[40] One morning he made the rounds of the French, Spanish, and Argentine embassies and discussed the Austrian situation with the well-informed and pessimistic French ambassador, Charles Corbin; that afternoon Kennedy called on the Russian, Brazilian, and Turkish embassies and "squeezed in" tea with Arthur Cardinal Hinsley, the archbishop of Westminster and primate of the Roman Catholic Church in England. Kennedy paid particular attention to the views of the cardinal, noting that he must have been informed by the Vatican's intelligence service, rumored to be the best in the world.[41]

Kennedy also managed to host a luncheon with Chamberlain's most vigorous opponent and ardent Eden supporter, Winston Churchill, and his son Randolph. The future prime minister and soon-to-be Kennedy critic deeply regretted Eden's departure from the cabinet because he believed it saved Mussolini from certain political collapse. It also strengthened the dictatorships in the eyes of the smaller countries, making them more willing to accommodate the dictators' demands. "That the Lion has had his tail wrung has lost them prestige,"

Churchill told Kennedy.[42] Churchill also heaped scorn on Chamberlain's policy of waiting for Britain to become stronger before negotiating with Germany. His information indicated that each month Germany was becoming ever stronger than Britain.[43] Kennedy's interviews with ambassadors and colleagues and officials affirmed his position: War is not likely and the United States should mind its own business.[44]

Within a week after the *Manhattan* docked, on March 8, 1938, Kennedy officially became a full-fledged ambassador in a show beset with pomp and circumstance fitting for such ceremonies.[45] He and the American embassy staff stepped into three British state carriages decked with top-hatted coachmen, footmen, and outriders in flowing scarlet cloaks and rode majestically through the streets of London. Kennedy and his associates were cheered by the crowds as they drove through the Yeomen of the Guard at the gates of Buckingham Palace and walked into the Forty-four Room to present his credentials to King George VI.[46] The boyish-looking king was distinguished, dressed in the uniform of an admiral of the fleet, and was "much more nervous than I was" during the simple fifteen-minute ceremony.[47] He "acts like a fellow that was doing all he could to keep people loving 'the king.'"[48] The chatty ambassador, unaware that protocol dictated that one not discuss royal conversations in public, told the press afterward: "I found the King a delightful and easy conversationalist." He informed Hull that their discussion covered a broad range of subjects on which George VI had been specially coached. Kennedy was impressed by the king's "remarkable insights into American conditions. He frankly surprised me with his knowledge of American affairs."[49] "The ceremony was short, but it was a happy one that lingered long in my memory," Kennedy wrote in his memoirs.[50] This time following traditional protocol, he wore a tie, tailcoat, and long trousers. Knee breeches were not required.

The question of whether he would bow to British custom and don silk stockings and satin knee breeches for Court functions had haunted Kennedy, who had already received a dispensation from the traditional dress. He was well aware that a diplomat who embraced the British custom would be charged with kowtowing to his hosts. He had been teased, especially by Roosevelt, who told him not to worry, he'd be a knockout in knee breeches.[51] As soon as Kennedy arrived in Plymouth, he was surrounded by reporters demanding to know whether he intended to wear them. "Not Mrs. Kennedy's little boy," he growled back.[52] "I had made up my mind that I would break that tradition. . . . It ill became either my experience or my personality."[53] It was the kind of gesture that Kennedy liked to make, not in the least discourteous, he reasoned, but simply an independent-minded American's expression of his right to maintain his own country's traditions by declining to show too much deference to his hosts.[54]

Kennedy's invitation to attend the season's first Court prescribed the customary men's attire: "Knee breeches, white waistcoats, decorations, riband and star and miniature medals."[55] Kennedy explained to Lord Halifax that he simply could not wear knee breeches. It would "ruin" him in America.[56] "Praise be to Allah," he exclaimed to Jimmy Roosevelt upon returning from Buckingham Palace with an agreement that he would not be wearing them.[57] On the evening of the first Court, May 11, 1938, Kennedy, in tails and trousers, approached the three-tiered throne dais to greet the king and queen. "Admittedly I was noticeable," Kennedy wrote.[58] It was said that Mary, the Queen Mother, frowned in disapproval of the ambassador's unprecedented dress.[59] The only trousers worn that evening were those worn by Kennedy and some of the "less important waiters," noted Randolph Churchill, writing for the *Evening Standard*.[60] The American press was delighted by the occasion, Kennedy observed; one editor gleefully wrote, "Joe Wore Pants." But the comment that Kennedy was proudest of was that made by a South Carolina journalist: "The main point about ambassadorial qualification . . . is not whether or not a man can wear knee breeches but whether, under stress of trying times, he can keep his shirt on."[61]

The incident illustrated the mischievous delight Kennedy took in irreverence and unconventionality; so too did his decision to abolish the tiresome annual custom of selecting American debutantes for presentation at Court. Driven to distraction by the flood of applicants, he complained vigorously and called the custom "distasteful," "invidious," and "undemocratic."[62] After consulting with the White House, the State Department, and British authorities, who were all like-minded, Kennedy decided to abandon the custom, thereby winning gratitude and praise on both sides of the Atlantic. Roosevelt, who heartily agreed with Kennedy's position, suggested instead that presentation should be reserved for the immediate family members of American officials living in London or long residing in England.[63] The Court, then cracking down on its own presentations, quietly added its approval.

The *New York Times* wrote that "Mr. Kennedy has done the sensible thing without giving offense to anyone except perhaps a few disappointed debutantes at home."[64] His decision won the approval of British cartoonist Sidney Low, who pictured debutantes trying to overthrow Kennedy and being set upon by the entire Kennedy family, who put them to rout. And the American press had a heyday. Kennedy proudly noted that "no act of mine has ever had such public acclaim," as the voluminous correspondence in the Kennedy Library shows.[65]

Kennedy had planned to break the story with Arthur Krock, who agreed to print the correspondence between the ambassador and Senator Henry Cabot Lodge of Massachusetts. In a "plot" before he sailed, Kennedy agreed to decline to present a candidate of Lodge's because she did not qualify under the new criteria, and to write to the senator explaining his decision.[66] Lodge was to insert the letter into the Congressional Record and to publicize it that way.[67] He was also to reply to Kennedy, praising his decision as "a truly democratic policy."[68] Unfortunately Kennedy's letter was published by the State Department, which had not known of the "plot," and before it notified Lodge of its release. The gaffe looked as if the Irish-American saloon-keeper's son had snubbed the blue-blooded Brahmin from the Back Bay. The error was corrected; Lodge published his letter of approval for Kennedy's decision, and the embarrassment to both men was "merry and short-lived," the ambassador recalled.[69]

At the season's first Court, Rose Kennedy and the two eldest Kennedy daughters were presented to King George VI and Queen Elizabeth. Only seven American women were chosen for the honor; all were wives or daughters of American officials in London or resident in England.[70]

Some Americans had whispered that this self-made millionaire who so desperately wanted social acceptance and responsibility would quickly be taken in by the sly and clever English. But Kennedy refused to be dazzled by English pomp, titles, and traditions. He greeted Fleet Street reporters at the embassy with his feet up on his highly polished desk.[71] "Boys, don't expect me to develop into a statesman overnight," he told them.[72] "I'm a baby at this diplomatic game."[73] The newsmen were impressed with his candor. "Right now the average American isn't as interested in foreign affairs as he is in how he's going to eat and whether his insurance is good." "Some, maybe, even are more interested in how Casey Stengel's Boston Bees are going to do next season."[74] "You can take it from me," he told the newsmen, "that I have no precise instructions from the President."[75] Reporters scurried off to write flattering descriptions of this authentic and frank American ambassador with a ready smile and a relaxed, breezy manner who quite clearly was not cut from the usual diplomatic cloth.

One observer wrote:

> The Londoners must have had reservations when he arrived. For he was not only the first Irish Catholic to defile the London Embassy but he was rambunctious and ill-tempered, worse than careless with his language, vulgar in the eyes of the nicer people, anything but bashful, and filthy with American dollars. He chewed gum. He put his feet on his desk and he called the 'pleased and flattered' Queen 'a cute trick.'[76]

Initially most British officials, too, responded warmly to Kennedy. Lord Halifax attributed the unusually large degree of sunshine to Kennedy's presence in London and, perhaps tongue in cheek, of his being "so representative of modern America."[77] Others like industrialist Lord Arthur Riverdale considered him an "intensive [sic] young man" who is "quite a new type" of diplomat. Lord Riverdale approved of Kennedy's self-reliance and independence and told Roosevelt not to worry about him, that Kennedy could take care of himself.[78] FDR's old friend Arthur Murray told William Phillips that "responsible" people liked Kennedy tremendously and that he was well thought of in every respect.[79] "Kennedy seems to have cleared the bar in one stride," Phillips wrote back.[80] The English had every reason to be well-disposed toward Kennedy. They believed him to be a shrewd businessman who could deal effectively with the negotiations about the Anglo-American trade agreements and to be a Washington insider who had Roosevelt's ear. Hence the English would ensure Kennedy's popularity and his success—or so predicted his old college teammate George Peabody Gardner Jr. They are "prepared for him to make a hit, which is half the battle."[81] One Englishwoman, Alice Head, described Kennedy as "a glorious man. He has taken England by storm. He is so straight, forward [sic] and outspoken, and not the pompous stuffy type of Ambassador we usually get."[82]

Not everyone was so enthusiastic. Stuffy traditionalists clucked their disapproval when Kennedy rushed across the ballroom floor to dance with the queen and defied Court protocol by inducing her equerry to invite him to dance with her.[83] Montagu Norman despised Kennedy "partly because he was an Irish-American, a Roman Catholic, and therefore 'of bad stock,' [and] partly because he [was] a man permanently 'on the make.'"[84] To Lord Francis-Williams, a Labour journalist, the new ambassador was "a tycoon who seemed . . . to combine all the disagreeable traits of all the very rich men I had ever met with hardly any of their virtues."[85] Said Sir Henry Channon: Kennedy's "chief merit seems to be that he has nine children."[86]

Although British officialdom may have given Kennedy mixed reviews, he was wildly popular with ordinary Britons. Ever since his arrival he had been surrounded by a storm of publicity, conquering the British press as he had conquered important members of the American. His "gift for charming newspapermen into writing such reams as are usually reserved for occupants of the White House or the electric chair" worked on both sides of the Atlantic, a high government official in Washington reported to Cyrus L. Sulzberger, an American freelance journalist living in London in 1938.[87] Boake Carter wrote that the British have discovered what Americans already knew, "that [Kennedy] is sincere, outspoken and completely American."[88] Photographers snapped pictures of him galloping on Rotten Row and listened to him brag with fatherly delight about the black eye Joe Jr. got while playing rugby at Harvard.[89] Kennedy's popularity with the sports-minded British soared when he, a nine-handicap golfer, teed off with an iron and shot a hole in one at the famous Stoke Poges golf course.[90] Dazed, Kennedy remarked to the British reporters: "Just fancy! I had to come all the way over here."[91] He tossed off a now-famous quip, which he used more than once in after-dinner speeches: "I am much happier being the father of nine children and making a hole in one than I would be as the father of one child and making a hole in nine."[92] His two eldest sons, at Harvard, cabled him: "Dubious about your hole in one."[93] By evening, Kennedy's lucky stroke was front-page news. And when Rose Kennedy and the children arrived in mid-March, the British press went wild. In London the size of his brood and its impending arrival made headlines. "Nine Children and Nine Million Dollars," wrote the *Daily Express*, awed by both feats.[94] Newsmen dubbed the family "the U.S.A. Nine-Child Envoy" and called Kennedy "The Father of his Country" and "Jolly Joe."[95] When the ambassador went down on the train to greet his family, he was mobbed by the children and scarcely got near his wife. Finding himself with only one ticket and no money, he had to borrow $120 from newsmen to take the family back to London. Reporters chipped in to lend him six first-class fares.[96]

As ambassador, Kennedy was made an honorary member of the most exclusive and prestigious clubs in London. "Look at this, Rosie," his wife recalled his telling her as he showed her a list that included "the Royal Thames Yacht Club, the Athenaeum, the Harlequin Football Club, the Queen's Club, the Monday Luncheon club, the Sunningdale Golf Club, the Phyllis Court Club and the International Sportsmen Club." "According to my count I am now a member of at least six exclusive golf clubs. I wonder what the people in Cohasset would think if they saw me now. It sure shows that if you wait long enough, the wheel turns."[97]

The height of Kennedy's reception and popularity among the British came in the spring of 1938 when he and Mrs. Kennedy were invited to spend the weekend at Windsor Castle with the king and queen. In the evening of Friday, April 9, the Kennedys drove to the castle for "one of the most fabulous, fascinating experiences of my life," Rose remembered.[98] She recalled that as they passed Eton, Joe had commented that so many young men from that famous place had died in the trenches in World War I.[99] The Kennedys arrived at seven o'clock and were greeted by the Master of the Household, who led them to their suite of two bedrooms and two bathrooms and a green sitting room filled with paintings of the royal family. It had once been the private chamber of Queen Victoria. "Look Joe," Rose said, as she found stationery with the royal coat of arms in the drawer of the desk. "Let's write to each of the children on it tonight. They will be so surprised and pleased."[100] The ambassador, sitting in a chair before a fire blazing on the hearth, mused: "Rose, this is a helluva long way from East Boston."[101] It must have seemed proper compensation for all the snubs and snobbery: Porcellian avenged!

After being served sherry and dressing in the requisite evening attire, at 8:20 the Kennedys were escorted by footmen to the Green Reception Room, hung with Gobelin tapestries and furnished in the style of Louis XV. There they met the other guests, including the prime minister and Mrs. Chamberlain and Lord and Lady Halifax. When the king and queen arrived at half past eight, they greeted each of the guests, who either curtsied or bowed, and they led them to the Garter Throne Room, where the table was set for ten. The royal couple sat opposite each other at the table covered with flowers so tall they could hardly see each other, making for much amusement and good-natured bantering. Throughout dinner a red-coated orchestra played. Kennedy sat on the queen's right, with the prime minister to her left, and Rose sat on the king's right, with Mrs. Chamberlain to his left. The ambassador was thoroughly taken with the queen, who impressed him with her intelligence and charm. Their conversation ranged from the anti-British bias in the American press, to the relations between England and the United States, and to Kennedy's attempts to get thirty-four nuns of the Convent of the Sacred Heart evacuated from war-torn Barcelona. Kennedy and the queen also talked about President Roosevelt's 100 percent support of Chamberlain's attempts to keep the peace. "What the American people fear more than anything else is being involved in war," the ambassador told her. "When they remember 1917 and how they went to make the world safe for democracy, and then they look now at the crop of dictatorships, quarrels and miseries arising out of that war they say to themselves, 'Never again!' And I can't say I blame them. I feel the same way myself." "I feel that way, too, Mr. Kennedy," the queen said. "But if we had the United States actively on our side, working with us, think how that would strengthen our position with the dictators."[102] The ambassador noted how animated her face became as she spoke so earnestly. The idea of a royal visit to the United States came to him as a way of improving Anglo-American relations. "You should go to the top-side people there, just as you are talking to me," he told her. "You would charm them as you are charming me."[103] She was immediately receptive.

Lady Halifax, sitting on Kennedy's right, asked him what President Roosevelt was like. The ambassador tried several words—"freedom . . . warmth . . . humor." He settled on "gallantry." "The man is almost paralysed yet he ignores it and this forces others to overlook it." Kennedy recalled seeing him pull himself up to his full height, bearing his weight only on his arms. "This always brings a lump to my throat, although I consider myself pretty hardboiled," the ambassador told her.[104]

As the evening ended, a Scottish bagpiper in a kilt walked through the room playing as the guests withdrew. The ladies remained with the queen, who stood in front of a fireplace in a drawing room as the men bowed to her and followed the king into another room.[105] Rose was fascinated by the Vandyck painting of the children of Charles I. Years later she could still recall her feelings:

> It was so incredibly beautiful. . . . There they stood, looking as if they had not a care in the world, and yet before their childhood was finished, two of them would die and the other three would be left to struggle for the crown in the wake of their father's beheading, an event which would bring upon their country a reign of terror and confusion beyond imagination. There was something about seeing those children frozen for that moment in time, blissfully ignorant of all the pain of the years ahead, that made me shudder inside and suddenly feel afraid.[106]

She might as well have been speaking of her own family: three sons and one daughter would die—two in plane crashes and two by assassination, causing social upheaval and civil unrest; one daughter would be lobotomized; and the remaining four offspring would be left to grapple with their grief.

The king invited Kennedy to sit with him on the sofa. In their fifteen-minute conversation, the ambassador again suggested a royal visit to the United States,[107] and the king told him about the music-hall joke that Kennedy was called the father of his country. In a more serious vein, the ambassador warned him that Britain suffered from unfavorable publicity and propaganda and suggested whom to contact to guarantee that the British would get a fairer hearing with the American press. When they rejoined the ladies, the company engaged in polite conversation while the red-coated orchestra played quietly. They discussed, among other things, the jewelry that belonged to Mary Queen of Scots, and the election in Fulham in which a Labour candidate defeated a Conservative. The royal couple withdrew at eleven, and the Kennedys finally went to bed at half past twelve.[108] A "very brilliant dinner party," Rose wrote on royal stationery to her daughter Pat, the next day.[109] "I lay in bed thinking that I must be dreaming that I, Rose Kennedy, a simple young matron from Boston am really here at Windsor Castle the guest of the Queen and two little Princesses."[110]

After breakfast in their sitting room the next day, the Kennedys went to Palm Sunday Mass in Windsor in a small Catholic church down a cobblestone alley while the other guests worshiped with the king and queen in the splendor of St. George's Chapel. After services, the Kennedys walked over the castle grounds. "We both felt the whole thing wasn't real, it was like playing soldier and turning back pages of history," Kennedy wrote in his diary.[111]

On the walk after lunch, Kennedy had a long talk about European affairs with both the prime minister and the foreign secretary. Chamberlain was pleased with the Italian agreement and the Italians' reasonableness in negotiations, he told Kennedy, and he found them a sharp contrast to the Germans—so rigid and too general. The prime minister also described the inconclusive conversation on March 3 between Hitler and Britain's ambassador, Sir Nevile Henderson, when Hitler presented his argument for self-determination for Germans. "I can see his point," Chamberlain said. "The German people have a right to self-determination." Nor would the British people support a government that went to war to prevent ten million Germans from having what is rightfully theirs, the prime minister told Kennedy.[112] "It seems to me," Kennedy said, "that the big question is whether Hitler means to limit his activities to helping his Germans or whether he has further objectives that will violate the self-determination of other nations." "Precisely," said Chamberlain. But the only way to find out is "to wait and see." So far all Hitler's demands have had to do with Germany, Chamberlain remarked. In *Mein Kampf*, Hitler argued "that Germany's future sphere of expansion lies in southeast Europe and the Ukraine. If he means economic penetration without force, we cannot very well object. Besides, war wins nothing, ends nothing. In a modern war there are no victors."[113] Europe's peace can be saved if the four major powers resolve their disagreements. But we must persuade the Germans and the Italians to be sensible, Chamberlain declared; that's the only way to attain a lasting peace, not the current "armed truce."[114]

"Do you think a failure to reach an agreement with Germany will mean war?" Kennedy asked. "No," Chamberlain answered, "for we are convinced that Germany is in no position as regards resources or reserves to go to war." In the meantime, we will try a policy of pacification that will be more advantageous than war and the destruction of civilization. These were opinions Kennedy was thoroughly in agreement with. Kennedy summed up his understanding of the prime minister's opinion: "There was in Chamberlain then no great sense of urgency, nor was there any such sense evident at Windsor Castle nor in the minds of the British public. My prophecy that 1938 would see no war was already a fortnight old. It seemed more secure than ever," he recorded in the memoir.[115] The Kennedys returned to the embassy by mid-morning to entertain guests of their own with happy recollections of their fabulous weekend.[116]

Nearly a fortnight after his arrival in London, Kennedy summed up his initial days in England to Roosevelt, who was surprised by his ambassador's immediate success and popularity.[117] "I think I have made a fairly good start here with people and seem to be getting along reasonably well with the Government so far"—as indeed he was.[118] Kennedy liked being liked.

He liked the warmth and informality of the king and queen and felt comfortable with them. He also liked having the goodwill and comradery of leading members of the government. He worked hard to cultivate Chamberlain and Halifax and to win the influence and favor of their coterie. It seemed to work. He was finally being accepted on his terms by the highest society in the English-speaking world. He relished every bit of it as he began to identify with the British political and social elite.[119] "I've got the best job in the world," he told Morgenthau.[120]

Yet Kennedy, initially the most popular American ambassador in living memory, would become the object of bitter hatred and ridicule on both sides of the Atlantic—particularly by those who had at first received him with such warmth—and his friendly relationship with Roosevelt would degenerate into barely concealed hostility. But for the moment Kennedy and his family were featured everywhere, and he and his boss were still chums. The president teased him: "When you feel that British accent coming upon you and your trousers riding up to the knee, take the first steamer home for a couple of weeks holiday."[121]

An ambassador has many roles. He is to be an accurate reporter to his home government, make his country and himself respected and liked in the host country, negotiate contractual interests, support and pursue his country's foreign policy, and illustrate vision and understanding in the international arena. An ambassador, Lord Halifax put it,

> act[s] as a two-way interpreter both of his own country to the country where he resides and of that country to his own. A good Ambassador must have a clear understanding of both. That is especially true of an American Ambassador in London and of a British Ambassador in Washington where contacts are facilitated and rendered closer by a common language and many common traditions.[122]

Kennedy originally seemed quite capable of carrying out such a mission.

Diplomacy, however, was an art he had no training and no background in. With great fanfare he had entered a world in which a man sometimes spoke more to conceal than to reveal, a world in which words were often chosen for subtlety and connotation, not clarity and precision. As ambassador, Kennedy no longer had the right to express his own views freely, however strongly he felt; he was only the spokesman of those in Washington who had the power to make the policy.[123]

In his previous public service, Kennedy was used to short-term jobs with considerable autonomy carried out under a nominal boss and intense and nearly continuous all-consuming effort, followed by rest and relaxation at Hyannis Port or Palm Beach. But the ambassadorship called for an undefined length of service with specific authority and limited responsibilities carried out under the watchful eye of the secretary of state and the president, who only occasionally called him home for consultation. Kennedy could not accustom himself to merely mouthing others' policies or resign himself to no longer being an autonomous actor only loosely answerable to Roosevelt.

Kennedy's new job called for unfailing discretion, uncommon shrewdness in assessing men and events, judgment unclouded by sentiment or prejudice, and a broad vision honed by education and experience—attributes that he, despite his Midas touch in business, did not possess.[124] Furthermore, he appeared on the diplomatic stage at a time of intense international turmoil, every bit as dangerous as 1914, as the last act in the drama of appeasement was being played out. Even those more experienced in international affairs than he had trouble believing Nazi ideology or comprehending the minds who created it. Few could predict the holocaust about to consume the world. But for a novice like Kennedy, the reality of the unfolding international events was even more incomprehensible and unfathomable.[125] He really was "just a babe" at the diplomatic game.[126]

As ambassador to the Court of St. James's, Kennedy did have a unique opportunity to influence the president's views on foreign affairs. Roosevelt and Kennedy's personal relationship, Roosevelt's respect for Kennedy's abilities, London's pivotal international position all gave Kennedy considerable credibility with Roosevelt, but to no avail. If ever a president needed sage counsel in foreign affairs, it was then; if ever there was an ambassador lacking the ability to give it, it was Kennedy.

The new ambassador had very definite views about his duties. He intended to be a working diplomat and to represent the attitudes of the average American, something that came naturally to him though it put him in conflict with the administration. Ray Atherton, a former adviser at the London embassy and a career officer, told Kennedy how efficiently the embassy was run and intimated that he could let the staff run the business of diplomacy while he devoted himself to social and ceremonial functions and to pursuing "contacts." Kennedy, however, had other ideas. The staff would continue to handle routine matters, but he insisted on keeping well informed. If anything important went on, the ambassador himself would handle it.[127] His fierce Irish pride would not allow him merely to accept the title but not shoulder the duties. Roosevelt's hunch had been right: Kennedy wanted to run things.

Kennedy got along well with the embassy staff of two hundred. After little more than a month in London, he told Anthony Biddle, American ambassador in Poland, "I like some of my colleagues of the Diplomatic Corps very much," and I can now "tell them apart." In particular Kennedy was impressed by their intelligence and perception.[128] Alan G. Kirk, the naval attaché at the embassy, also remembered the ambassador's expressing "confidence" in Herschel Johnson, his chargé and embassy counselor. Kirk thought that his own relationship with Kennedy "couldn't have been better." "I was loyal to him and he was very loyal to me." Reminiscing years later, Kirk said, "I have nothing but the warmest recollections of his conduct in our official relationships."[129]

One of the ambassador's many diplomatic duties was to prepare situation reports for use by State Department officials. Kennedy's procedural reforms helped to swell the flow of reliable information and ensured the smooth running of the embassy. He insisted that all reports be approved by him before being forwarded to Washington. This procedure sprang from the realization that poorly trained junior attachés were passing on to Washington cocktail-circuit rumors, lunch-table gossip, and chit-chat from teas and galas. Kennedy informed the staff that accurate reporting required "shirt-sleeve diplomacy"—rolling up your sleeves and trudging along, keeping in close touch with the sources.[130]

Despite his reforms, Kennedy's own assessment of events sometimes lacked solid analysis. His dispatches were self-described "quick," "newsy," "bulletins," more like a reporter's than an analyst's.[131] Before the war his reports were fairly factual, statistical, objective, impersonal, and unbiased, and even contained a few criticisms of Chamberlain, despite the similarity in their views and Kennedy's respect for and identification with him. Yet even then Kennedy's dispatches gave little information about what he was actually doing and were occasionally misleading, and so of doubtful value to department officials. They sometimes contained snatches of undigested conversation, untested opinions, gossip that indulged indiscreetly in personalities and "horseback opinions written at the gallop."[132] There were often glaring discrepancies between his interpretation and others' of the same event.[133]

When war did come, his dispatches became much more personal, pessimistic, and emotional—shrill, even, as he became incapable of keeping his own opinions from coloring his reports—and therefore doubtful as a basis for policymaking as he desperately tried to convince administration officials to adopt his policies. Near the end of his tenure in the fall of 1940 after Churchill had become prime minister, the official freeze on Kennedy was so complete that his access to information was sharply limited and ultimately necessitated circumventing him.[134] But so long as Chamberlain lived at 10 Downing Street, Kennedy's virtually complete access to the British government kept him well informed. If he came across anything dubious, he simply called "Neville" and asked him if it was true.[135]

Neville Chamberlain, the passionately rigid Tory prime minister, was one of the most important Englishmen with whom Kennedy cultivated a useful and pleasant relationship. That relationship with Chamberlain, who kept him better informed than official routine required and by whom he came to be treated as practically an honorary cabinet member, enabled Kennedy to establish a very effective diplomatic communication between London and Washington—so effective, in fact, that he received high praise from State Department officials like Sumner Welles. "I can't tell you how admirably you have been keeping us informed. It couldn't be better," the undersecretary wrote during the Munich crisis.[136] One *New York Times* reporter even claimed that Kennedy's contacts in the British government were as good as those of the classic Anglophile Walter Hines Page, the American ambassador during World War I.[137] Kennedy was thus in an excellent position to observe official British attitudes and intentions carefully and to be an informed reporter of the Chamberlain government. His reports impressed even FDR. "Old Joe has the damnedest way of getting information," he said admiringly.[138]

The gregarious ambassador enjoyed flaunting the personal relationship developing between him and Chamberlain, behavior not necessarily appreciated or reciprocated by the gracious but reserved prime minister.[139] At a dinner party Kennedy constantly referred to him as "Neville." As Kennedy did so, Chamberlain's Adam's apple was observed to quiver several times before he could spit out an unavoidable "Joe."[140] Soon after his arrival in London, Kennedy, with a kind of candor, told an acquaintance: "I'm just like that with Chamberlain. Why Franklin himself isn't as confidential with me as the Prime Minister."[141] How much of Chamberlain's friendship was politically motivated is unclear. Chamberlain's parliamentary secretary, Sir Alec Douglas-Home, contradicted Kennedy's glowing description of their friendship: "The relations between Mr. Kennedy and Mr. Chamberlain were not as I recollect very close." Another political intimate of the prime minister's, Sir Alexander Cadogan, the capable undersecretary in the Foreign Office, recalled that Chamberlain "had an almost instinctive contempt for the Americans"[142] and sneered at Roosevelt and his administration.[143] But one of Kennedy's biographers, David Nasaw, writes that

> Chamberlain, Halifax, and Cadogan were equally taken with the new American ambassador. They appreciated his frankness and intelligence and, from the moment he arrived in London, treated him not as the oddity he was—the first Irish Catholic ambassador ever and a blunt, plain-speaking businessman to boot—but as a trusted colleague with whom they could speak freely and candidly and occasionally share information gathered by British intelligence.[144]

Although Chamberlain may have had little personal regard for Kennedy, he encouraged him to presume upon their relationship and, for the sake of political expedience, to overestimate it. Both prime minister and president used the naive millionaire well.

Despite Kennedy's ready gift for getting information in his early days as ambassador, he failed to cultivate other "unofficial" channels of information or to develop a rapprochement with sources critical of the Chamberlain government such as Halifax's predecessor at the Foreign Office, Anthony Eden; or Winston Churchill; or Duff Cooper, the First Lord of the Admiralty. An exception was the socialist Ernest Bevin, who later, when Churchill was prime minister, became minister of labour and national service; for him Kennedy retained considerable respect and friendship.[145]

As a diplomatic neophyte, apparently without instructions from Washington, Kennedy could rely only on his own wits and judgment, making him vulnerable and receptive to the views of his host government. In the absence of Washington's direction and diplomatic initiative, he fell prey to Britain's appeasement-minded officialdom and became an agreeable understudy of their foreign policy. In particular, Kennedy became an eager pupil of Neville Chamberlain.

Political opponents like Winston Churchill dismissed Chamberlain as little more than a "town clerk looking at the situation in Europe though the wrong end of a municipal drain pipe,"[146] or, in the opinion of one Labourite, as "having been weaned on a pickle."[147] Lloyd George described him as "a good Lord Mayor of Birmingham in a lean year."[148] But the new ambassador was deeply impressed, even awed, by this Birmingham businessman with a reputation for being "masterful but magnanimous, dogged, but a first-class loser, a leader who fought better, and only for causes, not for himself," as one of Chamberlain's biographers, Keith Feiling, put it.[149] Kennedy came to share Chamberlain's realistic and practical approach to political issues and his attempts to review all the salient facts before making policy decisions.

Upon becoming prime minister at the age of sixty-eight in 1937, Chamberlain was "an old man in a hurry."[150] "It is a bit late in the day to become Prime Minister . . . and I can't expect a very long run," he wrote a friend. "[I am determined] to leave my mark behind me as P.M."[151] His austere, dark clothes, starched Edwardian collar, and black umbrella, relics of the Victorian age, conveyed circumspection and discretion and inspired trust and respect. His small, wiry stature one historian described as "assertively grey." He thought himself incapable of being wrong. He said of himself as prime minister: "I know that I can save the country and I do not believe that anyone else can."[152] Kennedy agreed. Chamberlain tried to rally the "virtuous passion" of ordinary British citizens by appealing to them over the heads of their political leaders and expressing their longing for peace. One of his colleagues said of him that "Chamberlain's hold over ordinary Englishmen stems from the fact that they see in him an ordinary Englishman: "decent, honest, but above all, supremely anxious for peace." He had immense public support.[153]

Chamberlain was hard to like; he had a manner too serious, seldom playful, and never cheeky. He was cultivated, hard-working, highly intelligent. But he was unable to distinguish between how he wanted things to be and how they were. He was unwilling to consider disagreeable evidence and looked for opinions that supported his. Lacking a university education, he was overly sensitive to others' opinions of him. His susceptibility to flattery, his self-righteousness and obstinacy enabled Hitler to exploit him and helped bring on his tragic failure in foreign policy. Whenever Chamberlain faced a choice with Hitler between conciliation and confrontation, he could only opt for conciliation.[154]

The self-made Wall Street speculator had much in common with the middle-class Birmingham manufacturer. Both were sensitive about their social origins and wanted social acceptance by their "betters," the blue-blooded Brahmins or the British aristocrats; both feared the destruction of capitalism, and both abhorred war and the radical institutional changes it would unleash.

Like Kennedy, Chamberlain believed in capitalism and its essential connection to peace, prosperity, and democracy. To maintain civilization, or at least their conception of it, the commercial ties between London and New York and the world's centers of trade would have to be preserved. To conduct a war, capitalism would have to give way to some kind of collectivism. And why fight to transform capitalism into socialism or, even worse, Bolshevism? Given the alternatives—communist Russia or a noncommunist Germany—both Chamberlain and Kennedy preferred the noncommunist Germany.[155] Although Kennedy "loathed Hitler and Hitlerism almost, though perhaps not quite, as much as he loathed Bolshevism," still a

Foreign Office official friendly to Kennedy said that he was "also a self-made man who had known poverty and he did not want to know it again."[156] Kennedy in fact had not ever "known poverty," and he never wanted to come to know it.

As for Russia, Chamberlain could in no way rely on its assistance. He confided to his diary in March 1938 his dislike and distrust of the Russians. He accused them of "stealthily and cunningly pulling all the strings behind the scenes to get us involved in war with Germany (our Secret Service doesn't spend all its time looking out of the window)."[157] Kennedy fully sympathized with Chamberlain's attitude at that time. "I wouldn't believe the Russians under oath," he wrote in his memoirs.[158] He told Roosevelt that he viewed Soviet Russia as an "imponderable in the situation." He saw absolutely no reason to think that the two English-speaking democracies could count on the Russians. Either Russia would come under Nazi domination even without an invasion, or the Soviet "doctrinaires" would withdraw into "splendid isolation" behind the walls of the Kremlin until "the pickings in Europe or West China were ripe."[159] Chamberlain's and Kennedy's shared hostility and suspicion of the Soviet Union led them to believe that Europe's peace could be maintained by appeasing Germany, a position not uncommon among diplomats and officials in the British Foreign Office and in the U.S. State Department during the interwar period. Writing to his sister Ida on March 26, 1939, Chamberlain said:

> I must confess to the most profound distrust of Russia. I have no belief whatever in her ability to maintain an effective offensive even if she wanted to. And I distrust her motives which seem to me to have little connection with our ideas of liberty and to be concerned only with getting everyone else by the ears. Moreover she is both hated and suspected by many of the smaller states notably by Poland, Rumania and Finland so that our close association with her might easily cost us the sympathy of those who would much more effectively help us if we can get them on our side.[160]

Furthermore, as good businessmen, they found it inconceivable that Chamberlain's negotiations with Hitler and Mussolini would fail to lead to mutually satisfactory compromises that would ease Europe's political and economic tensions. They assumed that the dictators' ambitions were limited to accommodating specific grievances, particularly self-determination for Germans, and that once these were satisfied, demands would cease and tensions would subside. But Chamberlain failed to see that his appeasement policy had the effect of increasing and strengthening the dictators' ambitions. The ambassador, too, was among the many who could not grasp the expansionist nature of Nazism or the demonic threat that Hitler posed.[161]

The prime minister was haunted by the pointless holocaust of World War I, which brought about the death of his beloved cousin, Norman Chamberlain, and he was determined not to repeat the mistakes of the past. He was thoroughly repelled by war because it "wins nothing, cures nothing, ends nothing," he told his Birmingham audience in April 1938. "In war," he said, "there are no winners but all are losers."[162] He intended, he vowed to Herschel Johnson, Kennedy's deputy at the embassy, to "strain every nerve to avoid a repetition of the Great War in Europe."[163] In practice that meant accommodate the fascist dictators' every demand. "As a result," historian Larry Fuchser wrote, "Britain backed resolutely into war with Germany with her eyes focused doggedly on the past. The case of Neville Chamberlain and appeasement therefore illustrates, in a particularly poignant way, the dangers of making public policy on the basis of unexamined analogies with the past."[164]

Kennedy applauded Chamberlain's opinions. War was "irrational and debasing," said the American millionaire. "War destroyed capital. What could be worse than that?"[165] Coupled with his fear for capital and capitalism and his dislike of collectivism was Kennedy's personal abhorrence of war. "I have four sons," he said, "and I don't want them to be killed in a foreign war."[166] Just as he had supported the New Deal in the early 1930s out of his fear of social revolution and concern for his family's security, so in the late 1930s he opposed the war out of concern for his family's welfare. His motive in both domestic and foreign policy was essentially the same—to protect his family—and his fortune, of course. Reminiscent of his earlier attitude of disgust at the waste and uselessness of the Great War, which had led him to spurn active duty and avoid the draft, so in his ambassadorship he remained unmoved by arguments about mystical patriotism or loyalty to the fatherland. In later crises, personal and emotional considerations, not nationalistic ones, led him to go much further than Chamberlain in refusing to recognize war as the ultimate weapon in statecraft.

As a willing ally, not only did Kennedy staunchly support Chamberlain's policy of appeasement, but by early spring he also began to urge Washington to endorse the prime minister's efforts—but only as far as they could be pursued without the collaboration of the United States. The appeasement policy was essential for Britain, Kennedy argued, as he later became even more of an appeaser than the appeasers. He frequently quoted the prime minister, who believed from 1938 on that Britain "had nothing with which to fight and she should not risk going to war with Hitler."[167] Chamberlain's policy could also be useful for the United States—or so Kennedy hoped—because it would prevent a war that might involve American interests. He was becoming more of an isolationist than Hull or Roosevelt.

Despite the similarity of their views, Kennedy disagreed with Chamberlain about whether political or economic solutions should take precedence in Britain's appeasement program. The prime minister believed that economic issues should be subordinate to political ones. The primary way to ensure peace was through political concessions, he insisted. "I disagree with those who think you can solve political difficulties by removing economic thorns from the flesh," Chamberlain told Sir John Simon. "Politics in international affairs governs action at the expense of economics and often of reason," he said.[168] But to Kennedy, whose vision was sometimes obstructed by the bars of the dollar sign, the equation was reversed. England has big debt; taxes are as heavy as can be, and the country is spending everything on armaments and, boy, when this stops, "they're in for it." The economic factor "will be the determining factor in writing the fate of the world rather than the political side," he told Jimmy Roosevelt, shortly after arriving in England.[169]

The ambassador also developed a good professional relationship with Lord Halifax, the foreign secretary, whom he frequently bragged about being close to, although Halifax may have thought otherwise.[170] He regarded Halifax as "the noblest figure in public life I have encountered."[171] The handsome, graceful, balding aristocrat with a false hand formed like a fist and a mobile thumb,[172] this "Uriah Heep–looking foreign secretary"[173] who was no "faithful Sancho Panza,"[174] struck Kennedy as "everything that an upper class Englishman who gives his life to public service ought to be."[175] A scholar, he was an Etonian who took a first in history at Oxford; a sports lover, he was the master of the Middleton fox hounds and had a country squire's interest in village cricket. Halifax could have lived his life on his ancestral estate in Yorkshire, but chose instead to enter public service: standing successfully for Parliament, serving as the president of the board of education and minister of agriculture in Baldwin's governments, becoming the viceroy of India, then Lord Privy Seal, and in 1938, after Eden's resignation, Chamberlain's foreign secretary and later the ambassador to Washington. His deafness lent him an air of preoccupation; his slight lisp encouraged his calm, slow thoughtfulness; his manner was pleasant, and self-deprecating. He seemed comfortably lethargic, was liked, admired, and underrated.[176]

Halifax, too, thought that war was stupidly destructive and had an abiding hatred of it. His parochial outlook and limited experience in international affairs led him, too, to believe that appeasement was the most effective policy to prevent war; like Chamberlain and Kennedy, he was willing to pay nearly any price for peace. (But he could never have foreseen the personal tragedy that would befall his family during World War II: Peter, his second son, lost his life; Richard, his youngest son, lost his legs.)[177] Despite the great gulf between the backgrounds of the two men—the old-monied, gently philosophical aristocrat with the air of religious asceticism, and the nouveau riche, pragmatic go-getter—they had one thing in common: neither was particularly qualified by training or temperament to serve in foreign affairs.

Other than Chamberlain and Halifax, the men Kennedy associated with most frequently were members of Britain's "Cliveden Set," the political officialdom and like-minded British businessmen, bankers, and financiers. His closest professional associates in London were the "arch-capitulators": Montagu Norman; Sir Horace Wilson, Chamberlain's éminence grise and chief industrial adviser; Sir John Simon, chancellor of the exchequer; and Chamberlain himself.[178] Kennedy also liked Sir Samuel Hoare, home secretary until 1939, then Lord Privy Seal through 1940; and Sir Alexander Cadogan, who considered Kennedy "very nice—frank, and, I should think, friendly."[179] Kennedy also "saw a lot" of his "great friend" Lord Beaverbrook, one of Britain's biggest press barons.[180] In fact, their friendship continued long after Kennedy resigned as ambassador.[181] Kennedy's relationship with other British officials seems to have been conducted on a professional basis.

At the embassy, Kennedy hosted a stag party that included the leading bankers in the city—"the Morgans, the Rothschilds, the McKennas—everybody," he reported to Morgenthau.[182] After dinner the guests and their host relaxed over brandy and cigars and had a "full," "frank," "dispassionate and friendly" discussion about Anglo-American economic and financial policies—their fears of a worldwide depression, their hope for a restoration of confidence in the business community, especially in the United States, and the embarrassment of Britain's default on its war debts.[183] Kennedy simply asked his guests questions and reported their conversation to Washington; he made no recommendations to the president vis-à-vis his economic policies.[184]

In the spring of 1938, the vivacious new American ambassador joined the weekend guests at Cliveden, the country estate of the Astors in Buckinghamshire, and charmed the dinner guests at the Astors' London mansion in St. James's Square.[185] The "Cliveden Set," the term coined by the left-wing editor Claud Cockburn of the *Week*, was a hodgepodge collection of politicians, editors, Oxford dons, and wealthy peers and peeresses, united under the roof of Lord and Lady Astor. It was rumored in the left-wing press to be a conspiratorial second Foreign Office and the power behind the scenes in the inner circle of the Chamberlain government. Reputedly the purveyors of appeasement, the Cliveden Set was accused of being too "friendly with both Hitler and Mussolini"[186] and of influencing His Majesty's Government in a pro-Nazi direction, accusations heatedly denied by Lord Astor in the *Times*.[187] Kennedy was accused of susceptibility to the "petticoat interference" of its leading hostesses, such as the Marchioness of Londonderry, Lady Austen Chamberlain, and the American-born Lady Astor. In a letter to Lady Astor, Kennedy made fun of the charges: "Well, you see what a terrible woman you are, and how a poor little fellow like me is being politically seduced."[188] Kennedy was decidedly not a member of the Cliveden Set nor duped by them, but he believed in the appeasement policy because he thought it was the best way, perhaps the only way, to maintain peace. Still, he would have been well advised to have kept his distance from the Cliveden Set.[189]

But Kennedy took the American liberals' and journalists' distortions of his friendship with the Astors much more seriously. By April 1938, Harold Ickes, a tireless Kennedy critic, dutifully noted that "Kennedy appear[ed] to have been taken in hand by Lady Astor and the Cliveden set," which Ickes described as "pro-fascist in sentiment."[190] The accusations were repeated by Drew Pearson and Robert Allen in their syndicated column "Washington Merry-Go-Round": "Joe has been taken in just a bit by the Clivedon [*sic*] charm, not on the Nazi-Fascist theories, but on the idea of cooperating with the Tories of Great Britain." But because he has lots of "Irish-American common-sense," he is likely to snap out of it.[191] Kennedy described the charges as "complete bunk" in a telegram to the journalists protesting the "great harm" and the "extremely bad" repercussions the falsehoods had had.[192] The columnists said that the charges came from "friends," both Kennedy's and theirs in the State Department, but they apologized to him and agreed to withdraw their accusations.[193]

Nevertheless, these personal and professional relationships among the British

Establishment must have had a considerable impact on Kennedy's conception of Anglo-American relations. His rapport with British officialdom enabled him to know their views and intentions and thus to remain a knowledgeable reporter of the government's policy; his role was that of an "absorbed bystander," reporting the events to Washington, but not a participant.[194] Further, as he associated with Britain's political and social elite—the opinion-makers, the industrialists, the aristocracy, the financiers—he began to accept and espouse their economic and political views. In fact, officials at the Foreign Office noted in their annual report of 1938 that Kennedy was "considerably criticized" for being "in the pocket of the Prime Minister with consequent subservience of the State Department to Whitehall."[195] Although it is unclear precisely who influenced whom, or to what extent the arch-appeasers gave Kennedy his political education, there was enough similarity in their attitudes to lead Roosevelt to wonder out loud during the Munich crisis: "Who would have thought that the English could take into camp a red-headed Irishman?"[196] But they did.

At daybreak on March 12, 1938, Adolph Hitler finally carried out his hotly debated and long-planned dream, "Operation Otto." German troops rolled across the frontier into Austria, and Vienna, that gay and cultivated capital, came under Nazi domination as the Austrian republic was incorporated into the Third Reich. Hitler's unbroken string of successes—the withdrawal from the League, rearmament of Germany, the remilitarization of the Rhineland, repeated violations of the Versailles Treaty—had given a certain inevitability to the takeover of Austria. The Nazi leader had long coveted this vast estate of Maria Theresa because he wanted to unite all the Teutonic races within the German Reich and because Austria was the gateway to Czechoslovakia and to southeastern Europe. If the Anschluss were allowed to stand, it would be extremely difficult to forestall further German expansion in Czechoslovakia or Poland or southeastern Europe. And beyond Vienna lay Prague, now isolated both economically and militarily, and hemmed in on three sides by German-controlled borders.

Europe acquiesced to Hitler's aggression. Mussolini reaffirmed his friendship and acceptance of annexation as he telegraphed Hitler: "My attitude is determined by the friendship between our two countries, as consecrated in the Axis."[197] Nor did Hitler have anything to fear from France or England; neither could do anything except protest. France, preoccupied with yet another cabinet crisis, lacked both a government and a policy. Chamberlain received the news of Nazi troop movements and of the ultimatum demanding cancellation of an announced plebiscite and the resignation of Austria's chancellor, Kurt von Schuschnigg, while Chamberlain was actually entertaining the German foreign minister, Joachim von Ribbentrop, and his wife at a farewell luncheon for him at 10 Downing Street—a "grim affair," recalled one guest.[198]

"The march of events in Austria made my first few days here more exciting than they might otherwise have been," Kennedy's March 21 private and confidential letter to Arthur Krock began, "but I am still unable to see that Central European developments affect our country or my job." Illustrating his ignorance of foreign affairs, the ambassador coolly concluded that "none of these various moves has any significance for the United States, outside of general interest," a position he staunchly maintained throughout the crisis. If in fact war did break out, he said, there would be time enough for American officials to review the events and decide on an appropriate course of action. Contemptuous of the "semi-hysterical attitude" of the surprised and anxious professional diplomats, he, by contrast, was not alarmed by the destruction of Austria's independence. Peace was still possible; war was not inevitable.[199]

Kennedy informed Washington of his conversations with several foreign representatives a few hours before the invasion and said that he was impressed with their description of the situation as "acute." Nevertheless, he wrote reassuringly, quoting the French ambassador: "Nothing is likely to happen except to have Schuschnigg eventually give in unless there is some indication that France and England are prepared to back him up." And that, Kennedy accurately predicted, they would not do. "My own impression is that Hitler and Mussolini, having done so very well for themselves by bluffing . . . are not going to stop bluffing until somebody very sharply calls their bluff," he said. "Nobody is going to fight a war over here unless Germany starts shooting somebody. Nobody wants it." Any American intervention was out of the question, he told Washington. Britain's "top-side people"—the heads of various governmental departments and leaders outside the government—"all feel that the United States would be very foolish to try to mix in," he told FDR. Their virtually unanimous recommendation was to remain prosperous and to build a substantial navy; beyond that, "time will take care of [Britain's] position with the United States," the ambassador cabled.[200] Measuring the crisis by his yardstick of his view of America's self-interest, Kennedy completely agreed with the advice of Britain's "top-side people." Blind to the political transformation in the balance of power and the increased vulnerability of Czechoslovakia, he interpreted Hitler's expansion as a move to secure markets and resources to alleviate Germany's economic situation.

Kennedy quickly concluded that the most urgent problem facing Europeans was not the political crisis but the economic crisis. The political maneuvering was simply "playing house," he wrote to friends back in the United States; it was not putting people back to work and it was not coming to grips with unemployment, the roots of the problem. To the jobless European worker with a hungry family to feed, it mattered little whether a swastika or some other flag flew over his roof.[201] If American business fails to improve and to increase its trade with Europe, "we will have a situation that will far overshadow any political maneuverings," he told Roosevelt.[202]

In a phone conversation a few days after the Anschluss, Kennedy emphatically repeated his economic views to the secretary of the treasury, Henry Morgenthau. "They can talk to me all they want about the political aspects of everything that's happening, Henry, but that isn't what the trouble is," Kennedy said. "The trend is definitely down unless they get together on some economic basis—to hell with the political." The British "[have] got an economic situation that's very much worse than anybody has pretended that it was . . . and it's going to get progressively worse," he predicted. "There isn't anything in the Christ-World that's going to save it." He foresaw a declining stock market in England, quite unrelated to the war scare, which would make America's market decline look very simple. Britain's insufficient trade, a lack of money, the lack of business acceleration, all reflected an unsound economy.[203] In a sweeping proposal he told FDR that "the time is going to come, after Chamberlain has made the political offers necessary, for you to make a worldwide gesture and base it completely on an economic stand." Do nothing at the moment, Kennedy advised, but eventually Europe will have a "mad desire" for increased trade and for new business and will welcome the president's initiative. Kennedy prophesied that FDR's proposal would be an unforgettable worldwide historical event. "It isn't something that may have to be done, it is something that will have to be done."[204]

Kennedy's do-nothing advice reflected the administration's position. Although FDR initially wanted to condemn the Anschluss, Sumner Welles and other officials in the State Department prevailed upon him, and the president was finally persuaded not to risk damaging appeasement possibilities in Europe by censuring the Germans.[205] The chief European adviser at the State Department, Jay Pierrepont Moffat, succinctly stated the American position: "We certainly can't be thought, whatever our sympathies may be, to assume any responsibility legal or moral, in Europe at the moment."[206] The only overt American response to the Anschluss was Secretary Hull's guarded statement on March 19, 1938: "The extent to which the Austrian incident . . . is calculated to endanger the maintenance of peace and the preservation of the principles in which this Government believes is, of course, a matter of serious concern to the Government of the United States."[207] He also closed the American legation in Vienna, raised the tariff on Austria's exports, and asked Germany to assume responsibility for Austria's debts, a request Hitler ignored.

Kennedy closely watched British reaction to the Anschluss and passed on conversations from social gatherings with financiers and businessmen to Washington officials and friends. Anticipating Chamberlain's condemnation of Germany's action in the House of Commons two days later, he cabled Hull that the British government was not disturbed by the Nazification of Austria but by the force used to effect it.[208] Nearly a fortnight after the annexation, the ambassador reported to the secretary that the British had a new and more "complacent attitude" toward the crisis, and he repeated his conviction that there would be no war. The British were not "going to let themselves into any kind of mess—and by a mess I mean a war—unless they had tried out every possible method to avert it."[209]

Kennedy also closely monitored the reaction of the British press and reported to Hull that it had been unanimous in praise of the government's condemnation of Germany's action. Although the press criticized the "ruthlessness" of the annexation, not one newspaper suggested that Britain should become involved.[210] On the day when the swastika was raised over Vienna, the Chamberlain government protested and then resigned itself, accepting the fait accompli, just as Kennedy had predicted.

Winston Churchill, "who seemed to most of official Britain the classical case of a man with a brilliant future behind him,"[211] vigorously criticized Chamberlain's policy. In a thought-provoking speech before the Commons on March 14, 1938, he proposed a "Grand Alliance," "a solemn treaty for mutual defense against aggression," organized by France and Britain.[212] Chamberlain, however, had already considered and rejected such a scheme. He viewed it as attractive but impractical.[213] Shaken by the Anschluss, he was more determined than ever to reach a settlement with the Axis allies. Although it was temporarily necessary to abandon conversations with Germany, he intended quietly and persistently to pursue talks with Italy. At the same time, he vowed to increase the rearmament program and show that Britain refused to be bullied.[214]

In the weeks following the Anschluss, Hitler seemed temporarily sated. He was like "a boa constrictor that had eaten a good deal and was trying to digest the meal before taking on anything else," Chamberlain told Kennedy.[215] Meanwhile, Kennedy continued to keep the State Department informed by providing summaries of the political situation from a wide range of British newspaper accounts and by passing on his conversations with key British officials.[216] The foreign secretary told him of Britain's intention to designate his office in Vienna as a consulate general and requested that the United States coordinate its announcement with Britain's. Kennedy offered to arrange for the announcements.[217]

Lord Halifax and Cadogan also advised him of the preparations for the prime minister's important statement on foreign affairs on March 24 in the House of Commons, establishing the government's diplomatic agenda for the months ahead and beginning its twisted and tension-filled journey toward Munich. Kennedy reported that the statement, after considerable tinkering, became more pro-French and less negative, and pleased British opinion by refraining from committing Britain to any specific action. It certainly pleased him too, as he sat spellbound in the diplomatic gallery listening to the prime minister pledge to work for a peaceful solution based on local autonomy and to urge the Czechs to grant more rights to their German subjects; but his statement also insinuated that if France were drawn into war, Britain would follow.[218] In an equivocal statement constantly quoted throughout the tense summer months of 1938, the prime minister warned Hitler:

> Where peace and war are concerned, legal obligations are not alone involved, and, if war broke out, it would be unlikely to be confined to those who have assumed such obligations. . . . It would be quite impossible to say . . . what Governments might become involved. . . . This is especially true in the case of two countries like Great Britain and France, with long associations of friendship, with interests closely interwoven, devoted to the same ideals of democratic liberty, and determined to uphold them.[219]

Chamberlain thus kept his options open. Britain now seemed to have a practical policy supported by the Commons and consonant with her worldwide position. But it remained to be seen whether France would accept the policy and whether Czechoslovakia would acquiesce to Hitler's demands.

A deeply impressed Kennedy described the prime minister's speech as a "masterpiece," a harmonious blend of "high morals and politics" such as he had never witnessed before. The Labour Party's leader, Clement Attlee, scored no points at all, Kennedy told Arthur Krock, in the second of his "Private and Confidential" series: Chamberlain "simply slew the Opposition."[220]

The speech also convinced the ambassador that no war was in sight as long as Chamberlain, whose popularity was growing daily, remained in power. "I can't see how anyone could (a) believe that a general war will break out during the remainder of this year or (b) could figure it would affect the United States very adversely if it did," Kennedy declared. To prove his point, he roamed over Europe's map, pointing out the potential tinderboxes and how the prime minister had shrewdly defused them: The Italians will get a deal, including a trade agreement and provisions for restricting a Mediterranean naval presence. The Czechs will appeal to Hitler as supplicants and ask him what he wants and then do his bidding; he will also get what he wants from Czechoslovakia without having to resort to any military presence there. The Czechs know that as long as Britain refuses to give France unconditional guarantees to reinforce their efforts, France will not act rashly to stop the German domination of Czechoslovakia; neither will the Russians, who are too far away and too disorganized—and thus the Czech situation will solve itself without any outside interference. The civil war in Spain is about to end in Franco's victory without either Britain or France aiding the government's forces—"so where is your war?" he asked.[221]

Still in a prophetic frame of mind, Kennedy foresaw an economic boom for Britain, particularly since Chamberlain had given the rearmament program priority and thus it would stimulate the heavy industries and increase trade. The United States should start an economic comeback to coincide with Britain's, the ambassador argued, especially since Britain could not prosper alone; otherwise we and everyone else will be so deeply in the doghouse that war might seem to be an attractive alternative. The British are "shooting the works in the hope that they can work out a general appeasement" whereby they can stand at the bargaining table with a few aces in their hands. It's a long shot, Kennedy said, but who has a better plan?[222] But there were some who did. Kennedy was deaf to those like Churchill who believed that Hitler could be stopped only by specific warnings that Britain would resist further German aggression.[223]

"I wish our fellows at home would attend to the worries they have on their own doorsteps and keep Europe out of their minds until they made some headway in their own country," Kennedy said. He found it ridiculous that "an American investor in his own country's securities should worry that war in Europe would tilt his apple cart further on the bias." Most of them "don't know a damned thing about foreign affairs and usually care less. Why are they concerned about them now?"[224]

After the crisis passed, Kennedy looked for an opportunity to explain his views on American political isolation and economic cooperation before an English audience. He wanted to explain matters of vital concern to the British and to disabuse them of any confusion about the relationship between the two English-speaking countries. "I feared that the admitted fact of Anglo-American friendship was being wishfully and perhaps artfully interpreted to mean that our common bonds also held us together in the fashioning of our national policies," he wrote in his memoir.[225] The forum Kennedy chose was the traditional debutante's coming-out party for the American ambassador, the Pilgrim's Club dinner, the first gathering for every new ambassador, always hosted by the premier Anglo-American Society. The event was held at Claridge's, the grand hotel in Mayfair, on March 18, six days after the Anschluss. Kennedy had been invited by the event's chairman, Edward Villiers Stanley, Earl of Derby, in late January, soon after his appointment.[226] Invitations were sent out to nearly four hundred British politicians, diplomats, and businessmen.

The ambassador knew he would have a receptive audience and spent several days working on his speech.[227] He submitted a copy to Hull for approval on March 11, and the secretary accepted it with minor alterations. Coincidentally Hull was preparing his own speech with a marked "internationalist" tone for the National Press Club. Hull, Jimmy Dunn, Sumner Welles, and Pierrepont Moffett [*sic*], according to Kennedy, all thought that Kennedy's draft was too isolationist.[228] While Hull was urging international cooperation among peace-loving nations and avoiding the extremes of isolationism and internationalism, Kennedy was arguing that "the average American has little interest in foreign affairs" and so it was difficult "to evolve any semblance of a long-range foreign policy," particularly given the endless combinations of various interest groups within the American public clamoring for special treatment. "I think it is not too much to say that the great bulk of the American people is not now convinced that any common interest exists between them and any other country. The burden of proof is on any nation that suggests collaboration"—statements that the cautious secretary deleted.[229] State Department officials, too, pruned Kennedy's draft, making it less isolationist in tone. Hull would have liked to cut even more, but other department officials restrained him, fearing an altercation between him and the ambassador. The suggested changes were sent to Kennedy. Perhaps concerned that he might appeal to the president over his head, Hull also informed FDR that virtually all the department officials agreed with him that Kennedy's original draft was too isolationist.[230] Dutifully Kennedy incorporated Hull's recommendation into his second draft and sent it to him for approval on March 14.

But Hull and Roosevelt both thought that even Kennedy's second draft was too rigid and likely to be misinterpreted. They suggested deleting vintage Kennedy phrases like "It is only when our vital interests are definitely affected that we are moved to action, and that is as it should be" and "We are still convinced in my country that the economic difficulties facing the world are more fundamental than the current political frictions" and "The United States . . . has no plans to seek or offer assistance in the event that war . . . should break out in the world."[231] Obediently, Kennedy complied with the requests for deletions in the twice-revised document and suggested a few more of his own, noting in his memoir that Hitler's seizure of Austria "was having an impact upon the Roosevelt-Hull thinking."[232] But Moffat remembered that the ambassador also had the gall to "beg" Hull to postpone his address, arguing that it could easily be misunderstood in Britain.[233] Lord Astor's warning to Kennedy that imminent war was more likely than "the leading men here" would like the public to know prompted him to call Hull and to urge him not to make his speech.[234] State Department officials, however, were livid at the ambassador's cocky request and interpreted it as an attempt to ensure that his more isolationist speech would receive a more favorable coverage than the secretary's.[235] Such behavior was hardly calculated to win Kennedy fans within the protocol-minded State Department and foreshadowed difficulties for him with Hull and FDR.

Both men gave their speeches as arranged. Hull's speech before the National Press Club on March 17 expressed America's concern that "the world was racing hell-bent toward destruction."[236] Hull argued that "isolation is not a means to security; it is a fruitful source of insecurity," and yet he reaffirmed the traditional American policy of no foreign-policy commitments. Hull's theme was that the United States should follow "a sound middle course" between internationalism and isolationism—a theme that Kennedy, sounding remarkably like Hull, would repeat in his own speech the next day.[237]

As the ambassador jokingly likened himself to a Pilgrim Father complaining about the woes of transporting a wife and nine children across the Atlantic in shifts, and drew laughs when he referred to the Boston Tea Party, the audience settled back in their seats, anticipating the usual rhetoric on Anglo-American friendship and common heritage. But within a few moments the listeners strained forward, determined not to miss a word of this astonishingly blunt lecture on American diplomatic self-interest. Because "our two countries enjoy a relationship which is unique," Kennedy said, he wanted to speak plainly, as one friend to another. The average American fears losing his job and fears getting into war. The Roosevelt administration intended to be "careful and wary" of commitments to foreign countries and to remain faithful to the traditions of no entangling alliances, he explained, echoing Hull. The attitude of the United States was frequently misunderstood. "In some quarters, it has been interpreted to mean that our country would not fight under any circumstances short of actual invasion." That attitude is inaccurate and dangerous, he emphasized. The audience applauded approvingly and then fell back into a thoughtful silence when Kennedy continued. "Others seem to imagine that the United States could never remain neutral . . . [if] a general war should unhappily break out." That was also a "dangerously conceived . . . misapprehension." The American government intended to "pursue whatever course we considered best for the United States." "My country has decided," Kennedy stated, "that it must stand on its own feet"—something of a spin on American public opinion.[238] His unsmiling audience understood the implication. However, the ambassador said, the American government would "join and encourage other nations in a peace program based on economic recovery, limitation of armaments and the revival of the sanctity of international commitments. . . . If the nations of the world would trade liberally and naturally among themselves a new kind of security would be born . . . based on intelligent self-interest and not on force."[239]

But such security was hardly likely in the face of Nazi aggression and widespread European economic dislocation. Although Kennedy closed his eyes to the former, he clearly saw the latter. His advice was a muddled blend of Roosevelt's public policy of isolationism—a doctrine that Kennedy really did believe in and carried to the extreme, pleasing even the most ardent isolationists—and Hull's sacred dogma of economic cooperation and free trade.

Kennedy had intended his speech for domestic consumption and to prove to his American audience that he had not gone British. It was only fair, he wrote to Arthur Krock, to tell the British the "unpalatable truth" that they could not assume that the United States would "come to their rescue if they get in a jam. I, personally, am by no means sure our people would consider it," he said to his friend. Although he noted that parts of the speech fell flat, he also appreciated the Foreign Office's favorable reaction to his "frank dealing" and thought that the speech was quite well received generally.[240]

In reporting the speech, the British newspapers—intentionally, Kennedy surmised in his memoir—deleted any reference to American neutrality if war were to break out and stressed instead the statement that no one should believe that America would fight only if invaded.[241] The *Times* even praised Kennedy for clarifying the European diplomatic situation and bemoaned that Britain lacked as articulate a statement from Chamberlain.[242] *The Economist* gave one of the most insightful interpretations of the speech. Although it was obviously disappointed with Kennedy's remarks and described them as "cautious," the prestigious magazine did comment that they illustrated how a government's policy in a democratic country "is confined within the bounds of public opinion which may be based on traditions that have little to do with urgent realities of the contemporary world,"[243] certainly an apt description of American isolationism in the late 1930s and of Kennedy's views on foreign policy.

The American press was quite laudatory in its assessment of Kennedy's address and touted it as a sound statement of American principles in foreign policy, even more sound than Hull's the night before.[244] Boake Carter of the *Boston Globe*, always a shrewd Kennedy observer, wrote that he was amused by Kennedy, "a two-fisted, hard-boiled market trader," pleading for better trade relations by arguing that "the more you trade with a fellow the more he's apt to like you." No such "namby pamby" principle exists in economic relations, the columnist said, and no one knows better than "Wall Street Trader Joseph P. Kennedy."[245]

Kennedy became an advocate for Secretary of State Cordell Hull's vision of economic internationalism embodied in reciprocal trade agreements. Both men believed that such trade agreements would be effective instruments for promoting cooperation and maintaining peace. "Wherever I go, and with whomever I speak," Kennedy assured the secretary, "I am stressing the fact that the economics of the situation need attention even more than the political aspects."[246] Sounding like Hull again, the ambassador, a few weeks after his Pilgrim

Club address on March 31, 1938, told the United Kingdom's Chamber of Shipping: "We want to see the channels of trade unclogged, so that goods may move freely between nations. Therein lies our hope of prosperity, not only for shipping but for other industries as well."[247] And therein lay Kennedy's credo for peace. The British press considered the ambassador's speech "uniformly favorable" and illustrative of Kennedy's typical "American approach."[248]

Picking up some of his earlier economic themes, Kennedy continued to emphasize the need for increased trade between the United States, Britain, and Europe to stimulate their economies, the source of "the real trouble in Europe."[249] Unless the Anglo-American nations strengthen their economic positions by providing solutions to unemployment and security for their workers, "nothing else will matter much," he warned the American Club on March 24.[250] His outlook for Europe was even bleaker. Europe's economic plight was "acute" and its standard of living deteriorating swiftly.[251] In another sweeping gesture, he proposed that "we are going to have a chance to come out with an economic scheme much broader than trade agreements to save the world, and that's the spot where I think the United States can earn the real respect of the world."[252] America must assume the leadership, he argued, since America has the manpower and resources.

Yet Kennedy's advocacy of American leadership applied only to economics; it did not imply an acceptance of political commitments or intervention. He remained a staunch nationalist, an isolationist in the tradition of Senator William F. Borah, a Republican member of the Foreign Relations Committee, an ally worth having. Borah regarded Kennedy as a very "sensible" foreign-policy spokesman. Like the senator, the ambassador believed that the United States should remain aloof from political alliances or entanglements in Europe's affairs. Political intervention in foreign affairs could only threaten America's economic security and her own democratic institutions. In late April, after Kennedy had been at his post a little over a month, he wrote to Borah: "The more I see of things here," he said, "the more convinced I am that we must exert all of our intelligence and effort toward keeping clear of any involvement. As long as I hold my present job, I shall never lose sight of this guiding principle." British political leaders had reassured him, he told Borah, that they completely understood American public opinion and were "going ahead with their plans without counting on the United States to be either for or against them." They did not "want or expect anything special from us." Now that this was understood, he could deal with them "in a frank and business-like manner."[253]

Although Kennedy had been caught up in the whirl of settling in and the drama of the Anschluss, by March 22 he had found a few minutes to catch his breath and to jot down his appraisal of his new home and new job to Hull. "I am still a little dizzy trying to meet Ambassadors and Ministers and newspaper men," he wrote, "and there isn't very much time to think, but I am hoping that the pressure will let up and we will have a chance to analyze some of these developments." "It looks like a very nice place, where one can make a lot of new acquaintances and become more educated in world affairs at his own expense.... I am sure I will have a fine time," he said, pleased with his positive reception. "I probably can do a good deal of missionary work" on the proposed trade agreement.[254]

Try as he might to retain his independence, the ambassador began to work more closely with Chamberlain and to urge American support for the prime minister's efforts, as he did when Chamberlain decided to extend the appeasement policy to Italy. The prime minister wanted to reopen negotiations about Mussolini's Ethiopian conquests, always a prickly issue between him and the president, who opposed the prime minister's desire to extend de jure recognition to Italy's new territory. The British told Washington that any lasting solution of Europe's problems would involve a general scheme of political and economic cooperation rather than the piecemeal approaches tried with Italy and Germany. Sir Ronald Lindsay, the British ambassador, asked Washington whether it might "assist or encourage such a development" by taking "independent but correlated action." Such help would be "of the greatest value," he said—a rather nervy request considering Chamberlain's attitude toward Roosevelt's conference proposal in January.[255]

Chamberlain's government kept Kennedy informed, and he in turn relayed information to Washington. He reported on his conversation with Count Dino Grandi, Italy's ambassador in London, who said that the Italians would "heave a sigh of relief" once the Anglo-Italian agreement was formalized. It would "relieve" Italy "of being so closely identified with Germany" and weaken the Hitler-Mussolini alliance. Kennedy added that it would indeed—all the more reason for supporting it.[256]

In early April, the wily British foreign secretary, using large doses of flattery to sweeten the gullible ambassador's judgment, solicited his help to get a public statement from Roosevelt endorsing the Anglo-Italian agreement. Halifax told Kennedy "that the United States was regarded by the world as having higher moral standards than his own country." If the president would "say some friendly word" in support of the agreement, it "would be an enormous help throughout the world," the foreign secretary said. "There is no question that Chamberlain and Halifax and the present British Government highly regard the influence of the president and yourself throughout the world," Kennedy wrote to Hull, applying his own brand of flattery. "There is no question about [the treaty] being the beginning of a step in the right direction," he said. "Ninety percent of the people in Great Britain will hail it with great acclaim," he predicted, quite agreeable to doing Britain's bidding.[257]

Perhaps to sway the opinions of influential officials and columnists who could affect administration policy, as well as to keep them informed of his own views, Kennedy, always a great publicity hound, sent another series of letters, written on April 14 and marked "Private and Confidential," elaborating on his opinions to a number of friendly newspapermen and politicians. "The Italians apparently realize that the Germans are essentially competitors and not allies and that Mussolini and Hitler cannot live long under the same tent," he wrote, "there simply isn't room." Whether the treaty would prevent or delay war is anybody's guess, Kennedy added, but right now "all I can say is that no immediate war is in sight."[258]

When the agreement was forwarded to Washington on the day before it was signed, April 15, Halifax repeated his request for a public endorsement, saying that he and the prime minister would be "grateful" if Roosevelt could "give some public indication of his approval of the agreement itself and of the principles which have inspired it."[259] Kennedy obediently forwarded the request, too, along with his suggested draft of a statement approving the agreement for the president's use at his forthcoming press conference. The ambassador urged Roosevelt's support of the agreement because he believed that "it was the high point in Mr. Chamberlain's foreign policy thus far."[260] Roosevelt remained chilly to the idea and reluctantly remarked to Sumner Welles of the State Department, "I suppose the last paragraph needs some answer."[261] Britain was "on the spot"; therefore Roosevelt and Welles decided to give her moral support.[262] Hull concurred reluctantly.

A weak "gentleman's agreement" was finally reached and signed on April 16, 1938, reaffirming the military status quo in the Mediterranean and the Red Sea, renewing the censorship of propaganda, and cautiously promising British recognition of Italian sovereignty over Ethiopia when Italy evacuated some of her "volunteer" troops from Spain. The agreement would not be binding until the touchy Spanish question had been settled to Chamberlain's satisfaction, a concession to American qualms as well.[263] By the end of the year, ten thousand of Mussolini's Black Shirts had been withdrawn from Spain, and the treaty became effective on November 16, 1938.

The cool, noncommittal press conference statement issued by Roosevelt on April 19 shied away from any overt endorsement of Italy's conquest of Abyssinia, which in fact never was extended; but it did applaud the treaty as an example of "peaceful negotiations." Was there any comment he might have on the Anglo-Italian agreement? a reporter asked FDR. "Yes, by Jove, there is," the wily president responded cavalierly. "I forgot it. I will see if I can find it. I have a perfectly good comment. Here it is right here."[264]

> As this Government has on frequent occasions made it clear, the United States, in advocating the maintenance of international law and order, believes in the promotion of world peace through the friendly solution by peaceful negotiation between nations of controversies which may arise between them. It has also urged the promotion of peace through the finding of means for economic appeasement. It does not attempt to pass upon the political features of accords such as that recently reached between Great Britain and Italy, but this Government has seen the conclusion of an agreement with sympathetic interest because it is proof of the value of peaceful negotiations.[265]

Except for the addition of the last line referring to "the value of peaceful negotiations" and a shorter, terser sentence structure, the presidential statement reflected Kennedy's almost verbatim.[266]

Thus, the president supported the method but not the contents of the Anglo-Italian agreement. "In one breath," Moffat said, "we praise the British for getting together with the Italians; in the next breath we imply that the Italians are treaty breakers."[267] Such was Roosevelt's strategy. He had devised a compromise between refusing and yet not endorsing appeasement, more like fence straddling than anything else. The upshot of this approach, however, was to leave him adrift in foreign policy and to leave his ambassador in London as an agreeable prop for Chamberlain's appeasement policy.

When the Anglo-Italian agreement was approved, its opponents argued that it would only lead to war. But Chamberlain defended the treaty as enhancing appeasement and thereby Europe's chance for peace. The prime minister also made good use of the president's ambiguous message of April 19 by selectively quoting Roosevelt's statement, an incident that continued to "rankle," Kennedy noted. Chamberlain maintained that it represented "sympathetic interest" on FDR's part, because it "affords proof of the value of peaceful negotiations," an interpretation that the opposition correctly called "a misrepresentation of President Roosevelt." It led Kennedy to speculate that Roosevelt and Hull may have thought that they had been taken in by Welles and perhaps by him as well, and that the president and his secretary might also believe that he, in turn, had been taken in by the British.[268]

The conclusion of the Anglo-Italian agreement was a personal triumph for Chamberlain and ended long-drawn-out, behind-the-scenes maneuvering consistently supported and applauded by his willing ally, Kennedy. The ambassador's appeal to Roosevelt to support Chamberlain's policy publicly may have been a factor in Roosevelt's decision to do so. His mild and vague expression about "sympathetic interest" and "the value of peaceful negotiations" was almost identical to Kennedy's. The ambassador received praise from Halifax, who told him how "very greatly I appreciate the help you have given us,"[269] and condemnation from American liberals like Secretary of the Interior Harold Ickes, who resented Kennedy's bad influence on Roosevelt. The critical secretary regretted "that the President made any such statements. It wasn't called for," he argued, "because the negotiations in question were between Great Britain and Italy." Ickes regarded Roosevelt's "unnecessary and regrettable"[270] endorsement as "an unusual procedure" since it implied his approval of Italy's militaristic policy toward Ethiopia and Spain.[271] Kennedy's later support of appeasement would continue to grate on Ickes and result in increasing enmity between the two.

The Anglo-Italian agreement set the stage for Kennedy's subsequent behavior as ambassador. He was willing to accept Chamberlain's political policies as temporary expedients that paralleled his long-range schemes for economic cooperation. He also appeared to have taken the initiative and enthusiastically urged on Washington a foreign-policy stance that the president reluctantly accepted. Like other American diplomats of the 1930s, Kennedy represented a nation confused and divided in foreign affairs, a virtually policyless nation in which Washington had not defined its attitudes toward European relations. In such a situation, a diplomat would be dependent on his own wits and convictions or be extremely susceptible to the fears and attitudes of his host government. Kennedy was both; the fault lay with Roosevelt.

The Anglo-Italian agreement had only been one facet of Chamberlain's policy for preserving the peace of Europe; another was to maintain the policy of nonintervention in the Spanish Civil War.[272] When the civil war in Spain broke out on July 17, 1936, as General Francisco Franco led an army revolt against the republican government in Madrid, Europe's leaders feared the fighting might escalate into a widespread European war. Franco's fascist rebels appealed successfully for aid from Berlin and Rome as the Republican Loyalists asked France for help. Bowing to pressure from Britain, who was ever fearful of enlarging the conflict, France refused aid and proposed instead a policy of general nonintervention. The United States, too, refrained from interference and was even unwilling to sanction the conventional international custom of trading freely and sending arms to the recognized government of Spain. Thus American foreign policy pleased the internationalists by allying the United States with Britain and France; it also placated the isolationists by refraining from intervention. It required no international commitments and therefore contained few domestic risks. Roosevelt's intention was to limit the war to a localized conflict, not to save Spanish democracy or stop a fascist takeover.[273] But as the war continued, FDR's principle of nonintervention in Spain aroused deeper passions and caused more dissension in the United States than any other foreign-policy issue.

To many a liberal, who pictured the Loyalists as heroically defending democracy and freedom and staving off fascism, this struggle was the supreme test of doctrinal orthodoxy. Nonintervention was a farce, they argued, and they pointed out that the arms embargo embedded in the Neutrality Act ironically aided the anti-democratic fascist forces. They were emphatic about lifting the arms embargo to aid the Loyalists and pleaded for the traditional policy of trading with the established government during a civil war, thereby reinforcing the embattled republican government. Liberal spokesmen like Ickes were boisterously indignant over America's "regrettable" Spanish policy. Ickes regarded it as "one of the black pages in American history."[274] Welles, the staid undersecretary of state, was also worried: he believed that Franco's victory would be tantamount to appeasement for Italy. It would advance Mussolini's interests in the Mediterranean substantially. Even some isolationists like Senator Borah and Norman Thomas, the head of the American Socialist Party, regarded FDR's policy as thoroughly unneutral, as "non-noninterference."[275]

Yet the opposition was no less vocal. To many a loyal American Catholic, the anti-clerical and socialist programs of the Loyalists were an affront. They insisted on steadfastly maintaining the current policy of nonintervention in cooperation with Britain, France, and a score of other countries. In addition, they could count on the support of Secretary of State Cordell Hull and a group of Anglophile career officers, staunch defenders of nonintervention. "In the absence of a general system of international security . . . it was difficult . . . to see how we could have followed any other course," Hull wrote in his memoirs. The nonintervention policy did not lead to a general conflict, he pointed out, and when European war did break out, not only did Spain remain aloof, but relations between Britain and France and the United States were "bettered."[276]

Thus Roosevelt was caught in the middle of a great national debate on foreign policy. Privately he was sympathetic to the Republic and considered lifting the arms embargo to Madrid in the spring of 1938. Domestic political realities, however, convinced him to refrain from repeal. It would be unwise and pointless, FDR argued, and agreed with House Democrats that repeal would cost them every Catholic vote in the fall elections.[277] "This was the cat that was actually in the bag, and it is the mangiest, scabbiest cat ever," wrote Ickes bitterly when he heard that Roosevelt had ultimately decided against revision. "This proves up to the hilt what so many people have been saying, namely, that the Catholic minorities in Great Britain and America have been dictating the international policy with respect to Spain." Nevertheless, the prudent politician in the White House could hardly afford to alienate such a large block of traditionally Democratic supporters. Even if the repeal did pass Congress, FDR told Ickes, "Spain would not be in a position to buy munitions from us."[278] Thus Roosevelt was willing to risk the wrath of his opponents by maintaining the arms embargo and to accept a fascist victory in Spain aided unintentionally by the United States, rather than undermine Britain or France and their support for nonintervention or chance a wider war in Europe.

Kennedy's position on revision and his influence on Roosevelt is a matter of debate. Some historians argue that Kennedy played a major, diabolical role and blame him for Roosevelt's decision to continue the embargo.[279] So, too, did Drew Pearson. He passed on to Kennedy the rumor circulating in State Department circles that Kennedy had been "rather vigorously urging" that the embargo be retained and that the insinuation, "naturally and unfortunately," was that Kennedy's position was due to his Catholicism.[280] It is true that privately Kennedy was "horrified at any suggestion that America or Britain should help in any way the 'bunch of atheists or Communists' he believed the Spanish government to be."[281] But when revision looked feasible, Kennedy carefully crafted his arguments in more general terms—perhaps, as some suggested, so that he would not do a disservice to his presidential ambitions by appearing "too Catholic."[282] In a dispatch to the secretary of state, Kennedy reported on Britain's Spanish policy, which he was in agreement with. It was designed "(a) to limit or prevent foreign intervention and (b) at all costs to prevent the internecine struggle in Spain from enveloping Europe in a general war." Kennedy supported Chamberlain's attitude and added that "with all its faults non-intervention has contributed towards the preservation of peace in Europe. Settlement of the Spanish problem," he wrote, "would seem to be an essential prerequisite to any scheme for general European appeasement. The injection of any new factor into this already overcharged and delicate situation," the ambassador warned, "might have far-reaching consequences."[283] It is also true that Kennedy cabled a vigorous protest upon hearing that Roosevelt was wavering about maintaining the arms embargo against Spain. Revision would help the Loyalists, he argued.[284]

Although the president and his ambassador ultimately agreed on the Spanish question, here, as on the Anglo-Italian agreement, it is unclear whether Roosevelt was strongly influenced by his ambassador's arguments or that he followed his advice in deciding to maintain the policy of nonintervention. Like Chamberlain and Hull, Kennedy viewed the

Spanish issue from the perspective of foreign policy; Roosevelt examined it primarily from the standpoint of domestic affairs. Kennedy's arguments may have affected Roosevelt's decision, but he was only one of the spokesmen arguing for a continuation of the existing policy. If Roosevelt was persuaded by anyone not to abandon revision, it was probably Hull who had the greatest influence. The president did not want to undermine the secretary's position on nonintervention. Hull's popularity in Congress often won victory in tough fights for the administration.[285]

Despite Kennedy's seeming popularity in London, Washington insiders criticized him chiefly for his flamboyant personality and style. Rumors were whispered about him back home—over his imminent resignation, his off-the-cuff views critical of the State Department, and his presumed presidential ambitions. "There is not one word of truth in that story," Kennedy said, in an exclusive transatlantic phone interview to the *Boston Evening American* as he emphatically denied that he was resigning. The *Daily Express*, Lord Beaverbrook's journal, declared that Kennedy wanted to quit his job in "a blaze of glory" by settling the British debt to the United States. "I have no intention of resigning," he said, and "I have no plans about the British war debt to the United states and . . . no intention of discussing [it] with President Roosevelt."[286] Asked at a press conference about Kennedy's settling of the British debts, Hull denied knowing anything about it. "In the case of Mr. Kennedy or Mr. Bullitt he always refers all inquiries to the White House," Morgenthau wrote, after a phone call to the secretary asking about rumors about Kennedy.[287]

Ickes delighted in undermining Kennedy with State Department officials. With his usual frankness, the ambassador had "inveighed eloquently against 'the career boys' in the State Department" to Ickes, a crotchety liberal who took it all in and mischievously repeated it to the department officials. Joe Kennedy, wrote Ickes, "insisted that the State Department did not know what was going on in Europe and that there was no use trying to keep the State Department informed. He complained that everything leaked through the State Department and that nothing got to the President straight unless he sent it to the President direct."[288]

Kennedy's general unorthodox behavior and his disregard for conventions, so amusing to the British, were treated less generously by the State Department. Its officials, originally neutral, were becoming more and more critical of the brash, tart-tongued ambassador. "The old libel that the State Department is made of 'cookie pushers' whose chief concern is the hang of their striped trousers," wrote *Time* magazine, "was just true enough to make many a grave, correct, dry-worded gentleman in the Department dislike the appointment of Joe Kennedy to London."[289]

Kennedy became even more controversial as rumors of his political aspirations were revived in the spring of 1938. Roosevelt was apparently indecisive and reluctant to break tradition by announcing his candidacy for a third term. Garner and Farley had an "understanding" to team up for the election, Ickes observed, prompting speculation from some Democrats that FDR might have to turn to Kennedy as his vice-presidential mate.[290] This would pit two

Roman Catholic vice-presidential candidates against each other. Ickes predicted that Kennedy's presence would strengthen the ticket since he would draw support from conservative business interests and provide for a well-financed campaign. The *Chicago Tribune* predicted that the conservatism of Kennedy "as compared with other Roosevelt followers will offset religious prejudice in the South."[291]

That Kennedy occupied a unique position, esteemed by both FDR and Wall Street, made some political supporters urge him to consider the presidency. But they got no encouragement. "I am not kidding myself about all this talk of candidate [*sic*] for President," Kennedy wrote to T. J. White, the general manager of Hearst Enterprises, whose boss, William Randolph Hearst, considered the ambassador a very viable candidate and said that others were looking seriously at him. Furthermore, if Kennedy "could get the country out of this mess he would have no right to refuse," said Hearst. Kennedy, however, promised White that he was "going to wrap up this job as best I know how and do as much good as I can and then I am going right back and go into business."[292] He also told a *New York Times* foreign correspondent that he discouraged the advances because "he [loved] his family too much. His present job [was] bad enough for the children without absolutely ruining them." And he also said, "I'm not a good candidate. I'm no good at going out and asking the public to vote for me. So far, I've managed to keep hold of my personal independence and I've never given the presidency a serious thought."[293] Kennedy believed that there were many reasons for him not to be a candidate in 1940, including that anti-Catholicism was still too potent a political force in the United States. But even more important was the president's attitude. "I knew the time was not propitious," Kennedy wrote in his memoirs.

> I knew that many of [Roosevelt's] closest advisors were urging him to break with tradition and run for the third time in 1940. There was little doubt that he had the matter under consideration. Mr. Roosevelt also had a quality—a failing, some have called it—of resenting the suggestion that he was to be succeeded and cooling perceptibly toward a man who might be considered, by his friends, a worthy successor. For many years Mr. Roosevelt had been my chief; he still was. I wanted no such false issue to arise between us and endanger both an official relationship of some importance and a personal association which to me had been heavy with meaning.[294]

Probably Kennedy's disavowal of his own presidential ambitions can be taken at face value. His political aspirations were, more likely, for his beloved son and namesake, Joe Jr., upon whose shoulders his family's enormous ambitions rested.

It is hard to find conclusive evidence of Kennedy's political appetites. Some of the Kennedy-for-President rumors grew from the press repeating itself. Boake Carter raved in his column that Kennedy was "sent to London to handle a dangerous job, at a most critical time." Those Washingtonians who wanted him banished because of his increasing popularity as "presidential timber" have fallen flat, the journalist wrote. Kennedy's forthright and sincere response to the events in Europe have won him his countrymen's praise. He has told the British that America is no longer "the tail on the end of the British kite." "So far," Carter chortled, "Kennedy has fooled 'em [his critics], by being simply a straight shooter which is something many citizens are looking for in 1940."[295]

Some of the gossip about Kennedy's presidential ambitions grew from maliciousness and a desire to foster friction between Roosevelt and Kennedy. One political observer claimed that the White House was particularly upset at how often Kennedy was mentioned as Roosevelt's successor.[296] Still, Kennedy's long-distance wooing of the American press appeared to confirm his supposed presidential ambitions. He continued to send several select correspondents "Private and Confidential" information that they published, much to the astonishment of the yet uninformed White House and State Department. One reporter, disconcerted by the intimate content of Kennedy's reports, collected his letters and handed them over to Roosevelt.[297] Some Kennedy watchers, not realizing that he had wanted the ambassadorship, believed that he had been exiled to London and argued that his actions were calculated to keep his name in the headlines. Another interpretation was that Kennedy was trying to prepare the public for his lack of success in settling the war debts and negotiating the trade talks and to absolve himself of responsibility for their failure.[298]

Concern over the situation in Europe, and his desire to see his son graduate, prompted Kennedy to cable Hull requesting permission to return to the United States in June. He wanted to meet with him and Roosevelt and discuss his "very definite impressions" about Europe.[299] The ambassador's mercurial spirits had sunk again. His discussions with Harold Ickes, newly wed and honeymooning in England, struck Ickes. "There was no doubt left in my mind that he is very nervous" and "full of the European situation." "He was greatly afraid that hell might break loose at any time over Czechoslovakia," Ickes wrote in his diary.[300] The ambassador spent the day before he left making the usual round of official calls on Chamberlain, Halifax, and a host of ambassadors and diplomats.[301]

"I'm just the same—you won't find me changed a bit," joked Kennedy as he welcomed a reporter on the telephone while the *Queen Mary* glided into New York harbor on June 20, 1938.[302] Jimmy Roosevelt, and the entourage of reporters accompanying him down the bay on the Coast Guard cutter, met Kennedy, who flatly denied that he was interested in the presidency. He pointed out that he had worked for Roosevelt since 1932. "I enlisted under President Roosevelt in 1932 to do whatever he wanted me to do. There are many problems at home and abroad and I happen to be busy at one abroad just now. If I had my eye on another job it would be a complete breach of faith."[303] In the good-natured banter between Kennedy and the reporters, the infamous knee breeches affair was brought up again. Was he trying to hide something by wearing long trousers? Both the king and queen understood his reasons for refusing to wear knee breeches, explained Kennedy. "[It] wasn't because he was bowlegged," but simply because he did not want to. To prove it, Kennedy spotted a pretty young lady reporter and, grinning broadly, offered to show her privately that he was neither knock-kneed nor bowlegged. His offer was declined.[304]

With fatherly pleasure Kennedy also announced that he would attend Joe Jr.'s graduation at Harvard while in the United States. There was even speculation in the *New York Times* that the Kennedy family would be doubly honored. It reported that, according to an "authoritative source," not only would Joe Jr. receive his bachelor's with honors, but the ambassador would be awarded an honorary degree at the June commencement.[305] Kennedy was thrilled by such talk since an honorary degree from Harvard symbolized the acceptance into that most elite Bostonian circle that had always eluded him. The repeated Brahmin snubs still stung, but this would be a pleasing compensation. Rose believed "it was an honor he wanted for the entire family, for it meant yet another door that would be opened to his sons and his daughters."[306] Once again the theme of the importance of family, for which he showed his most loving, hopelessly sentimental side, figured prominently in Kennedy's ambitions.

The hoopla may have been an instance of Kennedy's friends talking to each other. One source said that the nominating committee had indeed considered Kennedy but decided against it because of his bootlegging past.[307] He had gotten that "Yankee freeze." Another source said that the committee had indicated that it would consider it if he were a good ambassador. In any case, the degree committee headed by Charles Francis Adams, himself a descendant of a diplomatic dynasty at St. James's, did ultimately reject Kennedy. Perhaps the committee concluded that his ambassadorship was not a sufficient mark of distinction, or that the award was premature, or that he had a shady past. Or perhaps the committee was prejudiced against Irish Catholics. "It was a terrible blow to him," Rose told Doris Kearns Goodwin, when he finally learned that he would definitely not be receiving an honorary degree. "After all those expectations had been built up, it was hard to accept that he wasn't really in the running. . . . His mind ranged back and forth over the years and suddenly he felt as if he were once again standing in front of the Porcellian Club, knowing he'd never be admitted."[308]

But Kennedy feigned satisfaction. "There will be one honor degree in the family. That's pretty good," he told journalists at the Ritz-Carlton.[309] Years later, in his "Diplomatic Memoir," he adroitly managed to avoid having to own up to any great desire for the honor, instead of suggesting that he was deserving by telling that many Boston newsmen, indulging in the popular pastime of guessing who the recipients would be, assumed that he would be one. "Indeed, had I not known the contrary, I would have jumped to that conclusion myself for I could have thought that my varied and long services for the Government might have been suitably recognized in this manner."[310] Kennedy's plight delighted the White House. Harold Ickes wrote in his diary: "I remarked on a newspaper item . . . to the effect that Joe had declined an honorary degree from Harvard. The President said to me: 'Can you imagine Joe Kennedy declining an honorary degree from Harvard?' and I had to confess that I couldn't."[311] Despite the fact that he had returned to see his son graduate, Kennedy did not attend the graduation ceremonies themselves and told the press he was spending the day at Hyannis Port with his son

Jack, who was ill.[312] Jack was not ill, but Kennedy's sense of rejection must have been too great to allow him to swallow his own disappointment and celebrate his oldest son's graduation with him, an event Joe Jr. had to go through alone, without the applause of any family member.[313]

Despite the criticism he received from some quarters, there were still old friends, cronies, and Kennedy fans who were delighted with the ambassador. Arthur Krock, his lifelong friend, raved in his column, "Well, here is Mr. Kennedy back again, the rage of London, the best copy in the British (and Irish) press, his counsel steadily sought by the statesmen of the country to which he is accredited, his influence manifest and powerful in all matters in which the United States has an interest in Great Britain." He is still the same "old Joe," bubbled Krock, "undazzled by such a taking up socially and officially as no American perhaps has known abroad since Franklin's day, with his vocabulary unimpaired, his method unchanged and the British openly glad of his Irish connections."[314] Clearly, Krock said, it was the same high-spirited, wise-cracking Joe Kennedy who had left the United States four months earlier.

Kennedy was invited to Hyde Park to confer with Roosevelt the next day, June 21, about Britain and British foreign policy. The ambassador noted in his memoirs that the president still believed that at the appropriate time some "calm and rational approach" from him, though perhaps not his earlier plan of an international conference, could be an effective deterrent to war.[315] As they discussed the international scene, something happened that Kennedy believed signaled a new and more troubled relationship between them, something that would plague them and lead to misunderstandings and a lack of candor, something that was often to be manipulated by others for their own purposes.

The Machiavellian White House press secretary, Steve Early, who must have been acting at Roosevelt's devious instigation, informed William Murphy of the *Philadelphia Inquirer* and Walter D. Trohan of the *Chicago Tribune* that FDR was miffed at Kennedy about the rumors of his presidential ambitions and about Kennedy's "Private and Confidential" correspondence with certain members of the American press.[316] Early then showed the correspondence to Trohan. The two stories written by Murphy and Trohan appeared on June 23, 1938, and were similar, but the *Tribune* story was more detailed. It described "the chilling shadow of 1940" that had descended on the relationship between president and ambassador because of the "positive evidence that Kennedy hopes to use the Court of St. James [*sic*] as a stepping stone to the White House in 1940." It described Kennedy's letters to his friends as "political," containing much insider information and contrived in the hope of convincing them to support his candidacy for president. It accused him of hiring a press agent to keep his name in the political spotlight. It said that "Joe wants to run for President and is dealing behind the Boss's back at the London Embassy." Trohan's headlines blared: "KENNEDY'S 1940 AMBITIONS OPEN ROOSEVELT RIFT" and "President Turns Icy to Fast Friend." The *Tribune*, quoting from "unimpeachable sources" and engaging in wishful thinking, reported that Roosevelt's conference with Kennedy had been carried on "in a frigid atmosphere because Mr. Kennedy hopes to use the court of St. James's as a stepping stone to the White House in 1940." "Joe Kennedy never did anything without thinking of Joe Kennedy," the "soul of selfishness," replied Steve Early, masquerading as a "high Administration official." "And that's the worst thing I can say about a father of nine kids. He'd put them in an orphanage one by one to get himself into the White House."[317] The *Inquirer*'s story had little circulation beyond the paper's immediate territory, but the *Tribune*'s story was picked up by newspapers throughout the Midwest: in Michigan, Wisconsin, Indiana, and Iowa, and even Kansas.

Roosevelt's meeting with Kennedy did not lead to a split between the two. The president's concern was not that Kennedy might become a political rival, but that he might become a political critic. At best Kennedy was considered a long shot since he had never held an elective office and he had no power base. Besides, burly Jim Farley, a fellow Catholic, did have presidential aspirations and he controlled the political machinery of the Democratic Party. If Roosevelt subtly encouraged any political aspirations Kennedy may have had, it was only to ensure his loyalty.

As a critic, Kennedy could seriously damage Roosevelt's political future, especially by mobilizing the conservative anti-Roosevelt Wall Street sentiment. Any coldness that Roosevelt may have displayed during the interview must have been intended to convey his annoyance at Kennedy's indiscretions, but he made sure they parted as friends.[318] Although FDR made guarded replies to newsmen that afternoon about Kennedy's "pleasant and informative" interview, he also told them "that the international picture was not a particularly happy one. . . . All he could do was hope for the best"—an unfortunate and apt instance of America's weak response to the European crisis.[319]

On June 24, the day after the articles had been published, Kennedy was a dinner guest at the White House. On the next day, June 25, he learned who had leaked the story. Arthur Krock had inquired into the matter and sent Kennedy a confidential memo stating that one of the reporters present at Hyde Park confirmed to him that it was indeed Early who had told him and one or two others that "Roosevelt was annoyed with Kennedy partly because of the presidential boomlet" and also because he had given "inside information" on foreign affairs to correspondents before the president himself had received it.[320] The facts came from "an unimpeachable authority," Kennedy believed. "It was a true Irish anger that swept over me," he wrote in his memoirs. Kennedy tried to see the president; his request was denied. He tried to resign; Hull refused his resignation. The secretary tried to console him by telling him that Roosevelt did things like that; in fact, Hull said, "he treats me twenty times as badly." Kennedy finally had an interview with Early. Early offered a "half-hearted denial." In a further conversation with FDR, the president denied that he had anything to do with the goings-on. "In this way," Kennedy wrote, "he assuaged my feelings . . . but deep within me, I knew something had happened."[321]

Roosevelt discussed Kennedy's visit with Ickes, who was curious about the content and the viewpoint of FDR's comments. "I do not think Joe is fooling him very much," Ickes confided to his diary:

He said . . . he did not expect Joe to last more than a couple of years in London because he was the kind of man who liked to go from one job to another and drop it just when the going became heavy. . . . [Roosevelt] knows that Joe is enjoying his job in London, where he is having the time of his life although he cries "wolf."[322]

This illustrated a basic difference in the emotional makeup of the two men. Roosevelt was seldom anything other than undaunted, serene, gracious, relentlessly cheerful, "like the fairy story prince who didn't know how to shudder," wrote one close aide, yet a deeply lonely man unreachable by his wife and children, with no commitments to anyone.[323] Kennedy's personality fluctuated between bearish pessimism and bullish optimism. He was a hot-tempered, cold-blooded, "hard hitting, tempestuous and clever Celt," a man to be judged by what he did, not by what he said.[324] These innate temperamental differences would be further revealed during the succeeding crises and become a source of considerable friction between the two men.

Just before sailing on the SS *Normandie* on June 29, 1938, with his two sons, Kennedy once again had to confront two unsavory rumors circulating among journalists. Newsmen asked him about an article in the *Saturday Evening Post* by Alva Johnson, accusing Jimmy Roosevelt of using his connections with Kennedy to foster his insurance business. In return for Kennedy's business, the allegation was, the president's son had helped Kennedy get preferential treatment to import whiskey for his Somerset Distilling Company before prohibition was lifted. Furthermore, the article stated that Jimmy Roosevelt had been personally responsible for Kennedy's ambassadorial appointment. Since both allegations were untrue, Kennedy said that it was easy to deny them. "I would certainly like to be the best in anything I do," Kennedy cheerfully told the newsmen, but the rumor that he was the premier salesman of scotch whiskey in America "is a phony."[325] There is no record of who gave Johnson the story in the first place.

CHAPTER 3

Shirt-Sleeve Diplomacy: Trade, Treaties, Troubles

Kennedy returned to London, licking his wounds and recovering from Harvard's rejection and Roosevelt's betrayal. He left again for a brief respite in Ireland, where he was fêted and honored like visiting royalty. The journey lifted his spirits before he returned to London again to face the business of diplomacy—treaties, trade, and troubles over Czechoslovakia. The celebration in Ireland demonstrated his continuing support of appeasement, his susceptibility to British influence, and his shortsighted view of the significance of events. It also exhibited his need to claim credit for what he had done and for what he had not done, a trait that amazed and amused FDR and ultimately angered him.

Dominating Kennedy's return to England were political events: the summer-long crisis over Czechoslovakia, and the Anglo-American Trade Agreement, valued not so much for its economic as for its political significance. The trade agreement established him as a shrewd negotiator over trade but an inept interpreter of political realities and economic events. It also led to disagreements with the secretary of state. The Czech crisis showed Kennedy to be an ineffectual diplomat in his naive underestimation of the threat Hitler posed to central Europe and led Kennedy to flout the authority of Washington. Both events were ultimately costly to him by undermining him in the administration: The trade agreement led to the near collapse of his relationship with Secretary Hull, and Kennedy's view of the German threat to Czechoslovakia and his activities supporting Chamberlain's appeasement policy led Roosevelt to be distrustful of Kennedy's advice and suspicious of his intentions. His assessment of these events prevented him from being an effective voice in foreign policy in Washington circles and compromised his two goals of ensuring British appeasement and maintaining American isolationism.

A few days after his return to London, Kennedy, on July 7, 1938, accompanied by his eldest son, Joe Jr.; by Eddie Moore, his secretary; and by John B. Kennedy, a personal friend and journalist, survived an incredibly bumpy plane ride in the midst of a downpour to make a sentimental pilgrimage to Ireland, his first, to receive an honorary doctorate from the National University of Ireland in Dublin.[1] Kennedy told reporters at the United States Legation in Phoenix Park that he was so overwhelmed with emotion that he was afraid to speak; he might break down and weep.[2] But his broad smile and his sentimental feelings betrayed his intense Irish pride as he plodded across the "ould sod" and he and young Joe "follow[ed] rutted dirt roads and narrow country lanes" to "the ancestral homes of the Kennedys, in Wexford Field, and the Hickeys, in Clonakilty."[3] The visit was "one of the very pleasant occasions of my life," he recorded in his memoir; "I was happy to have this opportunity to see the land of my forefathers."[4] In the United States, Kennedy had quietly snubbed the Irish American organizations and was incensed when he was described as an Irish American. Once so labeled by a Boston paper, Kennedy later complained, "I was born here. My children were born here. What the hell do I have to do to be an American?"[5]

After the embarrassment of Harvard's rejection, the news of the Irish reward "came just at the right moment," Rose remembered.[6] The ambassador was emphatic in stressing to reporters its "nonpolitical" and "unofficial" nature.[7] He wanted the degree "for the sake of his children," he told John Cudahy, the American ambassador to Ireland, whose support he enlisted in seeking it. Roosevelt laughed "heartily" upon hearing that Kennedy "had not made up his mind whether to go to the trouble of accepting," wrote Ickes, always happy to pass along anti-Kennedy tidbits.[8]

The government of Eire, southern Ireland, must have looked upon the first Irish-Catholic ambassador to the Court of St. James's with particular pride. British Foreign Office officials considered Kennedy's trip "somewhat abnormal"—Kennedy was not accredited to Ireland. But after all, Cadogan said, the man was "of Irish extraction" and he had "publicly proclaimed his pleasure at the conclusion of the recent Anglo-Irish Agreement." "It seems to me," Cadogan went on, "that it would be a happy idea if he were now to accept the honorary degree from Dublin University, which would no doubt be conferred upon him at a ceremony where speeches would be delivered of a friendly character to this country." Sir Robert Vansittart, permanent undersecretary in the Foreign Office, argued that "even if we disliked the idea I don't see how we could possibly object. That being so, let us say that we shall be very glad if Mr. Kennedy agrees."[9] The Foreign Office followed Vansittart's advice.

The ceremony was presided over by Ireland's prime minister, Eamon de Valera, resplendent in black and gold robes and attended by members of the senate of the National University of Ireland. Kennedy was the fifth American to receive an LL.D. *Honoris Causa*. Sixty-five guests, including the diplomatic and consular corps, cabinet officers, members of the Dail and of Seanad Eireann, the Most Reverend Dr. Paschal Robinson (the papal nuncio), and other dignitaries toasted Kennedy at the state banquet at Dublin Castle on the 8th of July. "We welcome you for yourself and for your race. We are proud that men like you not merely do honour to your country, but honour to our race," said the prime minister.[10] As he addressed the dinner guests, Kennedy spoke eloquently on Anglo-Irish affairs and praised as "a step in the right direction" the recent treaty and the spirit that underlay its negotiation.[11]

The treaty Kennedy referred to was the Anglo-Irish agreement signed on April 25, 1938, in which he had a very strong interest.[12] Chamberlain regarded the agreement as another triumph for appeasement, and critics like Churchill viewed it as useless.[13] It also increased the tension between FDR and his ambassador as each claimed credit for it, and gave Kennedy's gleeful critics more ammunition to argue that the man had indeed been taken in by the suave and sophisticated British.

Before Kennedy's arrival in London, the president had written to de Valera and told him that he had asked his friend Mr. Joseph Kennedy, the newly appointed ambassador in England, to tell the prime minister that "Mr. Roosevelt had a very deep and personal interest in the successful outcome of these negotiations."[14] Kennedy relished the assignments, particularly pleasing to an Irish Catholic from Boston. Within days of his arrival in London, he phoned the office of Malcolm MacDonald, the dominion secretary who headed up the British negotiations. "Hello, Malcolm? This is Joe." MacDonald was not used to being rung directly, and he had no idea who "Joe" was. "Joe Kennedy, the American Ambassador. Can I come over and see you?" Kennedy presented himself at MacDonald's office and talked up the president's "keen" interest in the negotiations. Kennedy wanted to give MacDonald advice on how to get the most public mileage from the agreement in the United States and to explain how significant to American opinion "Dev's" approval of Anglo-Irish reconciliation would be. MacDonald quietly disregarded Kennedy's advice.[15]

Kennedy did see the prime minister on Roosevelt's behalf as well and learned that Chamberlain had gotten a general agreement on everything except Partition, the division of the island into Northern Ireland under Ulster's jurisdiction and Southern Ireland under Dublin's control, an arrangement his Tory government adamantly opposed.[16] Not only did the Anglo-Irish Treaty of 1938 provide for a complete trade settlement and a financial agreement about the long-standing Irish war debts, but it also contained a British promise to transfer to Southern Ireland the Irish ports of Cobh (formerly called Queenstown, in honor of a visit by Queen Victoria), Berehaven, and Lough Swilly. The ports had remained in British hands since Partition in 1921 because of the insistence of Churchill, who stressed their tactical importance to Britain's naval defense. Chamberlain, however, was willing to surrender them, arguing that they required the existence of a large military force and were redundant because of the bases in France and Northern Ireland.[17] He believed that the concession of the ports was nothing more than a symbolic gesture of goodwill and friendship between Britain and Ireland. "I am satisfied that we have only given up the small things . . . for the big things—the ending of a long quarrel, the beginning of better relations between North and South Ireland, and the cooperation of the South with us in trade and defence."[18] To Chamberlain, the Anglo-Irish agreement was a victory for appeasement; de Valera considered it mere payment of a debt and pledged that Ireland would not become a base for foreign powers during wartime.

Churchill, however, argued that it weakened Britain's strategic naval defenses. He attacked the treaty, particularly its port provisions, as "an improvident example of appeasement" similar to abandoning Gibraltar or Malta. "A more feckless act can hardly be imagined," he wrote.[19] The ports were the "sentinel towers" guarding the western part of Britain, protecting the food supplies of its inhabitants and the lifeline for refueling bases for ships guarding convoys. They were also useful bargaining chips for Britain's enemies. "The first step . . . an enemy might take could be to offer complete immunity . . . to Southern Ireland if she would remain neutral."[20] During World War II a neutral Ireland, as Churchill but not Kennedy had foreseen, did deny Britain access to Irish ports unless Britain surrendered Ulster, a stance that Kennedy attributed to de Valera's deep resentment over Churchill's display of venom and bitterness in his opposition to the treaty.[21]

Kennedy was delighted at the Anglo-Irish agreement. It might have an effect unlike anything during the last hundred years, and he urged the government to make the most of it. It reflected "great credit on the Prime Minister and the Secretary of State for Dominion Affairs," he said.[22] The treaty enhanced Britain's security and was another victory for the appeasement policy.[23] The ambassador thought "it now held as great a promise of enduring peace as did those [treaties] between England and the United States," he wrote in his memoir, seeming to dismiss the centuries of hatred, bloodshed, and cruelty between the two countries as inconsequential.[24] The treaty was "the best omen" for the prime minister's chances of negotiating a peace in Europe, the ambassador told reporters on his visit home,[25] certainly overstating its significance; but he added that he thought that de Valera overestimated the significance of the treaty's inability to solve the partition issue, and told Krock that the American press failed to appreciate its "far-reaching importance."[26]

Kennedy supported the treaty on domestic grounds as well because he reasoned that it could strengthen the relations between the United States and Britain by reducing the differences between Ireland and England. "There was no subject which had more influence of an unfortunate nature on Anglo-American relations than the Irish question," he stated.[27] The treaty would show the large Irish American population with its markedly anti-British attitude that a rapprochement between the two countries was actually possible.[28]

"From the point of view of the Anglo-American relations," Lindsay told Halifax, the Anglo-Irish Agreement "cannot fail to contribute to their further improvement."

> The O's and the Macs are still numerous in Congress, and throughout American political life, and politicians generally find it worth while to testify from time to time to their affection for Ireland and to their sympathy for Irish aspirations, even though with many it may be a somewhat academic sentiment, which may win a few votes and can hardly cost any.[29]

The extent of Kennedy's real influence is the subject of some debate. According to David Koskoff, a Kennedy biographer, a certain Englishman, unnamed, closely involved in the negotiations, said that Kennedy had "only marginal influence if any" on the British view: "we already wanted and appreciated the need for a treaty." Perhaps Kennedy tempered the Irish arguments with a winning presentation of the British position, the informant suggested.[30] When the agreement was concluded, the Foreign Office confidentially told Kennedy that he could pass along to Roosevelt that it would be signed on April 23.[31] Kennedy one-upped the messenger by saying that he himself had already learned about the signing ten days earlier—probably from the Irish, Koskoff believes.[32] Although Kennedy had previously notified the State Department of the event, he sent a cable confirming it.[33]

Two of the president's advisers, Morgenthau and Farley, mischievously spread the word that Britain had taken in Kennedy and he had "got himself into a little trouble" because "he had set himself up as the mediator on Anglo-Irish relations." Actually, these advisers said, Kennedy "had had absolutely nothing to do [with the settlement]," something of an overstatement.[34]

Ickes also knew that FDR thought of himself as the "determining factor" in the negotiations and claimed credit "for the success of this English-Irish agreement." Cudahy had initially been involved in the negotiations and Joe Kennedy had had "something to do with it," too, Ickes wrote in his diary, but the president was the real catalyst. Roosevelt told Ickes: "Probably history would never know what part he [Roosevelt] had played," because he had confidential letters in longhand to both Chamberlain and de Valera and sent them through Kennedy and Cudahy.[35] After the agreement was concluded, Roosevelt received a most appreciative letter from de Valera, which he proudly showed his advisers.[36]

Kennedy's inflated accounts of his own influence no doubt made prominent Irish Americans like Jim Farley jealous. Farley told Morgenthau that he, and not Kennedy, had called FDR's attention to the Irish situation.[37] Apparently the ambassador's role was only one more instance of Kennedy blarney.

If Kennedy's role in the Anglo-Irish agreement was overblown, his arbitration of the thorny Anglo-American trade negotiations was not. It illustrated his superb abilities as a mediator, his finely honed political instincts, his willingness to hunt tirelessly for areas of compromise, sometimes chiding Washington in blunt and unsettling language, all the while chipping away at areas of disagreement between British and American officials, quite in contrast to the secretary of state and to the "career boys" at the State Department.[38] Although the negotiations and their successful conclusion owed much to Kennedy's determination and skill in fulfilling the high expectations of him and enhancing his already glowing reputation among British officials, they nevertheless further weakened his position within his own administration, particularly with Hull and the State Department, who began to look upon him with suspicion and contempt.

The Trade Agreement Act of 1934 gave the president discretionary authority to "negotiate reciprocal tariff reductions with one nation and then . . . extend them to all other nations that gave most-favored-nation treatment to, or did not discriminate against, the United States."

The act appealed to both internationalists and nationalists. Internationalists applauded it because it lowered tariffs, expanded world trade, and allowed creditors to increase their imports to the United States; nationalists approved of it because it permitted the president to ignore a most-favored-nation approach and to increase American exports through bilateral negotiations.[39] By 1938 agreements had been made with eighteen countries—but not with the world's greatest commercial country and the United States' biggest customer, Great Britain. The significance of these agreements was political, not just economic, since they arrayed the signatories against the fascist powers, a factor hardly lost on Hull.[40]

Cordell Hull, for whom free trade was a fixation, had been arguing for lower tariffs since his maiden speech in Congress.[41] He believed that the Trade Agreement Act would lead to international tariff reductions and increased world trade and thereby reduce political tensions and ensure peace. He particularly wanted an agreement between the two great Anglo-Saxon democracies as a major contribution to world peace and a symbol of democratic unity.[42]

Kennedy agreed with him. "Personally I believed that the conclusion of a trade agreement was of immense importance not only to Anglo-American relations but also to the success of Secretary's Hull's general policies," Kennedy wrote in his memoirs. "It would, I believed, tend to make clearer the role that the economy of each of these nations should assume with regard to the other." Kennedy was banking on the personal relationships he had established to ensure his success in negotiating a proposal fair to all, and he was clearly looking forward to this assignment.[43]

The British Foreign Office, too, certainly valued an agreement, and wanted it particularly for its political significance in European affairs and its implications for war and peace.[44] Walter Runciman, Lord President of the Privy Council and former president of the Board of Trade, sensibly advised the Foreign Office to "make the most of any Anglo-American trade agreement." It would move the United States away from its policy of isolationism and gain the country's goodwill, vital for Britain's future. Above all, he argued, do not reject the U.S. initiative. The United States might then retreat behind its ocean moats and adopt a more extreme form of isolationism. But be careful, Runciman warned; do not move too fast or arouse the suspicion of isolationists. "Remember that the U.S.A. is at present only very slightly educated politically and internationally,"[45] an apt description of the state of American opinion on foreign policy. He also suggested that, upon the conclusion of deliberations, the prime minister himself go to Washington and sign the agreement. That would show the world how important cooperation with the United States was and how much the agreement was valued.[46]

Despite the widespread desire in both countries for an agreement, particularly as a political gesture, the negotiations with the British were among the most difficult and tedious and dragged on for nearly a year. As they lurched from haggling to stalemate to near breakdown, Hull appealed to Kennedy for help.

Hull's letter of introduction to the Court of St. James's described Kennedy as a former film producer, a man "unusually well qualified and informed" about the film industry.[47]

Soon after he arrived in London, the new ambassador went to work on his first assignment: trying to get concessions from Parliament on its import agreement about American motion pictures. Kennedy wanted to begin immediately, Hull wrote the British, and said that Kennedy was optimistic about his ability to negotiate, as part of the trade agreement, a settlement on films that would be acceptable both to the American film industry, which disliked the British restrictions on American films, and to the British government, which had legislation on films pending in Parliament and a deadline to pass it by early February. Controversy swirled over technical matters such as fixing quotas on the basis of film footage, the length of feature films, the definition of a British film as a film shot in Britain or the Dominions, and a number of other points of contention detailed by Will Hays at Hull's request.

Hull had tried to delay the discussions until Kennedy could take up his assignment in London, and even suggested enacting interim legislation in the meantime.[48] But the British refused the request. "We should hold firm," they argued, since the American film industry, which is getting a very fair deal," is trying to bluff by threatening Britain with the collapse of the trade discussions. "I cannot imagine for one moment that the U.S. Government would allow the negotiations to break down on the film issue," Lindsay wrote to Halifax.[49] But Hull made a terse threat to the Tory government:

> I am confident that the British Government will understand that an alteration to the disadvantage of the United States on the very eve of trade agreement negotiations in the status of so important a product as motion pictures could hardly fail to affect the attitude of my Government toward concessions to be offered certain important British exports to the United States.[50]

Even before he took up his duties in London, Kennedy had had preliminary discussions with Ambassador Lindsay and criticized the legislation before Parliament as detrimental to the health of the American film industry. Impressed, Lindsay told the Foreign Office: "With his energy and resourcefulness he would be at his best in attacking a complicated and difficult task like this and he might well do wonders."[51]

Kennedy's success seemed guaranteed. It looked so easy. Kennedy will be "shot with luck," Bernard Baruch wrote to Frank Kent, a Kennedy chum and fiercely independent columnist. "Our friend Joe will get a big medal because he is going to make another home run." Kennedy expected as much, too, and was optimistic about his job. In fact, he became such a vigorous advocate of American movie interests throughout his ambassadorship that he irritated many on both sides of the Atlantic. The British Foreign Office questioned his motives; so did the Americans. Among Washington insiders like Farley and Morgenthau, Kennedy became the butt of jokes. "Everyone knew that Kennedy was on two missions in England: movies and liquor," gossiped an American journalist in London.[52]

But Kennedy—brash, pragmatic, and practical—was ultimately shrewder and more successful, illustrating a better grasp of British political sensibilities and realities than Hull, with his rigid, doctrinaire approach, so offensive to the British. "Everything feasible is being done here," Kennedy wrote reassuringly, but he could see why the British refused to make more concessions. Oliver Stanley, president of the Board of Trade, told Kennedy that the British resented their financial loss and the success of Americans. Kennedy wrote to Hull, "You do not have to know much about the subject to make a convincing argument against any concession to the American industry."[53]

By mid-March Kennedy informed the secretary that the provisions of the bill as it now stood, with few exceptions, were fair to American interests and would allow the American film industry to continue doing business in Britain without losing substantial revenue. If a few more technical problems could be resolved, as Stanley hoped, then we would have a bill acceptable to American film interests. Take it, Kennedy advised Hull. This was the best the United States could hope for now. Still, the State Department continued to press for more concessions. The request for them has come too late, Kennedy reported, quoting Stanley. "It [is] impossible to work out." Kennedy predicted "an uproar in the House of Commons" if the British were asked to make even more concessions. "If we get what [Stanley] is trying to get in the film bill you [Hull] have not done a bad job for the industry," Kennedy concluded.[54] But by early June he recommended dropping the discussions on films legislation and returning the entire issue to Washington to be considered as part of the general trade-agreement package rather than treated separately, a suggestion Hull concurred with.

The significance of the negotiations on films was not the negotiations themselves, which had acquired a role out of all proportion to their value, but the difference between the ambassador and his chief. Kennedy, unlike Hull and the "cookie pushers" at the State Department, showed a willingness to compromise and to practice the art of the possible. Will Hays, president of the Motion Pictures Producers and Distributors of America, realized this. He wrote the secretary to express his gratitude and singled out Kennedy for particular praise. The "importance and value" of the ambassador's efforts cannot be overemphasized, he said, as he complimented Kennedy for having a firm grip and for his "complete understanding" of the situation.[55]

Kennedy's political skill was also illustrated during the months-long negotiations, which proceeded at a snail's pace, over the general Anglo-American Trade Agreement. During them Kennedy played salesman, critic, and mediator as representatives haggled over lumber, tobacco, rice, ham, lard, wheat flour, canned and dried fruits, corn, plywood, typewriters, cars, electric motors, toilet articles, and silk stockings. Like Hull, Kennedy grasped the political value of the agreement. "What leverage we possessed arose less from the economics of the situation than from such political advantages as might accrue to the British from an Anglo-American accord," he wrote in his memoir.[56] And he told them so. "The more the impression could be created in Europe that the United Kingdom and the United States were getting together, the less would have to be spent on armaments," he lectured Chamberlain, who repeated his arguments in his public statements. Not averse to using threats, the ambassador went so far as to warn the British "that some trade agreement between American and Germany might shortly come on the tapis."[57]

Kennedy also lambasted one of the president's speeches that had touched a sensitive British nerve. At Gainesville, Georgia, on March 23, 1938, FDR spoke out against "these economic royalists"[58] who give "little thought to the one-third of our population . . . ill-fed, ill-clad, and ill-housed." "When you come down to it," Roosevelt told his audience, "there is little difference between the feudal system and the Fascist system. If you believe in the one, you lean to the other."[59] To Tories who had been dubbed "pro-fascist" by their opponents, the president's remarks seemed to be an attack on class and privilege and a call to class warfare. Kennedy reprimanded the writer of the speech and accused him of nearly causing the collapse of the already tenuous trade negotiations. "This thing over here is going into a tailspin," Kennedy warned. If that happens, you will have "plenty of troubles," including "the possibility of war."[60]

He worked tirelessly, always hunting for areas of compromise, sometimes chiding Washington and patiently chipping away at British obstinance. He relished the idea that the situation required a type of trading beyond the capacity of the normal bureaucrat. "My experience in business, as well as the position that I had made for myself in England, fitted me, I thought, peculiarly well for the task of negotiation. I knew the men in the Cabinet who had to be prevailed upon and the influences that might be brought to bear, whereas Washington was dealing only with subordinates who were controlled by London."[61]

He was also shrewd enough to understand the importance of saving face. "It is not going to do anybody any good to appear to have driven a smart bargain. I therefore think they [the cabinet] will honestly make what in their opinion . . . are all the concessions they can make," he told Hull.[62]

Frustrated after months of negotiations with the "stubborn" British,[63] and rumors that they had almost reached a stalemate, Hull finally turned to Kennedy in late July and asked him to remind Chamberlain that the United States wanted a trade agreement not just for the financial advantages but "as a powerful initiative to help rectify the present unstable political and economic situation everywhere." Nothing could contribute more to international political and economic stability, he argued, than the announcement that Britain and the United States have concluded a broad trade agreement that could serve as a model for a new world order. It would be harmful and "tragic indeed," not only for Britain and the United States but also for world peace and economic growth, "if we, after months of haggling, should turn out a little narrow, picayunish trade agreement," Hull wrote to Kennedy. This "unprecedented opportunity" to contribute "to world peace and economic stability" we must not allow to vanish.[64]

Kennedy happily took up his assignment. He dutifully urged Chamberlain and Stanley to end the negotiations satisfactorily and repeatedly reminded them of "the larger view" that the agreement symbolized: Its importance was more political than economic.[65] The ambassador told Washington that the "stumbling point" for the British was their dogged intention to safeguard their preferred imperial status at the expense of American exporters, particularly in the competition between the United States and Canada in the British market over Douglas fir. Canadian lumber had a significant market advantage over the American product, which the Canadians were ready to concede. But the British absolutely refused to accept their position or concession.[66]

By mid-October, only Chamberlain seemed really interested in reaching a worthwhile agreement,[67] and even he felt it would be of limited value. The prime minister did not anticipate that the agreement had any kind of support from the United States; but he did expect that it would bring advantages "of a somewhat negative kind." And if the two English-speaking countries were not able to reach an understanding, "hard things would be said" on both sides.[68] They already were. Lindsay notified Halifax that the "absolute limit of American requests" had been reached and if agreed to would conclude the negotiations. But the negotiations left him bitter and exasperated. The administration's "delays and tergiversations have been intolerable," he wrote to the foreign secretary; "they can see no point of view but their own, and their demands cause His Majesty's Government loss of revenue and administrative difficulties out of all proportion to the benefits likely to accrue from American trade. We are being put through the mangle of American politics."[69]

Kennedy's blunt criticism of Hull's style, and his own resentment about the State Department's tendency to ignore his advice or to fail to keep him adequately informed, created even more friction between him and the prudent, decorous secretary. "The tone of the last document you handed the British was definitely in the nature of an ultimatum and the British so regard it," he told the secretary.[70] Kennedy happened to learn that the British were preparing to respond to Hull in the same manner and to cut off negotiations. He hurried to Chamberlain to urge him not to do so. Chamberlain agreed and the ultimatum to the United States was abandoned.[71] Kennedy also warned Hull that the Americans needed to move quickly to ensure the success of the negotiations; time was running out; opposition was growing. "If you can give me some inside advice as to what you will take to settle I will go to work on it."[72] But instead of sending him "inside advice," Hull repeated the administration's arguments. Kennedy felt hamstrung and received no instructions, he reported in his memoirs.[73]

"Far be it from me to make any suggestions as to how those handling the trade agreement should avail themselves of the Ambassador's services," he said to the secretary on October 18, "but it does seem to me that if they really want a trade agreement it might be well to have the man on the spot find out just how much further we could go without kicking the thing over." He continued: "I have said to you over the telephone I am not in a position to judge the value of the agreement or the terms of it. I merely know what some people are likely to do in a game of cards when they are called." He added: "I am assuming naturally that you want to get this deal through if it is at all possible."[74] Hull's cold reply sent the same day was:

"I cannot, of course, agree that the granting of our requests would make the agreement a farce from the British standpoint," and he refused to budge. He gratuitously appended, "I appreciate your interest in and efforts on behalf of the trade agreement."[75]

Undaunted, Kennedy tried a few days later. "In connection with this agreement, I think I know exactly what they are thinking," he wrote to Hull about the British. They all "have a severe case of the jitters" because of the gravity of Britain's economic situation. He then offered a set of practical suggestions: Confidentially let me know what requests we have refused the British but would make concessions on, tell me what they have denied us which we absolutely must have, give me a list of priorities, and then let me see how close I can come by using "fright more than argument." Besides knowing the priority of your demands, it is also important for me to know confidentially when you will break off negotiations. "Tell the boys," he added, that "it is unnecessary to make me tough by telling me you have to have everything, unless you must have everything, because I will be tough enough for lots more than your minimum." He would also go to Chamberlain for "a final clean-up," he promised. "It seems to me that every effort should be made to save the thing from a collapse." He also proposed using a dinner in honor of Stanley Baldwin, former Conservative prime minister, as an occasion to "shock" the guests by lecturing them on the importance of the Anglo-American treaty. This may be "presumptuous of me," Kennedy wrote, and perhaps "I should mind my own business," aware that "I have not been asked to mix into it," but I did want to try. This is "my last word and best judgment."[76] Although Hull cabled thanks to Kennedy for his help the next day, the secretary nixed his suggestion of a speech. He also wrote: "I think we should not take any action whatever and avoid any public discussion of the American-British trade position until the official reply has been received and our position has been formulated by me."[77]

On November 3, the secretary wired Kennedy that he had the president's approval to proceed with the deal as it stood. "I have reached the conclusion that the present offers represent the ultimate limit to which the British are prepared to go."[78] But Kennedy believed that this was "terribly unfortunate. . . . I knew I could get further concessions from the Prime Minister"[79] if the secretary "would only let me go to work on the matter," he wrote.[80] Hull dismissed his offer. "We have obtained about all that can be obtained," he told Kennedy in his cable to him the next day.[81] "I thought I knew better," Kennedy confided in his memoirs, "but there was nothing more that I could do."[82]

The signing of the Anglo-American Trade Agreement on November 16, 1938, was anti-climactic; no high-level representative attended the ceremony, and the official statements by the respective governments were routine. Hull described it as "mutually beneficial in every respect."[83] The British government's annual report for 1938 called it "the major event" that year in Anglo-American relations. Although the report described the negotiations as "protracted and difficult," the agreement did represent "the most outstanding achievement to date" of Hull's economic policies.[84]

Despite Kennedy's brash manner and constant profanity, thoroughly annoying to the staid secretary of state, that the agreement was completed at all owed much to the ambassador's persistence and to his pragmatic and professional approach. Hull's gracious tribute acknowledged Kennedy's efforts. "In reaching this decision," he wrote, "I have been influenced by your excellent telegraphic reports. . . . Your reports and assistance have been of great value and I am deeply grateful to you."[85]

Kennedy had been interested in negotiating the agreement from the beginning because he considered it a "meritorious policy."[86] It had the advantage of elevating tariff-making, a unilateral and political process, into a bilateral and semi-rational process of appeasement between our two countries, he argued. "The importance of the Trade Agreement lay in the fact that it demonstrated a capacity on the part of our two nations to mesh together more closely our economies so that they would become more complementary of each other and less competitive." But its drawback was "that it came too late." Had it been negotiated earlier, before the Anschluss or Munich, it could have symbolized the cooperation between the democracies and possibly could have influenced the policies of the dictators. But as its long, tortuous negotiations illustrated, such cooperation was not a major characteristic of their relationship.[87]

Kennedy had worked so diligently during the discussions because he shared Hull's dream of worldwide economic cooperation. "This is one form of international cooperation in which the United States is prepared to take an active part," the secretary said.[88]

In a luncheon address to the joint audience of the Manchester Chamber of Commerce and the Manchester branch of the English-Speaking Union on November 29, 1938, Kennedy referred to the trade agreement as "the greatest commercial arrangement of all time" and reiterated his economic thesis: "I am inclined to believe that we place too much emphasis upon the political side of international relations, and not enough emphasis on the economic side."[89] Not only did he once again reveal his blindness to political realities, but he even failed to grasp the real economic significance of the agreement. The chief effect of the trade agreement was national, not international; it enhanced America's economic affairs by expanding exports and almost doubling its favorable balance of trade rather than increasing imports and stimulating the world economy.[90] It also benefited American agriculture by eliminating duties on items such as "wheat, lard, and flour" and substantially reducing them on "rice, apples, pears and some canned foods."[91]

"As it was," the secretary bemoaned in his memoirs, "the agreement scarcely had a chance to operate."[92] But it did not come too late for Kennedy and others like him who sold liquor in the United States. They made a handsome profit when the tariff on liquor was cut in half.[93]

Another byproduct of the negotiations was Kennedy's growing admiration for Neville Chamberlain, whom he regarded as a kindred spirit. "I learned to think highly of Chamberlain," Kennedy wrote in his memoir, realizing how much they had in common. He too was a businessman. He was hard, as befitted a man who had been schooled by six years of a vain effort to grow sisal on an island in the Bahamas, and who had made a success of two struggling enterprises in Birmingham. But he was not narrow and could see the advantages that lay to business in fair and generous dealings. The gradual amelioration in the British position was due in large measure, I believe, to the influence of Chamberlain. He was not slow to realize that the negotiations of a trade treaty involved bargaining, but demanded an end to mere haggling.[94]

War debt was another issue about which Kennedy's shrewdness was quite apparent. The assumption that he had been sent to London to settle Britain's war debts with the United States created a flurry on both sides of the Atlantic. The Liberal Party in Parliament regarded their settlement as essential to improving Anglo-American relations. Despite rumors in the British and the American press in July upon the return of Kennedy from Ireland that he would meet with Chamberlain and other British officials, and even be joined by Bullitt and Morgenthau to discuss the debt issue, nothing happened. In fact the ambassador recorded in his memoir: "There was nothing to be done with the war debt problem."[95] The real fiscal issue, he reasoned, was not war debt, but whether with the rearmament program, the reduction in exports, and the increase in the unfavorable balance of trade, Britain could halt the decline in sterling.[96] Even when the questions whether Britain should acknowledge its obligations, or begin formal negotiations, or make token payments came up for debate in the House of Lords, Kennedy maintained a discreet silence officially and unofficially. He confided in his diary that any attempt to negotiate the debt would be seen in the United States "as prima facie evidence that England thinks it is going to get into another war and wants to be all set to borrow some more money."[97] Chamberlain agreed with Kennedy that silence was the best position: since there was no hope of solving the problem, the prime minister told the House, just keep quiet. Kennedy felt vindicated. "It seemed to me," he wrote in his memoirs, "that in remaining silent I had pursued the wisest course."[98] Indeed he had.

But naïveté and hyperbole, rather than discretion and silence, were two of the Kennedy hallmarks in his interpretation of international events. Both were illustrated by his analysis of the Phoenix Islands dispute, a relatively insignificant episode that he was asked to mediate in 1938. It foreshadowed his simplistic interpretation of international events, illustrated by his analysis of the crisis over Czechoslovakia and ultimately the causes of World War II.[99]

Shortly after he became ambassador, Kennedy was assigned to settle the conflicting British and American claims to the Phoenix Islands in the South Pacific east of the International Date Line. Both Britain and the United States coveted several islands, including Canton and Enderbury in the Phoenix group. The dispute arose in the spring of 1937 when both countries sent meteorological expeditions to Canton Island to observe a solar eclipse. The crew of His Majesty's Ship *Wellington* was surprised to discover the American minesweeper *Avocet* with astronomers on board already anchored in the harbor on May 27, 1937, and a claim to the islands under the Guano Island Act of August 18, 1856. The British government politely notified the American government that its ship was violating the Order-in-Council issued on March 18, 1937, incorporating Canton among other islands in the Phoenix group into the Gilbert and Ellice Islands colony. Roosevelt refused to accept the Order-in-Council. He authorized the occupation of the islands on March 3, 1938, and issued an executive order placing Canton and Enderbury Islands under the authority of the secretary of the Interior. The president also ordered that the American flag be hoisted on Canton, but not in such a way as to disturb the British flag already flying there. Through Kennedy, on March 10, the president proposed that Canton and Enderbury be held as a joint trust by the United States and the United Kingdom with equal rights and equal facilities for nationals from both countries for a period of twenty-five to fifty years, and leave the technical questions about their ownership in abeyance. On March 30, the British government "gladly accede[d]" to his recommendation "in principle."[100] Both governments made it clear that they wanted to deal with this "comparatively minor problem" through "frank and friendly consultation."[101]

The Roosevelt administration was particularly interested in these islands because it wished to forestall Japanese colonization and the establishment of Japanese military installations. It also recognized their strategic importance for transpacific air service for Pan American Airways, the leading commercial American aviation company, which wanted to build an airport.[102]

The negotiations were transferred from Washington to London upon Kennedy's arrival there. His instructions were to urge Chamberlain to accept Roosevelt's proposal for reciprocal occupancy and the postponement of ultimate sovereignty.[103] After several months of diplomatic haggling, in October 1938 an agreement was reached, although not finalized until April 6, 1939, on the basis of Roosevelt's proposal. Kennedy was given much of the credit. The *Daily Express* praised him for playing "a big part" in the negotiations,[104] and a *Washington Star* reporter claimed that the ambassador gave "Europe's leaders a tip today—to follow the example of the United States and Great Britain in settling their differences."[105]

Perhaps with the Czech crisis in mind, Kennedy interpreted the Phoenix settlement as a lesson for the world and, upon the conclusion of the negotiations on September 3, 1938, inferred and implied that the solutions to international tensions and crises required little more than goodwill. He praised the agreement as "a good-natured settlement of a profound difference of opinion, a cameo of what a world settlement might be if the same intelligent good neighborliness were always exhibited by different nations."[106] He confidently stated: "After all, the issues over which governments make such a fuss are generally small ones, or at least they start as small issues. . . . The difficulty seems to be that contending governments do not get together in a friendly and sensible spirit in the early months of controversy, before it has grown psychologically into a matter of real import."[107] In fact, the Anglo-American dispute over the Pacific Islands was not a "profound difference of opinion," as he described it, but a comparatively minor incident that caused suspicion and irritation out of all proportion to its significance. Kennedy's analysis of forthcoming crises was no less naive.

The crisis unfolding over Czechoslovakia throughout the spring and summer of 1938 that culminated in the infamous Munich Agreement in September tested the prime minister's policy of appeasing Germany, tested the grit of the American businessman-turned-diplomat, and found them both wanting. And once again, the prim Birmingham entrepreneur at 10 Downing Street could rely on the sympathy and endorsement of the self-made millionaire living at Grosvenor Square. Throughout the early months of the Czech crisis, the ever-faithful Kennedy supported Chamberlain's policies under the guise of reporting them to the American government. Kennedy's dispatches, detailed, well-informed, and impartial, with nothing of the hysterical tone they later acquired, indicated that he was in frequent contact with British policymakers and was a knowledgeable reporter of their viewpoint. Halifax, anxious to have Washington's "understanding," had kept his promise and made Kennedy privy to Britain's confidences[108] by telling him on the eve of Chamberlain's March 24 address the gist of it.[109] Chamberlain promised to undertake no further commitments to the Czechs and only insinuate that Britain would support France if France were drawn into the war. Kennedy felt reassured by Chamberlain's efforts to settle the dispute peaceably.

As with the Anschluss, Kennedy watched the Czech crisis unfold, an event he saw largely through the eyes of his host. Germany's annexation of Austria had foreshadowed the fate of Czechoslovakia, doomed by geography and politics. The lizard-shaped, elongated kidney, that polyglot nation that Mussolini dubbed "Czecho-Germano-Polano-Magyaro-Rutheno-Roumano-Slovakia,"[110] once part of the now defunct Austro-Hungarian Empire, stretched "like a bulwark athwart any drive that the Germans might make towards the southeast," as Kennedy described it.[111] It was landlocked, strategically located in Central Europe, easy to strangle economically, outflanked militarily, and surrounded by a sea of hostile neighbors: Germany, Poland, Rumania, and Hungary. Czechoslovakia was a state of diverse and seldom harmonious nationalities; the 7.5 million Czechs dominated 3.5 million Germans in the Sudetenland, 2.25 million Slovaks, and smaller numbers of Magyars, Ruthenians, and Poles.[112] Kennedy understood that its geopolitical position underlay its diplomatic arrangements with France; with the other members of the Little Entente, Rumania and Yugoslavia; and with the Russian-Czechoslovakian alliance. And it certainly underlay Hitler's support of the Sudeten Germans.[113]

The Sudeten Germans were deeply stirred by the Anschluss and closely tied to their Austrian cousins racially and historically. Konrad Henlein, a former gymnastics director, led the Czech Nazi Party and followed Hitler's orders to exploit the grievances of the Sudeten Germans by provoking a crisis in the spring of 1938, making unacceptable demands that compromised the country's political and military integrity. The Sudetens provided a convenient pretext for Hitler's twofold ambitions: to absorb all Germans living outside the Reich and to extend Germany's boundaries eastward. The Führer wanted not simply to incorporate the Sudeten Germans into the Reich but to crush the state of Czechoslovakia. That would not only give Germany the rich natural resources of that country, and mean the destruction of a potential Russian or Anglo-French military base, but also give Germany clear hegemony over Central Europe, as Kennedy had noted.[114]

Both France and Britain were keenly aware of Hitler's ambitions and wanted to avert a crisis and preserve peace. The French had an explicit obligation to aid the Czechs under the terms of their 1925 mutual defense treaty; their 1935 alliance with Soviet Russia operated only if France acted first. The British had, at most, a vague commitment to the Czechs as fellow members of the expiring League of Nations, and an obligation under the still valid Locarno Agreement of 1925 to aid France if France were the object of aggression. Since the end of World War I, every British government had resolutely refused to give specific, binding commitments to the eastern European countries or to promise to help the French fulfill their treaty obligations to their allies. The Chamberlain government was no exception. The prime minister's decision was to tell Hitler of his support for a peaceful settlement and to urge Prague to make maximum concessions based on granting local autonomy and more liberties to the German subjects, a policy that unintentionally encouraged Hitler in making his demands, and one that Kennedy was in complete agreement with.[115]

"Czechoslovakia is a tough bird," the ambassador told Hull, giving his initial appraisal on March 9, 1938, soon after he arrived in London. England would probably not make any direct attempts to stop Germany's progress in the east, he accurately predicted, provided that this progress was accomplished by "gentlemanly methods" like trade and propaganda. France, however, would definitely assist Czechoslovakia, and "that might put the fat in the fire."[116] But the British, he reported, believed that Hitler would take no steps to bring this about.

Kennedy's initial concern was that the United States might mix in and stir things up. "I wish our fellows at home would attend to the worries they have on their own doorsteps and keep Europe out of their minds until they have made some headway in their own country," he wrote to Arthur Krock in late March in a mind-your-own-business mood.[117]

But as the crisis careened out of control in early May and war seemed almost imminent, a now thoroughly worried Kennedy not only continued as a reliable reporter of Chamberlain's views but also initiated his own brand of "shirt-sleeve diplomacy" designed to prevent war. "The danger in Czechoslovakia is obvious," he cabled Hull on May 5, and "the British do not in any way minimize the danger of this situation which is heightened by uncertainty as to what Germany may do." They and the French had examined every possible avenue for helping the Czechs out of the impasse and were apprehensive about what could happen, fearing that the Sudeten Germans were becoming "more Nazi than Hitler himself" and quickly moving ahead of their leader, Konrad Henlein. Foreign Office officials feared that the Sudetens could cause trouble by behaving irresponsibly, Kennedy reported. Nevertheless, despite their apprehension, the British still refused to make any further commitments to the French or the Czechs beyond the prime minister's March 24 warning in the House of Commons, intended to impress upon Eduard Beneš, the Czech president, the importance of his finding a peaceful solution to his country's problem. They have agreed to tell him, "without saying so in so many words," that it is Czechoslovakia's responsibility to produce a solution "which will not give Hitler any ostensible excuse for intervening," the ambassador said.[118] In addition to pressing Beneš, the British intended to appeal independently to Hitler and emphasize their desire for a peaceful solution. Such an Anglo-German consensus could be a small step toward the larger step of a general understanding among the four great powers, a position that Chamberlain and Kennedy, too, had been advocating since Austria's annexation.

As the crisis continued into its second week in May, Kennedy reported that neither France nor Germany had produced any satisfactory results. After the Anschluss, the French thought Czechoslovakia's position was "hopeless," he wrote,[119] and the wary British, suspicious of Germany's real intentions, thought so, too, as they continued to try to prevent the issue from reaching a climax.[120]

Besides accurately reporting to Washington—thanks to Halifax, who in their frequent conversations kept him informed of all developments—Kennedy decided on May 14 to discuss the crisis with the Czech minister in London, Jan Masaryk, a man Kennedy considered quite charming but lacking the "realistic approach to affairs" characteristic of other diplomats. Kennedy was "determined" to consult with Masaryk about Henlein's visit and presumably to advise him about negotiating with Henlein.[121] The ambassador was increasingly willing to use his influence and his office to engage in personal diplomacy "shirt-sleeve style."[122]

Concern among British officials about Czechoslovakia reached fever pitch on May 20, 1938, as the crisis nearly dashed the prime minister's hopes for a peaceful solution. War impended; events succeeded each other quickly: London received reports of German troop movements; Sudetens armed themselves and sent 170,000 troops to the Czech-German border;[123] Chamberlain issued a two-fisted threat to Beneš on May 22—deal sensibly with Germany and "be reasonable because if you touch the spring it may well go off and then you may not do as well as you think."[124] Negotiations broke down between Prague and the Sudetens, war rumors circulated, reports of killings and woundings spread, panic broke out, another lightning German coup appeared imminent,[125] and Kennedy kept tabs on everything and reported to Washington.

The Czechs ordered a partial mobilization, and London sent a stiffly worded threat to Berlin warning against precipitous action and stating that if the Czechs were attacked and the French supported them, then Britain might enter the conflict too. After talking to Cadogan, whose passion for accurate detail earned his great admiration, Kennedy told Hull that the British believed that Germany was not ready for war and Germany's military command and staff knew this, but it carried no weight with Germany's political leaders. "The British feel that peace is more than ever at the hazard of an accident," Kennedy wrote in his memoirs.[126] It was inevitable, he said, that if Germany invaded Czechoslovakia and France attacked Germany, then Britain would be drawn in. "The real community of British and French defense against

Germany is too obvious to encourage any belief that Great Britain can afford to stand by in such a conflict," he cabled Washington on May 22.[127]

Kennedy described the confusion and the vehemence of the crisis in his memoirs by aptly quoting from *Vreme*, the government organ in Belgrade:

> Berlin protests; Prague prepares its defenses; London inquires in Berlin; Paris gives advice to Prague, Rome minds its own business; Budapest awaits developments; Bucharest watches Budapest; and Warsaw sympathizes with Berlin.[128]

The crisis passed quickly; there was no coup. The situation had "eased," the ambassador told Washington after a brief conversation with Halifax on May 23. Kennedy felt free enough to indulge in one of his favorite diversions that morning: He listened to Toscanini rehearse for a BBC concert.[129] "What a 'd—d close run thing' it was," Chamberlain was reported to have said about the crisis. He believed that his warning had dissuaded Germany from attacking Czechoslovakia. He concluded that the May crisis proved "how utterly untrustworthy and dishonest" Hitler's government was.[130] What followed was a period of "inaction from the public standpoint," as Kennedy characterized it,[131] although Hitler set October 1, 1938, as the date for military action against Czechoslovakia, as the captured German documents were to reveal in 1945. "No hint of such a definitive action was known to me," Kennedy wrote in his memoirs, "or, as far as I know, to our authorities anywhere. Hitler masked his determination to use force very cleverly."[132]

Unlike the Anschluss, the May crisis had plainly worried Kennedy, who was forced to consider seriously the prospect of war in Europe for the first time and America's role in relation to it. "The momentary lull in Central Europe has not caused anyone here to think that the Czechoslovak business is settled," he wrote to Jimmy Roosevelt at the end of the month. "The hard part lies ahead. . . . We seem to be living through one crisis after another these days, and no one appears to have any idea of how long this fumbling can go on without getting out of hand. . . . There is a certain fatalism in their attitude," he said of the British government.[133] Yet the lesson that both Chamberlain and Kennedy drew from this latest example of Nazi aggression was not to offer guarantees of assistance to any intended victim or to conclude any military alliances with likely allies, a kind of Churchillian Grand Alliance, but to do anything to prevent another crisis from erupting, fearing that the results could be far worse next time. They also learned, to Kennedy's utter relief, not to count on any support from the United States. If it should come, said Sir Darien Fisher, who headed the British Intelligence, "it must be considered as a wind-fall and nothing else."[134]

Like Chamberlain, Kennedy's initial analysis of the Czech situation proved to be blind and deaf to the warnings of men like Churchill who railed about the aggressive nature of Nazism and whom Kennedy accused of being jingoists and warmongers and of urging war on an unready Britain. Support for the prime minister's appeasement policy, Kennedy held, and his own advice to Americans to mind their own business were the surest protections against war.

Throughout the May crisis Roosevelt did mind his own business. He remained watchful, detached, quiet. The only overt act by the American government during its early stages was Hull's press statement of May 28, 1938, saying that the government regarded the Central European crisis as "critical" and that it had followed the recent events with "close and anxious attention." Hull also issued a warning that the outbreak of hostilities anywhere was likely to cause unpredictable and permanent damage "the ultimate consequences of which no man can foresee."[135]

Although the crisis subsided quickly, Hull wrote in his memoirs that the State Department "knew that the peril was greater than before. It was already a question whether 1938, only twenty years after the Armistice, would be the war year."[136] But without the forceful executive leadership in foreign policy that FDR was unwilling to give, there was little that the American government could do about the crisis in Europe, as its policy remained one of "pinpricks and righteous protests."[137]

Roosevelt's lack of leadership and firm diplomatic guidance allowed Kennedy—accustomed to leading, not following—once again to try a perilous form of personal diplomacy. He initiated a series of meetings with Herbert von Dirksen, the German ambassador in London, to try to create a better German-American understanding, and did so apparently without administrative approval and contrary to the practice of other American diplomats, busily distancing themselves from Europe's affairs. He must have assumed that improving relations with Germany would make a war with the United States less likely. In his attempt to win the Roosevelt administration's support for Chamberlain's policy, Kennedy was defining American foreign policy from Grosvenor Square and undertaking a diplomatic initiative that threatened both appeasement and isolationism, the twin pillars of his foreign policy.

In late May he told von Dirksen several times at social events that "he would like to do his very best to improve German–United States relations."[138] He planned to discuss European affairs in general with the president upon his return to the United States. The two ambassadors agreed to meet again before Kennedy left for the States in mid-June.

In a nearly hour-long meeting on June 13, Kennedy and von Dirksen discussed the "Jewish question," prejudice in the United States, Germany's position in Europe, relations with the United States, and the relationship between authoritarian and democratic governments, among other topics. Von Dirksen reported to Berlin that Kennedy had advised the Germans not to make so much "outward fuss" about the Jews. "It was not so much the fact that we wanted to get rid of the Jews that was so harmful to us, but rather the loud clamor with which we accompanied this purpose." Kennedy claimed to understand Germany's policy toward the Jews completely. After all, he said, he was from Boston, where many clubs had seen fit to exclude Jews for the past fifty years. And, because of anti-Catholic feeling, his father had not been elected mayor of Boston. Prejudice was commonplace in the United States, he said, "but people avoided making so much outward fuss about it."[139]

Kennedy also told von Dirksen that he intended to discuss the European situation in detail with Roosevelt and to tell him that the "United States would have to establish friendly relations with Germany." The president too, Kennedy said, wanted friendlier relations with the Germans, but no one had spoken favorably to him about Germany or the German government, something he intended to correct. Most people were silent about Germany either out of ignorance or fear of offending the Jews. The anti-German sentiment was strong only on the East Coast anyhow, Kennedy reported, where three and a half million Jews lived and had a strong influence on the American press centered there; elsewhere it was much weaker. He promised to use his considerable influence with the president and the press to reduce the "poisonous role" of Jewish influence, confident in his assertion that he would be believed because he was a Catholic. The ambassador bragged that he had already "set ['Johnnie'] Rockefeller right" about a report he received from a leading Jewish professor at the Rockefeller Institute. It claimed that the restriction of Germany's limited food supply for the army's use was causing suffering among the rest of the population. Actually neither FDR nor the American public were anti-German, Kennedy assured von Dirksen. Most Americans wanted "peace and friendly relations with Germany" and "had no prejudice" against Germany.[140] Nor did the average American have much affection for England, Kennedy declared. England had not paid her war debts and had forced King Edward VIII to abdicate because of his determination to marry a twice-divorced American. But if war were to break out, Kennedy agreed with von Dirksen, 90 percent of the American people would support Germany's enemies.

As for himself, citing Charles Lindbergh's report on the high morale of the German people as evidence, Kennedy said that "the present Government had done great things for Germany and that the Germans were satisfied and enjoyed good living conditions."[141] He reaffirmed his conviction that the key to world peace was economic appeasement and that "in economic matters Germany had to have a free hand in the East as well as in the Southeast." And he had a very pessimistic view, he said, of the situation in the Soviet Union.

Their discussion of the Czech crisis, during which von Dirksen put the total responsibility upon the Czechs and showed Kennedy pictures of their war preparations, led the American ambassador to ask what Hitler's future plans were and to inquire whether Hitler was propagandizing in countries in South America. Von Dirksen assured him that the Führer had no further territorial aims and that the question of the Polish Corridor would be settled between Germany and Poland.

The diplomats agreed with each other that authoritarian governments should have friendly relations with democratic countries; it was both "dangerous" and "wrong" to assume they were natural enemies. Like Britain, which had entered into discussions with Italy and Germany and was especially "anxious for a settlement with Germany," Kennedy reported, he and von Dirksen were of the opinion that other democratic countries should also negotiate with the totalitarian regimes. Furthermore, many countries—such as Poland, Rumania, and Yugoslavia—were a mixture of democratic and totalitarian systems. Even the United States in the years from 1933 to 1935 had become more totalitarian and was governed in an "authoritarian manner," Kennedy said; only after surmounting the economic chaos of the Depression did it resume its democratic and parliamentary institutions.[142]

Von Dirksen suggested that the American ambassador visit the "New Germany," an invitation he seemed interested in accepting. The two ambassadors arranged to meet again after Kennedy returned to London in mid-July.[143]

On the basis of their June conversation, von Dirksen believed that Kennedy was "sincere in his efforts to create a better atmosphere in German-American relations." He might be motivated by an "idealistic conviction" to bring about world peace as well as by political strategy having to do with the next presidential election, but not by personal political motives or a desire for personal prominence, the German ambassador concluded. Kennedy also impressed von Dirksen with the unassailability of Kennedy's own position. Nobody could undermine him, the cocky Yankee had bragged—not Hull, nor any Cabinet official, nor anyone of influence. The only superior he recognized was President Roosevelt, who was himself "on bad terms with the State Department," which he, like Kennedy, had little use for. The German ambassador reported that Kennedy was "favorably regarded in every way in diplomatic and Government circles here." He too had formed "a very good impression of Mr. Kennedy."[144]

Despite the fact that Kennedy often told people what they wanted to hear and that von Dirksen may have wanted to ingratiate himself with his superior and present Kennedy's comments favorably, von Dirksen probably assessed Kennedy's motives accurately. Judging European events by the single yardstick of their potential effect on his own family made Kennedy quite alarmed at the possibility of war. He really did believe that an American-German rapprochement would enhance his family's security. He may also have erroneously thought that his personal diplomatic initiative was necessary because Roosevelt was misinformed and unaware of the seriousness of the situation in Europe—something he blamed on "the career boys" in the State Department, whom he seems not to have informed about his conversations with von Dirksen.[145]

Kennedy's personal diplomacy produced mixed results. On the one hand, he demonstrated a certain amount of professional skill by developing a believable personal relationship with von Dirksen, who seems to have taken Kennedy's overtures at face value. If he intended to flatter the Nazi regime with his pro-German remarks and his seeming sympathy about the "Jewish question," then Kennedy was cynically acting like any diplomat who masquerades to the advantage of his own country and uses the means necessary to achieve the ends desired. His facility for feigning agreement with those he wanted to convince was well developed. And he liked being liked and savored the goodwill of prominent officials like von Dirksen.

On the other hand, the ambassador's conversation could have actually undermined the prime minister's efforts for a settlement with Germany. Kennedy's statements about the necessity for German freedom in the east and the southeast, especially from one who reputedly had the prime minister's confidence, might have increased Hitler's determination to expand and to achieve a settlement on his own terms. And Kennedy's attempts to strengthen

German-American relations could have weakened the American policy of isolationism that he so prized, a point seemingly lost on him. Not only did he mistakenly assume that U.S. support of Chamberlain's appeasement policy, without implying an American diplomatic or military commitment, would restrain Hitler, but he also believed that Hitler cared about the American attitude or that he could be deterred by American sloganizing and moralizing.

Kennedy's penchant for indiscreet behavior and his poor judgment, previously shown with Czech ambassador Masaryk as well as with von Dirksen, was repeated again in mid-June in a lengthy conversation with Germany's foreign minister, Joachim von Ribbentrop. The American ambassador promised "to do everything in his power" to stop the anti-German agitation in the U.S. press and "to keep America out of any European conflict." He would do "everything in his power to accomplish this," he reiterated—as if he could do something; as if Hitler cared.[146]

Kennedy's tendency to create his own diplomatic initiative and to act on his own authority as an autonomous public official only casually answerable to the president, rather than just to report the facts and let his government develop policy, was ultimately to get him into trouble not only with the State Department, which he was now openly contemptuous of, but even with Roosevelt himself. Certainly his naive and even bizarre statements leave one aghast at a diplomat willing to serve his own parochial self-interest by selling out everyone—the Jews, the Czechs, and anyone else—and by his narrow, unreflective perspective and wish to preserve peace at any price.

Kennedy returned to London in early July renewed and refreshed from his visit home and from his numerous conversations with government officials, including the president, businessmen, industrialists, former classmates at Harvard, and friends of his son. He immediately set forth on a brief speaking tour: celebrating the Fourth of July; unveiling a window in the Cathedral of Winchester dedicated to the memory of King George V for his assistance in World War I to the American troops—a "happy occasion," as Kennedy described it;[147] and dedicating an American room in Fydell House of the English-Speaking Union in the Lincolnshire town of Boston.[148] Over and over again his theme was the same: the superiority of democratic institutions and ideals over intolerant, undemocratic institutions that people filled with despair and facing injustice and lack of opportunity have turned to, and the "cheap talk" that only dictatorships are efficient.[149] He proudly noted the absence of a demand for radical change in the United States, he told an audience of the American Society at the Dorchester Hotel, and he spoke of Americans' faith in the future in the long run.[150] But we must not just talk about "freedom, civil liberties, [and] rights of individuals," he said. "To preserve democracy, we must make those things actualities. . . . We must make the system work."[151]

Neville Chamberlain, in his diary, noted Kennedy's sunnier mood. He had returned with "the most roseate accounts of the change in American opinion in our favor and of the

President's desire to do something to help," Chamberlain wrote after a meeting on July 5.[152] Halifax repeated the gist of Kennedy's rosy conversation to Oliver Harvey at the Foreign Office the next day. The American ambassador had assured Chamberlain that American opinion, formerly believing that Anthony Eden was the "second coming of Jesus Christ," now had developed a more positive view of Chamberlain. And Roosevelt was "very anxious to help us whenever he could." He considered sending the fleet to the Atlantic in the event of war and minimizing the impact of the Neutrality Act on the British. "I am inclined to doubt what Kennedy says about U.S. opinion and P.M.," Harvey recorded in his diary.[153] The wary prime minister also questioned Kennedy's views. Although the American ambassador gave him a needed "moral uplift,"[154] Chamberlain must have known from his own ambassador in Washington and other sources that Kennedy did not always reflect Washington's official views. Apparently nothing Kennedy said gave Chamberlain reason to change his long-term assumptions or mitigate his distrust of American policy.[155]

Kennedy's "roseate" mood also influenced his assessment of events in Europe. Chamberlain had reassured him in their July meeting "that nothing is going to happen [on account of Czechoslovakia] unless some unforeseen incident occurs."[156] Kennedy cabled Hull that the prime minister believed "that there is no real prospect of difficulty for some time at least."[157] Nor did Kennedy himself regard Europe's situation as "so critical." In mid-July, he wrote to Roosevelt that "there had been some fear that Germany might go berserk after the harvests are in, but the feeling now is that if this does not happen, war is not likely to come until next spring at the earliest."[158]

By mid-summer Kennedy's mood was fading. During his second "spirited" and "interesting" conversation with von Dirksen on July 20, he appeared to be "much more worried and pessimistic" than he had been, von Dirksen told Berlin. Economic considerations still dominated Kennedy's thinking, the German ambassador said. Although the American economy had somewhat improved, Kennedy was worried because the problems facing the world's economy—unemployment and lack of confidence—remained unsolved. He had talked with J. P. Morgan and Bernard Baruch, who were both "very depressed" and "pessimistic" about the economic situation.[159]

Kennedy was also gripped by his fear of a German declaration of war on Czechoslovakia; such an act would bring in England and France and then the United States either directly or indirectly. This idea "appeared to have a pretty firm hold on him," von Dirksen wrote. America's opinion of Germany had "deteriorated appreciably," Kennedy told him: The Americans were more and more confused and hostile. They blamed Germany for the general worldwide "insecurity," the poor economic recovery, and warmongering.[160]

Von Dirksen also reported that Kennedy told him that during his discussions of the international situation with Roosevelt, Roosevelt remained calm and unprovoked by mass sentiment. He proposed to give extensive support to encourage tranquility and to create better economic conditions. And von Dirksen reported—unbelievably—that Kennedy said

FDR intended "to support Germany's demands" with respect to England and to do "anything that might lead to pacification." It was "very obvious" from what Kennedy reported that the United States saw itself as "the protector and helper of England," von Dirksen wrote, and that England in turn owed "subservience and obedience" to the United States. Roosevelt's administration not only "supports the Chamberlain cabinet" but "assists it in overcoming all difficulties," he told Berlin.[161] Further ways in which the United States would assist Britain, Kennedy predicted, were to designate Eden as Britain's ambassador to Washington, to amend the Neutrality Act favorably, and to sanction Chamberlain's desire for a settlement with Germany with support strong enough to break any political opposition. The American ambassador also said that he intended to become a watchdog, making certain that the British did not use American aid to enhance their own position.

Although it was "obvious" that he was acting under Roosevelt's orders in his discussion, Kennedy "still made a good impression on me," von Dirksen cabled Berlin.[162] He had a hunch, confirmed by various sources, that FDR needed more economic successes before the next election and that Kennedy himself might even be a candidate for the presidency.

On August 16 the two ambassadors renewed their conversation about Kennedy's possible visit to Germany in September under the auspices of the International Wheat Conference, of which Kennedy was serving as president. Although the German foreign ministry had "serious doubts" about the proposed visit and believed that Kennedy's interpretation of American policy was "too optimistic" and that it might "create a false impression here," permission for the visit was extended.[163] The venture, however, never became a reality; the Munich crisis intervened.

Outrageous as Kennedy's plans were, they probably had little impact on Germany's view of official Washington. The German foreign ministry also received reports from their ambassador in the United States, Hans Dieckhoff, which they must have regarded as more reliable.[164] Kennedy's actions do illustrate his diplomatic ineptness and could hardly have helped the Allied cause.

There is no evidence that either FDR or Hitler knew or cared about Kennedy's plans. The ambassador's initiative, undertaken without the consent of his superiors, indicated his colossal arrogance and gullibility in believing that he could somehow independently and single-handedly establish better relations with Hitler and thereby secure the foundations of peace. His assumptions that he could pull off a personal diplomatic triumph by a visit to Germany certainly did raise serious questions about his gullibility. There would be other instances of Kennedy's credulous personal diplomacy.

Historians today know that Hitler had no intention of embracing armament limitations nor of negotiating peaceful settlements. They ask: Was either ambassador sincere in his statements? Clearly, von Dirksen was acting on instructions in telling Kennedy that Hitler was willing to negotiate an Anglo-German rapprochement. And Kennedy was enthusiastic and uncritical in his statements about von Dirksen. Although they seemed to have convinced each other, neither was able to convince his superior.[165] Years later when the captured Nazi documents were published and von Dirksen's dispatches made public, Kennedy would denounce what the German ambassador reported saying to him as "complete poppycock."[166]

In the course of his conversations with von Dirksen on July 20, Kennedy discussed the July 18 visit to London of Hitler's aide-de-camp, Captain Fritz Wiedemann, under whom Corporal Hitler had served during World War I.[167] Wiedemann had come on a "goodwill" mission on Hitler's behalf to meet with Halifax and to try to improve Anglo-German relations.[168] Kennedy was surprised to learn from von Dirksen that Hitler was willing to begin negotiations with the English over armaments and that now, July, was the time for them to offer proposals, provided, of course, that they added Russia, Poland, and Czechoslovakia to them. Include them, then an "armaments agreement can definitely be accomplished," von Dirksen stated.[169] Kennedy reported to Hull, perhaps the only one of his conversations he did report, that the German ambassador also "implied" that he "hoped there was some way that we could urge the English to start."[170] All for naught; the president still preferred to remain aloof.

Besides pursuing negotiations with the British, von Dirksen suggested that Reichsmar-schall Hermann Göring visit England. Kennedy told Washington that the English were cautiously "delighted"[171] but wanted the Czech situation to be settled first.[172]

Although Wiedemann's visit produced some garbled press accounts and grumbling among Foreign Office officials (who wanted to host Hitler's emissary at the Foreign Office rather than have Halifax receive him at his home), they believed that he spoke with the Führer's full authority. Chamberlain was reassured by Wiedemann's announcement giving him Hitler's "most explicit assurances" that if the Czechs were not provocative, the Germans "did not contemplate any coercive or violent move against Czechoslovakia."[173]

Wiedemann's visit produced no real results. British efforts to follow up and to urge a peaceful Anglo-German settlement about Czechoslovakia elicited nothing from Berlin. Nevertheless, Chamberlain felt reassured enough by Wiedemann's statement to take a country holiday in Scotland and go fishing.[174] Kennedy or von Dirksen must have been mistaken about Hitler's willingness to negotiate, or Kennedy misunderstood von Dirksen (whose English was poor),[175] or Kennedy was simply being toyed with. Nothing could have been falser than that Hitler wanted to negotiate with the British about anything.

Across the Channel in midsummer 1938, temperatures rose in Berlin and Prague. Hitler and Henlein found the Czechs remarkably stubborn. Negotiations were near collapse. To provide an impetus for a solution of the Czech crisis, and to seize the leadership in diplomacy, as one foreign official told Kennedy,[176] Chamberlain decided to sponsor the Runciman mission. He informed Kennedy of his decision before making the surprise public announcement to the House of Commons on July 26, 1938. Chamberlain told him that the Czech government, however reluctantly, had agreed on July 23 to have Lord Runciman, an expert in settling industrial disputes, investigate and mediate the crisis, acting as a private individual, independent of any government.[177] He was reputed to be "as wily as a serpent," one official told the ambassador.[178] Chamberlain's decision, Kennedy wrote in his memoir, made it clear that "England had accepted a prime responsibility for the settlement of the Czechoslovakian dispute"—as indeed it had.[179] Runciman referred to his mission to Roosevelt (whom he had met in 1937 when he was a guest at the White House) as being "set afloat in an open boat in a treacherous ocean . . . in the endeavor to reduce the points of friction between the Czechs and the Sudeten Germans and to guide that unhappy country into smooth water."[180]

Chamberlain clung to his hope that the Czech situation would be "adjusted without difficulty" and that that would open the way to a general appeasement agreement. The situation was "better," he told Kennedy, because of the Wiedemann visit, Austria's preoccupation with its international difficulties, and Germany's unpreparedness for war. America was "entirely out of sympathy, more so than ever, with the German cause." Despite the warnings of Chamberlain's advisers, this had encouraged Chamberlain "to go along with Hitler and see what can be done," Kennedy reported.[181]

The Foreign Office asked Kennedy, who agreeably complied without comment, to pass on its view to the State Department "that should the President or the Secretary feel that he could make some public statement expressing approval of Runciman's mission this would have a favorable effect on world opinion and Lord Halifax would naturally be much gratified." Sir Orme Sargent, the assistant undersecretary at the Foreign Office, supported the idea and told Kennedy that Roosevelt's support would be "extremely helpful."[182]

When the president, who had been on holiday, returned to Washington, he decided to ignore the requests for approval from London. Friendship aside, Roosevelt had no desire to comment on the mission. Washington had not forgotten how the president's tepid approval of the Anglo-Italian agreements had been used by Chamberlain to his own political advantage. Roosevelt also saw the fallacy in the argument that Runciman would or could act independently of any government, and resisted any action that could be interpreted as a sellout of the Czechs—views that Kennedy seemed not to share, so eager was he to support Chamberlain's initiative. But Roosevelt knew better and maintained his silence.[183]

As the stalemate continued, Kennedy continued to be kept informed and discussed the discouraging situation with Halifax, who told him that Runciman found the negotiations extremely difficult, that "he was not going through as he should," and asked Halifax "to twist Beneš tail."[184] Finally Beneš gave in and agreed to grant the Sudeten Germans virtually complete autonomy. Hitler ignored the offer from Prague.[185]

As Parliament went into summer recess, Britons enjoyed fair weather and sunned themselves on the beaches of Brighton and Bognor. Kennedy left London on August 4 to join his family already vacationing on the Côte d'Azur at Cannes, where they had rented a villa near the Hôtel du Cap. He relaxed on the Mediterranean by mingling with celebrities like Marlene Dietrich,[186] swimming and sailing with the Duke of Windsor, and writing to friends.[187] Kennedy flew back to the embassy refreshed and tanned. He arrived on August 29, 1938, ready to undertake what became the roughest six weeks of his diplomatic career. Throughout the Czech crisis he often worked late at night, often until three or four in the morning, and sent frequent, sometimes hourly, dispatches to Washington. The crisis was a major test of his diplomatic mettle, a test he failed.

During an hour-long conversation on August 30 right before leaving to join the king and queen at Balmoral, Chamberlain "was filled with uncertainty," Kennedy observed.[188] He surprised Kennedy with the news that there was a fifty-fifty chance of war since Hitler intended to have Czechoslovakia one way or another. Chamberlain told him he was "hopeful" that war could be forestalled by following his appeasement policy and exploring other alternatives for peace. Threats will not stop Hitler, Chamberlain said, and we are not in a position to make them. Kennedy loyally agreed. Would Britain join France if war broke out? Kennedy asked. We "might be forced into it," Chamberlain replied. Despite Britain's opposition to fighting, if France declared war, then an "aroused" public opinion could force Britain to fight. Still, he promised, "he definitely would not go until he was absolutely forced to."[189] "It will be hell," said Kennedy.[190] "My own impression," he assured the State Department, is that Chamberlain will use his influence to keep France and Britain out of war. If we avoid war, Chamberlain said, "something may happen for the good of the world."[191] "It is quite easy" to go to war, he remarked to Kennedy, "but what have we proven after we are in?"[192] This question Kennedy himself was later to echo. Giving him a strong vote of confidence, Kennedy described the "sick looking" prime minister as "worried but not jittery." He was still "the best bet in Europe against war."[193]

Upset by the war of nerves and worried about a general European war breaking out, the ambassador realized that the isolationist position of the United States would be extremely hard to maintain. If France and Britain entered the war, "the United States would follow." Is there anything that the United States government might do? he asked. Chamberlain said no. Despite Chamberlain's demurral, Kennedy, apparently without consulting Washington, impulsively offered him a blank check. The president would "go in with Chamberlain; whatever course Chamberlain desires to adopt he would think right."[194] If the prime minister wanted FDR to "do anything," then he, Kennedy, "would be glad to know about it."[195] Thus, Kennedy gave Chamberlain a sweeping assurance of support and conveyed a totally erroneous sense of approval and enthusiasm on FDR's part; he apparently meant that the president would accept either a sellout of the Czechs or war with Germany.

Chamberlain must have realized that Kennedy's reckless offer of a blank check was not a solid basis on which to establish a policy of bluff, and that Kennedy was not a particularly accurate or reliable spokesman for the administration. Actually there is little reason to believe that Chamberlain was any more receptive to Kennedy's views than the president was. The prime minister could not have taken Kennedy's diplomatic schemes seriously or thought he was a significant factor in defining American foreign policy. No doubt Chamberlain was willing to accept any support he could get from the United States, but there is no evidence that he expected it; quite the reverse. Kennedy's parochial diplomatic vision, his inexperience, and his fear of war prevented him from realizing that such a sweeping promise of American aid without guarantees of diplomatic and military support was meaningless and diametrically opposed to his oft-repeated isolationist position. Furthermore, were it to provoke Hitler, it could lead to the very thing he most feared, war itself.

Are the Germans "bluffing"? Kennedy asked Halifax in a conversation the next day, August 31, 1938. No, Halifax replied. Hitler intends "to get all he wants without a fight."[196] But Kennedy still refused to believe that a German invasion of Czechoslovakia was imminent; rather, Germany's policy was one of "bluff" and "intimidation." Despite his previous position endorsing Germany's expansion, Kennedy argued, "it was by no means certain or even probable that any expansion of territorial control would benefit those making it."[197] The Nazis might have difficulty imposing their economic system over a wider area. Even if they controlled southeastern Europe, Germany would still "find herself paralyzed by economic pressure" and limited by her financial resources.[198]

What would American reaction be if the Germans invaded Czechoslovakia and Britain did not fight? Halifax asked Kennedy during their meeting of August 31. That, Kennedy responded, would depend on whether the president thought Britain should fight.[199] Although American opinion would be "shocked" by German aggression in Czechoslovakia, that would not justify casting Europe into a general war, he said, withdrawing his blank check.[200] Kennedy turned to the secretary of state for advice. "I would appreciate some opinion from you as to [the] policy of handling the attitude of the British if Germany marches and the English decide not to."[201] So would the prime minister and the foreign secretary, he added.

Hull's stiff and noncommittal response to Kennedy's request for more guidance and advice read:

> I feel that the recent public speeches and public statements of the President and myself, which were prepared with great care, accurately reflect the attitude of this Government toward the European and world situation, and that it would not be practicable to be more specific as to our reaction in hypothetical circumstances.[202]

The recent public speeches and public statements to which Hull referred in his cable to Kennedy were Hull's radio address of August 16, Roosevelt's speech two days later at Kingston, Ontario, and Hull's anniversary statement on the Kellogg-Briand Pact on August 27. Hull's radio address, couched in the lofty, vague, self-righteous rhetoric he used astutely, repeated the usual on-the-one-hand, on-the-other-hand themes in American foreign policy that seemingly made for confusion but actually shrewdly allowed for flexibility and maneuverability.[203]

He intended to show the American public that an isolationist position would not necessarily protect them from a general war and to warn the Axis powers that even given American isolationism they could not rule out U.S. opposition to their aggression. On August 18, Roosevelt, speaking at Kingston, issued another warning by inserting into the State Department's text the promise "that the people of the United States will not stand idly by if domination of Canadian soil is threatened by any other Empire."[204] But this speech, too, restated the American aversion to foreign entanglements. It was intended to "embroider on the theme of the eternal question mark of American foreign policy," Moffat at the State Department said.[205]

Halifax told Kennedy he was delighted with the speeches and asked Hull to make a further statement on the Czech issue before the Nazi Party meeting at Nuremberg scheduled for September 12. It might have a "restraining effect on Hitler."[206] Hull obliged and issued a statement on August 27, the tenth anniversary of the Kellogg-Briand Pact, asserting that "on the observance or non-observance of the solemn pledges made ten years ago depends the preservation of all that is valuable and worthwhile in the life of each and every nation."[207]

Roosevelt was walking a tightrope. He encouraged the British to resist German aggression, but he would give them no assurance of American support if they did so. Thus it was safest to issue vague, high-sounding statements that required no backup. As for Kennedy, FDR seemed to determine that he could do only one of two things—"manage his London ambassador or cope with the hourly changes in Europe."[208] He opted for the latter. Thus the president kept up his tightrope act in foreign affairs and gave his ambassador enough slack to play out his role with little more than verbal hand-slaps and rebuffs from Hull that further undermined Kennedy's authority within the administration but had little influence on Roosevelt's foreign policy.

As before, the ambassador set himself at odds with the administration by ignoring protocol and going over the heads of the president and the State Department and acting as the spokesman for his own foreign policy. After his August 31 conversation with Halifax, Kennedy gave a transatlantic interview to a reporter from the Hearst-owned *Boston Evening American.* "Keep cool—things aren't as bad as they may seem," the ambassador counseled. "The thing to do here and in the United States is not to lose our heads." Does the English public support the cabinet in the crisis? the reporter asked him. "Yes, very strongly," Kennedy answered.[209] Two weeks later he ventured a prediction: "No war is going to break out during the rest of 1938."[210]

The president was livid over the interview and expected Hull to discipline Kennedy. A draft of the secretary's incensed reprimand to Kennedy accused him of causing "considerable embarrassment" by his transatlantic comments. Hull's final version, sent "with startling promptness" the next day, Kennedy noted—cold, but considerably toned down—was a do-not-do-it-again slap. It said that the ambassador's special telephone interview "will undoubtedly be regarded as unfair to other agencies." "Great confusion" would result if other diplomats followed his example.[211] Kennedy's apology was brief. "The only conversation they had with me was to the effect that people were very excited over there and I told them to keep cool." He added, "I manage to get along reasonably well with the agencies and have not heard any complaints."[212]

FDR joined Hull in scolding his ambassador: "As you know, we were all greatly disturbed by the appearance of an 'exclusive' message of advice" to the *Boston Evening American*. "It is not a question of 'getting along reasonably well with the agencies'—for, of course, you do that but it does involve the use of an American newspaper or a single news agency or 'special interview' or 'special message of advice' to people back here. I know you will understand."[213]

But he *always* answered phone calls from Boston, Kennedy wrote in self-defense in his diplomatic memoir. It was his habit to do so; his family lived there. Despite his having taken the precaution of immediately informing the State Department to explain the circumstances of the interview, Kennedy noted that "someone in Washington seemed greatly perturbed about the matter" and he blamed the reproofs he received from officials on his old association with Hearst: "I was suspect." In addition, Kennedy issued a denial of the rumor that Chamberlain had asked him to request a commitment of aid from the American government. But it did no good; Kennedy's denial did not drown out the chatter, particularly loud among journalists in isolationist strongholds like Chicago and Salt Lake City who accused him of having succumbed to flattery from the royal family, the Court, and the prime minister, and of having "gone English." The *Times*'s diplomatic correspondent, according to the ambassador, made the most accurate statement about his relationship with the British Establishment. It noted that during this troubling moment the "relations between the two countries [Britain and the United States] are at their most cordial. Mr. Kennedy has been kept informed throughout the discussions as has Corbin, the French Ambassador."[214] Even that failed to end the controversy, particularly in Washington.

Muckraking columnists Joseph Alsop and Robert Kintner joined in the chorus of accusers and observed in their joint column of September 19, 1938, in the *Washington Star* that "while Kennedy is loved in London, he is no longer popular at the White House." Citing "the highest authority," they charged that the president "knows of his private talk, resents it and rebukes it when he can"[215]—charges that loyal Kennedyite Arthur Krock called "lies."[216] But the ambassador's outspokenness continued to get him into trouble with Washington and continued to require many rebukes by the administration.

Kennedy's Chamberlainesque view of the imminence of war, or even a crisis in Central Europe over a problem as inconsequential to him as minorities, landed him in another dispute with the president over his draft of a speech. Initially he refused to be censored by the State Department, but he was forced to back down when department officials appealed directly to the president. Kennedy's speech contained a rhetorical question: "I should like to ask you all if you know of any dispute or controversy existing in the world which is worth the life of your son, or of anyone else's son." He went on to give his own answer: "For the life of me

I cannot see anything involved which could be remotely considered worth shedding blood for."[217] Roosevelt parodied it: "I can't for the life of me understand why anybody would want to go to war to save the Czechs" and ordered Kennedy to delete the sentences. "The young man needs his wrists slapped rather hard," FDR said, appalled by his ambassador's crassness.[218] During the difficult days ahead, the prime minister himself publicly lamented the menace of war "because of a quarrel in a far-away country between people of whom we know nothing," a sentiment Kennedy was to echo after the Munich Agreement.[219]

The occasion for the controversial speech on September 2 was the laying of a cornerstone in Aberdeen, Scotland, commemorating Samuel Seabury, the first Anglican bishop of the United States, consecrated in 1784. Appropriately, Kennedy's remarks were a defense of religious freedom and by implication a criticism of irreligion and of the persecution of Jews. "In certain parts of the world," said Kennedy, "the profession and practice of religion is being called a political offense. Men and women are being deprived of their natural born citizenship" and being thrown out of their homeland. In contrast he praised such "inalienable" Anglo-American civil liberties as freedom of worship, "the most precious of them all," along with freedom of speech, peaceable assembly, and trial by jury. These liberties distinguished the democracies from other forms of government. His conclusion, even once it was considerably revised by Roosevelt's intervention, must have pleased the appeasers. "We do not want war." We owe it to the peoples of the world "to leave no avenue unexplored in our efforts to prevent war. . . . I believe it can be done by the application of the principles we have been discussing—by faith, by spiritual courage, by loyalty to right dealing and by the exercise of common sense."[220]

Throughout the summer and into fall, Roosevelt had become more and more irritated by, and suspicious of, his outspoken ambassador, whose opinions he gave less and less credence to. "I do not think Joe is fooling him very much," wrote Ickes, who was curious about FDR's comments on Kennedy and happily recorded them in his diary. The president, as shrewd as they come, had predicted to Ickes that "Joe" would last no more than a few years in England. He preferred to go from one job to another as he had always done and move on when the going got tough. FDR also knew, Ickes wrote, that Kennedy loved his job and was having "the time of his life although he often cries 'wolf.'"[221] And perhaps too, the supreme White House politician resented that his Irish-Catholic appointee in London was being touted as a potential vice-presidential teammate for the 1940 election to oppose a possible Garner-Farley ticket, pitting two Roman Catholics against each other for the vice-presidency.[222] FDR was known to cool toward anyone who came too close to the throne or was regarded as a likely successor, and he jealously guarded his presidential prerogatives.

The president's annoyance led him to regard Kennedy, somewhat accurately, as having gone Walter Hines Page on him by trying to run America's foreign policy himself. Page was a staunch adherent of the Allies in World War I and disdained President Woodrow Wilson's policy of American neutrality. Ever noted for his pro-British position and for his admiration of British culture and civilization, Page was chided for being more British than the British. He ignored American neutrality in order to aid Britain before America's entry into World War I, and like Kennedy, he pursued his own foreign policy. Ultimately Page, because of his Anglophilia, became an ineffective advocate of American policy and, like Kennedy, lost the confidence of his president. After World War I, "a Walter Hines Page" became a mocking characterization of someone who advocated the interests of the country to which he had been sent, as Kennedy did, rather than those of the country that had sent him.[223] FDR accused his ambassador not only of becoming pro-British but also of having been taken in by the "slippery" Chamberlain.[224] He was "playing the Chamberlain game," the president said, by trying to force FDR's hand in his conversations with the press. Morgenthau confided to his diary: "Kennedy is playing with the British Foreign Office and the Prime Minister. He has spilled the beans and the President knows that."[225]

Not only had Kennedy courted portions of the American press and given exclusive interviews to the Hearst-owned *Boston Evening News*, but he also received extensive coverage in the British press. By playing up his frequent visits to British officials, he gave the appearance of continuous consultations between the United States and Great Britain, to the great distress of Washington. If we start "continual consultation," as Halifax requests, we will find ourselves becoming "'an associate power' before we know it," wrote Adolf Berle.[226] Moffat commented in his diary: "Joe Kennedy's star is not shining brightly these days. He cannot move without a blare of publicity, and in tense moments like these, publicity is the thing most to be avoided"—something a professional diplomat would have known.[227] But Joe Kennedy was no professional diplomat, and publicity was something he dearly loved and craved.

Hull, too, was dismayed. He accused Kennedy of pursuing his private foreign policy and of starting the rumor of a London-Paris-Washington peace axis. The secretary feared the resulting embarrassment to the United States if Britain and France went to war. He wanted to be informed but remain aloof from Europe's crisis.

It is entirely likely that Kennedy understood all this, but his support of Chamberlain's policy led him to act contrary to the wishes of the State Department.[228] But other than casual rebukes, there is little evidence that anyone tried to stop him or to explain to him that his personal diplomacy ran counter to the administration's policy. Neither FDR nor Hull nor any official warned him against involvement in Europe's emerging crisis or ordered him to cease his personal diplomacy, nor did they offer an alternative policy. Roosevelt, aware of his ambassador's unswerving devotion to peace regardless, may not have bluntly expressed to Kennedy his reservations about Chamberlain or his appeasement policy. For his part, the ambassador may have been unaware of the growing divergence between the president and the prime minister and himself.

Before Munich, FDR also regarded Chamberlain as untrustworthy and remained as suspicious and critical of his intentions as the prime minister was distrustful of his. "Chamberlain was playing the usual game of the British—peace at any price—. . . if he could get away with it and save his face," Roosevelt bitterly remarked. He resented the British government's repeated queries made through Kennedy, their all-too-willing mouthpiece, about what the administration's attitude would be under various circumstances. Chamberlain's and Halifax's queries to Kennedy were "designed to place the blame on us," the president said to Morgenthau, "so that if they went in it was on account of the support they would have gotten from us and, if they did not, it was because we held back."[229] "This is an old game," complained Moffat in his diary, "but Joe Kennedy seems to have fallen for it."[230] Neither FDR nor the State Department had. The administration saw the requests for what they were, attempts to shift to the United States some of the responsibility for Britain's decision about whether to go to war. But the American ambassador did not. He was either indifferent or blind to their implications.[231]

"The reports from the press on what Chamberlain has said do not gee [*sic*] with what Chamberlain told Kennedy," Roosevelt observed. "The press has deliberately distorted the British position, which is possible, or Chamberlain told two stories, one to Germany and France, and one to us. It is a nice kettle of fish," the president said. "It looks as though Chamberlain is lying."[232] The administration decided that "it would be a mistake to make any gestures, publicly or privately, at this time." FDR also wanted Kennedy publicly to deny the impression that the British had asked the United States what it would do in case of war. "They have us for the moment, stymied," wrote Morgenthau, who believed that "anything might happen" in the present crisis—"it is fifty-fifty." And the president, far from optimistic about Chamberlain's policy, as Kennedy thought, was more and more pessimistic. He told Morgenthau: "I'll bet three-to-one that the Germans will be able to accomplish their objectives" without a war.[233]

Thus, in the last days of August, Kennedy was quite willing to cooperate with Chamberlain and to support his appeasement policy, and willing to urge the Roosevelt administration to do so, too. Actually the foreign policies of both countries complemented each other, something that Kennedy may not have grasped: American isolationism reinforced Britain's appeasement policy but denied it the support needed for its success, and the appeasement policy encouraged the American belief that a more active foreign-policy role was unnecessary. The two great English-speaking democracies remained "unwitting and unwilling" allies.[234]

CHAPTER 4

Peace for Our Time

On the evening of September 12, 1938, Joseph Kennedy sat with Eddie Moore and several of his aides at the American embassy in Grosvenor Square writing to a friend and waiting for a broadcast from Nuremberg in which Hitler was expected to reveal his plans for Czechoslovakia. They could hear Hitler delivering his "boastful" and "threatening" speech in a shrill, whining voice[1] to a crowd of Nazi faithful aroused to fever pitch by a "week-long orgy" of drum-beating, passionate oratory, and patriotic pomp and spectacle. "Sieg Heil! Sieg Heil! Sieg Heil!" Kennedy heard the familiar frenzied chant growing louder and louder. Despite his optimistic prophecy that no war would break out in 1938 and his steadfast belief in Chamberlain's appeasement policy, Kennedy must have been filled with foreboding. He might send his family back to the United States, and he worried about whether he would ever see them again.[2]

The German chancellor reiterated his oft-repeated demand that the "oppression of Sudeten Germans must end" and the 3,500,000 "brothers" living under Czech rule must enjoy self-determination, thereby ensuring the annexation of the Sudetenland to Germany and the dissolution of Czechoslovakia.[3] Although the speech "contained highly offensive expressions," Kennedy wrote, Hitler had neither "closed the door entirely nor yet put his hand to the trigger."[4] "The gage of self-determination" had been tossed down, Kennedy noted, but Hitler had also promised the democracies a peaceful Europe once the fate of Czechoslovakia was settled.[5] The "madman" had decided to tease and taunt his prey a little longer.[6]

"Spontaneous" riots erupted in Czechoslovakia the next day, with clashes between the Henleinists and the Czech gendarmerie. Twelve people were reported killed.[7] The Czech president, Edvard Beneš, responded by establishing martial law in some of the Czech districts. German troop movements were reported. The "indecisive" French begged the British to find some way to prevent the invasion of Czechoslovakia even if that meant abandoning it. It was plain, Kennedy observed, that "the French were looking to the British to pull their chestnuts out of the fire."[8] British officials, too, were alarmed and feared that German troops were ready to pounce. Almost against their will, Kennedy observed, the British were getting pulled in. "I feel they sense great danger in the air," although they appeared quite calm, he reported to Washington.[9] Kennedy told Washington that for the first time in his conversations with English leaders "there was a slightly hysterical tone."[10] The inner cabinet—Chamberlain, Halifax, Simon, and Hoare—met constantly.[11] There was "a new glint in Neville Chamberlain's eyes and in those of Sir Samuel Hoare and of the others which I never noticed before," Kennedy remarked. "This time they mean business."[12] The many crisis-ridden months of fruitless negotiations and frenzied debate over Czechoslovakia appeared to be reaching a climax, and the long-pent-up quarrel was on the point of erupting.

Kennedy thoroughly enjoyed his role as an eyewitness to the historic and dramatic events of the Czech crisis and kept Washington informed of the prime minister's circuitous quest for peace, which led him from London, to Berchtesgaden, to Godesberg, to his final triumph in Munich. The ambassador gave his enthusiastic approval to the controversial Munich Agreement of September 30, 1938, which sold out the Czechs to Hitler and permitted the dismemberment of their state. Kennedy continued to give credence to the Myth of Munich after wiser heads saw its errors and retreated from their endorsement. Ultimately, he risked his career for Chamberlain's appeasement policy, which failed to bring peace. Furthermore, by willingly involving himself as an ally in the foreign affairs of the country to which he was posted, and by sometimes acting contrary to the policies of the country he represented, the ambassador's activities on behalf of the prime minister cost him his protective professional mantle of diplomatic impartiality and objectivity both with his host and with his home country.

Throughout the crisis, Kennedy frequently dashed back and forth between the embassy, the Foreign Office, and 10 Downing Street and loved conferring with officials at the highest level. If Chamberlain was too busy to see him, Kennedy was content to sit reading the newspaper at 10 Downing Street, to present a picture of sympathetic endorsement by the United States government.[13] One day he met the prime minister for business and then came back to see him again, so that it would be known that he had visited him twice on the same day during the crisis.[14] Chamberlain in return kept his faithful friend informed of his every move, even of his confidential cabinet conversations and his communication with Hitler that led to their meetings at Berchtesgaden, Godesberg, and Munich.

Kennedy also visited the king at Buckingham Palace for more than half an hour and conferred with diplomats from other countries.[15] He held weekend-long consultations with British officials like Halifax, Hoare, Cadogan, and Oliver Stanley, the president of the Board of Trade.[16] Kennedy continued his personal diplomacy in discussions with the German counselor of the legation, Edward von Selzam, and American aviator Charles Lindbergh, and met Roosevelt's personal emissary, Bernard Baruch. Kennedy also worried almost daily over the phone to his bosses in Washington and kept them posted on the events in Europe.

Sumner Welles at the State Department praised him: "I can't tell you how admirably you have been keeping us informed. It couldn't be better."[17]

Desperate to do anything to support Chamberlain's policy during the crisis, Kennedy kept up his ceaseless requests for some kind of action by Roosevelt on behalf of Chamberlain's efforts. He also counseled scare tactics, aided the government's censorship efforts, and may have arranged for American radio stations to carry a broadcast by the prime minister. The ambassador's efforts gave the appearance of American collusion with the British, a cooperation that did not exist and the very impression that Washington wished not to convey. Despite repeated British requests for gestures of support throughout the crisis, administration officials continued to refuse to assume any responsibility that might have compromised America's status as an indifferent neutral staying aloof from a potential European war.

For his part, Kennedy may not have understood—or cared, even if he understood, so great was his desire to maintain peace. Not only did his endeavors unintentionally undermine his own efforts to ensure American isolation and Britain's appeasement policy, but they also killed any credibility he might have had as a diplomat whose advice was worth listening to and respecting.

Incredibly, through his consultations with Halifax and von Selzam, Kennedy hampered his own strivings to bolster British resistance to Hitler. Halifax asked Kennedy yet again on September 10, before Hitler's speech, what America would do if Hitler went to war. "I had not the slightest idea," he said, "except that we want to keep out of war." Why did he think that Great Britain and not the United States should be the champion of democratic values and morality? the foreign secretary asked him. Kennedy's answer was that Britain and not the United States had made Czechoslovakia its business. Furthermore, the ambassador added, Americans failed to see why and where they should be involved.[18] His blunt remarks, though an accurate reflection of American opinion, were hardly likely to stiffen the British resolve to stand up to Hitler any more than his statements made to von Selzam would be likely to restrain or scare the Führer into backing down on Czechoslovakia because of the supposed strength of Anglo-American collaboration.

Kennedy told the German counselor two days later, on September 12, that he had believed that Britain would avoid war over the Sudeten question, and yet that he had completely changed his opinion because of conversations with Chamberlain and Halifax the day before, on September 11. The American ambassador was now firmly convinced, von Selzam told the German foreign ministry, that if France supported the Czechs, Britain would support the Czechs as well. In response to von Selzam's question about America's role if a European war broke out, Kennedy stated that his government would do everything possible "to keep America out of the war." He promised to "work for this" too, because he was the father of two sons of military age.[19] However, anti-German sentiment in the United States had never been stronger than it was at present, and he predicted that America would ultimately intervene if war broke out in Europe. It all depended on Hitler, he said. Apparently Kennedy, like most of his diplomatic colleagues, believed that the Führer wanted to avoid war. Had that been the case, a strong Anglo-American relationship would have given him pause and made him less belligerent and perhaps even have deterred him. But Kennedy and others misunderstood Hitler's determination: Hitler would have his war, regardless.

Another futile ambassadorial gesture designed to scare Hitler was Kennedy's suggestion, made to an obliging Roosevelt, to order two American cruisers, the *Nashville* and the *Honolulu*, to British waters simply for the effect on Germany.[20] The ambassador suggested to Halifax that "some political use might perhaps be made" of them. The foreign secretary also appreciated Kennedy's offer to call on the prime minister "in order to encourage German speculation" about Anglo-American collaboration, a thing Washington wanted to avoid.[21]

In the uncertain, fear-ridden days leading up to the Munich Agreement, the British cast "anxious looks" across the Atlantic as Kennedy repeatedly directed requests from Chamberlain to Washington in the hope that the United States might say "something helpful," recalled Sir Thomas Inskip, the minister for coordination of defense.[22] Roosevelt's only action was to urge peace in his messages to Hitler and to continue to refrain from any commitment to Britain in the event of war. He argued successfully for the contradictory twin aims of American foreign policy: to avoid war, because of America's military and psychological unpreparedness and political opposition to it; and to oppose Hitler's aggression firmly and not be seen to support Britain's appeasement policy. If the British succeeded in their opposition to Hitler, the Americans would claim credit for supporting Britain's resolve; if the British failed, the United States would refuse to accept any blame and affirm the policy of staunch isolation. Thus, the administration demanded that the British stand up to Hitler and risk a war for which they, too, were unprepared and could not win, and to do so without American support. Washington argued for "firmness" rather than "wise accommodation." Any attempt at compromise with the Germans would "bring about a certain let-down of American friendliness," Lindsay predicted on September 12 in a dispatch to Halifax.[23] For his part, Chamberlain believed that the United States would join the Allied cause if war broke out, but in the meantime his strategy was to respond to the crisis without expecting American aid.[24]

September 14 was a topsy-turvy day in the Czech crisis. Word spread of fighting in the Sudetenland as some two thousand Sudetens suffered heavy injuries in battles against the police. Henlein rejected the Czech proposals to solve the Sudeten problem and called for foreign intervention and fled to Germany. Beneš called off the negotiations.[25] War seemed so close that, only the day before, Morgenthau had ordered the return of American gold from London on American naval ships.[26] Late in the afternoon of September 14 came the announcement that Chamberlain would fly to Berchtesgaden to confer with Hitler the next day. Kennedy had learned of the plan only two or three hours before.[27]

The prime minister had interrupted a meeting to tell Kennedy about Plan Z, a daring and unconventional decision he had made without first consulting the cabinet. He had invited himself to Berlin to meet face to face with Hitler to discuss the Sudeten issue, perhaps the first instance of "shuttle diplomacy." Chamberlain suggested that the German army be demobilized and that the Sudetenland be given local autonomy for five years, after which an international body would determine a final settlement. If necessary, he told Kennedy, he would move the timetable up six months to placate Hitler. Chamberlain's theatrical gesture won the unanimous and enthusiastic support of the cabinet.[28]

"The great trouble with this," Kennedy shrewdly observed to Hull, "is that Herr Hitler will be winning a victory without bloodshed and make the next crisis whenever and about whatever it comes, much easier for him to win out." Chamberlain knows all this, the ambassador reported, but he wants Hitler to understand that his major goal is for a general conference to discuss international affairs. Czechoslovakia, after all, is but "a small incident in that big cause."[29] If the bribe of a conference is turned down, the prime minister told Kennedy, then we "will have tried everything" and made every proposal possible, after which we will fight beside France. Wish me luck and pray for me, Chamberlain asked him at the conclusion of their meeting.[30] Later that afternoon, Hitler's message arrived, agreeing to see the prime minister.

It must have been unusual for a British prime minister to keep an ambassador as well informed as a member of his own cabinet and for an ambassador to offer "great moral support," but it reflected how far Kennedy had ingratiated himself with Chamberlain, who continued to find him useful in trying to get some gesture of public encouragement from Roosevelt. Kennedy, agreeably, again passed along the request for some statement from the president about Chamberlain's trip just before his departure for Berchtesgaden on September 15.[31]

And again American officials maintained their silence, suspicious and wary of Chamberlain's motives and fearful of holding the bag for Britain. Chamberlain was for "peace at any price," Ickes quoted Roosevelt as telling him and the cabinet on September 16: By joining England and abandoning Czechoslovakia to Hitler's aggression, France would ensure the destruction of that country. After this international outrage, England and France would "wash the blood from their Judas Iscariot hands," predicted the president, who believed then that no war would break out.[32] Pierrepont Moffat, chief of the European division at the State Department, confided to his diary: "We did not know what Mr. Chamberlain was going to do . . . sell out the Czechs or not." So, there would be no "blank check." "Ever since the beginning of the crisis the British have been maneuvering to get us to give advice or to express ourselves . . . with the sole view of throwing responsibility on us in case their ultimate decision is an unpopular one," Moffat complained once again to his diary on September 14.[33]

At the press conference on September 15, Hull merely said: "The historic conference today between the Prime Minister of Great Britain and the Chancellor of Germany is naturally being observed with the greatest interest by all nations which are deeply concerned in the preservation of peace."[34] Beyond that modest statement American officials refused to go.

Around the globe, however, there was a sense of relief and admiration for Chamberlain. Kennedy noted his wife's diary entry:

> Everyone ready to weep for joy and everyone confident that issues will be resolved. Newspaper headlines read: "Empire Praises Decision—Australia Backs Mr. Chamberlain—Canadian Government's Deep Satisfaction—Relief in South Africa—New Zealand Firmly Behind Britain." Other countries were equally enthusiastic: "Danish Admiration," "Hopes in Hungary," "Roumanian Hope of Peaceful Issues," "Belgian Good Will and Hope," "Swiss Confidence in British Effort," "Istanbul 'most Noble Act,'" "Stockholm—'A Daring Task.'"

L'Osservatore Romano, speaking for the Vatican, wrote that Church officials promised to pray for the prime minister's efforts. Only Moscow disapproved—and the Czechs.[35]

The dumbfounded Czechs, anticipating a sellout, received the news of Chamberlain's journey. "Extra! Extra!" Prague newsboys reportedly yelled. "Read all about how the mighty head of the British Empire goes begging to Hitler!"[36] Chamberlain's journey to Hitler, like "Henry IV going to Canossa over again," destroyed the myth of impartial arbitration that Runciman had embodied, and amounted to Britain's direct participation in the crisis.[37]

"Tough and wiry," the sixty-nine-year-old prime minister embarked on his first airplane ride, a seven-hour flight in a howling rainstorm on September 15, and was greeted with an enthusiastic welcome from the rain-soaked Germans saluting and shouting, "Heil!"[38] Kennedy back in London waited anxiously for two days and kept Washington informed of the rapid-fire events.[39] He sent a barrage of dispatches—detailed, impersonal, dispassionate, unbiased—based on his extensive contacts with British officialdom, with Chamberlain, Cadogan, Halifax, Hoare, and Britain's labor leaders, Ernest Bevin, Walter Citrine, Herbert Morrison, and Hugh Dalton, as well as with the French ambassador, Charles Corbin, and with Walter Layton, the editor of the *News Chronicle*.[40] Kennedy's reports prompted a compliment from Moffat, thanking Kennedy for his invaluable wires informing Washington of the ever-changing nuances of British moods: "Your messages have equaled the highest level of political reporting," the State Department official wrote.[41]

Kennedy reported to Washington the gist of his earliest conversation with Cadogan on September 17 at 1:00 p.m., which detailed the prime minister's visit to Berchtesgaden. Chamberlain found Hitler in a "very bad" mood[42]—he had learned that three hundred Sudetens and forty Germans had been killed by the Czechs.[43] The incidents were nothing more than "ridiculous inventions," Chamberlain later told Kennedy.[44] An official British observer put the total number of fatalities at one.[45] The discussion between the two leaders centered on Hitler's insistence on the principle of self-determination, to which the prime minister refused to assent unless he consulted with his cabinet and perhaps even with Parliament about the transfer to Germany of districts in which the Germans were a majority. "My own opinion," Kennedy cabled Hull, "is that the issue is going to be self-determination or war," with the blame for war lying with the anti-Chamberlain faction.[46]

In a late-evening conversation that same day, the prime minister, who had quickly returned to London to confer with his colleagues over self-determination for the Sudeten Germans, met Kennedy and told him he believed that Hitler intended to invade Czechoslovakia within seventy-two hours after Chamberlain arrived at Berchtesgaden. Chamberlain had taken an "intense dislike" to the Führer, whom he judged "cruel," "overbearing," "hard," and "completely ruthless," Kennedy cabled Washington. But Chamberlain also believed that he had established a "certain confidence" in Hitler. "I got the impression that here was a man who could be relied upon when he had given his word," Chamberlain stated.[47] But the prime minister was suspicious of Hitler's solemn promise to respect the independence of the rest of Czechoslovakia and the integrity of Europe. "Of course, you have to take Hitler's word for that," Chamberlain remarked, but he never believed that Hitler was bluffing. "I will chance a world war if necessary," the Führer had told the prime minister, even after Chamberlain had warned him that if war broke out, Britain would feel compelled to join France against Germany. What would the United States do, the prime minister asked Kennedy, if all the other countries united to protect peace and order? Would it join them too? The ambassador relayed the question to Washington and asked officials to consider the issue.[48] No immediate reply was forthcoming.

Sunday, September 18, was the day on which France's prime minister, Edouard Daladier, and Georges Bonnet, its foreign minister, arrived "with their tongues out seeking for some excuse to avoid actual warfare," Chamberlain commented to Kennedy. Many "sad words" were said of the Czechs during the conference, the prime minister told Kennedy, but always the conclusion was the same: "We must be realistic."[49] The French accepted Hitler's demand for self-determination and recommended that Czech districts with a German population of over 50 percent be transferred to the Reich. Daladier and Bonnet also stipulated that an international commission that included the Czechs should supervise the population exchange and the frontier adjustments and provide for an international guarantee of the new boundaries.[50] A joint statement specifying those Czech areas to be transferred to Germany was approved and passed on to the cabinet and accepted, despite some strenuous objections, the prime minister confided to Kennedy. The next day, the Anglo-French proposals were presented to the Czechs. Initially Beneš rejected them, but after being subjected to intense British pressure, he gave way and assented to his country's dismemberment.

"My own impression," Kennedy cabled Hull after having come from a meeting with the worried and tired prime minister on September 19, "is that unless there is a terrific rise of public opinion all over the world, England does not propose to fight on the Czechoslovak issue." Chamberlain understood he was "going to be charged with the rape of Czechoslovakia," the ambassador reported, but he also said that he could "see no rhyme nor reason in fighting for a cause which, if I went to war for it, I would have to settle after it was over in about the same way I suggest settling it now"—Kennedy's sentiments exactly.[51] Winston Churchill, of course, saw otherwise. He protested against the surrender by the Western democracies to Nazi force and deplored their throwing a small state to the wolves. Although the public's reaction was mixed once the terms of the Anglo-French proposals were known, Kennedy noted, "there was little doubt the country as a whole stood behind Chamberlain. It was evident in the throngs gathered in Parliament Square and in the streets converging on Whitehall." Clenched-fisted demonstrators carrying signs reading "Stand by the Czechs—Stop Hitler and Stop War" were booed by the throng. Even Clement Attlee was heckled by a crowd chanting, "We want peace; Atlee [*sic*] wants war."[52]

The consensus among American officials and in the State Department was that the United States should remain a detached and silent observer even if Britain and France lost their prestige, Germany's hegemony grew, and the U.S. was accused of selling out Czechoslovakia. "Steer clear and keep quiet" was the State Department's advice.[53] Roosevelt watched and worried. His only overt gesture was to summon Ambassador Lindsay to the White House on September 19, without telling Kennedy, to discuss the Czech crisis in absolute secrecy, in an apparent attempt to encourage Chamberlain to stand up to Hitler. In a revival of his January 1938 proposal, FDR offered to attend a heads-of-state world conference, held in a non-European country, to achieve a general settlement, and if war did break out, to support an American blockade. He seemed "quite alive to the possibility that somehow or other in indefinable circumstances" America might again be drawn into war, although it was "inconceivable," Lindsay reported, that Roosevelt could send American troops across the Atlantic.[54] "You may count on us for everything except troops and loans," Roosevelt had earlier promised a French visitor. The British ambassador, preparing to go it alone, passed on the comment to Halifax and noted that FDR should have added the reservation: "subject to dictates of our public opinion and our own domestic politics."[55]

There is no evidence to suggest that Roosevelt's attempt to buck up Chamberlain worked or that the president was influenced by Kennedy's advice. The British response was a polite note to Roosevelt from Halifax, which Lindsay, the British ambassador, prodded him into writing, expressing Halifax's appreciation for Roosevelt's having taken Lindsay into his confidence. Halifax added that he was encouraged by the president's interest in these issues and doing his best to keep Kennedy informed.[56]

Chamberlain's seeming indifference to FDR's proposal illustrated the long-standing problem in dealing with even a sympathetic president. In effect Roosevelt was saying, "Open your mouth and shut your eyes and see what I will give you," observed a member of Lindsay's staff.[57] Thus ended the president's flirtation with convening a world conference or establishing a quarantine of Germany. The most the British could hope for from the United States on the eve of Godesberg was a benevolent neutrality. Although FDR returned to his do-nothing policy of maintaining silence and refusing to become Britain's scapegoat, the circumstances of the next week made him believe that war could be prevented.[58]

With consent wrung from the Czechs over the Anglo-French proposals on September 21, Chamberlain flew to Godesberg the next day to continue his discussion with Hitler. "Public opinion here, I think, is probably a shade against Chamberlain's plan and there is definitely opposition in the Cabinet," Kennedy told Washington, summing up the British attitude. In some of the meetings he attended, "the English are spending most of their time apologizing to us for the way England is acting." They assume that a future war is possible and would go to war if it were declared, although they are wholly unready for it. But they "would still be hollering murder because they had to fight [for] Czechoslovakia."[59] Further, the prime minister feared that war would end civilization as we know it and that communism or something worse would be likely to follow war—fears that Kennedy deeply shared. "You are damned if you do and damned if you don't," he wrote.[60]

As Chamberlain left for his second conference with Hitler, Kennedy, again displaying his supreme confidence in his diplomatic judgment and his penchant for engaging in personal diplomacy, ignored Hull's request for discretion and gave more than just moral support to the prime minister's quest for peace. "Representations" were made to the congenial ambassador, with Halifax discreetly hinting at the British government's displeasure over several anti-government scenes in a Paramount newsreel that had just been released, featuring potentially inflammatory speeches.[61] Kennedy graciously offered to look into the matter as Chamberlain flew to Godesberg on September 22. Acting unofficially and privately, no doubt without informing the State Department, he relayed the foreign secretary's views to Will Hays, president of the Motion Picture Producers and Distributors Association of America. Acting from a spirit of public duty, the London representative of the Hays office voluntarily withdrew the offending film, action that Kennedy thought "the right course to take."[62] The film showed an interview with Wickham Steed, a foreign-affairs journalist and former editor of the *Times*, and A. J. Cummings, the political editor of the *News Chronicle*, a Liberal journal. Both newsmen vehemently criticized the Chamberlain government for partitioning Czechoslovakia.[63] "Hitler has won an overwhelming diplomatic triumph," Cummings said, and even accused British statesmen of "a piece of yellow diplomacy" and of deceiving the public.[64]

The "Kennedy Incident," as the ambassador's intervention was called, became public during a debate in Parliament on November 23, 1938, when the opposition charged the government with censorship of newspapers and films. John Simon, the chancellor of the exchequer, told the House that Paramount News had decided to eliminate certain segments from the reel out of "a sense of public duty."[65] "It is interesting to find such an accommodating Ambassador," jeered Geoffrey Mander, a Liberal. He questioned the propriety of an American ambassador's willingness to aid the British government's censorship efforts. The strongest defense of Kennedy came from Sir Samuel Hoare. He reminded the Commons that the episode had occurred on September 22, the very day that Chamberlain flew to Godesberg. "If ever there was a day when it was necessary to exercise caution and say or do nothing likely to stir dangerous reactions, it was September 22." Halifax echoed the same line: "Believe me," he argued, "on September 22, faced with one of the greatest crises that ever confronted the world, we were not thinking about the fortunes of the National Government. We were thinking about much graver issues."[66]

Kennedy said he merely acted as an intermediary and passed along the British request to the Hays office. He protested that he had applied no pressure to change the content of the film. Nevertheless, he did record in his diary that he told officials that his "off the record" opinion was that some of the remarks were undiplomatic, given the precariousness of the international situation, and that the interviews should be eliminated.[67] Kennedy notified Halifax that he had turned the decision over to the Will Hays office. It—and not he—did "whatever was done.... I knew nothing about it," he wrote.[68] The interviews were removed from the newsreel. Despite the criticism in Parliament, this issue was not a serious matter of government policy but merely a small opportunity for Kennedy to use his influence as a friendly favor to his hosts. It also inalterably united him with Chamberlain and his policies and cost him the support of Liberal and Labour politicians.

To buttress Chamberlain's case for appeasement, Kennedy also used the arguments of two prestigious and influential Americans, Charles Lindbergh and Bernard Baruch, who realized how militarily unprepared Britain was. On September 21 the ambassador summoned to London the famous "Lone Eagle," Colonel Charles A. Lindbergh, America's lean, long-legged, boyish hero. Lindbergh had been impressed with Kennedy immediately upon meeting him in the spring at the Astors' and described him as having "great vanity" as well as great "ability."[69] The English like him, Lindbergh wrote, and noted that they were saying that "we have at last sent a real man to represent us."[70] He also noticed their lack of criticism of his Irish Catholicism. He is a remarkable type of diplomat, Lindbergh thought, impressed by his deep commitment to family values. "Kennedy interested me greatly," he said.[71] Kennedy was a rare "combination of politician and businessman"[72] whose opinions on Europe were "intelligent and interesting."[73] Anne Morrow Lindbergh found that her husband so enjoyed talking to the ambassador that she could barely pull him away. She too liked Kennedy and saw in him "an Irish terrier wagging his tail (a very nice Irish terrier)," she wrote.[74] Kennedy and Lindbergh were two of a kind.

During lunch at the embassy the next day, Kennedy asked Lindbergh to prepare a written report on Germany's air power and to meet with senior RAF officials to detail his reasons for his frightening account of German air superiority.[75] While the European democracies had slept, Hitler had created a Luftwaffe greater than the air forces of all other European countries combined. "For the first time in history," Lindbergh wrote, "a nation has the power either to save or to ruin the great cities of Europe." Germany was constantly increasing her margin of leadership with aircraft of excellent quality; her factories were capable of producing twenty thousand planes annually, and her extensive research facilities guaranteed continuous improvement in aviation design. He believed that only the United States was capable of competing with German aviation, and even it was already being challenged and surpassed by Germany. Furthermore, French aviation was in a "pitiful condition." Czechoslovakia had excellent machine guns and anti-aircraft guns and airpower that came from Russia, but everything else was antiquated. The Russians were buying American machines and copying

American factories. Although Russian military power was numerically "sufficient" and performed well enough to be "effective," it was inefficient and poorly organized. Lindbergh's assessment of England's military might was no less disturbing. England was in no shape for war and lacked the means to defend herself either by attack or counterattack, he argued; nor did England realize the military implications of aviation.[76] "I am afraid," he concluded, that "this is the beginning of the end of England as a great power. She may be a 'hornet's nest' but she is no longer 'a lion's den.'"[77]

Kennedy relayed Lindbergh's somber message to Neville Chamberlain, to the British Air Ministry, and to the secretary of state in Washington. He deleted Lindbergh's opinion that Europe should stay out of war, but that recommendation was apparent in his assessment.[78] Oddly enough, although the ambassador asked that Lindbergh's cable be sent to Roosevelt and the Department of the Navy and the Department of War, it was disseminated solely in the State Department.[79] Hull's memoirs mention that Kennedy spoke to him about Lindbergh's report, but there was no mention of the role that Kennedy had played in publicizing Lindbergh's views to the British, or of inviting Lindbergh to London, or of asking him to write the report.[80] Once again Kennedy apparently failed to inform Hull. Although the ambassador bragged to others that he had ensured that the prime minister received Lindbergh's report and that it had helped shape Chamberlain's opinions and his decision to stay out of war, there is no evidence that the report did so.[81]

Most contemporary historians think that Lindbergh's too gloomy and dismal views were the upshot of German propaganda and American gullibility and lacked factual accuracy and realistic interpretation. Nevertheless, by providing additional justification for the peace-at-any-price policy that Chamberlain had already embarked upon and his agreeably self-appointed American spokesman espoused, Lindbergh's views certainly had their desired political effect.[82]

The reports of the financier Bernard M. Baruch corroborated the frightening observations by Kennedy and Lindbergh. Supposedly taking his summer vacation in Europe, Baruch was actually on a confidential assignment for Roosevelt. Baruch's "mission" was to investigate the rumors of increasing Nazi military strength. His account was particularly depressing; he notified FDR that neither France nor England was prepared for war. Their airplane production was slightly over five hundred planes a month, while Germany's output was almost forty thousand planes a year.[83] "War was coming," he later said. "You could see it and you could feel it."[84]

Although Baruch shared Kennedy's horror of the military weakness of Britain and France, he differed radically with the American ambassador over the feasibility of appeasement. Baruch was to Winston Churchill what Kennedy considered himself to be to Chamberlain—a close personal friend and a tenacious exponent of his views. As a private citizen and personal emissary for Roosevelt, Baruch had considerably more freedom of movement than Kennedy. Unlike an ambassador sending confidential reports, Baruch could use his accounts to awaken the American public. That was Roosevelt's aim. "Put a burr under their tail, Bernie, and if I hear 'em holler, I'll know you're doing all right," the president instructed.[85]

Having succeeded in convincing all the parties to accept Hitler's Berchtesgaden demands to transfer the Sudetenland to Germany under the auspices of an international commission, Chamberlain flew to Godesberg on September 22 to continue the negotiations. Evidently Hitler was surprised and disappointed; no doubt he never imagined that Chamberlain could get the Czechs' agreement to dismember their own country. He also must have disliked being deprived of his dream of a military victory. To Chamberlain's surprise, Hitler informed him that the plan was moribund and demanded that the Czechs hand over the Sudetenland by October 1, fulfill the demands of the other nationalities within the country, and scrap the proposed international commission. Hitler moved the timetable up to September 28 and then back to October 1.[86]

After snatching a few hours of well-earned sleep, Chamberlain returned to London on September 24 heavy-hearted and convinced that there was no alternative but to do what he had told Hitler he would not do, to accept—or rather to persuade the cabinet, the French, and the Czechs to accept—the latest Nazi demands.[87]

Kennedy's days between Chamberlain's trip to Godesberg and his return from Munich were among the most crowded of his life and filled with "overpowering" suspense, Kennedy recalled in his memoirs. He was responsible for preparations to protect the embassy staff from air raids in a bomb-proof shelter in the basement, and for making arrangements to transport the hordes of Americans clamoring to return to the United States. He had to deal with the throngs in Downing Street, Whitehall, and Fleet Street desperate for any shred of information about War or Peace. He had to put up with vans cruising through Grosvenor Square warning people to get gas masks and blaring instructions about how to use them, with men working under glaring flashlights at night and hastily digging trenches in the parks, and with announcements in churches, at sporting events, and in theaters, telling people about the depots they should go to in case of attack. Kennedy endured crowded late nights and little sleep, sent hurriedly dashed-off dispatches hourly to the State Department, and held 2:30 a.m. phone conversations with Hull and Roosevelt urging them to call publicly for a peaceful resolution to the crisis.[88] Kennedy's efforts won high praise from Hull. "We appreciate your work over there very much. . . . You have been doing fine."[89]

As the government debated the prime minister's Czech policy over the next few days, Kennedy maintained close contact with British officialdom and foreign dignitaries and held nearly nonstop meetings with Cadogan, Oliver Stanley, and the Polish ambassador, Count Edward Raczyński. "The suspense is very marked," Kennedy cabled Hull. "The principal officials are in a state of depression."[90] He passed on predictions of a major fight over the Czech policy between the prime minister, who wanted "peace at any price," as Kennedy labeled it, and those like Duff Cooper, the First Lord of the Admiralty, who wanted to mobilize the fleet and not "take any more back talk from Hitler."[91] Even the ever-faithful Halifax, in a Dasmascus conversion, after a fitful night could not be convinced of the wisdom of Chamberlain's latest acquiescence to Hitler.[92] Not only could the prime minister not persuade his cabinet to join him, but he could not convince either the French or the Czechs to accept the Godesberg demands. Regardless, Chamberlain was still safe because no one could replace him, Kennedy believed. "In my judgment," he told Hull, "when England realizes just how unprepared she is, we will hear less talk of going to war and more talk of throwing out a Cabinet which could not predict the future any better than the present one."[93] But at least one Englishman could predict the future better—Winston Churchill, a name anathema to Kennedy and to Chamberlain. "Churchill had the worst political judgment in England," the prime minister said to Kennedy, "and really looked merely for the chance of making a speech on any subject rather than having any sound idea on the causes or reasons therefor."[94]

Finally on September 26 the ambassador secretly learned from Halifax that the cabinet had rejected Hitler's demands and that for the first time the British had made a commitment to the French. "If the French go to war the English will go with them," he reported.[95] The situation is "hopeless," Kennedy stated, as the October 1 deadline grew near.[96] The only "encouraging note" was War Minister Hore-Belisha's quip that he would "bet a hat that Hitler will back down."[97] Were the French equipped to fight, Hull asked Kennedy? Kennedy did not know, he reported, but the British "feel as they always do, that they can rise to the occasion."[98]

As the situation deteriorated, a desperate Chamberlain drafted a personal plea to Hitler, delivered on September 26 by the self-effacing, mild-mannered Sir Horace Wilson, an unrelenting appeaser. It asked Hitler to agree to an international tribunal in which Britain would oversee the transfer of Czech territory to Germany, and warned him that if the offer were rejected, then Britain would support France when war broke out. Hitler, in one of his "emotional steam-baths" in which he worked himself into "a lather rage" on the eve of a major address, astounded Wilson by behaving like a maniac during their fifty-minute interview: yelling at him, refusing to listen, threatening to walk out, and demanding that Chamberlain consent to the Godesberg ultimatum by September 28 at 2:00 p.m.—moving the deadline up two days.[99] If the Czechs refused, he would "smash" them, he shrieked.[100] "Figuratively speaking," Kennedy cabled Hull, "the door was slammed in Wilson's face by Hitler."[101]

In the wake of the deepening crisis, the American ambassador, apparently acting on his own and never doubting his diplomatic judgment, on September 25 told a now utterly depressed Chamberlain that he had prompted FDR to take some initiative immediately. Convinced by the events of that week that neither Britain nor France were ready for war, Kennedy reminded the prime minister of a commitment that the president had made to him back in July. If a crisis arose in which Kennedy believed that war was imminent, Roosevelt would do what he could to try to avert it. "I told [him] that in my judgment that time had come" and "I thought some message should be sent."[102] Yet Chamberlain neither accepted FDR's offer of help nor communicated directly with him. Perhaps Chamberlain's faith in his own policy, along with not believing that the president could really help, might explain his unresponsiveness.[103]

Roosevelt, now convinced that war might be prevented, decided to make a public appeal for peace. Over Hull's objection, he insisted on responding to Kennedy's request and decided upon a personal appeal to the European heads of state, to Hitler, Beneš, Chamberlain, and Daladier. "It can't do any harm," Roosevelt comforted Hull. "It's safe to urge peace until the last moment." The two men worked until the early hours in the morning on September 26 and finally hammered out the president's message: "For the sake of humanity everywhere I most earnestly appeal to you not to break off negotiations. . . . As long as negotiations continue, differences may be reconciled."[104] But once again his message contained the traditional statement of American foreign policy: "The United States has no political entanglements."[105]

Almost immediately responses came in from Chamberlain, Beneš, and Daladier that day, agreeing with the president and willing to negotiate for peace. Hitler's diatribe arrived later that night and blamed the present crisis on the obstinate Czechs. On Chamberlain's behalf, Halifax graciously thanked Roosevelt and stated that his government was doing all it could to ensure a peaceful resolution.[106] Roosevelt's appeal, a blend of eloquence and passivity, played well in British newspapers, according to Kennedy. He, too, was pleased and said it helped to offset British bitterness over the "terrific blast" they received from the American press over the "betrayal of Czechoslovakia."[107]

The next day, September 27, FDR sent a second appeal addressed only to Hitler, urging him to continue negotiations and suggesting an immediate conference in some neutral spot in Europe attended by all nations concerned about the Czech problem. But the president watered down even this vague modest gesture by stating that he would not commit the United States to political entanglements. He could be neither guest nor host of the conference, because that would anger the always vigilant American isolationists.[108]

Kennedy forwarded Chamberlain's request to be allowed to broadcast a message directly to the American people.[109] FDR feared that such a broadcast would be misinterpreted as an appeal, and he rejected the request.[110] Could the ambassador, determined not to be stymied, have arranged to have Chamberlain's address to the nation and the Empire carried by some American broadcasters?[111]

On the evening of September 26 or 27, the prime minister spoke of "how horrible, fantastic, incredible it is that we should be digging trenches and trying on gas masks here because of a quarrel in a faraway country between people of whom we know nothing. . . . I myself am a man of peace to the depths of my soul." But if war is declared, we must be certain "that it is really the great issues that are at stake," he said, his voice full of sadness and discouragement as he spoke of his loathing of war. To prevent another holocaust, Chamberlain promised, he "would not hesitate to pay even a third visit to Germany."[112] Kennedy was deeply moved by the speech.[113]

Finally the cabinet wore down the prime minister's resistance, and on the night of

September 27 announced that the fleet had been mobilized. Gas masks were clumsily tried on, the coastal defenses were outfitted, a statement was drafted for broadcast in the event of war; patients were removed from hospitals, their rooms were readied for casualties, schoolchildren were sent to the countryside. Churchgoing rose. Crowds knelt before the tomb of the Unknown Soldier and its long unfaltering flame in Westminster Abbey to pray that the Czechs would not be stubborn.[114]

Kennedy reported to Hull that on the way to the office that morning he had seen hundreds of men digging trenches and there were anti-aircraft machine guns in Hyde Park.[115] He ordered Americans in London to return to the United States and asked Rose to make plans for evacuating the family. "War [is] imminent," he told her.[116] In her memoirs, Rose Kennedy wrote poignantly of the "brooding, silence," the "un-smiling, un-emotional faces. Everyone unutterably shocked and depressed" and feeling that the "hopes for peace are shattered."[117] The pent-up summer-long tensions became almost unbearable as the pleasure-loving British tried to grasp at the glittering gaiety of a vanishing world—shopping sprees in crowded stores, holidays at the seashore, dancing in the great country houses, women laughing with men soon to be shot down in combat. "You had the feeling," Senator Jack Kennedy later reminisced, "of an era ending, and everyone had a very good time at the end."[118] The "long weekend" between the end of the Great War and the beginning of an even greater one was coming to a close.[119]

Just a few hours remained before the Godesberg deadline, 2:00 p.m., September 28, "Black Wednesday."[120] Kennedy was in despair and told Hull that he had spent three quarters of an hour the day before discussing the Czech crisis with the king, who was kept extremely well informed. He was "noticeably disturbed. . . . It was inconceivable to him that there should be another war especially when the memory of the Great War was still so fresh in everyone's minds," the king said to Kennedy.[121]

Parliament was to convene at 2:45 p.m. on September 28. At noon that day, the prime minister had telephoned Kennedy to inform him that early that morning he had sent a reassuring message to Hitler: "You can get all essentials without war and without delay." Chamberlain again offered his services. "I am ready to come to Berlin myself at once," he wrote plaintively. He had also sent a second message to Mussolini urging him to use his influence with the Führer to avoid war.[122]

Kennedy had received a pleasing but noncommittal cable from the president just before he departed to hear the prime minister address the House of Commons. "I want you to know that in these difficult days I am proud of you. Franklin D. Roosevelt."[123] Roosevelt sent the same message to the American ambassadors in Paris, Prague, and Berlin. As Kennedy hastened to Parliament Square, he stuffed the message into his pocket.[124] Throngs of people stood by as the police cleared narrow lanes for traffic. The quiet, unsmiling crowds cheered now and then when they spotted a familiar face or a well-known MP drove by, Kennedy remembered.[125]

That afternoon the House of Commons was filled to capacity as its members and other dignitaries assembled in anticipation of Chamberlain's answer at 2:45 p.m., forty-five minutes after the expiration of Chamberlain's ultimatum to Hitler. The well-known and the well-bred waited in dread, expecting Chamberlain to deliver an ultimatum similar to Sir Edward Grey's on August 4, 1914, which catapulted Britain into the Great War. The Queen Mother, Mary, was there along with other members of the royal family. So was the former prime minister, Stanley Baldwin, sitting between Halifax and the Duke of Kent.[126] The archbishops of York and Canterbury were there. The American ambassador, suffering from seven sleepless nights, squeezed into the diplomatic gallery beside the Italian ambassador, Dino Grandi, and near the French and Czech ambassadors.[127]

Kennedy watched as the audience broke into restrained applause when the worn and haggard prime minister entered the stuffy chamber, quivering with tension and passion at 3:00 p.m.[128] Slowly and carefully, fiddling with his pince-nez and barely glancing at his notes, Chamberlain, his face contorted by emotion, explained his negotiations with Hitler. As he reviewed what everyone already knew and he moved on to discuss recent events, those present leaned forward, grimly listening in silence. The stillness in that chamber was broken only by messengers delivering telegrams and messages to MPs. Then, at about 3:40, Cadogan at the Foreign Office ran to Parliament with a dispatch from Britain's ambassador in Berlin, Sir Nevile Henderson. Kennedy watched as a messenger raced up the steps to the Peers' Gallery and noisily announced that he had an important message for Lord Halifax. The envelope was hastily "passed over the heads of the peers" to the foreign secretary, who audibly tore it open, read the penciled note, and smiled broadly.[129] As Halifax rose to leave, he thrust it into Baldwin's face. "Sorry, excuse me," Halifax said as he pushed peers aside and stepped on their toes and made his way to the House floor. He gave the note to Sir Alec Douglas-Home, Chamberlain's private secretary, who looked astounded as he skimmed it and passed it on to Sir John Simon, who showed it to Sir Samuel Hoare, who took a quick glance at it, Kennedy recalled. Simon tugged at the prime minister's coat as he was nearing the end of his hour-long speech. Chamberlain turned around as Simon thrust the note into Chamberlain's face and ran his finger under the pertinent sentences. Sir Kingsley Wood, the secretary of state for Air, also "piled in" and glanced at the note. "There it is," he seemed to say.[130] There was a hush; the ambassador thought it lasted for at least a minute. As the tired prime minister read the message, his whole body changed—the tension and anxiety evaporated from his face; a flicker of a smile danced across it. He seemed ten years younger and victorious despite his too long and graying hair, wrote Harold Nicolson, MP and diarist, who witnessed the drama.[131] He was "the incarnation of St George—so simple and so unspoilt," single-handedly fighting the dragon, observed another. "I don't know what this country has done to deserve him."[132] Forgetting the microphone in front of his chair that carried his speech to a crowd spilling over into a nearby room, Chamberlain bent over and quietly asked Sir John Simon, "Shall I tell now?" Simon nodded. With a strained and hushed voice, the prime minister announced to the silent chamber: "I have something further to say to the House yet. I have now been informed by Herr Hitler that he invites me to meet him at

Munich tomorrow morning. He has also invited Signor Mussolini and Monsieur Daladier. Signor Mussolini has accepted and I have no doubt Monsieur Daladier will also accept." "I need not say what my answer will be."[133] Only for a moment was there absolute silence as the stunned audience just sat there. Then pandemonium erupted. "The cheers in the House from both sides were terrific,"[134] Kennedy told Hull, as practically the whole House rose to give Chamberlain a standing ovation, a tribute without precedent in that dignified old building. Papers were thrown into the air, handkerchiefs fluttered, Clement Attlee gave Labour's blessing to the plan, weeping MPs shook Chamberlain's hand (some, later, eagerly repudiated their reactions), one backbencher shouted, "Thank God for the Prime Minister!," and the American ambassador beamed and cheered.[135] Alec Dunglass later remembered ironically, "There were a lot of 'appeasers' in Parliament that day."[136] "Everyone immediately felt a vast relief and unspeakable emotion. From the depths of despair we were moved to a new hope," Rose Kennedy was to recall.[137]

Some in the audience realized what this meant to the Czechs; if Kennedy did, he cared little. Chamberlain had asked Hitler for a five-party conference; Hitler had invited only four parties. The Czechs would not be represented at a conference to decide their own destiny. In disbelief, Jan Masaryk, Czechoslovakia's minister and the son of its founder, looked down from his seat in the diplomatic gallery at the joyous throng. Was Czechoslovakia to be abandoned? He left the Commons—four years were to elapse before he returned.[138] A deeply ashamed Harold Nicolson believed he was watching "a Welsh Revivalist meeting" and glumly remained seated, despite an MP's admonition: "Stand up, you brute!"[139] Amidst the hysterical rejoicing, Eden stalked out of the room, white-faced with anger; Churchill remained seated in his place below the gangway, silently hunched over and brow lowered. Finally, he stood up and said "God-speed" as he shook the prime minister's hand.[140] He told the prime minister, "I congratulate you on your good fortune," and added, "You were very lucky,"[141] an interpretation that Chamberlain may not have liked hearing.

Kennedy loved the high drama and the roller-coaster emotions it produced. "I was never so thrilled in my life," he wrote.[142] He was now quite spoiled for theatre, he later told Cadogan. Never again would he be so entertained as he had been by Chamberlain's announcement of Hitler's invitation and the prime minister's departure for Germany, he cabled Hull in his dispatch.[143]

As Chamberlain prepared to leave for Germany, Roosevelt sent an ambiguous message, a terse "Good man!"[144]—a sincere statement of relief that no doubt applied more to the prime minister's determination to continue discussions with Hitler than to the actual terms themselves.

For Hitler's last-minute decision to call the Munich Conference, Roosevelt was given the credit because of his appeals to Hitler—a not so subtle reminder of historic precedent and America's alliance with the Allies in World War I, Kennedy recorded in his diary.[145] "The President can feel that God was on his side and he was on God's side," the jubilant ambassador wrote to Washington.[146] "The second message is the finest the President has written for a long, long time," he said of Roosevelt's message of September 27, addressed only to Hitler.[147] Hull, too, wrote that Roosevelt's actions "exercised considerable influence."[148] The English were deeply grateful. Cadogan told him that without question Roosevelt's appeal to Hitler "had done the trick," and a number of ministers and ambassadors also expressed their appreciation.[149] Halifax thanked Kennedy for FDR's timely intervention. The foreign secretary stated that he "had no doubt whatever that this had exercised a very powerful influence upon the course of events."[150]

The president's last-minute decision to issue his appeal indicated that he, like Kennedy, was convinced that Hitler was not bluffing. Though the belief was strong among Roosevelt and his advisers, British officials, and of course Kennedy, that the president's two appeals had been a major factor in influencing Hitler's decision, they were in fact of little importance.[151] The doubts of his Nazi advisers and his own people, evidence that Britain and France would eventually give in to his final demands anyhow, and Mussolini's influence and promise to him to come to Munich in person played the major roles in convincing the Führer to resort to negotiations rather than force. He no doubt looked at Roosevelt's appeals as signifying nothing more than the meaningless gestures of a politically impotent president.[152]

That afternoon when Parliament adjourned, the American embassy was mobbed by a sea of people cheering, laughing, and waving. The ambassador waded through the crowd and entered the embassy with a dazzling, triumphant grin: "Well, boys, the war is off."[153] "Everybody feels tremendously relieved tonight," he cabled Hull.[154] Charles Lindbergh ran into Kennedy when he went to the American embassy to get gas masks. "'You may not need them. There's some good news coming,'" the ambassador said, bursting into the room.[155] The "only discordant note," according to Kennedy, was from the Czech ambassador in London, Jan Masaryk, who rode back in a cab from Parliament with him. He said, "I hope this doesn't mean they are going to cut us up and sell us out."[156] That of course was precisely what it did mean. Kennedy gave no response. That evening as he collected his thoughts and wrote in his diary, an exuberant Kennedy summed up the day's events: "Tonight a feeling is spreading all over London that this means that war will be averted. If it is, it is quite likely that, with these four men around a table and with President Roosevelt always willing to negotiate, it may be the beginning of a new world policy which may mean peace and prosperity once again."[157]

At Simon's suggestion, the entire cabinet decided to surprise Chamberlain by coming to the airport to bid him Godspeed.[158] As he left for Munich, Kennedy told Halifax he had "good hopes" for the outcome of the conference and was "entirely in sympathy with, and a warm admirer of, everything the Prime Minister had done." Kennedy said to Halifax that he was also realistic enough to recognize "all the dangers and difficulties that still had to be surmounted." The European situation required "a spirit of realism," he said, which meant doing anything necessary to preserve peace.[159]

But perhaps "doing anything necessary to preserve peace" was not realism; perhaps "realism" dictated preparing as quickly as possible to go to war to stop Hitler's insatiable territorial acquisitiveness; perhaps it meant a policy of firmness such as Churchill argued for, not one of accommodation; perhaps it meant that the British realize that they had not achieved a great triumph but had only betrayed a small country with the only democratic government east of the Rhine by a policy not of appeasement but of blackmail.[160]

A very tired Chamberlain arrived in Munich on September 29, the city where Hitler had begun his own career in the midst of the seedy cafés and beer halls. The Führer put on a great show of friendship and gave the prime minister the two-handed handshake he went in for only on very special occasions. Daladier arrived as an uncomfortable witness; so did Mussolini, a self-styled mediator and the only one of the four who spoke the others' languages. The Russians were not invited, for fear of antagonizing Hitler. Although Chamberlain made a feeble attempt to persuade Hitler to permit the Czechs to attend, Hitler remained adamantly opposed. The Czechs waited quietly at the British hotel throughout the thirteen-hour meeting in which four non-Czechs carved up their country. "They had been invited," it seemed, "to expire with tact, and even, if possible, with gaiety."[161]

About two o'clock in the morning of September 30, 1938, the Munich Agreement was signed. All parties accepted that Germany would begin the occupation of the Sudetenland by October 1 and complete it by October 10. Czechoslovakia thus lost her border fortresses and was left defenseless. An international commission composed of the four powers and the Czechs would negotiate the final boundary between Germany and Czechoslovakia. Hitler would define the plebiscite areas that would be occupied by an international force. Voting procedures would be established. The inhabitants of the areas to be evacuated were allowed to take food, animals, household goods, and raw materials with them. Britain and France promised to guarantee what remained of Czechoslovakia against unprovoked aggression. The Führer had killed the French-Czech Treaty, isolated the Soviet Union from her European alignment, and laid the foundation for the complete destruction of Czechoslovakia—all without firing a shot.[162]

At 2:15 a.m. on September 30, Chamberlain and Daladier presented the agreement to the miserable, unconsulted Czechs. The atmosphere during the meeting was oppressive. Daladier was nervous and anxiously trying to preserve French prestige. Chamberlain, exhausted by his labors, yawned constantly, making no attempt to hide his weariness.[163]

The prime minister also asked Hitler to sign a statement: "We regard the Agreement signed last night, and the Anglo-German Naval Agreement, as symbolic of the desire of our two peoples never to go to war with one another again."[164] As the interpreter read the document in German, Hitler excitedly interjected "ja, ja," and agreeably signed the two copies Chamberlain had brought with him.[165] Before his meeting with Hitler that morning, Chamberlain had casually remarked to his parliamentary private secretary, Alec Douglas-Home: "If Hitler signed it and kept his bargain, well and good; [but] if he broke it, he would demonstrate to all the world that he was totally cynical and untrustworthy and . . . this would have its value in mobilizing public opinion against him, particularly in America."[166] Apparently the prime minister was not wholly oblivious to the opinion of the United States.

A mob of delirious Britons welcomed back their "flying messenger of peace."[167] "The thin figure in black, his smile more self-satisfied than usual, alighted from the plane carrying that ever-present symbol of British prudence, the rolled umbrella."[168] As Chamberlain stepped out of the aircraft he waved his paper to Halifax and shouted, "I've got it. I've got it,"[169] as Halifax cheered enough, it was said, to show his tonsils, a cheer fitting for any man with three sons of military age.[170] That evening from the window of 10 Downing Street, Chamberlain addressed the multitude. Holding up what Duff Cooper called "that miserable scrap of paper"[171] signed by Hitler, the prime minister yelled to the throng below: "This is the second time in our history that there has come back from Germany to Downing Street peace with honor. I believe it is peace for our time," he said as he stood at the very same first-floor window from which Prime Minister Benjamin Disraeli announced peace with honor after the Berlin Congress in 1878.[172] That "miserable scrap of paper" was to provide for the British people the rage that the "rape of Belgium" had provided in the Great War; it symbolized Hitler's treachery and steeled the British to endure the bombing, deprivation, and the heartaches of seven long years of war.[173] "This, it seemed, was the climax of Chamberlain's career, his moment of triumph," wrote the Chamberlain scholar R. A. C. Parker. "Chamberlain had won! He had brought peace!"[174] Appeasement had won. "The umbrella had been mightier than the sword," said Robert Graves, World War I veteran, poet, and novelist.[175] "There had never at any time been such a home-coming for any English statesman," Kennedy wrote in his memoirs.[176] Tens of thousands shouted themselves hoarse, running alongside the prime minister's car, thrusting their hands inside to touch him. The chorus of thanksgiving in Britain was led by the king, who invited Chamberlain to Buckingham Palace to receive his "most heartfelt congratulations on the success of your visit to Munich" and the thanks of the cheering throng below, with the king and queen on the palace balcony.[177] People all over the world were swept up in unrestrained joyful relief because war had been averted, Kennedy recalled.[178] When the Roman generals returned to Rome triumphant from their conquests, a slave rode with them in their chariots and held a golden crown over their heads and whispered in their ear: "All glory is fleeting." Or so the story goes. Chamberlain needed such a slave then. Andrew Roberts, Halifax's biographer, wrote that that was Halifax's role.[179]

Rose remembered Joe's wildly boisterous reaction. He was so thrilled by Munich that "he kissed me and twirled me around in his arms, repeating over and over what a great day this was and what a great man Chamberlain was."[180] And upon running into the Czech minister, Jan Masaryk, Kennedy remarked, "Now I can get to Palm Beach after all!"[181]—a comment that exhibited his colossal and unconscionable lack of compassion.

On September 30, President Beneš bowed to the Munich decision and resigned his office. Five days later he left the nation he had helped found and sought refuge in England. He told his countrymen: "I feel it is for the best not to disturb the new European constellation which is arising. . . . But this I will say, that the sacrifices demanded from us were immeasurably great and immeasurably unjust. This the nation will never forget, even though they have borne these sacrifices quietly."[182]

Both Joe and Rose Kennedy spent as much time as possible watching from the gallery as Parliament debated the Munich Agreement from October 3 to October 6; "singularly unimpressive," Kennedy thought the debate.[183] The still youthful-looking seventy-year-old Chamberlain, who had lost thirteen pounds during the ordeal, "looked thin," Kennedy noted in his memoirs. The ambassador's intense loyalty to the man and his policy, with which his own self-interest was so closely identified, led him to give a glowing and enthusiastic account of the style and substance of the prime minister's remarks to the House. "In a quiet and unhurried way," Chamberlain explained to the House that his actions alone had prevented war, wrote Kennedy.[184] The ambassador thought that the views of the prime minister's opponents, particularly Duff Cooper and Labour's Clement Attlee, were, in contrast, only ordinary and mediocre. The ambassador also opined that there were "men in every house of representatives in the United States that could make better arguments and advance their cause in much better shape" than Chamberlain's adversaries. "The great weakness in his armor," however, was that England had kept the expectant Czechs dangling too long before acting and that he had negotiated an agreement for world peace with Hitler but still urged a program of rearmament for England, a proposal that would "come back to plague him" in the months ahead by accelerating the arms race.[185]

Chamberlain graciously summoned his staunchest supporter for a half-hour meeting just before leaving for a short holiday in Scotland right after the conclusion of the debate in Parliament. Chamberlain told Kennedy that "he did not want to go away without thanking me for the help I had given him during the last month," Kennedy wrote in his memoirs, and "was kind enough to add that he had depended more on me than on anybody for judgment and support" and "insisted that I must stay on the job because he believed I could do much for world peace."[186] Could it be that Chamberlain, too, like Hitler, knew how to stroke the vanity of men?

But Roosevelt kept his own council. The president, whose reaction was shackled by the constraints of America's policy of isolationism, sent Chamberlain a congratulatory telegram that Kennedy dutifully delivered on October 5 during the debate in Parliament. "I went over to 10 Downing Street the day I received the cable, but instead of handing the cable to Chamberlain, as is customary, I read it to him. I had a feeling that cable would haunt Roosevelt some day, so I kept it."[187] And he was carrying out FDR's orders. The president wanted to protect himself and not risk embarrassing revelations later. He instructed the ambassador to read his carefully worded statement to Chamberlain: "I fully share your hope and belief that there exists today the greatest opportunity in years for the establishment of a new order based on justice and on law."[188] Although the Commons approved the policy of His Majesty's Government by a vote of 366 to 144—about three to one—profound disillusionment had set in both in and out of Parliament.[189] "Within a few days," Kennedy remembered, people in all walks of life and especially in the United States "were to turn against [Munich] and those who had any part of it."[190]

The long pent-up private quarrel in the cabinet erupted into a public argument. Duff Cooper resigned from the Admiralty after mobilizing the fleet and joined the chorus of critics in the Commons. They included Josiah Wedgwood, an old left-wing radical; the World War I author and diplomat Harold Nicolson; the future Conservative prime ministers Anthony Eden and Harold Macmillan; Labour's leader Clement Attlee, also a future prime minister, who characterized the Munich Agreement as "nothing but an armistice in a state of war" and denied that it gave "peace in our time";[191] the former World War I prime minister, Lloyd George; and of course Churchill. "We have sustained a total and unmitigated defeat," Churchill said of Munich on October 5. Pausing to let the storm of fervor and hissing in the Commons die down, he continued for forty-five minutes. "It is the most grievous consequence which we have yet experienced of what we have done and of what we have left undone in the last five years—five years of futile good intention, five years of eager search for the line of least resistance, five years of uninterrupted retreat of British power, five years of neglect of our air defences,"[192] he growled, "and do not suppose that this is the end. This is only the beginning of the reckoning . . . unless . . . we arise again and take our stand for freedom as in the olden time."[193]

Kennedy shared Britain's "mood of analysis" and reflection in the weeks after Munich and sent a dispatch to Hull on October 5, giving him his interpretation of why a European war was averted and what lessons America had to learn from that experience. Kennedy outlined some lessons: First, the German people did not want war. Their tumultuous reception honoring Chamberlain for his peacekeeping efforts impressed the Nazi officials and helped to preserve peace. Secondly, Chamberlain's "bulldog persistence" prevented the collapse of diplomatic efforts. Without his determination, "events would have been in the saddle and ridden away." Thirdly, Mussolini intervened and exercised a moderating influence on Hitler. Hitler felt obliged to Mussolini, who felt obliged to Chamberlain. Mussolini was indebted to Chamberlain for their Anglo-Italian agreement. Mussolini did not want war and wanted to protect Italy from an Anglo-French land-and-sea attack. Lastly, Kennedy credited Roosevelt's decisive intervention, despite its anti-Hitler bias, as being "effective," rather like the mobilization of the British fleet. His messages to Hitler "hit the nail on the head." It showed how quickly the United States would side with England and France if they were threatened. However, Kennedy warned, the exclusion of Russia from the conference was costly. But in their exclusion of Russia from their consideration, the democracies "lost a potential ally," something even more important to have in forthcoming crises when the New World would have to become the savior of the Old—as it did.[194]

Kennedy's assessment was broadly accurate. But it was Hitler's military and diplomatic advisers, not the German public, that made him hesitate. Joseph Goebbels and Hermann

Göring, fearing a wider general war with Britain and France, urged military restraint.[195] Certainly Chamberlain's tenacity brought the participants to the conference table, kept them there, and preserved peace. And certainly Italy's military unpreparedness as always and Mussolini's own ambitions in Czechoslovakia gave him pause and encouraged him to persuade Hitler to accept a diplomatic solution to the Czech problem. A peaceful cession of the Sudetenland would be triumph enough for Germany, Mussolini argued. Hitler, denied his war, grudgingly agreed to the Munich Conference. He regarded it as a "personal trauma" in which he had been tricked by Chamberlain into negotiations. At the last moment Hitler had "funked at war."[196]

But Kennedy overstated Roosevelt's role. Hitler had contempt for the American nation. It was a weak democracy whose mongrel population made it incapable of military superiority. He cared nothing about what its president said.[197]

Learn from Munich, Kennedy urged Hull. Return to "an unprejudiced" and "neutral" position vis-à-vis Europe (odd advice coming from someone who so thoroughly violated it) or face danger. Failure to do so, Kennedy warned, might lead fearful Britons to step up their armaments production, action not necessarily favored by their government. It could cause Hitler to see the Americans as potential enemies and to increase Germany's military production instead of exercising restraint and agreeing to armament reduction. It could also encourage Americans to engage in self-destructive and expensive actions "personally and materially."[198]

Kennedy's advice was odd in the extreme, given his own predisposition to interfere in Britain's foreign policy on behalf of Chamberlain—hardly neutral conduct. He was also apparently blind to the possibility that increasing Britain's preparations for attack would have been quite beneficial to the country if and when war broke out; so would arousing Americans to non-neutrality. That, too, could have made the country better prepared for war. In addition, his attitude toward the Soviet Union and his endorsement of its exclusion was utterly remarkable. Although he obviously realized that the very thing he championed, the rejection of Russia as a partner in European affairs, could bring about the very thing he feared, American involvement in the "Old World," he did not offer the obvious solution: embrace the Soviet Union; make it an ally. Instead, his conclusion was to urge the administration to play no role on the world stage but adopt a staunch, rigid policy of neutrality. As if it could; as if it should.

The ambassador's fierce loyalty and admiration for the prime minister led him to commit the great diplomatic blunder of failing to maintain professional distance from Chamberlain's policy. He completely and unequivocally staked his own diplomatic career on what many had come to believe was the wrong man, with the wrong policy, at the wrong time.[199] His heretofore unfailing acuity and nearly infallible intuitive grasp of timing in business and politics, along with an ample dose of Irish luck and pluck, began to forsake him in diplomacy.[200] It cost him dearly not only with his host country, as the British became increasingly critical of Chamberlain and his policies and by extension with Chamberlain's sympathizers like the American ambassador, but also with Chamberlain's own government, as Roosevelt's shrewder appraisal of the Nazi threat led him to disregard Kennedy's advice. Unlike the president, Kennedy never realized that there was a price for placating Hitler and maintaining peace beyond which the democracies would not go. That price had been paid at Munich.[201]

But FDR refused to provide anything more than "pinpricks and righteous protest"; a disbelieving public would not have accepted more vigorous leadership in foreign affairs. Thus the United States remained sunk in isolation. Throughout the Munich crisis the president was a detached observer, pursuing a policy of "no risks, no commitments"[202] as he worried and watched, hoping that the democracies would make a stand against Nazism over the Sudetenland. Both he and his well-informed State Department were dubious about the peace of Munich and uncertain about its future. Their skepticism made them unwilling and unable to give their ambassador definite guidance. Left to his own devices, Kennedy stumbled along on his complementary paths of supporting both appeasement and isolation, incapable of rising beyond his own narrow diplomatic vision and evaluating international events rationally or impersonally, or of analyzing them in their historical or international perspective.

Although Roosevelt bowed to his nation's mood, he still felt obliged to signal that American sympathies lay with the European democracies and that he deplored the aggressive actions of the dictators. Despite Welles's radio statement of October 3, made on behalf of the administration, that he hoped the Munich Agreement could create "a new world order based upon justice and upon law," Roosevelt, like Hull, actually had little faith in it.[203] To the president Munich was a lull before "the gathering storm" during which the democracies must rearm. Actually it was nothing more than a pause in Germany's expansion. Hitler had already made plans to swallow the rest of Czechoslovakia.

In the weeks and months following the Munich Agreement, Chamberlain's "peace for our time" ironically became a cry to use "our time" to rearm immediately. This stepped-up rearmament program lent credibility to Kennedy's belief that Munich bought Britain time—time to rearm, time "to create the means to permit [the British] to stand fast"[204]—as much time, of course, as it gave the Germans, who used it more shrewdly: Time was on Hitler's side.[205] As a totalitarian country, Germany could be mobilized more easily and more quickly than a democratic one, a point made by John F. Kennedy in *Why England Slept*, written in part with the dispatches and the advice of his father, but a point seemingly lost on the ambassador, who apparently failed to understand its implications.[206]

During the chaotic mobilization before Munich, sleeping Britons were awakened to the pitiably poor conditions of their defenses. During the eleven months that Munich bought, the British did expand their armament production slightly, but limited it primarily to radar and air-raid and anti-aircraft defenses.[207] In fact it was not until March 1939 that Chamberlain allowed any increases in British weapons acquisitions. He then scrambled to enlarge the military: new ships for the navy, with more planned; an increase in fighter aircraft construction and design; and an urgent demand for radio operations and radar—but leaving the army in worse shape than it had been a decade earlier.[208] Even so, British additions were not as great as those of the Germans, who were able to produce more arms than the British.[209]

With Hitler's two invasions of Czechoslovakia, on October 1, 1938, and on March 15, 1939, the British lost the friendship of the most democratic country in central Europe, the key to the rest of central and southeastern Europe, and a Czech force of nearly thirty divisions, a larger army than Britain had then. The Germans gained the big Skoda munitions factories in Bohemia and five hundred well-built tanks. The outbreak of war in September 1939 found Britain weaker in comparison with Germany than it had been in September 1938.[210]

"Munich today is far away and yet not far enough away for any accurate appraisal to be made of its significance," Kennedy wrote in his diplomatic memoir years later. His closeness to the event made it "impossible" for him to be an impartial judge. Kennedy defended the Munich Agreement, and shared the "profound thankfulness" of those who were involved in the dramatic events that averted war in the House of Commons on September 28. It had deeply affected him both personally and professionally, he wrote in his memoir. He was subjected to a "slanderous . . . vicious" assault and denounced as a coward. He was labeled the "most jittery" person in London, fearful of being bombed and accused of maneuvering to send his children to Ireland for their safety. Kennedy denied all charges.

Munich also affected Kennedy's own interpretation of diplomacy between the wars. It confirmed the unjust and unwise diplomatic assumptions of Britain and France that favored Germany in the 1930s, and illustrated the futility of the League of Nations. It was a "milestone" along the road to international and moral decadence that began with the crises in Manchuria, Ethiopia, and Austria and culminated in Poland and at Pearl Harbor. But Munich also provided Britain with an opportunity to reverse the troubling diplomacy of the interwar period. Thus, Britain could emerge as "the protagonist of right, justice and order" to play its "historic and customary role."

Unlike his opponents Churchill and Attlee, Chamberlain was a realist, Kennedy wrote.[211] The prime minister was realistic enough to accept Hitler's demands and to try to find a practical and just settlement of them through negotiations and appeasement, "the only hope for peace." Chamberlain held a realistic distrust of Hitler privately. Chamberlain considered Hitler "uncouth and certainly not the kind of fellow one would like to go around the world with on a two-wheeled bicycle."[212] Chamberlain was a realist when he called for doubling Britain's armament program upon his return from Munich. And even if Munich were a failure, Kennedy argued, it at least bought the democracies time—time to create the military means to ensure their survival.

Kennedy believed that Chamberlain's appeasement policy was far preferable to the views of his opponents like Churchill and Attlee. Kennedy feared that Churchill's bellicose demand for containment by an anti-fascist league would divide Europe into two camps and continue a cold war that could quickly turn hot. The ambassador was also contemptuous of

Churchill's willingness to use war as the ultimate diplomatic weapon, and would later go much further than Chamberlain in rejecting war as an instrument of statecraft altogether. On the other hand, Kennedy found Attlee's pacifist, socialist position commendable; so too was his assumption that the people of Europe were innately peace-loving. But even if Chamberlain were wrong and Churchill and Attlee right, and even if Munich were a diplomatic failure, it would still be beneficial, Kennedy argued; at the very least, it would buy the democracies time.

Although historians may well debate whether Chamberlain should have called Hitler's bluff at Berchtesgaden or Munich, Kennedy opposed it. No one, certainly not Hitler, believed that either Britain or France held a winning hand; nor did they. Kennedy accurately pointed out that Britain was diplomatically isolated; its public saw no merit in a war to save Czechoslovakia, and both Britain and France were militarily weak. France, torn apart by internal political dissension and teetering on the verge of bankruptcy, lacked the will to fight. Neither Britain nor France believed that Russia, the United States, or Britain's dominions could be counted on—a very realistic view of international affairs at Munich.

Russia was "an asset of dubious value," Kennedy thought.[213] Since it would be "wholly impractical" for Russia to aid Czechoslovakia across hostile territory, British officials early on deliberately chose to ignore her and to exclude her from discussions about Czechoslovakia. The British further realized that since the Russians regarded Czechoslovakia as essential to their security as a "bulwark" against German aggression, they would oppose any alteration in the status quo and instead remain "utterly but calmly intransigent." Why then invite her to compromise over a matter she considered vital to her security? Kennedy asked, in defense of the British decision to exclude her.[214] Russia's divisive diplomacy played the democracies off against the dictatorships; ultimately, Kennedy predicted unhappily, Russia would stand by and watch the two camps "tear each other to pieces." What the Russians really hoped for was war, Kennedy believed; but Russia's military had little ability to fend for itself. Her army and its officers had been demoralized and decimated by Joseph Stalin's recent purges. Russia wanted other nations to expend their armaments and risk their lives in her defense. She would then emerge triumphant from Europe's ashes and spread communism through a ruined continent. Chamberlain saw that, too, and "wanted no part of it. He preferred to gamble for peace," Kennedy said.

The Americans, hampered by their neutrality legislation, were unwilling to be even a little arsenal for democracy, let alone a bluff big enough to stop Hitler. And the British dominions, either hostile or indifferent to Czechoslovakia, would have refused to support Britain's bluffs and threats of war—inaction that would imperil the Empire itself.[215] Kennedy's argument was impressive; his assessment of Munich was credible.[216]

"There was no real answer to Germany's insistence upon self-determination in the Sudeten area," Kennedy pointed out, something that Chamberlain had swallowed in the aftermath of the Austrian coup, as Halifax, Henderson, and Lord Runciman finally did, too. Even if war did break out and was followed by a just peace, Germany's claim to the Sudetenland would still have to be recognized, Kennedy argued. Given the enormousness of the problem, the prime minister was right to consider all peaceful alternatives short of war, Kennedy believed, since war was a curse that would destroy the very civilization Chamberlain was striving to preserve. Writing in the post–World War II era, after the death of his beloved eldest son, the near death of his second son, and the death of his favorite daughter (whose own husband died on the battlefield in France), and surrounded by the menace of the Cold War that threatened to turn into a hot one, Kennedy poignantly concluded: "In the shadow of the broken homes of today, of the rubble of Europe and Asia, of a peace that is no peace and the threat of war even more horrible than we can contemplate, it is difficult to blame Chamberlain for a choice made long before the actual fact of Munich."[217]

A portrait of Joseph Patrick Kennedy,
c. 1892, in East Boston.

JOHN F. KENNEDY PRESIDENTIAL LIBRARY AND MUSEUM, BOSTON.

Joseph P. Kennedy Sr.'s
graduation picture from Harvard,
Cambridge, MA, 1912.

JOHN F. KENNEDY PRESIDENTIAL LIBRARY AND MUSEUM, BOSTON.

Joseph P. Kennedy throws a baseball during his years at Harvard, c. 1908–1912.

JOHN F. KENNEDY PRESIDENTIAL LIBRARY AND MUSEUM, BOSTON.

Joseph P. Kennedy seated at his desk at the Columbia Trust Company in East Boston, MA, January 1914.

JOHN F. KENNEDY PRESIDENTIAL LIBRARY AND MUSEUM, BOSTON.

Wedding of Rose
Fitzgerald and Joseph P.
Kennedy, in Boston, on
October 7, 1914.

JOHN F. KENNEDY PRESIDENTIAL LIBRARY
AND MUSEUM, BOSTON.

A gathering of the
Roosevelt Party by the
campaign train. Among
the crowd, Joseph P.
Kennedy and Franklin
Delano Roosevelt,
September 23, 1932.

JOHN F. KENNEDY PRESIDENTIAL LIBRARY
AND MUSEUM, BOSTON.

The Roosevelt Party
Oregon - California
Line
September 23, 1932.

Justice Stanley Reed swears in Joseph P. Kennedy (*left*) as U.S. Ambassador to Great Britain, while President Franklin D. Roosevelt (*seated*) looks on. White House, Washington, DC, February 18, 1938. JOHN F. KENNEDY PRESIDENTIAL LIBRARY AND MUSEUM, BOSTON.

Joseph P. Kennedy Jr., Joseph P. Kennedy Sr., John F. Kennedy. Arrival at Southampton, England, July 2, 1938.

JOHN F. KENNEDY PRESIDENTIAL LIBRARY AND MUSEUM, BOSTON.

OPPOSITE: A Kennedy family portrait at the London Embassy, UK, c. 1938. (*Back row, left to right*) Kathleen Kennedy, Joseph P. Kennedy Jr., Eunice Kennedy, Ambassador Joseph P. Kennedy Sr., Rosemary Kennedy, John F. Kennedy; (*middle row*) Patricia Kennedy, Jean Kennedy, Robert F. Kennedy; (*front row*) Edward M. Kennedy and Rose M. Kennedy, c. 1938.

JOHN F. KENNEDY PRESIDENTIAL LIBRARY AND MUSEUM, BOSTON.

German Führer Adolf Hitler shakes hands with British Prime Minister Neville Chamberlain (*left*) at the 1938 Munich Conference in which Chamberlain agreed to allow Nazi Germany to annex the Sudetenland, September 28–29, 1938. Note Hitler is using the double handshake he reserved for special occasions.

PHOTO BY © CORBIS/CORBIS VIA GETTY IMAGES.

British Prime Minister Neville Chamberlain (1869–1940) and his wife look down from a window at 10 Downing Street as crowds gather to applaud his peacemaking visit to Munich for the four-power conference, September 30, 1938. PHOTO BY TOPICAL PRESS AGENCY/HULTON ARCHIVE/GETTY IMAGES.

(*Left to right, back row*) Patricia Kennedy, John F. Kennedy, Eunice Kennedy, Rosemary Kennedy. (*Front row*) an unidentified Vatican guard, Kathleen Kennedy, Robert F. Kennedy, Rose Kennedy, Edward M. Kennedy, Jean Kennedy, and unidentified Vatican guard during the coronation of Pope Pius XII at the Vatican, March 12, 1939.

JOHN F. KENNEDY PRESIDENTIAL LIBRARY AND MUSEUM, BOSTON.

U.S. Ambassador to Great Britain Joseph P. Kennedy visits British dignitaries in Windsor. Photograph includes (*left to right*) Ambassador Kennedy, Princess Helena Victoria, an unidentified military official, and British Prime Minister Neville Chamberlain, April 16, 1939.

JOHN F. KENNEDY PRESIDENTIAL LIBRARY AND MUSEUM, BOSTON.

Ambassador Joseph P. Kennedy and his wife Rose Kennedy pose for a photo with King George VI and his wife Queen Elizabeth at the American Embassy in London. (*Left to right*) Rose Kennedy, King George VI, Queen Elizabeth, and Ambassador Joseph P. Kennedy, May 11, 1939. JOHN F. KENNEDY PRESIDENTIAL LIBRARY AND MUSEUM, BOSTON.

Joseph P. Kennedy receives honorary degree at Bristol with Winston Churchill and others present, May 25, 1939.

JOHN F. KENNEDY PRESIDENTIAL LIBRARY AND MUSEUM, BOSTON.

(*Left to right*) Joseph P. Kennedy Jr., Kathleen Kennedy, and John F. Kennedy walking to the Palace of Westminster in London, England, to hear Great Britain declare war on Germany, September 3, 1939.

JOHN F. KENNEDY PRESIDENTIAL LIBRARY AND MUSEUM, BOSTON.

Sumner Welles, Winston Churchill, and Joseph P. Kennedy in London, March 27, 1940.

JOHN F. KENNEDY PRESIDENTIAL LIBRARY AND MUSEUM, BOSTON.

American ambassador to Britain Joseph P. Kennedy with English statesman Winston Churchill outside Downing Street, London, October 1940.

PHOTO BY KEYSTONE-FRANCE/ GAMMA-KEYSTONE VIA GETTY IMAGES.

Kathleen Kennedy, American Red Cross, London, c. 1943.

JOHN F. KENNEDY PRESIDENTIAL LIBRARY AND MUSEUM, BOSTON.

John Fitzgerald Kennedy
and Joseph Patrick
Kennedy Jr. sit for portrait
in U.S. Navy uniform, 1942.

JOHN F. KENNEDY PRESIDENTIAL LIBRARY
AND MUSEUM, BOSTON.

President Kennedy
visits with his father,
Ambassador Joseph P.
Kennedy, while cousin
Ann Gargan looks on.
Hyannis Port, MA,
August 25, 1963.

JOHN F. KENNEDY PRESIDENTIAL LIBRARY
AND MUSEUM, BOSTON.

CHAPTER 5

Into an Abyss

During the rest of 1938, the disenchanted quickly fled from the appeasers. But among those still loyal and unwavering was Chamberlain's close friend and ally, the American ambassador.[1] He took advantage of the invitation to speak at the Trafalgar Day dinner of the Navy League to praise Chamberlain's struggle for peace and to honor his courage, devotion, and political wisdom in averting a holocaust—and to advocate for coexistence with the dictators. It was an occasion that proved deeply embarrassing to the State Department, led to considerable criticism of Kennedy, probably secretly delighted FDR, and thoroughly humiliated the talkative rogue ambassador, who was again called on the mat for this latest lapse in diplomatic judgment and discernment.

Following this debacle, and perhaps because of it, Kennedy became deeply involved in the European refugee problem. The "Kennedy Plan" to placate Germany's Jews and to quiet the uproar against their persecution by relocating them in parts of the British Empire, was designed to save Europe's peace. It was another ill-fated, offhand scheme and an example of Kennedy's personal diplomacy on behalf of his own interests, which Washington again met with indifference and stony silence. It further widened the rift between Kennedy and the White House and ironically contributed to his reputation for anti-Semitism and pro-fascism. It also led to a barrage of criticism against him by administration liberals and anti-appeasers who delighted in his growing unpopularity at the White House and exploited the presumed rift between the president and his ambassador and in creating his new negative diplomatic image.

As FDR began to reconsider ways to aid the democracies and America's probable role in a European war, he developed a hopeful policy of "methods short of war," never doubting the strength inherent in democracy. Although Kennedy supported Roosevelt's policy before Congress, in December 1938 he gave the president a memorandum that portrayed a dismal view of the European situation, particularly if the British Empire were defeated, and urged the creation of a new world order.[2] Nevertheless, the ambassador was steadfast in his defense of British appeasement and his support for American isolation. In a second memo, in March 1939, he urged that the United States become an isolated fortress by building an armed fence around North America with a huge arsenal and a two-ocean navy, and accept a form of fascism with economic restrictions and limitation of civil liberties: In order to fight fascism, the United States would have to become a fascist state.[3] This advice FDR simply ignored.

Despite FDR's expression of support for Kennedy's work, their relationship had become one of permanent estrangement masked by pleasantries and cordiality. Kennedy was a man FDR no longer needed but too potentially dangerous as a critic to let come home for good; the ambassador could be ignored, contradicted, and outwitted, Roosevelt reasoned, without too much political expense to himself. He therefore ordered Kennedy to return to London, safely out of the way, so that he could pursue the contradictions of his ambivalent foreign policy. As for Kennedy, although his authority and prestige were clearly in decline within the administration, he was still fulfilling his own diplomatic criterion of representing the views of the majority of his countrymen, if not those of his president.

Kennedy was extremely pleased to be the first ambassador ever invited to address the Trafalgar Day dinner, a rare tribute for any foreigner.[4] It was held in honor of Lord Nelson, the admiral and naval hero who decisively defeated Napoleon and combined French and Spanish fleets at the Battle of Trafalgar in 1805.

Anticipating criticism of his remarks, Kennedy spent several days polishing his draft and received Washington's official approval for his speech. Under the guise of putting up with Rose's wifely chiding about his choice of subjects, he told the audience that he had discussed several possible topics with her. Rose had in fact cautioned him about discussing diplomatically inappropriate issues. "Have you thought how this would sound back home?" she had asked. "You know, dear, our Ambassadors are supposed to lose all powers of resistance when they get to London and see things only through English eyes." She had also said: "You would have to produce concrete suggestions to bring home your point, and you know perfectly well that if you try to do that you will find yourself discussing issues which a diplomat should not raise."[5] Her husband did not follow her advice.

Mentioning much forethought and Rose's chiding, Kennedy launched into a lecture on the wisdom of coexistence with the dictators. Careful to label his plea as a "theory of mine," Kennedy argued that it is "unproductive" for democracies and dictatorships to exacerbate their obvious disagreements. "It is true," he allowed, "that the democratic and dictator countries have important fundamental divergences in outlook which in certain matters go deeper than politics. But there is simply no sense, common or otherwise, in letting these differences grow into unrelenting antagonisms. After all, we have to live together in the same world, whether we like it or not."[6] He devoted most of his speech to discussing the unique cooperative naval relationship between Britain and the United States, and to exploring how to achieve a similarly compatible relationship in merchant-marine shipping. He reassured his audience that it had nothing to fear from American maritime policy and urged that Britain and the United States become "friendly competitors."[7]

The *New York Times* emphasized Kennedy's "theory of mine" for coexistence with the dictators and described his speech as an excellent summary of Neville Chamberlain's recent Munich policy.[8] The pro-appeasement *Times* of London praised the ambassador for his references to "a relationship unique in the annals of naval history"[9] between the American and British fleets that "was an incentive not to discord but to peace."[10] What was "notable" and "encourag[ing]," the editorial said, was Kennedy's unqualified confidence that an increase in armaments would strengthen Britain's international influence.[11] "Confidence begets confidence and peace as fear begets fear and war," the *Times* declared.

Such a declaration "should do much in many countries to foster an atmosphere in which the policy of the Munich declaration can work itself out toward its proper consummation— the widening of the basis of common action, the renunciation of suicidal rivalry, and the final reestablishment of some better system of collective security for peace."[12]

On the other side of the Atlantic, Kennedy's speech and his hints of considerable reservations about the appropriateness of his topic created a major uproar in the press, among his countrymen, and within official Washington. His critics accused him of endorsing Nazi aggression.[13] One opponent, Heywood Broun, a Harvard classmate of his, advocated dropping him in Boston Harbor "among the alien tea," to restore his Americanism. Another accused him of talking too much and serving his own political ambitions, and still another was of the opinion that he had been seduced by the British and had neither the taste nor discretion of an ambassador.[14] "Mr. Kennedy should not be allowed to make such suggestions even as a private individual," two women members of the general public wrote to the White House.[15] Kennedy's supporters countered by saying that his plea was based on "common sense" and illustrated a "more realistic grasp" of international relations than the administration's.[16] Walter Lippmann in his October 22 column "Today and Tomorrow" took Kennedy to task for lacking "diplomatic discretion," of going far beyond his proper role, and concluded that Kennedy must have intended the speech for American consumption.[17] Lippmann also wrote that "amateur and temporary diplomats take their speeches very seriously [and] . . . tend to become . . . a little state department with a little foreign policy of their own"—an apt description of Kennedy's mindset.[18]

Incensed, Joe Jr. jumped to his father's defense in his "Answer to Lippmann Editorial against Dad" and complained that the columnist illustrated "the natural Jewish reaction." Would Mr. Lippmann rather the ambassador speak only about trivial matters—as if he were some "unemployed office boy"? Such a frank expression of opinion as his father gave, approved by the State Department in advance, would hardly increase his prestige in the United

States, given the country's current natural hostility toward dictators, and is hardly evidence of the ambassador's "being taken in" by the British. Furthermore, Joe Jr. loyally pointed out, if the ambassador were belligerent to the British, he would be cut off and find their doors closed and lose any opportunity to influence them. Ambassador Kennedy had advocated "the only possible policy to follow," Joe Jr. concluded. Unless you are prepared to destroy the fascist countries, "you might as well try to get along with them." This may be "extremely hard for the Jewish community in the U.S. to stomach," Joe Jr. wrote, no doubt echoing his father's views, and opening up both to charges of anti-Semitism.[19]

At Harvard, the second son weighed in. Son Jack told Kennedy that the speech, "while it seemed to be unpopular with the Jews etc. [*sic*] was considered to be very good by everyone who wasn't bitterly anti-fascist."[20]

Official Washington was stunned and hit with a barrage of questions about whether Kennedy's speech forecast a change in foreign policy. Was it a trial balloon that carried a hint that Roosevelt was retreating from his moral "quarantine" Chicago speech? Could it be that the department's consent was a "negative act of approval"?[21] State Department officials answered both questions with a resounding no. In his press conferences the next day, Hull said "he knew nothing new concerning American foreign policy."[22] Asked whether Kennedy's expressed views were his own, the secretary replied that that was his understanding. In an example of scholastic hair-splitting, the State Department offered the argument that Kennedy's emphasis on the differences between democracies and dictatorships referred to the domestic forms of government, and American foreign policy did not stress domestic differences. "Therefore Mr. Kennedy said nothing implying or advising any change in our foreign policy."[23]

Arthur Krock also dropped into the State Department to discuss the speech with department officials. Moffat assured him that the speech signaled no official change in policy. Any change would be announced by the president or the secretary. "We would [not] sound off through an Ambassador."[24]

Despite endorsing Kennedy's speech and remarking to Kennedy, "I think you have successfully avoided many pitfalls," the secretary of state, stunned by the public's criticism, beat a hasty retreat.[25] "Every time our foreign policy has run off the rocks it has been because of a speech made by one of our Ambassadors abroad," Hull fumed to Moffat. Regardless of this ambassador's claim to be setting out what was only his own pet theory, "we should have definitely called him off in advance."

The outcry in the United States started a fury of departmental buck-passing and a hunt for a scapegoat. Hull asked Welles why he had failed to see the problems with the speech. Welles replied that he had been preoccupied with Mexico and had absent-mindedly initialed the speech without editing it since he assumed that Hull had already approved it. Intent on preserving the reputation of the State Department, Hull cornered Moffat and demanded to know why he had not anticipated the problems the speech might cause. Moffat said that he assumed that there might be repercussions, but Kennedy's phrase "a pet theory of my own" would protect Hull and the State Department. He too had recommended no changes in the speech. Moffat confided to his diary: "A 'goat' is needed and I shall have to be the goat. In the long run, however, no one is going to be hurt unless it be Mr. Kennedy himself." He added:

> The truth of the matter is that the Secretary dislikes calling down Kennedy and Bullitt as they have a way of appealing to the White House over his head. The speech also came at a time when the trade agreement negotiations were in a most critical state and Kennedy was taking the ball and not inspiring the Secretary with the greatest confidence in the way he was carrying it.[26]

To counter Kennedy's foreign-policy blunder and to undo the misconception that the United States wanted a cozy relationship with the dictators, Roosevelt delivered a vehement denunciation of dictatorships. On October 26, a week after Kennedy's Trafalgar speech, the president in a radio speech said:

> It is becoming increasingly clear that peace by fear has no higher or more enduring quality than peace by the sword. There can be no peace if the reign of law is to be replaced by a recurrent sanctification of sheer force. There can be no peace if national policy adopts as a deliberate instrument the threat of war.[27]

Moffat's prediction was entirely accurate. Kennedy was incensed by FDR's public stab in the back. In a short address about a week after his speech, the ambassador, feeling sorry for himself, publicly mused to the Worcestershire Association about the reaction to it. He commented that he had been reading for about a week now about the remarks he supposedly made before the Navy League and had concluded: "If you preach democracy, you offend the totalitarian regimes. If you see anything good in dictatorships, you alienate the democracies. And if you should venture to suggest that the peoples of both groups go about their business and leave each other alone—well, then you catch it from both sides."[28]

In private, Kennedy was less restrained. "I am so god-damned mad I can't see." "Of all the insidious lying I have ever read in my life I have read in these columns the last two weeks," he incoherently wrote to South Carolina's Senator James Byrnes. The ambassador swore to the senator that this would be his last public office. "The only thing that could bring me into active political life again would be to hear that you were going to be a candidate for President and, with all the names I hear mentioned, why in the name of God you don't get busy is a mystery to me"[29]—an opinion that would no doubt have intrigued FDR as he mulled over the possibilities of a third term.

Still sending letters to pet correspondents, the ambassador vigorously complained to Doris Fleeson of the *New York Daily News* about the "poison" being spread about him at the White House. He told her about a note he received from his father-in-law that really got him down, a note telling him that Missy LeHand, the president's private secretary, was making unkind remarks about him. "I practically gave up. I thought Missy knew me well enough to know that I don't shift like the wind and that anything I have to say I say to the parties concerned."[30]

Joe Jr. noted that his father was not "too crazy about the job" and had lately spoken of quitting. "He is afraid that they are trying to knock him off at home, and may make a monkey out of him in some diplomatic undertaking." They already had. The administration had not informed him about the plans for the visit of the king and queen to the United States for the next year, and "he had to bluff his way through," his son said.[31]

Despite the barrage of criticism, Kennedy did receive one favorable letter from Roosevelt's son-in-law, John Boettiger. He told the ambassador that, regardless of all the "brickbats flying around," he had been doing a "grand job."[32] Kennedy grumbled in reply: "All I have been having poured into me for the last three months is how Roosevelt is off me, how the gang is batting my head off, and that I am persona non grata to the entire Roosevelt family." A lot of this was "hooey," of course, he wrote,

> but it is damned annoying three thousand miles away. When I add up my contributions to this cause over the past five years—and I do not mean monetary ones—I get damned sick that anybody close to the Boss finds it necessary to do anything but say a good word. It has taught me one lesson: I am going to stay on the side lines for a while and mind my own business and let the boys worry about their problems.[33]

But staying on the sidelines was not in his nature. Kennedy refused to be disciplined or to refrain from making caustic personal criticisms of FDR. Kennedy's memos continued to stream to pet journalists in the United States. In the Hearst-owned *New York Daily Mirror*, Boake Carter wrote that "the White House has on its hands a fighting Irishman, with blazing eyes and a determination to strip the bandages of deceit, innuendo and misrepresentation bound around the eyes of the American citizens," and prophesied a fight to the finish between the ambassador and his opponents in the administration.[34]

A *Wall Street Journal* columnist differed with the Hearst paper's prediction. Frank Kent wrote that the groundswell of criticism, especially in the liberal press, was particularly sweet to the mischievous boss in the White House. Kent thought that Roosevelt had been peeved at his ambassador's tremendously favorable publicity and a trifle jealous, especially because Kennedy's press fans were precisely those newsmen who habitually raised the "presidential blood pressure." It was not a secret, Kent wrote, that when Kennedy returned to the United States in June, "the White House crowd" planted critical stories in newspapers around the country. Roosevelt, Kent said, had also belittled Kennedy privately and accused him of hiring "high-powered" journalists to boost his own presidential ambitions. Precisely because the ambassador's Trafalgar Day speech was such a personal and political blunder, and because it did cause so much unfavorable criticism, "a Kennedy chastened and subdued by an embittering experience, a Kennedy nursing his bruises and licking his wounds, will be personally more popular around the White House when he next returns. Mr. Kennedy knows all this, Mr. Roosevelt knows that Mr. Kennedy knows it, and Mr. Kennedy knows that Mr. Roosevelt knows he knows it." But each man continued publicly professing his friendship and loyalty and preserving a veneer of cordiality because "each needs or wants what the other can give."[35] This was a very accurate assessment of the complicated Kennedy-Roosevelt relationship.

A highly indignant Arthur Krock, who resented the barrage of unfair and inaccurate charges his dear friend and patron Kennedy had been subjected to, summed up the controversy with his usual keen and fawning insights in a letter to Kennedy. You're doing "a wonderful job," Krock wrote Kennedy. Your bad press was due to your indiscreet and undiplomatic statement about trying to get along with the dictators, a statement that I would have urged you not to make, particularly under the strained diplomatic circumstances. It provoked a vehement reaction among the Jews that was echoed in the press; it angered Catholics because of the increasing sharpness between Hitler and the Church; it outraged liberals because of its practicality; and it delighted the White House crowd for any number of reasons. The outcry against your statement caused the State Department to pretend it had not given its approval and shaped the sharp comments the president made in his radio address. But behind most of the criticism was jealousy of your accomplishments, Krock loyally told him, and delight in finding "a peg on which to hang the charge that you have been seduced by British flattery, particularly Chamberlain's."[36]

In his memoirs, Kennedy devoted half a chapter to explaining the Trafalgar Day speech and to discussing its repercussions. He was particularly displeased with Hull for his Janus-like behavior and for stating that any approval of his was a "negative act of approval." Hull owed him an apology for withdrawing his approval of Kennedy's speech. None was forthcoming. Kennedy attributed Hull's about-face to isolationist-minded journalists like Dorothy Thompson. She argued that pursuing any idea like Kennedy's of coexistence with the dictators would involve the United States in commitments that would destroy our independence and our ability to live separately from conflicts in the Old World.

Kennedy was also disturbed by the vehement reaction the speech aroused among a number of Jewish publishers and writers. He sympathized with their deep concern for Germany's Jews, whose lives and fortunes were being destroyed. Compromise would not solve the problem; nor did Munich give them any hope—only the elimination of Nazism would. But he took issue with the tactics many of them used. Kennedy singled out Professor Max Lerner in particular as one who invented facts to suit his case. Lerner had told a Boston audience that Kennedy's "misinformation" that Hitler planned to go to war over Czechoslovakia was the incentive for Roosevelt's intervention with Hitler. The Führer actually had no intention of going to war, Lerner told the crowd, with full professorial authority, and said that Hitler had deceived both Chamberlain and Kennedy into betraying Czechoslovakia. The same theme appeared in the columns of the Communist paper, the *Daily Worker*. "I was naturally not the sole butt of their attack," wrote Kennedy, deeply upset by the criticism, "but I received my share of it. . . . I was hardly prepared, despite years in the public office, for the full viciousness of this onslaught."[37]

It was not just the uproar in official Washington caused by Kennedy's views that was noteworthy, but the unprofessionalism of his expression of them—its characteristic crudity and superficiality. In another "confidential" letter to T. J. White and W. R. Hearst, Kennedy defended his speech and told them he was glad he had made it—somebody needed to say what he had said, and he could afford to do so since he had no political ambitions for himself. In answer to the numerous charges that he had been taken in by the British, Kennedy said that they had only shown him "great courtesy" and nothing else to make him wish he was their friend. Nor have they "anything to offer the United States that is of any particular value to us," he said, apparently disregarding the shield of British sea and air power and the strategic value of Britain's overseas colonies. Unless the democracies were willing to threaten civilization by declaring war, "there is no point in . . . sticking your tongue out at somebody who is a good deal bigger than you are." His advice to the United States was always the same: "We ought to mind our own business." That means not kicking "the dictators' head off" one minute and urging them to cooperate with us the next. In business relations, whether individual or national, you must either stay away from your opponents completely or, "if you are going to stick your tongue out at them or slap them on the wrist, you have [*sic*] better be prepared to punch them in the jaw," he argued, without realizing that getting a punch in the jaw was just what Hitler wanted so that he could then punch everybody else in the jaw. Furthermore, Kennedy wrote, "I have no more sympathy with Hitler's ideas than anyone in America, but I asked myself, what am I going to do about it?" I could go to war to stop him or I could cut him off economically, "but, if I am just going to stick my tongue out at him, then I am not with it at all."

Other options such as Churchill's proposed Anglo-French bloc as a prelude to a European Grand Alliance or a policy for containment under the covenant of the League of Nations or even an attitude of cooperation with the Soviet Union, all were unacceptable to him. He ended his message with a prophetic and uncharacteristically sentimental observation: "My heart is almost broken watching us gradually lower ourselves into an abyss it will be very difficult to get out of."[38] Roosevelt was beginning to reap the harvest of his disastrous decision to play the "greatest joke in the world"[39] by appointing an ambassador who was not "with it at all" and who reduced the complexities and subtleties of international relations to sticking your tongue out and a fist fight. But the joke was on the president, who was no longer laughing.

One of Kennedy's favorite options for dealing with Hitler was economic cooperation. "I have an idea that maybe if Mr. Hitler enjoyed some good trade with us, he would be so busy trying to protect it he wouldn't have time to think about fighting with everybody"—a more appealing idea than his former ideas, except that Hitler did not want "good trade"; he wanted a good war.[40]

As the uproar over the Trafalgar Day speech died down and the strain between the ambassador and the president abated slightly, Kennedy became embroiled in Europe's refugee problems. He responded to the plight of the twenty-eight Spanish nuns by privately enlisting Lord Halifax's help in arranging for their escape from the Convent of the Sacred Heart in Loyalist-held Barcelona. Behind their rescue lay nearly five months of unrelenting red-tape cutting. Kennedy told Hull in confidence about his and Halifax's activities and added "that [they] should bring joy to your heart."[41] Kennedy had learned of the nuns' plight from the mother superior of the Convent of the Sacred Heart at Roehampton when he visited his three daughters at school there.[42] Working quietly and unofficially, he discussed the situation with Chamberlain and Halifax, who magnanimously promised "entirely unofficially" to "see what could be done"[43] and to "lend every help we could."[44] Kennedy offered to pay for the expenses of the nuns and accepted Halifax's suggestion, once again without approval from Washington, to request permission of the Spanish government on behalf of the United States that the nuns be allowed to leave. Halifax agreed to do so on behalf of the British government as well.[45] As a personal favor to Kennedy, Chamberlain dispatched the British destroyer *Hero* to Spain to transport the sisters to Marseilles. After receiving the promise that they would not return to Spain during the war or aid the rebels, the Spanish government finally granted permission for their departure.[46] The ambassador had a double motive for his involvement. His diary entry of July 20, 1938, reads: "I wanted to emphasize that the Jews from Germany and Austria are not the only refugees in the world, and I wanted to depict Chamberlain and Halifax as human, good-hearted men capable of taking an active interest in such a bona fide venture."[47] It was "a noble piece of work," Kennedy boasted to Hull.[48] For his efforts, 235 Chicago children from the Convent of the Sacred Heart offered a day of prayer for Kennedy and his "interesting" family. His correspondent proudly noted that Mrs. Kennedy and the Kennedy girls were also members of the Sacred Heart family.[49] But Kennedy could make no such arrangements for Germany's Jews, whose plight had become intolerable. His well-publicized but spur-of-the-moment scheme, labeled the Kennedy Plan, failed miserably, and his resentment grew toward some Jews who persistently whispered accusations of anti-Semitism against him.

On the night of November 9–10, 1938, Kristallnacht, "the night of broken glass,"[50] there occurred in Germany an orgy of government-sanctioned atrocities against Jews in retaliation for the assassination on November 7 of Baron Ernst vom Rath, the third secretary of the German embassy in Paris. He was shot to death by a Polish Jew, Herschel Grynszpan, a seventeen-year-old refugee whose father, mother, brother, and sister had been among the thousands deported to Poland from Germany. The killing provided the Nazis with an excuse for "spontaneous"[51] reprisals against Germany's 600,000 Jews and led to "hideous Jewish persecutions," Kennedy recalled.[52] Nazi gangs were ordered into the ghettos. Jews were raped, Jews were murdered, their businesses were burned and looted, their synagogues defaced, and thousands were arrested. The Nazi government imposed an incredible fine of one billion marks upon the Jews.[53]

Kristallnacht stunned Kennedy into silence by throwing into sharp relief the differences between the democracies and the dictatorships and by even threatening to undermine the Munich settlement and Chamberlain's appeasement policy. Chamberlain wrote in his diary: "I am horrified by the German behaviour to the Jews"[54] and lamented that "there does seem to be some fatality about Anglo-German relations which invariably blocks every effort to improve them." Kristallnacht brought an end to any further approaches to Hitler.[55] The Trafalgar Day doctrine of working things out with the dictators, Kennedy complained to Colonel Lindbergh,[56] seemed to be "out of commission," and made him "very sick at heart."[57] "The Jewish business"[58] made it nearly impossible to support any peaceful plan and threatened Western civilization itself: "So much is lost when so much could be gained."[59] No further public comment was heard from the ambassador about peaceful coexistence with the dictators.

After Kristallnacht, Hull virtually suspended diplomatic relations with the German government by calling home the American ambassador, Hugh Wilson, from Berlin. Germany retaliated by calling its ambassador home. Neither country was to have a diplomatic representative for the remainder of the peace. FDR told the press: "The news of the past few days from Germany has shocked public opinion in the United States. . . . I myself could scarcely believe that such things could occur in a twentieth-century civilization."[60] Kennedy completely agreed with Roosevelt's action. The pogrom was the "most terrible thing I have ever heard of," the ambassador said.[61] It also galvanized him into action on behalf of Germany's Jews—perhaps, as some New Dealers suggested, to atone publicly for his Trafalgar Day speech.[62]

Both Britain and the United States had previously been slow to respond to the plight of the German and Austrian political refugees. Initially Chamberlain was reluctant to discuss the touchy refugee issue publicly because he, like Kennedy, feared "snapping the thread of personal access" between himself and the German chancellor. And Chamberlain and his fellow appeasers had remained aloof from the problem.[63] The silence of some like Chamberlain and Halifax[64] was the result of anti-Semitism, the "callous insensitivity" of much of Britain's ruling class; the silence of others was a matter of political expediency, merely the cost of doing business with Hitler.[65]

Chamberlain wrote to his sister Hilda on July 30, 1939: "I believe the persecution arose out of two motives, a desire to rob the Jews of their money and a jealousy of their superior cleverness. No doubt Jews aren't a loveable people; I don't care about them myself—but that is not sufficient to explain the pogrom."[66] And "Halifax had, as he put it confessed in a letter to a close friend many years later, 'always been rather anti-Semitic.' Although inexcusable, especially in a practicing Christian," his biographer Roberts writes, "it was an anti-Semitism of the relatively mild form common to a number of his social contemporaries.

The viciousness and bloodshed of Kristallnacht was symptomatic of an altogether different species of anti-Semitism, and Halifax was genuinely revolted by it."[67]

Roosevelt, too, shied away from the problem. Beyond speeches, severing diplomatic ties, and easing the restrictions on visitors' permits for German and Austrian refugees, he refused to go. FDR had commented to Kennedy: "If there was a demagogue around here of the type of Huey Long to take up anti-Semitism, there would be more blood running in the streets of New York than in Berlin."[68] The State Department, too, feared that efforts on behalf of the refugees in Austria and Germany might exacerbate the situation by creating a new refugee problem and reduce the chances of resettling Jews in other countries.[69] American Jewish leaders themselves opposed any increase in Jewish immigration; it could lead to an increase in anti-Semitic feelings in the United States, a fear Kennedy shared.[70] It was "a very delicate problem" in America, Kennedy told Halifax. Latent anti-Semitic feelings could be drawn out and lead to "Ku Klux Klan–type activities," the ambassador predicted.[71] Nevertheless, Roosevelt, stirred by the application of the anti-Jewish laws to Austrian Jews after the Anschluss, resolved to try to help the Jews. He proposed to establish a committee of representatives from countries in Europe and Latin America to aid Jewish emigration.[72]

As early as March 1938, soon after Kennedy arrived in London, Hull had asked him to see whether the British would be willing to cooperate in an international effort at relocation.[73] The Chamberlain government feared that such a scheme might backfire: "Too great a kindness to the refugees might inspire the dictator countries to be even more severe," Kennedy noted in his memoir, "because they could then more easily unload their responsibilities to their own minority populations upon the rest of the world."[74] Poland, for example, could simply toss its Jews out, thereby augmenting the problem and probably causing a tremendous Jewish outcry in the United States.[75] This would make the Jews' problems doubly difficult to resolve.

Nevertheless, Washington went ahead with its plans for a relief agency, and Roosevelt announced that Myron C. Taylor would be the American representative on the committee.[76] By August 1938, the Intergovernmental Committee on Political Refugees had opened its headquarters in London, and George Rublee, a seventy-year-old retired diplomat and respected Washington attorney, a man of French Huguenot descent, had been elected its first director.[77] Rublee's aim was to go to Germany to negotiate for massive Jewish emigration. "I soon found that there was not much interest in British government circles or generally in the diplomatic corps in my work," Rublee told an interviewer years later. Nor was Washington particularly receptive. The president seemed to go along with the idea of helping the Jews because he believed that some action was appropriate, but he had little faith in its success. Roosevelt was essentially making empty gestures. "I felt that the lack of active support made my chances of success very difficult. It was an uphill job—I saw that," Rublee recalled.[78] Kennedy acted as a liaison between Washington and Downing Street and helped organize the first international refugee conference, at which he served as vice-chairman.[79] Despite Kennedy's reservations about the success of the mission, he promised the refugee committee "every assistance."[80]

Rublee asked Kennedy to help him win over the reluctant British. But Kennedy refused to lend more than moral support to Rublee's efforts. During the tense weeks of early September and the optimistic ones after Munich, Kennedy nicely but firmly staved off Rublee's pleas. Rublee told Welles that Kennedy was "personally sympathetic but he feels he cannot do anything." He was unwilling "to take a strong line" because he had "other matters he consider[ed] more important" and he believed "that our undertaking is hopeless."[81] Kennedy "did not seem interested and never gave me any real support or assistance," Rublee later recalled.[82]

The "other matters" were the negotiations over the Anglo-American Trade Agreement, in which the ambassador was deeply involved. No doubt he considered them to be of far greater importance than the refugee problem. Perhaps, too, Kennedy's cool response was triggered by his unwillingness to be upstaged. Ever since the summer of 1938, he had planned a visit to Germany and frequently discussed it with the German ambassador.[83] In the fall, he had again mentioned the issue to von Dirksen. Perhaps Kennedy refused to commit himself because he feared it might hinder Chamberlain's access to Hitler.[84] Or perhaps, as David Nasaw suggests, neither Kennedy, Chamberlain, nor Halifax, well aware of the geographical importance of the Middle East and of the support of Arab leaders, wanted to open the possibly sticky issue of Palestine's becoming a haven for Jews.[85]

Finally, on October 5, 1938, because of Rublee's prodding, the president personally intervened and directed Kennedy to convey to Chamberlain orally a message asking him to discuss the refugee problem with Hitler:

> I fully share your hope and belief that there exists today the greatest opportunity in years for the establishment of a new order based on justice and on law. Now that you have established a personal contact with Chancellor Hitler I know that you will be taking up with him from time to time many of the problems which must be resolved in order to bring about that new and better order. Among these is the present German policy of racial persecution.[86]

Kennedy wrote in his memoir: "Due to Chamberlain's preoccupation with debate on Munich in the House of Commons, I was unable to deliver the President's message personally to him, but I delivered it in writing to him and orally to Halifax."[87] Roosevelt asked Chamberlain to urge the German government to adopt a more lenient attitude toward Jewish refugees and to permit their orderly emigration. He suggested that they be allowed to take some of their property with them to make them more welcome to those countries who might accept them.[88] Two days later, Chamberlain agreed to Roosevelt's requests. He responded to Roosevelt: "I hope as you do that it will prove possible to persuade the German Government to make a practical contribution to the solution of the problem and I warmly welcome your suggestion that the first suitable opportunity should be taken of urging them to do so."[89]

Initially the British had been "very coy,"[90] Kennedy recalled, but then he learned, in strictest confidence from Halifax, who wanted to prevent an anti-Semitic outcry in the country, that they had been allowing seventy-five Jews a day into England without fanfare and publicity, nearly as many as the Americans permitted under their quotas.[91] Except for these few refugees, the British had not resettled any Jews in their empire.[92]

As the process lumbered on, going nowhere, Rublee became depressed over the inconsequential gestures made by the British, Roosevelt, and Kennedy, and with good reason.[93] Rublee could get neither the support of Kennedy nor that of the Foreign Office for his proposed trip to Germany on behalf of the refugees. As a guest of the ambassador's and seated at his table at a dinner party for the American Committee in London on October 13, Rublee reminded Kennedy of his promise to help him if he was in a "jam." "Well," Rublee told him, "I am in a 'jam' and I wish you would help me." Kennedy promised to speak to Chamberlain and Halifax, but he also told Rublee that he had spoken to the German ambassador earlier that day and he had informed him that "Hitler was not quite 'right' for this matter yet."[94] Even Kennedy became "disturbed and indignant" over the process. Restrictive legislation had actually increased, negotiations with Germany had not begun, and a mass of bureaucratic red tape allowed thirty-two nations to dodge their responsibilities hypocritically. Kennedy thought the problem essentially a simple one. His prescription was to find a "reasonably good area" for resettlement in the world and challenge Jews and Gentiles who were "touched in their pocketbooks . . . and in spirit" to fund fifty to a hundred million dollars to finance the emigration of Jewish refugees to that area.[95]

But no amount of red-tape cutting or personal intervention by Rublee, Roosevelt, Chamberlain, or Kennedy could save the German Jews. It was not until the universal uproar following the Nazi pogrom of November 9–10 that Chamberlain and Kennedy were finally spurred into action. Both prime minister and ambassador felt that the strained atmosphere left little likelihood of the immediate resumption of conversations between Britain and Germany over the appeasement program and issues like armaments and colonies.[96] An immediate solution had to be found. Thus Kennedy became a staunch advocate for a massive resettlement of Germany's Jews and met in a series of meetings after the pogrom with British officials—MacDonald, Halifax, Cadogan, and of course Chamberlain—to urge[97] the British "to do something . . . quickly" for Rublee's committee.[98] Rublee reported to Hull that for the first time since his arrival, British officialdom was realizing that "the mistreatment by Germany of a half-million oppressed people is a definite obstacle to general appeasement in Europe."[99]

Over lunch at Malcolm MacDonald's cottage in Essex on Sunday, November 13, 1938, the ambassador, his wife, and two other guests discussed the refugee problem in Germany and in Palestine. Kennedy gave the young dominion and colonial secretary a good "fight talk"[100] and asked point-blank

why England, which had all the land, did not show more interest in Intergovernmental relief. . . . [If the British would only do so] Rublee would have something to go on . . . then the problem of raising the money to get the refugees out would be secondary to having a place to put them.

. . . It looked to me like everyone was feeling sorry for the Jews but that nobody was offering any solution.[101]

Perhaps spurred by Kennedy's prodding, Chamberlain told the House of Commons on Tuesday, November 15, that there was a "deep and widespread sympathy here for those who are being made to suffer" and informed the MPs that an intergovernmental committee was discussing the possibility of resettling the refugees in Britain's colonial empire.[102] That same day the Commons scheduled a debate on the Labour Party's motion:

> That this House notes with profound concern the deplorable treatment suffered by certain racial, religious and political minorities in Europe, and, in view of the growing gravity of the refugee problem, would welcome an immediate and concerted effort amongst the nations, including the United States of America, to secure a common policy.[103]

At a dinner party that evening hosted by the king and queen at Buckingham Palace for King Carol II of Romania, a great-grandson of Queen Victoria, Kennedy had a long conversation with Chamberlain and urged "speed to get some place." Chamberlain told him that he had been informed by Halifax and MacDonald about Kennedy's proposal for the resettlement of the Jews and that he expected to do something.[104]

Kennedy called on Halifax at the Foreign Office the next day, who relayed the substance of their conversation to Lindsay. Kennedy warned Halifax, "by no very logical process," that the American government was growing "generally less sympathetic to His Majesty's Government" and emphasized the necessity of countering this opinion. Kennedy suggested that the British tell the United States government that they were prepared to make land available and provide financial support for the Jews.[105] Halifax could hardly contain his outrage, especially since the Americans were firmly refusing to let any more Jews in. He told Kennedy that he was "at a complete loss to understand by what process American opinion could properly blame us because the German Government chose to persecute Jews." Halifax hoped that Kennedy would persuade the United States to take a "more sensible line" on the matter.

Angered by American pressure and especially Kennedy's, the cabinet asked Halifax whether the American government would permit German Jews to come in under the unused portion of the quota of 60,000 British.[106] Halifax reassured Kennedy that the British government was diligently working on a resettlement scheme.[107] If it could be arranged, Kennedy said, it would have an immense "psychological effect" upon the situation. Kennedy also told him that Bernard Baruch had predicted that the American Jews could raise a hundred million dollars if an area for the resettlement of the refugees could be agreed upon. Anthony de Rothschild had predicted that English Jews would also make a major contribution to the enterprise, Kennedy said.[108]

"Things are moving,"[109] and "you can stop worrying about where to put the refugees now,"

Kennedy reported, despite all the obstacles. "That problem will be solved."[110] Word leaked out of a daring and simple plan of action devised by Kennedy, Chamberlain, Halifax, and MacDonald. Dubbed the "Kennedy Plan," its object was to rescue 700,000 German Jews and resettle them in sparsely populated areas in Africa and South America.[111] It was enormous in scope and called for generous financial contributions from private and public sources in the United States and Britain. This was pay-up or shut-up time. Now we will see, Kennedy said, if moral indignation can be transformed into ready cash. "The baby is tossed right into the laps of the people themselves for the real concern now is money," wrote Joe Jr.[112] An even greater Kennedy worry was that the outcry over the treatment of the Jews could stampede the United States into war. If people "can be roused to fever heat on this question, there doesn't seem to be much possibility of keeping them out of war," he said.[113] Regardless, the ambassador felt that he had done his bit.[114] He caustically remarked: "Now we will see how sorry the world is for them. It's a case of getting money now."[115]

Kennedy was given the credit for convincing the British to support the relief effort.[116] "Everyone thinks that it was largely due to his efforts that this gesture has been made," Joe Jr. proudly wrote, and credited his father for nudging MacDonald into action on behalf of Anglo-American friendship.[117] "It was Mr. Kennedy who started the ball rolling," said one impressed diplomat,[118] and Mr. Kennedy who convinced the British to seek colonial areas for resettlement of refugees in places like Kenya, British Guiana, Nyasaland, Northern Rhodesia, and Tanganyika.[119] One astonished newsman wrote, "What Mr. Kennedy has managed to do in the past fortnight is the talk of diplomatic circles in London at the moment." The British might have continued doing nothing if Joe Kennedy had not brought "all his energy and persuasiveness to bear." When one diplomat heard that the government was acting on behalf of the refugees, he said in amazement, "That man has Chamberlain eating out of his hand."[120] "Kennedy is rated the most influential U.S. Ambassador to England in many years," claimed *Life.* "If his plan for settling the German Jews, already widely known as the 'Kennedy Plan,' succeeds, it will add new luster to a reputation that may well carry Joseph Patrick Kennedy into the White House."[121] The *New York Times* attributed Chamberlain's change of heart and his newfound desire to do something "practical and generous" for Germany's Jews to his belief that "it brings [the British] good-will from across the Atlantic." Nothing improves Anglo-American relations like "a burning moral issue on which both nations think alike."[122]

Tony Biddle, the American ambassador in Poland, praised Kennedy's efforts and offered a warning. Your awareness of the rapidly growing Jewish problem as a global one and your attempts to improve it are "a grand piece of work—humane and timely," he wrote from Warsaw. Stationed in Poland, Biddle would know:

> I am afforded ample opportunity, as you may well imagine, to gain an insight to many aspects
> of what is fast becoming a tragedy. Recent pagan outrages in Germany against the unfortunate
> Jews are lamentable enough in themselves but the potential repercussions therefrom, which

I now discern in the making in eastern and central European states presage a turn from bad to worse.

Biddle feared that other states in eastern and central Europe like Poland, a country already "unhappy" with her own Jewish population and that feared becoming a "dumping ground" or a "hospitable retreat" from persecution in Germany as well as in Hungary and Romania, would "take a leaf out of Germany's book" and enact anti-Semitic legislation. His worry was not unfounded. He further warned that the Jews in eastern and central Europe and particularly the Zionists feared that Jewish emigration to other countries before the establishment of a Palestinian state might lead the British to postpone indefinitely the creation of a Jewish national home in Palestine.

Despite the widespread credit and publicity that Kennedy received from the press for the "Kennedy Plan," and Biddle's cable to Washington warning that other countries could enact anti-Semitic legislation in addition to Germany,[123] Washington officials played dumb and claimed no knowledge of the ambassador's scheme. Welles told Ambassador Lindsay that the government had sent no instructions to Kennedy, nor authorized him to present any proposal, nor been informed of any conversations the ambassador had had with Halifax over the refugee issue. The only agency that had any authority to deal with the refugees, Welles said, was the Intergovernmental Committee for Refugees, on which both Britain and the United States had representation.[124] Moffat wrote in his diary on November 16, 1938: "There seems no doubt that Mr. Kennedy is negotiating on his own with the British government, but he has never so much as reported a word to the President, the Secretary, or Mr. Rublee."[125] The next day, November 17, Moffat again recorded: "We are still in the dark as to what Kennedy is doing in London on refugees."[126] The State Department "got kind of peeved" and wired him "to find out what the hell was going on," Joe Jr. remembered. Kennedy maintained that all he was doing was urging prompt action.[127] Perhaps as a slap in Kennedy's face and a reminder to him to mind his own business, the president announced that henceforth Myron Taylor would be the U.S. government spokesman for the refugee situation,[128] a matter that Welles had emphasized in his conversation with Lindsay that day.[129]

The massive publicity surrounding Kennedy's refugee program, much of it planted by him, had a decidedly negative diplomatic impact. It was customary to share credit with others graciously and to claim to be acting on behalf of the American government. Kennedy angered many diplomats by his failure to do so. Moffat himself, usually a Kennedy fan, criticized his unrelenting pushiness and his grasping for publicity. The ambassador claimed so much credit for work done by Rublee and Taylor and their colleagues that it was hard for them to be polite about him.[130] Clearly this was a man unsuited to the traditional diplomatic role: As in his conversations with von Dirksen, he carried out his own diplomatic initiatives, not his government's; failed to inform his government of his actions; sought constant aggrandizement in the press; and acted on behalf of his interests, not the country's. The same Kennedy who refused to give the baseball to the team captain so many years ago.

Despite the fanfare and optimism, the "Kennedy Plan" was never implemented. It was little more than a haphazard response to a widespread demand for action. Of the thirty-two governments who sent representatives to Evian in July 1938 for the founding of the Intergovernmental Committee for Political Refugees, "it was plain," Kennedy later wrote in his memoirs, "that most of them, including us, were afraid of acquiring a minority problem of their own."[131] The Department of State saw little hope for increasing the quotas in the immigration laws.[132] Latin America, which had the best potential for receiving émigrés, actually increased its restrictions as the persecution continued. The French refused to open their colonies to anyone of German origins, the Dutch offered to settle one hundred families in Surinam, and the British dragged their feet. They wanted the Foreign Office, not the Intergovernmental Committee, to negotiate with Germany, and opposed Rublee's efforts to negotiate.[133] Britain was quietly permitting a few Jews to enter the country, as was the United States.[134] The only bright spots, Kennedy wrote, were Australia, which committed itself to taking in five thousand in the coming year, and the Philippines, which offered to take one thousand for several years, to increase the population of Mindanao.[135] Kennedy was impatient over the snail's pace and blamed the Jews in America for it. "The answer still seemed essentially simple," he wrote, years later after the war in his memoir: If overcoming the plight of the Jews were not always connected to Palestine, especially by American Jews, progress could be rapidly made, if funding could be found.[136] But of course the plight of the Jews was connected to Palestine, a very complicated issue. Halifax thought it would take an archangel to bring order to this chaos. The Arabs argued that they would only accept an Arab state or a partition presided over by the Arabs, the Jews, and the British. This prospect made him ill, Halifax said.[137]

The real coordinator was not the publicity-seeking ambassador, but the behind-the-scenes worker, Rublee. In early 1939, he went to Germany and painstakingly negotiated an agreement for the emigration of thousands of Jews, virtually all of whom were to be evacuated in five years. Germans like Hermann Göring, the head of Hitler's air force, who supported the Rublee committee, wanted to encourage emigration because it would speed up "the Aryanization of the economy" and possibly even strengthen Germany's export trade,[138] a policy that paralleled Kennedy's "Plan" for immigration. The German government would confiscate the Jews' property but agreed to pay their way to the border. After Rublee returned to London, Kennedy called to congratulate him. The ambassador was amazed. "How could it have happened? Why hadn't they done something like this before if they were willing to do such things?" "He thought it was very extraordinary," Rublee recalled.[139]

But then World War II erupted and Europe's Jews were stranded. The plan to evacuate the refugees became one of history's might-have-beens as Hitler imposed his own horrific plan, his final solution, and murdered six million Jews.

Commenting on the program, Rublee said, "I have no indication that the Germans are reluctant to talk." In fact, some Nazi officials had given serious consideration to the problem and had drawn up a list of proposals for discussion. "It is apparent to me, however, that the

British are reluctant to have me talk with the Germans."[140] Rublee accused the British Foreign Office of trying to "smother" the committee's efforts."[141]

But Rublee did not believe that anti-Semitism among Britain's political elite had hindered the program to evacuate the Jews.[142] Nor, perhaps, had anti-Semitism been a factor in Kennedy's motivation. One unnamed British negotiator said, "Kennedy was not anti-Semitic. . . . Nor, for that matter was he pro-Semitic, except when it suited his purposes. I imagine there was a bit of the cynic in Joe."[143]

Despite his probable sympathy for Germany's Jews and his undocumented (or rumored) efforts at working behind the scenes in helping many escape,[144] the ambassador faced considerable criticism from Jewish circles for his supposed indifference to the refugee program, for his defense of appeasement, and his alleged anti-Semitism. He told T. J. White that "75% of the attacks made on me" over the recent Trafalgar Day speech were by Jews; "yet I don't suppose anybody has worked as hard for them as I have or more to their advantage."[145] Just before Kennedy's return to the United States, a particularly revealing letter written on December 10, 1938, by Joe Jr., who so accurately echoed his father's views, described the ambassador's resentment of the Jews, especially toward the Jewish columnists in the United States. "With all the work he has done he is indignant that some papers have 'kicked his head off'" and erroneously claimed that Washington had to push him to get him to act on their behalf. Kennedy planned to give the Jewish journalists "a few blasts" for their "pile of lies" about him when he returned home.[146] Nasaw writes that Kennedy "had become the victim of his own prejudice. The more he exaggerated the extent of the Jews' political and media power, the more he worried about the future."[147]

Although Kennedy's true feelings about the Jews are hard to determine, he always resented his lifelong reputation for anti-Semitism.[148] He was genuinely shocked at the Nazi persecution of the Jews and was a frequent critic of the Nazi regime. It was "hostile to law, family life, even to religion itself," he remarked.[149] In an interview in 1944 with Joseph Dinneen, a correspondent from the *Boston Globe*, the former ambassador denied being an anti-Semite or a hypocrite, although he admitted disliking particular Jews. Kennedy accused them of being too sensitive to criticism and too apt to label critics as anti-Semites.[150] Many of his friends and business associates, he told a *Newsweek* interviewer years later, were Jews, and he belonged to a Jewish golf club in Palm Beach. "Pretty good for a guy who's supposed to be anti-Semitic, no?"[151] Nevertheless, his prejudices reflected the usual cultural biases of the time, and he habitually used epithets like "kike," "wop," and "mick."[152] Goodwin has an excellent analysis of Kennedy's social anti-Semitism. She writes that Kennedy "embodied many of the traits traditionally associated with the Jews. . . . As a 'money man' himself . . . he [could not] have seriously entertained the image of a vast international Jewish conspiracy dominating the financial world. It seems more likely that the roots of Kennedy's attitude toward the Jews lay in the social sphere. . . . For a man who had been held back all his life in this very sphere, Kennedy was not about to give up his own sense of possession and preeminence to yet another ethnic group."[153]

Jewish voices were not the only ones critical of Kennedy and his diplomacy; so were American liberals and Washington columnists known for being in the pocket of the administration. They greatly annoyed him by escalating their attacks on him and moving from mere sniping to vicious assaults after his Trafalgar Day speech and throughout the remaining months of 1938.[154] Not only did Kennedy's critics indict him for being pro-fascist in echoing Chamberlain's appeasement line, but they also judged him harshly for his social connections with the Cliveden Set. Administration liberals bruited it about that upon Kennedy's return to the United States, FDR would call him on the carpet for his advocacy of Chamberlain's policies and for becoming an intriguer treacherously scheming to seize either the presidential or vice-presidential nomination for himself in 1940. His critics found a most agreeable and receptive audience in Ickes and Morgenthau, who loved to stir up trouble between Kennedy and the president and delighted in the creation of this new negative image of the American ambassador.[155]

Ickes, a liberal, did not doubt the accusation that Chamberlain and the Cliveden Set catered to fascists and Nazis, a charge Lady Astor indignantly dismissed as "hog wash."[156] Since Kennedy was frequently on their guest list and shared many of their views, he was tagged with their reputation and regarded as their pawn.[157] The Cliveden Set was a loose assortment of Oxford dons, ambassadors and diplomats, men of letters, and society matrons; its reputation was as a monolithic pro-appeasement "second Foreign Office" known for cozying up to Hitler.[158] Kennedy met Lord Lothian, an intimate of the Cliveden Set, aboard the *Queen Mary* in early February 1939 as he and his son Jack were returning to England. An American foreign correspondent, Louis Fischer, an avid supporter of Republican Spain, was also on board. He noted that he and Lothian had "one good talk" in which they discussed the international situation and "wrangled about Spain." When Fischer told Lothian that he had just traveled the United States on a lecturing tour and found that most people were opposed to Chamberlain and appeasement, Lothian, perhaps feeling more than a bit defensive, said that he too had just crossed the United States and that the only people who disagreed with Chamberlain and his policies were "radicals, Jews and lecturers." "There must be millions of lecturers in America," Fischer wrote. He also disapprovingly recorded in his notebook that the outspoken ambassador and the disappointed appeaser, soon to be named the British ambassador to the United States, "spent much time together." Numerous associations like this stamped Kennedy with a new, unflattering image as a die-hard appeaser.[159]

In the White House, too, Roosevelt intimates gloated over how "terribly peeved with Joe" the president understandably was. Farley confidentially predicted to Morgenthau that Kennedy's next visit would "probably be the beginning of the end."[160] Furthermore, the "Palace Janissaries," liberals who opposed Morgenthau and Kennedy, had been spreading rumors again that Kennedy was about to retire from London and to succeed Morgenthau as secretary of the treasury, a position Kennedy still badly wanted.[161]

Criticism by Jewish columnists and liberal anti-appeasers the ambassador could shrug off, but not the accusations that he had lost favor with Roosevelt or that he was out of touch with American opinion. Kennedy had become concerned about the pro-war feeling in the United States and the American criticism of Chamberlain as "weak," "deluded," and a Nazi sympathizer. He was also worried about the rejection of Lindbergh's "acute observations" on the strength of the German air force. "I wanted no part of the European war then in the making," Kennedy wrote in his memoirs.[162]

Only by returning to the United States to confer with the president and to assess the country's mood for himself could he rediscover its viewpoint and assure himself that he was living up to his own standard of reflecting American opinion.[163] He told Lindbergh: "I am a little dizzy watching the present international situation and want to get to the United States to see what's happening there. . . . I am a little uncertain as to just where America is heading. Hence the trip," he wrote in a despondent mood on December 8, 1938, just a few days before setting sail.[164] As he boarded the *Queen Mary* on December 10, he assured the newsmen: "This is not a one-way trip. I never stay anywhere too long, but I am definitely coming back around February 1. . . . I am just going home to rest and do some thinking about America."[165]

The ever loyal Arthur Krock wrote that the ambassador was coming home to an "atmosphere of open attack and unfriendly gossip from the New Deal inner circle." Kennedy had been accused of being Chamberlain's "pawn," a "captive" of the Anglo-German Cliveden Set, a "sympathizer with the dictatorships," and a "public critic" of Roosevelt and his policies. Krock disputed the charges and praised Kennedy for his ambassadorial role. The New Dealers' anti-Kennedy campaign was a "great injustice" to Kennedy, Krock wrote, as he further noted that the Washington press opened fire after "unwise and well-wishing friends" began to engineer a "Presidential 'boom' for Mr. Kennedy." Krock said that he had closely observed Kennedy's work in London and believed "that these attacks and the stories do a great injustice to Mr. Kennedy." Krock also praised him for accomplishing his goals: "to render frequent and accurate reports, to achieve popularity and confidence at his post; to serve primarily his country's interest; to be watchful of blunders and indiscretions; and to conduct certain negotiations. All these Mr. Kennedy has done."[166]

Certainly White House devotees David Niles and Felix Frankfurter and liberals like Tom Corcoran, all part of Roosevelt's "Brain Trust," were adamantly anti-Kennedy.[167] Corcoran got "really violent" in his conversation with Morgenthau about Joe Kennedy and Arthur Krock. "Krock was running a campaign to put Joe Kennedy over for President; . . . if any prominent Catholic gets in the way, he's to be rubbed out. . . . Krock is the Number One Poison at the White House," Corcoran told Morgenthau.[168]

Kennedy's arrival in New York on December 15 was quite in contrast to the gala that had attended his homecoming of the previous spring. Reporters interviewed a gloomy Kennedy in his crowded suite on board the *Queen Mary*. It was no longer the same gay, wisecracking Joe Kennedy. A newsman's referring to him as "Your Excellency" produced one of the infrequent grins during the conversation. He frankly but somberly answered questions for nearly an hour and discussed Europe's situation and the pessimistic prospects for peace.[169] To reporters who asked him about "pro-German sentiment in England," Kennedy responded that England had never been "very favorable to Germany." To questions about his connection with the Cliveden Set, Kennedy responded, "I don't know what it is. It has not been my experience to meet any one who is pro-German." Asked his opinion of the Munich Agreement, Kennedy explained that Europe faced two alternatives at that time—chaos and war. "And if there is any way of doing better than either of those, then it is worth trying." "With me," the ambassador continued, "it is not a question of the strategy of the Munich Agreement. I am pro-peace. I pray, hope and work for peace." Although the prime minister's appeasement policy had not yielded the hoped-for results, Kennedy conceded, he still had no thought of abandoning it; it was still the surest way of maintaining peace and therefore safeguarding the position of the United States. Regardless of the outcome of the present European crisis, the ambassador said that he believed more than ever that the "United States should steer its course clear of European trouble" but increase its navy and army rearmament program as well. Roosevelt was "doing everything he can and he is admired for it abroad." A reporter kidded Kennedy about two of his previous predictions—that there would be no war and that the stock market would rise. Kennedy replied: "I had a couple of bad days with those predictions on my mind and I am going out of the prophecy business. . . . I'll still stand by both until the end of the year." But, he said, "on December 31, I am retiring from the prophet field."[170]

Newspaper columnists had reported that a substantial rift had developed between the president and his ambassador. Repeatedly, Kennedy "has bucked both the State Department and Mr. Roosevelt who is, of course, the State Department," wrote Boake Carter of the *Boston Globe*. The president has frequently either ignored or contradicted his ambassador's advice. "Kennedy has told Chamberlain one thing, only to have Mr. Roosevelt make a complete fool of the American Ambassador in London by himself announcing a different policy." An irate Kennedy, expressing his dissatisfaction in "language that he [Mr. Roosevelt] does not care to hear," Carter reported, plans on saying to the president, "Put up or shut up, but either way quit making a sucker out of me." But some of Kennedy's friends convinced him to calm down. "Mr. Roosevelt is slicker than you," they warned him. "He'll twist whatever you say and make himself appear with the credit and you with the discredit."[171]

Apparently Kennedy took their advice, swallowed his pride, and dutifully reported to Roosevelt. There seemed to be no hint of discord in their two-hour conversation on December 17. Kennedy followed his custom of reviewing the numerous irritants about his job and recited a litany of complaints: the White House was bypassing him—refusing to consult with him on the arrangements for the king and queen to visit the United States and on the negotiations over the trade agreement; FDR was undermining him by pursuing private contacts and letters, especially with Harold Laski, whom Kennedy quite opposed, particularly in the light of the "Jewish question." "I told him again that I was willing to step out any time that he wanted me to," Kennedy wrote in his memoirs, "but he insisted that I must stay." The rumors about him that members of Roosevelt's inner circle fed to the press were "of little importance to our relationship," as "Roosevelt dismissed the whole business with assurances of confidence in my objectives and my work."[172]

As they surveyed the "steady deterioration" of the European scene, Kennedy reported that there was a distinct possibility of war within the next few months. They spoke of the status of the Jews and the necessity of financial support by American Jews, of Chamberlain's hope that the United States would aid China, of Roosevelt's plans for saber-rattling, and of the difficulty of maintaining democratic institutions in the Western Hemisphere.[173]

Letting slip "a trace of impatience" about the prime minister's policy of watchful vigilance of Hitler, the president informed Kennedy of his intention to repeal the Neutrality Act, a move helpful to Britain and France, and to urge American rearmament, a program Kennedy supported, particularly in the air. It was the surest way of preventing American involvement in any European conflict, he believed. He offered to lend his help to "means . . . short of war" by meeting with Thomas Lamont, a Morgan banker, to gain the goodwill of business and banking interests toward Roosevelt's plan.[174] As Kennedy left the White House after the meeting that failed to live up to its spectacular billing by newsmen, he denied rumors that he would resign and that he had been summoned home by the president. Apparently neither had been anxious for a showdown. The ambassador told reporters that he had every intention of returning to London in February, unless there were some crises before then.[175]

Kennedy left Washington and flew to his sumptuous home on North Ocean Boulevard in Palm Beach for a six-week vacation with his son Jack.[176] Kennedy spent the days sunning himself; entertaining neighbors, including Colonel Robert McCormick of the *Chicago Tribune*; and talking on his poolside telephone with friends and journalists up and down the country. Kennedy gave Walter Winchell the "lowdown" on Lindbergh's report to Chamberlain about the strength of the German air force and took credit for bringing Lindbergh and Chamberlain together during the height of the Munich crisis. Kennedy's opponents now had further fuel for their criticism of him.[177] But Kennedy saw no reason to discontinue his support of Chamberlain and he found no widespread opposition to Chamberlain's policies. The people Kennedy spoke to also convinced him that his country was 100 percent behind a policy of isolation. Thus he was reassured and saw no reason to change or apologize for his views so thoroughly compatible with his countrymen's but no longer widely shared by Washington's policymakers; he was a diplomat with a new negative image and his influence was on the wane.[178]

As Roosevelt came to believe that appeasement was untenable and began to work toward a more active foreign policy for the United States after the Munich Pact, the differences between him and his ambassador became all too glaring. They realized they were working in opposition to each other. Kennedy later recalled the president's private sarcastic statement that "he [Roosevelt] would be a bitter isolationist, help with arms and money, and later, depending on the state of affairs, get in." "I'm very leery," Kennedy wrote in his diary. But while the president began to urge "methods short of war" and to regard intervention as a remote but real alternative, Kennedy's view was firm: Keep the United States out of any conflict abroad and cut American obligation in international affairs to nothing (or to zero).[179]

In his State of the Union message on January 4, 1939, the president spoke about "methods short of war" and suggested revising the Neutrality Act to allow European democracies access to American arms, ammunition, and implements of war, and strengthening national and hemispheric defense, particularly in airpower. On January 5, 1939, in his annual budget message to Congress, he asked for a whopping 1.3 billion dollars for defense and, a few days later, for an additional half a billion dollars, primarily for 5,500 planes for the army and 3,000 for the navy.[180] His design was to prevent war by calling for the greatest peacetime array of armed might in response to the dictator's challenge to peace.[181]

The Munich crisis also convinced Kennedy that the United States must rearm. So, he supported Roosevelt's drive for rearmament as well as the revision of the Neutrality Act and argued that the United States should become a beacon of tranquility and affluence in the West.[182] He tended to see Europe as "a kind of Miltonian Hell, inhabited by selfish politicians, fighting eternally for petty objects," and denied that any thread bound the United States to any other country. Thus he resisted any treaty with any nation, however short-lived, even though intended to stave off the war he so deeply feared, and he urged a circumspect role for the president, limited to offering advice and issuing vague statements, all in the hope of dodging the consequences of a conflict in Europe. He desperately wanted peace, but failed to see how the United States could add to the effort to achieve it, and advocated surrendering its shaping to other powers.[183]

A couple of days after his December meeting with the president, Kennedy gave him a gloomy memo with the earth-shaking title: "What would be the effect on the United States of the decline or collapse of the British Empire?"[184] Joe Jr. noted that his father wanted to have a study done to establish what would happen to the United States politically and economically if the empire were destroyed. "If we could possibly exist without them [the British] I think Dad would speak against us being drawn into a war."[185] Indeed he did, arguing from the memo's premises.

At Kennedy's instigation, Maurice Hankey, the recently retired secretary of the British cabinet who had served it for twenty years, examined the advantages of Britain's naval hegemony in a nine-page memo, and discussed the effects of the empire's collapse. He also analyzed three likely ways for the United States to respond. All had the advantage of allowing the United States to pursue a passive policy of isolationism and virtual pacifism and, when necessary, acquiescence to the totalitarian powers.[186] The memo concluded by urging the United States to establish a new world order. It asked "whether one of those rare moments is now at hand when prudence, foresight and self-interest combine in rendering action desirable which may change the history of mankind."[187]

Britain's control of the seas in the nineteenth century allowed freedom and democracy to flourish and kept the peace for more than a century, Hankey wrote. Until 1914 Britain's shield of naval supremacy and the growth of British liberalism had also allowed for the greatest expansion of freedom in history throughout the non-European and non-Asiatic worlds. Britain's sea power also provided the first line of defense for North and South America, which allowed them to develop internally without focusing on international affairs or war. Britain's naval supremacy was complemented by Europe's balance of power and the absence of any one country's domination of the Continent and had been reinforced by the United States in World War I. This defense system was currently being undermined by Germany's domination of central Europe, by Japan's threat to Britain in the Far East and to Singapore, and by airpower.

Hankey painted a bleak picture of the defeated empire. The victors—Germany, Italy, and Japan—would seize the British Navy, its naval and aerial bases, and cost Britain control of the seas. The British and French colonies in Africa and South America, valuable for economic and strategic purposes and for emigration, would be confiscated by Germany and Italy, included within their "Zollverein," and thereby give the conquerors naval and aerial hegemony in the Atlantic. This would jeopardize the enforcement of the Monroe Doctrine and threaten the security of the Western Hemisphere. Japan's occupation of Singapore would give Japan hegemony in the Indian Ocean and domination of Australia and New Zealand. Therefore, in the interests of the Monroe Doctrine and America's defense, the memo urged, the United States should expand its own sphere of influence by taking over British and French territories in Western Africa and the Pacific as well as French and British Guiana, by seizing aerial and naval bases in the Atlantic and the British West Indies, and by strategic spending on arms.

The memo outlined three choices for the United States if the British Empire did collapse. The United States could return to the Wilsonian thesis and "make the world safe for democracy," as it had done in 1914 by overthrowing the totalitarian nations militarily or by propaganda, by lowering tariffs, and by supporting the democratic control of the seas. Or it could stand by, quietly observing while the dictators gobble up Europe and Asia, and dominate the high seas and build a fortress around North America by occupying all strategic positions a thousand miles from her shores. Or the United States could create a "voluntary federation," or spheres of influence by the great powers designed to guarantee peace and security. These would include "the Monroe system, the Franco-British system, the Germanic system, Russia, and the Japanese-Chinese system." Economic and military advantages could develop from the relatively self-supporting federation—"long overdue," according to Hankey. A system of barter and free trade could be arranged among the members of the federation for essential resources unavailable in a particular sphere and necessary to a decent and peaceful standard of living. Inexpensive military collaboration among the democracies would also be necessary to make an attack on them impracticable. Such an arrangement would enable the world to "settle down," Hankey predicted, and enjoy a long period of peace and stability similar to that of the nineteenth century, and allow "the forces of freedom everywhere" to grow once again. The creation of the voluntary federation, the memo argued, would require the leadership of the United States, the only country strong enough for the task. "Whichever way we look the future of the world rests with the United States." It must become the guarantor of the democratic states or become a vestige of the past, engulfed in a hostile, totalitarian world, "the last really independent democratic state in the world—with what results on her internal condition none can predict," Hankey concluded.[188] Echoing Hankey's report, Kennedy wrote in his memoir: "Our concern should be primarily our continent and the support without resort to war of those who share the democratic idea."[189]

Each position allowed the United States to maintain its stance of isolation and avoid war and, at the same time, prepare for any emergency by rearming. But, in fact, following Kennedy's advice by withdrawing from global affairs, adopting a "live and let live" approach, urging the democracies "to attend to their own knitting,"[190] as Kennedy described it, and refusing to pursue a more active foreign policy merely allowed other countries to shape the future. Ironically, it may well have increased the chances of the war Kennedy so greatly feared.[191] William W. Kaufmann, a diplomatic historian, aptly described Kennedy's attitude.

> [It] . . . was akin to that of the weather prophet. He saw clouds on the horizon and he correctly predicted rain; but he hoped that the storm would either dissipate itself, or blow off in another direction. . . . He was content to watch, pray, keep his distance, and urge the purchase of umbrellas.[192]

However, Roosevelt and his advisers wanted a foreign policy that did more than urge the purchase of umbrellas, and he simply ignored the suggestion of a new world order under American leadership. There is no evidence that he or the State Department, already angry with their ambassador over his self-appointed role in the Kennedy Plan, took the memo's arguments any more seriously than they had his scheme for the resettlement of the Jews—further proof of his diminishing influence and the irreparable breach developing between him and FDR.

But FDR did want Kennedy's help before Congress. Both Kennedy and Bullitt received a presidential summons to come before a secret session of the hesitant House and Senate Committee on Military Affairs on January 10, 1939. Kennedy remembered that both he and Bullitt had told much the same story: that war was likely by spring or early summer.[193] Kennedy made Lindbergh's report the basis of his argument that "without the power to resist, the mere will to resist was futile. "It is just leading with your chin," he told the committee, "and when and where England will draw the line where she must resist . . . I do not know nor do I believe that [the English] themselves know." Kennedy took credit for distributing Lindbergh's study of German airpower and also claimed that Hitler's threat to use his overwhelming superiority in airpower was the major factor in Britain's and France's decision to support Munich.[194] Kennedy told Congress that the German military machine was "formidable"[195] and estimated that Hitler's air forces included an armada of 9,500 to 10,000 planes.[196] Kennedy's major recommendation was to increase American armaments in the air.[197] The best way to protect America, whose security was not directly threatened, was to rearm and to make the Western Hemisphere a peaceful and prosperous fortress, the ambassador stated, echoing the Hankey memo. But be wary of Mussolini's ambitions to imitate Hitler and to acquire a choice morsel of France's empire—Tunisia or a German expansion into Ukraine—Kennedy warned Congress.[198] And be wary, Bullitt told the committee, of Hitler's desire to acquire the smaller and less powerful central European states and possibly the naval bases in the West Indies in the near future.[199] An eastward advance, presumably into the Ukraine, could give France and Britain time to build up their armaments and might even keep them from having to enter the war; "but the rash could break out anywhere," Kennedy said.[200] His prophecy was nearly correct, though he couldn't comprehend Hitler's short-term policy for the Soviet Union.

Leaked to the press, excerpts from the memo and distorted paraphrases ran from the ridiculous to the relatively correct. The attitude of the press "is of interest," Kennedy wrote in his memoirs. There were certain obvious facts that many Americans simply refused to listen to, he believed, and he criticized the *Louisville Times*, the *Springfield Republican*, and the *Denver Post* for rejecting Lindbergh's advice. Attacks were made on Lindbergh's credibility, questioning his authority and accusing him of, if not being in the pay of Nazi officials, certainly being pro-Nazi, Kennedy pointed out.[201] Some newspapers derided Kennedy's testimony by calling him Roosevelt's mouthpiece, shoring up votes in Congress for the rearmament program; others predicted that his pro-British stance and criticisms of the president would bring about his early retirement.[202]

British journalists criticized him too. Kennedy denied the *Daily Express*'s statement that he had told the committee that "Britain's policy of appeasement was so deep-rooted that she would permit Hitler to build a German air base in Canada rather than resort to war." Kennedy countered: "I never said anything that could possibly be interpreted in such a way.... I never said it and I never thought it."[203] But he did paint a gloomy picture of Europe and predicted a European war in six months.[204]

On February 11, at Roosevelt's request, the ambassador returned to Britain, cutting his vacation short by two weeks.[205] Foreign Office officials told Herschel Johnson at the embassy that Chamberlain was anxiously awaiting Kennedy's return. Things were happening so quickly that the prime minister said Kennedy's absence was "dangerous" and could put him out of touch with events.[206] FDR had hurriedly called his ambassador two days before he left, to request his speedy return. "I told [the] President I didn't want to go to London unless I had his confidence," Kennedy recorded in his diary. "I wasn't the kind to be any good unless I was on good terms." "[I told him] I had never made a public statement against him or his policies and what I said privately wasn't as bad as [what] I had said to him personally." The president once again reassured him and said "he knew the way I felt about him.... He said that he knew all that and not to worry—people just liked to make trouble."[207]

Kennedy dutifully returned to London by the *Queen Mary*. While he was deeply appreciative of Roosevelt's many favors and susceptible to his charm and flattery, he doubted the sincerity of the president's commitment to peace and disagreed with the direction of his foreign policy. Kennedy also loved his job; for a man who enjoyed being at the center of things, London was the spot to be. So, he scurried back to his post, looking for new opportunities to shape America's foreign policy, hoping to restore himself to the president's favor and, despite his reservations, trying to convince himself of Roosevelt's assurances about maintaining a policy of isolationism and avoiding war.

Others, however, had their own explanations. The *Boston Globe* charged that Roosevelt knew that Hitler intended to swallow Czechoslovakia and deliberately sent Kennedy back to "force [him] out under [a] cloud of discredit so he could substitute for him a White House marionette." Kennedy, realizing that he had been "sold out," said the *Globe*, decided to foil Roosevelt's plans by returning to London to prevent him from appointing another "robot"— an interesting but rather implausible explanation.[208] Another theory was that the president had tried to get Kennedy out of London by offering him the post of secretary of commerce, but that Kennedy had refused it.[209]

Actually, Roosevelt decided to send him back to Britain because it was much safer than firing him. FDR was much too shrewd a politician to unmuzzle Kennedy and create a political monster by giving him an opportunity to criticize the foreign policy of the president publicly, especially if the president were to break precedent and run for a third term, as was rumored. Roosevelt might have to turn to Kennedy as a vice-presidential running mate to offset a possible Garner-Farley ticket. Not only would the ambassador's Catholicism counterbalance Farley's, but Kennedy's campaign would be well financed and especially attractive to conservatives.[210] Therefore, FDR's crafty strategy was to send Kennedy back to London and simply undercut his authority by going around him. Jimmy Roosevelt noted that "by 1939, Father knew that Kennedy had to go. But he did not want to make the change. He wanted it to evolve on its own."[211]

The ambassador was in a very "bullish" mood upon his return to London on February 17, Halifax noted.[212] Kennedy immediately made the rounds of British officials, making "even more generous use than usual of the American vernacular to emphasize his points."[213] Both Halifax and Chamberlain were "definitely encouraged, over the state of affairs, Kennedy told Washington, especially Chamberlain, who seemed so relaxed, healthy and "optimistic."[214] In general, although the prime minister did not ignore the fact that Hitler was "fanatical and impractical," Chamberlain saw no evidence of Hitler's moving toward the West or into the Ukraine. Hitler was in a quieter mood now because of Roosevelt's rearmament program and Chamberlain's own stiffer attitude toward him, Chamberlain said. His intention was to assume that he, Chamberlain, could do business with Hitler by taking him at his word and by going along with him; but at the same time—knowing full well that Hitler might not keep his word—Chamberlain would prepare the country for the future by rearming. He also believed that Hitler, not Mussolini, was the greater threat.[215] Oblivious to his own inconsistencies, Kennedy did at least catch a contradiction in Chamberlain's thinking: he told Hull that Chamberlain still hoped that appeasement could work out but at the same time also believed that Hitler was likely to cause a world war.

There was also greater political optimism for the prime minister. He "is stronger now than he has ever been,"[216] the ambassador cabled Washington. Even Churchill thought so too, and claimed credit for Chamberlain's success, of course. "The tide is running Chamberlain's way" right now, Churchill told Kennedy, because the prime minister is following Churchill's advice.[217]

Optimism prevailed among other British officials too. After talks with Hoare, Simon, and Lord Ernie Chatfield, along with Halifax, of course, and many others, on February 21 Kennedy cabled Washington that British officials were optimistic about peace. They "thoroughly believe England is on her way, that Germany will not attack, that conditions which forced them to do things last Fall that perhaps they would not have done" no longer prevail. Although they remain "distrustful of Hitler," they also "believe [that] chances for [an] explosion are small." Furthermore, the ambassador predicted, Britain would not declare war if Hitler attacked eastern Europe but would immediately if he moved westward.[218] However, Cadogan and some members of the Foreign Office were less optimistic.[219] And after dining with Chamberlain and talking with him for several hours on February 25, Kennedy cabled Washington that the upshot of their conversation was that Chamberlain still did not believe that war was imminent, despite all the evidence to the contrary.[220]

Chamberlain's assessment was so thoroughly contradicted by so many events and so much intelligence—the continuance of the Spanish Civil War, Germany's absorption of the Sudetenland, Germany's likely annexation of the remainder of Czechoslovakia, Germany's threat to Poland and the Ukraine, German influence in Hungary, Mussolini's threat to Tunisia, rumors that Germany would invade Holland[221]—"all of [it] grave and all of [it] alarming"—that Under Secretary of State Sumner Welles diplomatically inquired of Ambassador Lindsay whether there was "some explanation of Mr. Chamberlain's optimism." Lindsay said that the prime minister was "a remarkably unemotional, very logical, and very clear thinker who was reasoning out the situation on a basis of abstract logic perhaps rather than by taking into account the human elements involved and the mercurial factors with which he was dealing."[222] Lindsay also doubted whether the cabinet shared Chamberlain's reassurance about events, and knew that the Foreign Office most definitely did not. It was extremely apprehensive and tense; its views ran from one extreme to another from day to day.[223]

And yet nearly a week after his return on February 23, Kennedy cabled Hull that despite the optimistic attitude of many, "whichever way you look at it, the long-pull outlook is exceedingly dark for England." Although the English had made tremendous strides in defense preparations in the last six months, he said, they were still plainly worried. The "top-side" men in the government asked themselves nightly how much longer Hitler could economically afford to keep Germany at peace, he wrote, echoing the well-grounded fears he had expressed to FDR a few weeks earlier.[224] Kennedy's old bearish mood had returned: a world war was coming, he was certain about that; neither he nor anyone else could do anything to prevent it. It was Kennedy, not Chamberlain, who had it right.

The ambassador tried again. He sent FDR a rambling and repetitious eighteen-page memorandum, a "doomsday" memo[225] even more ardent than Hankey's December 1938 essay at persuading the president to adopt his isolationist views and urging him to construct an armed fortress to safeguard the United States. Kennedy's March 1939 memorandum examined the catastrophic consequences to American democracy if the British Empire were destroyed and if Britain lost her predominant position in Europe. The memo predicted that those consequences would lead inevitably to a totalitarian world, to an American form of fascism, and a policy of isolationism. Kennedy's memorandum was interesting because of its revelations about the psychology and political theories of the ambassador and his boss in the White House. But it, like the December 1938 Hankey memorandum, was met with the president's silence.

Kennedy argued that the military defeat of Britain and France, "the last bulwarks of democracy," would destroy liberalism both socially and economically and put their resources at the disposal of the authoritarian powers to be used against the United States. It would also alter the balance of world forces militarily, morally, and politically, to the great detriment of the United States, which would become a lonely, helpless hostage in a ghetto engulfed by a totalitarian world. The only recourse he could envision for the United States was a policy of extreme isolationism: build "an armed fence around North America by occupying all vital positions 1,000 miles from her shores" and construct a two-ocean navy and an air force to safeguard American interests behind its broad two "ocean moats."[226] Kennedy knew that such an undertaking would require enormous political risk and sacrifices by the American public, difficult for a popularly elected government to maintain, but he saw no viable alternative for preserving the country's independence.

He painted a gloomy picture if the United States remained isolationist and the fascist coalition were victorious in a global war. Three power bases could develop: the Rome-Berlin totalitarian Axis in Europe and Africa, Japan's domination in Asia and the Pacific, and a predominantly democratic group in the Western Hemisphere. The Soviet Union, always an imponderable, would "retire into splendid isolation" and look forward to ripe pickings in Europe and western China.

Kennedy's gloomy picture grew even gloomier: if Latin America fell to Axis control, there was only a fifty-fifty chance that America's democratic institutions would survive; if the American fleet were destroyed by a two-front attack, the independence of some parts of the United States would be in serious jeopardy; if she lost her role as the upholder of the balance of power, then her democratic institutions would be utterly wrecked and exposed to anti-democratic elements "boring from within." In addition, she would confront enormous spending on arms as well as increased taxation and national regimentation that would inevitably destroy democracy in an attempt to defend it from anti-democratic forces. All Americans would be affected by the restriction of civil liberties. Economic and industrial life would come to be regimented and government controlled, as in fascist countries. The American standard of living would decline, foreign trade would face disruption, and essential raw resources would fall into hostile hands. The self-destructive undermining of morale would provide "the proper soil in which foreign ideologies could take root," Kennedy's memo states. "Such centralization would tend to reproduce, possibly under other names, the basic features of the Fascist state: to fight totalitarianism, we would have to adopt totalitarian methods." "In short," he concluded, "America, alone in a jealous and hostile world, would find that the effort and cost of maintaining 'splendid isolation' would be such as to bring about the destruction of all those values which the isolationist policy had been designed to preserve."[227]

Despite his fatalistic conclusions and his awareness of the costs of isolation, Kennedy still refused to support any policy but isolationism, even though his arguments served only to illustrate its folly. His hodgepodge of a memorandum seemed to suggest that some form of fascism and economic control, however hard to swallow, might be necessary to guarantee the survival of the United States, and he quietly implied that the United States might have to accept totalitarianism itself in order to live with the totalitarian powers in Europe.

The significance of Kennedy's inconclusive memorandum lies in the differences it reveals between, on the one hand, the psychology and political philosophy of the White House optimist who put his faith in democracy and, however awkwardly, worked with its tangled and frustrating procedures and processes; and, on the other hand, the psychology and political philosophy of the pessimist in London who predicted a form of American fascism and advocated virtual pacifism.[228] Essentially no price was too high for Kennedy to pay for peace, and for safeguarding his family's welfare and fortune. On his growing roster of sacrificial victims were the Jews, the Czechs, the Poles, and democracy itself.

CHAPTER 6

Peace at Any Price

urope was to have only six more months of peace. Throughout this period, Kennedy's moods ran the gamut from exuberant optimism to utter despair and fatalism. He scoured the troubled horizons, ignoring the menacing omens and praying for miracles and finding reassurance in some of the most unlikely gestures and places. He grasped at them only to have them evaporate.

Kennedy found reason for optimism even in Mussolini's Italy and in the coronation of Peter's successor in the Church. Elated by his conversation after the papal coronation with Countess Ciano, Mussolini's daughter, the ambassador was convinced that the Italians wanted peace.[1]

Yet his optimism was quickly shattered by Hitler's next act of aggression, the absorption of the rest of Czechoslovakia, despite his promise not to violate the principle of self-determination by annexing any non-German population, and by Chamberlain's promise to guarantee the independence of Poland, as well as his later commitment to Greece and Rumania. Kennedy, of course, supported Chamberlain and continued to endorse his efforts and to work on his behalf, so it seemed, no matter what the prime minister did, even though it involved such a startling reversal of Britain's foreign policy, a new about-face troubling to the ambassador.[2] It also signaled the beginning of a divergence on foreign policy between the British appeaser who came to prefer war to Hitler's continued aggression and the American appeaser who wanted peace and virtual pacifism regardless of the Führer's actions. But so long as his good friend lived at 10 Downing Street, Kennedy seemed to believe that Britain was worth saving—up to a point, of course—provided that the expense to the United States was minimal and did not involve any kind of American military commitment.[3] Behind the protection offered America by two oceans and its policy of isolationism, he wished Britain well and was even willing to endorse the repeal of the Neutrality Act and to countenance the American military buildup and, furthermore, to acquiesce, if necessary, to an American form of fascism.[4] He also urged FDR, upon Britain's behalf, to warn Tokyo by transferring the fleet from the Atlantic to the Pacific.

After the scare over the Czechoslovakia crisis and Chamberlain's guarantee to Poland, Kennedy, to the dismay of Roosevelt, spent the summer before the outbreak of war developing a friendship with Hitler's financiers and economic advisers and urging political and economic negotiations between Britain, the United States, and Germany, steadfastly espousing Chamberlain's official foreign-policy line throughout the country and basking in the affection and goodwill of the British. Such activities not only increased the sniping about Kennedy in the United States, leading to sometimes unjust and unsavory comments, but they also encouraged FDR to snub him and to bypass him in favor of his own emissaries and left Kennedy fuming and increasingly outspoken and critical of his boss. The visit of the king and queen of England was simply too risky, the president judged, to allow Kennedy any involvement, known as he was to be a staunch opponent of any form of Anglo-American alliance.[5]

Although he was often bypassed by American officials, Kennedy was still on intimate terms with Chamberlain and his circle. He was kept extremely well informed about the government's actions, even ahead of the cabinet, and frequently briefed beforehand on the prime minister's announcements. The Roosevelt administration received thorough and prompt dispatches from its ambassador, describing Britain's attempts to establish a peace front, and its dreary and ultimately futile diplomacy with the Soviet Union. In the heat of the crisis in the last days of August, Kennedy sat in on the discussions of British officials at the highest levels of the government. He monitored events virtually moment by moment, would fire off two and three cables on the same day, and frequently put through transatlantic phone calls to the White House or the State Department, making dramatic pronouncements that did not always bear out their billing.

The unexpected announcement of the Nazi-Soviet Nonaggression Pact stunned Kennedy and sent him into a state of complete despair. Despite warning Roosevelt to proceed with extreme caution, the pessimistic and panicky ambassador urged him, on behalf of the British, to work for a Polish Munich and to press the Poles to acquiesce to Hitler's demands to preserve peace: peace at any price, peace by selling out first the Czechs, then the Jews, and now the Poles.[6] The American ambassador was one of the few people in government who still held that preserving peace was more important than opposing Hitler's aggression.[7]

There was a pause in Europe's drift toward war as the world's attention turned toward the Vatican. On February 10, 1939, Pius XI died. On March 2, 1939, Eugenio Cardinal Pacelli was elected by the College of Cardinals and became Pius XII. Even the coronation of Peter's successor was not without its political overtones. The German government sent no official representative. Moreover, Pius XII selected Luigi Cardinal Maglione as his secretary of state, a man noted for his pro-French and pro-democratic sympathies. Before his selection, both the German and Italian governments actively campaigned against Maglione's candidacy.[8]

Kennedy had predicted the election of Pacelli and was elated by it.[9] He enthusiastically wrote to Moffat, giving his impression of the new pontiff. "Besides being a most saintly man, he has an extensive knowledge of world conditions. He is not pro–one country or anti-another. He is just pro-Christian. If the world hasn't gone too far to be influenced by a great and good man, this is the man."[10]

Roosevelt conferred on Kennedy the distinction of being the first American to represent his country at a papal coronation.[11] He ardently wanted the appointment and lobbied hard for the honor. It would secure his position as his country's leading Catholic layman and add luster and prestige to his name and his family.[12] He asked FDR for permission to attend[13] and enlisted Welles to help him.[14] Finally, the president accepted Welles's suggestion and agreed to Kennedy's appointment as his special envoy.[15] Kennedy was ecstatic. It was "an honor that I personally appreciated," he wrote in his memoir. The honor was deeply meaningful to Kennedy as a Catholic, as well as a respectful gesture to the Church and the new pope. But it was also a personal matter: in 1936 the Kennedy family had hosted Cardinal Pacelli, then secretary of state for the Vatican, and entertained him in their Bronxville home. Kennedy had also escorted him to Hyde Park to visit the president. Kennedy's impression then was that the cardinal was a man of deep spirituality, wisdom, and kindness. When Pacelli was elevated to the papacy, Kennedy "wanted personally to honor the man who had already meant much in my religious life," he wrote in his memoir.[16] Thus, the Kennedy family, with the exception of Joe Jr., who was in Spain, was rounded up and sent off to Rome.[17] They were officially received by a delegation headed by the American ambassador to Italy, William Phillips, and including dignitaries from the United States Embassy and the Vatican, and the rector of the American Ecclesiastical College in Rome, where they were treated to a rousing reception and "boyish hilarity" from the students there, who snapped pictures and greeted Kennedy and members of his family as "from one Bostonian to another." Rose astonished the hotel clerk when she told him that her family and their entourage would require sixteen rooms.[18]

For his part, Pius XII was delighted by the presence of his former hosts and expressed his gratitude to President Roosevelt for sending a representative. Washington had not had official diplomatic relations with the Vatican for some sixty years—something Kennedy wished to remedy.[19] "I was intent on trying during the visit to make clear to others in the Church, as well as at home, the wisdom of maintaining a system of formal representation between the Vatican and Washington," he said. Kennedy reasoned that a formal relationship with the Vatican would permit a closer connection with the worldwide Roman Catholic community; it could allow American statesmen to understand Rome's aims and objectives better and to benefit from Rome's intelligence and influence, which could perhaps lead to a wiser exercise of the temporal powers of the "Chiefs of States." A tall order. It could also provide more inspiration and stability and enhance peace in these troubled times, Kennedy believed.[20]

On the day of the coronation, Sunday, March 12, 1939—a clear, sunny day—aides were sent scampering to correct a colossal mistake. The ambassador had discovered that there were no American flags to fly from his limousine and was irate. Rome was searched for hours—aides scoured shops and called on American residents to look in their closets. In vain. Kennedy was reduced to riding to the papal coronation in shiny black anonymity through streets lined with troops in olive-green livery and boys, some with guns, shivering in black shirts in the crisp morning air.[21]

At half past seven, the Kennedy family arrived at Saint Peter's in four cars, the women wearing the traditional black dresses and covering their heads with shawls or mantillas, the men in formal dress. The great square outside the basilica was packed with 400,000 people, and there were some 70,000 notables inside. The Kennedys were escorted to their places in the front row directly before the altar for the pontifical Mass to begin at 8:15. In front of them stood the Swiss guards like bronze statues holding their halberds and wearing shining armor and plumed helmets designed by Michelangelo. The family sat in the midst of European royalty: the Crown Prince and Princess of Italy, she wearing white satin with a silver brocade train; the Crown Prince of Luxembourg; Ireland's prime minister, Eamon de Valera; Italy's foreign minister and Mussolini's son-in-law, Galeazzo Ciano, Count of Cortellazzo; and the Duke of Norfolk.[22] Kennedy and de Valera chatted about the unreasonableness of England's opposition to the union of Northern and Southern Ireland, the prime minister practicing his oratory on his fellow Irishman, whipping himself up into a campaign mode for his upcoming trip to the United States.

The majestic procession began with Gounod's Papal March and shouts of "Viva il Papa!" as twelve attendants in red brocade carried the pope aloft in his *sedia* into the basilica. Flanked by two ostrich-feathered fans, he sat quietly, dressed in a huge white cape that draped the floor of the *sedia*.

In St. Peter's, Kennedy was seated in the front row next to Ciano for the five-hour ceremony. Ciano spent most of the time marching up and down St. Peter's with the other distinguished guests, bowing and smiling and giving the fascist salute as if trying to share honors with the pope.[23] "A swell-headed Muggo," the ambassador recorded in his diary.[24] He had also heard that Ciano was angry and believed that Italy had been "insulted" because England's representative, the Duke of Norfolk, marched ahead of him in the procession. After Mass and the coronation ceremony, the Kennedy family left for a reception hosted by the Colonnas, the first Catholic family of Rome. The ambassador was invigorated: "six hours and never tired," he wrote in his diary.[25]

Ciano was not the only guest to leave a disagreeable impression; so did the Kennedys. They caused a diplomatic glitch by occupying places meant for other dignitaries. Eight of the children plus their nurse, Elizabeth Dunn; their governess, Luella Hennessy; and Mary and Eddie Moore attended the ceremony in the basilica.[26] The size of the group and their usurpation of more space than the two seats allotted them caused Ciano to protest and to threaten to leave. One unhappy churchman, Giovanni Battista Cardinal Montini, later named

Pope Paul VI, recalled: "The situation was immediately resolved; but there remained in our memory the procession of the children of Ambassador Kennedy."[27] "Oh, will Joe ever learn!" wondered Boston's Cardinal O'Connell when told of the size of the Kennedy throng and the problems that caused.[28] But on anything disadvantageous to his family, their comfort and their status, Kennedy refused to learn.

The coronation was a ceremony more personal and more moving than anything Kennedy had yet witnessed officially. It was "a day overwhelming in its memory, in its magnificence, in its universal appeal," he told a *New York Herald Tribune* correspondent.[29] "The beauty of the [mass] that day was beyond belief," Kennedy wrote in his memoir. As he knelt in the hollow of the Dome of St. Peter's, listening to the chanting of the Kyrie and the Gloria by the pope and the responses by the Sistine Choir, and witnessed the papal appearance on the balcony and the crowning of the 262nd successor of St. Peter by the cardinal-deacon, Kennedy was overcome with emotion and fumbled for his handkerchief to wipe his eyes—but seeing that Rose's veil of black lace was thoroughly drenched, he passed the handkerchief to her. The ceremony was "a never to be forgotten experience."[30]

The next day the weather was "chilly and chillier."[31] Pius XII received the Kennedy family in a private audience.[32] As Kennedy entered the room and genuflected, to his "amazement," the pope broke custom and rose to greet him.[33] His Holiness was happy to see him, he said, and had "rejoiced" when he learned that the president had sent him to Rome.[34] Kennedy and the pope chatted about his visit to the Kennedys in 1936, when he was simply Cardinal Pacelli, and about the possibility of gaining the administration's formal diplomatic recognition of the Vatican. Kennedy advised him that the American hierarchy opposed it, fearing the loss of their power. He promised to help with getting Washington's approval. His Holiness told him he appreciated Roosevelt's efforts to ensure peace but found the tenor of the times deeply troubling. "The Church can only do so much," he told Kennedy, "but what it can do, it will."[35] Pius XII "was cheerful, most kind and showed a real affection for me," Kennedy proudly wrote in his diary.[36]

Kennedy's private audience with the pope lasted about twenty minutes, and then Mrs. Kennedy and the children, the ambassador's secretary Edward Moore, Franklin C. Gowen of the United States consular staff in London, Mr. Arthur Houghton, Mrs. Moore, Miss Elizabeth Dunn of Boston (the Kennedy children's nurse), Miss Luella Hennessy of Boston (the governess), and Rose's French maid were also presented to the pope.[37] Rose was so overjoyed by the pope's kindnesses and graciousness that her husband feared she would faint.[38] "Rose had achieved nirvana," wrote her biographer, Barbara Perry.[39] His Holiness gave rosaries in white cases to Rose and all the children, already loaded down with rosaries (twenty-two dozen) and religious objects for the pope to bless.[40] He patted the head of seven-year-old Teddy and told him he was "a smart little fellow." "I wasn't frightened at all," Teddy later declared.[41] Two days later, wearing a blue suit with a little white rose on his left arm, Teddy received his first communion from Pius XII, the first non-Italian ever so graced. His Holiness said, "I hope you will always be good and pious as you are today."[42]

The family met the new secretary of state, Cardinal Maglione, and visited the Sistine Chapel, had their picture taken, and returned to their lodgings "after the most thrilling day of our lives," wrote Kennedy.[43] He told Moffat: "The impression that the Coronation of the Pope and my private audience had upon me is not susceptible of description."[44] Pius XII was "awe-inspiring, majestic, kindness personified and with the humility of God"—these are examples of the ambassador's attempts at description.[45] Kennedy's press release referred to the pope as "a godlike figure . . . to whom the world could turn for sublime spirituality, for undaunted courage and for justice to all men."[46]

That afternoon the family took tea at the pope's summer residence, Castel Gandolfo. Kennedy was amused at the tea table, which besides tea was graced with Gordon's Gin and Canadian Club Whiskey. "It looked very funny in the Pope's house with fifty Cardinals around," he said.[47]

That evening, Kennedy joined the receiving line at the American embassy in Rome, along with William Phillips, the American ambassador to Italy. After dinner Kennedy talked for two and a half hours to Mussolini's attractive daughter, the Countess Edda Ciano. Count Galeazzo Ciano was there too, sitting across from them on a stool most of the evening. "I have no idea how able he is in his office, but a more pompous ass I have never met in my life," the ambassador cabled Hull.[48]

> Most of his time . . . he spent rushing girls into a corner for conversation, and he could not talk seriously for five minutes for fear that two or three of the girls who are invited in order to get him to come, might get out of sight. . . . As a result of my observations of Ciano . . . and the gossip that Mussolini now has a German sweetheart, I came away believing that we could accomplish much more by sending a dozen beautiful chorus girls to Rome than a fleet of airplanes and a flock of diplomats. If . . . Ciano becomes a great Secretary of State, then I have lost all judgment of men.[49]

The countess had acted as if she gave not a darn about her husband's behavior, the ambassador observed.[50] Would the United States fight? she asked Kennedy. "Positively," he had answered, believing there was no point in telling her otherwise.[51] But there was no reason for the democracies to fight fascist Italy, she had told him. Fascism had lasted seventeen years and had been good for Italians. Its major drawback was its alliance with Hitler, for which she blamed the democracies. "After all," she, Mussolini's daughter, had said, "if the United States, France and England all stuck together, there was nothing left for the Duce to do but play along with Hitler for his own protection." She had also implied that the Italians were "deeply concerned over the loss of the friendship of America."[52]

Apparently Kennedy took the countess's remarks to be an indication of a pro-American position and put great stock in them. He told Hull: "I believe there is a good deal in what she said."[53] More likely, Mussolini's daughter was merely telling the ambassador what she wanted him to think, and expecting him to pass it on to Washington, her pro-American remark just an offhand comment that Kennedy snatched at in the hope that it might be something more. He was also convinced that the Italians sincerely wanted peace and were unprepared for war, a view corroborated by the minister of agriculture.[54] Kennedy told Welles that he intended to follow up on his conversation with Countess Ciano and to try to gain the trust and goodwill of the influential people in the government and at the Vatican, and to discreetly use the influence of the pope for peace as well. Kennedy also hoped that there might be an opportunity for Roosevelt "to do the big job—peace for the world."[55] Aside from using his influence, Kennedy's only other suggestion for tearing Mussolini away from Hitler and preventing war with Italy was to recognize Abyssinia; this was not likely to happen, Kennedy admitted, since Italy had acquired Abyssinia by aggression, a means the United States condemned.[56]

Roosevelt, Kennedy cabled Washington, had an outstanding reputation among the Italians. "The speeches of the President drive them absolutely crazy. . . . Every time the President says anything, none of the members of the Cabinet or the Government in Rome are fit to converse with for the balance of the day"—another good omen, he thought, grasping at straws.[57]

The ambassador and his family left Rome delighted by the coronation, steadfast in their devotion to the Church and her interests, and persuaded that peace could be maintained. But the warnings were ominous; there was much to be pessimistic about. Even as soon as Kennedy arrived in Paris on March 16, 1939, to breakfast with William Bullitt, the American ambassador to France, he wrote: "Rome had suddenly become a memory and peace an even dimmer hope."[58] Few could believe that Hitler's appetites had been sated. But his next act of aggression came "as a complete surprise" to Kennedy and completely shattered his optimism.[59]

The two American ambassadors discussed the momentous news that on the Ides of March—March 15, 1939—Hitler, despite his promises, had swallowed up Bohemia and Moravia by nightfall and established a German protectorate for the remnants of the tottering state of Czechoslovakia. The newly "independent" state of Slovakia was declared a protectorate of the Reich, and Hungarian troops, with Poland's support and the Führer's blessing, seized Ruthenia. That evening Hitler himself triumphantly entered Prague and spent the night in the Hradčany Castle, the palace of the Czech kings and symbol of Czech nationalism. "Czecho-Slovakia has ceased to exist," he wrote from Beneš's table.[60]

The destruction of Czechoslovakia, Bullitt told Kennedy, "marked the end of our civilization." "Deplorable act," the ambassador recorded in his diary, as he flew back to London in a bearish mood to observe and report to Washington on the unfolding historical drama and still concerned about the future of American democracy. "I . . . thought we would eventually have to have some form of dictatorship in U.S.A. to solve our own difficulties," Kennedy confided to his diary.[61]

By annexing a non-German population, Hitler had broken his sworn word. In just six months, he had flouted international law, he had overthrown the Munich Settlement and its support for the rump Czech state, and he had violated the principle of self-determination, the basis for his previous actions against Czechoslovakia. Clearly, as Halifax said, Hitler's Reich would not be an exclusively Aryan empire.[62] These were events that not even Chamberlain could swallow. In addition, the smaller countries of eastern Europe, whether they had German minorities or not, were isolated, unprotected, and without British or French help and menaced by Hitler and his Nazi hordes.

On March 15, 1939, the prime minister dispassionately informed the House of Commons that Czechoslovakia "has become disintegrated" because of "internal disruption." He said that Britain's guarantee to Czechoslovakia was no longer valid.[63] His tepid statement aroused a barrage of criticism within his own party, in the press, and among Britons at large, and subjected him to intense pressure and led to a debate on foreign policy. Roosevelt, too, was indignant with the prime minister and likened him to Pontius Pilate.[64]

Kennedy saw Halifax on March 17 and reported that "American public opinion . . . was profoundly shocked. [But] the truth . . . was that nothing whatever could have prevented these recent events in Czecho-Slovakia except the decision to make war." Furthermore, present British policy had been stretched taut. Where does Britain go from here? the ambassador asked. Listen to Chamberlain's speech at Birmingham this evening, the foreign secretary responded. Both Kennedy and Halifax thought that revising the Neutrality Act would be extremely useful to Britain, action that Roosevelt was already in the process of taking.[65]

Chamberlain, feeling "not only a sense of national but also of personal grievance against Hitler," answered Kennedy's question[66] by deciding to launch a new direction in Britain's foreign policy and introducing it before the annual dinner of the loyal Birmingham Unionist Association on the evening of March 17. This Chamberlain was a very different Chamberlain from the one of two days earlier—one who had appeared stunned but unbowed by Hitler's brazen betrayal of his promise that the Sudetenland was his last territorial claim and by the tragedy he had inflicted on the Czechs. Chamberlain had finally realized that it was no longer possible to negotiate with Hitler[67] and knew that he could not rely on Hitler's word in any way. Hitler is "a madman," the prime minister said a few days after Prague.[68]

As Chamberlain boarded the train to Birmingham that evening, Halifax gave Kennedy the gist of the prime minister's speech and prepared him for the change in British diplomacy and the answer to Kennedy's question: Where do we go from here?[69] Before his fellow Conservatives, his voice indignant, Chamberlain reflected the mood of his audience. He bitterly condemned Hitler's aggression and vigorously announced his willingness to resist Hitler by force. He also told his audience that there was nothing he would not give for peace; nevertheless, "no greater mistake could be made than to suppose that, because it believes war to be a senseless and cruel thing, this nation has so lost its fibre that it will not take part to the utmost of its power in resisting such a challenge if it were ever made."[70] Chamberlain's speech was unusual for the forcefulness of his denunciation, Kennedy noted, and seemed to unite all Britain and the Commonwealth too, for the first time, as they had not been united at Munich in opposition to Hitler's dream to dominate the Continent.[71] It also marked if not the end of appeasement, as Kennedy claimed,[72] then at least its abatement and made it harder for the prime minister to implement that policy and to restrain critics who demanded more saber-rattling and bellicosity.[73] But it did ensure his continuous political leadership and won Kennedy's applause, despite the new direction it signaled in foreign policy. "I have been one with you in your striving for peace and have nothing but admiration for the convictions you so eloquently expressed last night," Kennedy wrote, loyal to the hilt, as he cabled Chamberlain "affectionate greetings" on his birthday the next day.[74] His touching personal devotion to his fellow appeaser, whom he referred to as "*my* Prime Minister," overshadowed what must have been his considerable discomfort at Chamberlain's change in foreign policy.[75] "Where do [you] go from here?" Kennedy asked.[76]

The Birmingham speech was "first rate," Kennedy told Halifax, but he also cautioned Halifax that it contained an explicit commitment to oppose further German aggression.[77] It "put the baby on their own doorstep," Kennedy said.[78] He added that he was surprised at the speed with which American opinion, led by the president, was moving toward resistance to any future German expansion, and noted that it was ahead of his own view on the matter, an unusual position for him[79] since his isolationist opinions had always been very much in the national mainstream. An American opinion poll taken on March 21 found that 66 percent of people polled supported selling armaments to Britain and France if they were at war with Germany and Italy, a position he, too, would later adopt.[80]

In addition to his Birmingham speech, Chamberlain answered Kennedy's question "Where do you go from here?" by personally drafting a bold four-power declaration to commit France, Russia, and Poland to joint consultations with Britain if Germany took further aggressive action in eastern Europe. Kennedy described it as "a proposal, in essence, to guarantee the integrity of Poland," with the port of Danzig and its 80 percent German population at the top of the Polish Corridor, one of the more outrageous creations of Versailles, and a prime Nazi target that represented Germany's strongest brief[81] and made it the next obvious victim on Hitler's timetable.[82] The French accepted the proposal, as did the Russians, but the short-sighted Poles, to the prime minister's very great relief, refused to associate themselves publicly with Russia and wanted Russia to have no part in the agreement.[83] They thereby excluded the only country that actually could defend them against Hitler's aggression and his demands for Danzig and the construction of an extraterritorial road across the Polish Corridor.[84] They thus ensured a Polish war with British support. The proposal would definitely have knocked the Poles "off the fence and put [them] in the Soviet camp against Germany," Kennedy reported,[85] but the Poles "do not like [the Russians] as bedfellows" and would be more than likely to refuse to join any program calling for closer ties with the Soviets. Furthermore, Józef Beck, Poland's foreign minister, feared that a commitment between Russia and Poland would cause a break with Hitler, and "war will be on," the ambassador told Washington.[86] Poland rejected the four-power proposal on March 24 and Chamberlain promptly declared it dead.[87] As Chamberlain reconsidered the proposition, he thought better of it and on March 26, 1939, wrote to his sister Ida: "Its [sic] like sending a man into the lions [sic] den and saying to him 'Never mind if the lion does gobble you up; I intend to give him a good hiding afterwards.'" As soon as Chamberlain understood Poland's position, he realized that it was unlikely that he would get the Poles to agree to the proposal.[88]

But the British still very much wanted an agreement as a warning to Hitler to desist from bullying, Kennedy told Washington, after a conversation with Halifax on March 24, and reported on the dickering among the parties behind the scenes.[89] They therefore devised a new plan whereby, as an alternative to the four-party proposal, Britain would ask France, Poland, Russia, Turkey, Greece, and Yugoslavia to join in a pact of mutual assistance to guarantee the independence of Rumania that Halifax deemed essential to Britain's national security. Chamberlain predicted that Rumania would be Hitler's next victim since he had always coveted Rumania's rich oil fields.[90] The replies of the six countries were polite but evasive and nearly hopeless, Kennedy noted. Suspicion of Russia's ambitions was rife in Poland and Rumania and to a lesser extent in Yugoslavia, Greece, and Turkey on many and diverse grounds.[91] The countries also feared that engaging in even an informal alliance with Russia would provoke Hitler into unleashing retaliatory action against them.[92] But nothing came of this plan either, despite the fact that Halifax thought that Greece and Turkey, "lying at Britain's imperial jugular," were as important to Britain's interests as Poland and Romania.[93]

Kennedy was skeptical of Britain's reliance on any of her eastern allies, such as Poland and Poland's "weak sisters" Russia or Rumania, and he did his best to persuade Halifax of his views. Kennedy warned Halifax, who remained unconvinced, that none of them would be able to give satisfactory assurances to Britain or France if war threatened. Kennedy predicted that the British would soon find it expedient to "wash their hands of the whole of Southeastern Europe."[94] "The great problem for all these European countries," the cynic in London wrote to Washington, "is to find out how they can get somebody else to come to their assistance for some other reason than 100% selfishness and that is impossible to my mind."[95] Issues of national independence or autonomy and the prevention of aggression were presumably examples of the impossible to his mind. But Halifax sincerely thought otherwise and kept dickering.

His dickering succeeded. On March 27 Chamberlain decided to pursue a formal treaty in which Britain and France would agree to give a pledge to aid Poland against an unprovoked attack by Germany, and Poland in turn would be obligated to assist Rumania against an unprovoked attack by Germany.[96] Does it mean "if Poland fights, Britain fights?" Kennedy asked Cadogan. "Of course,"[97] Cadogan retorted, finding the ambassador "very tiresome,"[98] and promised that there would be no hedging on Britain's part.[99]

Poland was of "vital" importance to Britain and a more valuable ally than Russia because of its ability to force Germany into a war on two fronts, "Germany's weak point," Chamberlain believed.[100] No one thought Russia trustworthy or competent: it was militarily impotent—its air force was too old, too weak, and too short-ranged; its army too poor, with "frightful" industrial backing. It was economically underdeveloped, politically isolated, and famously untrustworthy. The most anyone could expect from Russia, Halifax stated, was that Russia send ammunition to the Poles,[101] a rather plausible view in 1939 and one that Joseph Stalin himself shared. He, too, thought that Russia could aid Poland militarily and protect itself, but that Russia was not militarily strong enough to initiate operations. Russia was thus relegated to "a second line of defence."[102]

Although Halifax, for no apparent reason, believed that things were a bit quieter in late March, he also told Kennedy that he thought that the inevitability of war should be faced immediately—the very stance Kennedy wanted to avoid. The government wanted to lay down an imaginary line and tell Hitler that if he crossed it, war would be on. Kennedy observed that Halifax must be impressed by the fact that last year the British feared war but this year they feared tyranny more than war and were prepared to fight to oppose tyranny—an unhappy conclusion, in Kennedy's opinion.[103]

Kennedy too feared war and told American friends on the phone that the British public was well informed and accepted the radical change in official policy calmly—so calmly that Kennedy warned them not to be misled. Compared to the Munich crisis of the previous fall, "the danger now may be as great or greater."[104]

The rumors flying about at the American embassy in Warsaw and passed on to London on March 28 gave Kennedy even more reason to fear war. Ribbentrop was demanding an immediate German attack on Poland. The ambassador's news was corroborated by Ian Colvin, the Berlin journalist for the *News Chronicle*. His "hair-raising" anecdotal report that Hitler would refrain from attacking Poland only if he were certain that Britain would retaliate against Germany[105] was what Halifax needed to nudge Chamberlain to make a draft proposal to guarantee Poland's independence.[106] The prime minister, who may have been influenced by Kennedy's news, told his cabinet that the way to stop German aggression was to promise unequivocally to resist it by force. Consequently, he rashly decided to issue Poland a blank check by guaranteeing Poland's independence, and informed Kennedy so in advance of his official statement.[107] Kennedy called Hull with the news that Chamberlain would announce a "momentous,"[108] unilateral, open-ended guarantee to Poland on March 31 in the House of Commons.[109] The prime minister said:

> In the event of any action which clearly threatened Polish independence, and which the Polish Government accordingly considered it vital to resist with their national forces, His Majesty's Government would feel themselves bound at once to lend the Polish Government all support in their power. They have given the Polish Government an assurance to that effect.

"That statement," Kennedy observed, "marked a new shift in British policy. Never before had England guaranteed any borders [east] of the Rhine; never before had she so phrased her guarantee that the issue of peace or war was no longer in her hands but in the hands of the nation to whom she had pledged her full aid."[110] He also noted that "for the first time in the history of Great Britain, [that country] has left the final decision as to their fighting outside of their own country to the other power,"[111] a situation appreciated by Beck, Poland's foreign minister. In his conversation with Kennedy, he said that he was "more than happy" to have British support and to have Poland determine when she wants it.[112] On March 31, France also agreed to support Britain's gamble. Halifax's biographer, Andrew Roberts, writes in *The Holy Fox*: "Here was a deterrent with no inherent power to deter. . . . [Poland] was a more distant country of which [the British] knew even less" than they did about Czechoslovakia. "Halifax had attached British foreign policy to the cause of a nation whose name was synonymous with tragedy and which had spent much of the previous century being partitioned twice and under a foreign yoke," Roberts concluded.[113]

Washington seems to have had scant influence on Chamberlain's impromptu decision to guarantee Polish independence. Roosevelt, who had been getting more and more angry at Hitler, had come to be totally disillusioned with Chamberlain,[114] had only been able to manage the grimmest humor and to draw pessimistic conclusions from the latest example of Nazi aggression.[115] But now Roosevelt was utterly delighted at Chamberlain's action. "I talked about it that night to President Roosevelt," Kennedy wrote in his memoirs. "Chamberlain's plan 'is a good one but it probably means war,'" FDR predicted to his ambassador.[116] The president thought that the statement in the Commons was "excellent" and would be very effective with Americans.[117] Kennedy, by contrast, believed that Americans would regard Chamberlain's statement as a "subterfuge." But the news reports and popular reaction in the United States were highly favorable to the prime minister's guarantee.[118]

Halifax's nudging,[119] and his own distrust of Hitler,[120] finally led Chamberlain uncharacteristically, a few weeks later, to take a step unprecedented in Britain's peacetime history. He established universal conscription and required six months of military training for all twenty-year-old men and a ministry of supply to support the newly enlarged army—a demonstration of how seriously he intended to take the commitment to Poland.[121]

In his memoir, Kennedy reflected upon the differences between the England of March 1939 and the England of September 1938. Although the sense of panic, so palpable during the Munich crisis, and the "unreasonable fear" that asked for "peace at any price" had vanished, it was now clear that Hitler's growing menace—"as visible as a thundercloud," as Kennedy described it—could well provoke war. Every peaceful method possible to stop Hitler's aggression had failed, just as Churchill had predicted. Nevertheless, "England believed that it was still worthwhile to have tried them," Kennedy wrote.[122] Chamberlain had made much progress in rearming, Kennedy argued—so much progress that Britons believed themselves better prepared to fight in the event of war; the prime minister had gained much political advantage and support from his Birmingham declaration, and the guarantee of Poland had been overwhelmingly endorsed by every party in the House of Commons. The only thing left for his opponents to seize upon and criticize, Kennedy noted, was the prime minister's failure to secure Russia as a member of his coalition.[123] Halifax's biographer writes that "the logic of protecting Poland and Romania only made sense if there was some agreement with the Soviet Union, which would have to provide the logistical support, armaments and eventual back-stop to any war in the East." Chamberlain was a "definite drag."[124] In fact during the height of the negotiations over the original full tripartite alliance, Chamberlain was so exasperated with Russia that he threatened to resign rather than agree to an alliance with the Soviet Union.[125] Reluctantly Halifax had to acquiesce to this probably disastrous situation and was roundly criticized for agreeing to a policy to support Poland without a similar commitment from Russia. "It tied London's hand whilst freeing Moscow's. Stalin was left secure in the knowledge that a German attack in the East meant help from the West. A German attack in the West, however, was a war from which he could stand aside."[126] Chamberlain's outspoken opposition included Lloyd George; Churchill, of course; Labour's leader Attlee; and the other opposition voices, Hugh Dalton, Labour front-bencher, and Liberal leader Scotsman Archibald Sinclair.[127] Chamberlain's government has routinely been accused of negotiating in bad faith over Poland because they had no intention of going to Poland's aid. But an undated note by Halifax written in 1952 says that "neither the Polish Government nor the Roumanian Government were under any illusions as to the measure of concrete help that they might expect from Great Britain in the event of Hitler choosing war." Nevertheless, the guarantees "were the best chance, and indeed the only chance, of warning him off" the decision to go to war.[128] Chamberlain's biographer writes that had Chamberlain pursued an alliance with the Soviet Union, it would have been the best means, short of war, of restraining Germany. Yet he also argues that the alliance was unlikely because of mutual suspicion between the Soviets and the West. Furthermore, given Hitler's desire for war, only an assassin's bullet would have prevented it. Despite the conjecture, two things are certain: First, Chamberlain was personally responsible for obstructing the option despite growing cabinet and parliamentary support for it. His reluctance may have convinced the Soviets that the West lacked a sound commitment and usefulness to them. Second, a tripartite pact would probably not have deterred Hitler, but the Nazi-Soviet Pact, because it did remove the threat of a war on two fronts, did make war on Poland a certainty.[129]

For their part, the Soviets wanted an alliance with the West for self-protection and deeply desired peace, but they were also keenly suspicious of the Western democracies who had snubbed them at Munich and who they had long suspected were using them as a "cat's paw," only to turn aside and abandon them to Hitler's design. Stalin wanted peace above all and he might decide that Hitler was the best bet for getting it. It hardly mattered in the long run anyhow, Kennedy argued. Although he recognized the military importance of the Soviet Union, he said, it would still have to fight for Poland or Rumania regardless of whether there were a formal treaty with the democracies. "It was vital to Russia's self-interest," Kennedy told

Joseph E. Davies, the American ambassador to Moscow, whom he spoke to on April 3, 1939. Kennedy warned Davies that Hitler was wooing Stalin into an alliance in order to lock his back door before he attacked the West, a warning that Kennedy as well as Chamberlain dismissed, to their very great regret come August.[130] Kennedy wrote: "Neither of us [Kennedy or Davies] then contemplated that Russia would shortly unite with Germany in dismembering Poland. Davies at that time, however, shared my concern over the possibility that Russia might come to an agreement with Germany if Russia believed that her security could best be furthered by such action."[131] This was a possibility not lost on Halifax.[132]

In foreign policy, the six months left of peace were dreary, dismal months for both president and prime minister. Roosevelt kept urging Kennedy "to put some iron up Chamberlain's backside," and Kennedy's response was that "that . . . would do no good unless the British had some iron with which to fight and they did not."[133] Moreover, Chamberlain's efforts to restrain Hitler by some kind of peace front throughout the summer of 1939 were hampered by two issues: Poland's reluctance to join the Soviet Union in an anti-German pact and the mutual distrust that continued to plague the relations between the Soviet Union and Britain despite their vows for conciliation.[134] The "enigma of Russia" continued to be the dominant theme of Britain's foreign policy in Europe until the invasion of Poland in September.[135] In his frequent conversations with the prime minister, Kennedy noted, Chamberlain was unwilling to overcome his long-standing aversion to the Soviet Union and never found an alliance with it palatable. He never believed in the Soviets, never trusted them to refrain from trying to persuade Hitler to march west instead of east, and never thought they were militarily effective.[136] The job of Germany, even a dangerous Germany dominated by Hitler, was to serve as a buffer to offset "the Soviet bear," Chamberlain believed.[137] Chamberlain sounded very much like Kennedy.

The American ambassador shared the prime minister's deep suspicions of the Soviet Union. The Soviets were taking Britain "up a very dark road," he said.[138] Furthermore, it would be "the height of optimism" to expect Russia to befriend the United States after a victory of the totalitarian powers over the British Empire, Kennedy wrote to the president, after the fashion of his memo to him in March. The ambassador gave his opinion that it was just as likely that either Germany could dominate the Soviet Union by means of some action just short of an actual invasion or that the Soviet ideologues would withdraw into "splendid isolation" behind the Kremlin walls.[139]

Another alternative Kennedy envisioned, and his favorite, was that Hitler's attack be deflected eastward to the Soviet Union while the democracies stood aside, watching the two great totalitarian powers devour each other: Nazism versus Communism.[140] Such a scenario would have made a formal Anglo-Soviet alliance irrelevant, a position of some credibility in 1939 but failing to take into account what would have happened if Hitler had been victorious. The Continent would have had Nazi-dominated governments much like Vichy, France, in 1940.[141]

In any case, Kennedy believed that it was very unlikely that something would be worked out with the Russians. They "seem to be quite pleased with the way things are going, because it looks like a free-for-all with the Russians as the general beneficiary when it is all over."[142]

Years later, Kennedy recalled that the real stumbling block to an Anglo-Russian alliance in 1939 had been the Soviet demand to annex Estonia, Latvia, and Lithuania. Kennedy summed up what Chamberlain told him at Windsor Castle in mid-April of 1939: "[Chamberlain] can make a deal with Russia at any time now, but is delaying until he definitely gets the Balkan [*sic*] situation straightened away." To do otherwise would simply cause trouble.[143] Speaking in 1945, the ambassador remembered the major problem of the British had been "that if they backed Germany . . . they were then faced with a greater Germany, a weakened France, and a relatively defenseless England, whereas an alliance with Russia and the ultimate destruction of Germany would present England with precisely the problem that it now has, namely a vacuum of power in Central Europe into which Russian influence would flow."[144]

As Richard Whalen, one of Kennedy's biographers, points out, Soviet friendship would have been sordid and costly—unrestrained Soviet influence on the smaller states of northeastern Europe—but it was no uglier and no more costly than Munich, a price that Chamberlain had been willing to pay.[145] Thus the opportunity for an Anglo-Russian alliance was allowed to lapse until the Russians announced their agreement with the Germans on August 23, 1939, to the surprise and horror of Chamberlain and Kennedy.[146]

On Good Friday, April 7, 1939, the junior partner in the Axis imitated the senior and with no advance warning took his turn at rattling Europeans' nerves: Italy's black-shirted forces assaulted the water defenses across the Adriatic and invaded little Albania[147] and appeared determined to attack the Greek island of Corfu. As Rose and Joe Kennedy finished their round of golf at Addington, the ambassador received the news of the invasion. The situation made him tense and fearful of war, his wife recorded in her diary. "Everyone stunned and shattered by news of Italians [*sic*] advance, especially on Good Friday," she remembered.[148]

Kennedy was surprised by Halifax's "strangely optimistic" view that peace will hold—so surprised that he wondered to Hull whether the British had sources unavailable to others. Apparently the British believe that the Albanian situation "is not as hopeless as everybody else seems to think it is," Kennedy reported to Washington.[149] Mussolini's action, Halifax told Kennedy during their meeting on April 11, led the badly shaken Chamberlain to guarantee Greek independence[150] and later Rumania's too, if threatened by Italy, and to try to gain the assurances of the French and the Turkish governments as well.[151] Britain's interest in the Middle East, its oil fields, and the Suez Canal made a Greece friendly to Britain essential.[152]

Kennedy told Halifax that he thought the guarantees would be "greatly valued in the United States"[153] and help to offset concern over Britain's failure to denounce the Anglo-Italian agreement. When on April 13 Chamberlain informed the House of Commons of his guarantee to Greece and to Rumania, Kennedy congratulated him on his assurances.[154]

Thus by mid-April 1939 Chamberlain reluctantly found himself presiding over a dramatic shift in British policy, and setting up an elaborate system of commitments ranging from the Baltic Sea down to the Black Sea and the Aegean. Within this expanse were half a dozen countries, any one of which if attacked by the Axis powers could drag Britain and France into war. As for America's ambassador, despite his overwhelming desire for peace at virtually any price, he stood by "his" prime minister out of loyalty and admiration; thus, paradoxically and reluctantly, he found himself supporting the very thing that could bring about the very thing that he most feared: Chamberlain's system of commitments designed to prevent aggression actually increased the likelihood of war.

Across the Atlantic, Roosevelt and Hull debated foreign policy by the hour and groped for an appropriate response to the dictators' aggression. Since the neutrality bill was still bogged down in Congress, the president turned to the only other devices he had—the spoken word and saber-rattling. He sent a "Saturday surprise" message on April 15 to both Hitler and Mussolini, beseeching them to guarantee the independence of some thirty states, and referring to Finland, Estonia, Latvia, Lithuania, and so on down the map of Europe and the Near East. He also offered to act as an intermediary and to convene a conference to discuss outstanding problems. He ended the message by urging peace, a reduction in armaments, and increased world trade.[155]

Several days passed before the Axis replied to Roosevelt's message. In an outraged single sentence in a speech on April 20, 1939, the Duce said that he refused to be influenced by "press campaigns, convivial vociferations, or Messiah-like messages." The participation of the United States in any conference would reveal the American government in "its customary role of distant spectator," he correctly observed.[156]

Hitler's scathing and vitriolic reply finally arrived on April 28, 1939. Before the Reichstag he dramatically delivered another stinging harangue in which he abrogated the ten-year non-aggression pact with Poland, tore up the Anglo-German Naval Agreement of 1938, and denounced the Munich declaration. He mockingly said that he had polled each of the thirty-one states on Roosevelt's list and asked it whether it feared Germany. Each state said no.[157] Angered, Roosevelt fell silent.[158]

Although Kennedy had not known that the president intended to deliver his "Saturday surprise" message, nor that it lacked Hull's benediction,[159] he continued to declare that "our sympathies are against Hitler but you must not count on much more than that." Kennedy extended to the British America's promise of assistance in their mutual interests but with no "far-flung" obligations and only a vague commitment to giving material aid. Which "will be a long time coming." How much and when was anybody's guess.[160]

Nevertheless, Kennedy did act as an intermediary in Roosevelt's saber-rattling scheme intended as a warning to Tokyo. Half an hour after dispatching his message to Mussolini and Hitler, on April 15, 1939, FDR followed up by transferring the American fleet from the Atlantic to its home port in San Diego.[161]

The idea had originally been Halifax's. Half joking, Halifax and Lord Chatfield, the minister for coordination of defense, talked to Kennedy in mid-March and told him of Britain's promise to the Australians during the Italian crisis in 1936 that if international tensions increased, they (the Brits, presumably) would send a fleet to Singapore. Doing so now, however, would weaken Britain's position in the Mediterranean, where it was trying to contain Italy; but if the United States could transfer its fleet to the Pacific, that would reassure Australia, warn the Japanese, and allow Britain to operate in the Mediterranean.[162] This "gesture of value," as Halifax described it, should be done sooner rather than later, he advised Kennedy.[163] Lord Chatfield stressed to him that "this was psychologically important."[164] A couple of weeks later, Kennedy told Halifax that the president would announce his order on April 15 to return the United States fleet to the Pacific in May, ahead of schedule. "Thankful about Navy," Kennedy wrote in his diary.[165]

At the Windsor Castle weekend with the king and queen following the publication of Roosevelt's letter of April 15, Chamberlain greeted Kennedy uncharacteristically effusively. "That was a great job Roosevelt did,"[166] Chamberlain said, "immensely delighted" with the president's message and his order to send the fleet to the Pacific.[167] "You don't know how much I appreciate the President's efforts in the cause of peace. And that applies to you, too, Joe."[168] Although the prime minister was "a shade more hopeful of peace," Kennedy also saw the tremendous toll the strain was taking on the now seventy-year-old man. "He has failed more in the past week than he has in the past year," the ambassador told Hull. "He walks like an old man and yesterday talked like one."[169]

After the crises provoked by the dictators and the oratory in response to them, there were no major threats to Europe's peace until mid-August. During the brief interlude, in the diplomatic to-ing and fro-ing of threats and counter-threats and consultations going nowhere, Kennedy continued to work for appeasement, busy himself with speeches and travel, bask in British warmth and comradery with high and low, enjoy the concerts conducted by Toscanini and a weekend with the Chamberlains at Chequers,[170] advise FDR on neutrality legislation, make arrangements for the royal visit to the United States, and duck criticism on both sides of the Atlantic: all this before his August vacation on the Côte d'Azur.

Despite Chamberlain's change in foreign policy and Roosevelt's delight over it, Kennedy maintained his abiding faith in the necessity of appeasing Germany politically and economically and in viewing Hitler as a businessman he could bargain with. Kennedy led a throng of supporters on both sides of the Atlantic who thought it essential that the two English-speaking democracies maintain economic relations with Germany. Speaking for economic giants like Ford, Standard Oil, DuPont, Chase Manhattan, and the Bank of England, this is what James Mooney, the president of General Motors Export and vice president of the General Motors Corporation, said: "We ought to make some arrangements with Germany.... There is no reason why we should let our moral indignation over what happens in that country stand in the way."[171]

In the spring of 1939 Mooney went to Germany to discuss the Führer's request for a large loan with which to establish his New Order and enlisted Kennedy's support. In a spirit reminiscent of his personal diplomacy with von Dirksen, Kennedy was eager to meet German banker Emil Puhl and American-educated economist Helmuth Wohlthat, "Göring's right-hand man." Kennedy asked the State Department for permission to attend a private dinner hosted by Mooney in Paris.[172] The White House scotched the trip. Mooney then invited Wohlthat to come to London and to talk to Kennedy in early May, a conversation that seems to have been conducted without the president's knowledge or permission, behavior typical of Kennedy. The General Motors executive noted that Kennedy and Wohlthat "got along very well, seeing eye to eye on everything."[173]

They met again in mid-July. Kennedy reported his conversation to Hull and suspected, no doubt correctly, that he was once again being used for propaganda purposes as he had been with the von Dirksen episode. Wohlthat had told him that Hitler had no intention of considering economic problems at the present, regardless of their worldwide impact, because his primary interest lay in political and military issues. He had adopted a wait-and-see attitude toward Britain's mistakes. The Führer had every expectation of victory because of "British stupidity" and "bad tactics": their inability to reach an agreement with the Soviet Union, their failure to grapple with the interests of countries like Poland and Rumania, and the notion of Britain's encirclement of Germany inexplicably being propagated by English politicians. Neither did the Führer believe that Britain would risk war over such a trivial matter as Danzig, nor did he intend to take any action that would threaten a general world war. Wohlthat, himself a former member of the German General Staff, impressed upon the American ambassador that Hitler would not strike quickly because the British were daily strengthening *his* political position, and that when and if Germany did fight, he would have the complete support of the German General Staff who had become convinced that there was no alternative to going to war.[174]

After learning of Kennedy's conversation with a leading member of Göring's economic staff, FDR prohibited any further contact.[175] He saw something Kennedy was blind to: With war likely, it would not do for the American ambassador to cozy up to a leading Nazi. But the friendship between Kennedy and Wohlthat somehow continued. Writing after World War II to Morton Downey, Kennedy said that when he visited Paris in 1954, he saw his "friend Wohltat [sic], the German who was Hitler's Minister of Economics," and intended to go to Düsseldorf that fall to see him again.[176]

In the late spring of 1939, Kennedy took time out to have a little fun, to spread the Kennedy charm, flash that internationally famous ambassadorial grin, and kid the students and faculty at the several universities that awarded him honorary degrees. He proudly sent Hull a copy of the speech he intended to deliver in Edinburgh, in which he gave vent to his views on foreign policy, arguing that though the United States was isolationist, it also had a stake in foreign affairs second only to Britain's. The United States, he said, should look to its own national interest and support a peaceful resolution to the problems about to engulf Europe in war. He also wanted his speech to counter the growing criticism of him by some as another Walter Hines Page and by others as essentially an Irishman, displaying the Irish anti-British tradition. But Hull would have none of it, fearing unforeseen interpretations of his speech. He told Kennedy to stick with a gracious acceptance of the freedom of the city. "The only thing I am afraid of is that instead of giving me the freedom of the city they will make me queen of the May," he cheerfully cabled Washington as he jauntily set out.[177] Thus he dutifully espoused the official line of the British government in foreign policy, defended academic freedom, offered encouragement to students, and urged the audience to study American life and society. The warmth, affection, and thunderous applause at his reception at each university was in notable contrast to the snubbing he had had from Harvard and to the disdain that many Britons would have for him within a few months.

As he addressed an Edinburgh audience of three thousand on April 21, witnesses to his receipt of the Freedom of the City and the degree of doctor of laws, he received an ovation as he echoed the official guarded optimism of the British government. "Let us not forget that we still [have] peace," he said. "The fact that we [have] been able to escape war thus far should encourage us to hope that, somehow, we [shall] be able to win through to a just and durable peace."[178]

In a Manchester auditorium in mid-May, he received another degree of doctor of laws from Manchester University. "Our world today is in a sorry muddle," he said, stern-faced, and our fast-paced life casts doubts on traditional ways of doing things, not just moral concepts but also educational values embodied in universities. However, we must not dismiss our universities as outmoded and tradition bound; instead we should calmly and rationally use them to answer the new questions of today.[179] "By clarifying the past they could enable us to understand the present and give us the key to the future." He also suggested that a university education can be dangerous to the public welfare if it is misused by erratic and unscrupulous men.[180] His audience applauded his lecture loudly, and the editorial in the *Manchester Guardian* praised the speech for its "characteristic eloquence and good sense."[181]

The *Times* called Kennedy's focus on youth in his speech at the University of Liverpool on May 18 "the latest addition to the number of his wise, humane, and sincere speeches" and praised him for giving "encouragement without speaking smooth things and prophesying deceits." Kennedy, as the father of nine, the editorial said, well understands and sympathizes with the aspirations, the fears, and the impatience of youth who confront the challenges created by economic problems and the threat of war: These troubles are man-made troubles and man must resolve them.[182]

Kennedy was the first American ever to be awarded an honorary degree of doctor of laws by the University of Bristol and to receive it from the hands of Chamberlain's old adversary, Winston Churchill, the university's chancellor. During the ceremonies in late May, Churchill took the opportunity to lecture his audience on the propriety of Anglo-American relations. Nothing would be more injurious than to assume that the United States would fight Britain's battles for her. "It is not our business at the present time to ask favours of anyone. We have got to do our part ourselves," he said. Kennedy responded to Churchill's remarks by stressing that the English include the study of American history and culture in their schools, and arguing that "it [is] vital that English people should understand the changes going on in the United States."[183]

The ambassador was doubtless the first American ever to have conferred upon him the honorary degree of "Doctor of Fahrenheit" (representing the warm relations between the United States and Great Britain) while sitting beneath a banner inscribed "Hey, Hey, U.S.A.," and to ride to the ceremonies in the mayor's coach escorted by a posse of student motorcyclists followed by an odd assortment of motor cars. For those students nervous about their examinations, Kennedy joked that he had passed all his courses at Harvard except banking and economics—the very subjects he would make his career in. "A man would be an awful sucker to come here if you didn't like him," he called over his shoulder as he drove away. And indeed, the British most certainly did like him.[184] The *Bristol Western Daily Press* called him an "engaging personality" and "a delightful fellow."[185] He also received his fifth degree of doctor of laws, this one from Cambridge, later that same month.[186]

Besides his popularity among the British in general, Kennedy also relished his still warm relations with the king and queen and the government. He loved visiting the royal family at Windsor Castle and discussing Snow White and Dopey with Princess Elizabeth, passing along a ladybug on a gold spoon to the queen (who then put it on Chamberlain's shoulder as a sign of good luck), and traveling with members of the royal family to inspect a ballroom barrage in Hook, in Surrey, with Princess Beatrice (the great-aunt of George VI and last living daughter of Queen Victoria) and Princess Helena Victoria (the king's aunt). The ambassador broke protocol by telling the queen how beautiful she looked in the dress she was wearing; she blushed, accepted the compliment, and told him she would take the dress along on her trip to the United States.[187] Kennedy proudly recorded in his diary: "She told me that she had told Jimmy [Roosevelt] how remarkable it was the confidence that the British had in me and how it was shown today when the King and Queen and Chamberlain were to enter the *secret* room of the Ballroom Brigade the King immediately said 'Have Mr. Kennedy come in.'" "This gesture spoke more than words could ever speak."[188] The queen, after returning from the trip to the United States, also told him that she thought the president had a "real affection" for him, although she had heard that the two of them also had a volatile relationship.[189]

Kennedy certainly enjoyed the symbols of friendship and comradery extended to him by Chamberlain and Halifax. The ambassador spent a "quiet and uneventful" weekend with the Chamberlains at Chequers, the historic estate that had once belonged to Sir John Russell, the grandson of Oliver Cromwell. The Protector's sword and other memorabilia filled the historic estate surrounded on two sides by the Icknield Way, the oldest road in England, built before the Roman conquest. The remnants of the Castle of Cymbeline and an old druid altar could still be seen on the grounds. The estate was lovely in May; the forget-me-nots and bluebells, which Chamberlain was something of an authority on, were in full bloom. The prime minister, in one of his more optimistic and reflective moods, regaled his guests with his "skittish" willingness "to try anything for the cause of peace" during his trip to Italy by sending a bouquet of red roses to the Countess Ciano, Mussolini's daughter, and to give himself "a little protection by sending a bouquet to Madame Mussolini as well." "Butter would not have melted in [the Countess Ciano's] mouth." Madame Mussolini's bouquet must have wilted, as she was away at the time.[190]

Kennedy also liked being seen in public with the immensely popular Halifax. The ambassador enjoyed a small mishap when he went to 10 Downing Street to pick Halifax up after a late cabinet meeting on August 27. The bumper of his Chrysler got stuck under another bumper, and the bobbies had to ask eight or ten young men to lift up the other car to disengage the ambassador's amidst the laughing crowd cheering for the USA. "Quite a sight," Halifax said, laughing too, "the great British Public lifting the car of the American Ambassador to safety." Kennedy also recalled that people stuck their heads through the car window and poignantly said, "God Bless you!" "Please don't let us go to war," "You've saved us we know," and "I don't want to send my boy except to fight for Britain not for Poland."[191] But within a few short months, the universally popular Kennedy would become to most Englishmen the symbol of American duplicity and treachery.

Before the war, most of the English regarded him as Foreign Office officials did, as a "man with a vigorous and business-like personality, gifted with charm and a keen sense of humor," who possessed "every quality necessary for the success of his mission." Certainly, an official said, the ambassador looked at the British from an American angle, but he had acquired "an altogether remarkable understanding of [the British] outlook and a ready appreciation of their national qualities."[192] Such a sympathetic and vigorous defender of British interests as the American ambassador would be particularly valuable in the months ahead when the British needed American resources and aid to defend their besieged island country.

Besides espousing the official British line in foreign affairs, Kennedy's dispatches describing Britain's "battle of nerves" over Hitler's next action may have provided ammunition for Roosevelt in his renewed attempt to revise the neutrality bill by July, when the king and queen would arrive in the United States for an informal visit. "There is plenty of opportunity for trouble between now and the end of July," the ambassador cabled in late June, reporting on his conversation with Lord Halifax. "It all rests with Hitler." If he decides to "take on the

English, no olive branch will have any effect on him." There is a definite opinion that this is exactly what he has decided to do, the ambassador told Washington.[193]

As a way of keeping the United States out of war, Kennedy supported the administration's plan to repeal the neutrality legislation.[194] He must have quietly applauded as Roosevelt, still stinging from the dictator's rebuff, risked an isolationist filibuster and a delayed adjournment of Congress as he took up the fight for revision of the deeply embedded embargo provision lying at the heart of the neutrality laws. It prohibited the sale of all arms to any nation at war, regardless of whether that nation was the victim or the aggressor in the conflict. Roosevelt believed that only a quick show of aid to the democracies by the United States through the revision of its neutrality laws could prevent another war or at least make a victory of the dictators less likely; a do-nothing policy would only strengthen the hand of Germany's hawks.[195]

On June 30 the House approved a new version of the neutrality bill, but a late-night amendment that kept the embargo provision intact was passed by a vote of 159 to 157 in the absence of many Democrats. Undaunted, Roosevelt and Hull turned to the Senate and pressed Chairman Key Pittman of Nevada to bring the legislation to a vote before his Foreign Relations Committee. On July 11 the committee voted, 12 to 11, to reserve all consideration of neutrality legislation until January 1940.[196]

The Foreign Office noted that Kennedy, who had previously remained silent on the issue, was "greatly troubled" by the unwillingness of Congress to repeal the Neutrality Act. He feared that Hitler would believe that he could continue with his "adventure" because he supposed that the United States would not support Britain or France.[197] The bill's defeat caused American prestige abroad to "[suffer] a severe set-back," Kennedy wrote in his memoir. Critics proved him right. Some charged that Americans lacked the determination to stand against aggression. German editors blamed Roosevelt's lack of leadership for the gulf between the president and the American people, making it impossible for him to get his countrymen to join the "encirclement front" against Germany. The Italian press echoed the Germans: "Roosevelt and Hull Discomfitted [sic] for the Third Time; Roosevelt Definitely Bowled; President Does Not Know How to Resign Himself to the Idea of Not Aiding the Encirclement Powers."[198] In a bitter letter responding to Kennedy, Roosevelt wrote, "I feel, with you and the British Government, that the delay has given comfort to the aggressor nations." Although the Foreign Affairs Committee agreed to take up the matter in January, he informed Kennedy, "all we can do is to pray that another actual crisis will not arrive."[199] But of course it did, over Poland.

The British closely monitored Roosevelt's futile attempts to gain repeal, which they desperately wanted, but resigned themselves to following Lindsay's advice to refrain from any action likely to help the opponents of the amendment of the Neutrality Act and to "keep a stiff upper lip."[200] According to Kennedy, Halifax was not particularly concerned about the failure to revise the neutrality laws, considering it "satisfactory" simply to have the newspapers state that the United States would intervene if there were trouble.[201]

Actually Kennedy, like many diplomats and government officials on both sides of the Atlantic, was guilty of overestimating the importance of the United States in Hitler's thinking. Hitler contemptuously viewed America as "hopelessly weak" and "a mongrel society," and therefore incapable of cultural achievement or creating sound economic and political institutions. His plans for the invasion of Poland rested on Britain and France and his negotiations with the Soviet Union and not on the widely held belief that the repeal of the American neutrality law would be a major factor in maintaining Europe's peace.[202]

Amid the bitter controversy over the neutrality legislation came the visit in June 1939 of King George VI and Queen Elizabeth to the United States, the first visit ever by a reigning British monarch. Kennedy exuberantly adjudged the greeting between the king and the president as "perhaps the most important handclasp of modern times."[203] Their Majesties had been particularly eager to visit the Roosevelts, they told Kennedy, when he had first suggested the trip during the April weekend at Windsor Castle in 1938. As the ambassador was discussing the horrors of the Great War with the queen, it suddenly occurred to him that relations between the two English-speaking democracies could be improved by a personal visit to America by the royal pair and suggested it to her. "I only know three Americans," the queen had told him, apparently quite taken with the idea, "you, Fred Astaire, and J.P. Morgan and I would like to know more."[204]

It was he, so Kennedy claimed in his memoirs, who had persuaded the shy, hesitant king to accept the president's invitation, and who handled many preliminary details for the visit.[205] Kennedy distinctly remembered taking Roosevelt's invitation to the palace on a dreary, rainy September day in 1938 when the queen was christening a grand ship in her name and the king was deeply worried about the likelihood of war and of the return of the Duke and Duchess of Windsor to live in England.[206] The ambassador had been particularly anxious for the king and queen to visit the United States in order to boost their popularity among Americans and to dispel the mistaken impressions many had of them as a result of the abdication crisis. Kennedy was happy to inform Washington on November 3, 1938, that the king would announce his acceptance of the president's invitation on November 8 at the opening of Parliament in his Speech from the Throne.[207]

The Kennedys entertained the king and queen at the American embassy the day before they left for the trip. Excited and eager, the royal couple peppered the dinner guests with questions about various personalities, especially the Roosevelts, and asked about American manners and customs.[208] Rose went to great pains to create an atmosphere of American informality for the dinner. The menu was printed in English, not French, and featured American dishes: "Virginia ham, shad roe, and strawberry shortcake." Although the seating arrangements at the main dinner table followed protocol, with the king and queen sitting in the center of the table, the six younger Kennedy children were included and sat at a smaller table at the end of the long dining room. The evening concluded with two Walt Disney films followed by *Good-bye Mr. Chips*, an American movie made mostly in England. It made the queen and some of the other guests weep.[209] (Kennedy had had to use his considerable influence to acquire the film.) The royal couple were kind enough to invite Kennedy to don morning dress and a top hat to see them off from Waterloo Station on May 6 at 12:40.[210]

Roosevelt had first invited the royal pair at the time of the coronation of George VI in May 1937. A year later Roosevelt renewed his invitation through Kennedy when he learned that the couple would visit Canada in the summer of 1939. The president wrote, "I hope very much that you will extend your visit to include the United States. . . . I think it would be an excellent thing for Anglo-American relations." He requested, however, that any conversations about the visit be kept out of "diplomatic channels for the time being"[211] and, to signal the supposed apolitical nature of the visit, strongly preferred that, contrary to tradition, there be no "minister-in-attendance" other than the Canadian prime minister, MacKenzie King. Under the guise of a purely ceremonial visit, the president had every intention of pursuing diplomatic goals by educating the American public and by publicizing Anglo-American friendship and common interests and values under the noses of the dictators. He also wanted to emphasize "the essential democracy" of the royal pair by minimizing official Washington functions and inviting them to Hyde Park for its rustic naturalism and idyllic setting, complete with a picnic featuring beer and hotdogs, swimming, and a straightforward talk on diplomacy.[212]

To Kennedy, however, the visit of the king and queen became another example of the administration's circumvention of him. Not only was he not permitted to accompany Their Majesties to the United States, but he was even kept ignorant of many of the arrangements. He would know nothing about the trip, he complained to Hull, if it were not for the Foreign Office. "If the President wanted me to be aware of any discussion he is having I suppose he would inform me," he added with bitter sarcasm. His prestige "would be seriously jeopardized" if he remained ill informed. He felt "like a dummy," although he promised to carry on as best he could.[213] "Admittedly, I should have known by then that such are the ways of the State Department," Kennedy wrote in his memoir, resigned to his fate.[214]

Roosevelt tried to soothe Kennedy's pride by telling him that it was easier to sort out the details for the trip in Washington. One adviser recalled another motive: "The announcement of the royal visit infuriated the Irish at the White House. It signaled an impending alliance and we interpreted it to mean that America would soon be at war," Thomas Corcoran recalled.[215] It seemed too risky to allow Kennedy, known for his avowed isolationism and opposition to any alliance with any country, to participate in the arrangements. If FDR were to have an Anglo-American alliance in mind, Kennedy would be certain to oppose it.

Kennedy's hurt feelings aside, and the hair-raising car ride by Roosevelt at Hyde Park, which thoroughly frightened the queen,[216] the mid-June royal visit was a moment of friendship, goodwill, and glittering pomp and pageantry during a tense, crisis-ridden summer. It was an unqualified success and helped to store up goodwill for Britain in the tough months ahead. An editorial in the *New York Post* stated:

Great Britain is now engaged in an historic struggle to preserve democratic ideals. This endeavor has our undivided sympathy, supported by a tradition of Anglo-American friendship best exemplified by the 5000 miles of unfortified Canadian border. The Nazi press may sneer and wax sarcastic, but the clicking glasses at the White House banquet table were quite definitely audible in Berlin and Rome.[217]

The ambassador, swept up in the afterglow and given to overstatement, told his audience at the annual Fourth of July dinner of the American Society that Their Majesties had "made more friends for their nation than any other two people in history." Another exuberantly blunt New York businessman who never "threw his hat in the air over anything," now thoroughly smitten by the royal couple, wrote: "We liked them. We sure do!"[218] Although the visit produced no immediate change in congressional attitudes toward neutrality revision or in foreign policy generally, nor is its long-term impact possible to determine, it did create a firm relationship of mutual affection and genuine respect between the king and the president. And it pleased Kennedy: "I look back with some sense of pride in having suggested and arranged a visit that added something substantial to the building of a better understanding between our two peoples," he wrote in his memoir.[219]

During the royal visit Kennedy made up his mind to resign. While the king and queen were still touring the United States, he told American friends to expect him home soon and made a reservation on the first return flight of the new Pan-American Clipper. He had a long list of reasons for quitting: the toll on his family and fortune was immense; the younger children were becoming too British, his business affairs were being harmed, and the personal expenses of his ambassadorship were enormous.[220] Friends sensed a new note of irritation in his attitude toward the British. "A lot of people tell me that Britain is relying on two things today. . . . One is God and the other is the United States, and recently you [British] don't seem to have been counting too much on the Deity," he remarked in an interview.[221] Furthermore, Kennedy was homesick.

Even more important, perhaps, he was worn out and disenchanted by the stinging barrage of criticism he received from men of every political stripe at home and abroad. Snipers included administration liberals who sought to unseat him, grudge-holders irate because of imagined snubs, accusers who claimed that he used his office to fatten his pocketbook, progressives who criticized him for being undemocratic, Nazis who charged him with conspiracy, fellow isolationists who accused him of being too pro-British, and State Department officials who questioned his diplomatic judgment. Some of the criticism was accurate, much of it was exaggerated, and some was a vicious smear job.[222] All of it was in marked contrast to the rosy reception he still had in Britain—for the moment. He also had his adoring fans in the United States—fans such as Father Coughlin and Arthur Krock, whose support often drove the wedge between Kennedy and administration liberals even deeper.

The tale-telling secretary of the Interior, Harold Ickes, out to get Kennedy dismissed, delighted in exacerbating the differences between him and his boss. Ickes gossiped about him during a luncheon with John Cudahy, the American minister to Eire. "Joe Kennedy does some pretty loud and inappropriate talking about the President," Cudahy said, and described Kennedy as "vulgar and coarse and highly critical in what he says." When Cudahy chided him for talking so before the servants, Kennedy said he didn't give a damn.[223] Cudahy also admonished him that if he could not be loyal he ought to resign.[224] Roosevelt already knew that Kennedy didn't give a damn, but Roosevelt didn't give a damn either. He found Kennedy useful and that was good enough. Unlike the gossip-loving Ickes, FDR valued Kennedy because he was a well-informed and candid reporter. Roosevelt could afford to ignore his disloyalty.[225] When Ickes related his conversation with Cudahy to the president, the president told Ickes that he knew that Kennedy was disloyal but "as good as anyone in reporting carefully what was transpiring in England and in diplomatic circles." Roosevelt obviously had "[no] intention of removing him," Ickes noted in his diary.[226]

Undeterred and delighting in any kind of anti-Kennedy putdown, Ickes passed on to Roosevelt a cocktail-party quip made by Mrs. Ickes. "Mr. President, I had a talk with Senator Borah on the telephone today who, as you know, has better sources of information in Europe than the Department of State." FDR fell for it and asked, "Did you? Is he in Washington?" "No," Ickes replied with a straight face. "He tells me, from his confidential sources, that Chamberlain has decided to increase his Cabinet so that he can give Joe Kennedy a place in it." The president tossed his head back and roared.[227]

Nor was Ickes above gathering every malicious scrap of Kennedy criticism or showing the president smear jobs on him, particularly by Claud Cockburn, a former *Times* journalist in Washington and since 1937 a *Pravda* correspondent in London. Cockburn had made constant accusations of pro-Nazi intrigues at Cliveden, which provided much of the ammunition for the criticism of Kennedy's association with the Astors.[228] Ickes stayed behind after a Cabinet meeting to show FDR an article written by an exiled anti-fascist Italian diplomat, Count Carlo Sforza, which appeared in a Swiss Democratic Party paper, the *National-Zeitung*, and which Cockburn printed a crude translation of in *The Week* on June 14, 1939.

> The American Ambassador in London, Kennedy, is speaking with the Germanophile circle which is behind the London Times not only in a defaitistoc [*sic*] manner, but more in a way extremely hostile against President Roosevelt. He is sympathizing in such a way with General Franco—and means that he is doing a very good work for his church—that he often explains that the Democratic policy of the United States is a Jewish matter and that Roosevelt will disappear in 1940.[229]

FDR thoughtfully read the article and quietly replied, "It is true." Ickes believed that if the allegations were true, Kennedy ought to be recalled immediately. But FDR did nothing.[230] J. Edgar Hoover also sent him a copy of the article that appeared in the *Fortune Observer*, New

York City, on July 1, 1939. Writing on May 17 in *The Week*, the left-wing journal he edited, and quoted by Ludwig Lore in his *New York Post* column, Cockburn claimed to be puzzled by why Roosevelt kept Kennedy in office.[231] The ambassador's influence on the British government was so great that his opinions had even been quoted in the British cabinet, Cockburn said.[232]

Rumor had it, according to the president, that Bernard Baruch, another Washington insider, was put out by Kennedy because during Baruch's last trip to Britain, Kennedy had snubbed him. Baruch had called the American embassy and only a fourth assistant secretary turned up to help him. He was further outraged that he had to go through the regular line at customs along with the rest of his countrymen because the ambassador had not cleared him, the usual procedure with important visitors. Kennedy denied the first charge but said that he might have been at fault in the second matter. One of Baruch's friends had previously referred to the incident, but Kennedy had simply dismissed the remark as facetious. Baruch's temper could be smoothed, Kennedy was told, if he would seek his counsel on barter negotiations between the United States and Britain. "Well, I can't keep up with all this conniving. I have got too much to do with really important things and if the boys want to knock my head off, it's just too bad," he said.[233]

Indeed they did. Walter Winchell, the gossip columnist, contributed to the charge that Kennedy continued to gain financially from his position in London. Winchell wrote in his column that "there is no statute that prohibits our Ambassadors from speculating—get it?" Kennedy was livid over his "rotten insinuation" and told Wesley Winans Stout, the editor of the *Saturday Evening Post*, that it would be harder and harder to get good men to give up their "personal interests" and to go into public service. "I have never speculated in a share of stock in the last five years," he hotly retorted. "When I went to work for the Government in 1934, I made up my mind that I was through with stock markets, etc., regardless of what the cost might be and even during the year I was out of Government service I adhered religiously to that idea," he wrote Stout.[234]

Kennedy's critics even included progressives like Philip F. La Follette;[235] Hitler's propaganda minister, Joseph Goebbels; and Kennedy's fellow isolationist General Hugh S. Johnson. La Follette, the former governor of Wisconsin, accused Kennedy of being "sympathetic toward undemocratic elements in Great Britain" and had, like Kennedy, been the object of violent Nazi criticism. Goebbels described the ambassador as a "master conspirator" who plotted "to add the United States to an iron ring around Germany."[236] Johnson, the former head of the National Recovery Administration, lambasted the ambassador during his testimony on the revision of the Neutrality Act before the Senate Foreign Relations Committee. "Walter Hines Page was a British Ambassador to Washington," he said. "It would be a good idea to inquire whether we have not got another of those things at the Court of St. James [*sic*] now. The dowagers and the duchesses—not to mention the debs—are a potent pill."[237] Kennedy "has been taken in tow by the Social Lobby," chortled a columnist for the *New York Times*. "One more diplomatic American scalp dangles at the belt of the duchesses." Was there anyone "who may be trusted to go to London and not be led astray?"[238] The ambassador lightly dismissed Johnson's criticism of him as "one that is made on all ambassadors." One could not serve his country well without being on close terms with the host government, he told Stout. "They must respect and believe you, otherwise your efficiency is handicapped."[239]

The constant criticism of Kennedy by State Department officials continued as many questioned the soundness of his judgment. Adolf Berle reported that one of Kennedy's proposed speeches, in which he was going to urge Englishmen to boycott war, was "more than usually foolish." Berle convinced FDR to send his ambassador a cablegram telling him not to make the speech. Kennedy obeyed.[240]

Attacks against Kennedy became so intense that Hull, who had previously wondered whether the ambassador accurately represented the American position, came to his defense and told a press conference that he had "full faith" in Kennedy. Hull scoffed at allegations made by such politically diverse men as La Follette and Goebbels.[241] Hull said that he refused to believe that "there is anything serious about being attacked from a so-called Progressive, Liberal or similar angle one day and the next day being attacked by the opposite angle of reactionaryism."[242] Kennedy expressed regret that he had let critics get under his skin so deeply. But he felt handicapped by his position and could not resign and "hit back" against the "complete misunderstanding" of what is in the best interests of the United States. "I think the greatest shock many people have had is that they thought I could probably do a good job in business in America, but this one would be way beyond anything I had been trained for"—comments reminiscent of Boake Carter's wise counsel to Kennedy at the beginning of his ambassadorship. "Besides doing the ordinary routine of this job, I have had only one interest and that is, that the best interests of the United States are served by peace in Europe and not by war and my efforts have been toward that every hour of every day that I have been here."[243]

But Kennedy also had his defenders, who annoyed the administration's liberals and FDR himself and served to increase their resentment of the ambassador and to enhance his reputation for disloyalty to the administration. Father Charles Coughlin, a leading crypto-fascist Jew-baiting anti-Semite and editor of a right-wing national weekly, *Social Justice*, named Kennedy "The Man of the Week" in February 1939. Kennedy's family life exemplified "the ideal of an American home," Coughlin wrote. He also praised the ambassador for not being a "puppet of Barney Baruch in disrepute with his master." The ambassador was a "typical American," and under fire from the "newspaper 'smear brigade.'" He was about to be sacked, Coughlin wrote, because he supported Washington's policy of no entangling alliances and not some "Baruchian maneuver of international finance." Such statements from Coughlin, a fervent presidential critic, deepened the rift between Kennedy and the administration liberals.[244]

Roosevelt himself was not above indirectly launching a barrage at Kennedy by attacking his longtime friend and political booster, Arthur Krock. This correspondent had "never in his whole life said a really decent thing about any human being without qualifying it by some nasty dig at the end of the praise," the president said in a letter to Kennedy. Krock was "a social parasite whose surface support can be won by entertainment and flattery, but who in his heart is a cynic who has never felt warm affection for anybody—man or woman." "I suppose you know of the latest 'Krock' in the *Times* about you," FDR wrote to Kennedy. That "particular gentleman, with his distorted ideas of how to be helpful, has done you more harm in the past few years than all of your enemies put together," Roosevelt said, and referred to Krock's *New York Times* column of July 18, 1939, "Why Ambassador Kennedy Is Not Coming Home."[245] In it Krock accused the young New Dealers of waging a propaganda campaign against Kennedy, of asserting that he had fallen in Roosevelt's favor, and of leveling a host of incorrect charges against him—he had "gone British," he wanted to come to terms with the dictators, he was part of the Cliveden Set, and he had commented "less than adoringly" on Roosevelt's record.[246]

Actually there was little mystery about why FDR kept Kennedy in office. The president still found his temperamental, independent, wayward ambassador more useful and less dangerous at the Court of St. James's than in the United States. He was a good, candid, well-informed reporter, and he was an intimate of the Chamberlain government, a position that would be extremely helpful to FDR in the upcoming crisis over Poland. President and ambassador knew each other well and understood each other; each kept up his act of comradery and affection despite knowing about the mutual denunciations behind each other's backs. Besides, FDR could overlook faults in people he deemed useful. An unhappy Kennedy in London was less damaging to the president's possible third-term ambitions and his control of foreign policy than an unhappy Kennedy in Washington, where he might be able to mobilize forces critical to FDR in both domestic and foreign policy. Furthermore, the president could always circumvent his ambassador by sending his own representative abroad, as he had sent Bernard Baruch, or undermine the ambassador by refusing to keep him fully informed, as he had done with the royal visit. Keeping Kennedy in London out of harm's way was clearly the better course, the president reasoned, even though he had to spend a good bit of time administering large doses of presidential charm and persuasiveness to appease his ambassador and soothe his ego. "The trouble with Kennedy," Roosevelt told Morgenthau years before Kennedy became ambassador, "is you always have to hold his hand." Kennedy gets upset "at irregular intervals" and "he calls up and says he is hurt because I have not seen him."[247]

Once again, and yet again later, when the ambassador told Roosevelt he wanted to resign, Roosevelt administered a generous dose of charm and Kennedy changed his mind. I was just "telling several people the other day that I have complete confidence in you, that you have never mentioned leaving London, that you are doing a good job there, and that in these critical days I count on your carrying on."[248] Kennedy promised to remain at his job through the summer, at least, and canceled his reservations on the Pan-American Clipper.

Later, in a speech before the Pilgrim Club, Kennedy indulged in self-pity and described

London "as the most difficult place for an American diplomat to make a success." "Here you make good by what you prevent happening rather than cause to happen." He reassured his audience: "I am not planning to leave England, in spite of the fact that every morning when I get up I see either that my successor has been named or that I'm due to leave."[249] So instead of going home, in mid-July Kennedy wired Hull for permission to vacation in Cannes throughout August, noting that those in the British government were doing likewise. "In the middle of August it may be necessary for everybody to be back in London," he explained, promising to return within five hours "if anything should arise."[250]

Kennedy tidied up his own thinking, dashed off his latest views on the international scene, and made several calls on government officials before going on vacation. On July 20, 1939, he went to see the dour prime minister, who graciously told him that he would have been disappointed if he had not come to say goodbye.[251] After a long talk with the prime minister, the ambassador told Hull that the British were a bit more doggedly optimistic about the next thirty days. This optimism was echoed in the press and throughout the country. Yet Kennedy wrote, "The public is psychologically ready" for war.[252] Nevertheless, the prime minister had managed to convince himself and therefore Kennedy, too, that peace was still possible. Chamberlain believed that the country's conscription program and the recent naval reserves call-up had made Hitler, whom Chamberlain considered "highly intelligent," believe that England would fight if necessary, and might make him decide not to "gamble on a world war." Kennedy cabled: "We are witnessing the greatest and most expensive dress rehearsal that has ever taken place for a show that will never be produced."[253] But of course Hitler's plans called for a big dramatic production not at all to the liking of the two peace lovers.

After his conversation with Chamberlain, who was himself leaving for a two-week vacation in Scotland, from August 5 to August 21, the ambassador packed up and flew to the Côte d'Azur, to the Domaine de Ranguin, an estate above Cannes known for its beautiful rose gardens.[254] "For a lazy month, he swam from a rented yacht, played golf every afternoon, and coddled his stomach ulcer," and wrote to Roosevelt.[255] Kennedy enjoyed getting away from the bustle in London, and for the first few days he felt carefree enough to "let the world slip by"; and yet he never quite got away. He received daily dispatches from the embassy in London, and had the telephone at his fingertips.[256]

He was joined by his wife and seven of their nine children. Still he had trouble shaking off his mood of self-pity and despondency even in Cannes, with its warm sands and blue Mediterranean. Seeing his children again and having them close to him reminded him of "the kind of a world that some men were seeking to destroy and others were too divided to preserve," he wrote in his memoir.[257]

To Roosevelt he wrote a touching and sentimental letter proclaiming his loyalty. His friends did sometimes embarrass him, he acknowledged, in response to Roosevelt's digs about Krock. Although Kennedy wrote that he still enjoyed public service because it gave him the opportunity to work with Roosevelt, he felt dejected and unappreciated, little "more than a glorified errand boy" who worried that his experience and knowledge were being wasted. But of one thing Roosevelt could be sure, Kennedy said: "Regardless of any personal inconvenience, as long as I am of any assistance to you, I shall remain for whatever time you like." Citing his boyhood lessons of gratitude and loyalty, he wrote, "I have tried to live up to those two principles, and to you personally, I owe a debt on both counts." "Remember," he promised, "that whatever you want to do, I always 'stay put.'"[258]

Soon after Kennedy returned to London on August 22, 1939, Hitler dropped a "complete bombshell."[259] The news broke that the unbelievable had happened: the two mortal enemies, Nazi Germany and Soviet Russia, represented by their foreign ministers, Joachim von Ribbentrop and Vyacheslav Molotov, in the midst of a celebration with toasts and handshakes all around, signed a nonaggression pact on August 24, 1939, at l a.m. in Moscow. (By the time the treaty was actually signed, it was August 24, but it was dated August 23.) It ensured a German attack on Poland and ensured Soviet neutrality by conceding those areas that the democracies had refused to grant to Stalin. The Baltic republics and part of eastern Poland would go to the Soviets, and Germany would be allowed to dominate Lithuania. Hitler also recognized Stalin's greedy interest in Bessarabia and agreed not to claim any part of southeastern Europe. It seemed that Hitler had outbid the British and the French and offered Stalin a shaky peace and the illusion of security at a far higher price than the democracies could have afforded. And Stalin hoped for a long, devastating trench war from which he could remain aloof, just as Kennedy had predicted.[260]

Kennedy, who had been closely watching the developments, was shocked by the announcement of the non-aggression pact. But Washington was not. It had deliberately kept Kennedy ignorant of the negotiations.[261] Neither he nor Chamberlain had been aware that they had been going on; but Kennedy and Halifax, unlike Chamberlain, had foreseen that possibility.[262] Kennedy also believed that had he known about the negotiations, he could have prevented the pact by pressing Chamberlain and Halifax to step up their own negotiating with the Russians. Kennedy wrote in his memoir: "Indeed, the Russian-German accord of August 21 might never have occurred"—as if he could have prevented it; as if Hitler could have been prevented from making the pact.[263]

Pacing the floor of his private office in his shirtsleeves on August 23, the day after his return from Cannes, he told a caller, broadcaster H. V. Kaltenborn, "'You have come to me in one of the most important moments in world history!'" Although the ambassador realized that time was running out and that the opportunities for working out an accommodation with Hitler were slight, he also believed that "anything that keeps Britain at peace is in the interest of the United States." The United States will no doubt become involved, as "I believe we should," he told Kaltenborn, but financially, not militarily. "Chamberlain feels he cannot make too many concessions. Yet gaining time is the most important thing we can do at this point." Certainly time was what Chamberlain's government wanted, too—time to press the Poles into submission.[264]

The ambassador's advice to Roosevelt reflected his frantic determination to buy time to preserve peace, reminiscent of his advice over Munich. Buy time, he urged the president, on behalf of Chamberlain, press the Poles to submit to a Polish Munich, give in to Hitler's latest demands: Danzig, the Polish Corridor, and a plebiscite. As the father of two sons of military age, Kennedy's overwhelming desire for peace was less national or ideological than familial and financial. "I hate to think how much money I would give up rather than sacrifice Joe and Jack in a war," he once told his father-in-law, Honey Fitz.[265]

Propelled into a flurry of activity, Kennedy, in a state of despair, talked to both Halifax and Chamberlain and sent off to Washington his up-to-the-minute cables reporting on his conversations the day the news broke. That evening, August 23, at seven o'clock, Kennedy saw Halifax, who told him that war was inevitable. "England will definitely go to war if Poland starts to fight." "My reason shows me no way out of war, but my instincts still give me hope," Halifax said to him. Kennedy cabled Washington: "I have a distinct feeling that [the British] do not want to be more Polish than the Poles and they are praying the Poles will find some way of adjusting their differences with the Germans at once."[266] The "differences" included Russia's repeated request to allow its troops to pass through Polish and Rumanian territory, a request that Poland had adamantly refused to grant.

An hour later, Kennedy met the downcast and depressed prime minister, who "looks like a broken man," he wrote in his diary.[267] The situation looked "very bad," Kennedy reported in a second cable to Washington. Chamberlain saw no way to urge the Poles to accept Hitler's demands. Any attempt by him, he feared, would be "disastrous." "I have done everything that I can think of and it seems as if all my work has come to naught. . . . The futility of it all is the thing that is frightful; after all [the British] cannot save the Poles; they can merely carry on a war of revenge that will mean the destruction of the whole of Europe."[268] After millions of dead and the destruction of our financial and economic institutions, both sides would see, the prime minister predicted to Kennedy, that they had accomplished nothing and would seek peace on the same terms under discussion now.[269]

Chamberlain's mood was contagious; Kennedy, dubbed the Stormy Petrel,[270] became as gloomy as he. "I left with the feeling that the situation was dark and much worse than it was a year ago," he told Washington. The only hope he saw was for the Poles to use delaying tactics in their negotiations with the Germans. He implied that Roosevelt should use his influence for peace, perhaps in the hope of pulling off a Polish Munich. "The place to work is on Jósef [sic] Beck," Kennedy urged. "To make this effective it must happen quickly. I see no other possibility."[271] But even Poland would not bring much time, he feared. The most that could be hoped for was to get a short-term agreement.[272]

At ten that night, August 23, Kennedy sent a third cable to Hull. Everybody in Britain was "punch drunk" and incapable of planning any effective action, he reported. And, he said,

"I am not of the opinion that they are able to carry it and we are the only ones on whom it could be shifted." He warned Washington that the United States should remain aloof and evaluate the events calmly and dispassionately.[273] His advice to Hull was clear. "This is one bull whose tail we ought to go slow in seizing."[274]

Caution, delay, and gaining time by sacrificing the Poles was Kennedy's advice. But for what purpose? He was obsessed with gaining time. By his own admission, the situation was worse than it was a year ago: time had helped Hitler; after Munich he had increased his military preparations; more time would only help Hitler more. Time had worsened Britain's military position. More time could do little for the Allies. They probably had not even made war plans; nor would they unless war was declared, but continue in their unrealistic belief that somehow war could be prevented. Thus time would bring the Allies little benefit.[275]

As he had before, he now again urged a sellout—this time of the Poles: "I'd sell a hundred Polands down the river any day rather than risk the life of a British soldier or the loss of a British pound." Count Edward Raczyński, the Polish ambassador, later remarked that "Kennedy was generally sympathetic to Poland's plight, but Poland was of course a secondary concern to Kennedy."[276] His sympathy for Poland quickly evaporated when he thought of the global chaos it would cause. Nothing to maintain peace, peace at any price, peace for a while, actually peace for naught—peace was not on the Nazi agenda.

The next morning, August 24, Chamberlain's government approached the willing American ambassador with a very sensitive proposition: ask Roosevelt to put pressure on the Poles to acquiesce to Hitler's demands. It was a strategy that had succeeded once in preserving peace and might work again if the United States could be persuaded to go along with it. Sir Horace Wilson, on the prime minister's behalf, told Kennedy that "he saw no hope of avoiding war unless the Poles were willing to negotiate with the Germans." Put pressure on the Poles "at once," Wilson said, since Chamberlain believed that "the blow is fairly near."[277] Since Britain was in no position to press Poland, given its commitment to it, the only other likely actor was the United States.[278]

Kennedy called Washington that night to deliver Wilson's proposal. "The British wanted one thing of us and one thing only, namely that we put pressure on the Poles," the panicky ambassador told Sumner Welles as the president listened in. "They felt that they could not, given their obligations, do anything of this sort but that we could," Kennedy reported—his views exactly.[279] The proposal to press the Poles was unanimously scotched by FDR and his advisers. "As we saw it here," Moffat shrewdly assessed it, "it merely meant that they wanted us to assume the responsibility of a new Munich and to do their dirty work for them."[280]

Roosevelt did respond to the crisis, but not as Kennedy had advised. On August 23, 1939, the president sent a message to the king of Italy, Victor Emmanuel, requesting that he use his influence on behalf of peace. In his transatlantic call to Welles the next day, Kennedy pronounced the president's message "lousy," "a complete flop."[281] "The idea of anybody addressing anything to [the] King of Italy, whom people here had considered a nonentity for years, did not make the dramatic hit" that the president's messages usually did.[282] Only one thing would have made any difference, Kennedy told Welles, and that was to strongly urge the Poles to give in to Germany's demands. Such a message would have to begin: "In view of the fact that your suicide is required, kindly oblige by etc.," Adolf Berle, a seasoned State Department official, wrote in his diary. "Kennedy must have been sold a bill of goods, presumably by Sir Horace Wilson,"[283] but no such sale was necessary—Kennedy had already bought the goods some time before.

Again ignoring his ambassador's advice, Roosevelt also sent last-minute messages to Hitler and to Ignacy Mościcki, the president of Poland, the next day, August 24, and urged them to use every resource to settle their differences peaceably.[284] Adolf Berle said that these messages, typically illustrating American naiveté, would be about as effective as "a valentine sent to somebody's mother-in-law out of season."[285] When Poland's president immediately responded agreeably to Roosevelt's request, Roosevelt promptly sent off another cable so informing Hitler. "All the world prays that Germany, too, will accept," the president wrote.[286] This "put the bee on Germany," Roosevelt said, "which nobody had done in 1914."[287] He then sat back and waited for events to unfold.

Hitler's answer to Roosevelt's message came on August 25 in the form of a cable from Nevile Henderson, which Kennedy sent to Washington after meeting with Chamberlain, Halifax, Cadogan, and Wilson to discuss it late that evening. "Poland had no future," Hitler calmly told Henderson; Russia and Germany would see to that. He had every intention of getting "his rights in Poland" and was fully prepared to risk "a great war, from which England would suffer much more than Germany." He had only limited ambitions, Hitler said, and once the Polish issue was settled, he would "make a deal with England that would guarantee the British Empire forever."[288]

Henderson's cable contained a list of propositions regarding Poland that Hitler insisted Britain accept. Kennedy characterized them as "ridiculous" and said that they boiled down to one thing: Britain should abandon the Poles. Actually, he did not find Hitler's propositions so absurd. "Writing this out it looks like a ridiculous proposition to make Great Britain quit or cut away from the Poles but to hear the text as read it seems much more reasonable," he told Hull. After he had straightened out the Polish problem, Hitler intended, he told Henderson, to "go back to peaceful pursuits, and become an artist, which is what he wanted to be." That is what "he is now," Kennedy said in an aside, "but I would not care to say what kind."[289] Roosevelt was quite amused by his ambassador's cable and told Ickes that it was so unusual that he filed it away in his private file.[290] Kennedy still clung to the done-to-death policy of appeasement. And Chamberlain was seemingly willing to consider Kennedy's opinions and to allow him to sit in on policy deliberations, perhaps in the hope that he could succeed in winning Roosevelt's support to put pressure on the Poles.[291]

Upon hearing that Henderson's cable outlining Hitler's answer had been received and was being decoded, Kennedy called Wilson at ten o'clock at 10 Downing Street that evening,

August 24. "Any news?" Kennedy asked him. "A lot," Wilson answered, but he did not want to discuss it over the phone. "Would you like me to come around?" the ambassador asked. "Fine," Wilson replied. "I'll be there in 10 minutes," Kennedy said. He sped off in a taxi for the prime minister's residence and found a crowd waiting outside. "The American Ambassador," Kennedy heard people murmur as he was promptly admitted. He walked down a long corridor and entered Sir Horace Wilson's office. Wilson emerged from the Cabinet Room and met Kennedy in his office. And showed Kennedy the dispatches that Henderson had sent. "Okay," Kennedy said after he had read them. "Come along," Wilson commanded, and Kennedy followed him into the Cabinet Room, where he met Chamberlain, Halifax, and Cadogan, some of them still in their dinner jackets and evening clothes. Chamberlain invited Kennedy to sit next to him. Chamberlain asked Kennedy: "What do you make of it?" as the ambassador read Henderson's cable. The others made notes on Kennedy's comments or underlined the passages he was referring to. You can't "quit on Poland," Kennedy replied, "no matter what else happen[s]." Quitting on Poland would jeopardize Britain's honor and destroy your political party. "You must pass the hat before the corpse gets cold," Kennedy quipped, and suggested using the economic bait. Britain's response to Hitler should state that if a "reasonable Polish settlement" were negotiated, the United States and other countries might join in an economic plan far more beneficial to Germany than anything it would receive from Poland. After discussing the situation for another half hour, Kennedy prepared to leave to return to the embassy and send off his cable to Washington. As he walked past Chamberlain's chair at the end of the hour-long meeting, he affectionately patted the stiff and reserved prime minister on the shoulder and said, "Don't worry Neville, I still believe God is working with you."[292]

Kennedy's proposals amounted to little more than a huge economic bribe. He also advised the government to convene another Munich. The British listened and did nothing. Kennedy's proposals were immediately dismissed. They "defied the logic of events," wrote Nasaw. Hitler was not likely to be bought off with economic bribes. "It was even more preposterous to believe that the Chamberlain government, having failed in its attempt at appeasement at Munich, would try again less than a year later."[293]

His meeting with Britain's top policymakers over the Polish crisis was "probably the most important thing that has ever happened to me," Kennedy wrote in his diary. "Here I was an American Ambassador called into discussion with the Prime Minister and Foreign Secretary over probably the most important event in the history of the British Empire. I had been called in before the Cabinet and had been trusted not only for my discretion but for my intelligence. It was a moving experience," he said. "I felt greatly complimented to have been asked into that terribly important meeting."

Discussing the meeting the next day with Cadogan, Kennedy said how pleased he was to be consulted. "We are very happy to have an Ambassador here that we feel we can trust—whose judgment we respect and appreciate to give us another point of view," said the undersecretary, whose flattery was in marked contrast to Roosevelt's treatment of Kennedy and to British dealings with him after the outbreak of war.[294] Perhaps Ickes's joke that Chamberlain was making a place for Kennedy in the cabinet had not been so wide of the mark, nor General Johnson's about Kennedy being another Walter Hines Page.

An emotional and jittery Kennedy spent the twilight days of peace grasping at straws and searching for omens of peace only to have them float away like some will-o'-the-wisp. Hitler had not yet completely shut the door, Kennedy enthusiastically wrote to Hull on August 28, but peace was "balanced on the edge of a knife" as Hitler tried to squeeze and blackmail any advantage out of Poland.[295] Kennedy also cabled Welles an optimistic account of Joe Jr.'s trip to Germany, in which Joe Jr. concluded that the German people did not want war and that Britain and France had been psychologically paralyzed by the Nazi-Soviet Pact. However, Hitler had gone too far to back down with Poland. He would get his war, the ambassador's son predicted, but it would only last a week or ten days and not trigger a general European war.

How little the Germans understood the British; how little Joe Jr. or his father understood the Germans; how well the Americans understood the British.[296]

The ambassador paid rapt attention to events, meticulously observing them and making dramatic pronouncements that had no substance.[297] "The jig is up," he told Hull on August 27, adding that he had just sent him a cable—"the most serious one he had ever sent in his life." After Kennedy's guarded call, Hull sent for several aides, who sat waiting for Kennedy's cable for two or three hours on a hot, muggy Washington Sunday. His telegram did not bear out his sensational description. It was merely a rehearsal of the British cabinet's negotiation, which Washington viewed as an unrealistic play for time. It also made the administration suspect that the British were quite willing to leave Poland in the lurch.[298]

The unenthusiastic but still hopeful prime minister told Kennedy on August 30 that he was "more worried about getting the Poles to be reasonable than the Germans." The ambassador cabled Washington and reported that Chamberlain wanted to reassure the Poles about the future value of a settlement to them. He had also urged Henderson to tell Hitler that Danzig was really only a small matter: What really mattered was solving Europe's economic and political problems. The prime minister is not "kidding himself that this thing is settled" and sees "great difficulties ahead," Kennedy wrote.[299]

But Hitler had already set September 1 as the date for the invasion of Poland. In Washington, the "death watch" over Europe had begun once again.[300] One State Department official described it as "sitting in a house where somebody is dying upstairs. There is relatively little to do and yet the suspense continues unabated."[301]

On the eve of Poland's invasion, Kennedy whiled away the hours by writing letters. He wrote to Missy to ask her to do him a favor: contact an associate of his, Paul Murphy, from his New York office, and ask Murphy to send an "interesting" photo of Roosevelt and the king to her; then, "when everybody isn't too busy," get Roosevelt to inscribe the picture to him, Kennedy, and send it to him. He expected George VI to sign it too, he told Missy. He was not jesting.[302]

He also wrote to Mrs. Roosevelt, sadly musing about how quickly everything had changed. "This morning we are praying that, miraculously, war may be avoided, when only a month ago everyone thought things were definitely on the upgrade."[303] What most concerned him, he told her, was the inevitable devastating effect war would have on the political, economic, and social institutions of the United States. Her gentle reply was typical of her: "One cannot help but worry about one's own country. However, we must live from day to day and do the best we can. We cannot plan the future; that is for youth to do."[304] But Kennedy was inconsolable and could no longer be touched by soothing gestures. In a moving letter to Wesley Stout, Kennedy could not have been more explicit about his motives: "I have nine children and I have young friends and I regard them all as my hostages for my devotion to the interests of the United States, first, last and always."[305]

CHAPTER 7

It's the End of the World . . .
The End of Everything . . .

On Friday, September 1, 1939, "the news . . . came with a rush like a torrent spewing from the wires—German troops had crossed the border; German planes were bombing Polish cities and killing civilians; the Germans were using gas," Kennedy wrote in his memoirs.[1] Although information was sketchy and some accounts were exaggerated, Nazi troops were on the move once again. In a phone call to Cordell Hull that day, the ambassador predicted that Britain would declare war. "It's all over. . . . The party is on," he said. Any chance to prevent the war? the secretary of state asked. "Oh, unquestionably none," Kennedy replied.[2] But he was wrong; the party was not on. The Poles fought on alone for two more days while the French debated and the British temporized. Under the Agreement of Mutual Assistance signed between the United Kingdom and Poland on August 25, 1939, Britain was obliged to come to Poland's aid "at once" and to give "all the support and assistance in its power."[3]

Throughout this trying time, Kennedy kept his government well informed and anxiously waited for events to unfold. Britain and France had issued a warning to Hitler demanding the cessation of all hostilities against Poland, the ambassador wrote in his first dispatch on September 1 sent at 4:00 p.m. They also insisted upon the removal of all German troops from Poland; failing that, "the obligations of Great Britain will come immediately into play," the British warned.[4] Kennedy's second, third, and fourth telegrams sent at 5:00 p.m., 8:00 p.m., and 12:00 midnight that day said that a second note with an ultimatum with a time limit was being prepared and was to be sent that evening but was held up because of delays by the French. Kennedy thought the note likely to be ignored.[5] All Britain's armed forces had been mobilized, and Chamberlain had broadened his cabinet by inviting his constant critic and opponent of appeasement, Winston Churchill, to join it as First Lord of the Admiralty, and by asking former cabinet member Anthony Eden to become the secretary of state for the Dominions. The appointments were "hardly a surprise to anyone," and were necessary to make in order to consolidate the Conservatives, Kennedy noted.[6] Despite the war preparations, there was widespread suspicion and doubt about whether Britain would honor its commitment to Poland.[7]

Saturday, September 2, 1939, was "a day of ominous waiting silence," Kennedy remembered.[8] The delay was unavoidable, he cabled Hull, because the French chamber would not be convened until 3 o'clock that afternoon. The British wanted to coordinate the approach between the two countries and to avoid the impression of "dragging France into war," he wrote.[9] The British also wanted to demonstrate that they were not simply honoring their commitment to Poland; they were also supporting their French ally.[10] Chamberlain's announcement of aid to Poland was further confounded by Mussolini's unrealistic proposal of a Five-Power Conference between Britain, France, Russia, Italy, and Germany—a proposition that the British would only consider in the unlikely event that Hitler first withdrew his troops from Poland.[11] Regardless of the delay, Britain was "set to go," Kennedy told the secretary, since Chamberlain did not expect Hitler to evacuate Poland.[12] Thus, the next twenty-four hours were crucial, the ambassador predicted. London and Paris would ultimately decide whether or not to go to war.

Rumors and gossip ran wild throughout Whitehall that day. That evening, after an emergency meeting of the cabinet, members of the House of Commons nervously reassembled at 7:30 in a tense and suspicious mood, some with "flushed faces," fortified with "Dutch Courage," anxious to hear Chamberlain's decision.[13] They felt like a court summoned to hear the jury's verdict.[14] The prime minister rose to explain that he had had no reply from Hitler. As Chamberlain rambled through the chronology of events, MPs were stunned to learn that no time limit had been set; no decision had been taken. A moment of silence followed as Chamberlain sat down. Arthur Greenwood, the deputy leader of the Labour Party, sputtering, seething with anger, jumped to his feet to speak. Both parties cheered him, to his very great surprise. "*You* speak for Britain," Bob Boothby—some say it was Leo Amery[15]—called out; "I wonder how long we are prepared to vacillate," Greenwood demanded about the more than thirty-eight-hour delay. "We must march with the French."[16]

Kennedy listened with disgust as cheers thundered throughout the hall and the prime minister's most ardent supporters proclaimed their agreement with the opposition. The "smart people" in Britain and the United States who wanted Britain to go to war would very shortly "see what Chamberlain was trying to save them from," the loyal ambassador confided to his diary. The war itself would illustrate "what a great service Chamberlain did to the world and especially for England" at Munich in maintaining peace. A year ago, the government had not had the support of public opinion in the country, and especially in the Dominions, over the Sudetenland; the French had not wanted to support their allies, the Czechs; and the British military was "pathetic." "They couldn't have licked a good police force attack in the air." It would only have led to widespread slaughter, Kennedy wrote.[17]

Shaken and despondent, Chamberlain, Halifax, Wilson, and Cadogan met Charles Corbin, the French ambassador, and spent a frantic hour calling Daladier, Bonnet, and Britain's ambassador in France, Sir Eric Phipps, to try to persuade the French to give Hitler the shortest possible time limit.[18] Kennedy, too, arrived at 10 Downing Street to quickly confer for a couple of minutes with Britain's leaders and left as the cabinet—hungry, and all "scruffy and smelly" and on the verge of a "sit-down strike"—convened a short late-night session lasting until after midnight to discuss the time limit on the ultimatum.[19] They agreed to instruct Henderson to deliver to Hitler at nine o'clock the next day, Sunday, September 3, an ultimatum that would expire at eleven o'clock.[20] "Right, gentlemen, this means war," Chamberlain said in a "calm, even icy-cold" tone, as a deafening clap of thunder and blinding light lit up the cabinet room. "It was like something out of Oppenheimer," said Sir Reginald Dorman-Smith as he recalled the scene twenty-five years later.[21]

On September 3, Chamberlain showed Kennedy a copy of the speech written by the prime minister himself that he was to deliver a few hours later to the British Empire.[22] Tears filled Kennedy's eyes as he read it. He quickly returned to the embassy and sent Hull a triple-priority cable telling him that Britain would declare war at 11:00 a.m. that day, and he put an additional call through to Roosevelt.[23] A few minutes after 4 a.m. on September 3, the president's bedside phone rang. He could barely understand Kennedy, who was in utter despair, his voice choking as he gave him the gist of Chamberlain's remarks. Kennedy predicted that the victor would be chaos. The president tried to steady his old political ally, but Kennedy kept repeating, "It's the end of the world, the end of everything."[24] FDR roused his Cabinet to give them the news of war.

At eleven o'clock on September 3, Sir Nevile Henderson in formal ambassadorial attire gave Britain's ultimatum to a staff member of the German Foreign Office. The German ambassador, Ribbentrop, declined it.[25] The French had sent theirs at 10:20 in the morning of September 3 as well. It was to expire at noon.

Following his urgent call to Roosevelt, the ambassador cleared off his desk and hurriedly installed a small radio in his office so that he and some of his staff could listen to Chamberlain's 11:15 broadcast to the British people. "We were all terribly moved by the solemnity and tragedy of the occasion," he wrote. He was profoundly stirred. Unembarrassed tears stung his eyes as he heard his fellow appeaser so poignantly express his own feelings: "All my long struggle to win peace has failed."[26] "Everything that I have worked for, everything that I have hoped for, everything that I have believed in during my public life, has crashed in ruins."[27] Kennedy recorded in his diary: "I had participated very closely in this struggle and I saw my hopes crash too."[28] Just as with the assassination of the ambassador's son, President John F. Kennedy, on November 22, 1963, anyone who lived in Britain through this period can remember exactly where he or she was on that lovely Sunday morning, September 3, at 11:15, when Chamberlain solemnly announced: "This country is at war with Germany."[29]

When Chamberlain had finished, Kennedy telephoned him. To Kennedy's astonishment, the prime minister answered immediately. "This is Joe, Neville, and I have just listened to the broadcast. It was terrifically moving. . . . I feel deeply our failure to save a world war." "We did the best we could have done," the prime minister replied, "but it looks as though we had failed." Kennedy agreed and added "my best to you always." "Thanks, Joe, . . . and my deep gratitude for your constant help—Goodbye," Chamberlain said in a voice quivering with emotion. "Goodbye," Kennedy answered.[30] At 11:20 a.m. the ambassador cabled Hull that the Germans had not complied with the prime minister's ultimatum to withdraw their troops from Poland and so there existed a state of war between Germany and Great Britain.[31] Six hours after Britain, France, too, declared war on Germany.

Shortly after noon, Joe Jr., Jack, and Kathleen accompanied their parents to Parliament to hear Chamberlain read his declaration of war and listened to him describe his despair over his failure to preserve peace. It was a Sunday. Parliament had not been convened on a Sunday for nearly 120 years.[32] None of the Kennedys could have guessed just how long, how costly, and how deadly the war would be for their family.

Almost immediately, an air-raid warning sounded and everyone took refuge across the street from the embassy in the basement of one of Rose's favorite designers, Edward Moly-neux. The ambassador did what he could to cheer people up and to calm panicky, ashen-faced Americans hollering for boats. The air raid turned out to be merely a dress rehearsal. "This war is definitely not going to have the long run they predict," the ambassador wrote in his diary. The people at the home front in *all* the belligerent countries, especially the women and children, are going to exert a tremendous moral pressure on their fighting men to end the war quickly. "All countries will be damn sick of it pretty soon."[33]

At 2:30 in the morning on September 4, Kennedy was awakened by a phone call from the Foreign Office telling him the dumbfounding news that a British liner, the 13,581-ton Cunard White Star *Athenia*, under the command of Captain James Cook, having set sail to Montreal on September 1, before the declaration of war, with passengers including Americans who had boarded at Glasgow, Belfast, and Liverpool, had been struck in broad daylight on the port side without warning by a German torpedo, in violation of international law. At that moment the unarmed ship was rapidly sinking in the Atlantic two hundred miles off the northwest coast of Ireland.[34] It was the opening salvo of World War II in Britain. Its attack awakened memories of Germany's torpedoing of the *Lusitania* in 1915 with 1,195 passengers aboard, 124 of them American—an event that contributed to America's entry into World War I.[35] There were 311 Americans listed on the *Athenia* among her 1,347 passengers, most of whom were Canadian.[36] Of the 112 passengers killed by the explosion, twelve were Americans.[37] Kennedy called the American consulates at the ports of embarkation to get a list of names of passengers and then cabled FDR: "All on 'Athenia' rescued except those killed by explosion. Admiralty advises me survivors picked up by other ships. List of casualties later. Thank God."[38] Kennedy's intention was to "get them [the survivors] out as quickly and safely as we can with as much credit to the United States government as possible."[39]

The ambassador immediately told his son Joe Jr. to arrange for berths on other ships for survivors,[40] and sent his son Jack (with a large American flag, presumably as a comforting symbol of home[41]) and his old friend and aide Eddie Moore to Glasgow, where rescue operations were underway. Jack's assignment was twofold: find out what happened and help the survivors. The survivors portrayed a grim scene to the young interviewer: oil pouring from the exploding tanks, firemen thrown from a hatch, hundreds of seasick, half-clothed, oil-drenched passengers and crew crawling over dead bodies and slipping on oil and filth as they hurried for the lifeboats. Many of them had waited ten or twelve hours in the lifeboats, hoping for rescue. They had seen one boat swamped, drowning most of its inhabitants, and another smashed to bits by the propeller of a rescue ship. The conclusion was unanimous: the *Athenia* had been struck twice without warning by a German submarine's torpedo, although a Nazi radio broadcast from Berlin was already claiming that the First Lord of the Admiralty, Winston Churchill himself, had ordered a bomb to be put on the ship in order to inflame American passions between Germany and America.[42] The German press accused the British themselves and the First Lord of the Admiralty, in particular, of orchestrating a hate campaign against Germany and trying to turn the neutral countries against her.[43]

Jack tried to soothe the feelings of the outraged passengers. One college coed vented her anger at the nearest symbol of the American government, himself only a gaunt, twenty-one-year-old Harvard junior. Jack told his father that the hysterical survivors demanded a convoy. They were "in a terrible state of nerves," the ambassador said, forwarding his son's report to Hull, and prepared to launch into an "unbelievable" well-publicized diatribe against the government if they were sent home without a convoy.[44] The government said no to the convoy.[45] Jack relayed the government's answer to the survivors and explained to them that America's neutral status prevented Roosevelt from sending convoys for returning refugees. He told them that the American liner USS *Orizaba* would pick them up and take them to New York, but without a convoy.[46] After dealing with problems of overcrowding, reassuring passengers of their safety, and refuting charges of mercenary profiteering by the United States, Jack sent a full report to his father.[47] It had been a difficult experience. "I sent him up to Glasgow to handle the whole job of taking care of the survivors and finding out from them what had happened. And he handled it well, too," Joe Kennedy bragged with understandable fatherly pride.[48] The incident affirmed for him the importance of warning Americans to sail on ships under the American flag, something he had been valiantly trying to get them to do: wise advice with the danger of submarine warfare.[49]

An avalanche of cables from nervous relatives flowed into the embassy. Government funds could not be used to answer such requests, but the ambassador saw that the replies were sent promptly, and he paid for as many as 150 personal telegrams daily. When an aide reminded him that the ambassadorship was costly enough, Kennedy smiled and said, "It has to be done."[50]

During the first week of war, Kennedy's days as ambassador were hectic. He stoically endured London's blackouts and air-raid sirens and regained his composure by completing plans for his family's safety and burying himself in his work. Early every morning, the bobbies would recognize the ambassador's Chrysler sedan with the big "CD" (Corps Diplomatique) plate on it and wave him through the London traffic to the embassy.[51] As always, he entered his office, threw his coat over a rack, draped a chair with his vest, loosened his tie,[52] and rolled his shirt sleeves over his freckled forearms. He quickly went to work, all the while pulling at his black suspenders, swearing, talking to himself, and yelling orders. The windows of his office were always wide open, and the August page was still on his desk calendar. The three telephones, two radios, and two vases of freshly cut flowers were the only adornments in the otherwise plain blue room.

The ambassador's editor-in-chief friend, Henry R. Luce of *Time* magazine, featured a cover story on Kennedy as the "London Legman." He portrayed him as a complex personality: on the one hand, a "common denominator of the U.S. businessman," "safe," "middle-of-the-road," at heart "a horse-trader, . . . with one sharp eye on the market and one fond eye on his children"; on the other hand, a "super common denominator, uncommonly common-sensible, stiletto-shrewd," and as eminently "practical" as befits a small bank president. He observed the English war with a cool, detached eye and "as Ambassador Kennedy" asked the same question "as . . . Businessman Kennedy: Where do we get off?"[53] Indeed, that was Kennedy's basic question.

The embassy had been moved from the palatial building at Prince's Gate to an old red-brick apartment house seven stories high at 1 Grosvenor Square.[54] After exasperating delays, the State Department finally authorized an air-raid shelter in the house. Until it was built, however, the ambassador and his staff had to run several hundred yards to the shelter at the grand hotel in Mayfair, Claridge's.[55] The embassy staff, too, had been reorganized and put on a twenty-four-hour workday. One of Kennedy's aides, hoping to catnap after nightfall, optimistically brought in a collapsible cot, which he kept hidden behind the ambassador's black sofa during the day.[56] Kennedy spent a tense fifty-first birthday on the third day of war working in sweltering heat in his shirtsleeves at the embassy. That evening the family gathered around his birthday cake and then watched a new movie, *Bachelor Mother*. Only Jack was absent.[57] Few people got much sleep for the next few days.[58]

After the Kennedys had returned from France, the ambassador quickly moved his family to a closely guarded secret location: Wall Hall, J. P. Morgan's country estate, in Hertfordshire, a nineteenth-century "Gothic" castle with hundreds of acres of grounds and a considerable staff.[59] Over the next few weeks, the Kennedys were sent back to the United States as they had arrived, in shifts, three at a time, more or less. Rose (who always traveled separately from Joe for safety's sake) sailed on the *Washington* on September 14 with Kick, Eunice, and Bobby; Joe Jr. sailed a few days later on the *Mauretania* with a convoy and bragged to newsmen as soon as he disembarked about how helpful the Kennedys had been to the survivors of the *Athenia*, and echoed his father's views.[60] John flew to New York on the Pan American flying boat, the *Yankee Clipper*, arriving on September 19;[61] and the last installment of Kennedys—Patricia,

Jean, and Teddy—left on September 20 on the *Manhattan* with their lovesick governess, grieving all the way over leaving her English boyfriend.

All left for their newly opened house in Bronxville, New York.[62] Except Rosemary. Ever the adoring father, Kennedy paid meticulous attention to his children's welfare. He wrote to Rose in mid-September 1939 during the height of the Russian invasion of Poland telling her how terrible the war looked for Great Britain and urging an honorable peace before Britain was utterly destroyed, and in that same letter detailed his arrangements for Rosemary. The third of the Kennedy children was a nineteen-year-old developmentally disabled daughter who had been put in a Montessori convent school in Hereford under the capable eye of Mother Isabel, the mother superior. Kennedy had asked the Moores to remain in England to look after Rosemary and to take her out from time to time, Kennedy explained to his wife. "Between us all she will be really happy and enjoy herself," he wrote reassuringly, and told Rose not to worry.[63]

Once his family's welfare was secure, his greatest concern was the safety of the Americans in Britain on whose behalf he jousted with U.S. officials over the delays in their evacuation. The slower pace of peacetime Washington angered Kennedy; he grew impatient with business as usual and the tangle of bureaucratic red tape.[64] Even Joe Jr. had pitched in and tried to hasten the departure of nine thousand Americans still stranded in Britain by arranging for their accommodation aboard packed tramp steamers returning to the United States.[65] The ambassador's blistering attacks on Maritime Commission officials about delays in diverting the course of South America–bound cruise ships desperately needed for the throng of 1,500 Americans besieging the London embassy were overheard and quoted by a zealous newsman and made headlines back home.[66] It didn't bother Kennedy too much, he wrote. "I was too busy." But it did bother the State Department, which gave Kennedy a stiff reprimand.[67] The staid secretary of state told Kennedy that his charge that the reputation of the American diplomatic service was being damaged by the story about "dickering among crews for a war bonus and extra pay" and his recommendation that those responsible for delays in rescuing stranded Americans should "be hanged to the nearest tree" had made the front page of the *New York Herald Tribune*.[68] Kennedy vigorously denied issuing a public statement and blamed the report on the eavesdropping of *Herald Tribune* reporter Frank Kelly.[69]

Nor was the ambassador above taking potshots at other administration officials such as Secretary of the Treasury Morgenthau. Feeling slighted by Morgenthau's making "most extraordinary suggestions" for the payment of British and French war debts, Kennedy complained to Washington about Morgenthau's interference in matters beyond his jurisdiction. Just days after war had been declared, Morgenthau had proposed to both the British and French ambassadors in Washington that as partial payment for the war debts owed by their countries, both the *Normandie* and the *Queen Mary*, currently in New York, be transferred to the American flag. The State Department had begun conversations with Lord Lothian, the British ambassador in Washington. Kennedy found out about the scheme from the British two days after it was first proposed. "I heard of his suggestion first from the Foreign Office in London. Apart from its stark crudeness, I was outraged by this by-passing of the Embassy in London," he vented in his memoir, and confronted Morgenthau about excluding him from the talks.[70] "I feel that the man on the spot should certainly, in times like this, be kept currently informed," Kennedy wired him. He should not have to rely on the host government for information, he added sarcastically.[71] Morgenthau protested that he had never intended to exclude him, nor had he done so; he then asked Under Secretary Welles to explain the situation to Kennedy.[72] Welles did. He telegraphed Kennedy that he had informed both the French and British ambassadors that their countries were to regard the proposition "as not repeat not made. . . . Both of the Ambassadors, upon learning of the instructions given me by the President, expressed their deep satisfaction."[73] Morgenthau called Kennedy and told him that it had been the State Department's decision, not his, to open negotiations in Washington with Lothian. Kennedy told Morgenthau he held no grudge against him: "It's dead as far as I'm concerned, Henry, and I'm glad you called me up. And you know how I feel about it. . . . I know very well that I can save you a lot of bumps as far as this place goes . . . if I know what's going on, but this one struck me so between the eyes that I didn't know whether I was afoot or horseback."[74]

The ambassador also fought with British officials over their practice of censoring American mail, and seizing and detaining American vessels on the high seas and ordering them into ports in combat zones to examine their cargo. Initially the British censored only diplomatic and consular mail; Kennedy vigorously protested that, and the practice was discontinued. Then the British censored mail that flowed between the United States and neutral countries and passed through British territory like Gibraltar, as well as mail on board American and neutral ships. Kennedy protested that, too. Kennedy's problems were greatly increased when the British established their blockade. He had to deal with numerous complaints of unreasonable delays in examining American cargo. There were always protests, apologies, and promises, followed by more protests again, as the bureaucratic wheels creaked along. It took months to correct the situation.

The passage of the Neutrality Act and the creation of combat zones from which American ships were banned further increased difficulties for Kennedy and for the British officials. They would illegally order American vessels into banned ports to search their cargo. The State Department and American commercial officials were even further annoyed when the British ordered the seizure of all German exports on the high seas. "All of us knew little then of the meaning of total war and still held to the hope that there were rules governing the conduct of slaughter and the fight for self-preservation," Kennedy wrote in his memoir, after recounting his complaints against overzealous British officials.[75]

War touched everything in Britain, including Kennedy's position both in Washington and in London. He was struck by the decline in his status and told a confidant a few days after the declaration of war: "My days as a diplomat ended Sunday morning at eleven o'clock. Now I'm just running a business—an officer of a company. I'm back where I was ten years ago," he said, hiding his resentfulness behind a smile. "Instead of going up I've gone down."[76] Kennedy warned Washington "that the leverage of the present American Ambassador in London is due to lessen and that probably rapidly. . . . The boys think I am too hardboiled a nationalist."[77] "I will have to do quickly any really useful work," he wrote,[78] and yet even in the first week of war, he saw little evidence that war had come to London. Aside from the mad rush trying to get Americans out of Britain, the only other noticeable thing in London, Kennedy told Roosevelt, was the blackout and poorer service in the best hotels—otherwise "there is no real indication of war."[79]

Kennedy remained undaunted in his desire to advise Roosevelt. Despite his dustup with Morgenthau, and his own realization that his influence was fast declining, Kennedy was unwilling to believe or to accept that neither official Washington[80] nor members of Chamberlain's cabinet were paying much attention to him. Although British officials had less time for him with the outbreak of war, they still seemed to welcome him as much as ever, or so it appeared to him. After the declaration of war and throughout the fall of 1939, he continued his largely futile habit of making the rounds of British officialdom, of informing the administration of their activities, and of trying to influence Washington's decisions and policies.[81]

Kennedy told Hull about his conversation with Halifax on September 4, the day after the declaration of war. Kennedy asked Halifax how he felt about the outbreak of war. Relieved and refreshed, Halifax said, and ready for the struggle. "My feelings remind me of a dream I once had in which I was being tried for murder. I was finally convicted and, to my surprise, a feeling of relief rather than fear swept over me."[82] But Kennedy felt no relief; nor did he feel refreshed or ready for the struggle ahead. As they discussed the bleak military situation in Poland and speculated about how long Italy would remain "watchfully waiting," Kennedy began to grasp that this war could be akin to "total war." The major decisions would be made by politicians at home rather than by military leaders at the front, and political considerations would be major issues.[83]

The British, engaging in wishful thinking, were counting on a collapse inside Germany as a means of ending the war, which they expected to last no more than three years.[84] The only optimistic note Halifax mentioned was that British intelligence confirmed that economically, Germany faced some very hard times; she had only four months of oil and gasoline left. "That might be the beginning of the end,"[85] Kennedy wrote—more wishful thinking. It was also apparent to Kennedy that one of the reasons the British had not bombed Germany, or so they told the Poles, was that they feared killing noncombatants, especially women and children, and causing an unfavorable reaction of world public opinion, particularly in the United States. It would be detrimental to all the Allies.[86] Kennedy was dead on: "I think a good deal of this war's strategy is directed with one eye toward the United States," he wrote to Hull.[87] Indeed it was, an opinion he stated again and again.

On September 10, with war just a week old, Kennedy sent Roosevelt a long-winded, meandering letter labeled "Personal and Confidential," outlining his impressions of British attitudes, Britain's conduct of the war and its implication for economic and political policies, and his advice about America's role. Kennedy sang a verse from what was rapidly becoming his swan song: "There is no question that the war is going to be conducted with eyes constantly on the United States. . . . The English are going to think of every way of maintaining favorable public opinion in the United States, figuring that sooner or later they can obtain real help from America." As long as there is a possibility that we might come in, "England will be as considerate as she can not to upset us too much. Because, of course, she wants to drag us in. And my own impression is that if by any chance she should succeed, the burden will be placed more completely on our shoulders by 100% than it was in 1917."[88]

Intermixed with Kennedy's reports about British attitudes were his conversations with officials about military strategy, the potential effect of air bombardments and submarine warfare, the impact on Germany if Russia did or did not join her, and the resulting effect on Italy. These were coupled with Kennedy's observations on economic policy, the demise of Hull's Trade Agreement (now "completely out of the window"), and Kennedy's dire predictions about Britain's political transformation into a totalitarian country controlling her trade like any other totalitarian country in Europe and eventually resorting to barter or some other kind of compensation. Britain's political transformation and its economic consequences will have great implications for the American economy, he predicted. Kennedy urged that the United States proceed cautiously in passing economic reforms and trade legislation and carefully review their long-range financial implications for the American economy. He closed with one suggestion: "We should be on our guard to protect our own interests." The British are using their best brains to deal with their economic and financial situation and are focused on it 365 days of the year, twenty-four hours a day. The United States has "got to think, and to think most intelligently," about maintaining American trade interests and protecting the American financial system.[89]

On September 9, the ambassador also had a gloomy conversation over tea with King George VI and Queen Elizabeth. Kennedy reported to Roosevelt and to Hull that His Majesty was totally convinced of Poland's defeat and "worried desperately about" what Hitler would do next. The king's "unholy worry" was that the Führer would propose a peace settlement with Britain and France, probably within a month, an offer that no politician could support without risking political suicide and the wrath of the British public.[90] The king was very worried about what his position should be on the question of war or peace. Despite his own dire predictions of a future filled with suffering and misery, he said that "the British Empire's mind is made up. I leave it at that."[91]

The king tried to rid Kennedy of his pessimism and feared that it must influence his dispatches to Washington and his judgment of England's situation. The king wrote to Kennedy asking him to explain Britain's case to the American people. "As I see it," the king said, "the

USA, France and the British Empire are the three really free peoples in the World, and two of these great democracies are now fighting against all that we three countries hate and detest, Hitler and his Nazi regime and all that it stands for." As part of Europe, Britain has played a historic role as the policeman and defender of the liberties of the smaller countries, a role she was playing again in the current crisis.[92]

Although the United States does not regard herself as part of Europe, Kennedy responded, nevertheless the American people want to help England and France economically. The king's simple and courageous statement of Britain's role may have been beneficial to Roosevelt, who was beginning to urge Congress to repeal the arms embargo in the neutrality bill and to enact the cash-and-carry provisions.[93] Kennedy's letter closed with his promise: "Of this you may rest assured, whatever strength or influence I possess will be used every hour of the day for the preservation of '*that life*' we all hold so dear, and in which you and your gracious Queen help to lead the world."[94] Kennedy's subsequent ambassadorship was dedicated to doing just that, as he understood it.

In his diplomatic dispatch to Roosevelt and Hull on September 11, Kennedy reported that Hoare, in his lengthy conversations with him, too, echoed the king's views. Hoare painted a gloomy picture of the French military on land and on sea, an even gloomier one of the air war between the British and the Germans, coupled with the devastating cost of British diplomacy. France, Britain's ally, was likely to be a drain on her resources, Kennedy predicted to Hull. Hoare had told him that the French advance was "three steps forward and three steps back" and that Chamberlain's government feared that the French would ask Britain for bomber assistance. Giving such assistance, the ambassador learned, would quickly deplete the British bomber force and subject Britain to retaliatory and potentially devastating attacks on industries and civilian populations; failing to give such assistance could lead the French to criticize the British and to ask why fight to save them.

The most serious matter for the world in the next month, Hoare told Kennedy, echoing the king's worry, would be the proposal expected to be offered by the Reich to Britain to give up the struggle. Kennedy inferred from Hoare's statement that he meant that any British government that accepted Hitler's offer would be voted out of power; any government that refused it would face a long and devastating and perhaps unwinnable war expected to last three years. Neither option was acceptable. "The continuance of government on a war basis for that length of time will mean complete social, financial and economic breakdown and, in the end, whatever happens, nothing will be saved," Kennedy commented. "I agree," Hoare replied, "but if the war is stopped now, it would provide Hitler with so much prestige that you cannot guess how far he will be carried away for it. We can do nothing about it."

But Kennedy saw a third possibility, a unique American diplomatic initiative. Although the British public would find a peace proposal from Hitler unpopular and unacceptable, they might respond favorably to one initiated by President Roosevelt, the ambassador suggested to Washington. Just a couple of hours after his meeting with Hoare, Kennedy dispatched a rather incredible and unbelievable suggestion shot from the hip: "It appears to me that this situation may resolve itself to a point where the President may play the role of savior of the world," Kennedy cabled. "Having been quite a practical person all my life, I am of the opinion that it is quite conceivable that President Roosevelt can manoeuver himself into a position where he can save the world. . . . I am telling you this because I believe that the president should be considering beyond all other questions of worldwide importance, what action he might take "to bring peace to the whole world without increasing Hitler's prestige."[95] Thereafter his "savior of the world" proposal became Kennedy's constant refrain.

Washington's furious reaction was swift and blunt. Just two hours later a wire arrived from Hull informing the ambassador in no uncertain terms and in the strictest confidence on behalf of the president that "this Government, so long as present European conditions continue, sees no opportunity nor occasion for any peace move to be initiated by the President of the United States." Further, "the people of the United States would not support any move for peace initiated by this Government that would consolidate or make possible a survival of a regime of force and of aggression."[96] A desperately worried Kennedy added in his memoir: "The die was cast. It seemed now certain that it was going to be a long and bloody war. More, such being our official attitude, was there any real hope that we could stay out?"[97]

Although Kennedy was given this rather severe transatlantic slap, his proposal may not have been as reckless and "bizarre" as it might have seemed.[98] The president resented Kennedy's interference, perhaps because he had already been considering just such a duplicitous and cunning overture. Ever since early September he had been discussing becoming a backstairs peacemaker, a role most congenial to him, and not out of character, as his proposal to Chamberlain in January 1938 indicates.[99] Roosevelt had received a request from William R. Davis, who was sponsored by John L. Lewis, the leader of the CIO, the Congress of Industrial Organizations. Davis, an American businessman with extensive German contacts, was acting as a go-between on behalf of Field Marshal Hermann Göring to Roosevelt. Davis told Roosevelt that Göring wanted Davis to "influence the President not to revise the Neutrality Act, but support a German peace offer, in return for which the German Government would accord to the United States an absolutely free hand in the Far East."[100] The proposal had considerable support among the German generals and the diplomatic corps and was reinforced by Hitler himself in a speech on September 19, 1939, at Danzig. But FDR, although intrigued by Göring's proposal, would only intervene if asked to do so by the governments directly involved; otherwise he would wait and watch.[101] Berle's comment was to the point, as always: "Leaving aside the essential immorality of this . . . there is a delicious naiveté about it which would be amusing if it were not for the staggering realization that the life, peace, and happiness of millions of men are apparently in the hands of people who are behaving like half-ignorant children."[102] Davis also reportedly told Roosevelt that Göring wanted to prevent an all-out war with Britain and France and that either he or the German army might try to engineer a coup d'état against Hitler. But Roosevelt, more interested in removing Hitler from power than in mediating peace talks, was nevertheless willing to consider mediation if the parties involved officially asked him to do so.[103]

Roosevelt's jarring rebuke to Kennedy illustrated not only his displeasure at his ambassador, but also a growing difference in their attitudes. Unlike Kennedy, who viewed Nazism as a stabilizing force in central Europe and a bulwark against socialism—or worse, communism—and who saw no great harm in Hitler's domination of central Europe, the president saw Hitlerism as the threat it was and refused to play any role that would allow Hitler to remain in power or to retain Austria, Czechoslovakia, or Poland.[104] Nor was the president worried that Germany would develop a form of Russian communism. "They might blow up and have chaos for a while," he told his ambassador, "but the German upbringing for centuries, their insistence on independence of family life, and the right to hold property in a small way, would not, in my judgment, permit the Russian form of brutality for any length of time."[105]

Exasperated by his ambassador, Roosevelt scoffed at Kennedy's proposal to his advisers and rejected it out of hand. In discussing it with his old political henchman Jim Farley, the president accused Kennedy of having been "taken in" by the British. "He's more British than Walter Hines Page was," the president confided, a characterization not without basis. "Some weeks ago Joe had tea with the King and Queen, who were terribly disturbed about the situation. Afterwards he saw Sir Samuel Hoare and several others connected with the British government. They, too, were quite worried," Roosevelt summed up. "After his talks Joe sat down and wrote the silliest message to me I have ever received. It urged me to do this, that, and the other thing in a frantic sort of way."[106] Unlike Kennedy, who had come to identify with Britain's ruling classes, the Dutchess County patrician declared that "the trouble with the British is that they have for several hundred years been controlled by the upper classes." He accused them of devising governmental policies to protect and further their own self-interest, and of ensuring their control over Britain's economy. In the prewar days, Farley recalled, FDR had never been particularly fond of the British and doubted that Britain would ever go to anyone else's aid. He believed that "they were for England and England alone all the time."[107]

Henry Morgenthau, too, listened to the president disparaging his ambassadorial appointees over lunch and singling out Kennedy for special criticism. "Some of these people give me an awful pain in the neck. For example, Joe Kennedy," Roosevelt complained, warming to his topic. "Joe always has been an appeaser and always will be an appeaser. . . . If Germany or Italy made a good peace offer tomorrow, . . . Joe would start working on the King and his friend, the Queen, and from there on down, to get everybody to accept it . . . he's just a pain in the neck to me," FDR snapped. "The only thing that saves the information is I know my men."[108]

As FDR groped for some way to aid the democracies in the fall of 1939, he became deeply critical of his ambassador's opinions and simply ignored them. Kennedy was expendable, the president concluded. Perhaps as a further reprimand to Kennedy for his savior-of-the-world proposal, on the same day that Roosevelt received it, September 11, he sent a note of congratulations to Winston Churchill, the new First Lord of the Admiralty, whom Chamberlain had included in his cabinet: "I am delighted you are back at the Admiralty, takes me back to last war when I was with the U.S. Navy," Woodrow Wilson's former assistant secretary of the Navy wrote. He extended to Churchill and Chamberlain a unique opportunity: "Want you to feel if you want to send me anything personal just drop me a line and send it to me by pouch." Churchill, but not Chamberlain, gratefully accepted Roosevelt's invitation and immediately took advantage of it. The First Lord asked Kennedy to cable Washington that "the Naval person will not fail to avail himself of invitation and he is honored by the message."[109]

Roosevelt warmly cultivated his unique and confidential relationship with Churchill. It was without parallel in its range and impact in American diplomatic history and beyond the influence of the American ambassador. The president of the United States, the head of state of a country at peace and bound by strict neutrality laws, went behind the back of his ambassador and initiated a secret correspondence between himself and a subordinate minister of a country at war.[110] The "Naval Person" exploited his privileged position with relish, and took full advantage of the opportunity to bring to bear at least as much influence on Anglo-American relations as the ambassador in London, who dutifully if unhappily served as messenger boy for the two most influential political leaders in the English-speaking world.[111] The correspondence lasted until Roosevelt's death five years later and consisted of about 1,700 letters from each man. It was so secret that only a few of Roosevelt's and Churchill's advisers, including Chamberlain, were informed of its existence.[112] Had it been known by the president's opponents, it would have led to such severe criticism that it could have effectively ended his presidency and would without doubt have destroyed any chance for a third term. It might even have led to a call for impeachment.

Thus, as FDR began to search for a more active foreign policy with the outbreak of war in Europe, negotiations between the two great English-speaking democracies came to be centered in Washington, more often than not, instead of London. Once Churchill became prime minister on May 10, 1940, negotiations were conducted personally between him and the president as Kennedy was even further circumvented. Later the president again curtailed Kennedy's influence and access to official channels by sending abroad his own personal emissaries who bypassed the ambassador and reported directly to FDR. Kennedy, who learned about Roosevelt's invitation to Churchill three weeks later, on October 5—through Churchill, no less—was outraged by FDR's behavior. "It was yet another instance of Roosevelt's conniving mind," the frustrated ambassador sounded off in his diary. It's "a rotten way to treat his Ambassador" and "shows him up to the other people. I am disgusted."[113]

On September 17, as Soviet troops crossed into Poland to finish what the Germans had begun, Kennedy had a phone call from Lord Beaverbrook, the Conservative Fleet Street newspaper publisher, who was very distraught, informing him of the invasion. "Of course, you know I am against my country coming in and fighting," Kennedy immediately told him. Beaverbrook claimed that he expected no such thing, but he did want Kennedy to convince FDR to take the initiative to see what could be done to prevent further catastrophe, an issue about which the ambassador needed no prodding.

On the day of the invasion, Kennedy confided in his diary that "it is more apparent than ever [that] we must hold our position of strength, in order to be a determining factor in this peace settlement."[114] But, he wrote, we must not help create a settlement that leaves Germany victorious. These views he was to advocate repeatedly to anyone, anywhere, at any time, throughout the remainder of his ambassadorship.

Deeply stirred by the events, he wrote to Rose that the Russians' invasion of Poland would be "disastrous for the English . . . [but] if England has a chance to make an honorable peace she had better do it before she gets busted every way. . . . The difficulty is going to be to find a basis to settle on," an issue he spent the rest of his ambassadorship exploring. Then he cheerfully added: "This position at the minute is probably the most interesting and exciting in the world, and in addition I may be of some help in helping to end this catastrophic chaos."[115]

By September 28, 1939, the guns were silent as the two powers announced the fifth partition of Poland. The defeat of Poland was followed by a long, oppressive pause in which Hitler played a game of cat and mouse.

With the outbreak of war until his resignation as ambassador a year later, in November 1940, Kennedy's influence was on the wane. As Kennedy mulled over Britain's chances of winning the war in the fall of 1939, and for the rest of his ambassadorship, he was an unrelenting prophet of doom—gripped by fatalism and blinding fear—as he became certain of Britain's destruction and worried about America's involvement in Europe's war. Kennedy's conversations with Britain's leaders and his correspondence with Washington officials in the weeks immediately following the fall of Poland reveal his bleak but well-founded assessment of Britain's chances of winning and his disdain for British war aims. He so abhorred war that he doubted whether war was ever worthwhile, especially given the economic and material chaos it caused. He had a short-sighted view of the menace that Hitler posed and could not comprehend why Britain had little choice but to go to war. Since Britain had no great economic use for eastern Europe, Kennedy reasoned, why not let Hitler have it?

Kennedy's letters to Roosevelt show his doubts about the vitality and durability of democratic institutions, their political leaders, and their ability to survive and to cast off governmental restraints at the end of war—a not uncommon view in the 1930s.[116] Kennedy repeatedly pointed out to both London and Washington the wartime threats to Britain's economic system and the chaos that would surely follow as Britain and France were reduced to mere shells of their former selves. Until the end of his diplomatic career, his dispatches had a consistency and a prophetic quality in his assessment of the problems Europe would face after the war and in his vision of America's leadership in the postwar world; his was the voice of Cassandra.

But Kennedy, as well as many topside people in Britain, discounted Britain's many strengths—her bloody-minded will to resist under Churchill's incomparable leadership, her international and political experience, a surprisingly unified empire, and enough military reserves and strategic know-how to ward off defeat until powerful allies could come to her aid.[117]

Everything is "lousy," Kennedy told Hull. It was.[118]

Kennedy, despite Washington's putdown of his "savior of the world" proposal, was undeterred in his attempts to influence Roosevelt's decisions about the war and Roosevelt's role in ending it. Two days after the fall of Poland, on September 30, Kennedy sent Roosevelt three dispatches, two of which describe his views of wartime England and Allied diplomatic and military strategy, his political and economic predictions for England, and his recommendations about America's role in the war and in the postwar world. Some of Kennedy's recommendations were sound, some of them were overwrought, and some of them were simply wrong. All of them were intended to protect the United States from involvement in the war in Europe. Kennedy poignantly wrote in his memoir: "I never received a reply to . . . these letters."[119]

Almost from the start, Kennedy was announcing that Britain would lose the war and pointed out to FDR and Hull the weaknesses in her military strength and diplomatic alignments: British officials were already painfully well aware of these problems. Even her military experts doubted that the democracies stood much of a chance against Germany.[120] No military or naval expert Kennedy had spoken to at the end of the first month of battle believed that the present lineup of Germany and Russia and their prospective allies against France and Britain gave "England . . . a Chinaman's chance," he reported. The "topside people," Kennedy said, worry about Russia's submarines, airplanes and flyers joining up with Germany's naval and aerial fleets, while Italy, which Britain hoped to keep quiet in the Mediterranean, lurked in the background, poised, waiting to see whether Germany would be a winner. They also thought Germany might move into Belgium or Holland, or even worse, offer peace terms. Regardless, "England and France can't quit whether they would like to or not and I am convinced, because I live here, that England will go down fighting. Unfortunately," he told FDR, "I am one who does not believe that is going to do the slightest bit of good in this case."[121]

Even Chamberlain told Roosevelt: "We shall win, not by a complete and spectacular military victory, which is unlikely under modern conditions, but by convincing the Germans that they cannot win"—a position shared by the Allied generals.[122] They too believed that Britain and France would not lose the war, but they also thought that it could be hard for them to win it; they simply lacked the numbers. The generals reiterated Chamberlain's position that the Allies' best bet lay in convincing the Germans that they could not win it either,[123] a position Kennedy seems not to have considered. Russia's behavior in Poland was a vindication of Chamberlain's decision in delaying a deal with Russia, Kennedy wrote, and revealed the double-crossing tactics Russia would have used to gain her ambitions in the Baltic States.[124]

The outspoken ambassador argued with everyone in British officialdom—the king, Hoare, Halifax, Simon, and, of course, Chamberlain himself—over the wisdom of continuing the struggle and over what Britain's war aims were, proclaiming them muddled and ill-defined. For the life of him, Kennedy could see no sense in Britain's war. "Just what are you fighting for now?" Kennedy demanded of Halifax and Simon at the end of the first month of war. "You can't restore Poland to the Poles, can you?" "No, not all of it," Simon admitted. "Well, then," the ambassador declared, "that will be a failure; you can't talk about aggression and permit Russia to retain half of Poland and have its claw over the Balkan states as well as the Baltic states." "Possibly not," Simon responded.[125]

Aside from broad, basic themes, like those spelled out by Chamberlain in his broadcast of September 3, 1939, in the House of Commons, such as "the destruction of Hitlerism," its corollary, "a just and lasting peace," and the reestablishment of "a liberated Europe,"[126] and the king's statement to Kennedy on September, 12, 1939, that Britain was fighting against Nazi bullying by fulfilling its traditional role as "the policeman" and "upholder of the rights of the smaller nations,"[127] the ambassador told Washington that British officials had deliberately not developed more specific war aims and had particularly refrained from specifying territorial goals such as the restoration of the independence of Austria, Czechoslovakia, or even Poland. "Now there is no question in my mind," the ambassador continued, that "the British can see no way they can give up the struggle even though they are more and more confused in their own minds just what they are fighting for and what they will attain even if they win."[128] And what if Hitler were defeated, what then? Kennedy asked, dreading a new communistic social order in central Europe. Nazism, at least a stabilizing force in Germany, would give way to communism, which could become an even greater menace to Europe, he predicted, repeating the arguments he had used in the summer before the outbreak of war.[129]

Kennedy, of course, had his own ideas about the aims of the British. "For Christ sake," he'd tell them, "stop trying to make this a holy war, because no one will believe you; you're fighting for your life as an Empire, and that's good enough."[130] "The facility with which the Anglo-Saxon can play power politics while talking in terms of philanthropy is triumphing," he scoffed to Roosevelt at the end of the first month of war. "England is fighting for her possessions and place in the sun, just as she has in the past."[131] Despite the patriotic, moralistic, naive slogans his friends habitually mouthed, the ones he had found as unconvincing in 1939 as he had in 1914, this was not, he insisted, a moral crusade. He bristled when he heard such talk about how awful force was in international affairs and how it must be eliminated, "as if force hadn't always been the underlying basis in most all international dealings of any vital, life and death importance, and as if any means had been found for peacefully settling . . . international disputes. . . . But where there are two hungry dogs to eat a bone sufficient for one, arbitration doesn't decide the issue."[132]

His blunt assessment was right. As the leading defender of the international status quo that Britain had helped create and had benefited from, Britain was fighting not just to fulfill her commitment to Poland but to prevent the destruction of her empire, a near-impossible task, and her demise as a global power, already on the wane by the 1930s. Britain's war was a war of survival at all costs. Her governing elite shared Kennedy's anxiety and redoubled their efforts for victory, knowing full well that their world would be gone forever at war's end, something they did not want to hear the American ambassador constantly harping on.[133]

The ambassador's prescription for working with Hitler was simple: just give in to him and leave him alone, he advised the British. There was certain to be a change in political leadership sometime.[134] Even if Hitler were overthrown, the political crisis coupled with Germany's bleak economic outlook and the shortage of food would produce utter chaos. After all, "beating them isn't going to solve the problem of eighty million people who have no economic resources and nothing very much to look forward to," Kennedy insisted to Simon.[135] Although Kennedy described the behavior of the Nazis as "God-awful,"[136] he also thought that it was still tolerable and even preferable to the total chaos resulting from a holocaust. War was never worth it; nor could its impact justify it. His overriding goal was peace, even if it meant Nazi hegemony throughout Europe. Why not let Germany have eastern Europe? Kennedy asked,[137] showing his ignorance of the implications of his suggestion and his disregard for the lives and sensibilities of the peoples of eastern Europe.

Like Kennedy, Chamberlain abhorred war; but he also understood that any attempt by Britain to abandon Poland or any refusal to come to Poland's aid, especially after publicly pledging to do so in March 1939 and signing the Anglo-Polish Alliance in August, would result in the destruction of Britain's political and moral authority and the demise of her worldwide prestige and influence within the international community, a position unaccountably lost on the American ambassador.[138]

For Roosevelt, Kennedy painted a dismal portrait of the war's impact on the Allies. A long-drawn-out war would drain both Britain and France, he predicted, and relegate them to being mere shadows of themselves; nothing could be saved.[139] "I think that it will be a catastrophe financially, economically and socially for every nation in the world if the war continues and the longer it goes on, the more difficult it will be to make any decent rearrangements," he wrote in mid-October.[140] Even victory guaranteed defeat; they could win the war but lose the peace. If the Allies were to win, problems would still have to be solved and bills paid to keep Europe operating; if Britain and France were beaten, the consequences would be devastating for the United States. Our best customers would be finished. We would have to create a new world order with old enemies who know that we hate them—a plausible, chilling argument.[141] His conclusion was devastating: "I personally am convinced, that, win, lose, or draw, England never will be the England that she was and no one can help her to be."[142]

Kennedy had good reason for his despair: Britain's establishment had opened their balance sheets to him and convinced him of the accuracy of his views.[143] To be knowledgeable about

Britain's financial, military, and diplomatic situation in the days immediately following the attack on Poland was to be a pessimist. But only Montagu Norman, Kennedy believed, fully understood the seriousness of the situation.

"The financial and economic situation as far as Europe is concerned is worse than tragic," Kennedy cabled Hull and Morgenthau after a "bitterly bearish" conversation in Kennedy's office on September 29 with Montagu Norman, whose bleak views he shared. According to him, "England is now busted," Kennedy said, and could sustain a money economy only for two or three years.[144] He was right that Britain was near the end of her financial tether.[145] Europe would soon resort to widespread bartering, and Britain, with the collapse of the British Empire, would follow in the footsteps of once-mighty Spain and Portugal and become a has-been nation. Furthermore, Kennedy reported, Norman believed that England was moribund as a customer for America: she had no gold. If the war lasted much longer "there [would] be no hope for the world; . . . at least none for Europe," both believed.[146] In this prediction about the impact of the war on Britain's empire, Kennedy was correct: Britain did lose the empire after the war.

Although he told Roosevelt that democracy was "the only form of government that I want to live under," the ambassador questioned its viability and its durability. Faith in democracy as a form of government and confidence in the strength of democratic institutions had obviously worn thin during the interwar period; the fault lay with the democratic nations themselves who had allowed autocracy to flourish. The Allied powers had forced democracy on the defeated countries at Versailles at the end of World War I. The victors thereby aligned themselves with the status quo and opposed change.[147] The challengers to the international status quo in the interwar period, particularly Germany, Italy, and Japan, had adopted new autocratic and anti-democratic forms of government, he wrote. Their victory would ensure the demise of democracy outside the Western Hemisphere, a fear widely shared within political circles even in the United States in the 1930s. As Richard Overy has written in *The Road to War*, "It was not a question of a democratic world bringing fascist troublemakers to heel, but of a democratic retreat in the face of fanatical nationalism, military rule and communist dictatorship."[148]

Not even a month after the war was declared, Kennedy told Roosevelt that he saw widespread signs of decay and even decadence in both men and institutions throughout all levels of British society. Democracy, as Americans understood it, would be a casualty of the war in both Britain and France regardless of who was victorious, Kennedy predicted; it hardly existed now. Political power in Britain remained concentrated in the upper classes, as it historically had, but the political machinery was not producing able leaders. Even in Britain, Kennedy warned, it was likely that "extra-Parliamentary leaders" would be thrown up. Furthermore, inventions in technology like the airplane, and the industrial advance of foreign countries, along with the decline in British ability and forcefulness had caused Britain to peak as a world power and to sink into decadence.

Kennedy feared that even Chamberlain would become a political fatality, a possibility that left Kennedy distraught because he saw no politically viable alternative to Chamberlain. "For all Halifax's mystical Christian character and Churchill's prophecies about Germany," the ambassador wrote, "I can't imagine them adequately leading the people out of the valley of the shadow of death."[149] But Kennedy was utterly wrong: democratic institutions did survive in Britain after the war; there was no threat from "extra-Parliamentary leaders," and his strong dislike of Churchill led him to grossly underestimate the brilliance of Churchill as a wartime prime minister. But the president, with greater foresight and with a better grasp of history and international affairs, never doubted the resilience of democracy in Britain and elsewhere or its ability to shake off wartime constraints and to survive after the war. FDR was proven right.

Roosevelt tried to steady his gloomy ambassador by passing on a bit of the presidential optimism and good cheer: "While the World War did not bring forth strong leadership in Great Britain, this war may do so," he wrote on October 30, nearly two months after the outbreak of war. "I am inclined to think the British public has more humility than before and is slowly but surely getting rid of the 'muddle through' attitude of the past."[150] Always one to enjoy a hearty laugh, FDR passed on to Kennedy the latest joke making the rounds in Washington: "Suppose you had two cows. The Socialist would take one and let you keep one. The Nazi would let you keep both cows but would take all the milk. The Communist would take both cows."[151] The president's attempts at cheering up his by now habitually pessimistic ambassador were largely failures.

Kennedy advised Roosevelt to "curb our sentiments and sentimentality and look to our own vital interests"—those "lie in the Western Hemisphere."[152] This was a sentiment he had expressed in his March 1939 memo. The refrain ran throughout his dispatches repeatedly: Drive home to the American public the point "that we don't want any part of this mess,"[153] a view the vast majority of Americans shared.[154] At the same time, Kennedy argued, the United States should prepare itself for the leadership of the English-speaking peoples that it would undoubtedly assume in the postwar world.[155]

Despite Roosevelt's rebuke on September 11, Kennedy returned to his theme of an American-sponsored peace initiative at the end of the first month of war. He urged the president to be a "mastermind" and to consider how he could help the Allies "save face" by preventing the "world's greatest calamity" from befalling them and the United States, and at the same time, getting a top position as a result of his intervention.[156] Although everyone hates Hitler, Kennedy continued, writing to FDR on November 3, the second-month anniversary of the war, "it is by no means a popular war. Make no mistake, there is a very definite undercurrent in this country for peace." It will manifest itself in a demand for explicit war aims that will clearly show to everyone "that they are fighting for something they probably never can attain," Kennedy predicted. The British fear being "finished off," which they suspect will be their fate if they continue the war much longer. Kennedy's impression was that "if the war stays in the state it is now, this undercurrent [for peace] will get stronger and stronger here." He revived his "savior of the world" proposal, ignoring FDR's chilly initial reply, and hinted that the president should reconsider his refusal to mediate. Some of my English friends, Kennedy told him, believe "that only one man can save the world, not only in attaining peace, but in planning for the future, and that man is yourself. . . . You are a combination of the Holy Ghost and Jack Dempsey."[157] Still, FDR refused to budge. FDR, unlike Kennedy, almost dismissed the consequences of war, so intent was he on eliminating a regime he judged intolerable.

Despite Kennedy's advocacy of the winning combination of Holy Ghost and Jack Dempsey, Britain's perilous situation made him uneasy about America's role in wartime and led him repeatedly to urge the president to adhere rigorously to America's policy of isolation and neutrality. Kennedy's terror of the consequences of war all but led him to reject war as an instrument of national statecraft. Later he also contemptuously repudiated the Allied concept of "total war" and the demand for "unconditional surrender."[158]

Regardless of his ardent isolationism and advocacy of neutrality, Kennedy was not indifferent to Britain's plight. He had lived too long in Britain and liked the British too well not to be worried about their fortunes. He urged Roosevelt to "be considerate of our friends."[159] Friendship warranted revising the neutrality laws and *giving* the British limited material aid, the germ of Lend-Lease, a suggestion he made to Cordell Hull.[160] Later, some months after the evacuation of Dunkirk in 1940, gifts of guns and ammunition and fifty destroyers were not too costly for friendship's sake. He also thought that principle could be shoved aside in favor of Lend-Lease. But Kennedy's advocacy of "consideration" was only half-hearted. The interests of the English-speaking democracies could be better served if only Britain and Germany would agree to a compromise peace.[161]

With war more than a month old, rumors of a peace offer from Hitler had been in the news.[162] When it finally arrived mid-month (October), it was completely unacceptable to Chamberlain. Since Hitler refused to discuss the restoration of Poland's independence, the prime minister rejected the proposal. Hitler promised that the war would continue.[163] Kennedy announced to Rose that he expected a quick peace and complained to her and to Roosevelt that "the job is now a complete bore."[164] "I was amused and delighted to hear you say over the telephone that it was actually boring in London now that you have got rid of most of the returning Americans," the president kidded him. "Here in Washington the White House is very quiet. There is a general feeling of sitting quiet and waiting to see what the morrow will bring forth."[165]

As the president waited patiently, he considered ways to preserve America's peace and to aid the Allies quietly without provoking congressional opposition. In addition to opening up a confidential line of access to Churchill, the president also issued the proclamation of neutrality required by the 1937 Neutrality Act. It put an immediate embargo on the sale of arms and thus worked not only to the disadvantage of Germany but, to Roosevelt's great distress, to the detriment of Britain and France. The president further decided to help the Allies by taking up the fight to eliminate the embargo provision in the neutrality legislation by convening a special session of Congress on September 21. It became his first order of business in the fall of 1939. He wanted to keep the United States out of war and keep the peace at home. But he also argued that the bill as it now stood made the United States vulnerable to attacks and thereby jeopardized its neutrality and safety.[166]

Ever since the first weeks of war, Kennedy had sent the president polite but agonized appeals from the Allies about America's neutrality law. The ambassador wrote to the president on September 10, 1939, that British officialdom was "depressed beyond words" that the law still stood. In their opinion, "America has talked a lot about her sympathies, but, when called on for action, have [sic] only given assistance to Britain's enemy." All the British wanted was to buy equipment that was already ordered. Their feelings had not "yet reached the stage of bitterness," Kennedy noted, and anti-Americanism remained "carefully concealed."[167] He also passed on to the State Department the fears of the British secretary of war, Leslie Hore-Belisha, who was worried that the Soviet Union, Italy, and Turkey would side with Germany if the Neutrality Act were not modified. Britain's position would be "hopeless."[168] Roosevelt answered: "What you need to do is to put some steel up their backbone. That's what is necessary." Kennedy told in his diary: "I still don't believe he understands the almost desperate position of the British."[169]

Kennedy's mercurial spirits soared and sank as he listened sympathetically to British worries and considered the implications of neutrality revision for the United States. He too favored neutrality reform and giving Britain as much aid as possible and predicted that the position of the Allies would "be nothing short of disastrous" if the law were not revised.[170] Kennedy told King George VI that Roosevelt's decision to convene a special session of Congress for neutrality revision was exactly what many Americans hoped for. They wanted to aid the Allies economically but not militarily by sending troops.[171] However, wary Foreign Office officials also noted that Kennedy seemed to relish making off-the-cuff remarks at social occasions, or to Chamberlain, predicting that there was almost no chance that the Neutrality Act would be repealed or amended.[172] Always in the back of Kennedy's mind lurked the fear that after neutrality revision passed, the British would be spending every hour of every day trying to figure out a way to lure the United States into the war—as they would be.[173]

Roosevelt, sympathetic to Britain's pleas, sent Chamberlain a cheery note on September 11 reassuring him that revision was definitely part of the administration's policies. "I hope and believe that we shall repeal the embargo within the next month and this is definitely a part of the Administration policy," the president wrote to him, and at the same time invited both Chamberlain and Churchill to communicate with him.[174]

Roosevelt's argument to Congress was that the existing law supported aggressors and thus endangered American neutrality and peace; he made no mention of aiding the Allies. Neutrality reform, therefore, would ensure peace by preventing German attacks on American ships by prohibiting the United States from transporting war materiel in U.S. vessels and thereby reducing the likelihood of sending American troops to support the Allies. It would also aid the Allies by repealing the arms embargo and permitting the sale of goods on a cash-and-carry basis and requiring the Allies to transport their supplies in their own ships.[175] Roosevelt's strategy for revision convinced the Senate to pass the legislation by a vote of 63 to 30 on October 27. The House approved it by a vote of 243 to 181 six days later.[176] On November 4, 1939, the president signed the legislation into law, and a grateful Chamberlain told Kennedy that he could never thank him enough for all his efforts on its behalf.[177]

Kennedy's chronically pessimistic views, vigorously expressed and indiscriminately touted, led the once friendly British establishment to close their doors to him and cost him his influence within Chamberlain's administration, particularly after Churchill was included in it. Chamberlain, now the chief minister of a nation at war, could no longer acquiesce to Kennedy's unrelenting quest for peace or tolerate his defeatism. Their once close relationship was permanently changed. The ambassador's friendly relations with British officialdom and the Foreign Office were also broken as he received considerable criticism from its officials. Their growing hostility and resentfulness led them to accuse him of caring only about his own financial investments and political ambitions.[178] At one time associated with Chamberlain's inner circle, which had kept him one of the best-informed and influential foreign representatives in Britain, and once the toast of London and a great favorite with the British public, Kennedy was rapidly becoming useless and one of the most unpopular ambassadors in living memory, no longer accurately or adequately representing the views of his own government or sharing in his hosts' confidences. For his part, Kennedy began to curb his affection and admiration for the English and his concern for their plight. Affection would not get the better of his cold-hearted analysis.

The ambassador's defeatism, enunciated without reservation or discretion, became a source of great concern to British as well as American officials. It disturbed Charles Peake of the Foreign Office enough to meet with William Hillman, a former London correspondent of the International News Service and close Kennedy friend, to inquire about the ambassador's opinions on the war and to send Cadogan a memo describing their conversation. "'Bill, I'd sell 100 Polands down the river any day rather than risk the life of a British soldier or the loss of a British pound,'" the newsman quoted the ambassador as saying. Furthermore, he believed that if this war did not stop soon, it would bankrupt both the British Empire and the United States, which would be forced to enter it, leaving Bolshevism or at least socialism to emerge triumphant. Both were "dread specters" to him. Kennedy was currently obsessed with bankruptcy and defeat, Hillman noted: the ambassador was a "self-made man who had known poverty and who did not want to know it again."

If only the Allies had refrained from intervening in central Europe, Hillman remembered the ambassador wishing. After all, Kennedy argued, "Hitler and the Nazis could not last forever and, . . . there was bound to be a change in regime in Germany one day if we . . . only let it alone." Further, the ambassador was a practicing Catholic who "loathed Hitler and Hitlerism almost, though perhaps not quite, as much as he loathed Bolshevism," the correspondent remarked. Though he had tried to reason with him, Kennedy, Hillman told Peake, "was not amenable."[179] Though Hillman had accurately assessed the ambassador's political opinions and his fears for the future, either he or Kennedy had made too much of Kennedy's "poverty." Although a rags-to-riches story might have been politically advantageous for the ambassador, such a story was largely untrue. He had spent his boyhood and youth in considerable comfort and affluence.

The Foreign Office worried about what to do about this talkative ambassador and kept a close watch on him by starting a miscellaneous file—labeled "Kennediana"—of clippings, records of conversations, public statements, and even private telegrams, all secondhand, rather like a file the MI5 might keep. Foreign Office minutes reflected a growing wariness and increasing hostility to him and an awareness that he had lost influence with Roosevelt. A few weeks after the war began, Sir Berkeley Gage reported that a friend in the Coldstream Guards heard that Kennedy, at an informal dinner party where toasts were competitively exchanged, quite gleefully said that "we should be badly thrashed in the present war," an opinion that Cadogan said was probably based on Lindbergh's dubious views that the Germans knew where Britain's aircraft factories were but not vice versa, and that Japan and Turkey would enter the war on the Axis side and upset Britain's naval ascendancy. In addition, Gage wrote that Mr. Jack Kennedy, the ambassador's son whose opinions his father particularly valued, had recently returned from Germany and remarked that even the repeal of the Neutrality Act, a repeal that the ambassador thought unlikely, would not be helpful to Britain. Britain lacked sufficient gold reserves to make large purchases in the United States. The Foreign Office noted—warily, no doubt—that the ambassador was so impressed with his son's favorable views of Germany that he sent a description of them to the State Department.[180]

Gage's informant was probably Billy Hartington—William Cavendish, Marquess of Hartington and son and heir of Edward Cavendish, 10th Duke of Devonshire. Later Billy became Kennedy's son-in-law. The ambassador's vigorously expressed opinions were not due "to serious antagonism," Hartington said, "but rather to a delight inherent in most Americans in seeing the lion's tail twisted (and perhaps in twisting the lion's tail)." Gage underscored Kennedy's pessimism and wrote that the ambassador "is not optimistic about our chances of success in the present war," but he is "always friendly and helpful."[181]

Kennedy's indiscriminate opinions, freely offered at any opportunity, could be harmful, cautioned another official, because he is considered by some of his colleagues as "particularly 'in the know,' owing to his close contact" with British officialdom. Despite the considerable damage his talk could inflict, J. V. Perowne of the American desk pointed out, it could be useful in "jogging the Americans out of their 82% Gallup poll wishful thinking" about the Allies' chances of victory. Cadogan disagreed. The ambassador occupied a privileged position by virtue of his accreditation to the Court of St. James's and his access to the most influential people in the government, Cadogan wrote to his colleagues. "Surely the least we can ask in return is for Mr. K to exercise some discretion." But David Scott wrote that though this kind of talk is harmful in diplomatic circles, and will doubtless continue, there is only one way to prevent it and that is "to convince Mr. Kennedy that he is wrong."

Foreign Office officials discussed various options for reining in the ambassador, such as complaining to the State Department or to the American embassy in London or to Lord Lothian or talking directly to Kennedy, but they also realized that there was little they could do to muzzle him or keep him from indiscriminately expressing his opinion to whomever, whenever, about whatever he chose. Gage warned against approaching the State Department; the ambassador might still be converted, he wrote hopefully. Herschel Johnson, the chargé at the American embassy, was on close terms with the Foreign Office and often had to "take the brunt" for his boss's activities. Warn him, said Perowne. But complaining to Lothian or the embassy might cause even more trouble by silencing Kennedy and thus leaving British officials ignorant of what he was reporting to Washington, Gage countered.[182]

After much worry and discussion over how best to handle the troublesome diplomat, on October 3, 1939, the Foreign Office decided to send Lothian a letter, including newspaper clippings and Foreign Office commentary, warning him of Kennedy's indiscretions and defeatism. The ambassador's defeatist views were based on Britain's financial weakness, it maintained. Although officials found the ambassador's attitude "regrettable," they decided not to pursue the matter further for the time being, but to follow Cadogan's advice and ask Lothian "to drop a hint in the proper quarter" later, if necessary.[183]

British officials were also quite curious about and critical of Kennedy's motives. Sir John Balfour at the Foreign Office dismissed Kennedy as an ambitious man preoccupied with his own financial and political future, clearly inspired by "the wish to keep his own record clean with his countrymen."[184] Balfour accused Kennedy of relishing his diplomatic post because it gave him access to people in the highest authority, though he did not want to be "tarred with the pro-British brush." Scott also believed that Kennedy's focus on financial matters blinded the "poor man . . . to the imponderabilia which in a war like this will be decisive." Perowne mischievously passed on the gossip that there were "funny stories" currently circulating that the ambassador used his stock-exchange activities to advance his own interests and to make money that could be seen as evidence of his "anti-British proclivities"—accusations that had been made before and were widely accepted but remain hard to prove. Furthermore, Balfour reminded his colleagues not to forget that the ambassador was also an Irish American, and therefore well disposed "to twist the lion's tail, the more so when the animal appears to be in 'one hell of a jam.'"[185] They understood him well.

Kennedy's influence in official London circles was also lessened by Churchill's rise to power and his inclusion in Chamberlain's government in September 1939 after the attack on Poland. Without question, the new First Lord of the Admiralty stiffened the spine of the cabinet and represented the belligerent and bellicose mood of the British public. ("Winston is back" was affectionately flashed to the fleet upon his return to the Admiralty.[186]) He was an uncompromising foe of Hitler and Hitlerism and determined to see the war to its end;

he was also an unequivocal opponent of anyone who, like Kennedy, had been an appeaser, urged a negotiated settlement with Hitler, or gave a pessimistic appraisal of Britain's chances. Whalen, one of Kennedy's biographers, wrote:

> Churchill soberly acknowledged the long odds against England and the possibility of defeat, but he was inspired to fight the harder. The declaration of war had been an unwanted but resounding vindication of his unheeded warnings from the political wilderness. Now the shunned Cassandra wore a prophet's mantle and had a Cabinet minister's portfolio.[187]

The mutual suspicion and dislike between First Lord and ambassador was legend. Just as Churchill had looked coldly on Chamberlain's appeasement-minded American friend and his support of Munich, so Churchill adamantly opposed the ambassador's repeated peace efforts. He resented Kennedy's dismal accounts to Washington during the last summer of peace—accounts describing Britain's slim chances, which trickled back to Churchill through dinner companions like Walter Lippmann and friends, the president among them, in the United States.[188] Resourceful, ruthless even, Churchill intended to get what England needed, and he looked upon Kennedy as a barrier to be overcome. He abhorred Kennedy's policies of keeping the interest of the two countries in neat, tightly sealed compartments—an essential arrangement, the ambassador insisted, for keeping the United States out of war. Churchill worked indefatigably to create an Anglo-American partnership essential to his vision of a Grand Alliance.[189] He had once told Lippmann in the last months of peace that if Kennedy's prognosis about Britain's chances were correct and if Britain should be defeated, "It will then be for you, for the Americans, to preserve and to maintain the great heritage of the English speaking peoples."[190]

The ambassador was equally offended by Churchill. A friend had once asked him why he was at odds with certain Englishmen, an allusion to Kennedy's resentment of Churchill. Kennedy answered that he could not forgive those who had ordered the infamous Black and Tans into Ireland, a decision Churchill was responsible for as the secretary of state for both War and Air from 1919 to 1920 in Lloyd George's government.[191] Kennedy regarded him as "just an actor and a politician" and rather dangerous. "He always impressed me that he'd blow up the American Embassy and say it was the Germans if it would get the U.S. in. Maybe I do him an injustice but I just don't trust him," the ambassador confided to his diary.[192] Kennedy also told Roosevelt he looked warily upon Churchill's influence in the United States and cautioned him that "Churchill has in America a couple of very close friends who definitely are not on our team."[193] This should be kept in mind in case there is a change in government in the United States, the ambassador warned, keenly aware of the upcoming 1940 presidential election.

Kennedy was also deeply concerned about the emergence of a new prime minister in Britain. An undercurrent for a change in leadership was beginning, Kennedy told Rose, nearly a month after Churchill's cabinet appointment. He seemed to be the leading contender. If Churchill should become prime minister, "then I certainly think England's march down hill will be speeded up. Churchill has energy and brains but *no* judgment."[194] The ambassador's stinging indictment was one frequently made by Churchill's opponents throughout his long and colorful career, with some justification. Kennedy also noted that Chamberlain had as deep a distrust of Churchill as he did and realized that Churchill wanted the prime minister's job. Churchill "is better in the Cabinet than out," the prime minister said, "easier to handle." People are on to him now; no one would support him for prime minister, Chamberlain told Kennedy, sentiments that Kennedy recorded in his diary on November 8, 1939.[195]

The two discussed the prospects for peace and the role of the United States in the war. Chamberlain said that the government would seriously consider the appeal for peace proposed by the queen of the Netherlands and the king of Belgium the day before, most probably made to prevent the invasion of their countries; but he predicted that it would be rejected just as the proposal made by Hitler in the Reichstag on October 6 had been.[196] "Peace just is not practical as yet, because the German people have still not suffered enough to become disgusted with their leadership," the prime minister said. "When will the war end?" Kennedy asked him. Not much beyond next spring, was Chamberlain's guess, still expecting internal conditions in Germany caused by the blockade and the absence of any victories in the battlefield to lead to Hitler's downfall (wishful thinking again), as was his belief that Italy had no desire to enter the war. Chamberlain asked Kennedy to thank Roosevelt for his neutrality legislation. "That was helpful of America," the prime minister said. The Gallup Poll recently showed that 95 percent of the Americans polled supported the Allies, said Kennedy. "I don't want your soldiers," Chamberlain told him; "we need your resources but not your men"—words that Kennedy was pleased to hear as they supported his position.[197]

In this diplomatic tug-of-war over America's role, Kennedy, the political rookie, was at a considerable disadvantage in his duel with one of Britain's master politicians. Churchill had always complained about the shackles of America's neutrality legislation, but he did not just rely on pity. He made the most of the bleak picture and coupled it with a cunning appeal to American survival. He told Kennedy "that after all if Germany bombed Great Britain into a state of subjection, one of their terms would certainly be to hand over the fleet and if England attempted to scuttle the fleet the German terms would be that much worse; if they got the British fleet they would have immediate superiority over the United States and then her troubles would begin."[198]

Unlike Chamberlain, Churchill wished for American intervention, Kennedy's greatest fear. The ambassador's biggest worry was that if there were a long war, the United States would be dragged in. He could imagine a chivalrous but madcap USA gallantly dashing to save Britain. And inevitably American boys would be sent overseas to shed their blood on Europe's soil, a reality that Kennedy, ever mindful of his own two sons of military age, would do anything to prevent.[199]

Ignored, bored, and homesick, in the weeks following the outbreak of war after his family departed, Kennedy turned movie critic to escape the gloom of life in wartime England. A new comedy, *Mr. Smith Goes to Washington*, directed by Frank Capra and produced by Columbia Studios, had just been released. It starred James Stewart as a likable and naive Mr. Jefferson Smith, a former Boy Scout leader who was appointed to the United States Senate from some prairie state by a corrupt political machine headed by boss James Taylor and the governor and senator of the state. Newsmen, radio reporters, women, and handwriting experts, as well as politicians, were all under the control of the machine. Mr. Smith emerged as the hero in true American style after a one-man filibuster that lasted twenty-four hours and exposed the graft, greed, and corruption in the political system.

When the ambassador saw the film, he fired off an irate cable to Columbia Studios and sent a copy to the White House. "I consider this one of the most disgraceful things I have ever seen done to our country," he told the producers, who must have been astounded.[200] While praising the movie for its technical excellence, Kennedy argued that it gives a harmful view of American political life by conveying the impression that it is full of corruption and lawlessness, the very kind of erroneous impression that he had tried to correct as ambassador. He pointed out that Mr. Smith's filibuster was broken not by the inherent integrity of the United States Senate or by the institutional strength of the American government, but by the moral conscience of one man, Joe Paine. The other senator, an old friend of Mr. Smith's father who is overcome with guilt, tries to kill himself, and ultimately proves Smith's innocence. It was nothing less than "criminal," Kennedy scolded, to allow the film to be shown abroad and to give the impression that such corruption could occur in the United States Senate. Furthermore, Kennedy carried on, the well-established American muckraking tradition of violently criticizing public officials was much less acceptable to the English public and would offend its sensibilities. By conveying the impression that the United States was run by gangsters and crooked politicians, the film would also provide fodder for foreign critics of the American political system and do "inestimable harm to American prestige all over the world." The producers should be more responsible. After all, "the times are precarious, the future is dark at best. We must be more careful."[201]

One Columbia executive, Harry Cohen, and the director Frank Capra, as if guilt-stricken, jumped to the film's defense. They dashed off a reply to Kennedy explaining to him that the picture, far from being unpatriotic, developed the theme of Americanism by showing how the least experienced people could rise to the highest political heights, expose political corruption by using the existing Senate procedures, and "make justice triumph over one crooked Senator."[202] Enclosed in the cable was a long string of newspaper quotes praising the film. The uproar died down when Columbia remembered that the irate ambassador was just one more moviegoer who did not like a film.[203] The film was nominated for eleven Oscars, including the best director, and received an Academy Award in 1939 for best original story, by Lewis R. Foster.[204]

After the outbreak of war, Kennedy returned each night to the big old country house he rented near London, at Windsor Park. As he rambled through the empty rooms, the monotony and his loneliness were broken only by the frequent weekend visits of his daughter Rosemary and the Moores.[205] "The job is just a complete bore and with you all away, well it's just too awful. If I didn't have this house in the country I'd go mad," he wrote home in mid-October 1939.[206] "I'm sick of everybody and so I'm alone tonight by choice," he complained to Rose on their twenty-fifth wedding anniversary. "I love you devotedly." His sentiment was no doubt real, despite his numerous infidelities. The years together have been the kind of "happy years the poets write about," he wrote. Without her, he said, his job was "comparable with a street cleaner's at home."[207]

With much persuasion, he convinced Halifax that he could call home each Sunday and talk to his family for ten minutes without compromising Britain's security.[208] It took considerable organization within the family, Rose remembered, to talk to Daddy. Since there were ten Kennedys, each of them got one minute to talk. Rose and two of the older children organized the phone sessions, which ran like clockwork.[209]

The ambassador's frustration with wartime England affected him more and more. Even by November, there was little change in the slow English pace of doing things. Fumbling officials, in Whitehall and in the war office, working behind blacked-out windows, girding themselves for war, were grappling with Britain's basic problems as they desperately tried to make up for lost time.[210] "The English do not plan to plan; they plan to muddle," Gordon Jackson remarked.[211] But so far, few felt desperate or expected the tremendous sacrifices that the war would demand.

Although England's power to engage the enemy was gradually and haltingly growing stronger, its military machine had been unprepared for war, its economy was utterly unready for new stress, and its bureaucracy was without the essential plans and personnel necessary to meet the problems it was facing. Everywhere everything went awry, Kennedy grumbled in his memoir. He and his staff had their hands full as the embassy became the center for complaints against anything that left Americans' concerns unmet.[212]

Each day brought a new incident. The London embassy actively represented British interests in Germany. The embassy dealt with the repatriation of British and German consular officials and some 3,500 British citizens still in Germany when war was declared. Frantic British relatives sought word from their family members and friends from the Foreign Office, from the American embassy in London, from Brussels, and finally Berlin. The requests seemed endless, Kennedy reported, and once the phony war ended with the invasion of Holland and Belgium, attempts at repatriation were impossible for fear of fifth-column influence.[213]

Kennedy was already "sick at heart" because of the high cost of war, he told Robert Fisher, a Harvard classmate and football coach.

Seeing youngsters, whom you had to the house for dinner with your own daughters, going off to war and some of them already killed in airplanes; seeing business shot to pieces; seeing, with the vision or imagination I think I have, what's going to happen to America, even though they never get into the war . . . and of course they shouldn't. . . . When it is all said and done, no good can come from any agreement settled by a war.[214]

The job was taking a personal toll on Kennedy as well. He had lost fifteen pounds in two months; sleep was a luxury; the telephone rang nonstop; his doctor advised a thorough physical stateside.[215] Previous separations from his family had been compensated for by his sense of achievement and by considerable public acclaim for his efforts. But now Kennedy was getting restless and wanted to match his wits with something more challenging and less futile. His willingness to trade in his post for another position was well known and fodder for frequent press speculation.[216]

There was a position that intrigued him. Ever since he first came to London, Kennedy had compiled meticulous, detailed notes on England's mobilization and her wartime preparations.[217] One day his old friend Montagu Norman stopped by the embassy for a chat. "I see that you folks in the United States are contemplating industrial mobilization. Who's going to run it? . . . God Almighty?"[218] Kennedy looked forward to the opportunity to apply England's lessons to peacetime America.[219] His letters illustrated how keenly he observed the English scene and studied the wartime preparations. He was interested in the long-term implications of the evacuation of schoolchildren to England's countryside. It would reshape the distribution of population and the social structure, the ambassador thought. It would also improve the health of the underprivileged and broaden the horizons of the country folk. His letters included some touching and amusing stories of culture shock between city and country children.[220]

The restless, fervent Democrat must also have been itching to get involved in American politics again.[221] In 1940, the presidential election would be coming up, and certainly a major issue in the campaign would be America's role in wartime Europe. Because of his close observation of Britain's and Europe's problems, Kennedy was no doubt anxious to join the fray and debate American foreign policy with "the war hawks."[222] It was time to go home. Kennedy cabled Hull for permission.

In November the newspapers carried the story that Kennedy would return to the United States for "consultations" with the president and to spend the Christmas holidays with his wife and children. There was considerable press speculation about his recall and resignation, and his next appointment. The press reported that Kennedy "has made no secret of the fact that he is anxious to give up his post here" if the president decided he could be more useful elsewhere.[223] But the usual sources close to the president said that there was nothing unusual about Kennedy's return; he had not been recalled, he had merely requested permission to come home for a vacation. He was expected to return to his post in London sometime during the new year, but would fly back immediately if conditions in Europe warranted it.[224] Kennedy waited impatiently to leave. "I haven't been back in almost a year," he told a goodbye caller. "I'll bet anything that within an hour after I land I'll be in all sorts of arguments."[225]

As Kennedy prepared to leave, he notified Buckingham Palace that he was going on vacation. To his surprise and pleasure, he was invited to dine with the king and queen on November 28, 1939. After listening to the reading of the king's speech proroguing Parliament in the House of Lords in the morning, a much less stately ceremony than that of the previous year, Kennedy joined Their Majesties and the Duke and Duchess of Gloucester for a pleasant and informal lunch in their sitting room. The queen, her usual gracious self, chatted away amiably. George VI, however, looked thin and drawn. His stutter was more pronounced than usual, Kennedy noted. He was not certain exactly what the first course was—maybe melted fried cheese and egg. He ate it. After disclosing his dislike for hare and gallantly staggering through pheasant with potatoes and Brussels sprouts and not very good chocolate pudding (which the queen had ordered just for him, she told him), Kennedy joined in the general discussion about the United States and the war. He repeated his opinion that the United States should not send soldiers. The queen agreed and urged him to say so. She expressed disappointment with Lindbergh's statement that England was fighting only to preserve the Crown. Kennedy defended him—as well he might. He himself had been saying the same thing as Lindbergh. Lindbergh was an honest man, Kennedy said, and "not pro-Nazi." Would Roosevelt run for a third term? the king asked. "All of England hopes so." Apparently Kennedy gave no answer. Although the conversation was pleasant and gay, there was a new serious tone, scarcely hidden. "I think both of them conscious they might lose their throne if this war goes on too long," he noted in his diary.[226]

Upon departing the palace, Kennedy continued his round of meeting with the "top" people. He dropped in on Churchill at the Admiralty at five o'clock that afternoon. The First Lord was brimming with confidence, Kennedy observed. The ambassador had been keeping in touch with him because of Roosevelt's interest in naval operations. Churchill looked a little pasty, Kennedy thought, and a bit disappointed when his offer of a whiskey and soda was declined. Churchill wondered about the president's reaction to his plan to mine Norway's territorial waters as a way of preventing ore from Sweden going to Germany. He asked Kennedy to find out what the president's opinion was. They worked out a code to inform Churchill of the president's answer to his plan. If Roosevelt had no objections, then Kennedy would cable Churchill this message: "Eunice would like to go to party." If Roosevelt had objections, Kennedy would cable: "Eunice would not like to go to party."[227] Kennedy mentioned his shipping plans to relieve Britain of some of her naval runs between nonbelligerent ports and all long runs. Surely the United States could take over some of Britain's runs between North American ports and Pacific ports. Churchill enthusiastically endorsed Kennedy's proposal and promised him the Admiralty's support for it.[228]

At afternoon tea with Halifax, talk of war dominated the conversation. Upon hearing the foreign secretary's story about Hitler's telling Ciano he was "born an ass and would die an ass," Kennedy responded: "That proves two things to me . . . one that my own impression [of] Ciano is right and, two, that Hitler is a smart fellow."[229]

The dinner conversation at the Astors' with General Ironside the day before Kennedy left ranged around gentle gossip, about General Gamelin dyeing his hair, a discussion of Churchill as "the Great Optimist," predictions about Germany's next move, and Ironside's lack of fear of an attack on England's coastline. Kennedy found the general attractive and clearly courageous but lacking in imagination. Kennedy consoled himself with the idea that maybe generals are not supposed to have imagination. "Our situations will get steadily better," Ironside predicted. Kennedy thought Ironside's views about "how the war was to be won were interesting." The general believed that the neutrals would play the peacemaking role as their opposition to the Germans increased. As Hitler made no progress against the British and the French, the general prophesied, Hitler's prestige would decline. Peace would then become likely as trade with Germany was reduced and the neutrals' opposition to Hitler stiffened—a highly imaginative, delusionary scenario.[230] Kennedy was certainly on familiar terms with Britain's establishment.

On November 29, Kennedy crossed the Channel into Belgium, en route to Paris and then to Lisbon, where he boarded a Dixie Clipper for the flight to the United States. His well-tailored dark blue suits, his vigorously square-shouldered form belied the grueling pace that his prematurely lined face and his fatigue-rimmed eyes bore witness to.[231] Newsmen gathered around him and tossed questions at him as he alighted from the plane on December 6, 1939, in New York. Asked about his future plans, Kennedy bearishly replied: "I'm all through. This is my last public job. . . . I'll be dead and buried five years from now." But no one was convinced. What about running for president in 1940? one reporter asked. Kennedy replied ambiguously: "I haven't any idea." In response to a question about Britain's attitudes toward American foreign policy, he told reporters that the British were still trying to figure out "just what we mean." A similar thing might as well have been said by them about him. On the one hand, "we express great sympathy with their cause"; but, on the other, we reaffirm our "intentions to remain neutral. . . . It's like a fellow sticking out his tongue at a man and not being ready to punch him in the jaw."[232] But then he quickly added that the British government had no expectation that the United States would join the British war effort.

When Kennedy returned to the United States, he continued to peddle his philosophy of defeatism, a stance that offended British officials by whom he had been so well received. It offended Roosevelt as well. The president increasingly disagreed with Kennedy's assessment of Britain's chances as he listened to other voices and emissaries whose opinions were in stark contrast. Kennedy's diplomatic influence declined because he no longer represented his government's or his president's views and because his attitudes no longer coincided with those of the British, who he believed failed to understand America's policy. If so, Kennedy was as responsible as anyone for their failure to understand it.

CHAPTER 8

This Is Not Our Fight

Most astute observers believed that 1940 would be no ordinary year in American politics.[1] Would Roosevelt break with tradition and, despite his own personal wishes, seek a third presidential term? Would the "unreal quiet" of the war lurking in Europe burst into open warfare?[2] Would war have decisive consequences for the United States? Would the president recall his increasingly controversial and unpopular ambassador in London, whom he often undercut and bypassed and whose advice he all but ignored? Would Kennedy remain loyal to Roosevelt?

Kennedy tried to influence Roosevelt's decision to run for a third term. He vigorously endorsed him out of gratitude and self-interest and he helped make the case for Roosevelt's indispensability. Kennedy also tried to influence the outcome of the incipient war distinguished by the sitzkrieg in the west: he urged a compromise peace and staunchly supported the American government's policy of isolationism and neutrality. In both cases, Roosevelt arrived at his own conclusions not because he was persuaded by Kennedy's arguments, but because the course was one that Roosevelt had independently decided upon as a response to events in Europe. They, and not his ambassador's urging, led him reluctantly to inch along the road to an unprecedented third term and to parry with many, Kennedy included, but ultimately to decide to run again in 1940.

In the spring of 1940, Kennedy's little influence with Roosevelt was further undercut by Roosevelt's decision to establish the Welles mission to explore the possibility of a peaceful resolution of the war. Roosevelt concluded that peace in 1940 was not possible but that aid to the Allies was, and he began to veer more and more in their direction. Moreover, Kennedy alienated the British public, who had come to think of him as their defender and as one of their own. His blind fatalism and his shocking statements about Britain's chances would cost him his privileged position with British officialdom. The year 1940 was also when the most popular American ambassador at the Court of St. James's would resign his post in disgrace and destroy any further chance for a career in public service.

Kennedy was elated to see New York again when his Dixie Clipper landed on December 6, 1939. The mood of gaiety pulsating in the city and the blazing lights in Times Square seemed to shine even more brilliantly in contrast to the drabness of wartime London. Kennedy, the first passenger to alight from the plane, was delighted by the hearty greeting from curious newsmen milling about, anxious for his opinions on the war and the third term, and from Rose, who pushed through the crowd at the airport to greet him with a kiss.[3] Even the stock market appeared to rally on his return; newsmen credited him for its bullish performance.[4]

Kennedy remained noncommittal as he chatted with reporters about the war. Chamberlain's government has an "excellent" morale he said; it "perk[s]" up each time a British ship is sunk. It "understands our position perfectly" and "does not have the slightest belief that the United States will get into the European war." And yet the British are confused and have reason to be: on the one hand, we say we sympathize with their cause, but at the same time, we are determined to remain neutral.[5]

"How do you stand on the third term, Joe?" one old Bostonian friend asked him, pulling Kennedy aside during his airport press conference after his return from London. "I can't go against the guy," Kennedy replied, one Irishman to another. "He's done more for me than my own kind. If he wants it, I'll be with him."[6]

Two days later, on December 8, 1939, Kennedy officially endorsed Roosevelt for the presidency. He paused to chat with reporters as he made his way up the steps to the White House and commented that "the problems that are going to affect the people of the United States—political, social and economic—are already so great and becoming greater by the war that they should be handled by a man it won't take two years to educate." But it was the president's repeated promise to maintain peace that most influenced Kennedy. "First and foremost, we know from what we have seen and heard that President Roosevelt's policy is to keep us out of war, and war at this time would bring to this country chaos beyond anybody's dream. This, in my opinion, overshadows any possible objection to a third term."[7]

Kennedy's strong endorsement of Roosevelt for a third term, and his reasons for it, "burst like bombshells," Arthur Krock wrote in his column on December 12, 1939. It was invaluable to the doctrine of indispensability that the president's supporters had been spreading ever since the outbreak of war. But anyone who had listened to the ambassador's almost continuous litany of complaints against Roosevelt, Roosevelt's appointees, and aspects of the New Deal must have been baffled. Kennedy "was almost the last man in the Administration from whom anti–New Dealers and New Dealers alike expected such a statement," Krock said. "Shell shock" was the explanation given for Kennedy's endorsement by bitterly disappointed Democratic moderates and businessmen who had counted on his vigorous support for the two-term tradition, who well understood his opposition to certain New Deal policies, and who knew that he predicted an impending Dark Age for humanity. "Joe is usually a bear, but this time he is a whole den," his anti–third term critics claimed, particularly those who had discussed international affairs with him.[8]

Kennedy may not have been such a surprising recruit to the doctrine of indispensability after all. He may have had no reservations about FDR's becoming a third-term candidate. He probably did sincerely believe that the seasoned, experienced president, who did at least say the things that Kennedy wanted to hear, was essential to the country. Perhaps the ambassador was also trying to prove his loyalty to his chief by his endorsement and to curry his favor in order to win another post in Roosevelt's next administration. As one who knew him well, Arthur Krock had assessed Kennedy as a pragmatist whose "lifelong formula has been to attain objectives by use of the personal equation," and not to be excessively preoccupied with principle.[9]

After chatting with reporters that morning, December 8, 1939, the ambassador was swept upstairs in the White House elevator to meet the president at 9 o'clock for a two-hour-long conference, the coveted first appointment of the day, an indication of the esteem Roosevelt wanted Kennedy to believe he held him in. His bulging briefcase led newsmen to speculate on whether it held a peace proposal from Chamberlain. No hint was ever given.[10]

As the president sat regally in bed eating his breakfast and pouring coffee from a thermos, he received his ambassador most cordially. Roosevelt looked extremely tired but listened intently to Kennedy's wide-ranging and "very bearish" lecture. Kennedy told Roosevelt about his conversation with White House reporters that morning and that he'd endorsed a third term. But Roosevelt declined to run; he would not be a candidate, he said, but a solid, winning candidate would be found. Kennedy responded: "Absolutely no."[11] They then went on to other matters.

Kennedy told him of his plan, blessed by Churchill, to have idle American ships trade with British possessions in nonbelligerent ports and to transport American lumber in American-flagged ships to countries whose supplies of Scandinavian pine had been curtailed by the war. Mapping out water routes with his finger on the mahogany highboy in the president's bedroom, Kennedy explained Churchill's plan to disrupt German ore shipments by mining Norwegian waters. The First Lord hoped for Roosevelt's approval. Since the United States had laid 350,000 mines during World War I, Roosevelt saw no objections and agreed to the plan. Kennedy cabled Churchill the president's approval: "Eunice would like to go to party," the coded message said.[12] FDR was particularly interested in Kennedy's concern that the sale of British securities might have disastrous consequences in the American market right before the election and wanted to discuss it further.[13]

The president invited Kennedy to accompany him to his press conference. There Kennedy sat quietly and listened to Roosevelt give him "a good break," praising him to the press about his plans for shipping. Again Kennedy noted the president's fatigue and his lack of "flash," but he was impressed with his wide-ranging knowledge. Certainly Roosevelt knew his business.[14]

Kennedy was again honored by his meeting with the president in the last appointment of the day, at 4:30, the second-most-coveted hour of the day.[15] Kennedy had sandwiched in visits to the State Department, too, and the Maritime Commission. In his meeting with the president, he again broached the subject of the third term. "What about this 3rd term; you'll have to run," the ambassador said. "Joe, . . . I can't. I'm tired. I can't take it. What I need is one year's rest. That's what you need too. . . . I just won't go on unless we are in war," the president declared. Mindful of Kennedy's ardent isolationism, he added, almost as an afterthought, "Even if we are in war, I'll never send an army over there. We'll help them with supplies."[16] "I'm willing to help them all I can but I don't want them to play me for a sucker."[17]

As the two old gamecocks swapped stories and discussed potential presidential candidates, FDR appeared to boost a variety of men, including Kennedy, but refrained from giving anyone a specific endorsement—his old technique of divide and conquer. What about Hull? Kennedy asked, although he thought the secretary was indecisive. Won't do, Roosevelt answered. Hull had delayed getting information out about Russia's attack on Finland until the Russians were on their way to bomb the Finns, causing a real blow to American prestige. The president suggested the new head of the Federal Security Agency, Paul McNutt, a real "go-getter" if he's given a specific task; then there's Harry Hopkins, who has "gained sixteen pounds and hasn't got cancer, in spite of what Mayo's [*sic*] said; there's Attorney General Frank Murphy, who is 'doing a swell job'" there's Robert Jackson, a fine fellow and most able; "yourself," Roosevelt graciously added; and Bill Douglas, Kennedy's pick of the bunch. The president did not want the job himself, Kennedy confided in his diary, but he was convinced that Roosevelt wanted his own man, whom he would train and help after a year of rest.[18]

They talked about other subjects: Roosevelt's Cabinet, finances, and Winston Churchill. What was the "Naval Person" correspondence with Churchill all about? Kennedy asked. "I always disliked him since the time I went to England in 1917 or 1918," Roosevelt said. "At a dinner I attended he acted like a stinker. . . . I'm giving him attention now because of his possibilities of being P.M. and wanting to keep my hand in."[19] Kennedy must have felt heartened to hear the president so emphatically express the views that he, too, so strongly held.

Missy LeHand came in with a stack of papers for the president's signature. The three of them chatted briefly. "I want to see you soon again, Joe," Roosevelt called out as Kennedy prepared to leave. "Meanwhile, get the rest you came back for, and give my best to Rose."[20] The afternoon had faded away as the ambassador emerged from the president's office at six in the evening dazzled by the presidential charm, all skillfully crafted to keep Kennedy in line. Kennedy marveled at his boss's mastery of men and affairs—admiration that was not returned. Nothing in Kennedy's opinions surprised him, FDR later told Ickes. "As might be expected, Joe Kennedy was utterly pessimistic." He predicted "that the end of the world is just down the road."[21]

Only after the ambassador left the White House after his second meeting with Roosevelt did he acknowledge to newsmen his view of the seriousness of the European situation. Did the British and French expect the United States to "help" them in their war? a newsman asked. "Nobody over there wanted war and so they can't find any fault with America when she insists she wants to remain neutral and stay out of war. The British were never misled as to our position," Kennedy said, flashing his famous grin, as he left for Boston to join his family.[22]

During his brief stay in Boston, Kennedy underscored his fervent isolationism in his first public address since the war began, on December 10. Two days after his conference with Roosevelt, Kennedy, along with his two elder sons, spoke extemporaneously at a reunion of parishioners at the seventieth anniversary banquet of the Church of Our Lady of the Assumption, where he had served as an altar boy. He strongly urged America to "keep out of war." "As you love America, don't let anything that comes out of any country in the world make you believe you can make a situation one whit better by getting into the war," he admonished the parishioners. "It is going to be bad enough as it is."

In an interview following the speech, he said, apparently indifferent to the presence of reporters who jotted down his words, that one of his greatest fears was that the "sporting spirit" of the American people and their desire not "to see an unfair or immoral thing done" could bring America into the war. "There is no reason—economic, financial, or social—to justify the U.S. entering the war. . . . This," he said plainly, "is not our fight." Asked about the likelihood of peace, Kennedy replied, "It [is] anybody's guess . . . when there will be peace."[23]

Kennedy's speech pleased the Boston Irish, with their ingrained, fervent Anglophobia.[24] But when the speech was circulated in Britain, Englishmen reacted with anger and dismay, hearing for the first time the ambassador's unmitigated isolationism. The conservative British weekly *The Spectator* regarded the ambassador's advice as "something of a shock." There are, it argued, plenty of American isolationists giving bad advice without the ambassador to the Court of St. James's, who knows all our worries and vexations, joining their number.[25] Kennedy defended himself in his memoir, writing that England, as *The Spectator* itself had observed, had "perhaps been a little spoiled" by American ambassadors like Walter Hines Page who put English interests above those of his own country. Kennedy continued: "I could already see . . . the beginning of the drive to bring about our entry into the war, headed in the Cabinet itself by Churchill. It was my purpose, however, to resist that type of entanglement and to try to make certain that whatever our destiny, it would be of our own seeking."[26]

But British Foreign Office officials, by now quite used to Kennedy's pessimistic remarks, greeted his comments with relief. Sir Berkeley Gage wrote: "It would certainly not have helped us if he had said the opposite, in view of the present state of American public opinion." Cadogan jotted on Foreign Office notepaper, "I don't think these utterances are too bad in the circumstances. I should not have been surprised by worse." J. V. Perowne attributed Kennedy's words to political ambition and calmly rejected them altogether. "I don't see what else Mr. Kennedy could have said. Perhaps [Kennedy is] trying to stave off possible indiscreet questions regarding his own candidature for the Presidency," Perowne wrote. "I don't believe anyone here [would] give the utterances a second thought."[27]

But there were those in Washington who might. On December 15, 1939, the ambassador tried to persuade a group of State Department officials and army and naval officers to embrace his philosophy of isolationism. Only by isolating herself from Europe's problems and strengthening her own position to withstand Europe's collapse could America save herself, he said—a position well received by many in Roosevelt's Washington. He reported that British and French morale was dangerously low and that Germany was France and Britain's superior economically and militarily. The British expected an attack on Belgium or the Maginot Line in the spring, he stated, and he doubted whether the democracies, who yearned for an early peace, could stand the strain for another year. "By the end of this year, if not before, people in England and France, and all over Europe will be ready for communism," he predicted, a view reflecting his own lack of faith in democratic institutions.[28]

Kennedy and his family spent Christmas in Palm Beach, where his December vacation was prolonged into late February 1940. He had been having "a very rotten time" of it, he wrote the president, but now he was feeling much better. Kennedy entered the Lahey Clinic for a physical examination. He was having biweekly checkups, he had lost fifteen pounds since the outset of war but his weight had stabilized, and the constant pain he had been experiencing had now become intermittent. He asked Dr. Lahey to write to Roosevelt directly and to vouch for the seriousness of his stomach illness and explain that he, Kennedy, needed two months of quiet and rest. But he also promised that if a European crisis arose, he would ignore the doctor's orders and return to Europe immediately. Roosevelt called Kennedy to insist that his first concern should be his health.[29]

The Palm Beach home that Kennedy had bought many years before from the Wanamakers, Philadelphia's first department-store family, was his favorite vacation spot and where he liked to spend much of the winter. Built in the 1920s in the Mediterranean style and designed by resort architect Addison Mizner, it faced the ocean and had a huge sea wall that offered shelter to the many palm trees in the garden from the worst of Florida's storms. Kennedy shunned the social life associated with Palm Beach and spent lazy days living a simple life: sleeping fourteen hours a day, relaxing in the sun, swimming in the pool or the ocean, perfecting his tan, playing golf in the afternoon, and watching movies on the patio at night. For a change of pace, he might drive to the race track in Hialeah. He also entertained a houseful of distinguished guests: Britain's new ambassador, Lord Lothian; Sumner Welles of the State Department; Arthur Krock, of course; and the new appointee to the Supreme Court, Bill Douglas. The Kennedy children, after their Christmas break, returned to their schools in the north.[30] The announcement of the Welles mission on February 9, 1940, made Kennedy's return to Britain essential. He was feeling much better, had gained a little weight, and had the Lahey Clinic's approval to return to London within the next few weeks.[31]

Kennedy's extended stay aroused speculation that he might resign and accept a position campaigning for the president's reelection. "I'm certainly not going over there for the ride," the ambassador told reporters when informed of rumors that he might resign his London post. "The fact that I am going back to my post should be sufficient answer to all resignation rumors." He told reporters he planned to sail for Genoa on the *George Washington* on February 24, 1940, and then take a train to Paris and fly to London.[32]

Meanwhile, rumors of a Kennedy-for-President movement had sprung up in Massachusetts. Without his consent, a campaign to elect Kennedy-pledged delegates was underway.[33] Certainly Kennedy could have counted on the support of the Massachusetts delegation,[34] and seemingly on the support of Roosevelt, too, who suggested at their meeting of February 13, 1940, that Kennedy run in Massachusetts. Surprised, Kennedy told him flatly that he would not run and issued a statement to the press that evening denying his candidacy, an announcement that the Farley delegation greeted with considerable satisfaction.[35] Although he was flattered, Kennedy told the press, he felt compelled to decline the honor. His present post dealt with such "precious" matters that "no private consideration should permit my emergencies or interests to be diverted."[36] Few in the United States or in Britain could have taken that with a straight face. However, the timing for a Kennedy candidacy was wrong, as Kennedy himself surely knew. Roosevelt might run again; if he were to do so in 1940, other candidates would have no chance of getting the party's nomination. Furthermore, the president was known to sour swiftly on any possible rival for his job. So why should Kennedy undermine his own position with FDR and within the party to take a shot at something that could probably never materialize in 1940?[37] Despite Kennedy's refusal, John F. McCarthy Jr., a Boston lawyer, said he would continue to put forward Kennedy-pledged delegates.[38]

Although the party faithful were ready to support Roosevelt if he chose to run again, Jim Farley, an Irish Catholic, was also a favorite Bay State candidate. Among his supporters was young Joe Kennedy Jr., one of the most active Farley men in Massachusetts. Joe Jr. was beginning his political career by running as a delegate to the Democratic national convention and remained, with his father's backing, a steadfast Farley man. The younger Kennedy announced Farley's candidacy two days after the elder Kennedy's statement to the press denying his own candidacy. Regardless, the elder Kennedy maintained his support for Roosevelt.[39]

Kennedy emerged from his Palm Beach estate in mid-February 1940, healthier and heftier, to return to Washington before leaving for London. He met with Roosevelt for an hour-and-a-half conference. The president was in an ebullient mood, eagerly looking forward to his several weeks of vacation cruising in the *Tuscaloosa* on the Caribbean. He had been reading up on the region, he told Kennedy, and talked about its economic problems and its importance for naval and aerial strategy. But it held little appeal for the United States. Roosevelt laughed off the idea of acquiring any Caribbean possessions in exchange for any obligations, a position he would later change his mind on.[40] "It would just be enlarging our biggest poorhouse," Roosevelt said, referring to Puerto Rico. Their wide-ranging discussion included the spring offensive in Europe, certain to come; the president's distrust of Mussolini, whom he accused of lacking the courage to stand up to Hitler; and Kennedy's suggestion of a loan to make it easier to liquidate British-held securities. Kennedy left the meeting still convinced that Roosevelt had not decided whether to run for a third term despite Farley's annoying attempts to push him into making a decision.[41]

In addition, he held discussions with State Department officials[42] about the increase in anti-British feeling and managed to embroil himself in arguments with Ambassador William Bullitt and Secretary of the Treasury Morgenthau over Roosevelt's conduct of foreign and fiscal policy. On February 17, Kennedy met Breckinridge Long, the newly appointed assistant secretary of state, and told him he was struck by the outpouring of anti-British feeling, a significant factor in America's isolationism. The ambassador said that he had "taken the pulse" of the people who went to his chain of movie houses throughout the country. About 80 percent in his unofficial survey were anti-British, he said. Long suggested that Kennedy inform the British authorities of his findings and detail a long list of American gripes against them: tampering with American mail, ordering American ships into prohibited areas, searching American ships en route to neutral ports, and preventing Red Cross supplies from reaching the grief-stricken Poles. The sooner the British realized how much antagonism their actions were causing, the undersecretary said, the sooner they could improve their relations with the American government and the American people.[43]

The president, too, was concerned about the growth of anti-British feeling and about British search and detention of American ships. He had already written to Churchill in early February, protesting Britain's behavior and informing him of the considerable public criticism it aroused: "The general feeling is that the net benefit to your people and to France is hardly worth the definite annoyance caused to us."[44] When Kennedy returned to Britain, he did his best to straighten out misunderstandings between the two governments. He soon boasted to a friend that the "exchange of rude notes has stopped." Problems were discussed orally now, and left "much less sting."[45]

Kennedy's defeatist reports about Europe's fate were echoed by the American ambassador to France, William Bullitt, who had also returned to the United States for the holidays. Although he and Kennedy had similar views on the European situation, they advocated different solutions and different roles for the United States, positions that echoed the divergent views within the State Department, which Kennedy described as "hunting for some basis upon which to fashion a policy." Kennedy acknowledged that he was a pessimist. He feared that war would break out "on a furious scale" by early spring and bring economic and social disaster and defeat to Britain and France. Germany would be sustained by her considerable economic resources and her substantial military equipment: her submarines, her raiders, and her magnetic mines would greatly cripple Britain's trade.[46] Bullitt thought that America's interests warranted doing everything possible to bolster the Allies and called attempts to bring about peace "fruitless."[47] American material support could tilt the European balance in favor of the democracies, he hoped, so that American military intervention might not be necessary. Nevertheless, the United States should prepare for that necessity, Bullitt argued. He believed that Britain and France were clearly winning the war and that within the next three months Germany would be forced to her knees. "I feared that these predictions of his were likely to be as far wrong as those he had made to me on the eve of the war," Kennedy recorded in his memoir.[48] But Kennedy, of course, urged the United States to look out for its own national interests by maintaining its isolationist policy and by urging a compromise peace in Europe.[49]

They also disagreed about financial aid to the Allies: Bullitt wanted to grant the Allies uncollateralized loans so that they could buy supplies; Kennedy wanted to require the Allies to exhaust their own financial resources first, and then to give and not lend them money. A loan could not be repaid by a bankrupt country, a fate certain to befall both France and Britain, he believed; their bankruptcy would poison relations between the United States and the defaulting country for many years. Kennedy's proposal would also clarify matters to the American public about what we were doing and what it cost. Why pretend that we were making a loan to a bankrupt country? he asked.[50]

The long-standing rivalry between the two ambassadors was egged on by Roosevelt, who loved to pit them against each other by feeding their competitiveness. "I talk to Bullitt occasionally," Kennedy told Rose. "He is more rattlebrained than ever. His judgment is pathetic and I am afraid of his influence on F.D.R. because they think alike on many things."[51]

The differences between the two ambassadors boiled over into a loud, angry feud one afternoon in early March 1940 in Bullitt's State Department office. Bullitt recounted the incident to the irascible Ickes. Bullitt had been in the midst of an interview with Joseph M. Patterson, the publisher of the *New York Daily News*, and his Washington correspondent, Doris Fleeson. Kennedy invited himself in and cheerfully butted in on the conversation. Before long, he was emphatically saying "that Germany would win, that everything in France and England would go to hell, and that his one interest was in saving his money for his children."[52] He then launched into a thundering attack on the president, whereupon Bullitt interrupted and disagreed. Their discussion became so vehement that Patterson and Fleeson discreetly left. Bullitt, considered to be "the soul of indiscretion, was more anti-Kennedy than pro Roosevelt"[53] and accused Kennedy of disloyalty. He told him "that he had no right to say what he had" before the two reporters. Kennedy replied "that he would say what he Goddamned pleased before whom he Goddamned pleased." Bullitt then accused him of being "abysmally ignorant on foreign affairs" and having no "basis for expressing any opinion." As long as Kennedy was a member of the administration, "he ought to be loyal—or at least keep his mouth shut."[54] The two ambassadors parted furious. Whatever else Kennedy's latest flare-up with Bullitt indicated, it clearly showed that despite Kennedy's endorsement of Roosevelt, Kennedy still remained sharply critical of his boss.[55]

Besides colliding with Bullitt, Kennedy ran headlong into Secretary of the Treasury Morgenthau over Kennedy's presumptive role as Britain's economic adviser. Kennedy believed that his status as the American ambassador would be undermined were he not allowed to advise the British on their finances; exactly "what the president definitely doesn't want," Morgenthau informed his staff. Morgenthau also told the British embassy that the president wanted the discussions to take place in Washington, but Kennedy continued to interfere from London.[56] At the end of November 4, 1939, the Exchequer put off its prearranged requisitioning of stocks and met its exchange needs by selling $50 million of gold, acting on advice from Kennedy.[57] Roosevelt told Morgenthau that Kennedy wanted the British to sell securities instead of gold, but he was also worried that it would be unwise to dump securities on the market, a rather curious position that alarmed Morgenthau. He told London that the Treasury was concerned about the shift from the sale of securities to gold because it would weaken the American position and was contrary to U.S. financial interest.[58] On April 29, 1940, Morgenthau met with his staff in a confidential meeting to discuss buying gold from Britain. In "one of these typical asinine Joe Kennedy letters," Morgenthau said, the ambassador asked the president to get congressional legislation to stop the further purchase of gold. Harry White of the Treasury, who advised the secretary on monetary policy, regarded Kennedy's suggestion as "absurd," as the ambassador himself knew. It would mean the sale of so many securities on the world market that the SEC would object vigorously. White wondered what Kennedy's motives really were.[59] He was out for personal financial gain, Morgenthau concluded, a charge for which he had no evidence. "The only thing that has explained Joe Kennedy to me for the last couple of years is that he has been consistently short in the market." If this were correct, said the secretary, "that would explain this thing. Every move he makes is to bear down on our market . . . to depress our securities and our commodities."[60] "This whole proceeding has left a very bad taste in my mouth," Morgenthau complained, as he reassured Britain's financial attaché that Kennedy had expressed "his own personal opinion, . . . not the opinion of the Administration."[61] Their disagreement ended with the predictable presidential hand-slapping of his rambunctious ambassador. Roosevelt, under prodding from Morgenthau, curtly informed Kennedy that the United States Treasury, not the ambassador in London, would decide about gold purchases, and Kennedy, by implication, was to refrain from interfering in the matter.[62]

The British were plainly worried about Kennedy's return to London. The Foreign Office file labeled "More Kennediana" contained comments written by officials in January 1940 and showed the depth of officials' hostility to him. They had been keeping tabs on his "défaitiste" campaign while he was still in the United States. J. V. Perowne accused the ambassador of spreading it all around the States that "the British were whopped in this war" and that "they didn't stand an earthly chance of winning." "The rigours of life in London in war time are so considerable that they induce illness in certain ambassadors some 2 months after they have returned to their native lands!" he sneered.[63] "Gastric trouble contracted no doubt at the dining tables of Mayfair," wrote J. Balfour,[64] and he described Kennedy as "malevolent and pigeon-livered." "I don't believe we can (alter his views)."[65] Appropriating a bit of *Hamlet*,

Balfour referred to the ambassador as one part wisdom and three parts coward.[66] In particular Sir Robert Vansittart, an ally of Churchill and a major adviser to the cabinet, was worried that the ambassador had returned to press for a negotiated peace.[67] "Mr. Kennedy is a very foul specimen of double-crosser and defeatist. He thinks of nothing but his own pocket," Vansittart wrote.[68] "I suppose we shall have to have him back again, but if he does come I hope he will be estimated at his true value—which is heavily minus—both here and at No. 10."[69] T. North Whitehead, who had just returned from the United States, questioned the wisdom of letting Washington know, even informally, of British objections to Kennedy. He would, after all, be a valuable asset to the president's upcoming campaign, especially among the Irish along the east coast, Whitehead wrote.[70]

Nor were British officials and journalists happy to have him return to Britain. The Foreign Office, dreading his arrival in late February, decided to be much more reserved in front of Kennedy and spread the word that he was no longer to be "treated like an honorary member of the cabinet."[71] Cadogan passed the word on in highly secret notes to other departments and heads,[72] and one responded by promising to give "oral warning" to any department officials.[73] Several Foreign Office officials suggested that either Halifax or the prime minister might have "a firm talk" with Kennedy.[74]

Harold Nicolson, writing in *The Spectator*, blamed Kennedy's social intimates for his pessimistic views. "Were I to frequent only those circles in which Mr. Kennedy is so welcome a guest, I also should have long periods of gloom." Upon his return, Kennedy would be warmly received, Nicolson predicted, "by the bankers and isolationists, the knights and baronets," by the "shiver-sisters of Mayfair" and the "wobble-boys of Whitehall," by the "native or unhyphenated rich" hoping for a "little raft of appeasement on which they can float for a year or so" before they drown. Few ambassadors would receive a welcome of such bewildering diversity. But if the ambassador could only go in disguise to Leicester and Glasgow, he would realize that "the lisps of the pushing popinjays of Belgravia, the signs of the ageing egoists of Mayfair, are but as the ripple of water in the reeds." He would see how tough the British are. They understand that there can be no lasting peace until Prussian military might is destroyed, until the boundaries of France and the Low Countries are protected against invasion, and until the map of Eastern Europe is redrawn and its countries are able to defend themselves.[75]

Ever since the early days of January 1940, the wily pragmatist in the White House had been mulling over what "helping the British in the war"[76] meant and what, if anything, he could do to prevent the holocaust that seemed to be about to engulf Europe.[77] As if he had accepted Kennedy's suggestion of "[saving] the world"[78] by being "a combination of the Holy Ghost and Jack Dempsey,"[79] the president announced his decision on February 9, 1940, to send his personal emissary to Rome, Berlin, Paris, and London to examine the possibility of a permanent, just peace. Perhaps, the president reasoned, it might convince the Germans to postpone their western offensive in the spring and thereby give the Allies time to reinforce their defenses, and perhaps it might even prevent Mussolini from entering the war. The mission was to be disguised as a fact-finding mission. Deception was necessary so as not to create false hopes in London or Paris or Berlin, or to agitate American isolationists who were already suspicious of FDR's commitment to peace and might oppose his candidacy for a third term.[80]

The Economist understood the Welles mission as a reflection of domestic American politics and the upcoming presidential election. It was designed to ease the fears of the voting public by offering something to everyone: to the isolationists it would show that the president was trying to shorten the conflict; to those demanding a more aggressive American role, it would show American leadership in the peace process. "The United States does not want to be drawn in to Europe. Neither does it want to be left out. The Welles mission exactly expresses this paradox."[81]

For the mission, Roosevelt chose Sumner Welles, his boyhood friend with the same white-gloved, prep-school upbringing at Groton and Harvard, the urbane, sophisticated undersecretary of state. He was to be accompanied by Jay P. Moffat, the head of the European section in the State Department. Welles was to have authority to deal directly with the heads of government, offer no dramatic peace proposals, make no suggestions, and accept no commitments; he would only wave the old bait—postwar disarmament and trade expansion. "My mission," Welles correctly assessed, "therefore was a forlorn hope."[82]

Originally Kennedy welcomed it, unlike Bullitt, who deeply resented it and saw it as a rebuke of himself. He remained in the United States sulking instead of hurriedly returning to France to greet Welles.[83] Kennedy, however, regarded Welles as the most able man in the State Department. Writing in his memoir, he said that he would only be "too happy" if an enduring plan for peace could be found. "More than this, I believed that a bad peace was preferable to the shooting war that was certain soon to break. The threat of Nazism, . . . could eventually be overcome by a program for the economic rehabilitation of Europe in which America should take an active part. War seemed to me to hold no real answer for the future." "It was worth trying anything to bring the war to an end,"[84] he believed, consistent in his oft-expressed views.

But Kennedy's resentment knew no bounds when he learned that Welles had authority to bypass him and deal directly with the British. The ambassador complained that he had not been consulted, as he had not been, and protested that he was being superseded, as he was. Although he might have been delighted by Roosevelt's willingness to consider a compromise peace, the very thing that Kennedy had been urging on him, the ambassador saw Welles's mission as one more example of a public putdown by the president and more evidence to the British of Kennedy's disfavor in Washington. He found a sympathetic listener in Myron Taylor, the newly appointed American representative to the Vatican, to whom he complained upon landing in Rome on his return to his post. Taylor told Kennedy that he had advised the president back in January to consult with the ambassadors of the countries involved before sending anyone, for fear of belittling the ambassadors and undermining their influence. But Roosevelt ignored Taylor's advice. With his usual disdain for administrative procedure, Roosevelt "cut right through the normal diplomatic procedures." "I think the President wanted to make a stage play," Taylor surmised. Kennedy nodded in agreement, thinking of his own treatment by Roosevelt in the Roosevelt-Churchill correspondence. "That's hardly the way to build up an organization," Kennedy mused. "It's like Roosevelt though; he does those things"—a comment that Roosevelt could just as well have made about Kennedy.[85]

Kennedy also commiserated with Robert Murphy at the American embassy in Paris about his unhappiness over returning to London, his conviction that a $50-a-month clerk could do anything he did, that he ought to quit, but that to do so before the election would look graceless. Repeating his by now constant refrain, Kennedy added that "the United States would be crazy to go into the war, and . . . he didn't mind telling the British that they were kidding themselves if they believed otherwise."[86]

Kennedy told Rose that the trip over on the *Manhattan* was made more agreeable by the presence of Clare Boothe Luce and Margaret Case, the society editor of the American *Vogue*. When they landed in Naples on March 4, 1940, they took a sightseeing trip to Pompeii and "looked the place over" before leaving for Rome. The next day Kennedy saw Bill Phillips, Myron Taylor, Cardinal Galeazzi, and a "lovely" 50th anniversary performance of *Cavalleria Rusticana* in Rome with Mrs. Luce. The excited audience was very dressy, he told Rose, and the queen was in attendance, but "I never saw so many homely women in my life and there wasn't one smart dress or more than five thousand dollars worth of jewelry in the whole place," a comment that must have pleased the fashion-conscious Rose. The next morning Kennedy went to Milan and finagled a private tour of the Cathedral and da Vinci's *Last Supper* before leaving on the train for Paris. As the train crossed into France, Kennedy noticed the presence of many French detectives, a sure sign that Sumner Welles was on the train. Kennedy dashed back to greet him and the two journeyed together to Paris.[87]

Kennedy landed at Heston airport, west of London, on March 7, 1940, with a wide grin and a Palm Beach suntan, and was met by a group of reporters asking about the "war boom" in the United States. He denounced charges that the United States was like "Uncle Shylock," and dismissed as pure "poppycock" any criticisms that Americans were getting fat on the world's misery. Asked about isolationist sentiment in the United States, Kennedy expressed his opinions freely, as usual, and defended American policy. "If you mean by isolation a desire to keep out of war I should say that it is definitely stronger. I think it is stronger because the people understand the war less and less as they go along,"[88] an opinion that was misconstrued in the British press: "America didn't know what the war was all about." His remarks caused an uproar in London.[89]

"My Dear Ambassador—Why Didn't You Tell Them?" asked A. Beverley Baxter, MP, writing an open and friendly letter in the *Sunday Graphic* and gently chiding Kennedy for not informing his countrymen. If anyone should understand what the war is all about, it is the American ambassador to the Court of St. James's, Baxter wrote—you, "My dear Joe," an eyewitness to the events leading up to the war, an observer of Britain's unrelenting attempts to maintain peace, and one whose instincts rebel at the viciousness of the Nazi regime. It is being fought for our children and our children's children, so that they "may live in a world where there is decency and light instead of the darkness of war and scientific barbarism. . . . This is what this war is about."[90]

In his memoirs years later, Kennedy wrote: "Remarks [of mine], which I believe correctly summarized American thinking at that time, were not received graciously by the British press. In fact, the press lashed out at me quite bitterly." He accused Baxter of misunderstanding his role. His role was American ambassador to Great Britain, not British ambassador to the United States. That was Lord Lothian. Kennedy noted a coolness toward him in those circles that wanted to involve the United States in the war.[91]

The officials at the Foreign Office were initially resentful of the Welles mission, Roosevelt's "awful, half-baked, idea," as Cadogan called it.[92] Perowne blamed Kennedy and "his défaitiste campaign" for inspiring it.[93] They regarded it as an intrusion and as a grandstand play by the president to inaugurate another peace initiative at Britain's expense. The equation according to foreign officers: Roosevelt believed that Britain could not win and the United States could not let her lose; either the U.S. would come to Britain's aid and declare war on Germany, or the U.S. would force Britain to accept peace. Roosevelt's timing of the mission was significant, they reasoned; it was the last moment before Hitler's expected spring offensive and the most opportune moment before the election to strengthen Roosevelt's hand politically. The Foreign Office also assumed that regardless of what Welles reported to the president, Roosevelt would inevitably lobby for peace. We must be certain, officials told each other, that when Welles arrives he be told the "right sort of tales, associate with the right sort of people, and [have] the right kind of impression conveyed to him."[94]

The British poked fun at the Americans with gibes and scorn. Vansittart urged the government to "warn Mr. Roosevelt off any undesirable grass, before we have to receive the grass-snake Mr. Welles."[95] Anthony Eden sarcastically said to Kennedy: "We're going to be very polite to Sumner Welles; that will surely be appreciated in America."[96] But Chamberlain, "his usual gracious self," according to Kennedy, warmly welcomed the ambassador when they met the day after his return to Britain, March 8. Kennedy was pleased and assumed that the newspaper articles about his remarks in the United States and on the day of his arrival had had no effect on Chamberlain's regard for him. The prime minister told him that he had originally been "disturbed" by the trip because he feared that its purpose was to "put over a peace plan." But now he welcomed the mission, Chamberlain said, because it would make Britain's war aims "more articulate" to Americans.[97] The home secretary, Sam Hoare, told Lord Lothian that he thought that Welles's mission was politically valuable; it could prove a "useful antidote against the defeatism of people like Kennedy."[98] The British reserved their snide remarks and hostility for Kennedy. They snubbed him by failing to invite him to the palace for tea with the king and queen. Welles quickly smoothed over the incident and made certain that Kennedy got an invitation.[99]

Despite his unhappiness over Welles's mission, Kennedy met Welles and Moffat at the airport on the morning of March 10, Sunday. It was a warm spring day, Moffat noted, and aside from the many uniforms, there was little to indicate that Britain was at war. It seemed as if everyone in London was enjoying a leisurely stroll in the parks. Kennedy gave the guests his hastily gathered impressions of only four days as he took them for a drive through the city and a stroll in Kew Gardens.[100] The rundown that Kennedy gave Welles indicated that there had been little change in Britain's position—or in the American ambassador's—since the war began. "England will only accept a peace if they are convinced that it is a sure one," he explained to Welles. "There can be considerable give so far as its details are concerned but they must somehow be assured that they will not be required in a short time to hop in again. Only yesterday both Halifax and Chamberlain stressed this angle in my talk with them."[101] He then dropped Welles and Moffat off at the Dorchester instead of their initial destination, Claridge's. Scotland Yard had agreed to the change in hotels because it feared that Welles's rooms would be bugged by the Italian Fascist manager. (Moffat wondered whether the move was made because the British wanted to bug the rooms.)[102]

Kennedy had worked hard arranging the details of the trip, and for the next two weeks accompanied Welles and Moffat on their visits to British officials.[103] Kennedy had been "spinning ever since" their arrival, he told Rose. They made the rounds and had two or three conferences with Chamberlain and Halifax and met Churchill and Eden and other cabinet members, retired Liberal politician Lloyd George, party leaders, opposition leaders, and the royal family. The British behaved "exceptionally well" toward Welles, Kennedy wrote Rose. They were well-mannered, featured Welles prominently in the press, and assured him that there was "no hope" of peace until the Nazi regime was destroyed. Kennedy described Welles as working very hard to find some plan to save the world. But "the chances look like about one in a thousand," Kennedy told his wife.[104]

Kennedy and Welles arrived at the palace for tea the next day, March 11, at 4:30. The king and queen had closed most of the rooms of Buckingham Palace for the duration of the war and had been living in one of its wings. The king, dressed in an army uniform, greeted his guests cordially and sat in what he laughingly called the "Ribbentrop chair," the chair Ribbentrop had sat in during his last visit to the palace almost two years before, on the day when Germany invaded Austria.[105] Welles was struck by how much graver the king's manner was and how more forcefully he spoke than he had on the trip to Washington the previous summer, a vivid event of a fading world that seemed long ago.[106] Kennedy noted how charming the queen looked, and she wore a diamond bracelet and five strings of pearls that set off her purple dress. She poured tea as they chatted about how much good the royal visit to the United States had done, Göring's magnificent estate and his poor taste in modern painting,

Ribbentrop's refusal to speak to Welles in English (a language Ribbentrop was fluent in), the queen's recollection of Kennedy's refusing to eat hare, and the wartime sugar ration the royals stuck to. Their conversation was pleasant and charming, Kennedy noted in his memoir, but not particularly substantial, quite appropriate for a tea party lasting slightly over an hour. Welles and Kennedy left the palace to cheers at 5:45 and went directly to 10 Downing Street to see Halifax and Chamberlain.[107]

As they waited for Halifax to join them, Welles gave Chamberlain a handwritten note from Roosevelt that Welles had previously shown Kennedy.[108] It stated that Roosevelt had sent Welles, his boyhood friend, on a fact-finding mission and explained that Roosevelt would support no temporary or inconclusive peace.[109] Upon Halifax's arrival, they went into the historic cabinet room on the ground floor with windows facing the park, in the back of the prime minister's official residence. Kennedy noted how poor the lighting was: there were only two ceiling fixtures, and he made a mental note to send Chamberlain a good desk lamp from the United States. They sat at a long green baize table that nearly filled the room.[110] Halifax and Chamberlain reviewed the dispatches from Finland, in the grip of an invasion by the Soviet Union and fighting for its independence. "More complications," Chamberlain muttered, shrugging his shoulders and making no reference to any Allied offensive in Scandinavia. Kennedy asked whether Finland's problems would cause any for the Allies. "It's hard to tell what is going to happen," Chamberlain responded.[111] He then explained his position regarding Germany and the war. In contrast to Kennedy, who saw no immediate alternative to Hitler, Chamberlain, speaking in "white hot anger,"[112] made it clear that he vigorously opposed a negotiated peace. "It [is] impossible to make any kind of a deal with the Hitler regime." "Our quarrel is not with the German people"; if some other group were in power, "it might be possible to get somewhere." In that case, he said, he would be "more than willing to be reasonable" on the Polish and Czech issues. But it was not possible "to do business on any terms with the existing regime," he reiterated. Halifax agreed and added that he did not want a peace that would allow Hitler to save face with the German people.

"I just don't see that," Kennedy blurted out. If a proper solution could be found for Poland and Czechoslovakia, if Europe were peaceful and secure, and if Hitler convinced the Germans that he had done something great for them, "Why should you object?" the ambassador asked. "Based on these facts, I fail to see a good reason for continuing the war." "Perhaps," the prime minister replied, and said that there were groups in Germany that would create a new regime. Even though "in my heart and soul I am for peace, I can see no real peace without the restoration of confidence, and, of course, without that we cannot even contemplate disarmament," he told his American guests, expressing the same position he had held since the outbreak of the war. But Kennedy, who would put up with virtually anything from the Führer and his Nazified Europe to preserve peace, disagreed with Chamberlain's insistence that the end of Hitler's regime was essential to peace. "That isn't much of an offer for you to work on," he said to Welles as the two men quietly walked back to the Dorchester in the dark. Kennedy thought that the interview was courteous and sincere but it had not been a happy one; it had been over almost as soon as it began. Breaking the silence, Welles observed that the prime minister seemed to be "a tired man whose mind is not too elastic."[113] In all the conversations I had with him, Welles later wrote, "neither courage nor determination were lacking, nor the frankest admission of his own mistakes."[114]

Welles and Kennedy had a busy day on March 12, meeting with the Labour leaders, Attlee and Greenwood; Sinclair, the Liberal leader; Cadogan at the Foreign Office; and Churchill at the Admiralty. Kennedy noted in his diary that none of the political figures thought that the current Nazi regime could be trusted. They knew that "war would be hell," he wrote, but "they were going to see it through." Churchill's comments were the most emphatic. Sitting in a big chair before his fireplace, smoking a cigar and drinking a scotch highball, he lectured his guests upon the necessity of the complete military defeat of Germany and the confiscation of her industrial plants. The Nazi government was a "monster born of hatred and of fear.... We will of course win the war and that is the only hope for civilization," he said, speaking eloquently and gesturing as though before thousands. Kennedy, however, still deluded himself that "if Roosevelt could get out a plan that was fair and made peace secure for all, regardless of governments, the people would accept it."[115]

On March 13, Welles and Kennedy spent practically the whole morning with Lloyd George. Lloyd George urged making peace, if at all possible. More than anyone, he knew the horrors and the futility of war. All the totalitarian governments have brilliant leaders, he said, whereas the democracies have none. The only exception was Roosevelt. Welles and Kennedy spent the rest of the day with High Commissioner S. M. Bruce of Australia, who represented the Dominions, and with Anthony Eden and James Maxton, the Socialist leader.[116]

Upon returning to the embassy that day, Kennedy and Welles reflected on their impressions from the interviews of the last few days. "One thing sticks in my mind," Kennedy told him. "The old men who run the government are all so near the grave that they run the war as if there were no generations to follow them. The young ones look at it as a job and they love it and will not give it up. There seems [*sic*] no real fire anywhere, no genius, no sense of the shambles that are to come." Welles agreed with him.[117]

The second interview at six in the evening on March 13 between Welles and Kennedy and Chamberlain and Halifax seemed to Kennedy to produce a slight shift in Britain's position. The British had requested the meeting in the belief that, though the first meeting had been futile, perhaps something positive could still come out of the mission. Chamberlain immediately said to Welles: "I am more and more convinced that we could not enter into an agreement with the present regime in Germany. Confidence must precede and not follow disarmament and confidence is lacking. . . . Hitler and his group are not to be trusted." Regardless of what the terms of the proposal were, "I would feel that Hitler had in the back of his mind a way of getting around the agreement." Welles, carefully measuring his words, replied:

Do I understand, that, assuming the Germans were willing to withdraw from Poland and help reconstitute it, that they would set up Bohemia and Moravia as a separate unit, that they would hold a plebiscite in Austria and that they would express a willingness to disarm along lines that Hitler told me he had been willing to do for the last four or five years and which he had suggested to the British some years ago—a form of disarmament that would be coupled with a central authority consisting of the nations of Europe—that then you would still be unwilling to make an agreement with the present Germany?

"The trouble with all that, Mr. Welles, is that we could not believe Hitler," Halifax interjected; "we would suspect that in a few months we would be back in essentially the same position we are in now." We never want Hitler to tell his people that he has been diplomatically victorious. "Well then, Mr. Prime Minister," said Welles, assuming that all the things I said can be done and I have reason to think they can be done, do I understand that you still would refuse to treat with the German Government?" Chamberlain hesitated and finally stated: "From my point of view, yes; but I have never discussed this with the Government and I cannot tell you what their reaction would be." Kennedy, not convinced by his "yes," interjected "that the position of the British Government would be untenable . . . if a peace [could] be brought about that was not merely temporary and precarious." If you continued to oppose it, then "I myself would like to lead the opposition to the Chamberlain Government," Kennedy said, partly in jest. "I would hate to have to take you on, Joe," Chamberlain rejoined. As the conversation came to a close, Chamberlain said to Welles that "if what you suggest can be worked out with Hitler it will be nothing short of a miracle. But I am perfectly willing to see a miracle happen and willing to pray to God that it might." "[Although] the chances are one in a thousand—better, one in ten thousand," Welles said, "I must explore every possible angle." Kennedy sensed that Welles had been encouraged by the exchange and by Chamberlain's more flexible position. He had drawn back from his previous position of a military victory over Germany. Kennedy considered it "a step forward." "Even if nothing comes of it," Kennedy said to Chamberlain, "the record will show that England was at least willing to try." The prime minister was pleased by Kennedy's statement.[118]

That evening, at a stag dinner for Welles and Moffat attended by Britain's leading political figures, Kennedy showed his considerable diplomatic skill by maneuvering the conversation around to the touchy war issue. Under the guise of good-natured bantering and needling, he got across to the British many distasteful truths about Anglo-American relations. He made it plain that certain actions like taking American ships into combat zones would risk a major blowup between the two countries. He had even told Hull that if the *Manhattan*, on which he was sailing, were to be blown up, it would not be a sufficient cause for war. "I thought that would give me some protection against Churchill's placing a bomb on the ship," the ambassador said. "Not I," said Churchill, who had to have the last word: "I am certain that the United States will come in later anyway."[119] Because of Kennedy's persuasiveness, even

Churchill understood more clearly how British actions irritated the Americans. The party ended on a light note: Churchill, who had done most of the talking, said that he believed that he well understood the average British workman. "His back is up. He will stand for no pulling punches against Germany. He's tough." "Well," Kennedy responded, "if you can show me one Englishman that's tougher than you are, Winston, I'll eat my hat." Kennedy's performance "was superlatively done," Moffat, a former Kennedy critic, wrote in his memoirs.[120] Writing his account of the trip in 1944, Welles remembered a comment Churchill had made that evening.

> [Churchill] said to me that he was now sitting in the same office in which he had sat twenty-five years before, confronted by exactly the same situation. This was because British governments during the past twenty years had refused to follow a realistic policy toward Germany. The objectives of the German people had not changed and would not change. These were world supremacy and military conquest; objectives which endangered the security of the United States as much as they imperiled the safety of the British Empire.[121]

Churchill, of course, had been right.

As Kennedy anxiously watched Welles's plane take off on March 14, 1940, in a blinding snowstorm that had grounded all other planes, he reflected on the Welles mission. "The chance [for peace] was . . . one in a thousand." "But it was worth playing, . . . for thousands, perhaps, millions of lives hung on that chance."[122] Indeed, that was so, and the lives of his own sons and daughters as well.

Actually the Welles mission was futile. There was no chance of any successful negotiation for peace now. The only peace settlement that the Axis wanted was one they themselves imposed. Welles had made no peace proposals; he received none from any source. At the end of March 1940, Welles completed his mission and returned to Washington. None of the leaders to whom he had spoken—not Mussolini, not the pope, certainly not Hitler, not Daladier, nor Chamberlain—had offered any hope for peace. Roosevelt drafted a nebulous statement on March 29 in which he said the information Welles had gathered would be of the greatest value when peace was established. The president's statement proved to be too optimistic. And when the time for peace came five years later, almost all the heads of government whom Welles had visited in Italy, Germany, and Britain were dead. France was the exception, and its head of government was no longer in office.[123]

Roosevelt thought the mission had done no harm. But it had done no good. It had left a trail of bitterness in some English quarters. Suspicions lingered toward American attitudes and ambassadors, suspicions that continued to plague Kennedy, who was still unable or unwilling to understand the aggressive nature of Nazism and who could conceive of no other leader for Germany.

The man who had been the most warmly received American ambassador in living memory was finding London chilly. He had retreated behind America's ocean moats and drawn the line at national self-interest, even parting company with Chamberlain. At one of the few English parties Kennedy did go to soon after his return, he noted that the atmosphere was distinctly anti-American. Hostess Nancy Astor, his fellow American, denied the increase in anti-Americanism, all the while reflecting in her well-placed barbs the critical English attitude toward their former colonies.[124] Kennedy advised Rose not to let any of their children return to Britain just now because of the pronounced anti-American feeling and the anti–Ambassador Kennedy sentiment.[125] It would destroy their happy memories. "If the war gets worse which I am still convinced it will, unless Welles and Roosevelt pull off a miracle, I am sure they will all hate us more," Kennedy predicted to his wife.[126]

George Bilainkin, the "ubiquitous diplomatic correspondent for the Allied Newspapers" with whom Kennedy had a confidential and respectful relationship,[127] noted in his diary: "K. does not go out to any dinners nowadays." "In the old days he wanted as much as a month's notice for a luncheon or dinner appointment." Now he reads and works hard. Despite his unconvincing protestations about not caring "'what the hell they say,'" he was hurt and dismayed by the change.[128] "The British had come to think of him as one of their own," wrote one correspondent from London. "They expected him to plead the British cause when he went home. Joe was shocked by the changed atmosphere. He spent more time with embassy people and American friends since the British social invitations were not as numerous as in pre-war times."[129]

Even Kennedy's reception in the American embassy was cool. He had always kept his distance from the embassy crowd, which even before his vacation had demonstrated a distinctly anti-Kennedy feeling. One official there grumbled to a member of the Foreign Office that he deplored the ambassador's holiday speeches.[130] Another defended his boss against the biting criticism of a conservative English politician, but in doing so gave "the impression of agreeing" with his critics' charges.[131] By the time Kennedy returned to London, he had become so unpopular with his own staff and the American press corps that American newsmen "wax[ed] indignant at the mere mention of Kennedy's name."[132]

In order to get away from the formality of London dinners and to provide a retreat for himself and his staff, Kennedy moved rent-free into St. Leonard's, a seventy-room English castlelike country estate near Windsor owned by Horace Dodge, one of the auto magnates of Detroit. The furnishings were formal, giving the impression of having been decorated by a professional but unimaginative interior designer, Kennedy thought, and requiring about a twenty-five-person staff. It had all the modern conveniences like a bathroom for each of the bedrooms and oil heat. Its yellow roof and its proximity to a factory and an airfield a few miles away made it an easy bombing target. Kennedy had to have the roof painted gray to help conceal it. Regardless, a few months after he took up residence, after a particularly heavy raid, he found the tail of a burned-out bomb on the lawn. It had his initials on it—JPK. The enormous grounds with shrubs and flowers included a nine-hole golf course and a stable. While Kennedy was horseback riding in Windsor Park one morning, he encountered the king, looking very tired, and the two princesses, looking exceptionally well. They stopped and chatted with him for about fifteen minutes. Princess Elizabeth asked about Mrs. Kennedy, and Princess Margaret Rose just smiled and looked cute.[133] But many English quite resented Kennedy's three-month absence and were insulted by his decision to live outside London. As before, Kennedy blamed the criticism on the Jews, bemoaning that Walter Lippmann had been saying "he hasn't liked the US Ambassador for the last 6 months. Of course the fact he is a Jew has something to do with that. It is all a little annoying, but not very serious."[134]

Even the German news agency took potshots at Kennedy. In a story released from The Hague in mid-March, the Nazi press claimed that Kennedy had "lost the good will of the British Government" because he had given Washington a pessimistic assessment of the Allies' ability to win on the western front. The report claimed that he blamed the British for their diplomatic blundering over Poland and for the ineffectiveness of their air power and armaments manufacturing, and that British officialdom was rife with pessimism and feared that a lengthy war would weaken their leadership. The news story was labeled "a fantastic Nazi lie" and was completely denied within an hour by Kennedy himself as well as by British officials. Hull issued a statement that the story is "absolutely untrue. Clearly intended as a troublemaking story." No such diplomatic dispatch had ever been made, the State Department said flatly. Kennedy called the charges "the best fairy tale I've read since 'Snow White.' Not a word of truth in it."[135] But there was; Kennedy's dispatches in the fall and his reports to Washington officials indicate that there was truth in the story. Apparently neither in Washington nor in London did the administrations want the ambassador's pessimism known. He might damage British morale and undercut chances of getting greater American support for the Allies.

A few weeks later, the publication of a series of documents bound in white, *Polish Documents Bearing on Events That Led up to the War*, or the *German White Paper*, gave reporters even more ammunition with which to attack the ambassador. The German publication allegedly contained documents confiscated from the Polish government during the Nazi invasion of Poland during the first few weeks of war in September 1939. These documents contained records of frequent conversations the Polish ambassador in London had supposedly had with Kennedy, and talks held with Bullitt and the Polish ambassadors in Paris and Washington.[136] They "prove[d]" that not only the Allies but also the United States had encouraged Poland to reject adamantly the Nazi demands for Danzig.

One dispatch from the Polish embassy in London to Warsaw stated that Kennedy would intervene with Halifax to ensure that the Poles received the loan they had requested from the British.[137] Jan Wszelaki, the Polish commercial councilor in London, reported that he had spoken with Kennedy on June 16, 1939: "The ambassador agreed that cash was of the greatest importance, saying that if England would now withdraw its help in this matter they would have to give ten times this amount later in order to obtain the same effect. He added that he was going to see the Premier [*sic*] Lord Halifax, and that he would mention the necessity of helping Poland immediately with cash." Kennedy confirmed the first statement but could not recall the second. In his memoirs, he wrote: "I could very probably have told Halifax that . . . the Poles . . . [needed] cash and not sterling credits." Another document claimed that in March 1939 Kennedy had said to the Polish ambassador in London: "England would go to war if the Poles resisted a German attack, particularly on Danzig." This was Kennedy's opinion, he wrote later, and "I very probably voiced it." The *German White Paper* also included a document that cited Ambassador Kennedy as saying that his two elder sons had recently traveled throughout Europe and learned a great deal. They intended to give a series of lectures in the United States on what they had seen in their travels. Their plans went awry when the war broke out, Kennedy said. A further document of June 16, 1939, reported that Joe Kennedy Jr. "had recently visited Poland and other European countries and had views on their problems," and that the elder Kennedy had boasted that young Joe had "the ear of the President and was listened to by him probably more than I. With considerable paternal pride, I had sent some of young Joe's observations to the President and I could easily have bragged about the interest that I thought the President took in them."[138]

The publication of the documents caused a major uproar within the administration and in the American press as editors accepted them as evidence of American officials contravening the nation's interest by involving themselves in Europe's affairs. Roosevelt insisted upon a categorical denial. Hull, deeply concerned about the allegations, repudiated the documents, saying that they did not warrant "the slightest credence." "They have not represented in any way at any time the thought or the policy of the American Government."[139] Despite its categorical denial, the State Department had "just a sneaking suspicion" that there was "more truth than fiction in some of the reported conversations." They had the "ear-marks of authenticity," wrote Assistant Secretary of State Breckinridge Long, who feared their domestic impact more than their international effect and worried that they could be useful to Republicans. "They indicate actions which are characteristic of both Bullitt and Kennedy." Hull, long critical of both men, deeply resented their custom of "going over his head and talking to the President," Long recorded in his diary. Hull had to get Roosevelt's consent to their instructions before they were sent in order to maintain harmony between the president and Hull and the State Department. Long also feared that there were other documents, particularly involving Bullitt, known to be drinking heavily and behaving in unorthodox ways—documents that might be even more revealing than those already published.[140]

A short-lived isolationist howl went up, threatening a congressional investigation. Kennedy, convinced of the authenticity of the *German White Paper*, maintained a discreet silence. He thought that the documents were not forgeries and that the Polish ambassador had reported the conversations reasonably accurately. Not only were the statements made about himself true, Kennedy recalled, but the allegations attributed to Bullitt—for example that the United States would not initially join the Allies if war broke out over Poland but would come in later—were identical with the views he had so frequently expressed to Kennedy.

He wrote Rose that he would welcome a congressional investigation, both from his own personal standpoint and for the country's welfare.[141] He might also have relished a thorough investigation of his by-now archenemy William Bullitt, considered by some diplomats to be "the most dangerous man in Europe"[142] and "an unbalanced war monger"[143] whom Kennedy continued wrongly to blame, along with the president, for pushing the Allies into accepting the Danzig issue as a casus belli, even forgetting that the British had made their own decisions quite independently of any American advice. The *German White Paper* could have been cited by Kennedy as "proof" of this theory that the Allies should have left Poland alone to negotiate as best she could with the Germans.[144] But the storm created by these events was soon consumed by a larger storm that broke out in Norway.

Sumner Welles, too, agreed with Kennedy's assessment of the documents and believed that they did accurately represent Bullitt's views. When Welles was in London, he told Kennedy that he was "amazed" at what the documents contained. Bullitt did not just limit his promise of assistance to the Poles; he also gave the French assurances of American support. "Bullitt, you know, has been mixing into almost every phase of the French Government and has even been advising them on military strategy," Welles told Kennedy. Bullitt had even complained to the president of being worn out "because he had been practically running the French Government."[145]

Kennedy briefly discussed the German documents and the whole range of Anglo-American relations with George Bilainkin. "I have been scrupulously careful all the time I have been here never to say what I could, or might not, do, in my relations with your Government." For his part Bilainkin dismissed the "allegations" against Kennedy as mere "nonsense." "Perhaps a *diplomat* [*sic*] *de carrière* might have been more aloof, but then we must pay for having business celebrities as ambassadors; and surely, if Kennedy did speak in the way suggested, it was no heinous crime," Bilainkin wrote in his diary.[146] Perhaps not, but it did illustrate the problems in having persons untrained in international relations occupying key diplomatic posts in precarious times, especially those well known for indiscretions and for representing their own views rather than those of their governments. Roosevelt knew his man well and realized that ultimately Kennedy evaluated everything on the basis of "the personal equation." And yet Roosevelt kept him on. The blame lay with Roosevelt.

CHAPTER 9

England at Bay

T he only stirring in the "unreal quiet"[1] in the West during the "twilight war," as Churchill called it,[2] had been the Soviet invasion of Finland launched on November 30, 1939. The Soviet dictator, Joseph Stalin, feared that Finland, which he regarded as part of his sphere of influence, might fall under German domination. For several years he had repeatedly discussed the possibility of territorial adjustments with the Finns to protect Leningrad, Russia's second largest city, only twenty miles from the Finnish border; but no agreement had been reached. He wanted the Finns to cede part of the Karelia Isthmus and part of the Rybachi Peninsula to the Soviets, in exchange for territorial concessions in eastern Karelia. He also wanted a thirty-year lease on the port of Hangö, one hundred miles from Helsinki, the Finnish capital, for the Soviets' use as a naval base. The Finns refused. Determined to get what he wanted and certain of victory, Stalin ordered a force of thirty divisions and six tank units to invade Finland in the Winter War.[3]

The Red Army attacked in winter, with heavy snow and temperatures as low as 50 degrees below, Celsius. Their mechanized forces were ill-equipped for this type of warfare. The troops ran amuck and got bogged down in the Finnish terrain with its thick forests, frozen swamps and lakes, and a few nearly impassible roads. Under inspired leadership, the nine Finnish divisions, wearing snowshoes and skis, in white uniforms, fought back. The Finns cut Soviet supply lines and ambushed their columns, which stretched out in long lines for miles. The Finns decimated five Russian divisions and halted the Russian offensive. It was a disaster for the Soviets, and by January 1940 it was obvious that the Soviet assault had been a miserable failure.

In February, Stalin initiated a new military offensive under new leadership with an expanded army of 50 to 1 and massive amounts of equipment. Under intense artillery bombardment, the Soviets slowly clawed their way through the Finnish line and by March 14, 1940, the Red Army forced the stunned Helsinki government to accept a dictated peace. The severe terms demanded the surrender of the entire Karelian Isthmus, territory on Lake Ladoga, a lease on Hangö, and no territorial compensation for the Finns. Technically the Finns still had their independence, but their ability to defend their country was considerably weakened.

The Finns had fought well, but they had received no aid from the Allies, despite appealing to the League of Nations. The French so resented their government's failure to support the Finns that Daladier was kicked out of office for not coming to their rescue. He was replaced by Paul Reynaud on March 20, causing "only a slight ripple in England," Kennedy noted.[4] The British were more restrained about their government's do-nothing response as Chamberlain, in the middle of the Welles talks, shrugged off the invasion as if his mention of it was an afterthought and supported a Finnish/Soviet peace. The government had been reluctant to send British troops to aid the Finns because, Kennedy noted in his memoir, Halifax feared that such action would strengthen the relationship between the Soviets and the Germans.

The Soviet Union benefited from the new territorial arrangements. They removed any border with either Norway or Sweden and thus insulated the Soviet Union from any future conflict in the region. Although victorious, the Soviet Union, a country of 175 million, had been completely humiliated by a country of not quite 4 million. The collapse of the Soviet's military might and its decline in prestige convinced Hitler that the Soviet military was incapable of defeating his Wehrmacht.[5]

The campaign in Finland was "more than a severe set-back to the prestige of the Allies," Kennedy believed.[6] It was also something of a setback in Anglo-American relations. Upon his return from the United States in March, Kennedy sensed a distinct rise in anti-American feeling. He endured taunts even from Lady Astor as well as her guests at Cliveden. Eden tried to smooth things over by denying that there was any anti-American feeling, but he also told Kennedy that if there were, the United States was at fault. Eden blamed the United States for its failure to assist the Finns in their courageous struggle.[7] "Nuts," Kennedy recorded in his diary,[8] knowing all "too well . . . the cold calculations of Halifax and Chamberlain," who always considered the question of aid to Finland subordinate to Britain's interests.

The Finnish campaign made all of Scandinavia a possible theatre for military operations and forced the Allies to reassess their military strategy for an offensive against the Germans.[9] Throughout the fall and winter, the Allies had been preparing three possible offensives. Two involved Norway and one involved the Rhine; all were enthusiastically endorsed by Churchill, who was largely responsible for them, Kennedy noted.[10] The Allies were plotting to blow up the Leads in Narvik, a sheltered passage between Narvik and the sea. The Allies were also planning to occupy Narvik and other major Norwegian ports along the Atlantic coast like Stavanger, Bergen, and Trondheim, in order to obstruct German ore shipments. They also intended to mine the Rhine to delay the Germans' expected spring offensive by thwarting their communications at the home front. But Finland's peace initiative undermined the pretext of aiding Finland as an excuse to seize the ports. The Norwegian proposals would now have to rest on their own merits as the Allies debated which plan to use and when and how.[11]

Following the campaign in Finland, Kennedy turned his attention to the political drama in London and did his best to keep Washington informed about the events there. He attended sessions in the House of Commons, spoke to the principal political figures of all parties, and passed on his insightful and shrewd opinions about Britain's political turmoil to Washington. His balanced, sound, up-to-the minute, and well-informed dispatches were filled with admiration for the British and advice on how to protect America's self-interest. They gave the administration a box seat for London's responses to Hitler's productions on the Continent.

The end of the Finnish war brought about "a certain lull" in London and an increase in tension and boredom, Kennedy wrote in his memoir.[12] He attended a session in the House of Commons on March 19 and witnessed an acrimonious exchange between Chamberlain and his opponents, who "needled him" by challenging the accuracy of his statements as he bitterly defended his policy. He revealed a nasty temper, so unlike the man Kennedy had known and admired. "The strain of these days was already obviously taking its toll," Kennedy lamented, and was spilling over inside and outside of Parliament and onto the streets.[13]

By late March, Kennedy noted that "the phony war had ceased to be popular." People were confused and restless over the seeming lack of direction and inaction by the Allies; even the people who made the decisions seemed to have no answers about what to do and how to do it. Halifax told Kennedy that there was also a lack of consensus among the French and the British. The French "were somewhat cool" to Churchill's proposal to mine the Rhine, but Reynaud strongly supported mining the Leads and seizing the Norwegian ports. The British simply acquiesced to French pressure on the Norwegian strategy. Halifax also told Kennedy that except for Churchill, the British were waiting for Hitler to attack and wondered whether his inaction was a deliberate attempt to undermine Allied morale. If so, it was working. The morale of the French military was quickly deteriorating. Kennedy cabled Hull: "The real complaint of the British against Hitler is that he is not cooperating with the British in helping to win the war for them."[14]

"Missed the bus," Chamberlain jeered, taunting Hitler in a speech to the Conservative Central Council on April 4 over his failure to launch an assault on the west.[15] General Ironside bragged the next day to journalists: "Frankly, we would welcome an attack. We are sure of ourselves. We have no fears. . . . We are ready for anything they might start. As a matter of fact, we'd welcome a go at them." The Germans had already been given the "go" and were sailing for Norway on April 3. "It was to break in all its fury only four days later," Kennedy wrote.[16]

It was not until April 5 that the Allies finally made the decision to mine the Leads; to land British troops at the Norwegian ports of Narvik, Stavanger, Bergen, and Trondheim; and to inform the governments of Norway and Sweden of their intent. Kennedy, too, was told of the plan and shown the note to the governments. Hitler knew about the plan, too. German intelligence was "generally aware" of British plans but lacked their exact details. He was particularly worried about threats to Germany's iron-ore shipments from Sweden. Hitler therefore decided on a preemptive invasion of Norway and Denmark and thereby forestalled by a few hours an Allied plan almost identical to his. "Nothing was said at the time" of the similarities between the two plans, Kennedy noted in his memoir.[17]

In the foggy morning of April 9, 1940, and just a few hours after the British had finished mining the Norwegian inland waterways and were still nearby, Denmark's army of 15,000 men was overwhelmed by the Germans, who took the Danes by surprise. The Germans overran the country in a few hours and the Danes surrendered that same day. An initial Nazi invasion force of ten thousand also invaded Norway a few hours later, carrying troops across the Skagerrak and along the Atlantic seaboard for disembarkation at all the major ports in Norway, an extremely dangerous and daring plan that Hitler enthusiastically endorsed. The Germans had gained control over the resources of Denmark, the Baltic Sea lanes, and the sea and airway routes to Norway in less than a day.[18]

Kennedy had stopped at the Foreign Office that afternoon to confer with Halifax and Cadogan and was shown a copy of the speech that Chamberlain was to deliver to Parliament that day. A little before four o'clock on April 9, Chamberlain announced to the nerve-wracked House of Commons that German troops had conquered Denmark and had landed at important Norwegian ports. Fighting had erupted in Oslo and Trondheim. Chamberlain promised to give full aid to the Norwegians and announced that the British navy was already under sail.[19]

Everywhere the invaders caught the small, inexperienced, and inept Norwegian forces off-guard. The Germans showed early in the war the superiority of land-based airpower over sea power. They were thus in an excellent position to attack the British, French, and Polish units fighting alongside the Norwegians. In the first few days of the campaign, the Germans were victorious. The Norwegian resistance simply collapsed, and the Germans made full use of their control of the air as they moved from Oslo throughout the country. They had superior strategy and greater precision and fighting ability than the Allies on land, but not at sea, particularly at Narvik, the port farthest away from Germany and the hardest for their navy to get to. The British navy destroyed ten of Germany's destroyers in the fjords off the coast of Narvik, half of the German fleet, and ultimately sank or damaged most of Germany's large surface ships, an ominous upset for Hitler, who planned to invade England in the summer and fall of 1940. Faced with military disaster on land, the Allies agreed to withdraw to the south of Narvik on April 26. In May they first seized Narvik in a lackadaisical campaign and then evacuated it on June 8. The German offensive underway in Western Europe convinced the Allies of the necessity of withdrawing all their troops.[20]

Kennedy observed that the British public was slow to realize the extent of the defeat in Norway. It took a while for reports of the ruthless bombings of British troops by the Wehrmacht to dribble back to London, of naval action canceled because of lack of air support, and of poorly trained and poorly equipped troops unprepared to survive in Norway's weather. It took a while for the European capitals and finally London, too, to realize that the Norwegian campaign was a disaster and "to question the Churchillian thesis that Hitler's attack on Norway was one of his great strategic errors," Kennedy wrote from his vantage point in

London.[21] Norway had been conquered within two months, a dramatic ending to the phony war and "the prelude to a real shooting war."[22]

The Allies had been soundly humiliated in a situation they should have been victorious in. Their deeply flawed plans were based on mistaken Allied troop estimates, on an overestimation of Britain's naval power, and on a guess that Hitler's most likely pathway for invading Norway would not be along the Atlantic seaboard but through the Skagerrak, between Denmark and Norway.[23] It was as Churchill, its architect, described it: the "ramshackle Norwegian campaign" in which the Allied effort was "too little, too late;"[24] in which "we have been completely outwitted."[25] It led Chamberlain to conclude that "Churchill's impatience, impetuosity, and lack of consistent purpose over Norway suggested that he had learned nothing from the Dardanelles disaster in 1915 with regard to the dangers of improvised large-scale combined operations."[26] The Norwegian debacle led to Chamberlain's resignation. It had been a costly campaign: Norway lost its independence, Chamberlain lost his government, and Hitler lost most of his surface fleet.[27] The outcome led Chamberlain's critics to ask just who had "missed the bus."

Hitler's invasion "shocked the world," Kennedy wrote. Its daring, its quickness, and its success against overwhelming odds was used by Allied politicians against the Nazi regime who made much out of Germany's brutal violation of neutral rights.[28] It was a "staggering blow to the British," Kennedy wrote Rose on April 26, 1940. They "are not making a very good job of it." Kennedy predicted that the real danger of a German victory in Denmark and Norway would be the disastrous effect it would have on the neutral countries in the Balkan states as well as on the Low Countries. Moreover, he said, it might convince Mussolini to join the victors and thereby create "another bad mess for the Allies," for whom "this war means absolute chaos."[29] It did mean that: the Allies simply did not have the numbers in men or in matériel to win.[30] Although "my sympathies are completely with the Allies," Kennedy told Rose, yet "we may have to fight Hitler at some later date over South America, but we had better do it in our own back yard where we will be effective and not weaken ourselves by trying to carry on a fight over here"—Kennedy's persistent prescription for America's foreign policy and one that Roosevelt would disagree with.[31]

The botched British landings in Norway, in disarray from beginning to end, only deepened Kennedy's gloom. On April 26, 1940, he sent off a long, bleak report to the president and the secretary of state, describing British unpreparedness and military inefficiency and the widespread undercurrent of dissatisfaction it was fostering, something he had not seen before. "You know that this bearish streak of mind started before Munich and is not a new one," Kennedy told Washington. "A great many people here tonight are beginning to realize that unless there is a terrific change and quickly things will be as serious as one can imagine because England lacks efficient leadership from top to bottom." But the ambassador could see no alternative to the present government and called the manpower "terribly limited."[32] He dismissed Churchill, as did many in his own party, as little more than a has-been whose judgment has been called into question. "Mr. Churchill's sun has been caused to set very rapidly by the situation in Norway which some people are already characterizing as the second Gallipoli,"[33] the Dardanelles debacle in 1915 that Churchill as First Lord of the Admiralty had been responsible for. Kennedy passed along a remark making the rounds at the embassy: When is America coming into the war? an Englishman asked an American friend of Kennedy's. "When is England coming in?" the friend replied. "Never mind about America."[34]

But FDR was no longer sympathetic to his ambassador's by-now habitual fatalism over Britain's military status or its lack of leadership and his unrelenting predictions of disaster. Even so, the busy president took time out to offer words of comfort. "These are bad days for all of us who remember always that when real world forces come into conflict, the final result is never as dark as we mortals guess it in very difficult days."[35] Kennedy turned a deaf ear to Roosevelt's soothing words.

For comfort, Kennedy looked instead to Rose, always his staunchest supporter. The thought of her coming over for several weeks or perhaps for a month in May cheered him up immensely; but she should come without the children, he advised in a letter to her on April 5. There would be nothing for them to do except waste their time in nightclubs and get into lots of arguments about American foreign policy. "Conditions in England haven't changed much at all," Kennedy warned Rose. Nor had he. The English dislike that Americans criticize the Allied conduct of the war and resent that Americans make money from it. And Kennedy was still the same: "I haven't changed any of my bearish opinions." He was worried about where and when the battle between the Allies and the Germans would be joined, but he had no doubt that it would come. The unstable political situation in France and the change of leadership in England[36] led him to predict that Hitler, who had not yet felt the sting of the Allied blockage, might be willing to gamble on an economic war for the rest of the year and to be content with attacking only the convoy system. "Of course, all of this is subject to change without notice," Kennedy warned Rose, but if Hitler decides to invade Holland, "the fat will be in the fire."[37]

Kennedy was also uncertain about how much longer he would hold his ambassadorship, no longer the "best job in the world." In early April "the news all seems to be Roosevelt won't run so automatically I'm out," he told Rose. The only thing is how soon? . . . The [Germans] want Roosevelt licked because they feel they couldn't be worse with anyone else."[38].

Kennedy also told Rose that he had been worried about the welfare of Eddie Moore—he was sick with a bad case of the "flu" in Paris. Kennedy had flown over to bring Eddie and his wife, Mary, back to England. Eddie did not want to return to the United States just yet; he assumed they would all be leaving soon anyway and could all go home together.[39] While in Paris Kennedy visited with Clare Boothe Luce for a couple of days,[40] went off his diet, upset his stomach, and complained to Rose about it. He ended his letter like a dutiful husband, with a loving comment: "Well darling I guess it's right nothing is perfect in this life and I just don't like being so completely away from you. . . . Maybe old age and a bad stomach will change me. I don't know. I guess I'm a restless soul: Some people call it ambition. I guess I'm just *nuts!* Nevertheless, I love you so much."[41] Despite being homesick and missing his family, Kennedy turned his attention back to England's fate.

Kennedy attended the closing session of the two-day debate on Norway in the House of Commons on May 8, 1940. Sitting in the gallery near Ivan Maisky and Charles Corbin, the Soviet and the French ambassadors, Kennedy noted the tone of despair and hopelessness over England's military situation and the belligerent mood regarding Chamberlain's leadership. As First Lord of the Admiralty, Churchill, "Chamberlain's loyal, if impulsive, lieutenant,"[42] whom he believed to be "absolutely loyal,"[43] deserved and received the lion's share of the harsh condemnation and gallantly shouldered the blame for the largely naval war in Norway. Kennedy was impressed with Churchill's speech and able answers. He handled the critics and constant interrupters well and lost his temper only a couple of times. One also had the impression, Kennedy wrote in his diary, that Churchill saw the mantle being lowered on his shoulders sometime in the near future and he did not want anyone to be angry with him.[44]

Churchill was responsible for the Norwegian disaster, but it was Chamberlain who paid for it politically.[45] The ambassador watched a furious political revolution erupt as the charges of inefficiency and unpreparedness over the Norway campaign reached their height in an acrimonious and historical parliamentary debate. Chamberlain's party led the attack against the government—"a very painful affair," he told his sister Ida[46]—with taunts about Hitler having "missed the bus." Leo Amery, a privy councillor and Chamberlain's long-standing friend and colleague from Birmingham, dealt the unkindest cut of all. He rose from the Tory benches behind the government and to the ringing cheers of the Commons delivered a "body blow"[47] by quoting Oliver Cromwell's dismissal of the Rump Parliament: "You have sat too long here for any good you have been doing. Depart, I say, and let us have done with you. In the name of God, go."[48] Lloyd George, the Liberal Party leader in World War I who seldom attended the House and had been through all this before, gave vent to his twenty years of Chamberlain-hating with "an attack whose bitterness was as raw as a whip," and struck a deep blow against his enemy.[49] In a spellbinding twenty-minute speech with his arms flailing, the former prime minister delivered his "last flicker of destructive genius." The present prime minister "has appealed for sacrifice. The nation is prepared for every sacrifice so long as it has leadership. . . . I say solemnly that the Prime Minister should give an example of sacrifice, because there is nothing that can contribute more to victory in this war than that he should sacrifice the seals of office."[50]

The prime minister's own party deserted him to join the Opposition. The majority in the House of Commons on May 8 shrank from over 200 to a mere 81 during the vote of confidence. Forty-one Conservatives, including Anthony Eden and a weeping young officer in uniform, an admirer of Chamberlain, voted against the government. About sixty abstained,[51] including Lady Astor; it was a virtual rebellion. Pandemonium broke out as the vote was announced and jubilant Tories howled themselves hoarse shouting, "'Resign' and 'Go' . . . and singing 'Rule Britannia.'" The vote was a "mortal blow" and destroyed Chamberlain's government. It was the only time a majority government was removed from office by a vote in Parliament in the twentieth century.[52]

Britain was tottering toward chaos, Kennedy reported. "Everybody was shocked." The prime minister was "in very bad shape mentally and physically" and looked "stunned" and "beaten."[53] "Chamberlain, Halifax and Churchill are unquestionably tired men." "While stolidity may be a British characteristic, they leave sinking ships here as well as in any other country." Rattled, resentful, and stubborn, Chamberlain might slug it out before he resigned, Kennedy speculated. But neither Chamberlain nor his noisy critics had plans to give purpose and direction to the war, Kennedy told Washington, as he watched Chamberlain trying to run a war without public backing and over the angry protests of a bickering party. The press, too, was clamoring for a change in leadership and demanded either a much broader cabinet, one strengthened "by new blood," or a new prime minister, or both. After talking with members of the British establishment from all parties, Kennedy concluded: "Everybody is mad. They all want to do something and go places; but nobody has the slightest idea of what should be done."[54]

Worried that the Chamberlain government would not survive, Kennedy called the president at midnight and gave him a brief summary of what had happened. Roosevelt was surprised at the number of Conservatives who deserted Chamberlain and sorry about the bad feeling that had developed. And Roosevelt "had just learned that Germany had delivered an ultimatum to Holland." Did Kennedy know anything about it? No, Kennedy said. Subsequently he called Churchill, Halifax, and Hoare to see whether anyone had any information; no one had. John Cudahy in Brussels had a vague understanding that there had been some kind of action by the Dutch, but he didn't think they had had an ultimatum, nor did he expect the Germans to do anything that night or the next day. But there was a strong possibility that something would happen in the next fortnight, Cudahy told Kennedy. The next morning, May 9, the Foreign Office asked Kennedy about the information he had. He told them what he knew, and they had nothing to add. The British seemed resigned to the hopelessness of their situation. "A terrible world this is getting to be," Churchill remarked, upon hearing from Kennedy about the ultimatum.[55]

Chamberlain's defeat could not have come at a more dramatic moment in history, with the ending of the phony war by the long-expected Nazi invasion in the west. The prime minister had two choices, as Kennedy saw it. Chamberlain could remain as prime minister only if he drastically reformed his cabinet, the very least he could do. That would satisfy his supporters. However, even if he did so, Kennedy feared that Chamberlain could still be in for difficulties; he would be blamed for any Allied reverses and those would be likely to lead to his dismissal. And even if he remained as prime minister, he would still lack the country's confidence.[56] Something more than a drastic reorganization of the cabinet was essential to placate the politicians in Westminster and London's clubs, the Fleet Street press, and public opinion, Kennedy told Hull.[57]

Chamberlain's second option, Kennedy reported to Roosevelt, was to resign and recommend a successor. Chamberlain had two choices: Halifax, no doubt Chamberlain's first choice and the choice of the Conservative Party and political establishment, including the king, or a completely galling prospect—Churchill, popular with the public. However, Kennedy recalled his conversation with Chamberlain several months back when they were discussing the possibility of Halifax's becoming prime minister. Chamberlain was worried that as a Peer of the Realm, Halifax's membership in the House of Lords would make it hard for him to provide leadership in the House of Commons, even with an enabling act to allow him to speak from the House floor. In addition, Churchill's close friend and associate Brendan Bracken informed Kennedy that Churchill would refuse to join any cabinet headed by Halifax, "a rather bad start for the new Government." Kennedy also heard that Arthur Greenwood and Clement Attlee, Labour's leaders, would refuse to join a new Chamberlain cabinet as well.[58]

Kennedy learned later in the evening on May 9 that at six o'clock that day Chamberlain had convened a meeting at 10 Downing Street to assess the political situation. Halifax, Churchill, Attlee, and Greenwood attended. Chamberlain asked the Labour Party leaders two questions: would they join a new government headed by him, or if not, would they join a government headed by Churchill? "Our party . . . won't have you and I think I am right in saying the country won't have you either," Attlee responded; but he and Greenwood did promise to consult their party's national executive.[59] Churchill made an impassioned plea for Labour to join a Chamberlain government; Labour remained unmoved. When Halifax was asked his opinion about becoming prime minister, he said: "Perhaps I can't handle it being in the House of Lords." Hearing the hesitation in his voice, Churchill delivered the coup de grâce: "I don't think you could," and that was that.[60]

There was more jockeying throughout the afternoon on May 10 about Chamberlain's willingness to resign and about who was to be in the cabinet. Any hope that he may have had about remaining as prime minister was quickly removed by Attlee's phone call to Chamberlain at 5:00 p.m. After consultation with his executive committee, Labour's answer to Chamberlain's questions were no and yes. Labour was determined not to join a cabinet headed by Chamberlain, but it would join one headed by Churchill. An hour after Attlee's call, just a bit short of his third anniversary as prime minister, Chamberlain went to the Palace to surrender his seals of office to the king. In the midst of accounts flowing into London describing heavy fighting in the Lowlands, he reluctantly recommended that Churchill be his successor.[61] "Private Secretary of Mr. Chamberlain confirms that he has resigned and that Mr. Churchill is now Prime Minister," Kennedy's cable to Washington May 10, 1940, reported.[62] "At 9:00 pm on 10 May 1940 Chamberlain announced his resignation in a radio broadcast and urged the nation to rally behind its new leader." The queen told Chamberlain that his address was so dignified that it caused Princess Elizabeth to cry as she listened to it.[63]

Churchill described the events in *The Gathering Storm.* That evening, May 10, he received the traditional summons to Buckingham Palace to kiss the king's hand. George VI received him graciously and invited him to sit down. After looking at him "searchingly and quizzically" a moment, His Majesty said, "I suppose you don't know why I have sent for you." Churchill returned: "Sir, I simply couldn't imagine why." The king laughed and said, "I want to ask you to form a Government." Churchill said he would certainly do so.[64] He formed a national coalition and a five-man war cabinet and assumed the offices both of prime minister and minister of defence. He insisted that Chamberlain, as leader of the party, and Halifax, as foreign secretary, remain in the cabinet.[65] "Thus the path was clear for the more pugnacious, more dynamic, more determined and more strong-willed—though more unpredictable—Churchill."[66]

That evening as Churchill was driven back to Admiralty House, where he was living for the time being, he was uncharacteristically silent. His bodyguard, Inspector W. H. Thompson, thought it appropriate to congratulate him. "I wish the position had come your way in better times for you have an enormous task." Churchill's eyes filled with tears and he said, "God alone knows how great it is. I hope it is not too late. I am very much afraid it is. We can only do our best." He entered Admiralty House and climbed the stairs with his jaw set, determined, the master of his emotions.[67] Churchill went to bed at three in the morning. He felt a sense of profound relief: "I felt as if I were walking with Destiny, and that all my past life had been but a preparation for this hour and for this trial."[68]

Kennedy called Churchill to offer his congratulations on the evening of his appointment and jokingly to refresh his memory that he—Kennedy—was responsible for his new position. He reminded Churchill that he had been the one to inform him of Roosevelt's consent when Churchill as First Lord of the Admiralty had conceived of the infamous mining of the neutral Norwegian waters. "Eunice went to the party," he said, a reference to their coded message about mining the Leads, "hence Norway, hence Prime Minister."[69] Never outdone, Churchill replied, "Eunice should have gone to Party 3 months earlier."[70] Kennedy said, "She was willing to." Most probably, Churchill was not amused. Koskoff points out that in addition to Kennedy's claiming credit for Churchill's becoming prime minister, what seems to have amused Kennedy was not the "majestic self-sacrifices involved, but rather, the irony inherent in what he took to be the undeserved windfall of the successor."[71]

"Saw Chamberlain today," Kennedy wrote in his diary a few days after Chamberlain's resignation. "He is definitely a heartbroken and physically broken man. He looks ghastly; and I should judge he is in a frightfully nervous condition." In their brief conversation, Chamberlain did not seem bitter, just heartbroken.[72] That did not keep Kennedy from asking him to autograph a picture for him. I want to hang your picture in my house, Kennedy wrote to him, "to remind me constantly of a man who worked with all his capacity to keep peace in the world, and with whom I am most happy to have been associated with in the 2 most eventful years of my life."[73] "I value your friendship most highly," Chamberlain had told him. "You have been a great help to me."[74]

Chamberlain continued to serve in Churchill's war cabinet as leader of the party and Lord President of the Council. He resigned on October 3, 1940. Little more than a month later, on November 10, he died of bowel cancer.

Suddenly, without warning, at dawn on May 10, 1940, 5:35 a.m., an "all hell has been let loose"[75] Nazi offensive against the Western Powers erupted as Germans shattered the quiet of the twilight war, just as Kennedy, "tearing his hair" out over the events, had feared.[76] With astounding speed, the Germans struck treble blows in neutral Holland, Belgium, and Luxembourg, and readied themselves to goose-step through the streets of their capitals. "Imagine the drama of the situation," Kennedy wrote to Hull. "Churchill was realizing his life's ambition to become Prime Minister, spending the night forming his Cabinet so as to announce it at 6 o'clock tonight, and Hitler invades Holland."[77]

Kennedy was awakened by a phone call at 6 o'clock that morning from Hull, who asked Kennedy whether he knew anything about what was happening. "Nothing," Kennedy replied, but he promised to find out. He promptly called the Admiralty and learned that the only news the British had was that Holland had been invaded. The Admiralty apparently knew nothing about Belgium or Luxembourg. "It struck me that they didn't have the slightest idea of what was going on."

Kennedy got dressed and went to his office to call the American embassies in the capitals. Acting as a go-between, he inquired about the military situation in each city and about the fate of Americans there and passed his conversations on to Welles in Washington, who greatly appreciated his efforts. Welles had not been able to get through to Brussels, The Hague, or Paris, and he was very anxious to know what was happening. Things were "very bad" at The Hague, the American ambassador, George Gordon, told Kennedy; he expected a battle there within the hour. The Germans had laid mines in all the Dutch harbors and at Rotterdam and were landing in parachutes and sea planes, Gordon said. It was impossible to evacuate Americans and British survivors. Just as Cudahy, the American ambassador in Brussels, was telling Kennedy about the large concentration of German planes over Luxembourg around two o'clock that morning and describing the bombing of Brussels at 5:30, there was an air raid warning in Brussels. The Belgian government had no warning of the assault, Cudahy said. Kennedy called Edward Reed, the counselor of the U.S. Embassy in Rome. He had no news. His only source of information was the radio; there had been nothing in the morning newspapers. Kennedy then spoke to Halifax, who told him that the British were moving in every direction—from the sky, sea, and land.[78]

On May 13, three days after the invasion, Churchill met Parliament to ask for a vote of confidence for the new national government. The cheers from the Conservative benches in the House of Commons that day were for Chamberlain when he entered the House, not Churchill.[79] Churchill's maiden speech as prime minister, a paraphrase of Garibaldi's famous remarks, was brief but moving, with members giving him a standing ovation, Kennedy wrote. Churchill said: "I have nothing to offer but blood, toil, tears and sweat. . . . You ask, what is our policy? I will say: It is to wage war by sea, land, and air. . . . You ask, What is our aim? I can answer in one word: It is victory, victory at all costs, victory in spite of all terror, victory however hard and long the road may be, for without victory there is no survival." The House voted unanimously to support the government: "Ayes, 381, Noes 0," Kennedy reported, and adjourned until late May.[80] Britain now had a leader fully equal to the arduous task ahead, one for whom defeat was utterly unthinkable, one whom Kennedy disliked intensely and frequently misjudged, one whom Kennedy equated with worldwide financial chaos, bankruptcy, and Bolshevism. Their antipathy was mutual.

In his order of the day, May 10, Hitler bragged to his troops: "The hour of the decisive battle for the future of the German nation has come." The battle would "decide the destiny of the German people for a thousand years."[81] And it looked as if Hitler might be right. In just a few weeks he managed to achieve a spectacular victory. "A holocaust of German fire and steel" rained down on the Dutch and Belgian borders as Germans dressed in Dutch uniforms landed in Luxembourg the night before and caused confusion among the Allies. Screaming dive bombers roared through the air, and parachutists landed in airfields, seizing airports and towns as the blitzkrieg rolled on toward France. Behind the assault forces were 120 infantry divisions, with twenty in reserve, and six thousand planes ready to do battle. The Allies had about 112 divisions near the German and Belgian border and planned to add twenty-five more Belgian and Dutch divisions to them. Kennedy, who had been told of the Allied military plan, noted that the Dutch and the Belgians had refused to hold staff talks with the British or French. Consequently, the Allies had no idea when or where they would connect with the Belgians.[82]

The Dutch opened their floodgates, hoping to drown the enemy in a swampy morass. The Allies moved up their half-million troops to buttress the brave though ineffectual Belgian army, but failed to coordinate their forces with the Belgians.[83] Within five days German troops in their massed armored units broke through the barely defended, rugged Ardennes gap and began their sprint down into northern France. They smashed their enemies like matchwood with such astonishing speed that even they were amazed.[84] Their masterful terror tactics caused chaos and despair among the frantic hordes of civilians swarming the roads and obstructing the Allies' military operations. Death was everywhere: men, women, children, horses, wasted towns. "For the Germans everything went according to the book, or even better than the book, in the unfolding both of strategy and of tactics. Their success exceeded the fondest hopes of Hitler," William Shirer wrote.[85]

The assault on May 15, 1940, surprised the Dutch army, which had not fought a European war for a hundred years and was ill-equipped for motorized warfare. The Dutch were forced to surrender to Germany after only five days of fighting. On two British destroyers, Queen Wilhelmina, the royal family, and the entire government fled to England. They intended to carry on the war from there,[86] much to Kennedy's surprise and dismay. He feared its demoralizing effect on the Dutch.[87] Roosevelt sent a personal telegram to Queen Wilhelmina telling how proud he was of the "splendid resistance" the Dutch military had shown against "impossible odds" and inviting her to come to the United States. Kennedy went to Buckingham Palace, where the Dutch queen was staying, to deliver the message in person. She looked like any other "nice middle-aged lady."

After discussing the president's offer with the royal family and members of the Dutch government, M. Van Kleffens, the Dutch foreign minister, informed Kennedy that Queen Wilhelmina and Prince Bernhard would remain in England, but that Princess Juliana and the children would go to Canada. If anything happened to the queen, the princess would have to function as head of the government, an impossibility in the neutral United States. The princess and her children made the trip to Canada in a Dutch cruiser and arrived on June 11.[88]

The nightmare continued: Brussels overrun, Rotterdam's old city leveled, Cambrai, Arras, Boulogne, Abbeville—all besieged; the Nazi breakthrough across the Meuse. The lines of communication from the northern armies had been severed, and the Allied forces lured into Belgium isolated and surrounded, its King Leopold about to surrender. The race to the Channel was on, pinning the Allies' backs to the sea; the demoralized French army collapsed.[89] The Allied disasters were the result of unpreparedness, little military innovation, and incompetence.[90] Only a few Allied strongholds remained—Boulogne still, Calais, Dunkirk. "We expect to be attacked here ourselves," Churchill wrote to Roosevelt through Kennedy, and "if necessary . . . we shall continue the war alone."[91]

Throughout the "hurricane of events" Kennedy maintained close contact with British officials and dutifully passed on their views to Washington.[92] He sounded his familiar themes and staunchly argued for supporting the Allies with matériel but not with men, for fighting in our own backyards, for a version of the Jack Dempsey and Holy Ghost scenario, and for a peace negotiated by Roosevelt. And he grew more and more disgruntled with his role as messenger boy between the two heads of government.

Kennedy met with Halifax at the Foreign Office on May 13. Winning this war is going to be a question of whether one has enough airplanes, Kennedy said. Was there anything that the United States could do? he asked. Was there anything that he personally could do? Could Britain have airplanes? Halifax responded. Have the prime minister consult directly with the president, Kennedy said. "You must pass the hat now," he advised, "while the corpse is warm."[93]

Kennedy noted approvingly the enormous about-face in American public opinion after the Nazi invasion of Holland and Belgium, and applauded the new desire of the American people to aid the British with everything except troops.[94] But his admiration and affection for the British did not dispel his doubts about the effectiveness of American aid. "My sympathies are completely with the Allies," he told Rose, but "I don't know just how [giving aid] could be done." What can we help them with? he asked. We have nothing to spare. His list was a realistic assessment of Allied and American strengths and weaknesses: the Allies don't need credit from us because they have more than two billion dollars in American securities, plus their gold reserves; we can't send an army because we haven't got one ourselves; we can't send the navy—it protects the Pacific and keeps the Japanese from walking off with the Dutch East Indies and everything else out there; but we can send airplanes with the latest technology and we're doing so as quickly as possible. Let's not weaken ourselves by taking part in Europe's fight; we may have to fight Hitler ourselves. If so, let's do it in our own backyard and not overseas. "So it is easy enough to say we should do something but the real difficulty is—what?"[95]

But Churchill knew what and wasted no time. He invited Kennedy to meet him on May 14 at midnight, not an uncommon hour for Churchill to hold meetings; he often held meetings late at night or in the wee hours. It seemed that he never slept. He expected everyone to come when summoned. Everyone did. When Kennedy arrived at Admiralty House, Kennedy noticed that it had been completely blacked out and was guarded by 175 soldiers. He was ushered into Churchill's office. Churchill, seated in a comfortable chair with his colleagues around him, cigar smoke encircling him, greeted Kennedy warmly.[96] As he listened to Churchill talk, Kennedy was unnerved by Churchill's poor physical state. The ambassador noticed the tray nearby loaded with liquor and the scotch highball Churchill was drinking, clearly not his first. "The affairs of Great Britain might be in the hands of the most dynamic individual in Great Britain but certainly not in the hands of [the one with] the best judgment in Great Britain," Kennedy wrote in his diary.[97] Churchill asked him what he knew about the "Barbary Coast Pirate" (meaning Mussolini).[98] Kennedy told him he had just learned from Ambassador Phillips in Rome that Mussolini had decided to enter the war. It will gravely affect Britain's position in the Mediterranean and in the Atlantic, Churchill remarked. Italy's subs added to Germany's could mean heavy losses for Britain and could increase the Allies' chances of defeat. "Things are bad, as you know," the "almost desperate" prime minister said to Kennedy. The German advance is overwhelming; the French are just barely holding on and are pleading for more British troops, which we cannot send; and we expect to be vigorously attacked here within a month.[99]

"If that is the case, what do you think the United States could do? . . . It isn't fair to ask us to hold the bag for a war that the Allies expect to lose," Kennedy put it to him. "If we are to fight, under these circumstances it seems to me we would do better fighting in our own backyard"—an argument echoing the one he made to Rose. "What do you expect of us?" Kennedy asked him. "Thirty or forty old destroyers and all the airplanes you can spare," Churchill answered. We will also need steel and chrome. "I am going to ask the President for these." "We will have to turn to the United States for nearly all our supplies." Churchill paused and then said: "Regardless of what Germany does to France, England will never give up so long as I am in power even though England is burned to the ground. The Government will move if it has to and take the fleet to Canada and fight on." Churchill clung to the belief that Britain would never be defeated. The bleak prospects seemed to have deepened his bloody-minded determination to fight.[100]

"The Former Naval Person" handed Kennedy his cable to be transmitted to Roosevelt the next day. It was a forthright, urgent appeal for aid of every kind short of military participation, and he hoped Roosevelt would give aid even when Britain could no longer pay for it. "The scene has darkened swiftly," Churchill began, as he gave a dismal survey of the war: the enemy have a large air presence; the land battle has just started. "We must expect that Mussolini will hurry in to share the loot of civilisation. We expect to be attacked here ourselves . . . by parachute and air-borne troops, in the near future, and we are getting ready for them. If necessary, we shall continue the war alone." Churchill told Roosevelt:

> But I trust you realize, Mr. President, that the voice and force of the United States may count for nothing if they are withheld too long. You may have a completely subjugated, Nazified Europe established with astonishing swiftness, and the weight may be more than we can bear. All I ask now is that you should proclaim non-belligerency, which would mean that you would help us with everything short of actually engaging armed forces.

The prime minister specified Britain's immediate needs: the loan of forty or fifty old destroyers; several hundred of the latest kinds of airplanes, anti-aircraft equipment and ammunition; materials like ore and steel; and assurances that the British would still be given the equipment when they could no longer pay for it. Churchill also suggested that there be more Anglo-American naval cooperation in Ireland and in the Pacific, to keep "the Japanese dog" quiet.[101] His order was a tall order. The very thing that Kennedy feared was Churchill's intention of equating Britain's survival with American security and giving Roosevelt a choice: either declare war or watch Britain burn to the ground.[102]

In his cable to Roosevelt and Hull at two in the morning on May 15, describing his conversation with Churchill, Kennedy marveled at the determination of the British. "The shadow of defeat was hanging over them and their spirits were low," but "they are tough and mean to fight on." He offered to explore Churchill's unequivocal and defiant promise of moving the government and the fleet to Canada. "I think this is something I should follow up," Kennedy wrote.[103]

Churchill, impatient for news, followed up his conference with Kennedy on May 14–15 by a phone call at twelve midnight on May 15. Had Roosevelt got his message? Churchill wanted to know. Kennedy reassured him: he had sent the message instantly. What would Roosevelt do? the prime minister asked. The president would try "anything he could do that wasn't a complete violation of the law," Kennedy replied. When would we get an answer? the prime minister asked. "As quickly as [the president] could possible send it," Kennedy said.[104]

On May 16 around midnight, Kennedy received Roosevelt's reply to Churchill's message. It was discouraging. "I am of course giving every possible consideration to the suggestions made in your message," Roosevelt wrote. A possible loan of forty or fifty of our older destroyers could not be made without the specific authorization of the Congress. But "I am not certain that it would be wise for that suggestion to be made to the Congress at this moment," Roosevelt said, nor could the United States spare them even temporarily. Even if the United States could lend destroyers, it would still take at least six or seven weeks before they could sail under the British flag. He also assured Churchill that he was doing everything possible for Britain to get the latest anti-aircraft equipment and ammunition; but that, too, was subject to the needs of the American military—and here, too, Roosevelt was not too specific. Satisfactory arrangements, he said, have been made for the British to purchase steel and other anti-aircraft material. He promised to give serious consideration to the suggestion of sending an American squadron to Irish ports, but in the meantime the American fleet would remain in Hawaii. Roosevelt closed with jaunty words: "The best of luck to you."[105] As if a postscript were needed, Roosevelt called Kennedy the next day to ask him to reassure Churchill that he was doing all he could to help, as indeed he seemed to be.[106]

Despite this "nightmare of frustration," as Welles called the events consuming the Allies, across the sea Roosevelt remained "serene, confident, alert, ebullient, almost nonchalant."[107] On May 16, the day after Roosevelt received Churchill's plea for help, he rode up to Capitol Hill in the pelting rain to address members of Congress, many of whom were wearing buddy poppies, a tribute to the soldiers who had fought in Flanders Field in the Great War.[108] There was an unusually large number of city police, plainclothes detectives, and Secret Service patrolling the Capitol Plaza as several hundred spectators applauded and waved umbrellas when the president and his party approached the Capitol. He was accompanied by Mrs. Roosevelt and a few military personnel. Inside the chamber, guests were stuffed into the galleries that had long been filled to capacity. Lord Lothian, Britain's ambassador, sat in the diplomatic gallery not far from Mrs. Roosevelt and her guests. It was his first time there. He surveyed the scene carefully. There were several other diplomats, too.

The president, wearing a dark blue pinstripe suit, made his way to the rostrum, walking slowly from the well of the House up the long ramp to the deafening cheers and ringing applause of its members and guests. Seldom had he received such an ovation by a joint session of Congress. Roosevelt's expression was grave as he began; he spoke in a calm, low, firm voice. Newsmen could see his white knuckles as he grasped the podium in the House during the tense half-hour address; the House listened in somber silence. "These are ominous days," the president warned the joint session: we are no longer an impregnable fortress. While we pray for peace, we must also prepare for the worst. No attack is unlikely. Not only does Germany appear to have more planes than the Allies combined, but it has the ability to turn out more planes weekly than the United States and its allies. The president electrified Congress by asking it to challenge the Nazi threat boldly and cripple it. He requested over a billion dollars ($1,182,000,000) to make the country's defenses impregnable and made a dramatic appeal for the production of a whopping fifty thousand planes annually to create an aerial armada equal to none. A cheering Congress, both Democrats and Republicans, applauded wildly and agreed to grant FDR's request and more, in a show of national unity during an international crisis.[109] Rather than accept his ambassador's advice to protect the United States by "fighting in our own back yard," the president came to a different conclusion. He decided that the wiser policy was to "keep the fighting away from our own back yard." This could be done, he reasoned, by guaranteeing an Allied victory, essential to American security, and by helping Britain and France stand on their own two feet.[110]

A grateful Churchill interrupted a cabinet meeting on the morning of May 17 at the Admiralty to tell Kennedy how pleased he was by Roosevelt's response to his message. The prime minister spoke "feelingly and appreciatively" about the president's request to Congress and for omitting that England would have to pay for the equipment.[111]

In the early morning hours of May 15, Churchill was awakened by his bedside phone. "We have been defeated. . . . We are beaten; we have lost the battle. . . . The front is broken near Sedan; they are pouring through in great numbers with tanks and armoured cars." It was France's badly shaken premier, Paul Reynaud, speaking in English.[112] Churchill was dumbfounded.[113] The next day Kennedy notified Washington that Churchill had journeyed to Paris to prop up sagging French morale. Kennedy gave his latest somber assessment of the situation: "deadly acute." A "crack up can come like a stroke of lightning. . . . Any action must be conceived now if it is to be effective. . . . The President might start considering . . . what he can do to save an Allied debacle." Only he, with "some touch of genius and God's blessing . . . can do it."[114] Exactly how the president might prevent an Allied debacle Kennedy did not say, nor was God's blessing forthcoming. But as the military situation continued to worsen, the ambassador's dispatches to Washington repeatedly urged the president to negotiate a peace settlement. Implicit in Kennedy's remarks was his assumption, one commonly held by many Britons, that Britain's cause was lost, and that the United States was justified in shoring up its own defenses to make the Western Hemisphere an impregnable fortress.

After returning from France on May 17, Churchill stepped up his request for aid from the United States. The situation here is very grave, but we will "persevere to the very end" regardless of the result of the battle in France. We expect to be attacked here soon. "If American assistance is to play any part it must be available soon," the ambassador cabled, quoting Churchill.[115]

Churchill put even more pressure on Roosevelt by showing how the interests of the United States would be jeopardized if France and Britain were conquered. He played his trump card: the British fleet. In a telegram to FDR on May 20, Churchill set out a grim scenario. Were the Germans to gain control of Britain's fleet, they would rule the waves, the European Continent, and the Western Hemisphere as well; so much for the Fortress Americana. If the United States left Britain to its fate and if other political figures came to power, the prime minister continued, the "sole remaining bargaining counter with Germany would be the fleet." One could not "blame those then responsible if they made the best terms they could for the surviving inhabitants. Excuse me, Mr. President, putting this nightmare bluntly," but we need not dwell upon such matters at present. Roosevelt needed no convincing.[116]

Kennedy lapsed into hopelessness and despair. Churchill's warning about the surrender of the British fleet greatly "disturbed me," he wrote in his memoir. "It was not difficult for me to perceive the importance of keeping the British Navy out of Hitler's hands."[117] The disheartening news from the front also deepened his mood. Despite his deep admiration for the Allies, Kennedy doubted their ability to stave off disaster. Everything he had predicted had happened. "The jig is up," he wrote to Rose himself on May 20, not asking the secretaries to type what he had written. "The situation is more than critical. It means a terrible finish for the Allies. . . . The English will fight to the end but I just don't think they can stand up to the bombing indefinitely. What will happen then is probably a dictated peace with Hitler probably getting the British Navy, and we will find ourselves in a terrible mess. My God how right I've been on my predictions. I wish I'd been wrong."[118] Indeed, Kennedy had been right—so far—but he would be wrong in underestimating the determination of the British rallied by Churchill's superb rhetoric and brilliant wartime leadership. But he was not wrong yet.

Disasters collided with each other. The Belgian army, making up nearly a third of the Allied force, surrendered unconditionally to Germany at 4 a.m. on May 28, after only eighteen days of fighting. King Leopold chose to remain in Belgium against the advice of his government, which went into exile, and despite the denunciations of betrayal by the British and French. Kennedy defended him and applauded his bravery: "Leopold saw his army collapsing, no hope whatever of relief. . . . He was a human being, who could not stand useless sacrifice."[119] The king became a virtual German prisoner throughout the war and was deposed by his people after its end.

Belgium's surrender left tens of thousands of French and British troops trapped in north-eastern France, pinned down, backs to the sea, and about to be overrun. Kennedy's cables cataloged their fate. "The situation according to the people who know is very, very grim," he told Hull after a conference with Halifax on the evening of May 23. Kennedy was amazed that the English seemed incapable of grasping that they could be beaten. "This country has plenty of guts and courage which I do not underestimate," Kennedy wrote, "but . . . it is going to take more than guts to hold off the systematic air attacks of the Germans." Again, he urged the United States to be ready to broker peace on behalf of the desperate Allies. "If anyone can save an Allied debacle, it is the President," Kennedy wrote, quoting Halifax. The Germans fear his influence. But if the French could hold out, maybe Hitler might be willing to make peace.[120]

Halifax had already drafted a telegram to Roosevelt, probably written on May 25, unsigned and never sent, suggesting that the president approach Mussolini on behalf of the British and the French and ask: What is his price for staying out of war? Would he participate in a four-power conference between Britain, France, and Germany to end the hostilities? But Churchill carried the day, and after intense debate lasting several days, he convinced the cabinet not to follow Halifax's advice.[121] Churchill had carefully considered Halifax's suggestion, he told the cabinet, and has refused to enter into negotiations with "That Man." The Nazis would demand that Britain become a "slave state," with a puppet government, and surrender her fleet and naval bases. Yet because Britain had such immense advantages and resources, Churchill said, he refused to consider parley or surrender. "If this long island story of ours is to end at last, let it end only when each one of us lies choking in his own blood upon the ground." There were immediate cries of joy and approval all around, Churchill wrote in his memoir.[122]

Hull instructed Kennedy to ask Kingsley Wood, the new chancellor of the exchequer, and Montagu Norman, the governor of the Bank of England, whether plans had been made to ship Britain's gold and securities to Canada for safekeeping. The cabinet had not considered the idea, Kennedy learned, but Kingsley Wood said he would talk with Churchill about it. Churchill vetoed the suggestion and argued that people might think the government was panicking. Surprised by their lack of foresight and worried about Churchill's warning that another government might use the fleet as a bargaining chip with Hitler, Kennedy argued that plans could at least be made for such an eventuality. He reasoned that if the British government had a stake in Canada, such as gold and securities, or the royal family, the government might also send the fleet there to protect them. Kingsley Wood just shrugged the idea off. "I was learning rapidly that one can become unpopular by offering advice that people don't want to hear," Kennedy wrote in his "Diplomatic Memoir." "My contacts with the Churchill cabinet were certainly far less friendly than with the old government. Yet my first duty was to the United States and I had to tell them that they could not count on us for anything but supplies. And the worse the situation became, the harder it was to tell them."[123]

And again: "My impression of the situation here now is that it could not be worse," Kennedy cabled Roosevelt on the eve of Dunkirk. "Only a miracle can save the British expeditionary force from being wiped out." Talk of peace is "in the air." Of course the Germans would consider it on their terms, but that would be much better for Britain and France than if the war continued, Kennedy opined—a nudge to the president to negotiate "terms" for Britain and France.[124]

On the evening of May 26, 1940, the British Admiralty ordered "Operation Dynamo" to commence: Churchill's "miracle" was on; the first soldiers were evacuated that night.[125] A pensive and sober throng stood watching the news flash around Times Tower in Times Square.[126] Few believed that more than a fraction of the 350,000 Allied troops on the beaches of Dunkirk could be saved. Always a seafaring people, the English responded in droves with anything that would float—lifeboats from liners docked in London, pleasure boats and yachts, barges, Thames tugboats, ferries, and fighting craft like destroyers and minesweepers: anything, sail or steam. That evening a great tide of small craft—the "Mosquito Armada," as Churchill called the more than eight hundred small boats—left England's southern shore to rescue the British and French troops trapped on the sand dunes and blood-stained beaches of Dunkirk and to carry them back to England to fight again.[127]

The evacuation ended on June 4, 1940: 338,226 men—most of the British Expeditionary Force, and over 100,000 French—had been saved. But their military equipment—heavy tanks, trucks, guns, and ammunition, two years of production—was now in German hands. The campaign in Flanders that the evacuation so gloriously ended had been a complete disaster, and the British would soon be left to fight Hitler alone, as were the several thousand soldiers left behind at Calais.[128] Churchill approved the order requiring them to remain in place to prevent the Germans from reaching Dunkirk; the troops at Calais would not be withdrawn. After making this "grim decision," Churchill spoke uncommonly little at dinner that evening, eating and drinking with manifest lack of appetite. He told Eden he felt "physically sick." In Parliament months later he honored the men at Calais for their sacrifice and called them "the bit of grit that saved us."[129]

When Parliament met on June 4, Churchill acknowledged the catastrophe of Dunkirk: "We must be careful not to assign to this deliverance the attributes of a victory. Wars are not won by evacuations." Regardless, the prime minister flung scorn and defiance at the enemy:

We shall not flag or fail. We shall go on to the end, . . . we shall defend our island, whatever the cost may be. We shall fight on the beaches, we shall fight on the landing-grounds, we shall fight in the fields and in the streets, we shall fight in the hills; we shall never surrender, and even if . . . this island . . . were subjugated and starving, then our Empire beyond the seas, armed and guarded by the British Fleet, would carry out the struggle, until, in God's good time, the New World, with all its power and might, steps forth to the rescue and the liberation of the old. As the House roared its approval, Churchill muttered to a colleague, "and . . . we will fight them with the butt end of broken bottles, because that's bloody well all we've got."[130]

To the British, Churchill's speech was a solemn commitment; to Kennedy, it must have seemed a hideous promise. Such a definitive statement in favor of continuing the war regardless was abhorrent to the American ambassador. So too was the prime minister's appeals for the New World to liberate the Old; they played upon Kennedy's deepest fears of American involvement in the war.[131] And to the French? The French were surprised by the "tactical error" in Churchill's speech, his stating that Britain would fight "the menace of tyranny, if necessary for years, if necessary alone."[132]

But before Hitler could attack England, he first had to gain control of the Continent. At dawn on June 5, 1940, the morning after the fall of Dunkirk, a great wave of German troops marched from the Somme toward Paris to begin their siege. They were running into each other and causing confusion because of their overwhelming numbers and the swiftness of their assault. The next day, near Paris, German tanks cut at two places a 150-miles Front—the Maginot Line. By June 10, the Germans were on the outskirts of Paris. The government fled Paris for Tours; the French army was routed.[133] France near collapse, Paris readied itself for a siege, a fight to the death.

"Days before Paris is snatched," Kennedy predicted to George Bilainkin, a British diplomatic journalist and friend who dropped by the ambassador's office to discuss the events in France.[134] Kennedy was ill at ease, playing with his tie, shirt sleeves rolled up, no suspenders, no vest. The veins stood out on his neck as he railed away at Bilainkin in an I-told-you-so mood about how right he—Kennedy—had been. "I always told your people you were not ready last September. . . . You'll remember my words, putting out the tongue when you must be able to hit the other man in the jaw. . . . Through Munich you gained a year in which to prepare—and yet, nine months after that, you are in the position of having only two or three divisions fighting in France." I always told you that we had nothing to give you, he continued. "I could have easily said the usual blah and poppycock, but what's the bloody good of being so foolish as that? . . . What the hell are you worth if you just mislead them?" This war will spread, and "the Germans will be after the Russians next." "How in God's name, have you English been so foolish, and so stupid . . . not to have taken a better measure of the enemy than you have done? Is it not just fantastic?" Bilainkin asked: Is there anything that the United States could spare? Kennedy must have been thinking about the same thing; he responded thoughtfully and frankly: "We have little to give you and it's no use pretending that we have." "But we are anxious to help . . . to do something while there is yet time. Tell me what we can do, and we will try it. We want to help the democracies, for our own sake as much as theirs."[135]

On June 14, the Nazis broke through the Maginot Line. That same day, they captured Paris and hoisted the swastika over the Eiffel Tower. On June 16, the French and the Germans signed an armistice. Kennedy had been right about Britain and France, as he would be about Russia.[136]

Watching from the sidelines, Mussolini eyed the spoils and then in a craven act, after being certain that the French were decisively beaten, slithered into war with France.[137] Bullitt had known that war with Italy was coming. He had cabled Roosevelt on May 29: "Al Capone will enter war about the fourth of June, unless you can throw the fear of the U.S.A. into him."[138] Roosevelt *had* been trying "to throw the fear of the U.S.A. into him" and had repeatedly beseeched him to refrain from going to war. Roosevelt even offered to mediate between Italy and the Allies and to ensure personally the execution of any agreements. But Mussolini wanted war and told Hitler so. The Duce told his generals: "I need only a few thousand dead to enable me to take my seat, as a belligerent, at the peace table."[139]

On June 10, at six o'clock, standing on the balcony of the Palazzo Venezia in the heart of Rome, Mussolini spoke to a group of a hundred thousand or so fascist followers hastily gathered and jammed together in the square. In his usual bombastic style, bouncing around on the balcony like a "jack-in-the-box," he proclaimed that destiny had required Italy to enter the war. Italy's war was "the struggle of a poor people against those who wish to starve us with their retention of all the riches and gold of the earth." His speech was greeted with thundering applause right on cue.[140]

On that same day, FDR was to deliver a speech at the University of Virginia in Charlottesville, proposing to send all available aid to Britain. Just before he was to board the train for Charlottesville, he received a message from Bullitt telling him that Mussolini would declare war on France that day. The French termed it a "stab in the back."[141] FDR fumed all the way on the three-hour train ride, accompanied by Mrs. Roosevelt and their son, Franklin Jr., whose graduating class from the Virginia Law School the president was to address. FDR kept turning a phrase over in his mind as he made last-minute changes to his speech. "Don't use it," discretion warned; "Use it!" the "old red blood" commanded. Bloodlust won and Eleanor approved. FDR inserted the sentence in the speech. When the party arrived in Charlottesville, Roosevelt was relaxed; color had returned to his cheeks. He smiled and waved to the throng as he rode to the Memorial Gymnasium to don cap and gown and give the commencement address. The crowd of several thousand were packed into the gym and applauded enthusiastically as the president led the procession of dignitaries to the platform. After giving a lengthy explanation of his efforts to restrain Mussolini, Roosevelt lashed out at him, contempt in his voice, and calmly and firmly delivered his "impromptu" denunciation: "On the tenth day of June, 1940, the hand that held the dagger has struck it into the back of its neighbor."[142]

This was an eloquent, resolute, militant speech—more militant than any before. It guaranteed aid to the Allies and it was decidedly unneutral. The United States was taking sides; there would be no more vacillation, no more hope that the United States could remain a Fortress Americana in a totalitarian world, as Kennedy had urged.[143] The only issue now was how to get on with it. "Signs and signals call for speed—full speed ahead," Roosevelt had said.[144]

On the other side of the Atlantic, "a deep growl of satisfaction" erupted from Churchill and his officers as they worked late that night at the Admiralty War Room and listened to the president.[145] Roosevelt's pledge to rearm quickly and to provide material resources to the Allies was a statement that Churchill later mistook—perhaps deliberately, perhaps not—to be a commitment by the president to provide military aid to mortally wounded France.

When Kennedy met Churchill that evening in the cabinet room, they observed their cocktail ritual: Churchill was drinking a highball, as always; he offered Kennedy one, as always; Kennedy declined, as always. Churchill was roundly cursing Italy's dictator. "Words fail me" in "repeating what the Prime Minister, whom I have just seen, thinks of Mussolini," Kennedy cabled Washington.[146] Compared to Mussolini, whom the prime minister pronounced "a jackal and a betrayer of all things good and fair, Hitler is a gentleman," Churchill told Kennedy.[147] Churchill repeated to Kennedy his litany for victory, now his standard line. And Kennedy relayed Churchill's views to Hull: Britain would fight to the death and Hitler would find her a very fierce adversary; Britain desperately needed destroyers, especially with the threat of imminent invasion and Italy's entry into the war; his government would never surrender the British Fleet, but it could not legally bind another government not to surrender the fleet. After the presidential election and the bombing of so many well-known places in England from which so many American cities and towns drew their names, the American people would rise up and demand war.[148]

Churchill wrote to Roosevelt in the early hours of the morning before going to bed to tell the president that he and his advisers "were fortified by the grand scope of your declaration." Your promise of aid "is a strong encouragement in a dark but not unhopeful hour." We must do all we can to keep the French in the fight; your speech gave them hope and strength to continue. Hitler will soon turn on us. "Nothing is so important as for us to have 30 or 40 old destroyers"; "not a day should be lost," he pleaded. "I send you my heartfelt thanks . . . for all you are doing and seeking to do for what we may now, indeed, call a Common Cause." His Churchillian rhetoric was dramatic and hasty, but not necessarily groundless.[149]

Stunned by the Nazi victories and by Britain's "pitiful" and "appallingly weak" preparations for war, the ambassador believed that Britain's real defense "will be with courage and not with arms." It would be "fallacious" to assume that the English have anything else to fight with, he confided in his diary on June 12. If France falls, it will be nothing "short of a miracle" if Britain holds on; but she'll do so in the hope that the United States will enter the war, he wrote, believing that Britain's cause was practically lost anyhow—as it very nearly was. Kennedy was more realistic about Britain's chances than was the prime minister.[150]

But Britain did hold on until the United States entered the war. Churchill's leadership and aid from the United States, the destroyer deal and Lend-Lease, which Kennedy sanctioned, were all part of that miracle. And when Americans did demand war, they did so not because of their anger over the bombing of towns and cities in England with American namesakes, as Churchill predicted, but because of their outrage over Japan's attack on the U.S. fleet anchored at Pearl Harbor.[151] Kennedy may have underestimated British doggedness under Churchill's inspired leadership, but the ambassador had the better understanding of his fellow Americans both in Congress and throughout the country, the majority of whom still overwhelmingly supported isolationism, as he did.[152]

Distinguished Harvard economist and later President John Kennedy's ambassador to India, John Kenneth Galbraith, gave a balanced perspective of Ambassador Joe Kennedy's views.

> To be fair to Kennedy it should be understood that anyone reporting on Britain after the fall of France who didn't say there was little hope would be doing a bad job of reporting. In purely rational terms, Kennedy's dim assessment of British prospects was correct. Yet this was one

of those rare occasions in history when romantic and heroic optimists managed to be right. Why? Because Hitler didn't realize his full strength after Dunkirk. Because he turned on the Soviet Union first before finishing Britain off. Because Churchill's rallying of the intrinsic strength of the British was remarkable. And, of course, because the U.S. finally got involved.[153]

Although Kennedy deeply admired the guts of the British, he cared enough to keep the record straight and to guard against incipient anti-Americanism and scapegoating. Many British were buoyed by the American press reports implying that it would only take an "incident" for the United States to enter the war. If that were so, "desperate people [would] do desperate things."[154] The vast majority believe that the United States should be fighting on the Allied side, he told Hull. If we do not come to the aid of the Allies and things go badly for them, they will blame the United States. The British will ignore the fact that they for years failed to prepare and, instead of blaming the Baldwin and Churchill governments, will severely criticize the United States, thus poisoning Anglo-American relations for years to come. There is a very marked anti-American feeling here. "We are well on our way to becoming the 'patsies,'" a worried Kennedy cabled Washington. "This is entirely unjustified to me."[155] We do not want a hostile people united against us. Implicit in his stance was the fact that he felt the United States was justified in not taking major steps to come to England's aid.[156]

He suggested to the secretary that some official explain the limitations put on extending aid to the Allies and offered to do so himself.[157] Hull endorsed Kennedy's "admirable" suggestion and discussed the issue with Lord Lothian. Lothian intended to ensure that the British purchasing agent in Washington be given authority to publicize the "considerable amount" of military equipment the Allies had received and to state that the amount would probably be increased in the future.[158] But Kennedy was dissatisfied with the release and suggested that the secretary give the matter "much more serious attention." The paltry statement issued that morning by the British Purchasing Commission was not at all satisfactory and failed to explain that the United States had little war matériel to aid the Allies with.[159]

Although Kennedy was convinced of Britain's imminent defeat, he softened his mid-May position and began urging aid to the Allies, but not to the extent of jeopardizing American self-interest—as he understood it.[160] Kennedy joined Bullitt in advocating the sale of war matériel to the Allies and called for quicker production.[161] After the hasty retreat by the British expeditionary forces at Dunkirk, Kennedy urged the speedy sale of military equipment from America's reserve supplies or storehouses. Adding his own voice to the growing British chorus led by Churchill pleading for destroyers, the ambassador argued that fifty destroyers were not too much to give an old friend. "Their psychological effect could be of even more value than the actual help," he said.[162] Indeed it was, as both Roosevelt and Churchill understood.[163]

American rifles, ammunition, machine guns, fifty destroyers—all would be helpful to the Allies and all met with Kennedy's approval, as did the winking at principle in favor of a moderate form of Lend-Lease in the fall.[164] But he believed that there should be no statement implying any further military commitment to the Allies, a position he shared with Roosevelt, despite Churchill's persistent appeals to Roosevelt to give a further commitment.

While Paris was under siege from June 5 to June 15, 1940, and Churchill was flying back and forth between Paris and London trying to buck up his sagging ally, there was a confusing tug of war between Churchill and Roosevelt and Reynaud over American aid to the Allies. On June 10, Reynaud had asked Roosevelt for material help for the Allies. On June 13, Churchill met Reynaud in the City Hall at Tours. The French government had been forced to relocate there because German forces were marching on Paris. On June 13 the government moved again, to Bordeaux. The situation was horrible. France was facing death and destruction. The army was refusing to fight and lapsing into anarchy; it wanted to negotiate an armistice. Reynaud insisted that Churchill release him from the March 28 pledge not to sign a separate peace. Churchill vigorously argued against it in "the greatest oration made in the history of the world," according to Beaverbrook, who accompanied the prime minister to Tours and heard his delivery. Churchill said NO! in unambiguous terms. The French "must stick"; England would and did.[165]

In the meantime, also on June 13, Roosevelt asked Kennedy to hand-deliver to the prime minister a copy of his response to Reynaud's requests of June 10. It was extraordinarily vague and ambiguous. "Your message . . . has moved me very deeply," the president began. "As I have already stated to you and to Mr. Churchill, this Government is doing everything in its power to make available to the Allied Governments the material they so urgently require and our efforts to do still more are being redoubled." Roosevelt added that he was doubly impressed by French efforts to fight on, even if it meant withdrawing to North Africa and the Atlantic. He also told Kennedy to tell Churchill that he would not send an American squadron to Ireland as Churchill had requested, and that the U.S. fleet would remain in Hawaii.[166]

Kennedy swiftly arranged for an appointment with Churchill at Admiralty House upon his return from France around 8:30 that evening, June 13. While Kennedy was dining at the Coq d'Or, he received a phone call telling him that the prime minister would see him at 9:30 p.m. sharp, just before a cabinet meeting. When the ambassador arrived, the prime minister and his family were beginning dinner. Kennedy read Roosevelt's message to him as Churchill quickly devoured a very large four-course meal. He became "visibly excited," "visibly moved," as much by his interest in Roosevelt's response as by the Champagne he was drinking, the ambassador noted. Churchill read and reread Roosevelt's message himself, three or four times. He thought that this was the answer to Reynaud's plea.[167] It was the "light at the end of the tunnel."[168] It was a promise "that America assumed a responsibility if the French continued to fight" and implied a commitment for the United States to enter the war. "I felt, as Churchill did," Kennedy wrote in his diary, "that this was a commitment and that Roosevelt knew what he was doing,"[169] but Kennedy also saw it as "a great danger."[170] The prime minister rushed off to inform the cabinet of Roosevelt's message, as Kennedy went home to a meager meal of milk and sponge cake and to take a nap.[171]

Roosevelt's statement was probably as far as he could go without congressional consultation, Churchill told his cabinet. The president "could hardly urge the French to continue the struggle, and to undergo further torture, if he did not intend to enter the war to support them." Churchill also explained that Kennedy had assumed that Roosevelt "must have authorized" the publication of the statement even if the president had not explicitly said so.[172]

At 11:00 that same evening, Kennedy once again received a phone call from the prime minister summoning him immediately to 10 Downing Street. Upon his arrival, Churchill, in a highly excited state, interrupted the cabinet meeting to ask Kennedy to call Roosevelt right then and there to get his permission to publish his message to Reynaud. Kennedy did call the president, but Roosevelt gave a weak no; Hull had objected, the president explained.[173] Kennedy asked Roosevelt whether he knew about the conditions in France and about the meeting of the Allies at Tours. The president said no. Kennedy offered to send him a report on those events; the president could then decide whether he wished to publish the message. Churchill asked to see Kennedy's report.[174] Churchill thought that Roosevelt just failed to grasp how serious the situation was. Kennedy returned to his office to prepare the report and the minutes of the meeting at Tours.

Once again, that same night, Kennedy was rousted by a phone call from Churchill summoning him to 10 Downing Street. Kennedy dashed over to pick up the prime minister's own statement for the president. It dramatically and vigorously argued that the publication of Roosevelt's message to Reynaud could be the necessary ingredient in keeping France in the war. It would "deny Hitler a patched-up peace with France" and could "play the decisive part in turning the course of world history." Once Hitler realizes that he cannot dictate peace to France, Churchill predicted, he will turn his full fury on Britain.[175] Kennedy told him he would send the statement to Roosevelt and also suggested that Churchill call the president around 2:30 a.m. Churchill declined; he expected to be sound asleep by then.

Kennedy returned to the embassy around 1:45 a.m. and gathered the necessary staff to code and send the message. Then he went home and again tried to sleep. About 4:30 a.m. the president called Kennedy. Roosevelt was adamant; he did not want his message to Reynaud published in any form and asked Kennedy to tell Churchill. "As I asked Ambassador Kennedy last night to inform you," the president said, "my message of yesterday's date addressed to the French prime minister was in no sense intended to commit and did not commit the Government to military participation in support of Allied governments." Only Congress had the right under the Constitution to make such commitments. He also told Kennedy to tell Churchill that if the French navy cut itself off from the government before the armistice, the American government would feed and supply them. Kennedy was to give Churchill both pieces of information in the morning. "I was a little sleepy," Kennedy wrote in his diary, "and this is the best recollection of the conversation." To reinforce his decision, Roosevelt repeated his instructions in a cable to Kennedy the next day. Kennedy was able to relay his instructions to Churchill at 9:20 a.m. on June 14 during a phone call from Churchill. Churchill, visibly affected by Roosevelt's refusal, said quietly: "All would be lost in France." "My impression is that all would be lost in France anyway," Kennedy wrote in his diary, "and I am sure that the publication of the President's reply would have only delayed the demise very slightly and merely temporarily."[176]

In addition, there was a vague sort of Declaration of Union between France and Britain for an "indissoluble union of our two peoples and of our two Empires. . . . We . . . resolve to continue the struggle at all costs in France, in this Island, upon the oceans and in the air. . . . We shall never turn from the conflict until France stands safe and erect in all her grandeur." The two governments and the two armies would act and fight as one,[177] a "what you have is mine and what I have is yours" partnership, as Kennedy described it. "A noble sentiment but just does not mean much," he cabled Hull.[178] Kennedy opposed any such statement and argued that it could leave the United States holding the bag for the defeat of France. "Though I realize the tragedy of the present moment and how important it is for the success of these poor people that their morale should be bucked up . . . I nevertheless see in the message a great danger as a commitment at a later date," he cabled the president.[179]

Not one to accept no, Churchill, unable to sleep, sent a telegram to Roosevelt on June 14 repeating his earlier warnings about how critical for France this moment was and that a declaration of war by the United States might save France. He stated that "in a few days French resistance may have crumpled and we shall be left alone." He also wrote: "If we go down you may have a United States of Europe under the Nazi command far more numerous, far stronger, far better armed than the New World."[180] The president no doubt arrived at his own conclusion without paying much attention to either Kennedy's or Churchill's advice.[181]

Even as these discussions were going on in London, the Germans occupied Paris unopposed on June 14. The French had withdrawn their troops from the city and its suburbs and declared it an open city to protect it from bombardment or street fighting. It was the sixth capital to fall to the Nazis within the year.[182] Churchill had to face the imminent defeat of his ally, no doubt with some relief and the expectation of a German invasion.

The British are beginning to realize for the first time this morning, June 14, that "they are in for a terrible time with little hope for eventual victory," Kennedy cabled. Some are even questioning the use of fighting. If they thought there was a chance of a decent peace, they might well rise up and throw the government out for going to war in such a state of unpreparedness in the first place. Kennedy's bleak pessimism could hardly get any worse or be more mistaken.[183]

The prime minister had the better understanding of his countrymen, who were stoically preparing to fight to the death in a crusade to defend their homeland.[184] "The people of England would tear [me] to pieces," Churchill told Kennedy, if he failed to tell them that their government would fight on until ultimate victory. "I don't agree with this," the ambassador reported to Hull; "it is too early to make predictions; it depends on what happens to the French fleet,"[185] one of the bargaining chips in the terms of a French armistice. There were two options for the fleet: scuttle itself or sail to English ports or to North Africa. The British did agree that the French could negotiate an armistice provided that their fleet would sail to British ports. They also welcomed the French air force and all troops: come to Britain or go to North Africa.[186]

But Kennedy was dubious. Why assume that the French fleet would scuttle itself or could join the British fleet? he asked in his report to Hull. More likely, the French fleet would be turned over to the Germans. He also speculated, doomsday fashion, about what could happen if the Germans got their hands on both the French and the British fleets. With most of the American navy in the Pacific, there was no telling what Hitler would do. "He might insist on occupying Canada while an indemnity was being paid." That would force our hands, too.[187]

The final act in France's tragedy came on June 16, when Reynaud resigned and advised the president to send for Marshal Pétain, who formed a cabinet. "We must cease to fight," Pétain told his countrymen, and requested an "honorable" armistice that night.[188] On June 22, 1940, at 6:50 p.m. the armistice was signed in Marshal Foch's old dining car, which Hitler had ordered to be brought from the Musée des Invalides in Paris to the Forest of Compiègne to the exact spot on which Germany had surrendered to France on November 11, 1918. The Franco-Italian armistice was signed on June 24 at 7:35 p.m. in Rome. Six hours later the guns fell silent.[189] The swastika had been hoisted over Warsaw in September 1939, Copenhagen in April 1940, Oslo in April 1940, The Hague in May 1940, Brussels in May 1940, and Paris in June 1940.[190] Britain and her Dominions were alone and had to face the might of two countries whose European population was three times as large as Britain's. Historians will no doubt ponder the question of how the two richest and largest empires on earth could bungle everything, Bilainkin wrote.[191]

Churchill addressed the House of Commons on June 18, the anniversary of Britain's victory at Waterloo 135 years earlier. He took his countrymen into his confidence, quite unusual for any politician. He was tired and spoke for half an hour detailing the desperate situation Britain faced; ironically, his staff thought his delivery uninspiring and much too long. Britain must prepare for the worst, he warned. "The Battle of France is over. . . . the Battle of Britain is about to begin. Upon this battle depends the survival of Christian civilisation." But his conclusion was exhilarating: "Let us therefore brace ourselves to our duty and so bear ourselves that if the British Empire and its Commonwealth lasts for a thousand years men will still say, 'This was their finest hour.'"[192] As they did, for it was. Churchill's statement became a rallying cry that seemed to unite the people in a holy war in which the alternatives were victory or death; it made one feel that he could beat up the whole world full of Nazis.[193]

That afternoon, the *Evening Standard* published a cartoon by David Low. It showed a solitary British soldier in full battle array standing on a rocky shoreline pounded by menacing waves and looking out across the sea. He holds a rifle in one hand, shaking his fist with the other and hurling defiance at an angry, dark sky as if to ward off the unfriendly airplanes approaching. The caption: "Very well, alone."[194]

Ultimately, as Bentley Gilbert wrote, "Britain's place as the only survivor of the Allies seems to have brought to the nation, and clearly to Churchill, a kind of exhilaration. Decisions became simpler, as they always do in war, but in coalitions allies must be consulted. Now there were none." Churchill was obviously relieved by the elimination of the "dead weight" of the French.[195]

And the French fleet about which Kennedy had been so concerned? On the evening of June 26, he went to the Foreign Office for an update on Britain's plans for the French fleet. "I was not only briefed, I was shocked," Kennedy wrote in the memoir. "Halifax intimated that the next battle would be at sea between the British and French fleets." He also made mysterious statements about Britain fighting from Canada, but the two ideas made little sense to Kennedy. However, eight days later, "sense and purpose was given to everything," Kennedy said.[196] After giving the French fleet fair warning to sail to British ports or to face an assault, a warning that was ignored, the prime minister ordered the fleet of their ally blown up in the harbor of Oran, Algeria, on July 3, 1940. The attack, in full public view, lasted for nine minutes and killed 1,297 Frenchmen. The flower of the French fleet was destroyed by British guns. One battleship escaped. It was a stunning new display of Churchillian ruthlessness and impressed the American president as it was designed to do. Roosevelt had been notified in advance by Lord Lothian and approved of the action.[197] Churchill's action showed that this was no gutless leader heading a cringing nation crying for peace. It also impressed the Conservatives in Parliament. When Churchill appeared in the House of Commons to report on the operation, he was cheered by them for the first time since becoming prime minister. The first time he entered Parliament as prime minister, on May 13, the Conservatives had applauded Chamberlain, not Churchill.[198]

Against Churchill's inspiring rhetoric and indomitable courage, and the stoicism of the British, Kennedy was no match. He viewed the struggle between the Allies and Germany halfheartedly, continually urging the president to pursue a compromise peace or at least to keep the fighting confined to Europe, even if that left Hitler in control—not an uncommon view in Roosevelt's Washington before Pearl Harbor. But the president was by now becoming immune to his ambassador's pleas for peace and deaf to his dreary predictions of destruction and desolation. The moment for Kennedy to practice the arts of diplomacy was quickly drawing to a close.

CHAPTER 10

Very Well, Alone

William Shirer writes: "All that stood between him [Hitler] and the establishment of German hegemony in Europe under his dictatorship was one indomitable Englishman, Winston Churchill, and the determined people Churchill led, who did not recognize defeat when it stared them in the face and who now stood alone, virtually unarmed, their island home besieged by the mightiest military machine the world had ever seen."[1]

Winston Churchill had a small, pink, cherubic face, was a roly-poly and undistinguished-looking man, who stood five foot six and a half inches tall, who "waddled rather than walked," who had a mushy voice and a speech defect, something between a lisp and a stutter (no one could exactly categorize it; he always had trouble pronouncing *s*). This impediment made it hard to understand him and sometimes gave the impression that he was drunk, but he nevertheless mesmerized audiences and inspired nations with his oratory.[2] He looked ever so Victorian in his immaculate silk shirt, bow tie with polka dots, winged collar, short black coat, and striped trousers, along with props: gold-knobbed cane, hat, unlit fat cigar, and small silver snuff box.[3] Even his prose style gave the impression that he was from an earlier century, more romantic, more leisurely, more cultivated.[4]

At sixty-five Winston Churchill was too old to be prime minister by the standards of his age. He began life in a hurry, it was said, born two months "premature," according to the *Times*, a ruse most in his circle would have understood and something of a medical miracle were it true. He arrived unexpectedly on a "bed covered with the feather boas and velvet capes of guests who had come for the ball." He was born in a small room serving as a ladies' cloakroom, "on the ground floor just outside the Great Hall" near the grand ballroom, in the wee hours on Saint Andrew's Day, Saturday, November 30, 1874, at Blenheim Palace, the family estate of the Marlboroughs.[5] Bells from Woodstock Church rang out the next day to announce the birth of another Marlborough. His distant ancestor was John Churchill, the first

Duke of Marlborough, who assembled the Grand Alliance in the seventeenth and eighteenth centuries during the reign of King William III and Queen Anne to defeat the nemesis of his day, France's Louis XIV. Churchill's cousin was the ninth Duke of Marlborough, "Sunny" Churchill, with whom Churchill was close. Winston's father, Randolph Churchill, was the second son; he never inherited the title or the palace. Randolph served in Parliament from Woodstock, a small borough that included Blenheim. He rose to be the chancellor of the exchequer and leader of the House of Commons in the Tory government of Lord Salisbury, but ended his political career by resigning over a petty dispute. He suffered from paralysis and insanity perhaps from a brain tumor, or perhaps not—or perhaps, as his son thought, from syphilis acquired from a prostitute after a night drinking Champagne as an undergraduate at Merton College, Oxford. He died at the age of forty-five in 1895. His death was a blow to his adoring son, whose dreams of comradeship and political collaboration died with him. For the rest of his life Winston would pursue but never catch his father's ghost.[6]

Churchill's mother, Jennie Jerome, was a spirited, raven-haired beauty whose father was a millionaire. She was a New York socialite with a silver-spoon upbringing and a legion of lovers. Her ancestors had fought in Washington's army for American independence from King George III. Through his mother, Churchill inherited an affection for and affinity with her countrymen.[7]

As a child Churchill found solace from the indifference of his parents by staging imaginary battles in his nursery with the toy soldiers from Germany that Mrs. Everest, his beloved nanny (whose picture later hung in his study at 10 Downing Street), had introduced him to. He had an army of fifteen hundred lead soldiers, always at attention and arranged into divisions and brigades on his floor. Later he enacted battles with his brother, cousins, and anyone else he could commandeer against "the enemies of England." They had to obey two rules: Winston was always the general and no one was ever promoted.[8]

When he was eight, Churchill was sent to boarding school, St. George's, where he continually rebelled against authority and was routinely beaten by a sadistic headmaster. The beatings nearly broke him. When Mrs. Everest saw the marks of the beatings, she told Lady Churchill and he was removed from St. George's. Churchill was an indifferent pupil at Harrow, the famous old English "public" school. But he loved literature, especially poetry, and history. The seeds were sown for his later success as a journalist and for him to receive the Nobel Prize in Literature for his multivolume history of World War II. He was sent to the Royal Military College at Sandhurst because his father thought him too dull to become a lawyer. The son became a politician who wanted to be a soldier. He had a lifelong desire to be a great general-hero like Napoleon. Churchill never rose above the rank of lieutenant colonel. He served in World War I in France, and he went on to direct the military affairs of his nation. He combined a nineteenth-century view of Britain's imperial greatness, as the grandest and most powerful nation on the globe, with a Victorian's romanticized zest for soldiering where casualties were small and victories immense.[9]

Churchill had been born and bred for war. It was "the greatest of all stimulants," he said.[10] In response to a comment made by his secretary after World War II that life was just not as exciting as it used to be, Churchill said, "You can't expect a war all the time."[11]

Known for eccentricities in his personal habits, Churchill drank too much. Doris Kearns Goodwin describes his daily doses of sherry, scotch and soda, and Champagne topped off with ninety-year-old brandy.[12] Churchill was a two-fisted drinker.[13] And he smoked too much. Beside his chair in the smoke-filled cabinet room, there was a bucket he tossed cigar butts in. The Royal Marines guarding his room sold them as souvenirs; Churchill never knew.[14]

Off and on throughout his life, he suffered from severe depression—his "black dog," as he called it.[15] He was a very lonely, remote, self-absorbed figure, indifferent to everyone. He was a bully, even to his mother; never took no for an answer; and had a formidable temper and never quite apologized.[16] He demanded the near-impossible, barked or growled orders at his terrified but devoted subordinates eager to do his bidding.[17] He had a vicious tongue. He described Chamberlain as "the narrowest, the most ignorant, most ungenerous of men." Of Stanley Baldwin, another former prime minister, Churchill said: "I wish [him] no ill, but it would have been much better if he had never lived."[18]

Churchill was a man of action and enormous energy. When he was not sleeping, he was working; he wasted no moment. He worked everywhere: in the car, in the bathtub, in bed stroking his cat Nelson, or prowling the corridors of No. 10 in a soldier's "tin hat," his crimson dressing gown embroidered with a golden dragon, and monogrammed slippers adorned with pom-poms,[19] or in his office wearing one-piece blue siren suits that zipped up the front and made him look like a teddy bear. His children called them "rompers." He designed them himself.[20] As prime minister he worked outrageous hours, often in the middle of the night, sometimes to two or three a.m., dubbed "the Midnight Follies" by his exhausted staff and officials dropping with fatigue; and he expected everyone else to do the same. His aides stumbled to his bedroom and stood there while he stripped naked and "scratched his back with his back-scratcher" as they reviewed the day's events.[21] He refreshed himself by taking a daily hour-long nap in the nude—the equivalent of three hours of sleep at night, he told Kennedy—and by eating hard in order to work hard.[22]

Despite Churchill's manifold talents and immense political experience—as home secretary, as First Lord of the Admiralty twice, as minister of munitions, as minister of War and Air, as colonial secretary, as chancellor of the exchequer (proudly wearing his father's robes), and then, finally, as prime minister and as minister of defence—there was still a sense among his fellow Conservatives that his political judgment could not be trusted. "More than a few would have agreed with the private verdict of Stanley Baldwin, then Prime Minister: 'When Winston was born lots of fairies swooped down on his cradle with gifts—imagination, eloquence, industry, ability; and then came a fairy who said, "No person has a right to so many gifts," picked him up and gave him such a shake and twist that with all these gifts he was denied judgement and wisdom.'"[23] Labour's leader Clement Attlee said, "Fifty percent of Winston is genius, fifty percent bloody fool."[24]

But Winston Churchill had a most profound understanding of the threat Hitler and Nazi Germany posed, far more than anyone else, and stridently predicted the course of events during his wilderness years. When he became prime minister, "he wiped out everything that had gone before," and started the war all over again.[25] Churchill's policy was simple: beat Hitler.

His son, Randolph, described the moment when his father realized how Britain would win: "I went up to my father's bedroom. He was standing in front of his basin and was shaving with his old fashioned Valet razor. . . . 'Sit down, dear boy, and read the papers while I finish shaving.' I did as told. After two or three minutes of hacking away, he turned and said: 'I think I see my way through.' He resumed his shaving. I was astounded, and said: 'Do you mean that we can avoid defeat?' (which seemed credible) or 'beat the bastards'? (which seemed incredible). He flung his Valet razor in to the basin, swung around, and said: 'Of course I mean we can beat them.' Me: 'Well, I'm all for it, but I don't see how you can do it.' By this time he had dried and sponged his face and turning around to me, said with great intensity: 'I shall drag the United States in.'"[26]

Churchill deserved as much credit for Britain's victory as anyone; he had an indomitable spirit and simply refused to give up or give in, traits well honed throughout his long, tempestuous life. He later remarked, "Some people pretend to regard me as The British Lion. But I am not the Lion. I am simply the Roar of the Lion." He became the symbol of defiance for his besieged nation. He acted on instinct and said that the war required "a man utterly blind to reason, a man who refused to see the sound and compelling reasons for despair and surrender."[27] Churchill told Kennedy: "I would be telling you wrong if I said I didn't think we had Hitler licked. . . . We are going to beat this man."[28] His was a voice for steadfast resolution, despite all the evidence to the contrary. Such a man Kennedy was not.

Upon hearing that Churchill had been appointed prime minister, Roosevelt told his Cabinet, "Churchill was the best man that England had."[29] To ensure the continuation of their private comradery, Churchill wrote to Roosevelt on May 15, 1940: "Although I have changed my office, I am sure you would not wish me to discontinue our intimate, private correspondence."[30] The president responded the next day: "I am sure it is unnecessary for me to say that I am most happy to continue our private correspondence as we have in the past."[31] The president began to listen with sympathy and admiration to the new prime minister, whose determination to defeat Hitler he so admired.

Churchill's political ascendancy and his growing closeness with FDR had a significant impact not only on Anglo-American relations, but on Kennedy's position and influence as well. Although he thought that Churchill had "much more drive than Chamberlain,"[32] the ambassador missed the old camaraderie and intimacy. No longer could he enjoy the confidences and the casual access that he had had with Chamberlain. With a man like Churchill, an aristocrat, an imperialist, a writer, most likely an alcoholic, and definitely a warmonger, Kennedy simply had no common ground.

The two men also clashed temperamentally. Kennedy, by now habitually pessimistic, was thoroughly convinced of Britain's doom and saw Churchill as an adversary, as cunning, scheming, unscrupulous, desperate, and suffering from "slightly cockeyed" judgment;[33]—no doubt a reference to Churchill's being hell-bent on dragging the United States in somehow.[34] Churchill's barely veiled threats about Britain's fleet falling into Hitler's hands worried the pacific-minded Kennedy, as did Churchill's dire predictions that "after us, you will get it."[35]

On the surface the two were cordial; underneath, their suspicion and dislike grew. Perhaps jealous of Churchill's direct relationship with Roosevelt, Kennedy seemed at times to be attempting to turn the president against the British leader. The ambassador suspected that the prime minister communicated with pro-war elements in America, "notably, certain strong Jewish leaders."[36] When Churchill heard rumors that there was an uneasy feeling in some circles that he did not like the United States, its peoples, or their president, Churchill vigorously denied the accusation and launched a constrained tirade about Ambassador Kennedy, whom he held responsible.[37] Churchill aroused the Irish in the ambassador when he referred to Cobh, an Irish port in Eire, as "Queenstown," its traditional British name.[38] The plain-speaking American envied Churchill's eloquent oratory, and regarded his moralistic view of the war as offensive, as holier-than-thou, and maybe a dig at himself.[39]

Kennedy was offended by Churchill's personal slights. He suspected that Churchill did not keep him fully informed[40] and that Churchill was not quite candid with him. He resented it when Churchill rescheduled and cancelled their meetings. Kennedy blamed Randolph, Churchill's infamous son, known to be an "s.o.b." whom even his father accused of having "a poisonous tongue,"[41] for turning the prime minister against him. Churchill's drinking was legend, and was something Kennedy frequently noted in his diary, almost as if he intended to keep a tally of just how much Churchill drank. When Kennedy, a teetotaler, repeatedly declined the drinks offered him,[42] Churchill would simply help himself to another glass of scotch or whiskey or Champagne, and kept fresh drinks waiting on his table to be drunk at the conclusion of their meetings.[43] After one such round of offers, Kennedy rather pointedly said he had sworn off drinking and smoking for the duration of the war. "My God," Churchill complained, "you make me feel as if I should go around in sack cloth and ashes."[44] Kennedy never made a secret of his disapproval. When someone asked him what kind of man Churchill was, the ambassador replied, "Churchill is a remarkable man, or as remarkable as any man can be who's loaded with brandy by ten o'clock in the morning." When he finally succeeds in dragging America into war, "he'll reach for that brandy glass, lift his hand on high and say 'I have discharged my duty. Victory is ours! This is my crowning achievement. God save the King.'"[45]

Despite Halifax's assurances that Churchill saw few people other than the military staff,[46] Kennedy felt isolated, snubbed, out of favor not only with Roosevelt's administration but with

Churchill's. For his part, Churchill simply ignored Kennedy, going over his head and dealing directly with FDR in their "Naval Person" correspondence.

Much of Britain's success in ultimately getting American aid depended on Churchill's ability to communicate candidly with Roosevelt. Had their blatantly unneutral correspondence become public, revealing Roosevelt's growing closeness with Churchill and the greater possibility of America's entry into the war, it would have created a major domestic and international uproar. Roosevelt had not, after all, favored any other political leader with such privileged correspondence, not even Reynaud, and certainly not Hitler or Mussolini or Stalin. Public knowledge of the Roosevelt-Churchill correspondence would have raised a hue and cry among the isolationists in Congress, to say nothing of the American people, most of whom were still noninterventionists. It would also have led to charges that Roosevelt was engaged in a diabolical plot, despite his promises of neutrality, to draw the United States into war. Congressional opposition probably would have destroyed Roosevelt's prospects of a third term and discouraged him from running, something that he was still evaluating in the spring of 1940. If Roosevelt had decided not to run, the field would have been left wide open for another presidential candidate, possibly someone much less concerned about Europe's affairs, whose election would have had serious consequences for the Allied cause by altering the nature of Anglo-American relations and changing the course of the war itself. Revelations of the president's conduct could also have thrown a wrench into American-German relations, and perhaps led to military action against the United States. So the Roosevelt-Churchill correspondence had to be kept secret.

But for a brief moment, Tyler Kent, a code clerk in the American embassy in London, could have changed the course of world history by revealing the correspondence, had it not been for the decisive actions of Ambassador Kennedy and British Intelligence MI5. This incident ensnared Kennedy in a cloak-and-dagger spy episode, with "a Mata Hari–like narrative,"[47] unique in Anglo-American diplomacy and without equal in the history of the United States.[48] Kennedy, acting contrary to his own oft-expressed views about American self-interest, ironically emerged as the guardian of the Roosevelt-Churchill correspondence by shielding it from public scrutiny, and an accomplice in a scheme to keep the American Congress and the public ignorant of the implications of the president's foreign policy. No part of Kennedy's life is shrouded in more secrecy, Kennedy's biographer, Richard Whalen, wrote.[49]

The Roosevelt-Churchill dispatches bypassed the usual Foreign Office channels and the British censors and were delivered to Kennedy, who usually read them and then sent them on to the code room where clerks worked around the clock coding the messages. The messages were sent in the Gray Code, a supposedly unbreakable cipher system. One of the clerks handling the Gray Code was Tyler Gatewood Kent, a code clerk, like a technician, trusted completely with the highest security clearance possible. Kennedy vaguely recalled him as one of his 200 employees in the embassy. Kent was in his late twenties, about five foot nine, clean-cut, with wavy brown hair, and smartly dressed by Brooks Brothers. He was a loner, quiet, reserved, resentful of authority, and deeply discontented because he felt he was working far below his station. The State Department had rejected his application to the Diplomatic Corps. It judged him "brilliant but neurotic," and frowned upon his lack of discretion in flaunting his affairs with married women.[50]

Kent coded and decoded the most sensitive messages, including the correspondence between the prime minister and the president. As he read and pondered the messages between Roosevelt and Churchill, Kent thought that "this is obviously something which ought to be called to the attention of the proper authorities in the United States," he told Robert Harris, a reporter for the *Times*, many years later.[51] He began stealing about fifty documents weekly from the embassy and copied anything that could be interpreted to mean that Roosevelt was intending to draw the United States into the war. Although he thought he owed loyalty to the American ambassador, he "had a higher loyalty to the people of the United States," he said. "I intended to show the documents to the U.S. Senate," particularly to sympathetic members of the Senate Foreign Relations Committee and to members of the America First Committee who deeply opposed Roosevelt's policy.[52]

Kent was an unlikely informer. He had all the WASP credentials for a career in the diplomatic corps. He was a descendant of a seventeenth-century Scotch-English blue-blood Virginian family. His mother doted on him, and her family pulled strings for him at the Virginia State Assembly. His father had been a career official in the American consular service and a friend of Cordell Hull, who urged William Bullitt to take Tyler with him to Moscow. Kent had accompanied his father to his various diplomatic posts, had been educated at elite schools in Europe and the United States, and was fluent in French, Greek, German, Russian, Italian, and Spanish. He taught himself Icelandic as well. After the outbreak of war, he had been transferred to London from the embassy in Moscow, where he had served as a code clerk for two years and became known as a philanderer there too, with a long succession of mistresses, married and unmarried.[53] He had become rabidly anti-communist and vehemently anti-Semitic. "The Jews," he believed, "are basically responsible for the establishment of world communism." He also thought that the Allied resolve to go to war with Hitler was "a tremendous mistake," he told Robert Harris, and that Roosevelt's policy of aiding the Allies was not in America's best interest.[54]

Mid-May was a frightful time for the Allies; they were confronted with military disasters and feared imminent invasion. The small countries on the Continent were being cut down by the Nazi scythe; the Germans were chasing the Allied armies to the sea across the broken British and French lines; the French armies to the south of the British Expeditionary Force had simply "melted away." As the news from France worsened, Churchill went to Chartwell, his home in Kent, on Saturday morning, May 18, to prepare his first speech as prime minister. After lunch he learned that the Germans had arrived at the Channel. He quickly returned to Downing Street to call an emergency meeting of his War Cabinet at 4:30.[55] In the midst of all this frenzy, the European-wide communication system at the American embassy in London was jeopardized and ultimately shut down by an espionage incident.

That same day Kennedy was at St. Leonard's, his Windsor residence, dining with Clare Boothe Luce, when he received a phone call from Herschel Johnson at the embassy. Johnson told Kennedy that Scotland Yard had notified him that the Yard believed that one of the code clerks in the London embassy had passed on confidential information to Nazi allies.[56] Kennedy was outraged when he learned from Captain Maxwell Knight of MI5, an agency responsible for counterespionage from Scotland Yard, that British security service had had Kent under surveillance for seven months, beginning just days after his arrival in England from Moscow, on October 5, 1939. The Yard had delayed arresting him in order to use him as bait to implicate as many other subversives as possible.[57] "I was naturally distressed by the incident," the ambassador wrote in his memoir, "and by the failure (that I had no hesitancy in commenting on) of the Scotland Yard officials to bring their suspicions about Kent to our attention months before." Their unwillingness to do so, Kennedy complained, meant that Kent continued to be employed for months at the embassy in the most sensitive of positions and led him to divulge privileged information throughout Europe as well as to be able to compromise the integrity of the most secret diplomatic codes.[58] "We would never have left the man in the code room if there had been the slightest ground for suspicion against him," embassy officials protested.[59]

Ironically, Randolph Churchill, the prime minister's son, knew that MI5's delay in arresting Kent also allowed them to keep the American ambassador himself under electronic surveillance for several months. Kennedy's well-known defeatist views, his advocacy for a compromise peace, and British wariness about what he might do next, given that he had acted on his own initiative without Roosevelt's sanction and contrary to his administration's policies, made him a worrisome suspect to British security officials.[60]

The ambassador learned that Kent had come to the Yard's attention because of his relationship with members of the Right Club, a pro-Nazi, anti-Semitic fifth-column organization with international contacts. It was led by Captain Archibald Ramsay, a graduate of Sandhurst, an openly anti-Semitic Scottish Unionist MP and a "little crazy" on the subject, a wounded and decorated World War I veteran, a member of one of Scotland's most distinguished families, and distantly related to the British royal family. He was described as a "sincere but thoroughly muddled English patriot."[61] He had often visited Kent's flat and had been shown copies of the Roosevelt-Churchill correspondence. Ramsay intended to inquire about it in the House of Commons, thereby exposing it to public scrutiny.[62]

Ramsay's associate, Anna de Wolkoff, was a rabidly anti-communist White Russian.[63] She claimed to have been "suckled" on anti-Semitism from birth, as members of her background were.[64] The daughter of an ex-admiral in the Imperial Russian Navy, her parents were czarist émigrés who had fled to London in 1919 after the Bolshevik Revolution, and ran the Russian Tea Room, well known for its caviar. She had become a British subject and worked in a fashionable dressmaker's shop. She blamed her family's social decline on Jews, communists, and Freemasons, and was a "soul mate" for Kent.[65] The Yard believed that Anna de Wolkoff also frequented Kent's flat and read secret embassy documents—dispatches, telegrams, and letters between Roosevelt and Churchill—along with confidential information about naval operations off the coast of Norway, superb grist for Nazi anti-British propaganda.[66] Scotland Yard also had Kent under surveillance because of his association with Ludwig Ernst Matthias, a member of the Gestapo and a naturalized Swede of German origin.[67] And Kent was suspected of having connections to a spy ring run by Italians in which the Soviet Union and Germany, allies at the time, were involved. The information he gave them went from London to the German foreign ministry through the Italian foreign ministry, which represented a country not yet at war.[68]

Scotland Yard needed Kennedy's permission to waive Kent's diplomatic immunity in order to allow the Yard, as representatives of a foreign government, to conduct a search of an American citizen for documents that were American property. In his diplomatic memoir, Kennedy wrote that "neither of us [Herschel Johnson or Kennedy] had any hesitancy about permitting such a search and we notified the Foreign Office to that effect," thereby giving the British jurisdiction over Kent, a move that Washington fully approved.[69]

Under Secretary Welles, acting for the ailing secretary of state, immediately sent Kennedy "a very secret cable" dismissing Kent from government service as of May 20 and authorizing Kennedy to waive Kent's diplomatic immunity.[70] Two days later Hull cabled his ambassador: "'This Government has no objection to formally charging the offender with violations of British law,' and 'in the circumstances, publicity in connection with such charges might not be helpful.'"[71] Indeed not, especially to Roosevelt. Kennedy assured Hull that British officials had informed him that a veil of official silence had been thrown over the case and recommended that Washington also maintain secrecy, since "this case stinks to high heaven." Indeed, at a press conference on May 25, Hull denied any knowledge of the matter; London simply passed the buck, and even the most astute journalists in the business were unable to uncover anything. A few days after Kent's arrest, the British Home Office did release a statement approved by the State Department: "In consequence of action taken by the American Ambassador in co-operation with the British authorities, Tyler Kent, a clerk who had been dismissed from the employment of the American government, has been under observation and has been detained by order of the Home Secretary."[72]

Kennedy's waiver and the State Department's complicity guaranteed that the trial, with its proceedings, testimony, and evidence, particularly the correspondence between president and prime minister, would be kept secret. The litigation would be held in a country at war that had enacted sweeping legislation to restrict the centuries-old freedoms of its citizens.

If Kent's diplomatic immunity had not been waived, he would have been deported and tried publicly in the United States for breaking his oath of loyalty, for committing a felony by stealing confidential documents, and for violating the Yardley Act by showing stolen embassy documents to Anna de Wolkoff and Captain Ramsay, among others. The Yardley Act prohibited any employee of the American government with access to any official diplomatic code from publishing or giving to another any unauthorized diplomatic correspondence from the United States government to any foreign government. If convicted, the felon would face a fine of $10,000 for each document and/or be imprisoned for ten years. Thus, Kent could have been fined $19,290,000 and sentenced to 19,290 years if convicted under the American law. A trial in the United States would have guaranteed disclosure of the secret Roosevelt-Churchill correspondence to a still overwhelmingly isolationist Congress and American public in the months before the 1940 election and make Kent something of a hero to the American Right as the man who destroyed the president and saved the country from war.[73] The case remains the only known instance of an American's diplomatic immunity being waived by an American ambassador.[74]

When Captain Knight, along with two officials from Scotland Yard and the American embassy's second secretary, armed with search warrants, knocked on Kent's door at 47 Gloucester Place, London, on May 20, 1940, they heard a voice twice shouting, "Don't come in!" They broke down the door and found Kent inside wearing striped pajama bottoms and standing beside his unmade bed. His mistress, a scared, dark-haired young woman of Russian nationality and married to a British citizen, was wearing the pajama top and doing her best to compose herself. Despite her costume, she claimed to be going to Kew Gardens for a picnic and that she had stopped by to invite Kent to accompany her. When the investigators searched Kent's flat, they found in a battered leather suitcase over fifteen hundred documents stolen from the embassy. Some were telegrams sent between the embassy and the State Department and letters and telegrams to other embassies throughout Europe. There were letters in confidential codes about secret subjects, and some others were just a miscellany. Some of the material had been copied and coded by Kent himself and filed under such headings as "Germany," "Russia," "Churchill," "Halifax," and "Jews."[75] Many of the documents were not particularly significant, but others were extremely important because of their requests for aid and candid descriptions revealing the shaky military and political conditions facing England. One particularly outspoken letter from the prime minister to the president had been written only hours before the raid. Kent had a penciled copy of it in his pocket. It described Britain's military situation as "full of danger" and pleaded for destroyers and fighters, a plea coupled with the blunt nightmare warning that if the present government were to fall, and another came to power, "the sole remaining bargaining counter with Germany would be the Fleet." Kent also reported that in May 1940 Kennedy had told Roosevelt that the conditions in England were "so bad that serious internal trouble might be expected at any time," implied that Britain might capitulate, and urged that the United States fight in its own backyard—information extremely valuable to Germany.[76] In addition, officials found two very fine photographic plates of cables containing correspondence from Churchill to Roosevelt sent by Kennedy, a list of the members of the Right Club, a set of duplicate keys to the Code Room,[77] and stickers declaring "THIS IS A JEW'S WAR."[78]

The evidence contained the entire history of the American government's diplomatic correspondence since 1938. Not only had the diplomatic codes been cracked, but Germany and Russia knew America's diplomatic strategy.[79] Worried State Department officials believed that Kent's arrest, along with leaks from London to Copenhagen, Berlin, and Bucharest, made it clear that he may have had colleagues in other European embassies and that there could be more unfriendly groups representing unfriendly governments within them.[80] State Department undersecretary Breckinridge Long described the damage to the confidential American diplomatic communication system as being "a terrible blow—almost a major catastrophe."[81] "Nothing like this had ever happened in American history," he said.[82] It took weeks before the situation could be restored. But in the meantime, Kennedy wrote in his memoir, the embassy had to devise new ways of transmitting the information flooding in at the very moment when the Germans were racing to the Channel, Europe was reeling under the Nazi assault, the new British prime minister was trying to prop up a France teetering on the brink of collapse, and Hitler was pondering an invasion of Britain. No secret correspondence could be sent or received—a state of affairs that lasted for two to six weeks until a new code could be set up and distributed by special couriers outside the service to the U.S. embassies abroad.[83]

The ambassador, who ironically shared Kent's desire to keep America out of war and had his own brand of anti-Semitism, and was himself under surveillance by MI5, joined the interrogation in his own embassy office. He thought the interview was "not too deftly conducted," but it did provide enough evidence to detain Kent longer.[84] "Send the traitorous bastard in," Kennedy ordered Knight, and berated Kent for his behavior. "From the kind of family you come from . . . one would not expect you to let us down," the ambassador "snarled." Throughout the entire interview Kent was "cool, contemptuous, and arrogant,"[85] Kennedy recalled, and explained Kent's incredible self-assurance and sneering, supercilious attitude as evidence that he did not comprehend the seriousness of the situation. Kennedy believed that the worst thing Kent expected was that he would be deported to the United States and the political implications of his case were so extreme that they would protect him from prosecution. Answering questions in a thin, nasal voice,[86] Kent "played up and down the scale of an intense anti-Semitic feeling, showed no remorse whatever except in respect to his parents," the ambassador said, "and told me to 'just forget about him.'"[87] Kent's defense, which Kennedy found unconvincing, was that he had taken the documents "for his own information," and because he had found them "interesting."[88] Additional evidence, Kennedy noted, showed that Kent and other colleagues in Moscow had smuggled furs and jewels into the United States. Furthermore, the embassy's records revealed that he had recently applied for a transfer to the American embassy in Berlin, presumably to be in a better position to provide information for German officials.[89]

Kennedy concluded "that the whole matter deserved a very thorough investigation that could only be effectively carried out by the British police and that evidence pointed to an offense under British law."[90] He therefore waived any further immunity for Kent. Kent was arrested by Scotland Yard and incarcerated in Brixton Prison. With the State Department's approval, and no doubt to its relief, the British held him incommunicado, awaiting charges for five months. The British government, according to Kennedy, purposely did so to avoid embarrassing Roosevelt or allow Kent to influence the 1940 presidential election.[91] Hull urged Kennedy to "take appropriate steps to ensure Kent will have a competent counsel . . . and that his trial will be fair."[92] For the next four years, Washington maintained a deafening silence about Kent except for a brief statement issued on June 2, 1940, in the *Chicago Daily Tribune*: "In consequence of action taken by the American Ambassador, in cooperation with British authorities, Tyler Kent, a clerk who has been dismissed from the employment of the American Government, has been under observation, and has been detained by an order of the Home Secretary."[93]

In the Kent case the British government found the justification for the detention of anyone who was thought to have undermined the war effort. Within forty-eight hours of Kent's being taken into custody, his accomplices, Captain Ramsay and Anna de Wolkoff, and members of the Right Club were also arrested and imprisoned. So too were Sir Oswald Mosley, the head of the British Union of Fascists, and some eight hundred of his followers.[94]

The four-day trial, *Rex v. Tyler Gatewood Kent*, began on October 23, 1940. It was held in camera in the Old Bailey courtroom, with heavy brown paper covering the windows in the locked courtroom doors guarded by police. The press was excluded. Lawyers and jurors were sworn to secrecy. Witnesses arrived at the Old Bailey in closed cars and were led down corridors reserved for criminals, to protect their identity. Kent was charged and convicted under the Official Secrets Act of 1911 on the grounds that it "*appears* that his purpose was a purpose prejudicial to the safety or interests of the State" and under the Larceny Act for stealing documents.[95] The three-day debate was of considerable legal consequence. It dealt with the issue of diplomatic privilege by which any diplomat in any country is protected from the judicial system of that country. The central question was who, if anyone, could waive diplomatic privilege and thereby subject a diplomat to the judicial system of the host country? Did diplomatic privilege belong to the ambassador or to each member of the diplomatic corps?

Kent's barrister, Maurice Healy, argued that the court had no authority to try Kent. It was, he said, "'a monstrous thing'" and "entirely contrary to the general principles of international law and the comity of nations that an ambassador should hand over one of his own subjects out of his own protection into the hands of the country in which he was arrested."[96] Sir William Jowitt, the solicitor general representing the prosecution, argued that the privilege of immunity was the prerogative of the ambassador and not the individual and therefore Kennedy had the right to waive it; consequently Kent could be subject to British law, a position accepted by the judge. Although Kent had been employed in the Foreign Service in the State Department, he was not an officer; he was one who served at the pleasure of the ambassador. In addition, Max Knight provided evidence that he had served Kent with his discharge papers from Kennedy in prison. Since Kent had been discharged from the Foreign Service by the ambassador as of May 20, the court ruled that the privilege of immunity did not apply and Kent could stand trial in Britain.[97]

Kent pleaded not guilty to the seven counts against him, four for acquiring documents "for a purpose prejudicial to the safety or interests of the State. . . . which might be . . . directly or indirectly useful to an enemy," one for transmitting them to Anna de Wolkoff, and two for stealing "the property of His Excellency the American Ambassador."[98] Throughout the trial Kent steadfastly defended his loyalty to the United States and argued that he was acting as a responsible American who wanted to protect his country from Europe's war. Since he believed that the American public had a right to know about their president's decidedly unneutral conduct, he planned to smuggle the documents into the United States and to give them to Roosevelt's isolationist opponents to use against his pro-British policies, a position not likely to be appreciated by the British jury.[99] British officials requested access to some of the documents during the trial, but the State Department denied permission on the grounds that there was already enough evidence to convict Kent.[100]

It took the English jury twenty-five minutes to find an American citizen guilty on all counts of violating British law by *appearing* to jeopardize Britain's security by stealing American property. Kent was sentenced to serve seven years at the windswept internment camp built at a monastery at Camp Hill on the Isle of Wight, with the terms running concurrently on each of the Official Secrets charges, and twelve months penal servitude on the larceny charge.[101] Kent's two accomplices—Anna de Wolkoff and Captain Ramsay—were also sentenced to prison.[102] Ironically the first major espionage trial of World War II involved not a German or Japanese or Italian subject, but an American citizen who was tried and found guilty in a British court under British law.[103]

"If we had been at war," Kennedy later stated, "I wouldn't have favored turning Kent over to Scotland Yard or have sanctioned his imprisonment in England. I would have recommended that he be brought back to the United States and been shot." "The only thing that saved Kent's life," the ambassador said, "was that he was an American citizen and we were not yet at war."[104]

Not until November 7, two days after Roosevelt's reelection, when the need for secrecy was past, was the press granted access to the court to see Kent sentenced. Right before Christmas of 1945, he was deported to the United States.[105] Considering the charges against him and the impact his actions had on the diplomatic codes and corps, the State Department displayed surprisingly little interest. "We do not give a damn what happens to him," an official said.[106]

On September 2, 1944, before Roosevelt's fourth election to the presidency, the Kent case just happened to gain attention in the United States. Arthur Sears Henning, a *Washington Times-Herald* correspondent, reported on November 12, 1941, that Richard R. Stokes, a Labourite MP and opponent of Churchill's, had asked in the House of Commons about the communications between Roosevelt and Churchill in 1939 when Churchill was the First Lord of the Admiralty in the Chamberlain cabinet. The whispering within official circles questioned whether Roosevelt and Churchill had been acting behind the back of Prime Minister Chamberlain and whether they had agreed that the United States would aid Britain more vigorously despite the limits that the Neutrality Acts and the Johnson Act put on aiding Britain. There were also suspicions that Captain Archibald Ramsay had been held in detention for four years without charge under the Defense of the Realm Act because Kent had informed him about the Roosevelt-Churchill correspondence. Henning's dispatch somehow escaped the censors and was sent to Kent in prison. On May 15, 1944, he confirmed that the article was "essentially correct."[107]

An outcry erupted in Congress over speculation about whether Kent had evidence to prove that Roosevelt and Churchill had colluded to bring the United States into war. For a moment, it seemed that from prison Kent might sabotage Roosevelt's campaign for a fourth term, but the writ of mandamus seeking Kent's return was denied by the Supreme Court without comment.[108] In response, the State Department issued a press release on September 2, 1944, in which the facts of the case were reviewed. The press release explained vaguely that Kent's immunity had been waived because Britain's interest was "preeminent."[109]

Two days later, Kennedy, now resigned from his ambassadorship, granted an exclusive interview to Henry J. Taylor, a reporter from the *Washington Daily News.* Kennedy told Taylor that Kent had not been "railroaded" by Scotland Yard to keep him from revealing any commitments made by Roosevelt to Churchill to aid the British before America's entry into the war. Nor was Kent a special liaison between the two. But he did know the content of their messages because he decoded them himself. Since the war began, Kennedy, and Roosevelt in turn, had received weekly briefings from Churchill and other officials describing Britain's strength in complete detail. "We had to assume that week by week this same data went to Berlin by way of Kent," Kennedy explained, implying that Kent was a traitor who passed the information on to Anna de Wolkoff and the Italian embassy to Germany.[110] The State Department's press release and Kennedy's interview had the effect of derailing the Kent case as an issue in the campaign and of causing anti-Roosevelt critics to distance themselves from it.[111] As Kennedy described Kent's activities, he made several incorrect statements, and embellished events, making Kent appear more treacherous than he actually was.[112]

"Arrant lies, . . . Kennedy's statements were arrant lies," Kent replied upon seeing a copy of the 1944 Kennedy interview.[113] His mother, Ann H. P. Kent, had tried for years before her son's return to gain Kennedy's assistance, but he continued to ignore her, returning her letters unread. Having spent her life in diplomatic circles, she was well aware of the unusual circumstances of her son's trial and launched a tireless campaign to have him returned to the United States and tried under U.S. law.[114]

One day, according to Kennedy biographer Richard Whalen, Kennedy happened to run into Kent's mother in a hotel lobby in Washington. She pleaded with him to help her. Although he considered her "a really wonderful woman," he could do nothing, he gently told her. She persisted. "This might strike one of my sons," Kennedy reportedly said, ending the conversation.[115]

The Tyler Kent case continued to stalk the former ambassador as Kent tried to sue Kennedy for libel. It also continued to arouse the wrath of the anti-Roosevelt right-wing press against Kennedy. A few months after the end of the war, in October 1945, Kennedy wrote to his Boston counsel urging that some official body reopen the case. Kent himself would never do it. "Of course, the fellow was absolutely a bad one and he will never dare bring anything to trial because they've got too much on him," Kennedy wrote. Kent's sympathetic reception by the anti-Roosevelt press is based on his supposed knowledge about the relationship between Churchill and Roosevelt—"all pure unadulterated bunk!" said the ambassador. As for apologizing for anything he had said about Kent, Kennedy's response was an unequivocal "nuts."[116]

Even five years later, Kennedy was still concerned about the case and the attacks made against him by newspapers critical of Roosevelt. In November 1950, Kennedy wrote to Lord Beaverbrook to ask for his help in the matter. "One of these days I've got to put the whole case out," in order to correct the story, Kennedy told him. "The anti-Roosevelt press has always made something terribly diabolical about the Tyler Kent case." It was not able to smear Kennedy, he claimed, because "I was able to smash back at Kent rather strongly." But to protect himself, Kennedy asked Beaverbrook to get various newspaper articles and documents pertaining to the trials of Kent and de Wolkoff and Ramsay's detention. "Whether I use it or not is a different matter," Kennedy told him.[117]

In 1963, Kent tried to sue Kennedy for defamation of character on the grounds of Kennedy's comments in his 1944 interview.[118]

In 1985 the publication of the correspondence between Roosevelt and Churchill, 1939–1945, discredited the wild charges against Roosevelt. There was no evidence to prove that Roosevelt and Churchill had colluded to get the United States to enter the war before Pearl Harbor. Ultimately the Tyler Kent case did not amount to much, but it could have.[119]

The puzzling Kennedy-Kent case has continued to provoke the curiosity of historians and journalists because of its possibly historic impact on the election of 1940 and the war. As Robert Crowley writes in the introduction of *Conspirator*, by Ray Bearse and Anthony Read, their book provides a comprehensive account of "a junior American clerk who, for a brief time, held the prospect of diverting the course of world history by his actions."[120] Peter Rand, on the cover flap of *Conspiracy of One*, declares that Kent "stood at the crossroads of history."[121] John Costello, *Ten Days to Destiny*, calls Kent "a silent, but far from insignificant, pawn on the political chessboard" between two kings, Roosevelt and Churchill.[122] Had he succeeded in checkmating Roosevelt by revealing their correspondence, the course of history could have been altered substantially.

The case is also intriguing because of what it may reveal about Kennedy's character. Why did Kennedy refrain from ruining the president's chances for a third term and perhaps his own for becoming a presidential candidate, and why did Kennedy refrain from trying to cripple a foreign policy with which he was in such profound disagreement? Several Kennedy scholars and historians of Anglo-American relations offer explanations. Richard Whalen wrote:

> In 1940 the Ambassador served as an accomplice in maneuvers designed to deceive the American people as to the ramifications of Roosevelt's foreign policy. Moreover, he persisted in this duplicity long after any apparent purpose of state was to be served. Throughout the Kent episode, Kennedy was faced with a choice between acting on his professed beliefs or on his immediate personal interests. Unfailingly he chose the latter.

But Whalen does not explain why.[123] Neither does Joseph E. Persico in *Roosevelt's Secret War*. After noting with irony the similarities between Kennedy's and Kent's views on American foreign policy, Britain's grim chances of survival, and their anti-Semitic bias, Persico states that Kennedy did what he always did "when his principles collided with his survival. He pulled the rug on Kent."[124] Michael R. Beschloss, in *Kennedy and Roosevelt*, however, suggests that Kennedy "was unwilling to influence American policy at the cost of an act that seemed illegitimate and disloyal."[125] Bearse and Read believe that Kennedy may have been in accord with Kent's public reasons for stealing the documents, as he too was collecting copies for his own purpose. However, he was not able to use them to charge Roosevelt either with "warmongering" or with conspiracy with Churchill—a"real bonus," they write. In addition, "as ambassador, [Kennedy] was outraged at actions that he regarded as disloyal to himself. The chief of mission is ultimately responsible for overseeing security precautions, so Kennedy found Kent's treachery a deep personal embarrassment.... In Kennedy's eyes, therefore, Kent was a traitor as well as a thief," Bearse and Read wrote.[126] Consequently Kent was not in the least deserving of the ambassador's support. John Lukas, in *Five Days in London, May 1940*, wrote that "it is interesting to note that there was nothing unconstitutional in the contents of the Churchill-Roosevelt correspondence. It was fortunate for Roosevelt that Kennedy, whose political preferences were similar to Kent's, chose to wash his hands of Kent and would not insist on his immunity. Kennedy the politician chose not to break with Roosevelt before the 1940 election campaign; he did not think that this was the right occasion or the right time to cause open trouble for Roosevelt."[127]

Perhaps Kennedy's actions regarding Kent's betrayal and Kennedy's failure to disclose his knowledge of the Roosevelt-Churchill correspondence can best be explained by Kennedy's sense of loyalty to the president and Kennedy's own self-interest. Putting his loyalty to the president and his own political ambitions ahead of political ideology might be a way to make FDR feel indebted to him, and a way to incline the president to bestow his blessing on the political ambitions of the Kennedy family.[128]

Throughout the spring and summer of 1940, Kennedy's fortunes were at a low ebb. Alone in London, the subject of much criticism and many snubs from the British establishment, Kennedy was feeling sorry for himself—he was homesick and looking for a way to make a graceful exit. "The big difficulty, of course, is being lonesome," he wrote to Rose, "but I have to keep my mind off that or I'd throw up the job and go home."[129] "Not even work interests me," he told Rose. "I just need my family."[130] He turned to them and reveled in their unconditional love and adulation, which he fully returned, taking comfort in his belief that his position as ambassador at such a significant time in world history might bring prestige and advantage to them, sometime, in some way.[131] He wrote candidly to Rose: "After having worked as hard as I have the last six years and a half, I don't want to do anything that would reflect on the family. After all that's why we went into this and I don't want to spoil it for the sake of a month or two."[132]

His lonesomeness led him to continue to dither with Rose over the possibility of her returning to London—only a fifty-fifty chance, he acknowledged in a letter on April 26. "It's terribly interesting, but it's Hell to be here without all of you. I get blue about once a week and then I am most unhappy."[133] But Kennedy put a stop to the plans for his family's return because of the very great possibility of trouble erupting on the Continent and because of the strong anti-Americanism developing among the Kennedys' friends. "It's silly for you or the children to come over. It might spoil your pleasant impressions."[134] So Rose resigned herself to not returning to Britain, which had been scheduled on the Clipper of May 10 as Hitler devoured France.[135] Joe wrote, "I'm heartbroken, but you just couldn't be here." He added that he planned to get Rose and the Moores out of England quickly because he expected a "terrific bombing pretty soon." "Well darling it's certainly been a great adventure. It's getting near the finish."[136]

Kennedy's letters to his wife were filled with affection and warmth: "I get news that you are more beautiful than ever,"[137] or "I just don't like being so completely away from you."[138] And they always ended with something like "I love you and miss you all the more."[139] Hers to him were filled with loving references to praying for him and gently needling him to go to church.[140] "But you are so important to me—my darling—so do take care of yourself the best way you can & we shall just keep on praying."[141] "All my love" or "All my love dearest" or "All my love always" were her standard closings.[142]

Kennedy maintained his role as the proud paterfamilias, as the ever-loving father whose word was still everything to everyone. He presided over his large brood with tenderness and interest, taking pride in their success and savoring the details of their lives even if he was an ocean away. To his children, his good opinion and his attention to them were the most important considerations in their lives.

Rosemary had remained in Hereford and had earned a certificate in teaching. "I am very proud of you and I love you a lot," he cabled.[143] She much enjoyed his twice-weekly phone calls and loved serving as his hostess at Windsor. But she was concerned because her father thought she was fat;[144] seven-year-old Teddy was fat too, and not concerned.[145] But he found a dead skunk in the pool and told his father in poor grammar and original spellings that he had to swim in a sulphur pool elsewhere.[146] Jack bragged about his success with southern girls. "I did better than usual," he told his father.[147] Pat was thrilled by her father's wire on her sixteenth birthday,[148] and Bobby reported on the songs the family was making up about her new, extremely tall boyfriend: "6 feet 7 Straight from Heaven . . ."[149] Bobby had become much stronger, looked "100% better," and had improved immensely at his new school, the Portsmouth Priory in Rhode Island. "Everybody has noticed," Jack wrote.[150] Bobby had had some boils on his knee but they were almost healed, he told his father, and he was not getting yelled at in the middle of Mass anymore, because Father Downing had been in an accident.[151] Eunice was the captain of her winning swimming team and played in a tennis tournament in Ohio. She was escorted off the tennis field twice by a coach during her match because she was wearing the wrong attire. Eunice had borrowed an outfit that was too short, leaving a gap that exposed her leg between her stockings and her shorts, much to the chagrin of the nuns and the amusement of the spectators, her mother noted.[152] Eunice also went to the circus with a chum and bought a "lazy lizard." At the performance, she peeked into the box and the lizard jumped out, landed on a nearby shoulder, hid under a skirt, and sent a friend of Eunice's scrambling onto a railing. Amidst shrieks and hysterics, someone found the lizard. Eunice demanded her 35 cents back because she had been tricked.

Rose took their "three darlings"—Rose, Eunice, and Bob—to Class Day at Harvard and then to Jack's commencement, where they had the worst seats in the place because Jack got them at the last minute. But they were able to see all the dignitaries and the graduates since they passed by them on their way to the platform. The commencement speaker got hissed when he suggested that the graduates might have to go to war. Jack looked tanned, healthy, and handsome in his cap and gown, with "a wonderful smile," his proud mother wrote her husband. Kick went to the boat race in New London after her brother's graduation and stayed for the weekend in Long Island. Joe Jr. was getting ready to go to the Democratic National Convention in mid-July, but his mother wanted him to go to Anne McDonnell's wedding to Henry Ford II first, touted as the social event of the century.[153] The Kennedy family letters certainly give a view of a loving, close-knit clan; no wonder their father missed them.

The elder Kennedy could also take fatherly pride in the success of his two eldest sons. "I am sending you my thesis," Jack Kennedy wrote to his father in the spring of 1940.[154] The title was *Appeasement at Munich: The Inevitable Result of the Slowness of the British Democracy to Change from a Disarmament Policy*. The second son was a senior at Harvard and a candidate for an honors degree in political science. In her memoir, Rose Kennedy explained that Jack's interest in the issue of appeasement grew from his experience in London meeting the prominent men of the time, touring Europe, and observing the approach of war.[155] He spent hours at Harvard's Widener Library thumbing through parliamentary debates, newspapers, periodicals, Foreign Office minutes—all the usual research documents—besides absorbing a constant flow of advice from his father, admonishing his son to check his spelling and his word usage, get his dates right, and improve his writing style.[156] Jack even managed to get the thesis in before the deadline, just barely, with the help of five stenographers and much rushing madly around during the last week—so his brother Joe informed their father in a March 17 letter. Joe, who had read a draft of the thesis, was dismissive and unimpressed with his younger brother's efforts. It "represented a lot of work but did not prove anything." But Jack said that he fixed it up in the last days and the final version "seemed to have some good ideas so it ought to be very good," Joe Jr. told his father.[157]

Jack's efforts got him a magna cum laude on his thesis, which enabled him to graduate from Harvard cum laude in political science in June 1940. His proud father sent him a check and cabled: "Two things I always knew about you one that you are smart two that you are a swell guy love Dad."[158] Jack's professors urged him to have the thesis published;[159] so did Arthur Krock. Still the final word rested with the father: on whether he thought it worth the effort and whether it should be published while he was still ambassador. "You can judge after you have seen it," Jack wrote to him. "I thought I could work on re writing [*sic*] it . . .—as it stands now—it is not any where [*sic*] polished enough although the ideas etc. are O.K. I think. . . . Whatever I do, however, will depend on what you think is the best thing."[160] I want to conclude with something about the best policy for the United States modeled after Britain's experience but "of course don't want to take sides too much," the diplomat's son wrote. What would be a good title? he asked his father. Arthur Krock had suggested *Why England Slept*, a play of words on Churchill's *While England Slept*. Will Churchill mind? What about a publisher? What about an agent? "Can you fix it?" Jack asked.[161] His father's opinion was everything.

"Thanks a lot for your wire. Worked it in," he wrote, in response to his father's cable.[162] The elder Kennedy urged Jack not to be too easy on the appeasers, an ironic piece of advice considering how well his son echoed his own views. In his early draft, Jack, like his father, excused the appeasement of Germany at Munich as necessary because of Britain's slowness to rearm, and defended it as an acceptable way to buy time to strengthen her military. Jack blamed appeasement not on the misguided leadership of Baldwin and Chamberlain but on "underlying factors" like too much confidence in the League of Nations, pacifism, and the parochial views of capital and labor, as well as the incapacity of democratic institutions to provide for quick rearmament. Jack's conclusion expressed doubt about the ability of democracy to provide adequately for national security. Dictatorships, by contrast, could deal with problems with a long-range perspective more efficiently and effectively, he argued. So, democracy had less ability to confront global problems, he reasoned, a view commonly held in the interwar period when democratic institutions were being severely challenged. At Munich, Chamberlain simply had no choice; the pacifistic and anti-militaristic British public had refused to invest in or to modernize its military, nor would it have supported a war against Germany.[163]

In a long letter of May 20, the ambassador praised his son for doing a "swell job." But several of the people to whom the elder Kennedy had shown Jack's thesis had said that he had been too magnanimous in pardoning Baldwin and Chamberlain as the leaders responsible for England's position at Munich. On the one hand, "no good purpose can be served by making scapegoats out of Baldwin and Chamberlain; on the other hand, . . . you have gone too far in putting the blame on the British public . . . and . . . letting Baldwin off too easily," the ambassador said. "I believe that the basis of your case—that the blame must be placed on the people as a whole—is sound," his father wrote; nevertheless, "don't give the appearance of trying to do a complete whitewash of the leaders . . . [I]n a Democracy a politician is supposed to . . . look after the national welfare, and to attempt to educate people. . . . It may not be good politics but it is something that is vastly more important—good patriotism." No other position is workable in a democratic society, he opined.

The ambassador suggested that Jack offer another argument: that "the National leaders failed to rearm, and they were caught at Munich. They had to shut up because they couldn't put up. . . . Britain is a democracy and at that time Britain was definitely a pacifist democracy. . . . Why not say that British national policy was the result of British national sentiment and that everyone, leaders and people alike, must assume some share of the responsibility for what happened. . . . For some reason, Britain slept." You can point out that Roosevelt has had to face the same problem in trying to educate the American people about the dangers of aggression, the ambassador wrote. "Democracy in America, like democracy in England, has been asleep at the switch. . . . We should profit by the lesson of England and make our democracy work . . . right now. Any system of government will work when everything is going well. It's the system that functions in the pinches that survives. . . . [P]ractically everybody is now convinced that we had better be strong as hell if we want to survive in the world of to-day," he concluded.[164]

"Will stop white washing Baldwin," Jack obediently replied,[165] as he incorporated whole sections from his father's letter into his revised conclusion. Instead of speculating that democracy's inability to respond quickly might make it irrelevant, Jack's final conclusions offered a strong defense of democratic institutions and argued that rearming was essential to their defense. "We can't escape the fact that democracy in America, like democracy in England, had been asleep at the switch. . . . We should profit by the lesson of England and make our democracy work. . . . It's the system that functions in the pinches that survives," Jack wrote, all virtually word for word from his father's letter.[166]

Prompted by his father, Jack consulted Arthur Krock, who recommended an agent and advised Jack on rewriting the manuscript to have it ready for publication in the spring, in

May or June 1940.[167] Jack managed to transform into a bestseller a piece of work that "half a hundred seniors do . . . as part of their normal work in their final year" at any good university, as Harold Laski, one of Joe Jr.'s professors at the London School of Economics, put it. Laski wished that Jack had not published the book and offered well-intended criticism. Although it is "the book of a lad with brains, it is very immature, it has no real structure, and it dwells almost wholly on the surface of things." Most people don't publish their senior thesis because they have little to say. The value comes in having done the work. Furthermore, Laski added, no publisher would have accepted the manuscript if the author had not been your son and you the ambassador, insufficient reasons for publishing. Please understand, Laski told Kennedy, "these hard sayings from me represent much more real friendship than the easy praise of 'yes' men like Arthur Krock." I care about your sons and I don't want them to become spoilt rich boys.[168] Kennedy ignored Laski's advice and asked Henry R. Luce, of Time Inc., to write the foreword. The book was hastily brought out in July by Wilfred Funk, Inc., sponsored by the Book-of-the-Month Club, and published on the eve of the Blitz in England. What better evidence for the failure of appeasement?

Why England Slept sold 80,000 copies in the United States and Great Britain. Jack received around $40,000 in royalties and gained some celebrity. He bought a Buick with his American earnings and gave his English royalties to the bombed city of Plymouth.[169] His mother boasted to her diary that Jack's book "was widely heralded, became a best seller, and was acclaimed by no one less than the British Ambassador, Lord Halifax, as one of the best books written about the months preceding the War."[170] His father bragged that Chamberlain was anxious to read the book.[171] Montagu Norman (governor of the Bank of England) also asked him about it, Kennedy told Jack. "You would be surprised how a book that really makes the grade with high-class people stands you in good stead for years to come," his father wrote him. "Get a good rest," he advised his son. "You have the brains and everything it takes to go somewhere."[172] His father's pride in his twenty-three-year-old second son was quite justified; so was his pride in his eldest son.

Young Joe Jr., his father's namesake, was the elder Kennedy all over again. He was handsome, tall, robust, friendly, and intensely loyal to his family. He echoed his father's opinions on nearly any subject. "Ask my father," Joe Jr. said, citing his ultimate authority, during a tempestuous debate.[173] As a student at Harvard, he helped to establish a campus organization, Keep America Out of War, and argued for isolationism, sounding just like his father. "Are we going to fight for the liberties of the people of the world when [it] is really none of our damned business but is up to the people in those countries themselves?" he wondered in "Notes," written in June 1939 when he and Kick were touring Europe. "I know it is terrible the way the Jews are being prosecuted [*sic*] . . . but . . . that is none of my business unless my country wants to dominate the world and impose its conditions of justice on all people." "America might be a deciding force in preventing war only if she is prepared to back up her statements"—a view also reminiscent of his father's. Echoing Ambassador Kennedy's infamous Trafalgar

Day speech, young Joe once asked: "Are we going to continue to accept newspaper reports which always try to state the worst of all the dictatorships?" "Is [it] impossible to live in a world with the dictator countries?"[174]

As the eldest son, he was anointed the surrogate parent, an assignment his father took very seriously. On the eve of Joe Jr.'s twenty-fifth birthday Kennedy wrote him: "You [now will] take over your interest in the Trust and . . . become owner of a considerable amount of securities and money." He reminded him of "his responsibility to the family." "You don't know what a satisfaction it is for me to know that you have come along so well, . . . I have such confidence that come what may, you can run the show," his unabashedly loving father wrote to his favorite son[175] as he asked him and Jack to show particular attention to Bobby and Teddy, as he would do were he at home. It would mean a "great deal to them."[176]

As the standard-bearer for the Kennedy family, Joe Jr. was being groomed to fulfill his father's presidential ambitions. Rose thought that "it has been tacitly agreed that Joe . . . would be the one to devote himself as a member of government," she wrote in her diary.[177] During Joe Jr.'s student days in London in 1933–34, Professor Harold Laski remembered that the younger Kennedy sat in his study "and submitted with that smile that was pure magic to relentless teasing about his determination to be nothing less than President of the United States."[178] His father suggested that his son establish the proper foundation for a political career. So young Joe dutifully enrolled at Harvard Law School.[179]

In the spring of 1940, only a few days shy of his twenty-fifth birthday, Joe Jr. also launched his political career as a delegate to the Democratic National Convention from the poor, staunchly democratic West End of Boston. He ran as a Farley candidate, completely opposed to a third term for Roosevelt. His family connections as Joe Kennedy's son and Honey Fitz's grandson should have ensured an easy victory. But like any good ward politician, he campaigned vigorously, meeting people, shaking every shakable hand, rapping on doors.[180] He came in second and won one of the two seats. "The Kennedy name is a pretty good vote getter," the victorious delegate happily wrote to his father. "Over all the result was very satisfactory. . . . Grandpa was very pleased about it and he knows the situation pretty well."[181]

At the convention in Chicago in July 1940, the president's men, determined to win a unanimous convention vote on the first ballot for a third term for their non-candidate, cornered young Joe Kennedy and reminded him of the many honors the president had bestowed on his father. Surely his gratitude and loyalty dictated that he switch camps, they argued. They also hinted that his political career would be short-lived if he continued to back Farley; so would his father's. Young Joe sought refuge and advice from the ever-faithful Arthur Krock. Your father would expect you to do the honorable thing, Krock said, as you expect to do, too. "Don't worry about the old man. You will neither make nor break him. He'll do either by himself."[182] FDR's frustrated supporters even put through a call to London to ask the ambassador whether he would talk sense to his boy. "No," Kennedy firmly replied. "I wouldn't think of telling him what to do."[183] Acting on Krock's advice, whenever the Massachusetts delegation was canvassed, a determined young voice announced: "James A. Farley."[184] After the first vote was done and the tally was 946 for Roosevelt and 72 for Farley, Farley did the gentlemanly thing and moved that Roosevelt's nomination be accepted by acclamation.[185]

After Roosevelt's renomination at Chicago, Farley wired Kennedy his thanks for his son's dogged support of him. A grateful father returned the thanks and added: "After all if he [Joe] is going into politics, he might just as well learn now that the only thing to do is to stand by your conviction. Am most happy to say he needed no prompting in this respect."[186] Joe Jr. left the convention feeling that he had done "the right thing," he told his father; his father thought so too.[187] "I think the incident will stand you in good stead," Kennedy wrote to his son.[188] Kennedy's children were his investment in the future and the means by which this unusually ambitious man would create a political dynasty and soar to even greater heights.

The British had kept a close eye on the convention proceedings. "Of course, we want [Roosevelt] to run," the prime minister had told Kennedy, "but we must take care that the United States does not know that. But if we stirred up some action here in July, which seems more than likely, FDR might then be more inclined to run."[189] Indeed, on July 3 the British "stirred up some action." They sank the French fleet to impress the Americans. It did. Roosevelt had approved in advance of this act of "self defense"; most Americans approved, too.[190]

Americans across the seas were gearing up for the presidential election of 1940. After a tumultuous convention in Chicago and Roosevelt's renomination by the Democratic Party, Jim Farley immediately resigned as its national chairman. Roosevelt offered the job to Senator Jimmy Byrnes, who firmly declined but suggested Kennedy's name.[191] Arthur Krock, whose advice Kennedy had sought about resigning and seeking another position within the administration, had been trying for months to convince Kennedy that the chairmanship of the Democratic Party would be just the ticket out and provide the graceful exit for which he had been searching for months.[192] In London Kennedy heard from Joe that Kennedy's name was being floated for the position. But Byrnes, in an apparent change of heart, told Joe Jr. that Kennedy should remain in London. "It doesn't look like it is going to be easy to get you back over here," Joe Jr. wrote him.[193]

Another post for which he had been frequently touted by Arthur Krock and badly wanted was the chair of the nation's yet to be created Advisory Defense Commission. Kennedy had for years taken copious notes from Britain's wartime experience to prepare himself for the position. But in this too his hopes were dashed; the president said no.[194]

By late July Kennedy was fed up. "After we have a good bombing here, . . . I am really going to go home. . . . My activities thereafter will be most limited. . . . I will not be making any contribution either to the country or to myself by remaining here, but of course that will depend entirely on how gracefully I can make an exit," he told Joe Jr.[195]

But FDR weighed in and called Kennedy in London on August 1 to give him "the dope straight from [him] and not from somebody else." The Democratic Committee had suggested that Kennedy return to the United States and run the 1940 presidential campaign, FDR said, but the State Department had vetoed the proposal. The president, administering lots of "applesauce," as Kennedy called it—a Kennedy euphemism for "bull shit," according to Nasaw[196]—told him that he "would be happy to have him in charge, but the general impression is that it would do the cause of England a great deal of harm if you left there at this time." Thank you but no thank you, Kennedy said. The job did not interest him, he told Roosevelt. "I wouldn't take the job even if it were offered to me." Out of respect for his current position, "I should stay as long as there [is] any prospect of the British going through a bad bombing." But if Hitler has not started a bombing campaign by the end of the summer, he might just as well go home. "As far as I can see, I am not doing a damn thing here that amounts to anything and my services, if they are needed, could be used to much better advantage if I were home." His comments were largely true. Spreading on still more applesauce and trying to soothe his ambassador's injured pride, the president responded: "That's where you are all wrong. I get constant reports of how valuable you are to them. . . . It helps the morale of the British to have you there. . . . They would feel they were being let down if you were to leave. . . . The people in our country . . . feel well satisfied with you being in England." Roosevelt's argument was irresistible. "Things are better there now, are they?" the president asked. Kennedy's usual gloomy reply was "Yes, if you mean they are willing to fight with broken bottles." The conversation ended on a somber note: They both felt "damn sorry" that Roosevelt had agreed to be a candidate again, but he could see no alternative. So, Kennedy stayed put.[197] The president's transatlantic praise must have surprised his ambassador, but it was vintage FDR—at once charming and cunning, all choreographed for him to get what he wanted.

But Kennedy was no fool either. He told Rose the next day that he had been "damn fresh" to the president, who had called him because "he is afraid I will walk out because of my dissatisfaction with things and he wanted to 'soft soap' me." FDR feared "I might say: The Hell with it. If this is the way you want to run the place, I will go home." It would be quite embarrassing if I did. "I am not fooling myself about all this 'applesauce' and I haven't the slightest doubt that they would turn around tomorrow and throw me in the ash can," Kennedy wrote to his wife. In a rare moment of reflection Kennedy added: "The trouble is that people think you do a great deal more than you really do and that you are much more important than you are and therefore they would expect you to stay, thinking your task is Herculean, whereas the truth of the matter is, I could name a hundred people who could carry on the detail of the office. As to the psychological effect, both here and abroad—that I don't know."[198]

Kennedy had it right—applesauce and soap were just two of Roosevelt's tools. Since Kennedy thought that the Germans were unbeatable, a view at odds with Roosevelt and his administration, they thought Kennedy incapable of objectivity about Britain's military status and morale. Roosevelt would have been justified in dismissing him from the ambassadorship and replacing him with someone the administration did have confidence in. But this was not politically possible; with the presidential election looming, too much was at stake. The administration feared that Kennedy might use his considerable clout with his fellow Irish Americans, important for the success of the Democratic ticket, by whipping up their Anglophobia and telling them how militarily unprepared the British were. Or he might simply sit out the election, or worse, support Roosevelt's opponent, Wendell Willkie. Kennedy was just too dangerous to have at home. So, Roosevelt decided to keep him tucked away in London until after the election. Roosevelt would simply work around him as he had done before; hence the phone call of August 1 and the applesauce and soap.[199]

During the summer months after Dunkirk and the collapse of France, Britain found itself virtually unarmed, isolated, and alone, daily dreading a German invasion, which was not to come. Kennedy anticipated an invasion of Britain, too; throughout the summer of 1940 he issued dire predictions of Britain's defeat in candid letters to his family and friends, a more receptive audience than Washington. "Either the 8th or 9th of July or the 15th" was the expected invasion date, the ambassador told Washington as he passed on information gleaned from Halifax. "This I realize, is a day out of the sky."[200]

The Luftwaffe would easily gain air supremacy over the Channel, given its domination of the air bases on the west coast of Europe,[201] and then quickly turn against the Royal Navy and Army, crippling them both, the ambassador wrote to his son John on August 2. All the plans for Britain's defense only amount to a "tinker's damn [*sic*]," as Kennedy described them to Joseph Patterson, editor of the *New York Daily News.* As soon as the Germans achieve supremacy in the air, they will invade Britain at their convenience.[202] And the British, overwhelmed by hopelessness and despair, would surrender, he predicted to Rose.[203] So far, Germany's air attacks had been "piddling affairs," he told John, in a letter on August 2, 1940.[204] Nevertheless, Kennedy further explained to his fourteen-year-old son Robert, "we are expecting that Hitler will really go to work and bomb the whole place out this week." It was to Hitler's advantage to try to end the war quickly in order to quell the potential threat of unrest and instability among the millions of conquered, starving people in Europe and to forestall the thing Kennedy feared most—that a chivalrous America would come dashing to Britain's aid in regrettable and unforeseen ways after the 1940 election. We shall know soon, the ambassador continued, expecting Britain's invasion momentarily, and feeling "like the fellow sitting in the theatre waiting for the curtain to go up."[205]

At the same time that the British expected an invasion of their island homeland, they were locked in a frantic battle at sea with great losses. The success of the German U-boats and dive-bombers in the Battle of the Atlantic was causing the British rapidly to lose their destroyers, severely endangering their imports and exports and creating the near-certainty of a food shortage in Britain the next winter.[206] The long-term perspective was "frightful," he told Rose.[207]

But the British saw it otherwise and rejected Kennedy's doomsday scenario. They believed that their island fortress, made invincible by their navy, their air force, and the rest of their large military contingent, could fend off any invasion.[208] Their morale is "excellent," Kennedy marveled to his wife; since they believe that Hitler can't conquer their air force, he can't invade their island.[209]

At the end of July, Kennedy repeated his frequent warnings to Washington: be wary of Britain's overtures for aid. "Do not let anybody make any mistake; this, from Great Britain's viewpoint, is a war being conducted from now on with their eyes only on one place and that is the United States," he advised Hull. "Unless a miracle is performed they realize that they haven't a chance in the long run," he cabled, expecting Britain's collapse in the fall.[210]

It was to Kennedy's credit that he was such a hard-headed realist in assessing Britain's grim prospects for survival; considering Britain's lack of weapons—destroyers, tanks, planes, guns—and money—qualities of character seemed to matter little; Britain simply lacked the resources to halt the Nazi juggernaut.[211] Kennedy's prediction about Britain's survival was astute; it would indeed take a miracle, and a miracle did come to pass. Despite Kennedy's foreboding, Roosevelt began to believe that Britain's cause was not lost and that aid from America could play a decisive role between victory and defeat.

By the summer of 1940, Roosevelt had come largely to ignore Kennedy's dire warnings about the invasion and defeat of Britain. Roosevelt had also decided to disregard the advice of his military experts. Over the unanimous opinion of his most trusted military advisors such as army chief of staff General George Marshall; key congressional and Cabinet leaders, including his own secretary of war; and vocal opponents like Senator Gerald Nye of North Dakota, Senator David Walsh of Massachusetts, Charles Lindbergh, and General Hugh Johnson—and Kennedy, of course, as well as the bulk of the American public—FDR, acting quietly but decisively, overruled their advice and extended aid to Britain.[212]

In his Charlottesville speech on June 10, 1940, the president had promised to help Britain's cause by supporting "methods short of war," by granting the resources of the nation to the opponents of force and by organizing and speeding up the process by which those resources could be used in the United States in its own defense against any emergency.[213] From mid-June to late August 1940, he took several measures to implement that sweeping promise. FDR reorganized his Cabinet by introducing bipartisanship and bringing in two ardent internationalists, thereby weakening the influence of isolationists like Kennedy. Roosevelt also accepted the British invitation to send his own unofficial envoys to London and did so without Kennedy's prior knowledge or approval. Their assessment of Britain's chances for military success differed markedly from Kennedy's and helped to convince FDR that American aid to Britain could be crucial. Roosevelt also agreed to Churchill's request for destroyers, action Churchill had been urging for some months and Kennedy seemed to give tepid support to.

For several months the president had been considering introducing bipartisanship into the Cabinet. On June 19, 1940, he replaced two of the staunchest isolationists in the Cabinet, Secretary of the Navy Charles Edison and Secretary of War Harry Woodring, with two of the most ardent pro-Allied Republicans: Colonel Frank Knox, a former newspaper publisher and the Republican vice-presidential candidate in 1936, and seventy-two-year-old Henry L. Stimson, previously William Howard Taft's secretary of war and Herbert Hoover's secretary of state, who became the secretary of war again. Both Knox and Stimson were unyielding opponents of Nazism and all that it stood for and supported generous aid to Britain, including the repeal of the Neutrality Act, compulsory military service, an increase in the army to one million men, the creation of the world's largest air force, and the immediate shipment of a substantial number of outdated airplanes and American convoys to aid Britain, a policy far more sweeping and far-reaching than anything Kennedy supported.

In addition, FDR accepted Britain's invitation in mid-July and sent to London Colonel William ("Wild Bill") J. Donovan, his classmate at Columbia Law School and Republican contender for governor of New York. Donovan was a self-made man, a Catholic, an Irish American, a distinguished World War I commander of the "Fighting 69th" Regiment, a winner of the Congressional Medal of Honor, a successful New York lawyer who maintained an avid interest in international and military affairs. He was destined to become the head of the secret Office of Strategic Services, the forerunner of the Central Intelligence Agency. A man of great ambition, energy, and immense personal charm, Donovan never permitted political differences to interfere with his friendship with the president. His assignment was to ascertain the strength of Britain's will to fight and to evaluate her military capabilities.[214] Kennedy had protested Donovan's mission because Kennedy felt that he was being undercut by it; he was.[215]

When Donovan arrived in Britain on July 14 accompanied by Edgar Mowrer, a respected foreign correspondent from the *Chicago Daily News*, his hosts warmly received them, treating them with great respect and graciousness, no doubt hoping that these Americans would affirm Britain's ability to ward off invasion and report more favorably than Kennedy had done. The British had long been worried lest Kennedy's pessimistic cables lead even Americans sympathetic to the British to balk at contributing ships to a navy that might soon be confiscated by the Nazis.[216] Donovan scouted defense equipment, factories, and military installations; he talked candidly with King George VI, Churchill, members of the cabinet, military experts, and ordinary citizens. He saw secret dispatches, intercepted German documents, and the war bunker underneath Whitehall from which military operations were directed. He met everyone and everybody in an attempt to size up Britain's strength and morale—everyone, that is, but Kennedy. Donovan's snub was intentional.[217]

The White House had deliberately not informed Kennedy of Donovan's arrival. Kennedy was doubly offended because he had learned about the visits of Donovan and Mowrer from the British, who had known about the arrangements for about a week.[218] Kennedy was also surprised to learn from the British War Office about the special military mission headed by

Admiral Robert Ghormley and General George Strong and scheduled for late August. They were sent to London for staff talks and to "observe" for the president. They were assigned to the ambassador as his military attachés. Ambassador Lothian had "cooked" the scheme up and "sold" it to the president about three weeks earlier. Even the State Department didn't know about it. Kennedy strongly criticized this "back-room procedure." His criticism was ignored.[219]

Kennedy sent Hull a terse, sarcastic dispatch on August 7, 1940, complaining that he could not do his job because of a lack of information: "Now there is probably a good reason why it is necessary to go around the Ambassador in London and take up the matter with the British before he knows about it. However, I do not like it and I either want to run this job or get out." The delicacies of diplomacy require me to be informed before the British are, Kennedy argued, whom he accused of leaking information to the press. When I am not informed, it is embarrassing and confusing.

These are interesting comments from an ambassador known for his unconventional diplomatic ventures himself. "Not to tell me, is very poor treatment of me, and is bad organization," he grumbled to Hull. In addition, the ambassador warned, the presence of generals and admirals assigned to the embassy to hold staff talks will be used as evidence that the president has been trying to get the United States into war. No one will believe that they are my military attachés. At least let us all collaborate on a story that is believable and suits the occasion, Kennedy said.[220] Despite his self-pity, wounded pride, and loud protests that he had been "slighted," and that Donovan's trip would be "disruptive" to the embassy and that Ghormley's visit looked like war and would create confusion for British authorities, Washington maintained its unyielding and determined silence.[221]

"While I am thoroughly disgusted with the way Roosevelt is handling this situation [Donovan's trip] as far as this Embassy goes," Kennedy groused to his wife, "there is nothing much I can do about it." FDR had no understanding about organization; despite my protest, he sends people over here to tell him what he already knows. Under ordinary circumstances, I would resign, Kennedy said; but then these are not ordinary circumstances.[222] But he, like many Washingtonians in the administration, failed to see the method in Roosevelt's casual style. Assigning various people to the same task allowed FDR to be nimble and cunning, if he so chose, and beholden to no one. It let him try different policies and ultimately left him in charge to make the decisions when and as he saw fit, a kind of divide-and-conquer approach.

In contrast to Kennedy's constant predictions of the imminent invasion and inevitable destruction of Britain, Donovan's report to Roosevelt was optimistic: "Doing fine," he reported.[223] Grit holding; morale still good. British preparations for defense were excellent, he told the president. The airfields were scattered throughout the country and cleverly camouflaged, the army and navy operated effectively, and the coastal defenses bristling with machine guns and barbed wire were strong. Thus, a concentrated attack on the Royal Air Force would be extremely difficult. Donovan put the odds of Britain's surviving an attack by Germany at more than fifty-fifty, more like sixty-forty. Hitler would pay a huge toll. Britain could make it with more American aid, Donovan cheerfully predicted. Roosevelt thought so too and agreed with Donovan's assessment, provided that the president was willing to disregard American neutrality.[224] The mission had been extremely "useful," the *Spectator* wrote approvingly. Donovan took home with him "a picture of Britain substantially different from that drawn officially by the pessimistic Mr. Kennedy."[225] In fact, the British were so delighted with Donovan that when Kennedy resigned his post, the Foreign Office officials considered "dropping a hint" to the State Department that the appointment of Donovan as ambassador would be most welcome.[226] Thus, the road to greater and more far-reaching commitments like the famous destroyer deal and Lend-Lease had been paved.

Kennedy met Admiral Ghormley, General Strong, and Major General Delos Carleton Emmons, whose mission he had vigorously opposed, at the railroad station on August 15. He invited them and his military attaché, General Raymond Lee, to his estate before they could meet with British officials. Kennedy spent the meeting criticizing Churchill for his military strategy in Norway and in Western Europe and told his guests that he "saw dynamite in their visit." Staff talks "meant that we were getting ready to go in." Ghormley informed Kennedy that he, too, was annoyed with Roosevelt for sending him. Ghormley had met with the president in Washington and had asked him point blank if the United States was going to war. "Positively not," Roosevelt replied. Regardless, the delegation was hastily sent off to London. Kennedy left the meeting completely confused about Roosevelt's intentions. "I don't understand Roosevelt, I feel all the time he wants to get us into war and yet take what he says to Ghormley—I just can't follow him." Kennedy's attempt to do an end run around the British War Office officials apparently had little effect on Ghormley's assessment of Britain's military prowess or her chances of surviving a German onslaught.[227]

The Battle of Britain, begun on August 13, 1940 (the date Germans have traditionally assigned to it), was the first stage in Operation Sea Lion, the ultimate invasion of Britain. Hitler intended to engage the entire British Fighter Command so that the Luftwaffe's numerical air superiority could destroy it.[228] His "fat Reich Marshal," Hermann Göring, launched Operation Eagle on August 15. It was the air battle against Britain designed to destroy the RAF so as to establish the first condition for the invasion of Britain. So certain of victory was Göring that he believed that within four days he could shatter Britain's fighter defenses in southern England; within two to four weeks the Luftwaffe alone could annihilate the RAF. England would be on her knees, and a land invasion would not be necessary.

Hitler very nearly succeeded.[229]

Goodwin writes:

Night after night, German planes pounded the southern coast of England, damaging airfields, dockyards, communication lines, and radar stations. (In a single night, the Luftwaffe hit six radar stations, but, not realizing how critical radar was to Britain's defense, the Germans did not pursue the attack.) Meanwhile, hundreds of German barges were moving down the coasts of Europe, convoys were passing through the Straits of Dover, and tens of thousands of German troops were gathering along the northern coasts of France. . . . The sky in southern England had become "a place of terror, raining blazing planes, shell splinters, parachutes, even flying boots."[230]

By the end of August, the RAF was stretched almost beyond endurance; Hitler was nearly able to achieve his goal of mastery over southeast England. Only if the British failed to accept a compromise peace, as Hitler fully expected them to do, did he plan to issue Directive No. 16, "Operation Sea Lion," and to set the target date for the invasion of Britain sometime in late September 1940. Thus the British gained a brief respite in the land war but continued their frantic struggle in the Atlantic. Britain had lost more than half of its company of destroyers at Dunkirk; in July alone eleven more had been crippled.[231] The island nation, so completely dependent on imports, desperately needed destroyers to protect its commerce, as Kennedy was well aware.[232]

On July 31, 1940, just before the Battle of Britain began, Churchill, who had refrained from nudging Roosevelt about the destroyers for several weeks, renewed his request for them in a "former Naval Person" communication sent through Kennedy. "It had now become most urgent for you to let us have the destroyers, motor-boats, and flying boats for which we have asked. . . . The whole fate of the war may be decided by this minor and easily remediable factor," the former Naval Person and new prime minister told the president. We have destroyers and anti-U-boats under construction, but they will not be ready until late fall or early winter. In the meantime, the air attacks on our island have inflicted many casualties. Your destroyers could tide us over for a few months. Now that you know where we stand, Churchill pleaded, I am confident that you will do everything possible to help us at once. Fifty or sixty of America's reconditioned destroyers would be invaluable and replenish Britain's declining fleet of warships. "Mr. President, with great respect I must tell you that in the long history of the world this is a thing to do now," the desperate prime minister wrote.[233] Even King George VI made an urgent personal appeal to the president. "The need is becoming greater every day if we are to carry on our solitary fight for freedom to a successful conclusion."[234] The president assured the king that he was considering his appeal but unfortunately had not yet found a way to accommodate it.[235]

Initially Kennedy seemed to favor the destroyer deal. Halifax told Churchill that the ambassador had "promised to back it to the best of his ability. He quite agreed about the importance and urgency of the matter."[236] The prime minister was so pleased that he ended his letter on July 31 to FDR by praising Kennedy, who he knew would read the message before it was sent, as "a grand help to us and the common cause."[237]

But Kennedy resented British pressure and thought that Churchill "was overplaying his hand."[238] The ambassador chided Halifax about it in a dispatch: Roosevelt knew all he needed to know about destroyers and will "settle it in his own way in his own time; to try to give him the hurry up or to point out again the dangers to America was not likely to influence him much." In all the years that he had known him, Kennedy said, he had never seen him submit to a "rush act."[239]

Roosevelt faced a dilemma throughout the summer of 1940: he could not legally send destroyers to England unless the navy certified that they were not needed for America's defense and unless America's neutrality was not jeopardized. But five months earlier, naval officials had already testified about their potential value to American security. And if the president tried to get special legislation through Congress, Senators Walsh, Wheeler, Nye and Co., the guardians of isolation, would raise a major fuss that could result in endless delays and perhaps defeat for the bill.

At a Cabinet meeting on August 2, Navy Secretary Knox suggested offering the destroyers in exchange for access to British navy bases in the Americas. The Cabinet endorsed the idea, but it still assumed that congressional legislation would be necessary and that it would probably fail in Congress. The Cabinet also agreed that the British would be approached through Lord Lothian, Britain's ambassador to the United States, to see whether they would guarantee that the British fleet would not fall into enemy hands should Britain be defeated but instead sail to North America or to ports in the British Empire.[240]

A group of four distinguished lawyers and president's men had been mulling over the dilemma as well and presented a masterful and resourceful scheme to FDR. He immediately accepted it. The *New York Times* published it in the letters-to-the-editor section on August 11, 1940. Congressional sanction is not necessary for the president to aid countries resisting aggressors, its authors argued; the president already had plenary authority from his powers as commander in chief and head of state. He could constitutionally establish an executive agreement for a quid pro quo arrangement to swap fifty World War I battleships in exchange for ninety-nine-year leases on British air and naval bases for the hemispheric defense of the United States.[241]

Donovan began lobbying Cabinet officials and senators to gain support for FDR's counterproposal to Churchill to swap destroyers for naval bases for ninety-nine years. When the deal was completed, FDR acknowledged his debt to Donovan.[242]

Still, FDR needed to "feed [Congress] molasses," he told Lothian, to stave off the anger of congressional isolationists and other critics.[243] Kennedy delivered the molasses in FDR's telegram of August 13, 1940. It asked that Britain approve of the acquisition of its bases in Newfoundland, Bermuda, the Bahamas, Jamaica, St. Lucia, Trinidad, and British Guiana by the American military for ninety-nine years in exchange for destroyers. It also requested, as Kennedy had urged, that the British guarantee never to surrender their fleet to Germany but scuttle it or sail it to ports within the British Empire if Britain's survival seemed imperiled. Both assurances were necessary, Kennedy explained to Churchill, for Roosevelt to justify to the American public that extending aid to Britain was essential to the security of the Western Hemisphere and to offset congressional and public criticism.[244]

"We will let them have anything they want on these Islands," Churchill told Kennedy, but he balked at the required molasses. Accepting some obsolete destroyers in exchange for Britain's imperial possessions could have an oppressive effect on public opinion, Churchill warned. Better to give the bases in Bermuda and Newfoundland outright as a gesture of friendship.[245] It was a matter of national pride, of sustaining Britain's "splendid" morale, Churchill explained. As concerned about political ramifications and face-saving as Churchill was, Roosevelt was too, and insisted on swapping the rest of the bases for the destroyers. Churchill sternly warned FDR two days later: "In any use you may make of this repeated assurance [that the fleet would not be surrendered] you will please bear in mind the disastrous effect from our point of view and perhaps also from yours of allowing any impression to grow that we regard the conquest of the British Islands and its naval bases as any other than an impossible contingency."[246]

Despite Kennedy's initial support for the destroyer deal, his enthusiasm waned as he grew anxious about his old fear, American aid to Britain. He was worried about two things: the distribution of the Royal Fleet and a long-term, open-ended commitment by the United States to aid Britain. If Britain were defeated and Churchill's government were dismissed from power, Kennedy reminded Washington, the prime minister's promises to scuttle the fleet would not be binding upon another British government. It would seek peace on terms most favorable to it and use the fleet to its greatest advantage. "I therefore think it might be well to decide how we can protect ourselves in this event," Kennedy wrote to Hull.[247] In addition, the argument that the first line of defense is the English Channel would be used to justify any action taken by the American government and could involve the United States in a war for which it could end up "signing a blank check" and holding the bag for everything.[248]

Kennedy also resented being left out of the destroyer deal negotiations. They had begun in London and involved Kennedy, but they were quickly transferred to Washington, where FDR and Churchill haggled over the details through Lord Lothian and ignored Kennedy.[249] Excluded from the discussions, ignorant of the negotiations, unhappy that the British had information that he did not, Kennedy protested to Washington on August 14: "It would be helpful to me here if I could know the gist of Lothian's message of August 8."[250] Washington responded by turning a deaf ear.

Kennedy tried again. Surely you know about "the very embarrassing situation" I am in regarding the destroyer negotiations, he cabled the president on August 27, 1940, about a week before the details were finalized. There is "no commonsense explanation" for my lack of knowledge of the arrangements. Lothian had been informed about the details; why haven't I? If not for Churchill's cables and some additional information sent through the London embassy, Kennedy said, I would have known virtually nothing. With only secondhand information, it "has been impossible for me to make any contribution to the destroyer-bases discussion," but I maybe could have made one. "Frankly and honestly I do not enjoy being a dummy, I am very unhappy about the whole position and of course there is always the alternative of resigning, which I would not hesitate to do if conditions were not as they are," he complained to Roosevelt.[251]

Roosevelt sent a swift, soothing reply the next day:

> The destroyer and base matter were handled in part through you and in part through Lothian. . . . There is no thought of embarrassing you and only a practical necessity for personal conversations makes it easier to handle details here. . . . Don't forget that you are not only not a dummy but are essential to all of us both in the Government and in the Nation.[252]

Despite the presidential pat on the head, Kennedy continued to feel aggrieved, and FDR continued to ignore him. "Now, of course, as I told you, I know nothing about the background in the United States for all these negotiations," Kennedy wrote with sarcasm to Hull as the negotiations were nearing their end. "England never gets the impression they are licked and therefore they never can understand why they should not get the best of the trade." Grumbling and griping had grown in Britain over swapping bases for well-worn destroyers, "but because I had no background I have not been able to do anything about it."[253]

"Explain" to the prime minister, FDR told Kennedy, that the American public would only be convinced that their defenses had been strengthened if the destroyers had been exchanged for bases and not given as gifts. Kennedy was pleased to have been given a job to do. But a few days later he learned that he had once again been cut out from the negotiations and had not even been notified of the signing.[254]

Certainly Roosevelt was notorious for circumventing his nominal top people, but possibly no one was ignored so consistently as Kennedy. FDR wanted to run his own foreign policy in his own way without his ambassador's constant naysaying and interference. Kennedy had, after all, conducted his own brand of foreign policy without Washington's sanction. In addition, he had a reputation well known to FDR for leaking information to the press. Kennedy believed that Roosevelt's motive in bypassing him was to prevent his conversations and commitments to the English from being published and read by disapproving eyes.[255] The president had every reason to be wary of his high-strung, independent-minded ambassador with whom he strongly disagreed on foreign policy, and Kennedy had every reason for supposing that Roosevelt intended to bypass him.

On September 2, 1940, the day before the deal was to be announced, a group of English and American officials including Churchill and Lord Beaverbrook, his influential minister of aircraft production, and the American military observers accompanying Admiral Ghormley, whose mission Kennedy always opposed, assembled at the "Destroyer Dinner," so christened by Churchill, to celebrate closing the deal.[256] "A good dinner with important company is a familiar British trick to take Americans into camp," Kennedy noted in his memoir, and it seemed to work.[257] Kennedy, who had peevishly kept tabs on when and how much Churchill drank, had a new gripe about Churchill's behavior—the frequency with which his long daily afternoon naps made him inaccessible or late or were inconvenient for officials or turned Whitehall topsy-turvy and stalled government business, matters of little concern to Churchill. The prime minister had not even been available to see him at 3:30 on August 14, the day after Roosevelt had sent him the telegram about his offer to furnish the British with destroyers. It had interfered with his nap, the prime minister explained as he apologized to Kennedy. "Imagine," Kennedy confided to his memoir, "this was the message Churchill had been waiting for for weeks, and on which he said the fate of Civilization might well depend, and he had to have his afternoon nap!"[258] And on the evening of the dinner party, Kennedy gleefully noted in his diary, his sleepy host must have just awakened from his nap and was fifteen minutes late to his own party.

The guests sat back enjoying a box of Churchill's favorite cigars, a gift from Kennedy, "to even up the destroyer-bases deal," he told them.[259] Their wide-ranging conversation concerned the negotiations over destroyer bases and their implications for the American and British elections; the Blitz, the success of night bombing, and the estimates of the number of people killed (780, according to Churchill); the likelihood of Hitler's attempting an invasion at Dover; Churchill's willingness to repudiate the 1918 war debts; and the training of British pilots in American airfields. They also discussed Churchill's belief that Hitler would not gain air superiority and could not successfully invade Britain.

Churchill told his guests that he had promised Roosevelt that he would not embarrass him before the presidential election by publicly discussing Churchill's original proposal to hand the bases over as gifts, nor did he want the newspapers to speculate about American entry into the war as a result of the deal. But he owed it to his own electorate to explain to them before their next national election why he had agreed to a swap of Britain's naval bases for a few dozen decrepit vessels. The arrangement made the British look "very silly," said Lord Beaverbrook, who had always opposed the deal.[260]

What shape were the destroyers in? Churchill asked Kennedy. Kennedy did not know, but it seemed to be an "as is" deal. Had they been "overhauled"? Had they "submarine detectors" or "depth bomb machinery"? Churchill asked Ghormley. Ghormley did not know. "Will they be able to come across the ocean on their own power?" Beaverbrook asked. "Perhaps," Kennedy replied.

Kennedy's long-standing suspicions about Churchill's apparent generosity and specious guilelessness in the deal were finally confirmed. Churchill wanted a blank check from the United States, as Kennedy had long suspected, although he was surprised by the prime minister's frankness. The prime minister told his American guests: "I always expected if I made such a gesture [giving the bases], you would have to give us something and of course I believe that the something is going to be, sooner or later, big financial credits or gifts." Had he been prime minister after World War I, he said, he would have repudiated Britain's debts to the United States. Britain's contribution in 1918 had been manpower, and hence that of the United States should be money. It was obvious to Kennedy that Churchill could easily have repudiated Britain's current debt to the United States[261] and that he had no reluctance to ask for anything from the U.S. without paying for it. The United States would have little choice but to grant Britain's request since the British would argue that they were fighting the war for us, Kennedy wrote. "I know the American people," Churchill had told Kennedy, "and they wouldn't be so low-down as not to appreciate the importance of this gift when we want something later on."[262] The destroyer deal would enhance the president's prestige, Kennedy predicted, so long as the American public did not learn that we could have had the bases for free.

Ghormley, who had been informed by the British, told Kennedy that the agreement was to be announced at six o'clock on September 3, 1940, the first anniversary of the war. "Of course nothing had been said to me about it," Kennedy complained to his diary; Roosevelt had been as "inconsiderate" as always.[263] By mid-day on September 9, the destroyers were decommissioned by the United States Army; a few hours later they were sailing to the Atlantic, ready to do battle against the Nazis.

The British were "inordinately happy" about the deal, Kennedy cabled Hull.[264] The king wrote Roosevelt two days after the announcement was made: "I cannot tell you how much I have appreciated your efforts to help us, and admired the skill with which you have handled a very delicate situation."[265] Kennedy was right. Roosevelt did gain a lot of prestige from the deal. The American public overwhelmingly approved of it and praised the president for his shrewdness in getting the better part of the bargain. Even FDR's opponents, who criticized him for bypassing Congress and accused him of flirting with dictatorship, were silenced when he shrewdly likened the destroyer deal to the Louisiana Purchase.[266]

Kennedy appeared to be delighted too. The agreement threw a ring of impenetrable steel around the United States to protect it from the German navy, Kennedy told Hull. What could possibly be better than this? Regardless of any criticism, the president could at least say: "I have conducted the affairs of this country in such a manner that it has been possible to obtain these important bases for 99 years with no real loss of anything worthwhile to America."[267]

But that was not quite so. In his delight over a shrewd Yankee horse trade, Kennedy, still the diplomatic rookie, may not have realized that he had just lost another joust with Britain's masterful, resolute, and cunning prime minister. The United States had sacrificed its prized neutrality and was now on a limited war footing. The agreement had irrevocably committed the United States, without any formal treaty, to aid Britain by "methods short of war" and had dragged a grudging United States halfway into armed conflict with bellicose Germany.[268]

Churchill, of course, did realize how much Britain had gained. In his six-volume memoirs on World War II, he wrote that the destroyer deal marked America's transition from neutrality to non-belligerency. It "was the first of a long succession of increasingly unneutral acts in the Atlantic which were of the utmost service to us." By all historical standards, the German government would have been entirely justified in declaring war upon the United States, he concluded.[269] The symbolism of the destroyer deal was more important than any material object.

Just what effect the destroyer deal had on Hitler's plan is unknown, but it meant that Germany could no longer ignore the United States. It might have been one factor in his decision to forego Operation Sea Lion, the invasion of Britain, and to focus his attention on the invasion of the Soviet Union in the spring. It also hastened the negotiations that created the Tripartite Pact between Italy, Japan, and Germany in September, aimed at keeping the Unites States out of the war.[270]

By December 1, 1940, when Kennedy had returned to the United States to resign and his fatalism was once again firmly entrenched, he spoke his mind to Arthur Krock, his lifelong friend, about the deal. The ambassador told him that he believed that it was "the 'worst ever,' that we have no contract for the bases, and that when 'all the facts are known,' they will 'shock the American people.'"[271]

In his attitude about the destroyer deal, as in later legislation for Lend-Lease, Kennedy wanted to give and not give the destroyers to Britain. The ambassador's was a vacillating, muddled, equivocal position reflecting his affection for Britain coupled with his desire to keep the United States out of conflict, a *sic et non* approach seen more fully in the debate over Lend-Lease.

On September 3, 1940, Ambassador Kennedy and Winston Churchill and members of the cabinet attended a service in Westminster Abbey commemorating the outbreak of the war. Churchill "somehow contrive[d] to look more confident every day," noted the *New York Times* correspondent James B. Reston. As they waited for the service to begin, screaming sirens echoed throughout the historic abbey, warning of an imminent attack. The prime minister stood up, walked over to the cloisters, and talked at length to the dean. Churchill called the king and advised him not to attend the service. It would not do to see the king leave the service after the raid had begun, Kennedy surmised. While waiting for the decision about whether the service would proceed, Halifax and Eden were conversing with Kennedy. Eden told Kennedy that if a bomb hit during the service, it would probably be the only way he, Eden, could be buried in the Abbey. Churchill returned to his seat and an announcement was made that the service would be resumed. The Luftwaffe had attacked London three times that day and fought fiercely all over southeast England. Kent and Essex had been particularly hit hard. But the RAF's red and black Spitfires diving out of the clouds escorted by Messerschmitt fighters had broken up the Nazi fighter patrols, attacked their bombers one by one, and then driven them back toward the Channel. By the day's end, the RAF had downed twenty-five Nazi planes. Britain lost only fifteen.[272] A grateful nation gave thanks.

"There's hell to pay here tonight," Kennedy cabled Washington on September 6, 1940, his fifty-second birthday, as he rode horseback through the fields at St. Leonard's during an air-raid warning and saw bombers in the sky.[273] London survived its most extensive air raids to date. The Battle of Britain entered a new phase, the Blitz, which lasted until the eve of Hitler's attack on the Soviet Union on June 22, 1941. On September 7, instead of ordering Operation Sea Lion, Hitler ordered his bombers to attack the world's biggest city, partly in retaliation for Britain's bombing of Berlin on August 25. For fifty-seven nights Londoners endured unrelenting, massive bombing raids by the Luftwaffe, designed to destroy their morale and to reduce their great city to uninhabitable rubble. France's General Maxime Weygand predicted that Britain "would have its neck wrung like a chicken."[274] To which Churchill was later to respond in Ottawa, December 30, 1941: "some chicken; some neck!"[275] But on October 12, Hitler postponed the invasion for the winter and on October 20 canceled the daytime bombing of London and was to follow it with nighttime bombing runs.[276]

"All indications point to an attack coming," Kennedy notified Washington on September 11, 1940. RAF reconnaissance photos showed that there was a "terrific" lineup of ships and barges and harbors with magnetic mines around the battleships, all in anticipation of an invasion. British officials from Churchill on down were hoping for it, they assured the ambassador; not only would it be a major setback for Hitler, but it would also give them a clear indication of how extensive his power was and how successfully Britain could cope with it.[277] Kennedy was doubtful—rightly so. Hitler's preparations were too obvious, the ambassador argued, and Hitler still had not defeated the RAF, a necessary precondition for his attempting an invasion.

Politically, Churchill—"the God of all," as Kennedy sarcastically dubbed him—was still strong and popular; but if the Blitz should undermine Britain's morale, unrest would follow, with untold consequences. The British are simply unaware of the real dangers they face, he said; thus among them there is an unrealistic optimism.[278] They refuse to take the German menace seriously, and censorship of the news keeps them ignorant. Kennedy sounded his familiar refrain: Despite the government's "stiff upper lip" and cheerful impression "that all is well," unless the United States signs a blank check and provides the financial means for Britain's struggle, something he continued to oppose, "I do not believe that [the British] have a chance," he told Hull.[279] At present, the government is coping with the sleeplessness, poor transportation, and poor health of the Britons.[280]

Certainly the facts supported Kennedy's well-informed skeptical view of Britain's future. Despite Kennedy's views, Roosevelt was ultimately convinced that Britain was a worthy investment and did provide a blank check and the essential financial means Britain needed. Further, Hitler was thwarted in his design; he did not win air supremacy over the Channel or the British Isles, and Britain's morale did not collapse; qualities of character like guts, discipline, and unflinching, bloody-minded determination, which Churchill embodied and was able to muster among the British, did matter in the fall of 1940. But most significantly, Hitler himself changed his mind. On September 17 he shelved his invasion plans for Britain and on October 12 called the invasion off for the time being. His Luftwaffe had been stretched beyond its limits; London was simply not within its fighting range. He decided that the Soviet Union, long his ideological enemy despite their diplomatic marriage of convenience consummated on the eve of war, was more suitable prey.

If not as accomplished a diplomat at the Court of St. James's as Washington might have liked, Kennedy succeeded in honing the art of diplomacy in his own little world at Hyannis Port, where his beloved family lived and to whom he longed to return. Kennedy's letters to his family during this time were like a course in diplomacy, similar to the dispatches he sent to Washington, a rich mix of his pessimistic assessment of the horrific perils Britain faced, the bombing and invasion it expected, Hitler's victory on the Continent, and how right Kennedy had been about everything.[281]

As for the English, Kennedy noted, there were many angles to this war that they do not yet fully understand, he wrote to his son John. Their censors prevent them from being well informed by covering up and by rewriting newspaper copy about the war, something the Germans are doing as well. So, what should you believe or disbelieve? "I don't know," he told John. "I am feeling very well" and "haven't had the slightest touch of nervousness," Kennedy wrote, but he remarked that other people were beginning to break. All and all, "it is a great experience. The only thing I am afraid of is that I won't be able to live long enough to tell all that I see and feel about the crisis," he wrote, in an I-told-you-so mood. "When I hear these mental midgets . . . talking about my desire for appeasement and being critical of it, my blood fairly boils. What is this war going to prove? And what is it going to do to civilization? The answer to the first question is nothing; and to the second I shutter [*sic*] even to think about it," Kennedy said.[282]

Kennedy's letters home were filled with charming personal anecdotes about his own often harrowing experiences and sympathetic descriptions of the sufferings of the stoic Londoners enduring the Blitz. He had grown to admire their steadfastness in the face of adversity and the threat of invasion. "The last three nights in London have been simply hell," he wrote to Rose on September 10. The night before, he had donned his steel helmet, climbed out on the Chancery roof, and stayed there until two o'clock in the morning watching as the German bombers set London ablaze, running in relay teams to the French coast every ten minutes, back and forth in twenty-five-minute shifts, for seven to nine hours a night, paralyzing any attempt at normality. Kennedy could see the silhouette of St Paul's dome against the inferno fed by the incessant German bombers. He even slept in the Chancery air-raid shelter and "did very nicely for myself."[283]

The bombing inflicted terrific damage. The Germans wrecked London's communication system and bombed power plants, docks, and railways. He saw seven huge fires in London one evening and worried that the Air Raid Precaution Group and the firefighters would soon be physical wrecks. Manufacturing had "gone to pot."[284] Prince's Gate just escaped being hit when a bomb exploded in the barracks across from Rotten Row, and another fell on the bridle path across from the house. Even the Natural History Museum in Kensington was practically gutted by bombs and fire.[285]

A bomb made a direct hit on a house fifty yards from Herschel Johnson's, destroying it completely and killing six. Johnson barely escaped but is well and hearty, Kennedy reported.[286] His own garage was bombed twice, and the car he was riding in was tossed up onto the sidewalk by a bomb.[287] As he returned from the Foreign Office, a time bomb blew up about fifty yards from his car near Piccadilly and Bond Street. "Boy, this is the life," he told Washington.[288]

The American embassy urged Americans to move out of London. Despite the fact that it made him vulnerable to charges of cowardice and failure of nerve by officials in the Foreign Office, Kennedy followed the embassy's advice and returned every night to his Windsor Great Park country home near Windsor Castle.[289] "I thought my daffodils were yellow until I met Joe Kennedy," Churchill scoffed.[290] Even Halifax noted that a bomb had fallen very near Kennedy's house outside of London. "Everybody is no doubt inclined to think [it] a judgment on Joe for feeling he was likely to be safer there than in London."[291] In a chatty letter to his daughter Jean, the ambassador wrote that the Air Ministry complained that his house was so colorful that it made a superb landmark for the German pilots. It would have to be camouflaged, the ministry insisted.[292] Even camouflaging his house failed to prevent several near misses. During one raid, a bomb landed only three hundred yards from the house and cut a beech tree in half.[293] On another occasion, he narrowly escaped being hit by a Messerschmitt 109 that had lost its propeller in a dogfight. Apparently the pilot tried to make a forced landing on Kennedy's front lawn, just grazing his house, gliding over the tops of the trees, and finally alighting at the royal park close by. He was so close that "we could see the fuzz on the pilot's face and almost count his buttons," the ambassador joked. "I don't know what else they [the Germans] can do unless they come in my front room."[294] They almost did. Two bombs destroyed several cottages on the estate and injured eleven people as Kennedy lay in bed and felt the walls of his house trembling and saw the lampshades flying across his bed.[295] His colleagues found a bomb near his Windsor house with his initials on it. "Initials don't count," the ambassador cheerfully declared.[296]

Kennedy kept a running tally of all the air raids he went through and came up with the impressive total of 244.[297] Yet only on two occasions was he in an air-raid shelter, once on an inspection tour at the embassy and again in the House of Commons when Churchill's speech was interrupted by the drone of the Luftwaffe and everyone was herded to safety. Dubbed the "'most-bombed' diplomat" by the press, he said that the bombs did interrupt his sleep, but that was "nothing new to married men who, like myself, have many children." He wearily complained that London's great problem was lack of sleep.[298]

The chances of anything happening to him are "one in a million," he told Rose. "I am completely a fatalist about bombing accidents. I don't think anything is going to happen to me, and for that reason it doesn't worry me the slightest bit. I am still riding horseback every morning. I play golf on Saturdays and Sundays. My stomach is quite good. The only thing that gives me any concern at all is getting home." But, he said, "I feel that I must see this through."[299]

His letters also revealed his boundless love for his wife and children, written to one or more of them nearly every day, especially his two elder sons, whom he had sent to elite Protestant and secular schools, the better to prepare them for their careers.[300] Kennedy's letters included paternal advice and admonitions about every aspect of their lives, jokes at his own expense, and gossip about their friends. He deliberately spread the news around to encourage his children to exchange letters and to show each child an equal amount of attention and make them all feel equally loved and important.[301] "I have tried to divide up all the news among the children, so after you have read all the letters you will be up to date," he told Rose.[302]

After telling Jack how homesick he felt when he heard Jack's voice on his birthday record on September 10, he advised him to let his book have a long run rather than to write articles that critics might attack. There was plenty of time to do that, his father said.[303]

In his letter to Bobby, Kennedy gave a long description of his assessment of the likelihood of Britain's being invaded, its political situation and Churchill's clout, censorship vis-à-vis the United States, and a fatal scenario in which Germany, allied with Italy, would move into southeastern Europe, defeat Turkey, and gain control over the oil wells and the Suez Canal. "Should they get control of these oil fields, the prospect for England becomes darker by the minute."

But he ended his lecture on diplomacy on a more paternal and affectionate note:

> Well, I am terribly sorry I have not had a chance to see you this summer Bob, but I do hope you will put in a good effort this year. It is boys of your age who are going to find themselves in a very changed world and the only way you can hold up your end is to prepare your mind so that you will be able to accept each situation as it comes along, so don't, I beg of you, waste any time. Do all the things necessary to get yourself in good physical condition and work hard.[304]

The ambassador admonished Teddy, his youngest, for failing to write all those letters he had promised his father. He compared Teddy unfavorably to his sisters, who managed to write once a week at least. He and Bobby were the poorest correspondents among the Kennedys, their father chided. But he did appreciate Teddy's heartfelt cheerleading "Hip! Hip! Horray!" on the family recording. "Couldn't have been better," his father wrote. "Well, old boy, write me some letters and I want you to know that I miss seeing you a lot," his father told him and expressed the hope that their swimming in Palm Beach the next winter would make up for his not swimming with the boy at Cape Cod that summer. "After all, you are my pal, aren't you?"

Kennedy passed along a good laugh at himself when he told Teddy that as he waited at the embassy for a dinner party in his dinner jacket, he just happened to realize that he had forgotten to shave for a couple of days. "So you can see how busy I am." He also described the guns shooting and bombs exploding throughout London, the fires set by the Luftwaffe, and the abysmally noisy conditions of life in air-raid shelters at night. "I'm sure, of course, you wouldn't be scared . . . but you might get a little fidgety," he told his eight-year-old son. The sight of the poor women and children and the homeless people in the East End, the most bombed part of London, is really pitiable, Kennedy wrote. After enduring four days of bombing and seeing everything they had go up in flames, they looked like refugees. "I hope when you grow up you will dedicate your life to trying to work out plans to make people happy instead of making them miserable, as war does today," his father told him.[305]

Kennedy gave Rose his social news and gossip in his letter to her of September 10 and described his dinner with Churchill and Beaverbrook and the American military observers, General Emmons, General Strong, and Admiral Ghormley, and several nights later, one with the Duke and Duchess of Kent. Kennedy told his wife that Nancy Astor was getting "nervous and quite a bit fidgety," although "she is still terribly nice." She gave him a valuable antique snuffbox for his birthday and he gave her quite a licking on the golf course, he boasted: "she won't dare talk golf to me any more."[306] "Well Darling, I've dictated the news but I want you to know that I love you and miss you terribly," he told his wife. He promised to take care of himself and to do his job, but "I just wish I could be with you and help with the children." It would not be long before he was home now.[307]

Even while London burned, Kennedy found time to acquire keepsakes for his family to remind them of their adventures during his ambassadorship. When Charles Corbin, the French ambassador, closed up his London house, Kennedy reported to Rose that he took over Corbin's French chef as well as Corbin's wine cellar. The chef could "puree a bale of hay and make it taste like chocolate ice cream." Kennedy shipped the wine along with some champagne to the United States, to be drunk at family weddings.[308] But then he had to tell Rose that the Germans had sunk the ship on his birthday, September 6—"so that's that."[309] He also bought four "very lovely little pictures" by "a very good man" as well as silver selected and appraised by Christie's, and the royal tea set donated by the queen, for which he paid double at the Red Cross sale, because "I thought it would be most interesting for the family." Queen Elizabeth wrote Kennedy "a very sweet note" in which she explained that she feared that the set would look lonesome, so she had a tray made to go with it. She presented it to the Kennedys as a token of friendship from her. Nor were home furnishings too mundane for the ambassador's attention; he obediently did Rose's bidding and looked for "bright and cheery" material to match her scheme for their Palm Beach living room; he figured it would be a real savings at $2.00 or $2.25 a yard.[310]

The loot was carefully selected to appeal to his family's interests: books on Napoleon and his family from the Red Cross sale; a volume on the Duke of Wellington and other great statesmen, which "will be of intense interest for the boys"; plus a variety of other valuable old books at prices so low it was ridiculous.[311] Even in the midst of the threat to Britain's survival, Kennedy didn't refrain from asking the prime minister for a personal favor for his family: autographed posters, one for each of his nine children, and excerpts from his two famous speeches—"otherwise I will get into plenty of trouble."[312] "I think they will become important historical documents," Kennedy told his wife. The treasure trove was sent in two separate mailings, half in each mailing, lest everything be lost at once.[313] Nothing was too good for his family, and no obstacle or inconvenience to anyone too great to accommodate them.

He spent his fifty-second birthday in war-torn London listening over and over again to a recording of his children's somewhat off-key but peppy voices and to Rose accompanying them on the piano. "Your piano touch was never better," he wrote her.[314]

He talked with Beaverbrook, Halifax, and Montagu Norman about going home. They all told him they regarded his leaving as tragic and recommended he go home, rest up, and then return—suggestions Kennedy rejected. "That doesn't suit me at all," he told Rose. "When I go home, I want to stay home. I don't want to do anything which will harm the British, but on the other hand I have no misgivings about finishing my job here as soon as it is clear whether or not Hitler plans to invade." After six years devoted to public life, "I am tired."

Look for me to return toward the end of the month, he told Rose in a letter on September 10, 1940; by then he would have been through so much bombing that "nobody in America could think I had left before I had seen a big part of the show," or challenge his courage or his reason for departure.[315]

A brooding Kennedy remained in London, ignored, bypassed by his boss, and out of sorts with the administration. He was thoroughly dissatisfied with the liberal clique surrounding the president and miffed at being ignored and undercut by the State Department and the administration. Moreover, he had long suspected that FDR and his administration were taking steps to drag the United States into war, despite Roosevelt's assurances to the contrary.[316] Privately, Kennedy belonged with the isolationist critics on Capitol Hill; publicly, however, he was still tied to Roosevelt's "provocative" policies,[317] which had escalated from neutrality into "non-belligerency."[318]

Kennedy's equivocal acceptance of the president's more vigorous methods in foreign policy—the president's methods short of war, Kennedy's self-pity and desperate loneliness for his family, his irritation and embarrassment over FDR's repeated slights and slipshod style, his boredom and his resentment of British snubs, all led him to insist upon returning to the United States despite Washington's objection. Rumors swirled that he would endorse Roosevelt's opponent, Wendell Willkie, in the 1940 election and resign his position. British Foreign Office officials were relieved about his possible resignation despite the praise and the many tributes Kennedy received. They feared the influence he could have on the upcoming presidential election and the subsequent course of American aid to Britain. They viewed him with contempt, labeling him as little better than "a Fifth Columnist."[319]

For his part, Roosevelt apparently believed that his talkative and pessimistic ambassador could sabotage his foreign policy and undermine his reelection chances less if he remained abroad on a tight diplomatic leash, restrained, if not by loyalty, then by fear of public chastisement as an unfaithful, self-serving ingrate. But FDR, as it turned out, was wrong.

By early October, Kennedy had told reporters: "This is my last public job."[320] One crisis after another had kept him in London despite the speculation about when he would resign. But by the fall of 1940, Kennedy had decided to go home. He "looks mentally exhausted; physically tired, lacks interest," wrote George Bilainkin, a British journalist for the Allied correspondents with whom Kennedy maintained a friendly relationship. He had had enough of England, her war, and her diplomacy.[321]

But exhaustion was not the only motive for Kennedy's return; he also wanted to come home before Election Day. "I know more about Europe than anybody else in this country because I've been closer to it longer," he boasted. "I'm going to make it a point to educate America to the situation."[322] He wanted to tell Americans that Britain could not survive without a massive amount of American aid that could never be repaid; that war meant bloodshed and hardship; that finally "American boys in uniform might be compelled to follow American dollars across the Atlantic and into battle."[323]

Speculation raged on both sides of the Atlantic about Kennedy's return to the United States. The British Foreign Office minutes revealed that officials despised him and were worried about his "defeatism" and hoped that Washington had "the Ambassador's number."[324] They took potshots at him, vented their disgust and contempt, questioned his courage, and accused him of "going to pieces"[325] and of being little more than "the biggest Fifth Columnist in the country."[326] They also reported conversations with "a highly reliable member of the American Embassy" who believed that the ambassador "had lost his nerve."[327]

Officials also speculated on the ambassador's influence on Britain's future negotiations with Washington, the success of which was essential to Britain's survival. They discussed Kennedy's influence on Roosevelt's chances for reelection and worried about Kennedy's rumored endorsement of Wendell Willkie.[328] They must have heard the rumors circulating in diplomatic circles and among journalists that Kennedy would officially lead a peace offensive when he returned to London.[329]

The British had good reason to be concerned. A secret memorandum from the American embassy in London written by Graham Hatton on October 18, 1940, and part of the Foreign Office file, reported on Kennedy's conversations with Hull about his retirement. It referred to a "sensational and influential" article written by the ambassador in which he endorsed Roosevelt's opponent. Hatton interpreted Kennedy's action as a direct attack on Roosevelt's attempt to prepare the country for war. Since Kennedy could be extremely dangerous in his present mood and could threaten Britain's negotiations with the Roosevelt administration,

Hatton suggested that Kennedy be denied access to Britain's financial records. "He might make damaging use of them," Hatton wrote, "both against Mr. Roosevelt and, indirectly of course, against us."[330]

When Kennedy paid a courtesy call on Halifax to announce his resignation, Kennedy described his article as a stinging indictment of the Roosevelt administration for having "talked a lot and done very little." The ambassador was "very much out of temper with the United States Government and the President" for failing to inform him—Kennedy—of their policies or activities for the last two or three months, the foreign secretary wrote in the official minutes. If by some chance Kennedy did not return to the United States, he told Halifax that the article would be published by November 1, the eve of the election—a rather heavy-handed piece of blackmail. Kennedy, little comforted by his host's attempts to soothe his feelings, left their interview "a very disappointed and rather embittered man."[331]

The impact of such an article by Kennedy "would be of considerable importance," Halifax warned his colleagues.[332] It confirmed their worst suspicions: that Wall Street had won Kennedy's loyalty again; therefore, like Wall Street, he had decided to favor Willkie. Given that Roosevelt's support would be useful if not necessary to any political ambitions that Kennedy had for himself or his sons, his support of Willkie was not likely; but the article did work to the ambassador's advantage by giving him the appearance of impressing the British within the administration.

However, an unsigned note in the Foreign Office minutes on October 19 reported on a conversation in which Kennedy said that although he thought it would be disastrous if the United States joined the war, he intended in no way to embarrass Roosevelt or to interfere with the supply of arms to Britain. He also stated that the United States should recognize Britain's commitment to fighting the war by *giving*, not lending, the British money for supplies when their treasury ran empty, a reassuring position for officials, reminiscent of Churchill's, and the germ of Lend-Lease.[333]

Rumors and speculation on the other side of the Atlantic increased as the chess game between king and pawn played out. Press hounds asked Hull on October 15 whether or not Kennedy would return to the United States on October 23. The secretary vaguely answered that the ambassador would be returning "before long," but he declined to say when or to confirm the rumor that Kennedy's resignation was imminent. The White House, too, was silent. Roosevelt has heard the rumors, his press secretary said, but "I don't know whether there is anything new as between the present and the old reports."[334]

The contest between president and ambassador climaxed the next day. Kennedy sent FDR a cablegram demanding that FDR allow him to come home. Other ambassadors had been permitted to come home, he argued, whereas he had heard that he was to remain in Britain until after the election.[335] Even so, he still needed official authorization to return or face accusations from his critics that he had run out on the British during the Blitz.[336]

Kennedy called Under Secretary Welles on October 16 and told him that he was coming home or else. If he was not home before the elections, the ambassador informed Welles, he had instructed his ever-faithful secretary, Edward Moore, to release a statement to the press in which Kennedy complained about Roosevelt's treatment of him during the last three months: the appointment of Donovan and other military officials, failing to give Kennedy information about the destroyer deal—"the worst ever," as Kennedy described it—and ignoring him in general. This not-so-veiled threat worked; just a few hours later the ambassador was authorized to come home.[337] An announcement from the White House simply said that "Ambassador Joseph P. Kennedy will return soon from London for "consultations" with President Roosevelt, but he will not resign."[338]

The president wrote to Kennedy to invite him to come home to recover from the "severe strain" of his ambassadorship and to meet with him to discuss his reactions to Britain's wartime experience. But Roosevelt also requested that his ambassador not make any statements to the press and that he come directly to the White House for "consultations."[339] Taking no chances on the administration's change of heart, Kennedy immediately told the press that he would leave for the United States on October 23. "It is doubted he will return as Ambassador—and it is certain he will not if he has his way about it," a *New York Times* correspondent wrote.[340] Columnists Joseph Alsop and Robert Kintner surmised that Kennedy's story about his impending retirement might have been orchestrated by the "mercurial" and gloomy ambassador himself and might be the last move in his "exciting little game" with Roosevelt.[341]

Many astute observers had been plainly baffled by FDR's obvious reluctance to allow Kennedy to return right before the election. Roosevelt wanted Kennedy to stay in London as long as possible to keep him quiet and out of the way. Kennedy wanted to come home as soon as possible to express his opinions to anyone willing to listen, and intended to do so convincingly and persuasively the moment he got through customs.[342] The *New York Post* speculated about a row brewing between the president and his ambassador. It reported that the ambassador was angry because the administration had underfilled its commitment to help Britain and because FDR insisted on sending military missions to London that circumvented him. Upon his return, it reported, Kennedy would officially or unofficially lead a peace offensive.[343] The International News Service out of Washington asserted that Kennedy was "profoundly pessimistic" about Britain's military situation, and in profound disagreement with the president over Britain's chances and with the administration's policy of extending all aid short of war to Britain.[344] Both the news service and the *New York Times* suggested that the president intended to keep Kennedy in London until after the election, fearing that he might undermine support for Britain—or more likely fearing that he might undermine support for Roosevelt. Alsop and Kintner believed that Kennedy's gloomy views about the weakness and near defeat of the British Empire, about its little value as an ally—even if correct—could undermine a basic tenet of American foreign policy: the British Empire is "our only ally and our only protection against world catastrophe." "If Kennedy does come home," they warned, "it will be well to listen to him carefully but to take his jeremiads with a grain of salt."[345] Arthur Krock wrote in his *New York Times* column that the ambassador's "gloomy" views about the war's outcome might give the impression that the administration is "backing the wrong horse, which won't be helpful in November," and could reduce the present public support for aid to Britain "short of war." Even if Kennedy had been "gloomy," Krock reminded his readers, he had also been right.[346]

Rose saw it that way, too. She offered to go right up to the White House as any wife would and tell everyone there that she was worried about her husband's health and that he had done enough and should be sent home. She also promised to chloroform him until after the election was over to keep him from expressing his defeatist views and undermining the president's chances for reelection.[347]

But FDR knew his man. He realized that his ambassador was best kept at a distance until he had simmered down, and that his diatribes were so much verbiage, not to be taken seriously. Although Kennedy meant every syllable of abuse at the moment, he forgot it all quickly. If reminded of an unkind remark later, he would either deny saying it in all deceptive sincerity or claim he meant nothing of the sort, even if he had said it.[348]

Throughout the week before his departure, Kennedy shrugged off press inquiries about his rumored resignation and busied himself in a round of official goodbyes. He lunched with the king and queen at Buckingham Palace,[349] had his picture taken shaking hands with Winston Churchill at 10 Downing Street,[350] and called on Halifax to say goodbye. Kennedy expected a close fight between Roosevelt and Willkie, he told the foreign secretary, and "was breathing threats of brutal speech to Roosevelt" upon his return. However, Halifax, who did not particularly like Kennedy, knew that "his bark was much worse than his bite" and predicted that he would not make things harder for FDR and would help him in the end.[351]

Kennedy's last days as ambassador ended as his first days had begun, in a flurry of courtesy calls. He called on the Chinese, Brazilian, Portuguese, Chilean, Argentinian, Egyptian, and Spanish ambassadors. He also saw the Japanese and Russian and Turkish ambassadors. With few exceptions, their views were the same and to Kennedy's liking. Most were "very pessimistic" about England's chances of surviving the war. The Portuguese ambassador thought England's situation was "terrifically bad," as did the Chilean ambassador. He called England's situation "grave." The Argentinian ambassador expected a short war and claimed, on account of the destroyer deal, that America had already entered it. Despite Britain's courage and high morale, "the prospects are bad," he said. The Egyptian ambassador, "a very smart fellow," Kennedy wrote, thinks that the main struggle will be in Egypt. Britain must stop seeing it as a secondary issue and send troops and equipment there as soon as possible. The Spanish ambassador said little except that his people wanted neutrality and no more war. Both the Russian and the Turkish ambassadors predicted that the United States would soon enter the war. Without America's entry, the Turkish ambassador told Kennedy, the war would be lost for England, and would quickly spread to the United States. Only the Russian ambassador was at all "optimistic about the outlook for Britain," so long as there was an arranged peace, Kennedy noted. He must have been pleased by their views since most of them agreed with his own. "We are probably going to have trouble," Kennedy predicted, but we'd better get ready to fight to protect ourselves where we can, and not where somebody would like to have us."[352]

During his round of goodbyes, Kennedy discussed Britain's postwar government with other British officials and political leaders. He envisioned worldwide economic instability after the war and saw only incompetency in the current political leadership, including the "socialist crowd" that he accurately predicted would come to power at the end of the war. He thought that it would reject the obligations of the former government, including the repayment of the billions of dollars that it had borrowed from the United States. Kennedy feared what it would all mean for the United States. "Unless we handle our affairs with more vision than I think we are going to, we shall be getting ourselves deeper and deeper in the mud," he wrote in his diary.[353]

"Point-blank," Kennedy asked the Labour Party's Herbert Morrison, the newly appointed home secretary, "just what type of government he visualized in England at the close of the war; at what point did he think he could stop short of National Socialism?" Morrison said that although he thought that the old British form of government would be gone, Britain could still retain its democracy and have all the advantages of national socialism without its negative features like the Gestapo. How? Kennedy asked. Morrison had no answer. He was at a loss as to how. But Morrison, like the other socialist leaders, believed that when they came to power, they would be able to create a form of socialism that would be agreeable to the British. They could also learn new economic and financial lessons from Hitler. "Hitler has managed to get along without gold, and he has managed to keep his people busy; and in spite of all the predictions, Morrison said, . . . Hitler has not had a crash."

Ernest Bevin, Churchill's minister of labour and national services, told Kennedy that the ruling classes had no understanding of the "social problem." None in the Foreign Office had ever dealt with "the people" or considered social problems, Bevin said. Kennedy regarded him as politically ambitious, as one who wanted to be a great British leader who would develop a program reflecting the "new thought," but not one related to National Socialism. When Kennedy asked him what needed to be done to achieve a desirable social order, Bevin, like Morrison, said he was "stuck."[354]

Clement Attlee, the future postwar Labour prime minister, told Kennedy that he was trying to work out an appropriate form of government for England after the war. Kennedy sensed that those in authority believed that they needed to have an answer soon "to sell" to the British so that they will know "what they are fighting for." "Oh boy! I'm beginning to see National Socialism budding up so fast that these fellows don't recognize it," he wrote in his diary.[355] Kennedy believed that the unregulated free market capitalism through which he had made his fortune was doomed. It was a relic of the past. This had been his basic reason for initially supporting Roosevelt for president in 1932 and for urging his reelection four years later. The man who had written *I'm for Roosevelt* in 1936 was the same Joe Kennedy in 1940. He feared that if the United States entered the war, its economy would be subject to regulations and controls that would destroy capitalism. That had been Britain's fate. War was the death knell of capitalism. "American capitalism would not survive the coming of war. . . . Here, in a nutshell," wrote David Nasaw, "was the most basic reason he was committed to doing everything he could, . . . to keep his country out of war."[356]

Kennedy also made a painful farewell in calling upon the dying Chamberlain, whose bowel cancer Kennedy had learned about in July.[357] Chamberlain, in a reflective mood about the choices he faced and the decisions he made as prime minister, said to Kennedy: "A Democracy will not wake up until the danger is imminent." "Leaders have to wait until public opinion is formed and then try to be a little ahead." I could do that with conscription, Chamberlain said, but to withdraw money and resources from commercial life, "the life of England," and invest it in the military would not have been politically acceptable.[358] Chamberlain's statement was reminiscent of John Kennedy's argument in his book *Why England Slept*; that is to say, it echoed Kennedy's opinion as well.

Kennedy found Chamberlain's comments "touching. . . . We've always seen eye to eye," the retired and retiring prime minister told him. "I haven't had many successes in my life, but I've made real contributions I think. . . . I want to die. . . . Nothing to look forward to," Kennedy recorded in his diary. As Chamberlain clasped Kennedy's hand in both of his, he said, "This is Goodbye, we will never see each other again." They never did. Kennedy left him, feeling terrible; he almost cried.[359]

The British press, mindful of the need for "hands across the seas," rather disingenuously heaped praise on Kennedy. "Forever in deeds if not in written words, we are Allies. Largely that is Joseph Kennedy's work. Good-bye Joe! Heaven bless you! Your job is done," gushed the *Daily Herald*. The *Evening News* wrote rather self-servingly that "it is Mr. Kennedy single-handed who has strengthened Anglo-American friendship in London."[360] "He is so refreshingly cheerful, so efficient, and so human that the war effort undertaken through his Embassy is never irksome, and he can usually suggest an inspiring viewpoint on most subjects," flattering words from the *Liverpool Post*.[361] The *Times* tribute was the most gracious. He would "be missed here by his many friends," its editor wrote. "Nevertheless, Mr. Kennedy has been careful to avoid one of the pitfalls which yawn before all representatives of the United States and England. He never allowed his private friendship to turn him into an Englishman and thus weaken his influence with his own people"—an opinion most definitely not shared by his own government.[362]

As a British souvenir, Kennedy took home an air-raid siren, which he intended to use at his Cape Cod house to call his children ashore in time for dinner. His leave-taking was a time for mutual praise and back-patting: "I did not know London could take it," he said of Londoners' courage during the Blitz. "I did not think any city could take it. I am bowed in reverence."[363]

On October 22, 1940, Kennedy left London. After nearly three years of service the ambassador and his staff at the American embassy bade each other a tearful farewell. He was "an exceptionally hard task-master," remarked one admirer. As he walked down the steps of the embassy, Kennedy met a barrage of reporters. "Turn this way and that. . . . Shake hands. Face the Chancery," they commanded. Suddenly the ambassador was alone. As he walked down Grosvenor Square

> the steps seemed shorter and shorter. There he was turning the corner, and looked just an ordinary man. . . . He was only a figure whom none turned round to study, none noticed. This was Kennedy whose labours in the United States, whether he be in complete accord with Roosevelt or not, may change our political pages decades hence. The man whose counsel may implant in the United States a keener desire to help British endeavors in the war, or may equally force a compromise Peace. Who knows?[364]

Kennedy never returned to Britain as ambassador. He was consumed by hopelessness and despair over Britain's fate and scared that the United States would be dragged into war by the Machiavellian prime minister and his willing accomplice, the American president. He believed Britain's cause was lost; still he did not think the country was a stock to be dumped simply because its value had fallen. He supported—at least some of the time—the destroyer deal, provided that it was not too costly to the United States or undermine America's military position, and he protested all of the time that it would do no good. He also favored giving Britain money and military equipment as its reward for bearing the brunt of the war: America should provide the matériel for war but never become an active participant. He kept silent about his earlier suggestion of a compromise peace and never uttered a word urging Britain to refrain from resisting Germany's aggression. To prevent what he feared most, Britain's destruction and America's entry into the war, Kennedy could offer no consistent counsel. "That we can be of any assistance to the cause in which [the British] are involved, I cannot get myself . . . to believe," he cabled Hull.[365] "This war won't accomplish anything," Kennedy had said to Chamberlain. "Absolutely," Chamberlain had responded. Kennedy wrote in his diary: "How fortunate it might be for civilization if, instead of making enemies of every country in the world for the United States, we had made friends; then our influence would have amounted to something. As it is now, as it has been ever since I arrived here, they all regard us as a terrific influence but in their hearts no country likes us at all."[366] Kennedy's heart was simply not in the fight.

CHAPTER 11

To Be *and* Not to Be

The big blue and silver Pan American Atlantic Clipper flying from Lisbon landed at LaGuardia Airport on October 27, 1940.[1] It was carrying Ambassador Joseph Kennedy, a man in a position to undermine FDR's quest for a third term by endorsing Wendell Willkie, the Republican nominee, and to jeopardize American aid to Britain by publicly criticizing Roosevelt's foreign policy. Both the president and Prime Minister Churchill were keenly aware of Kennedy's troublemaking potential and his ability to cause serious damage to their plans. But once again the crafty president was able to appease his mercurial ambassador, whom he needed to save the Catholic vote, and won him over by appealing to his vanity and his ambitions for himself and his family.

It had happened just as FDR had wished: Kennedy endorsed the president for a third term in a major nationwide radio address, arguing for the doctrine of indispensability and allaying fears that the president would take the country into war. Kennedy's speech had considerable influence on the election, in which FDR won a decisive victory and left a tired and happy president indebted to his ambassador. But their personal relationship deteriorated, especially after Kennedy's indiscreet interview with the *Boston Globe*. Actually the interview confirmed many of Kennedy's private statements and opened the gates for an avalanche of criticism of him on both sides of the Atlantic. His love of publicity and his outrageous candor with the press, once so advantageous for him, proved to be his undoing and cost him a graceful exit from the administration, as well as incurring the resentment of the British. The testy relationship between president and ambassador, growing for more than a year, culminated in a crescendo of abuse during a meeting at Hyde Park. But even after that, they appeared to mend their rift, if only superficially. They publicly posed as friends and colleagues because they found each other useful.

Following his notorious interview with the *Boston Globe*, Kennedy began a one-man crusade to keep America out of war. He made impromptu eye-popping remarks to Hollywood moguls and his hosts in California, comments immediately reported back to FDR, and winning him further animosity from the administration's liberals. Kennedy seemed to argue for coexistence with the dictators, a position that highlighted the vast difference between the intemperate and pessimistic views of the ambassador and the views of the more measured and optimistic president. He consistently out-Hamleted Hamlet—to be and not to be—in his confusion and his contradictions about the administration's foreign policy, in his fence-straddling Lend-Lease testimony, in the radio address in which he tried to clarify his views, and in his speeches at Oglethorpe University and Notre Dame in which, within little more than a week of each other, he argued for isolation and then for intervention.

Slowly Roosevelt severed his relationship with Kennedy by undercutting his position, leaving him angry and bitter. Henceforth Kennedy played no major role in the great national diplomatic drama and was relegated to a bit part. His break with FDR cost him plenty: the president's goodwill, a dignified exit from his inner circle, a diplomatic career, and another job on the administration's payroll.

During his journey to the United States, Kennedy was surrounded by the sights and sounds of war; they formed the backdrop for his trip just as they formed the background for his views on America's foreign policy. He left London on October 22, 1940, to the blast of an air-raid siren giving him a noisy sendoff. He was accompanied by his secretary, Jack Kennedy, by his valet, Frederick Stevens, and by William Hillman, a newspaperman from *Collier's*. The quartet flew to Lisbon in a private plane granted to them by the British government the next morning, after an hour-and-a-half delay due to a malfunctioning magneto on their flying boat. The delay made them miss the fighter escort that was to accompany them, and made them easy prey to a German attack. They were further delayed at Lisbon for twenty-four hours because of unfavorable weather. But the delay gave Kennedy a chance to catch up on his correspondence.[2]

On October 19 he had received Chamberlain's last letter, in which the former prime minister expressed his gratitude for the closeness of their relationship: "I should imagine there can have been few cases in our history in which the two men occupying our respective positions were so closely in touch with one another as you and I. I found in you an understanding of what I was trying to do," Chamberlain wrote.[3] The day before he left, Kennedy sent a heartfelt response conveying his deepest admiration and respect for him: "I have met . . . two men whom I felt had dedicated their lives to the real good of humanity without any thought of themselves. The first was the present Pope, the other was you," Kennedy wrote. "Your conception of what the world must do in order to be a fit place to live in, is the last sensible thing we shall see before the pall of anarchy falls on us all," the ambassador told him, loyal to the last to their shared belief in the policy of appeasement, now such a painful failure, and the views that Roosevelt did not share. "For me to have been any service to you in your struggle is the real worth while [*sic*] epoch in my career," Kennedy said with complete sincerity. "Mark my words the world will yet see that your struggle was never in vain. My job from now on is to tell the world of our hopes"—a self-appointed mission that Kennedy took up with relish, particularly in his testimony before Congress about Lend-Lease, and in speeches and correspondence throughout 1941 before Pearl Harbor. "Good luck, Neville, may God watch over you and bring you the peace you richly deserve: Now and forever, Your devoted friend"—as indeed Kennedy was and remained.[4] And when Chamberlain died on November 9, 1940, Kennedy issued a gracious tribute to the press in honor of the prime minister whom he regarded as "misunderstood in America." Kennedy predicted that "the world will miss his sane counsel. He really gave his life that England might live." He had been "closer to Neville Chamberlain than I was to anybody in England," Kennedy said. Such a claim of intimacy was not reciprocated by the retired and retiring prime minister.[5] Henceforth, whenever he could, Kennedy would say that if Britain survived defeat in war, it would be due to Chamberlain's actions at Munich and not Churchill's rhetoric or wartime leadership.[6] Kennedy often said that the British should erect a bust in Chamberlain's honor for his activities at Munich, which bought an unready Britain time and preserved peace.[7]

On the afternoon of October 23, the ambassador and his party arrived in Lisbon, the last but best "listening post" in Europe, as Kennedy described it. One could become privy to much reliable information from the many well-informed French and Germans streaming into it, the ambassador observed, and advised Washington to "have a lot of bright fellows there" to hear the latest information.[8] Kennedy was met by Warden Wilson, who served as the first secretary of the U.S. Embassy in Lisbon. He gave Kennedy a note from the president requesting him to make no comments to reporters, to refrain from discussing his resignation, and to come immediately to the White House. "I was, of course indignant, but could understand Roosevelt's position," Kennedy confided in his diary, and obediently complied.[9] "I have nothing to tell you boys,"[10] he said to the scores of reporters waiting for a statement at the Lisbon airport.

The administration became increasingly concerned about keeping Kennedy under wraps when he and his entourage arrived in Horta, in the Azores, a day late because of unfavorable weather.[11] When officials realized that he would not arrive in Washington for at least another day, the first act of Welles's drama began to unfold. Welles had been put in charge of staging a production to keep the disgruntled ambassador quiet and to deliver him safely to the president before the man could sound off to anyone—a tactic initially suggested by Arthur Goldsmith, one of Kennedy's closest friends.[12]

Goldsmith recommended that FDR send Kennedy a note instructing him to make no statements to newsmen and to have him met at the airport by "somebody important" from the State Department—all necessary, Goldsmith believed, to pacify Kennedy and to show him that his stature was honored and respected.[13]

On October 25, Kennedy and his entourage arrived in Bermuda and were greeted by another message from the president. He invited Kennedy and Rose to spend Saturday night at the White House. "I should like to have the opportunity of seeing you both Saturday so that I can talk with you," the president wrote. Kennedy called the White House to tell Roosevelt that he would be delayed. Although Roosevelt explained that he was going to New York the next day to campaign and would not be able to see him then, he urged the Kennedys to come to the White House immediately upon their arrival anyhow.[14] Kennedy also received a Roosevelt-inspired wire from Senator James F. Byrnes inviting him and Rose to dine at the White House that evening and asking him to keep quiet until he had seen the president. FDR had called Byrnes to inform him of Kennedy's arrival and to pass on the rumor that Kennedy might switch horses and endorse Willkie. "Apparently the Ambassador was dissatisfied about something," Byrnes drily wrote. Byrnes and his wife were also invited to the White House for dinner that evening.[15]

Kennedy arrived in New York at 2:30 in the afternoon on Sunday, October 27, two days late. He received yet a third message from Roosevelt, hand-delivered from Max Truitt, an old Kennedy colleague who was accompanied by Robert Stewart—apparently "someone important" from the State Department's British Empire desk. Stewart was under orders to chaperone Kennedy until he was safely in Washington.[16] "Thank the Lord you are safely home" the president warmly began and informed the Kennedys that "we expect you both at White House" immediately.[17] The ambassador and his wife obediently took the five o'clock flight to Washington that evening.

In an effort to dodge reporters at the airport when the plane landed, Kennedy, clutching the air-raid siren and a well-worn, bulging briefcase, nearly missed his family welcoming committee: his wife Rose, and daughters Jean, Kathleen, Patricia, and Eunice.[18] Rose Kennedy called out, "Oh Joe!" He replied, "Darling!" and they embraced. The six Kennedys, all on the verge of tears, formed a huddle in which each one practically smothered the other, embracing and hugging whoever happened to be closest. "Where's Teddy? I don't see Teddy," the ambassador exclaimed, looking around for his youngest child. The car Teddy was riding in had been delayed by traffic.

"Mr. Kennedy looked for all the world like a man bursting with things to say," wrote one reporter. "Do you intend to resign?" "How do you feel about a third term?" "Will you campaign for the President?" "How [are] the British . . . faring?" newsmen asked him. "I have nothing to say until I've seen the President," he told reporters as flashbulbs exploded. "I am going right to the White House, and I'll talk a lot when I'm finished with that," he promised, smiling like a Cheshire cat. Kennedy and his family were escorted by policemen through the cheering crowd of Foreign Service officers, friends, and other dignitaries, as he waved to the applauders, shook hands, and posed for pictures. A press conference was arranged for eleven o'clock the next morning at the Waldorf Astoria Hotel in New York City.[19]

The president had also enlisted the support of the shrewdest and most effective ally he could muster, the ambassador's wife, Rose. "I suspect he had [her] come down because of her great influence on me," Kennedy noted in his diary.[20] Her persuasiveness worked, he later admitted to Krock, making Kennedy susceptible to Roosevelt's plans.[21] Rose found her husband tired, embittered by bureaucratic duplicity, and disinclined to support FDR in the upcoming election. With the well-honed political instincts of a loyal politician's daughter, Rose felt deep gratitude for Roosevelt's attention and was well aware of the many favors he had heaped and could continue to heap on the Kennedy family. No doubt as Roosevelt had hoped, she, as if on cue, quietly lectured her husband and reminded him of Roosevelt's generosity: "The President sent you, a Roman Catholic, as Ambassador to London, which probably no other President would have done. . . . He sent you as his representative to the Pope's coronation. You would write yourself down [as] an ingrate in the view of many people if you resign now."[22]

The ambassador and his lady were picked up by a White House limousine when their plane landed at 6:30, and they were whisked away to the White House to dine with the president at 7:15. It was to be one of the most momentous meetings in Kennedy's career.

The president greeted them graciously. He was seated at his desk mixing drinks in a cocktail shaker and reaching for ice with his powerful hands, Rose Kennedy remembered.[23] They were joined by Missy LeHand, Roosevelt's personal secretary, acting as hostess, and by Senator Jimmy Byrnes and his wife, all props in the carefully staged drama directed by the president and designed to win Kennedy's public support for FDR's reelection. Kennedy later remarked that the presence of other guests "prov[ed] that Roosevelt didn't want to have it out with me alone."[24]

The dinner was relaxed and informal, Kennedy recorded in his diary, and served off the president's study on the second floor, with the usual Roosevelt family Sunday fare: scrambled eggs, sausages, toast, and rice for dessert.[25] The ambassador reported on his final visit with Chamberlain and showed Roosevelt the last letter he had received from him. The group at the White House chatted on for a while, discussing economic and wartime conditions in Britain, Kennedy recalled. Suddenly, halfway through the meal, Byrnes, acting as if he had just been struck by lightening, blurted out: "I've got a great idea, Joe. Why don't you make a radio speech on the lines of what you have said tonight and urge the President's re-election?"[26] Kennedy finessed the issue, remaining noncommittal. Byrnes continued to press his point and to argue that the ambassador's public endorsement for a third term was "absolutely essential" and "most necessary for the success of the Roosevelt campaign." FDR also agreed. Network time had already been arranged by the Democratic National Committee on Tuesday evening, but still Kennedy refused. His heart was simply not in it, he later wrote in his diary,[27] still feeling particularly aggrieved, as he had not talked privately with the president and "got off his chest" the things that were bothering him.[28]

Undaunted, FDR then turned his considerable charm on Rose and regaled her with stories about her father. "The President worked very hard on Rose," Kennedy observed,[29] quite aware of Roosevelt's ploy. She later wrote in her memoirs: "I was as susceptible as most people to Roosevelt's charm and blandishments. He was undoubtedly a genius in his personal relationships. . . . Even while I knew I was being charmed, the charm was difficult to resist." "He knew that one of the easiest ways to get around me was to tell me complimentary things about my father."[30]

After dinner the group returned to the president's study; still they refused to leave Kennedy alone for his much anticipated showdown with Roosevelt. Seething, Kennedy finally blurted out: "Since it doesn't seem possible for me to see the President alone, I guess I'll just have to say what I am going to say in front of everybody." There were butterflies in her stomach, Rose recalled. Byrnes was appalled. The president turned pale, his eyes nervously snapping, as he gave the floor over to his smoldering guest.[31] Hardly bashful, Kennedy needed no prompting and began to unburden himself, making his arguments "in his most forthright way—which was *very* forthright," Rose recalled in her memoirs.[32]

"In the first place I am damn sore at the way I have been treated," Kennedy stated. "I feel that it is entirely unreasonable and I don't think I rated it. . . . Mr. President, as you know, I have never said anything privately in my life that I didn't say to you personally, and I have never said anything in a public interview that ever caused you the slightest embarrassment." The Navy Day speech, which the State Department had approved in advance, was the only speech of his that had ever been criticized, Kennedy reminded the president. When it was, the department turned tail and refused to support him, leaving him holding the bag. Further, the ambassador continued, when there were many people last year who doubted whether or not you should have a tradition-shattering third term, "I definitely came out for you for a Third Term."[33] And besides, he noted, the president often turned to him whenever he or a member of his family were in a scrape.[34] "In spite of all that, you have given me a bad deal."[35]

Then Kennedy went after the State Department. He was always "a forceful talker," and his vocabulary included "many words not found in dictionaries," Byrnes wryly commented, most of which he used in denouncing the State Department and its treatment of him.[36] Kennedy enumerated his grievances: particularly aggravating were the presidential envoys like Welles and Donovan who left him cooling his heels and conducted their business by going over his head. Then there was General Ghormley, whose mission he learned about from the British, not the State Department. Even the destroyer deal had been carried on through Lord Lothian and not him. And the State Department never informed him of anything. "All these things were conducive to harming my influence in England," he insisted to Roosevelt. Kennedy told the president that he demanded that the British tell him what was going on; if they did not, he threatened to become "most unfriendly" toward their interests. "So I smashed my way through with no thanks to the American Government."[37]

Kennedy went on and on: besides his troubles with the State Department, there had been leaks in the American press that compromised his position and made the British refuse to give him additional news about the war. Portions of a cable of Kennedy's even turned up in one of Joseph Alsop's syndicated columns, "Capital Parade." Where did the leaks come from? Kennedy demanded. Breck Long of the State Department, a likely source of the leaks to Alsop, even had the gall to call the ambassador at 2 a.m. and put Alsop on the phone to discuss with him the evacuation of children, Kennedy reported to Roosevelt. Besides, Kennedy concluded emphatically, he would not return to London.[38]

Throughout Kennedy's long recital of victimization and abuse perpetrated by the State Department, Roosevelt listened sympathetically, nodding his head, as was his habit, and saying "yes, yes," gestures that those pouring out their hearts to him usually took as signs of approval but actually meant only that he was listening. Finally, it was Roosevelt's turn. He took everyone by surprise when he not only offered no defense of the State Department but blamed it for everything and expanded upon Kennedy's criticism. The president entirely understood his ambassador's position, he said; in fact, Kennedy was being "charitable." The president "had put up with similar treatment" himself, he told the astonished group, but only because of the war. After the election there would be a "real housecleaning." The meddlesome "desk men" were all to blame for the whole deplorable mess. "They" would never be allowed to treat "friends of his, like Joe" so outrageously again.[39] The president went on and on giving everyone involved a "verbal blistering"; Rose described it as a "harangue."[40]

None of it had been his fault, Roosevelt assured his ambassador. The president blamed everyone else, denied Kennedy's charges, and proclaimed his friendship. It had been Knox's idea to send Donovan to England, FDR said, while it was he who told the State Department to clear the matter with Kennedy first. That was news to Welles. Roosevelt couldn't understand why they had failed to keep Kennedy informed. Rose, according to the ambassador's diary, chimed in and tactfully said that it must be hard to fully comprehend events some three thousand miles away. But Roosevelt would have none of it and continued his scathing attack—an award-winning performance. He was surprised about the leaks; he simply could not understand that. Why would Breck Long call Kennedy at 2 a.m.?, the president asked, most indignant; he could not understand that either. Neither could anyone else, apparently. "Those career men always did things wrong," he said in disgust. He had not realized how cavalier their treatment of his friend Joe had been, a proposition Kennedy quietly disputed and warily recorded in his diary: "Somebody is lying very seriously. . . . I suspect the President."[41] Byrnes thought that Kennedy seemed to be a bit uncomfortable and to feel "a touch of sympathy for the State Department boys." After Kennedy had railed against his treatment and spoken his mind, he became noticeably more cordial, Byrnes noted.[42]

FDR then turned the conversation to Kennedy's eldest sons and their extraordinary achievements, a subject upon which he had obviously been coached. He congratulated both Rose and Joe for producing such fine boys. "I stand in awe of your relationship with your children. For a man as busy as you are, it is a rare achievement. And I for one will do all I can to help you if your boys should ever run for political office," a tantalizing statement that must have warmed the hearts of both parents and offered them every incentive to do whatever was necessary to ensure Roosevelt's support.[43] It was a subtle bribe by one of the most skillful political artists in the country, the implications of which could be disastrous if Kennedy turned Judas Iscariot.[44]

With a masterful sense of timing, the president again asked Kennedy whether he would publicly endorse him for a third term. Kennedy said yes. "I will make the God damn speech for you."[45] "I would write the speech without saying anything to anybody and say just what I felt." But first he "wanted the situation cleared up between us," he told FDR.[46] Kennedy agreed, he wrote in his diary, out of his sense of duty. But he did refuse an invitation to accompany the president on his train the next day to Madison Square Garden and to go to a rally that night. His appearance as the president's guest, Kennedy told Roosevelt, would spoil the surprise of his speech and would give the impression that he was not likely to oppose him. Not a former Hollywood mogul for nothing, Kennedy also heightened the drama and suspense by asking Byrnes to tell the press that he would be speaking under the sponsorship of Rose and his nine children and that he would pay for the radio time himself.[47]

As soon as the ambassador agreed, Missy, without missing a cue in the carefully scripted drama—which, unknown to Kennedy, had been planned days before—jumped up and called the National Committee to set up time on the radio. He only found out later that his major role in the reelection production was "to save the Catholic vote," which was rapidly deserting the president. Kennedy was apparently unaware that he had again been had by the masterful politician/director/producer Roosevelt, who once again had outmaneuvered him.[48]

The reporters covering the White House were left to draw conclusions on the basis of circumstantial events at the White House. As the evening progressed, word was prematurely passed to those outside that Kennedy had been invited to campaign with the president in New Jersey and New York. Most reporters assumed that he would accept, and many drifted away. By 10:15 that evening, when Kennedy emerged, the few reporters still remaining were surprised to learn that he had declined the president's invitation and was noncommittal about future events later in the week. He had already given out the information that at the Waldorf Astoria the next day there would be a press conference in which "he would say anything he had to say." As Kennedy stepped into a White House car to take him to the Washington airport, he told reporters that he intended to fly to New York that evening to work on his speech for the following Tuesday evening.[49] Unbeknown to the reporters, Rose had accepted Roosevelt's invitation to spend the night in the White House. She slept in the bedroom used by the queen of England on her visit in 1939.[50]

"One doesn't send 'regrets' to an invitation to a White House event," wrote a *New York Herald Tribune* columnist—that just "isn't done"—and concluded that a rift must have developed between the ambassador and the president. Rumors of a dispute spread throughout the capital and were carried over the late-night news wires. The next morning the headlines in the *New York Herald Tribune*, the leading Republican newspaper, read: "Kennedy Sees Roosevelt amid Signs of a Possible Break." The reporter wrote that "Mr. Kennedy's seeming intention to absent himself from Mr. Roosevelt's impending major political speeches, led immediately, of course, to speculation as to the possibility of a break." The reporter also commented on "reports from London that Mr. Kennedy intended to come home, tender his resignation to Mr. Roosevelt, and then make public his views on the Administration's conduct of foreign policy, with which, it was stated, he did not agree."[51]

The next day suspense heightened as reporters waited at the hotel for Kennedy, who never appeared. Instead Edward Moore showed up with a press release: "Ambassador Kennedy will speak over the nation-wide Columbia network on Tuesday at 9:00 P.M." He was speaking under the auspices of Rose and their nine children, and he himself had paid $20,000 for air time.[52] Kennedy, who loved the theatrical, was always a showman and had devised the melodrama himself.[53] Throughout the day he maintained his silence as he remained sequestered in his hotel.

An excited *New York Times* reporter said that "in view of the rumors that [Kennedy] was not entirely in sympathy with the Administration's foreign policy and is planning to resign from his Ambassadorship his present reticence is provoking excited speculation."[54] The jubilant Willkie supporters believed that Kennedy was breaking rank; the Democrats dismissed such rumors and believed he would discuss Britain's critical situation and announce that he was for Roosevelt.[55] Clare Boothe Luce, an ardent Willkie supporter, thought that Kennedy, her "hero," would probably "turn the trick" for Roosevelt if Kennedy came out for a third term in his speech, but doing so would be a "terrible disservice" to America and drive a rift right through her heart.[56] And an upset aide in London believed that his boss might be "giving the works." He warned the ambassador in a phone call: "Do be careful, do be careful!" he kept repeating, apparently worried about the ambassador's loose tongue and shoot-from-the-hip style. "For Heaven's sake do not say anything before you see Roosevelt at the White House, for, if you do, it will mean, politically, gravely damaging things."[57]

On the evening of October 29, 1940, a week before election day, Kennedy went on the air at 9:00 p.m. to argue for Roosevelt's reelection. Kennedy's half-hour speech, a rambling, repetitious, pedantic lecture, was a "character reference"[58] for Franklin Roosevelt and his desire to keep the United States out of war, an explanation of how the president intended to do so, and a defense of Kennedy's own views. The ambassador assured the American public that Roosevelt's foreign-policy objectives were aiding the British and rearming the United States as quickly as possible.

"Good evening, my fellow Americans," Kennedy said over the national radio hookup of 114 CBS stations. "On Sunday I returned from war-torn Europe, to the peaceful shores of our beloved country renewed in my conviction that this country must and will stay out of war." He proceeded to outline the world situation from his "ringside seat" as the ambassador to the

Court of St. James's since 1938, to assure the American public that Roosevelt's foreign-policy objectives were sound and in agreement with his, and to argue that the election of Franklin Roosevelt was the best assurance for maintaining peace.

Certain facts are clear, Kennedy said: the American people want peace and a resolution to their own problems. They repudiate the philosophy of force. They want to make themselves strong by rearming. Three thousand miles of ocean will no longer protect them; they must rearm fast enough to stay out of war and to maintain peace.

After defending Chamberlain and the Munich Agreement for avoiding war in 1938 and for buying the Allies time, and after having witnessed the failure of diplomacy in 1939, Kennedy again asserted: "I am more convinced than ever that America should stay out of this war." The American people overwhelmingly support avoiding war and want to do so by giving all aid possible to Great Britain. The candidates of both political parties and the American people agree on that. The most harmful thing we could do from the point of view of either the United States or Great Britain would be to declare war, the ambassador insisted. Were that to happen, our own military forces would be in control; all military shipments to Britain would cease; America's responsibilities to protect the Western Hemisphere under the Monroe Doctrine would expand; and American military aid to Britain would be curtailed. Most of all, we would lose the precious time we need to become militarily strong. Our navy and Britain's gallant fight are protecting us and buying us time to do that. Thus from either the American or British point of view, the most "foolish" thing we could do would be to declare war, he repeated again and again. "There is no valid argument for putting America into war. We can be strong, unprovocative, resolute, fair with the democracies, hostile to the aggressors, and sympathetic with the oppressed without bringing to our shores that miserable thing that does nothing but destroy—war."

Throughout this campaign, the president's political opponents have made the "wicked" charge that President Roosevelt wants to involve the United States in the war. "Such a charge is false," Kennedy asserted. There are no secret commitments to involve the United States militarily. "I, as the Ambassador of the American people in London, . . . can assure you now with absolute sincerity and honesty that there has been no such commitment." It "is completely absurd" to suggest that American troops will be sent to war.

The best evidence of the president's intention, his ambassador steadfastly argued, was his desire to provide every possible assistance to Great Britain to ensure that the British Navy and the British nation can continue their "gallant battle" and thereby guarantee the security of the United States. Britain's resistance buys us "precious time" to build up our own defenses—an argument reminiscent of Munich. In addition, the president has strengthened the defenses of the United States by securing a promise from the British that their fleet, important to our own national security, would never be surrendered or sunk but instead be sent overseas to defend the Empire.

After defending Roosevelt's policies and motives against his critics, Kennedy turned to the charges against himself, his address being as much a rebuke of his critics and a defense of his views in foreign policy as it was of Roosevelt's. Of course, the president and I have disagreements, but on issues and methods, not objectives, Kennedy said. On the fundamental questions of foreign policy, economic policy, and America's future, there is little disagreement between us.

Kennedy acknowledged that he was often accused of being "steeped in gloom," but "gloom . . . is nothing more than 'facing the facts,'" he said. What is the reason for gaiety? Much of the world's productive capability is used to kill: millions will starve; millions more will suffer disease. "The greatest war machine in the history of mankind . . . serves a man who believes that war is a noble cause and that world domination is his destiny." Gloom is reality. The only way to avoid war is to be militarily strong, a difficult proposition in a democracy. As Jack Kennedy showed in *Why England Slept*, the ambassador said, plugging his son's book, the strengths of a democratic society—vitality, voluntary cooperation, and a capacity for sustained effort—quickly become weaknesses in preparing for a war that might never happen. We must all share in the blame for the shortsightedness and inherent weakness of democracy in Britain as well as in the United States, for the failure to appreciate the threat to both countries, and for their failure to adopt adequate methods to ensure their safety.

Thus, in this militarily charged atmosphere, rife with war and worldwide social revolution, the American people will make a grave decision: which of the two candidates do they want to lead the nation in the next four years. Roosevelt's experience best qualifies him to be president, Kennedy argued. The "staggering" worldwide problems and inequalities developing from the world crisis that the next president will have to face make the arguments against a third term "insignificant" by comparison, Kennedy said. It will take two years to train any newcomer, and two years is too long. "We do not have the time to train a green hand even though he comes to his task full of goodwill and general capacity but lacking in vital governmental experience"—an apt description of Willkie.

"As a servant of the American people," as well as a father and the head of his household, Kennedy said, "my wife and I have given nine hostages to fortune. Our children and your children are more important than anything else in the world. The kind of America that they and their children will inherit is of grave concern to us all. In the light of these considerations, I believe that Franklin D. Roosevelt should be re-elected President of the United States."[59] The speech was as thoroughgoing an endorsement of an office holder as possible, and a statement hard for anyone to spurn.

Kennedy eagerly awaited the critics' reviews of his performance. They were stunning. The president sent him a telegram that evening: "We have all just listened to a grand speech many thanks. . . ." And he must have heaved a great sigh of relief.[60] Byrnes, too, was pleased; he thought the speech was "most effective."[61] Kennedy's family was delighted. Jack appreciated the plug his father gave his book and told him that he was "proud to have sponsored you."[62] Kathleen sent a telegram: "It's great to be famous—Goodnight from your 4th hostage."[63]

Coming from one whose antiwar views were so well known, the speech was particularly persuasive to the American electorate. Telegrams of praise poured into the White House. "If possible," said one message to the president, "have Ambassador Kennedy make more talks. Next to you he is the best vote getter."[64] If the ambassador "made radio addresses everyday [sic] and night for the rest of the campaign," we could carry forty-eight states, said another.[65] One "converted Republican" urged that Kennedy's speech be rebroadcast every day.[66]

The ambassador's address received rave reviews from the press. *Life* magazine described it as a great vote getter, "probably the most effective of the campaign. For more than anything else, it allayed fear that Mr. Roosevelt would 'take this country into war.'"[67] Even the *London Daily Mail* praised the speech and suggested that Kennedy's "intervention at this stage may sway the approaching election decisively in favor of the President." And the ambassador "clearly and accurately" expressed the British opposition to an American declaration of war. Britain is America's first line of defense. In exchange, for Britain's efforts on behalf of her own defense as well as her non-belligerent ally, the *Mail* said, we want all the military equipment we can get, we want more of it, and we want it sooner. "An American declaration of war at this stage would be of no help to us"—exactly what Kennedy had said in his address.[68]

Why had Kennedy agreed to make an about-face and give the speech? Had he been duped? His speech was totally "out of keeping" with his private views and with his "earned reputation as one of the most forthright men in public life," wrote Arthur Krock in his memoirs. The newsman believed that Kennedy, unimpressed by Willkie's presidential qualifications, had intended to sit out the campaign except for a speech warning against American involvement in war. As surprised as anybody, Krock attributed his about-face to "the overwhelming pressures to which Kennedy had been exposed" and noted that FDR, without batting an eye, had seemed to sacrifice the State Department "to keep Kennedy on the reservation."[69] Perhaps the officials in the State Department had been warned beforehand to expect a "sell-out." Richard Whalen argues that the quickness with which Missy LeHand ran to the telephone to give the Democratic National Committee the go-ahead indicated that the performance had been staged. But the real "dupes" had been the Willkie supporters, believing that Kennedy would denounce FDR and endorse Willkie.[70]

Probably one major reason for Kennedy's change of heart was that he really did believe that FDR was indispensable. A year earlier he had argued: "The problems that are going to affect the people of the United States, political, social, and economic, are already so great and becoming greater by war that they should be handled by a man it won't take two years to educate," a sentiment identical to the one expressed in his radio address on the eve of the 1940 election and reminiscent of his stance in 1936 when he endorsed Roosevelt in his campaign book, *I'm for Roosevelt*.[71]

Kennedy not only believed in the president's indispensability, but he "in all sincerity," according to his wife's memoirs, really was in complete agreement with FDR's program in foreign policy at that time: support England as thoroughly as possible to prevent the United States from becoming Hitler's next intended victim, rearm and make the United States impregnable to attack, and refrain from war unless the United States is besieged.[72]

Being Kennedy, political considerations were always paramount for himself and his family. Certainly he realized that he was a candidate for chairman of the newly created Advisory Defense Commission, a post he wanted and was eminently qualified for.[73] He had to know as well that his name was circulating in political circles as a potential presidential nominee and that Roosevelt encouraged him. "The reason for the switch to FDR was simple," Stewart Alsop later wrote in the *Saturday Evening Post*: "Roosevelt offered Kennedy—or so Kennedy firmly believed—the Presidential nomination in 1944. When instead Roosevelt ran for a fourth term, Joe Kennedy was understandably bitter."[74]

Years later, Clare Boothe Luce told Michael Beschloss in an interview that she and her husband had fully expected Kennedy to endorse Willkie and were astonished when he endorsed Roosevelt. She told Beschloss that in 1956 she had asked Kennedy why he had changed his mind. Flashing his famous grin, he said, "I simply made a deal with Roosevelt. We agreed that if I endorsed him for President in 1940, then he would support my son Joe for governor of Massachusetts in 1942."[75]

Another factor was undoubtedly the Roosevelt charm, which few could withstand. Certainly Kennedy caved in to it; he was too ambitious, too opportunistic, and too much of a sycophant; he simply could not say no. He had never been able to stand up to his chief in any confrontation since they first met in 1917 at Fore River Shipyard. Besides, he wanted another job in government.[76]

Certainly a major influence, by Kennedy's own admission, was his wife Rose, Honey Fitz's favorite child. The ambassador himself admitted that her advice "carried the greatest weight." "Rose was far more capable of thinking of the effect, of the political leverage" than was her husband, her biographer wrote. "She may also have been thinking well into the future, when her sons would enter politics. An affront to Roosevelt at this moment might have undermined Joe's position in the Democratic Party; it might have crushed Joe Jr.'s chances of rising, should Roosevelt win the election; it might have soured the electorate on Catholics in high places. Rose was no doubt aware of all these possibilities." Her husband did well to listen to her.[77] Finally, it was a relatively easy decision for him to make: Willkie was not qualified; Roosevelt really was indispensable and might be able to prevent war; and it was good politics for the Kennedy family.

The next evening, October 30, 1940, after the ambassador's radio address, Roosevelt campaigned in Kennedy's hometown. In Boston Garden that night, the president gave a major speech to a cheering audience of 22,000 in which he announced his decision to allow the British to buy 12,000 more war planes and to place orders for billions of dollars for other arms and munitions. It would bring to the United States, still recovering from the Depression, more jobs and greater prosperity, an advantage that might offset any criticism about the clear violation of America's neutrality.[78] The speech was so isolationist that Wendell Willkie cried: "That hypocritical son of a bitch! This is going to beat me!"[79]

The president also made a solemn promise that would later come back to haunt him: "And while I am talking to you mothers and fathers, I give you one more assurance. I have said this before, but I shall say it again and again and again: Your boys will not be sent into any foreign war," a promise that must have seemed increasingly hollow even to such an optimist as him,[80] and one that must have increased Kennedy's bitterness toward him. In 1944 the ambassador's own beloved son Joe Jr. would be lost when the plane he was flying across the Channel exploded, leaving no trace of him. His father later demanded of the vice-presidential candidate in 1944, Harry Truman: "What are you doing campaigning for that crippled son of a bitch that killed my son Joe?" "If you say another word about Roosevelt, I'm going to throw you out the window," the loyal Truman replied.[81]

In addition, Roosevelt gave an approving nod to the Boston Irish that night by welcoming back to America "that Boston boy, beloved by all of Boston and a lot of other places, my Ambassador to the Court of St. James' [sic], Joe Kennedy."[82] His speechwriters protested at the use of the personal pronoun "my" and suggested using "our Ambassador"; but FDR would have none of it. "My" was correct, he insisted. He was wrong and right.[83]

By the next day, Republican orators had seized upon the word "my" as evidence of FDR's overwhelming egotism and dictatorial aspirations. "The United States was approaching 'one-man rule,'" Willkie told a Republican ally in New Jersey. "It used to be 'my friends,' now it is 'my Ambassador.' Pretty soon it will be 'my generals,' then it will be 'my people,'" he declared, trying to make political hay out of Roosevelt's choice of pronouns and linking him to Caesar, Charlemagne, Napoleon, and Hitler.[84] Actually, the president was technically correct. An ambassador is the personal representative of one head of state sent to another, said the Department of State in a clarifying statement. The president as the head of state confers credentials upon his ambassadors in a form letter to another head of state; in Ambassador Kennedy's case, his credentials were from Mr. Roosevelt to King George VI.[85]

On November 5, the nation voted and gave Roosevelt a decisive third-term victory. The popular vote was slim, 27 million for FDR to 22 million for Willkie, but the electoral vote was sweeping, 499 to 82.[86] Kennedy, whose radio address had given FDR considerable credibility and probably saved the Catholic vote for him, dropped in for a five-minute meeting at noon the day after the election and congratulated the happy but tired-looking president: "Well you've got it—I certainly don't begrudge you the next four years," the ambassador said.

During his White House meeting with FDR, Kennedy celebrated the president's victory by offering his resignation as ambassador, a customary gesture for public officials.[87] But his was no mere formality. "I've told you how I feel being Ambassador without anything to do," Kennedy explained. I'd return to England in twenty-four hours if there were a chance of peace or of something threatening the United States, he said, but otherwise I'd rather be home. The president did not blame him, he said, especially after all the suffering the State Department had caused him, a position Kennedy took exception to. It was not all State's fault, he wrote in his diary—much was the president's. But Roosevelt did ask Kennedy to retain his title of ambassador until his successor was appointed. Thus, Kennedy's resignation was not formally accepted until February of 1941. The president also asked Kennedy to "stay around U.S. until I have a chance to look into this situation over here," a hint that Kennedy understood to be a follow-up comment to one FDR had previously made to Rose implying that he intended to find another job for her husband in Washington, something Kennedy himself was looking forward to with relish.[88]

That same day Kennedy stopped at the State Department, where he held a lengthy conversation with Cordell Hull, Sumner Welles, and Breckinridge Long, "the desk men" against whom he had so railed to Roosevelt. Welles had warned Kennedy not to resign in a snit; he would be back in the government soon. Hull, on the other hand, wanted to be rid of Kennedy and urged him to be stiff and resign now. Hull was quite bitter and blamed people like Hopkins for Kennedy's treatment. Take care of yourself, he told Kennedy.[89] Long, an assistant secretary of state for European affairs, was himself a former ambassador to Italy, a sometime fan of Mussolini and his fascist regime. Long had a well-deserved reputation for anti-Semitism, anti-Catholicism, anti-liberalism, anti-everyone who was not a white patrician Protestant southerner of his stock.[90]

Unlike official Washington, Kennedy took no satisfaction in the recent Allied successes in Europe: the RAF had knocked the Luftwaffe out of the skies over England; Hitler had "postponed" Operation Sea Lion indefinitely and would soon turn eastward; Franco's Spain was still neutral; the British still controlled the Suez Canal; the Middle East had not been invaded by Italy; and Britain and the United States would soon be producing more airplanes than Germany.[91] Long was alarmed by Kennedy's defeatism, which Long interpreted as a kind of shell shock from Kennedy's having lived through wartime London. Kennedy "is quite a realist and sees England gone," Long recorded in his diary. There was little reason for Kennedy to return to England or to continue as ambassador, he told the trio; there was nothing "real" to be done and no policy to ensure victory in the war. Kennedy repeated his usual litany: England is broken; she will have to go off the gold standard and then will not be able to meet her obligations to us; the British Empire is crumbling and maybe the British Navy is gone, too; Britain will soon be forced into an understanding with victorious Germany; Churchill will be dismissed; Lloyd George will become the British Pétain, exactly what Churchill thought and Hitler wanted. The "spirit and the morale of the world is broken," Kennedy concluded; "people have lost their faith in God."

Kennedy "does not believe in our present policy . . . [nor] in the continuing of democracy," Long wrote. Unlike Roosevelt, Kennedy doubted the strength and resilience of democratic institutions to right themselves, and predicted that the United States would have to "assume a Fascist form of government here or something similar to it . . . to survive in a world of concentrated and centralized power," sentiments Kennedy had voiced before in the December

1938 memo to Roosevelt, and Long himself might have uttered—a view sharply contrasting with the president's and a major source of the ideological differences and conflict between president and ambassador.

Kennedy would not exactly appease Hitler, Long noted, but the extent to which Kennedy would cooperate with Hitler "is undefined." Kennedy's opinions about how best to proceed "are nebulous." "Some uncharted way [must be] found," Kennedy believed, for "a realistic policy" of economic collaboration by the United States with Germany and Japan. How this was to be done he was at a loss to explain, since the U.S. lacked anything to trade with and feared industrial competition; but the existing policy was wrong, he told the secretaries, and could not be corrected—of that he was certain.

Kennedy also told Long that he intended to undertake a mission to see Hearst, to "try to set him right," and other publishers like Robert McCormick (*Chicago Tribune*), too. And, he might have added, to spread his thesis of doom and gloom. Don't talk to the press, Long warned. Don't scare people on foreign policy. Americans need "education in foreign affairs. To thrust it upon them too suddenly would be disastrous," Long said, advice Kennedy agreed with and then ignored. But he would have done well to heed it.

The two ambassadors continued their discussions the next day, November 7, at the White House after the swearing-in ceremony for the president and his triumphal procession up Pennsylvania Avenue. Kennedy told Long that Hitler had twice invited him to come to Germany for a conference, but Kennedy had twice declined the invitation. "Hitler must have got the impression Kennedy had views which Hitler might use as an approach to us," Long recorded, an opinion that Germany's Ambassador von Dirksen had also supposedly shared.[92] Kennedy had changed little since he wrote the memo to the president in March 1939 predicting that to fight fascism, the United States would have to adopt many features of fascism, an opinion that continued to put him at odds with the president.

Several days after Roosevelt's reelection, and before his California trip, Kennedy had reason to be pleased. He returned to Boston for a physical checkup at the Lahey Clinic and was given an excellent bill of health. No doubt also delighted with the happy turn of events resulting from Roosevelt's reelection and the possibility of a new job with him, Kennedy expressed his opinions to anyone who would listen.[93]

One reporter in particular was interested in Kennedy's views, Louis M. Lyons of the *Boston Globe*. Lyons was an effective, cautious, and sensitive reporter, one of the best, who had joined the *Globe* staff in 1919 and became its expert on international affairs. He was a Nieman Journalism Fellow at Harvard and a curator of the Nieman Foundation. Laurence Winship, the managing editor at the *Globe*, urged Lyons to get a piece on Joe Kennedy appropriate for a Sunday feature story. Lyons wrote to the ambassador on November 8, 1940, requesting an interview from him "as a traveler home from the wars, not political talk." Lyons reminded Kennedy of the very laudatory article he had written about him in 1936, "Kennedy 'Sticks His Neck Out,' Asks Business to Back New Deal," which was published before Kennedy's own campaign piece for FDR, *I'm for Roosevelt*.[94] Winship followed up Lyons's note with a telegram to Kennedy supporting Lyons's request for an interview.[95] Kennedy consented to the interview, to be held on Saturday, November 9, 1940, at one in the afternoon in his room at the Ritz-Carlton Hotel.

Lyons was joined by Ralph Coglan, the speaker at the Nieman dinner the night before. He liked Kennedy the minute he saw him, and believed him to be a kindred spirit. Charles K. Edmondson, himself a Nieman Fellow at Harvard on leave from his newspaper, was also present. He had been showing his boss, Coglan, around town.[96] Both were editorial writers for the *St. Louis Post-Dispatch* and as staunchly committed to isolationism as their newspaper was.[97] Under the criteria of the fellowship, only Lyons could report the interview, which he understood to be on the record.[98] Kennedy also agreed to give Edmondson and Coglan a background briefing on American foreign policy and on the English war effort. Kennedy had secured their agreement beforehand that his remarks would be off the record, but he had failed to do so with Lyons, clearly a grievous oversight as events unfolded.[99]

It all began so harmlessly. The newsmen waited for Kennedy in his suite in the Ritz. Upon his arrival, Lyons introduced him to his two colleagues, and after they had asked Kennedy questions, Lyons got out his pencil and pad and began his interview, hoping that they would leave. Instead they remained, listening appreciatively to Kennedy's rapid-fire, tough comments, the very ones he had been putting in his dispatches since the war began, delivered as though he were giving a campaign speech for the isolationist senator from Montana, Burton Wheeler of America First.[100] He was a "buddy" of his, Kennedy told them, and boasted that he had financed his campaign with Robert La Follette.[101]

Kennedy chatted amicably for an hour and a half in a homey setting well known to any reporter, "as American as apple pie," interviewing a local dignitary from the Rotary or Elks Club in his best "hail-fellow-well-met" manner. Kennedy sat in his shirtsleeves with his suspenders flopping around his hips, spearing apple pie topped with American cheese. His mind flowed like "the free, full power and flood of the Mississippi River," a better representative of "the great heart of America," Lyons wrote, than any other diplomat sent to London in modern times. Kennedy's stream-of-consciousness monologue roamed from England's war effort to Eleanor Roosevelt to American foreign policy, and to the queen. Kennedy was surprisingly candid, even for Kennedy, obviously assuming that the whole interview was off the record.[102] But occasionally he held up his finger to caution Lyons that what he had just said was "off the record," as if his other remarks were on the record. Lyons always honored his specific request for confidentiality.[103]

Lyons and Coglan dashed for a cab, eager to return to their office to compare notes and savor every morsel of Kennedy's comments. "I wouldn't be in your shoes," Coglan remarked. "How do you know what you can write? He just puts it up to you to follow your own conscience and judgment and protect him in his diplomatic capacity." "Well, the last time I interviewed him in 1936," Lyons recalled, "he poured himself out just like this, without laying any restriction on me, and I wrote every bit of it, and it went all over the country—the interview in which he said why he was for Roosevelt. And he said it was the best interview he'd ever had. But he wasn't an ambassador then." "It all depends on how you handle it," Coglan said. "Any story can be told if it's told right."[104] But telling it "right" was precisely the problem.

Lyons also reviewed his notes with Edmondson. "Don't forget," he reminded Lyons, Kennedy had said "Lindbergh's not so crazy either"—a statement Lyons added to his article.[105]

Kennedy never saw the story in advance and he knew nothing about it until the next morning, Sunday, November 10, 1940, when Joseph Dinneen, an old friend and reporter for the *Boston Globe*, called him in Bronxville, New York. Dinneen, who was filling in as Sunday editor, asked Kennedy for a statement about Neville Chamberlain, who had died that day. Kennedy told him that Rose was waiting to go to Mass, but he promised to prepare a tribute and asked Dinneen to call him back. By the way, Dinneen casually said, "'That's quite an interview you gave Louis Lyons for this morning's paper." 'Why? What did he say?' Kennedy asked. 'What did he say?' Dinneen repeated. 'He wrote everything you told him. I've got it here. '"The Queen is one of the most intelligent women you ever met. It will be the Queen who will save what's left of England and not any of the politicians,'" he read aloud, skimming through the long story. "'She's got more brains than the cabinet. . . . Democracy is finished in England. The country will go Socialist. . . . You'll spend everything you've got to keep us out of the war. If the United States gets into it with England, we'll be left holding the bag.'" A hush fell over their conversation for a moment. 'Do you want me to keep going?' Dinneen asked, wondering whether they had been cut off. 'He wrote all that?' Kennedy asked in amazement. 'All that and a lot more,' the reporter replied. 'Anything wrong with it: You said it, didn't you?' A pause—finally Kennedy replied: 'I said it. . . . I want you to read the whole thing to me, but not now. Rose and I have got to go to Mass. I'll be back in an hour. Call me.'"

In the meantime, the *Globe* received a request from London for a copy of the interview. Dinneen called Winship and repeated Kennedy's admission that he had been quoted accurately. Kennedy's confirmation was passed on to the reporters as their deluge of inquiries poured in from wire services and newspapers. When Dinneen tried to call again, Kennedy's phone was jammed up for hours by calls from London's *Daily Mail* and *News Chronicle*, New York reporters, UP, AP, and INS requesting confirmation and asking for a complete text of the interview. After filing his request with the operator and waiting for hours for his turn, Dinneen finally got through and spent the next half hour reading three full columns of Kennedy's uncensored views to him.[106] "Well the fat's in the fire," Kennedy said, "but I guess that's where I want it."[107]

But that was not where he wanted it. The publication of his indiscreet, candid remarks made his private views known to everyone. Although they were no different from those he had uttered confidentially to Hull, Welles, and Long, as well as friends and colleagues in Washington and London throughout his tenure as ambassador, they were not the sort of thing that a diplomatic diplomat said in public. Everything he said offended somebody.

The story set off a firestorm of protest against Kennedy on both sides of the Atlantic and cost him the gratitude of Roosevelt and the affection of the British that he had done so much to gain.

The article ran on page one of the *Boston Sunday Globe* and began with the sensational headline "KENNEDY SAYS DEMOCRACY ALL DONE IN BRITAIN, MAYBE HERE," but it failed to expand on that dramatic statement, as if the author, aware of its politically charged nature, was afraid to touch the issue again until halfway through the article. It was followed by the most unusual headline: "PINCH COMING IN U.S. TRADE LOSS." As if the *Globe* were uncertain how to handle that, too, forty-one paragraphs later Kennedy's statements elaborated on the headline. "It's the loss of our foreign trade that's going to threaten to change our form of government. We haven't felt the pinch of it yet. It's ahead of us." The next headline was equally unrevealing: "AMBASSADOR ASKS AID TO ENGLAND BE VIEWED AS 'INSURANCE': BEGS AMERICA WAKE UP, GIVE MORE POWER TO MOBILIZE INDUSTRY."

The story unfolded in a leisurely way, in rambling "feature" fashion under Lyons's byline. He described Kennedy in shirtsleeves, eating apple pie, and noted the quick rapport he developed with Ralph Coglan. Six paragraphs later, the political dynamite exploded with the sensational revelation of Kennedy's personal crusade against American intervention. "'I'm willing to spend all I've got left to keep us out of war. . . . There's no sense in our getting in. We'd just be holding the bag. . . . I know more about this European situation than anybody else, and it's up to me to see that the country gets it.'"

Henceforth Kennedy's personal views were made public for all the world to read. Lyons quoted Kennedy's expression of great admiration for the queen. "The Queen was one of the most intelligent women I ever met . . . and when it comes to a question of saying what's left for England, it will be the Queen and not any of the politicians who will do it. She's got more brains than the Cabinet"—opinions that revealed his low opinion of the British political establishment and no doubt did not endear him to them.

Following Kennedy's generous remarks about the queen, Lyons quoted the ambassador's views on Eleanor Roosevelt. "She's another wonderful woman. . . . And marvelously helpful and full of sympathy. Jim will tell you"—a reference to James M. Landis, dean of Harvard's Law School, who arrived as the reporters were leaving—"that she bothered us more on our jobs in Washington to take care of the poor little nobodies who hadn't any influence than all the rest of the people down there together. She's always sending me a note to have some little Susie Glotz to tea at the embassy." When Kennedy's remarks were quoted, usually out of context, his praise for the graciousness and thoughtfulness of Eleanor Roosevelt was often omitted; instead his words appeared to insult her: "she bothered us more . . . to take care of the poor little nobodies . . . [like] Susie Glotz."

Kennedy had equally candid opinions on the future of democracy in England and America, also infuriating to both governments; these opinions were often quoted out of context. "People call me a pessimist. I say, 'what is there to be gay about? Democracy is all done.'"

"You mean in England or this country, too?" one of the reporters asked. "Well, I don't know. If we get into war it might be in this country, too. A bureaucracy would take over right off. Everything we hold dear will be gone. They tell me that after 1918 we got it all back again. But this is different. There's a different pattern in the world. . . . national socialism is coming out of it," Kennedy observed.[108] A little later in the interview he said again: "'Democracy is finished in England. It may be here. Because it comes to a question of feeding people. It's all an economic question'" stemming from our foreign trade, he told the newsmen.

He was often quoted as having said, "Democracy is finished in England," a stark, inflammatory statement standing alone without any context, a statement that angered Englishmen in 1940 desperately fighting against Hitler's onslaught. But when the war ended in 1945, the British elected a socialist government under the Labour Party prime minister, Clement Attlee. Upon taking power, Attlee did establish a socialist economy by nationalizing the major industries in Britain. This perhaps was the upshot Kennedy feared—not the end of democracy, but the end of plutocratic capitalism and the institution of socialism, even democratic socialism.

Kennedy offended the English with other indiscreet statements: "'The whole reason for aiding England is to give us time. . . . England is doing everything we could ask. As long as she is there, we have time to prepare. It isn't that she's fighting for democracy. . . . She's fighting for self-preservation, just as we will if it comes to us.'" His statements were reminiscent of those he had already made to British officials more than a year before when the war began, and more recently to State Department officials like Breckinridge Long.

What about Canada if Britain were defeated? one of the newsmen asked. Kennedy replied tactlessly: "Well, we're sucked in on that, and the Monroe Doctrine and all." We must make the most of the next six months; it would be fatal to do otherwise. "Nobody could handle industrial mobilization but Jesus Christ," but we must educate America to the need for it, and fast, too. What if Hitler were to be victorious, Coglan asked Kennedy, would the United States refuse to trade with Europe? "That's nonsensical," the ambassador emphatically stated.

Would aid to Britain draw us into war? Edmondson asked. "'No,' said Kennedy positively. Not if we know the answer. Not if we are coldly realistic and for America all the time. . . . What would we be fighting for?" he asked. Apparently a Nazi-free Europe would be an insufficient motive.

Returning to a familiar theme, he said: "But the thing now is, aid England as far as we can; that's our game. . . . give her what it takes . . . and don't expect anything back." Let her pay for what she needs, but when she can't pay, "give it to [her]. Mark it off, as insurance," he urged, a position of self-interest he had held ever since the war began.

Ending as he began, as a man on a crusade, he insisted: "'I say we aren't going in. Only over my dead body. . . . I'm going to make it a point to educate America to the situation,'" he told the reporters.

"Well, I'm afraid you didn't get much of a story," he laughed, with unintended irony, as the reporters left the suite.[109]

At the close of Dinneen's lengthy telephone conversation, Kennedy quietly replied, "He didn't miss a thing. He has destroyed me as an Ambassador. There is nothing left for me now but to resign." "Why did you say it, Joe?" Dinneen asked. "I understood that I was merely giving them background and that it was all off the record," he said. That's why I apologized for failing to give them much of a story.[110]

The next day, November 12, 1940, Kennedy went to Washington and spoke to the president.[111] Neither party made the conversation public, but when Kennedy left the White House, his career in Roosevelt's Washington was over. Despite Kennedy's public denial about the accuracy of the interview, FDR told Ickes a couple of weeks later that he believed that the Lyons interview was "authentic" because Kennedy had been quoted making similar comments in Hollywood and elsewhere.[112]

Kennedy issued a formal announcement on November 12 cavalierly repudiating his *Boston Globe* interview, despite the fact that he had earlier confirmed it. "I have read the interview that I am supposed to have given to Mr. Louis M. Lyons of the *Boston Globe*," Kennedy's press release began. "When Mr. Lyons came to see me in Boston, I made it clear in the presence of Mr. Coglan and Mr. Edmondson . . . that I should be very happy to give them my thoughts off the record, but I would make no statements that should be printed at this time." Throughout the conversation, Mr. Lyons made no notes and wrote entirely from memory, Kennedy said; consequently the story contained many "inaccurate" remarks. "Many statements in the article show this to be true because they create a different impression entirely than I would want to set forth." Were I to give out information on important diplomatic matters, I would insist on making certain that all the facts were correct so there would be no inaccuracies or mistakes. The interview was the "first serious violation of the newspaper code on an 'off-the-record' interview I have ever experienced. I may be guilty of errors of judgment, but I hope never guilty of errors of good taste."[113] Actually, he was guilty of both; and certainly errors of taste are of smaller importance than errors of judgment.

Lyons refused to comment on Kennedy's charges and issued a release saying, "I don't think it's up to me to make a statement." Ask the *Globe*, he said; they know everything about the story.[114] The *Globe*, having sworn that the story was accurate, had no alternative but to defend its reporter and issued a press release doing so. The *Globe* "regrets that Ambassador Kennedy takes exception to publication of the interview" and explained that Lyons believed he was free to use any of the ambassador's statements, except those the ambassador specifically stipulated were "off the record." The confidentiality of those was honored, the *Globe* said.[115]

The remaining events in this episode conferred little glory on Kennedy. Outraged, he indulged in some irrelevant and senseless face-saving tactics. He demanded that Lyons publicly confirm that the conversation had been off the record. Lyons refused. Kennedy then demanded a retraction from the *Globe*. A retraction was prepared and approved by

Kennedy, but Laurence Winship, an editor of considerable integrity, stood by his reporter. "I'll quit before I print this," he told the management. Kennedy then demanded that the publishers print a front-page editorial in their own names stating that he had been victimized by Lyons. The editorial, too, was written and sent to Kennedy, who accepted it, but it was also withdrawn because of Winship's opposition.[116] Winship also phoned Lyons on Monday, November 11—Armistice Day—and told him that FDR had called his close friend Archibald MacLeish, the librarian of Congress, to check up about Lyons and his story. Despite Kennedy's demand for Winship's and Lyons's scalps, Winship, the managing editor, asked Lyons to write something for the next morning "to keep your name in the paper." In revenge, Kennedy withdrew all his liquor advertising for Somerset Importers for years and continued to believe that his confidences had been betrayed.[117]

Lyons resigned from the *Globe* to become the curator of the Nieman Foundation at Harvard, in accordance with arrangements made several weeks before the infamous interview.[118] He continued to insist that his version of the incident was accurate. David Koskoff, one of Kennedy's biographers, interviewed Lyons in July 1961. Lyons explained to Koskoff that "he had been proceeding quite innocently, thinking that all the story amounted to was a colorful feature article—'Hometown boy comes home.'" But Lyons also said that he was politically naive at that time and was unaware of the implications of the story. He had no expectation that it would create the uproar it did.[119]

Writing in 1971 in *Newspaper Story: One Hundred Years of the Boston Globe*, the official history of the newspaper, Lyons said that "the only trouble with the story is that it blew up." He had run it as a feature story using wartime England as a backdrop against which he painted Kennedy's dramatic personality with all its intense passion, pungency, and vitality. The quotes were standard Kennedyisms that Kennedy had often expressed to officials on both sides of the Atlantic. They formed the body of the story and revealed his unrelenting opposition to America's entry into war.

Lyons insisted that he had honored the ambassador's request to respect privileged material and that he had left out some undiplomatic references. He also disputed Kennedy's claim that he, Lyons, had made no notes. "Actually," Lyons wrote in *Newspaper Story*, "I had made notes, though sparsely." Kennedy's talk outran him, but it was the kind of talk that is unforgettable and if you can get to your typewriter immediately after it, you can reconstruct the whole story from an outline, Lyons maintained. "Diplomats always do it that way." Had he exercised "more diplomatic caution," a wiser Lyons wrote in 1971, or if Kennedy had stipulated beforehand that the interview had been off the record, or claimed that he had been misquoted, the more commonplace ambassadorial alibi, "it would have saved both of us a lot of trouble." But Kennedy did neither; neither did either. "One can hardly misquote a man through two or three columns," Lyons said wryly. The dynamite that destroyed Kennedy's career "was his, not mine."[120]

James Landis, however, who had been present for part of the conversation and came in late to break it up, believed that Lyons really had misunderstood the terms of the interview.[121] On the other hand, Ralph Coglan criticized Lyons for not exercising discretion and protecting Kennedy, but he also put part of the blame on Kennedy himself. He should have stated clearly that his opinions were off the record, Coglan said.[122] Despite the fact that Coglan was an editor at the *Saint Louis Post Dispatch*, its publisher, Joseph Pulitzer Jr., wrote a letter to Kennedy in which he said he regretted the publication of the interview and denounced it "as a breach of faith."[123]

The greatest impact of this unhappy episode was on Kennedy himself. His ambassadorship to the Court of St. James's, the height of his public career, was now drawing to an inglorious close. The very directness and candor that had always made Kennedy such good copy had finally ruined him; small wonder it had not happened before this, given his penchant for shooting off his mouth into any available ear. Since Kennedy had already resigned, the interview did not cost him the ambassadorship. But it did make his departure graceless.

The publication of the Lyons story brought a storm of protest in Britain within government circles, the House of Commons, and the Foreign Office, and among journalists who for some time had been worried about Kennedy's defeatism and its effect on morale. The *News Chronicle* wrote that members of the House of Commons of all political parties, many of whom were friends of Kennedy's, had been "puzzled" and angry about statements he made about the death of democracy and the ascendancy of National Socialism in Britain after he left London. They preferred to accept Roosevelt's opinion: "Britain is the last line of democracy."[124]

J. V. Perowne of the Foreign Office wrote that "the American Department [of State] sometime ago exposed the hollowness of any belief that Mr. Kennedy was a friend to this country."[125] Long anti-Kennedy, officials commented in their minutes of November 13 that his interview had had a "bad press" but noted that privately he had been making statements that sounded very like those attributed to him by the *Boston Globe* reporter. However, they were dubious about Kennedy's denial and took umbrage at his statement that Great Britain could "make peace on very reasonable terms at the present moment."[126] Lord Lothian, repudiating Kennedy's *Globe* comments, said that he had "never seen a country more democratic than England is today."[127]

British journalists took whacks at Kennedy, too. A. J. Cummings, who had had a run-in with Kennedy over his request that Cummings censor his anti-appeasement statements in a 1938 newsreel, wrote in his column "Spotlight on the War" for the *News Chronicle* that Kennedy "deceived many decent English people." "His suave, monotonous style, his nine over-photographed children and his hail-fellow-well-met manner concealed a hard-boiled business man's eagerness to do a profitable business deal with the dictators." "It is all to the good," Cummings wrote, "that the British people now know where Kennedy stands." His "greatest cause in the world" was keeping the United States out of war, whereas Roosevelt's was helping the British defeat "the criminal activities of the Nazi gangster."[128] British newsman George Murray, in a scorching letter to the London *Daily Mail*, wrote: "You have said things about us that we regret to hear. They are things which in time, I think, you will regret having said. . . . Perhaps you were always a defeatist and never owned it in public. . . . We can forgive wrongheadedness, but not bad faith."[129]

The Economist accused Kennedy of "making statements about British weakness and insincerity which no friend of Britain or lover of the truth would permit himself."[130] Even the staid *Times* of London was critical of Kennedy's habit of "distilling the sort of gloom which he has apparently adopted as his second nature."[131] Bilainkin, by contrast, one of Kennedy closest friends and a diplomatic correspondent, argued compassionately that judgment be suspended. "Let us be just to Kennedy, wait till fuller records are available. I have never doubted his friendship for the people of this country."[132] London's *Sunday Dispatch* expressed similar sentiments. It defended Kennedy for "being England's No. 1 friend in the US. . . . Mr. Kennedy is doing as much for Britain as any man in America."[133]

The barrage of criticism startled Kennedy, apparently oblivious of the callousness of his remarks. Once the darling of London and British society, heralded as the most popular American ambassador in memory, he had come to be despised, distrusted, and reviled. He was surprised and hurt. He issued a statement to the American press denying—untruthfully—that he made anti-British remarks and repudiating the "gossip" in London that he expected the British to lose the war. "This is nonsense," he said. "If an interview, which was repudiated by me, and a story in a gossip column are going to be sufficient to wipe out the broadcast I made, coupled with my two years and nine months in London, then I am beginning to wonder if I ever had very much standing in London."[134] Such unwise self-pity and surprise at the English reaction to his remarks reflected even less credit on Kennedy's judgment than his remarks themselves. He had in fact repeatedly predicted England's defeat; now he was denying having done so. In a letter to Bilainkin dated December 11, one month after the infamous interview, Kennedy said: "Much to my amazement was the fact that the English would use that as an excuse to write attacks on me, and when that was followed up the other day by _____ on the children, why then I can't understand it. To be attacked here by columnists, and bitter partisans, that's understandable, but to have England jump into the fray is beyond me."[135] Kennedy cabled James Seymour, Kennedy's secretary at the embassy in London, that he did not mind the attacks on him but resented the "personal observations on [his] family. . . . As far as I am concerned, I don't give a damn."[136] But of course he did give a damn. "I can't take criticism: I don't see how you can," Kennedy told Senator Burton Wheeler a few months later.[137]

In the weeks after the *Globe* interview, Kennedy spoke out frequently and intemperately against the British and their war. On November 13, 1940, he left for the West Coast on his antiwar crusade. While in California, he stopped off in Hollywood to visit his former motion picture colleagues Harry Warner, Samuel Goldwyn, Louis B. Mayer, and others. They welcomed their former colleague back to Hollywood by hosting a lavish luncheon in his honor at Warner Brothers. After dessert Kennedy made a mind-boggling, thundering, impromptu three-hour address that horrified the audience, a private informal gathering of some fifty movie magnates, most of them Jews. Although his remarks were off the record, word of them quickly spread throughout Hollywood.[138]

The famous actor Douglas Fairbanks Jr. "tattled" on Kennedy by sending FDR a letter that was too "hurried and probably too passionate" but contained the gist of Kennedy's remarks—remarks that he and many guests found disturbing. Kennedy emphatically stated that Britain had not yet lost the war but neither had she won it. There was no reason in *any way* (emphasis by Fairbanks) for the United States to enter the war. We should continue giving Britain aid but not to the extent that it compromises our neutrality. As in the infamous Lyons interview, Kennedy said again that Lindbergh and his appeasement groups "were not so far off the mark when they suggest that this country can reconcile itself to whomever wins the war and adjust our trade and lives accordingly." Like Lindbergh, Kennedy seemed almost willing to believe a dictator's promise and to claim that the United States was in no peril.

Kennedy "threw the fear of God into many of our producers and executives by telling them that the Jews were on the spot, and they should stop making anti-Nazi pictures or using the film medium to promote or show sympathy to the cause of the democracies versus the dictators," Fairbanks wrote Roosevelt. The film industry had a "dangerous" influence on the public and was abusing its power, the ambassador had said. Its members, and its Jews in particular, "would be in jeopardy" if they continued to do so. Anti-Semitism was increasing in Britain, and British Jews "were being blamed for the war." Fairbanks disputed the accuracy of Kennedy's statements and added that His Excellency was the butt of many jokes because he seemed to be "the most frightened man in the realm" when the bombing began in Britain.

Fairbanks also believed that Kennedy had been "violently influenced by strong Catholic appeasement groups and is in favor of a negotiated peace." The Catholic Church wanted peace "at any cost" because it would bring people back to the Church. It would use every means it had to preserve peace.

Kennedy's talk made a very strong impression; many found it quite persuasive, Fairbanks wrote. Because Kennedy was still accredited to Roosevelt as ambassador, Fairbanks thought that "many people . . . feel . . . he is voicing new Administration thoughts," despite the denials by many who refused to believe this. Fairbanks urged Roosevelt to made a strong statement stating the administration's position, and to remind people that our freedoms "cannot be taken smugly for granted." He should also accept Kennedy's resignation.

Kennedy's remarks were so unsettling and so unnecessary that many people speculated about his motives. Fairbanks said that Hollywood leaders thought that Kennedy was trying to promote a new contract for Will Hays, and that Kennedy himself wanted to clean house and scare the Jews out of Hollywood so that he could return to the film industry and take control.[139]

Kennedy's sensational remarks slowly appeared in the newspapers. Critics like the syndicated columnists Drew Pearson and Robert S. Allen made much of Kennedy's remarks and his visit to William Randolph Hearst. The newsmen reported that Kennedy had told the movie moguls

1. That England, although fighting heroically, faced overwhelming odds, and the United States might as well realize that England was virtually defeated.

2. That the United States should carefully limit its aid to Britain so as to gain time to become fully armed, in order to be in a better position to do business with the Axis victors.

3. That Hollywood producers should stop making films offensive to the dictators.[140]

Two anti-Nazi films, *The Mortal Storm*, starring Jimmy Stewart, and *The Great Dictator*, featuring Charlie Chaplin, had recently been released. Kennedy feared that their success would encourage the production of similar films.[141]

Kennedy, accompanied by his son Jack, a student at Stanford, flew to William Randolph Hearst's retreat, Wyntoon, outside of San Francisco. "I feel I know the situation abroad, and am in the best position to answer anybody . . . in America," he told Hearst. Kennedy also had the fullest answer to Britain's request for financial aid, he said, as well as a great many other problems that would involve the United States.[142] At a cocktail party at the Hearst retreat, Kennedy spoke with FDR's daughter Anna and his son-in-law John Boettiger, who took offense at Kennedy's opposition to Roosevelt's policies and tried to stick up for FDR. "What right have you to go against the principles of my father-in-law?" Boettiger demanded. Kennedy responded: "Now, wait a minute. I have not in any way said I'm not in accord with what your father-in-law says. Let's not argue now. . . . I'm not going to stoop to argue with you," Kennedy said as the tension mounted between the two. Despite hostess Marion Davies's attempt to dampen their quarrel with offers of drinks, which Kennedy declined, the two men squared off as Anna and Marion agreed to let them fight it out as the two sensible women retired to the powder room.[143] Boettiger sent a letter to FDR, warning him: "After our talk with Joe in California, both Anna and I were considerably worried about what we thought were Fascist leanings."[144]

Kennedy critics like Harold Ickes believed that "Kennedy is out to do whatever damage he can" and passed on to Roosevelt a report that Kennedy not only repeated his statements from the *Globe* interview about Britain's defeat and the demise of democracy in his Hollywood remarks, but went even further.[145] Apparently Kennedy told Hearst that he intended to begin a campaign for appeasement in the United States. He also planned to work with appeasement-minded journalists Roy Howard and Joe Patterson of the *New York Daily News*, the paper with the largest circulation in the United States. The team of Kennedy, Hearst, and Howard could become a formidable trio, Ickes predicted, with Kennedy's money and ability to raise even more, combined with the newspaper empire of the Hearst and Howard chains. If they were to be joined by the *Washington Times-Herald* and the *Chicago Tribune*, their publicity range would be enormous and potentially very devastating to Roosevelt's foreign policy and for aid to the democracies, the very thing that Roosevelt had always feared from his outspoken, maverick ambassador.[146]

"I'm just the same—you won't find me changed a bit," Kennedy had said after returning from London for the first time in June 1938.[147] And that was exactly the problem. Even at this late date, November–December 1940, he seemed to have forgotten nothing and learned nothing during his stay in London about what was at stake for Europe—or for the United States—or understood the nature of the Nazi regime. Kennedy's California statements had echoes of his Trafalgar Day speech, Chamberlain's defense of the Munich Agreement, Kennedy's question "why fight to save the Czechs?," and his memo arguing for a Fortress Americana, views that continued to put him at odds with Roosevelt.

Actually, Kennedy had said nothing that was a departure for him. His defeatist views were identical to those he had recited to Roosevelt only a month before, similar to his views expressed to Breckinridge Long, to those in the *Boston Globe* interview, to William Randolph Hearst, and to the Hollywood crowd. But the election was now over, FDR had won, and he was now free to end his game of cat-and-mouse with Kennedy and to cut the ties with him—something he had been postponing for some time. But he would not do it just yet, not so long as Kennedy could still be useful. Their relationship unraveled slowly, not abruptly, but irretrievably and conclusively, and culminated in a crescendo of abuse during a meeting at Hyde Park on November 20.

While Kennedy was on the West Coast, the Roosevelt family went to Hyde Park to spend a quiet weekend before Thanksgiving. They spoke of Kennedy, his interviews, his travels to California, and his visit to William Randolph Hearst. "We'd better have him down here and see what he has to say," FDR remarked. Mrs. Roosevelt met Kennedy's train at Rhinecliff and took him immediately to meet the president in his little study on the ground floor. Ten minutes later an aide told the first lady, "'the President wants to see you right away.' This was unheard of," Mrs. Roosevelt recalled. She rushed into the office. FDR asked Kennedy to step outside and said to her in a "glacial" and "shaking" voice, "I never want to see that son of a bitch again so long as I live. Take his resignation and get him out of here!" But "we've got guests for lunch and the train doesn't leave until two," she reminded him. "Then you take him around Hyde Park, give him a sandwich, and put him on that train!" Mrs. Roosevelt took Kennedy to her cottage at Val-Kill for lunch. Only when she began to listen to Kennedy's pessimistic assessment of the Allies' chances fighting an invincible and omnipotent Luftwaffe did she understand her husband's fury. Years later Eleanor Roosevelt described her husband's outrage at Kennedy as "the most dreadful four hours of my life."[148]

Even so, for public consumption, at least, the two men were still willing to pose as friendly colleagues rather than as adversaries and to appear to mend their rift, if only superficially. Kennedy still needed Roosevelt for another job in government and his blessing for anything he or his sons might do in politics, and Roosevelt still needed Kennedy's support or at least his acquiescence in the coming congressional debate over the Lend-Lease Bill.

"Very pleasant and agreeable," Steve Early, the White House press secretary, told journalists as he described Kennedy's long and leisurely meeting with the president on Sunday afternoon, December 1, 1940. Kennedy had gone to the White House for an unscheduled meeting to discuss his resignation as ambassador and his possible successor. Early reported that Roosevelt made "no objection whatsoever" to Kennedy's resignation, nor his determination to stump for peace, nor the Lyons interview, nor the Hollywood diatribe, and the president did ask Kennedy to stay on until his successor was named, just in case.[149]

Roosevelt, clearly suffering from a cold, a fever, and possibly pleurisy, Kennedy noted in his diary, seemed quite worried about the future, more than usual, as they discussed Britain's dire predicament. "Possibly, he recognizes the truth of what I have been telling him," Kennedy wrote, and again warned Roosevelt about Churchill. "Mr. President—Churchill is keeping the fight going only because he has no alternative as Churchill the fighter," Kennedy said. It was Churchill's fondest hope to get the United States to enter the war to share Britain's problems. "Mr. President, there is no doubt in my mind that Churchill has no particular love for the U.S. nor in his heart for you." "I know," FDR replied. "He is one of the few men in public life who was rude to me. (This is the story he told me last year)," Kennedy recorded. Roosevelt, however, was under no illusions about Churchill's motives, nor did he disagree with Churchill about the threat that Hitler posed. FDR needed no warning from Kennedy.

The president also told Kennedy that he had reviewed the financial situation of the British: "They're all right for quite a while," he said, a statement that put him at odds with his ambassador's predictions of imminent bankruptcy. But the president also realized that Britain would soon need financial support and he wanted to come up with a workable plan. Kennedy pointed out the danger to England if the Germans closed England's western ports and cut off her imports. Kennedy told FDR: "With England licked, the party is all over. You've got to help England *now* and you've got to get the defense up *now*," a position Roosevelt completely agreed with and embodied in his soon-to-be-announced landmark Lend-Lease legislation. "'As I see the picture,' Kennedy told FDR, 'you have 2 alternatives—To become greater than Washington or Lincoln or to become a horse's ass.' He said: 'I have a 3rd alternative—to be the one responsible for making the U.S. a small and unimportant power.' I said, 'That puts you in my second class.'"[150]

That evening Kennedy delivered a press release announcing his resignation as of November 6, 1940. It read: "Today [December 1, 1940] the President was good enough to express regret over my decision, but to say that, not yet being prepared to appoint my successor, he wishes me to retain my designation as Ambassador until he is," adding the last phrase to please Roosevelt. "But I shall not return to London in that capacity." Kennedy also told the press that after taking a short vacation to Palm Beach, he would begin a crusade and devote his energy to "the greatest cause in the world today, . . . to help the President keep the United States out of war" and to preserve "the American form of democracy."[151]

Although Roosevelt had described Kennedy's job performance in glowing terms to Sumner Welles, who predicted to Kennedy that he would soon be back in the government, this time the president did not publicly welcome his former ambassador back into the fold.[152] There was no "Dear Joe" letter thanking him for his service or a request to consider himself part of the administration. Those days were over and that relationship was finished.[153] After saying his goodbyes to the State Department, Kennedy said: "I'm out of a job now and off the payroll here."[154] His associates within the State Department, "now visibly relieved to be his associates no longer," according to journalists Joseph Alsop and Robert Kintner, confidants of the White House,[155] resolved to make his unemployment permanent. Since Kennedy had offered to work on any international problems after his resignation,[156] a reporter asked the president's press secretary whether Kennedy might serve in some other government post. "I don't see anything like that in the picture right now," Early replied,[157] as Kennedy left for Palm Beach for a vacation.

So long as Kennedy wore the president's protective mantle, his opponents were careful about their comments; but once he resigned as ambassador, the dam broke over his ill-considered remarks on both sides of the Atlantic. A host of critics with hatchets raised accused him of almost everything, with some justification—being a Nazi admirer, pro-fascist, an anti-Semite, a turncoat, a Roosevelt hater, a reactionary. Ickes, always an arch-critic of Kennedy, dubbed him a "wet blanket . . . defeatist."[158] Other critics labeled him a "defeatist propagandist" and likened him, not unnaturally, to Lindbergh.[159] The columnists Joseph Alsop and Robert Kintner, staunch interventionists, noted that wherever Kennedy went "there have been sudden crops of defeatist rumors and appeasement talk!" They marveled at Kennedy's denial of defeatism. "Let there be no mistake about it," they wrote. What he really intends to do is "to peddle appeasement all across the United States." His advice is deserving of about the same amount of "respectful attention as would be accorded, say, to Sir Horace Wilson in London," Chamberlain's appeasement-minded accomplice.[160]

Those praising Kennedy were every bit as partisan as his critics. Representative Louis Ludlow told the House of Representatives: "Thank God for Joseph P. Kennedy." In contrast to other ambassadors, he "stands four square, first, last, and all the time for America." Ludlow likened the former ambassador to "a great Rock of Gibraltar" in his advocacy of peace and America's noninvolvement in war, giving hope and cheer to millions of his fellow Americans.[161] The former president, Herbert Hoover, also praised Kennedy and remarked of him that "all the things he'd said and done in the last ten months had been of more help in keeping America out of the war than anything else."[162] The editorial writers of the *Washington Times-Herald* bemoaned the smear campaign against Kennedy and found nothing disloyal about his argument favoring a negotiated peace: "Kennedy has gone on unofficially and without undue publicity expressing the opinion that a negotiated peace would be better than a fight to a finish and that we ought to stay out"—precisely their own view.[163]

The ever loyal Arthur Krock defended Kennedy vigorously and praised the "good work" he did in London on behalf of the American people. He described his endorsement of Roosevelt's "aid short of war" as "hardly the plan of an 'appeaser,' though it can still be the program of a noninterventionist."[164] Even Krock recognized that Kennedy's service was tainted by off-the-record interviews for which he could only blame himself. "Unguarded talk" was also a serious defect; another was faith in his "hunches" rather than hard, cold facts and analysis. But those who knew Kennedy well, the journalist explained, knew how to ignore his "ingrained gloom." Unfortunately, the British did not. That is why they labeled him a "defeatist," Krock wrote.[165]

As an influential force in American politics, Kennedy was through. He was no longer a participant in the inner circle of men surrounding Roosevelt who made the decisions that so deeply affected people's lives. Most of what he could do was to conduct a rear-guard action by leading a wobbly crusade on behalf of peace and to undermine the president's foreign policy and at the same time court him to regain a position in his administration. As early as January 1941, before the hearings on Lend-Lease, Kennedy was looking for a back door by which to reenter the administration. His name had been mentioned as a possible emissary to Ireland to help the British in their relations with that stubbornly neutral country.[166] Such an assignment would present him in a positive light and no doubt bring him much needed favorable publicity. It was the bait that Roosevelt used to keep Kennedy in line.

Roosevelt viewed his victory in the election of 1940 as a referendum on the foreign policy of the United States and its role as the great "arsenal of democracy." In the weeks following the election, Roosevelt and his speechwriters, Sam Rosenman and Robert Sherwood, who had moved into the White House to write the speech, had gone through seven drafts. But it was Harry Hopkins who suggested the memorable phrase "the arsenal of democracy," a concept embodied in the Lend-Lease legislation. The public was introduced to the concept in a famous fireside chat on the evening of December 29, 1940, in which Roosevelt urged his fellow citizens to become that arsenal by demonstrating the same resolution, patriotism, and sacrifice it would if the country were at war.[167] The speech called for a dramatic piece of legislation that sprang from Roosevelt's creative mind and heralded the cessation of America's neutrality. The legislation would establish the arsenal and empower the president to give all aid short of war—to sell, transfer, lend, or lease military equipment, weapons, and supplies to nations whose security he deemed necessary to the United States. It left the issue of reimbursement up to the president's discretion.

"This is not a fireside chat on war," the president began. "It is a talk on national security." He criticized the widespread belief that the United States would not be seriously threatened by events overseas. Not since the days of Jamestown and Plymouth Rock has the security of the United States been so threatened, he emphasized. It is threatened by the expansionist program of three powerful countries—Germany and Italy and Japan. They have united to dominate the world and intend to destroy the United States if it interferes with their plans for expansion. Some say that the European and Asian wars are not a source of concern to the United States, Roosevelt said. They are wrong. The survival of the United States depends on the survival of Great Britain. If Britain were to be defeated, the Axis powers would control Europe, Asia, Africa, Australia, and the high seas—and be able to draw upon and use enormous military and naval assets against North America. We "would be living at the point of a gun—a gun loaded with explosive bullets economic as well as military," he said. To survive, we would have to become a militaristic power with a wartime economy. He ruled out the argument by the isolationists and advanced by Kennedy of a "negotiated peace," instead insisting on sending to the opponents of aggression all aid possible. "There can be no appeasement with ruthlessness." There is far less chance of the United States getting into war if we do all we can now to support the nations defending themselves against attack by the Axis than if we acquiesce in their defeat, submit tamely to an Axis victory, and wait our turn to be the object of attack in another war later on.

"The people of Europe who are defending themselves do not ask us to do their fighting. They ask for the implements of war, the planes, the tanks, the guns, the freighters which will enable them to fight for their liberty and for our security," Roosevelt asserted. To aid them, "we must have more ships, more guns, more planes—more of everything. . . . I want to make it clear that it is the purpose of the nation to build now with all possible speed every machine, every arsenal, every factory that we need to manufacture our defense material. We have the men—the skill—the wealth—and above all, the will." To protect the United States and to help Britain, America must become "the great arsenal of democracy," he urged. "I believe that the Axis powers are not going to win this war. . . . We have no excuse for defeatism. We have every good reason for hope—hope for peace, hope for the defense of our civilization and for the building of a better civilization in the future."[168]

The address could not have come at a better time for the British. As the president was speaking that evening, Londoners were being hammered by the heaviest bombing since the war began. The sky over London was thick with pungent smoke and looked like daylight as flames fanned by wind served as beacons for enemy aircraft and lit up the sky. The bombs destroyed much of the old city, including the Guildhall, dating from the days of William the Conqueror and the center of the city's government. Dr. Samuel Johnson's house in Gough Square off Fleet Street, eight of the churches built by Christopher Wren, and the Old Bailey were also burned. St. Paul's was endangered by rings of fire, but they were put out in time to save it. Homes, shops, offices, hospitals, and warehouses were destroyed or damaged. Eighty horses were killed when a bomb landed on a brewery. The devastation, according to one witness, was surpassed only by that caused by the Great Fire of London in 1666. The city was saved from greater destruction by the heroic efforts of firemen and civil defence volunteers. Women were heroic too; they served as ambulance drivers and messengers and handed hot drinks to red-eyed firefighters. There were few casualties. London went on with work as usual. The bombing was intended to break the morale of Londoners and to undermine Roosevelt's message. It did nothing of the kind. On December 30 at 3:30 a.m. Londoners were listening intently to Roosevelt's message on their radios, his address inspiring their determination and optimism.[169] And when Churchill and his wife visited the smoking ruins on a two-hour walking tour the next day, they were greeted with cheers as firemen and demolition workers paused in their work. Churchill smiled and doffed his hat. "Good luck," the crowd cried out; "Good luck to you," the prime minister replied. The morale of Londoners was as great as it had been in the early days of the Blitz in September, Churchill wrote in his memoir. "I thank you for testifying before all the world that the future safety and greatness of the American Union are intimately concerned with the upholding and the effective arming of that indomitable spirit," Churchill told Roosevelt on December 31.[170]

Americans were listening, too. At nine that evening, the hour for Roosevelt's address, there was a noticeable drop in the numbers of theatergoers in New York City. People stayed home to hear their president.[171] Opinion polls showed that 80 percent of Americans listening to the speech approved of Roosevelt's policy; only 12 percent opposed it.[172] But to carry out his plan, Roosevelt needed to gain Kennedy's support, or at least his acquiescence, since the crusading former ambassador could still do great damage to the president's plans. What he got instead was Kennedy's muddle-headedness, almost as good as his silence—or maybe even better, since it made him look confused, contradictory, and thoroughly ineffectual on foreign policy.

On January 14, 1941, Kennedy was invited by Hamilton Fish, Roosevelt's own congressional representative from Dutchess County, a staunch Republican isolationist and avid presidential foe, to appear before the Foreign Relations Committee of the House of Representatives and to testify on the Lend-Lease Bill, H.R. 1776. Opponents like Fish argued that it gave the president essentially dictatorial powers to conduct a kind of unauthorized war that the United States would inevitably be dragged into. Supporters, on the other hand, believed that it would do exactly the opposite: it would prevent American involvement in war by providing military aid to Britain against Germany.[173] Fish told Kennedy that he assumed that he would speak in opposition to the bill. "No comment," Kennedy replied, no doubt enjoying the suspense.[174]

Uncertain about the protocol, Kennedy asked Sumner Welles for advice. Welles said he would speak to Hull about the congressional invitation. Kennedy also informed the undersecretary that he intended to deliver a radio address on January 18, 1941, in which he would answer his critics and clearly explain his position on America's foreign policy. He was "sore" about "the strange things [that] had happened," he told Welles, indignant about the attacks against him by both sides, and still plagued by the president's "Hatchetmen," whom FDR refused to rein in. Welles tried to soothe Kennedy and asked him to do nothing until he had reported back to him.[175]

The president's promise never to see the former ambassador again after their Hyde Park interview was ignored in the face of Kennedy's avowed intention to lead an isolationist crusade against Lend-Lease. After speaking with the president, who expressed no opposition to Kennedy's congressional appearance, Welles relayed Roosevelt's invitation to Kennedy to come to Washington for a talk. No doubt "to butter me up," Kennedy replied. "Oh, no," the undersecretary answered.

After a brief meeting at the State Department on January 16, 1941, Kennedy called at the White House for an appointment with the president that was to last an hour and a half and made him nearly an hour late for his other appointments, something that delighted Kennedy. After waiting a quarter of an hour, he was finally ushered into the president's bathroom. Kennedy perched on the toilet seat while FDR, still wearing his gray pajamas and seated in his wheelchair, started to shave. The wily president could not have been friendlier or more engaging in this most intimate and informal setting clearly designed to take the edge off of his disgruntled former ambassador's resentment. It worked, as always. Roosevelt's charm completely disarmed Kennedy. After getting the formalities out of the way, Kennedy, as always, poured out his heart over the poor treatment he had received from both sides and especially from the president's "Hatchetmen." Roosevelt sympathized with him, as always, but interjected that he had fared worse, worse than anyone else in the last eight years except for his son Elliott.[176]

Why were so many people convinced that he and the president were not friends? Kennedy asked several times. Ignore the "kissers" and the "termites," as they were called; the president always did. Kennedy privately questioned this comment. Roosevelt couldn't ignore them; it "wouldn't have been human," Kennedy wrote in his diary.[177] It was unfair, he complained, "to wind up seven years of service in his Administration with a bad record" after fully supporting Roosevelt's agenda. "This time, I had to do something for the Kennedy family."[178]

They spoke about Kennedy's radio speech. He intended to explain his position on foreign policy and to urge every form of aid to Britain except military intervention; Roosevelt voiced no opposition. They discussed Lend-Lease. People were uncomfortable with the president's request for such vast powers as contained in the bill, Kennedy told him. Although the president probably could force the legislation through Congress, it "would leave a very bad taste." Besides, the American people "are not sure you want to keep out of war," Kennedy said. "For the last seven years," the president remarked, "I have been going to get them into every war that has taken place in Europe—and I haven't done it yet. I have said it 150 times at least. . . . I have no intention of going to war," he repeated. "I don't know whether it was due to my own suspicions," Kennedy wrote in his memoirs, "but it [did not] sound as convincing as it did before when he said that same thing."

They talked of old times: of Kennedy's possible successor, of Japan's interest in Manchuria and access to oil, of Germany's morale and rumors of Germany's desire for peace, of Roosevelt's son Jimmy and his adventures in Hollywood, of the British whom Kennedy did not think Roosevelt was "sold on . . . at all" and about whom Kennedy warned the president to be "gun-shy."

The president said that he "would like to have a long talk with me about the Irish situation," Kennedy recorded in his diary, and repeated what Welles had already told him, that Roosevelt thought "I was the only one who could help straighten [it] out." But their talk about Ireland never came to pass; "that was all that was said on the subject," Kennedy wrote.[179]

FDR, of course, was only playing with his ambassador, enticing Kennedy with the likelihood of his rejoining his inner clique and the likelihood of an appointment to Ireland. Nothing could have pleased Kennedy more. The president's strategy might also serve the greater good of keeping Kennedy's radio address and his testimony on Lend-Lease favorable or at least inconsequential—a shrewd and successful ploy by the president, reminiscent of his courtship of Kennedy just before the 1940 election by which Kennedy was seduced into giving a resounding radio address urging the president's reelection. It worked again. Kennedy's visit with FDR had the desired effect: it placated Kennedy and kept him in check. His radio address and testimony on Lend-Lease were harmless.[180]

Both in his radio address on January 18, 1941, and in his appearance before the hearings on Lend-Lease held by the House Foreign Affairs Committee two days later, Kennedy tried to court Roosevelt by fostering the illusion that they saw eye to eye on foreign policy. Kennedy argued for giving the greatest amount of aid to Britain and for staying out of the war. Both policies "can be applied without confusion and without . . . contradiction," he said.[181] He straddled the fence to such a degree that it could have pleased both ardent isolationist Senator Burton Wheeler and President Roosevelt if they only listened to half of it, journalist Dorothy Thompson of the *New York Herald Tribune* wrote.[182]

Egged on by critics, Kennedy's nationwide thirty-minute radio broadcast on January 18, 1941, his first as a private citizen, was described by the *Christian Century* as like a defense attorney's summation to the jury against charges of treason against the president.[183]

His son Jack, having earned his bona fides in his father's eyes with the publication of his book, served as consultant to him. On their San Francisco trip, they spent considerable time discussing how the ambassador might respond to the increasing attacks on him after the Lyons interview. Take the high road, Jack suggested; do not respond in kind to the personal attacks from Alsop and Kintner. Don't be defensive. But do say "you don't give a damn what they [Alsop and Kintner] say about you personally."

Use a thoughtful and judicious tone and correct the impression that you are still an "appeaser." Ask what the word means; dissect it, analyze its meaning; challenge your critics to define it. "I don't mean that you should change your ideas or be all things to all men," his son shrewdly advised, "but I do mean that you should express your views in such a way that it will be difficult to indict you as an appeaser unless they indict themselves as warmongers." Remember, too, that businessmen have always been suspected of being appeasers, particularly in England, since this was the group that supported appeasement. Thus, you must reject any similar beliefs. But also explain why you are not an isolationist. "*It is important that you stress how much you dislike the idea of dealing with dictatorships,*" Jack told him, underlining his opinion in his letter to his father. Stress that you hate dictators, you hate dealing with them and distrust every word they utter. Say that you have been successful under a system of democratic capitalism that you want to maintain. The way to maintain it is to stay out of Europe's war and to build up the United States economically and militarily. Say "it's not that you hate dictatorship less—but you love America more," his son said.

Subtly imply that you have been right all along but do so without opening yourself to criticism as a know-it-all. Say that you have been close to the situation for three years and had an eyewitness view of events. State that you always told the truth as you understood it, to the British and to the Americans.

With respect to the "gloom charge," say that you do not like gloom for gloom's sake but it may be of some advantage to be gloomy. You have seen plenty of optimists in the stock market and in diplomacy who got cleaned out. But offer some hope, too. Say that by preparing for the worst, you can deal with it. State again that "you don't care what people think—you are interested only in the long-run point of view of what is best for this country." Draw on your own experiences. That will make the speech interesting and give it authenticity.[184]

It was sound advice. His father listened and then delivered the speech his own way.

Kennedy spoke in a studio in the National Broadcasting Company in the RCA Building in the presence of Mrs. Kennedy, their daughter Patricia, and Edward Moore. The ambassador told his audience that he had decided to give the address because he intended to clarify and correct the many false statements that had recently appeared about his opinions on foreign policy. "The saddest feature of recent months is the growth of intolerance. Honest men's motives are being attacked," he said. He wanted to oppose those intolerant, "ruthless and irresponsible Washington columnists [who] have claimed for themselves the right to speak for the nation" and whose smear tactics against their opponents are a menace to our free institutions—a jab at Alsop and Kintner, despite his son's warning.

Kennedy particularly deplored the columnists' "false and malicious" charge against him as an "Apostle of Gloom" and vigorously denied that he was either a "defeatist" predicting Britain's defeat in the war, or an "appeaser" looking for a German peace offer contrary to British interests, or sympathetic to "Isolationists." Predictions about the war's outcome, he declared, could only be based on the knowledge of the strengths and weaknesses of both adversaries. Since he did not know about Germany's military strength or the "toughness" of her morale, especially after eight years of tyranny, he could not predict victory or defeat for either country. Those listening to his broadcast must have had trouble suspending their disbelief. Kennedy cheerfully added that he was an "appeaser," as he broadly redefined the term, "because I oppose the entrance of this country into the present war." So must all of you be, too, "who want to keep America out of war." The real defeatists were those who saw no hope for peace for the United States, he said—a rather confusing and muddled assertion.

Kennedy took pains to debunk the arguments of those who predicted dire consequences for the United States if it remained at peace and if Germany were victorious. He scoffed at the idea that Germany would lead a successful totalitarian attack against a peaceful United States. Just as it would be impossible for Germany or any other country successfully to invade the United States, to transport troops and ammunition over three thousand miles of ocean without shipping or airplane bases, and to sustain a force of military occupation over the North American continent in the face of a hostile citizenry aggressively defending their country, so would it be impossible for the United States to invade Europe, he said. The United States could not possibly send into Europe an expeditionary force large enough to make up the difference between the German and the English military forces. But of course it did, both in World War I and in World War II.

The United States should not go to war, Kennedy said as he explained why. It is true, he allowed, that worldwide German domination would be terrible to consider; but even that did not mean that the United States should enter the war. Presumably Kennedy believed that defeating Nazi Germany or preserving democratic Britain would not be sufficient war aims to go to war; he saw no such thing as an allied fight for democracy. How would going to war preserve our ideals? he asked. What would our war aims be? We should not enter just to support another country's war aims or to write a blank check. If we did enter, we would have to underwrite the entire effort. And at the war's end with the Allies victorious, our treasury would be empty and the fabric of our civilization destroyed. With the United States "standing guard," we would be obligated to reorganize Germany and the other European countries as well as ourselves to prevent them from going Communist—as the United States was to do. "Are our children's and our grandchildren's lives to be spent standing guard in Europe while Heaven knows what happens to America?" The answer to the question was yes.

Kennedy reminded his audience that he had always urged the American government to pursue two policies: "give the utmost aid to England" and avoid war. Aiding Britain is definitely in America's self-interest, he explained (sounding very much like Roosevelt himself), but not to the extent that we endanger American defenses or enter the war ourselves or undermine our own democratic institutions. "England is not fighting our battle." "This is not our war," he emphasized, willfully blind to any special Anglo-American relationship.[185] But because Britain's "spirited defense" is advantageous to us as a means of maintaining American ideals and interests, we ought to "arm to the teeth" and give Britain all possible help because it will give the United States the most essential thing it needs: "time—time to rearm,"[186] the refrain from Munich again.

But how could the United States buy time? Kennedy's confusing and contrary answer at the end of his address "may and may not" be to enact the Lend-Lease Bill, H.R. 1776 into law. On the one hand, he said that his observations of the British war effort led him to support centralized responsibility, a statement in support of Roosevelt's legislation. But then, inexplicably, and to the delight of Roosevelt's opponents, he stated his objections to the bill, saying that the immediate peril was not sufficient to justify surrendering an amount of congressional authority and responsibility "unheard of in our history." There were other "less dramatic ways" of securing the authorization Roosevelt needed than those proposed by the legislation, Kennedy said.[187] But what they were, no one, including Kennedy, was quite sure. Kennedy closed his radio address by issuing a clarion call: "America must unite—*now.* America must sacrifice—*now.* America must work—*now.* Then and only then can we hope to spare ourselves and our children from the dismal destiny of blood and tears."[188]

Kennedy "'had out-Hamleted Hamlet.' Instead of 'To be or not to be,' he had managed 'to be and not to be,'" journalist Dorothy Thompson of the *New York Herald Tribune* wrote. It was an example of "Mr. Kennedy vs Mr. Kennedy," which left everyone quite baffled. "It seems to me," she wrote, "Mr. Kennedy having taken a vote in his own mind . . . balances at zero."[189] Harold Ickes, who listened to the speech on his radio, thought that "Kennedy gave all of us the impression last night that he was doing some tightrope walking. He would seem to take one position and then to reverse himself. The speech was not impressive."[190] Kennedy's disastrous performance on his self-appointed mission made him appear irrelevant as he tried desperately and ultimately unsuccessfully to keep America out of the war that he feared Roosevelt was inching toward.

But unite behind whom or what? Kennedy's inability to explain himself effectively undermined his own argument.

Two days later, on January 20, 1941, Kennedy appeared before the twenty-five politically and geographically diverse members of the House Foreign Relations Committee in the Ways and Means Committee Room to begin the national debate on Lend-Lease or the "dictatorship bill" or the "blank check"—the terms depending on one's political orientation.[191] By ten in the morning the airy gallery was packed with several hundred spectators jammed in anywhere especially to hear him: inaugural visitors, congressional wives, dozens of interventionists and militant pacifists who, like a cheering squad, applauded when Kennedy took the stand.[192] The retiring ambassador, tanned, trim, and fit, argued for "Help-Britain-but-stay-out-of-war" as the first opposition witness in the hearings. They were convened by ranking member Hamilton Fish, a grandson of President Ulysses S. Grant's secretary of state. Other witnesses representing a wide variety of political perspectives included Norman Thomas, the chairman of the Socialist Party; isolationist Charles Lindbergh; General Hugh S. Johnson; and members of the State Department and the administration, including Secretary of the Treasury Henry Morgenthau, Secretary of State Cordell Hull, Secretary of War Henry L. Stimson, and Secretary of the Navy Frank Knox.[193]

Kennedy's only prepared text was his radio address, from which he did not deviate. He testified for five hours in an atmosphere of formality intermixed with levity and applause for his "Irish wit" and "Boston straight talk" against Lend-Lease.[194] Some of the questions asked of him were important; others were too silly or insulting to be taken seriously. He repeated the themes of his radio address on January 18 and offered such fence-straddling testimony that not even his friends on the committee could untangle him.[195] He was visibly torn between isolation and intervention; between loyalty to FDR and doubts about the wisdom of the bill's sweeping language and its broad delegation of power to the president. Kennedy reasoned that the present danger did not constitute an emergency for the United States. And yet he said that "to get things done, you have to have power in one hand—and to that extent, I am one hundred percent for granting," and then warned of the necessity of consulting Congress even during emergencies. He argued for a committee acting as a liaison between the executive and legislative branches of government.[196] Although he stated his opposition to the bill's present form, he was unable to be specific in his criticism or to explain how to improve it. And in one humorous moment he admitted, "I don't want to make any suggestions because I don't know what I'm talking about."[197]

Fish asked him what about this sixty- or ninety-day crisis we've heard so much about. Britain has been in a crisis ever since September 3, 1940, Kennedy replied; the crisis became particularly acute in June 1940, but there is no way of determining when Britain will fall, if that is what you mean by crisis. Did he know Britain's war aims? he was asked. No, he replied; nor did they matter in aiding Britain or in the congressional debate over Lend-Lease. Is it in the best interest of the United States to give the utmost aid to Britain? he was asked. "That's right," he shot back. Will the United States be worse off if Britain falls? "Yes, sir," he responded. The problem, according to him, was not financing the British, but "how to make the stuff and get it to them." They desperately need ships this year; otherwise their own shipping and food supply will be "serious and vital" problems.

One moment Kennedy railed against America's involvement by arguing that it was not America's war; the next he stressed America's stake in England's victory. Aid to Britain should be determined on the cold-blooded basis of American self-interest and would give the United States that "precious and indispensable element of time," he stated repeatedly. What would be done after the United States became fully armed remained unstated. The audience broke into sustained applause at the day's end when Hamilton Fish praised the ambassador as "the one man, who more than any other is trying to keep the United States out of this war."[198]

He seemed blind to the obvious—that Lend-Lease, like the destroyer deal, was an irreversible commitment that clearly revealed the "unwritten alliance" between a bellicose Britain and a peaceful America—the very thing he most feared.[199] But he also revealed his motive in his memoir. He knew "full well that England couldn't survive without Lend-Lease" and so he chose not to get too tough in his testimony or to make any public statements in opposition to it.[200]

Despite his testimony, the bill passed both houses of Congress on March 11, 1941, by 60 to 31 in the Senate and 317 to 71 in the House, a vote that reflected the will of the American people.[201] A Gallup poll showed that 62 percent of Republican and 74 percent of Democratic voters favored the Lend-Lease Bill in theory.[202] A jittery but still willing nation followed Roosevelt's leadership as it slid from neutrality to non-belligerency to intervention capped by its unwritten alliance with Britain, but it stopped at the last irrevocable act.[203] Kennedy's crusade to keep America out of war, by contrast, was stalled. By May 1941, 68 percent of the American public favored helping Britain even at the risk of war, and 85 percent thought that the United States would become a belligerent anyhow. Even so, 79 percent wanted to remain at peace, and 70 percent thought that the United States had either done enough or more than enough to aid Britain. At this stage, the American public seemed to have become as confused and contradictory as Kennedy.[204]

Now that Kennedy had lost his privileged place within that influential clique advising the president on foreign policy, he could speak out publicly and without reserve. But once again his message was Hamlet-like, contradictory and confusing, arguing both for isolation and intervention. On the one hand, at Oglethorpe University on May 24, 1941, Kennedy gave a brilliant, candid, downright isolationist commencement address; on the other hand, at Notre Dame on June 2, 1941, he delivered an address making the case for intervention.

At Oglethorpe, Kennedy told the audience of graduates and their families that as ambassador in London he had worked for peace. When war broke out, he supported aid to Britain because it bought us "the precious element of time," but he did not support intervention in war. The issue the administration now faced was how to make aid to Britain effective. He warned, however, that "we should not let our aid to Britain become the argument for direct involvement"; we should not go to war "just because we hate Hitler and love Churchill." From an economic point of view, a British victory would be helpful, but it would be "nonsense to say that an Axis victory spells ruin for us," he argued, oblivious to the implications for Europe's Jews or any conquered nation under Axis domination.

Criticizing Roosevelt by implication and sounding distrustful of him, Kennedy said, "There are some among us who sincerely believe that the welfare of the United States requires us to become a belligerent." They give us slogans and stir our emotions, but facts, along with "the completest candor," "the fullest disclosure," "the freest debate," are what the people who must suffer and die deserve to have before they can support the interventionist cause; it is the democratic way, he affirmed. The instincts of Americans are solid; "they want no part of this war" despite their hatred for National Socialism. "If America can hold firmly to her faith in herself, can continue to build a more permanent system of social, economic, and political justice, such an accomplishment will be far more impressive to the world than speeches, promises, or even armed intervention." Kennedy's summation of American foreign policy was succinct: "It is to rearm as swiftly as possible, to give every possible aid to Great Britain, but to stay out of war," as he had said in his radio address. As a father with two sons in their twenties who would soon enter military service and alter the Kennedy family's warm, rich, protected world completely, Kennedy's conclusion was particularly poignant:

> For you young Americans entering adult life in such a distorted time, the usual advice seems
> hollow. The ancient platitudes sound empty. Of course, you must have the qualities of greatness

of heart and soul. But today your generation needs character and faith more than all those who have gone before. . . . When the history of these times has been written, I hope and pray that it will show that the American lads of 1941 . . . contributed mightily to giving to all our people a sounder basis for orderly living and that all this was accomplished with the essential liberties still substantially unchanged. May you bring honor to your families and to your college by the measure of wisdom you will give to the serious problems of tomorrow and by the degree of self-sacrifice with which you face your solemn obligations.

It was a moving speech, one of Kennedy's best.[205]

The Notre Dame address given on June 2, 1941, was the only other public address Kennedy delivered between the Lend-Lease hearings and the bombing of Pearl Harbor. In the intervening week between the two addresses, on May 27, 1941, Roosevelt had declared a state of unlimited national emergency in a radio address, his first since the "Arsenal of Democracy" speech. It called for increased aid to Britain short of going to war and contradicted Kennedy's Oglethorpe speech. The ambassador dutifully changed horses, unwilling to publicly contradict the president. His address at Notre Dame on June 1, 1941, must have delighted the interventionists and Roosevelt supporters as much as the Oglethorpe address had put them off. He told the commencement audience at Notre Dame that FDR's proclamation of an unlimited emergency was a "most historic and most solemn" one and required the "unlimited loyalty" of Americans, and he urged cooperation with the president. The remainder of the speech was rich in Catholic morality. He concluded that there was much in our culture that should be repudiated: "A monopolistic capitalism, as defined by the Papal encyclicals, which freezes credit, concentrates wealth in the hands of a few, excludes labor from a share of the profits, and considers the right to property as so absolute as to be unbounded by its use, is not worth preserving. . . . An economic system which . . . permits subversive groups and racketeers to infiltrate into its ranks. . . . A system of education which ignores, sometimes repudiates, religion and morality is not worth preserving." But there was also much that should be preserved. "The essence of *Americanism* [Kennedy's italics] is . . . the recognition of the sacredness of human personality and the inherent inalienable rights which every man possesses independent of the State."[206]

The two commencement addresses illustrated two conflicting points of view; by canceling out each other, they had once again virtually destroyed any influence Kennedy might have had on the conduct of American foreign policy.

Throughout 1941, between the hearings on Lend-Lease and the bombing of Pearl Harbor, Kennedy generally remained out of the public arena and refrained from joining in the isolationist campaign against the president. Kennedy spent much of the year with his family—the last one they would ever have together. But he still desperately wanted to rejoin the administration and have another job. Because Roosevelt wanted to keep Kennedy under his control, he did shrewdly dangle several jobs in front of Kennedy after his resignation and the attack on Pearl Harbor, but he did so knowing that the jobs were beneath Kennedy's dignity and that Kennedy would refuse them. A Kennedy dependent on Roosevelt for a position, still teeming with ambition and hungry for the political limelight, gave the president the best opportunity for managing him. But nothing came of it: from a variety of people there was too much opposition to Kennedy's reappointment. But the major reason Kennedy was not offered anything suitable was that Roosevelt did not want it; when he was through, he was through. He had had it with Kennedy. When Kennedy left his post in disgrace and embarrassment in February 1941, the doors of government service closed behind him permanently.

On December 7, 1941, Kennedy, vacationing in Palm Beach, turned on the radio and heard the stunning news of the Japanese attack on the United States' fleet at Pearl Harbor. This meant war. In his diary he wrote: "When you consider the Japanese situation, our attitude toward them, and that Roosevelt knows they have been preparing for 20 years, our unpreparedness is nothing short of insanity."[207] But swept up in a wave of tumultuous patriotic anger, he quickly put aside past grievances and immediately cabled Roosevelt five hours after the attack: "In this great crisis all Americans are with you. Name the battle post. I'm yours to command."[208] Two days later Kennedy received a form letter from Stephen Early thanking him for his offer of assistance.[209] Then, again nothing. As if to remind Roosevelt of their correspondence, Kennedy sent him several bottles of Champagne for Christmas. He received a polite thank-you note. Again, nothing.[210]

Nearly a month later, on January 5, 1942, Kennedy heard from the House Majority leader, John W. McCormack, who had spoken to Roosevelt and urged him to employ Kennedy in the defense program. FDR remarked that he was surprised at not hearing from his former ambassador, whom he claimed to have "great affection for" and described as "a tough Irishman and very stubborn." He "was practically the only important man in the country" who had failed to offer his services after the attack at Pearl Harbor, the president told McCormack. McCormack repeated his conversation to Kennedy, and urged him to write to Roosevelt again and to remind him about his telegram and to ask to see him and offer his services. Then again, nothing.[211]

Disturbed by the apparent misunderstanding that festered for several months, Kennedy finally swallowed his pride and wrote to FDR on March 4, 1942, to straighten out the problem. He asked Grace Tully, the president's secretary, to deliver it to the president personally.[212] The ambassador told the president that not only John McCormack but Senator Alben Barkley as well had said that Roosevelt seemed surprised at not hearing from him. "I don't want to appear in the role of a man looking for a job for the sake of getting an appointment," he told his former boss, "but Joe and Jack are in the service and I feel that my experience in these critical times might be worth something in some position. I just want to say that if you want me, I am yours to command at any time." Kennedy also forwarded copies of his telegram of December 7 and the perfunctory White House reply from Steve Early.[213] He then waited for Roosevelt to respond.

Several days later, on March 7, 1942, Kennedy finally received a reply from the president. "It is mighty good to get your letter and I am very certain that I did not get your telegram of December seventh. This was probably because several thousand came in at the same time and were handled in the office without my ever seeing them," FDR wrote in his most charming, nonchalant manner. He also mentioned that he was "of course, sure that [Kennedy] wanted to do everything possible to help," and added that, given Kennedy's former experience in shipbuilding, he might be useful in the shipping industry.[214] Unaccountably, Kennedy seemed to accept Roosevelt's description of the chaos in the White House as the legitimate explanation for his non-response despite the fact that Steve Early had written to Kennedy immediately upon receipt of his December 7 letter and said that the president was pleased by his offer of assistance.[215]

Kennedy called Rear Admiral Emory Scott Land, the head of the War Shipping Administration and Kennedy's successor at the U.S. Maritime Commission on March 11, 1942, to inquire about the kind of job that Land envisioned, what the expected results were, and what authority Kennedy would have. Land explained the options: set up a new shipbuilding company, help manage four or five of the weak shipyards, or manage a wage board. None of the suggestions appealed to Kennedy. In none of the proposals was there a position "in which I could get you any real results," he told Roosevelt in a letter the next day, March 12. Nevertheless, Kennedy continued, "I think you know that if I am given a job clearly and concisely I will work hard to get you the results you want, but running around without any definite assignment and responsibility, I'd just be a hindrance to the program." Even so, it will be "a great satisfaction for me to know that you will use me if the proper occasion arises. I'll be there when it does."[216]

Joe Eastman, the director of Defense Transportation, offered Kennedy a position in charge of all rubber transportation. "Definitely a rotten job," Kennedy wrote in his diary, "I know nothing about transportation,"[217] but he told Eastman he would think it over. Kennedy decided to discuss the offer with Roosevelt and made an appointment with him to do so.

When Kennedy arrived at the White House on April 15 for an appointment for the 12:45 slot on the calendar, usually a dead time, he was met by Steve Early and Grace Tully, who ushered him into the president's office graciously. Roosevelt, looking "badly," but "gay," Kennedy noted in his diary, glanced up and smiled at him but was too busy writing at his desk to shake his hand or to inquire about the family, a not so subtle rebuff. Throughout their thirty-five-minute meeting, Kennedy continued to feel snubbed. Roosevelt made a dig at Kennedy by seeming to criticize a journalist who wanted a job but refused to say he was sorry for all the misunderstanding he had caused for Roosevelt. "He had not taken me back to the fold," Kennedy confided to his diary, nor was he, Kennedy, sorry. Roosevelt did not seem to have read Kennedy's letter of March 12 and "had no friendly feeling" for him, Kennedy noted, believing—correctly, no doubt—that the president was only meeting with him because it was "good politics." "He will put me to work not particularly to help the war effort, but to help his politics." But the president could not even help his politics, as he could find nothing suitable for Kennedy. Eastman's proposals "would be no good";[218] nor would the job with the rubber program, the president said.[219]

Newsmen asked FDR at his press conference on April 21, l942, a week after Kennedy's visit to Washington, whether Kennedy would be returning to the administration. "No, no," was the president's reply. "I had a very pleasant talk, that was all."[220] Indeed, that was all.

Certainly Roosevelt understood Kennedy. Kennedy had to have a considerable job in keeping with his considerable opinion of his considerable talents, one befitting a man who had headed two federal agencies and held a top diplomatic post. FDR also knew that Kennedy was temperamentally incapable of serving as a subordinate to anyone except the president himself.[221]

In addition to Roosevelt's opposition, there was strong private and public hostility to any consideration given to Kennedy for a government position, so much that there was really no likelihood of an important position for him in FDR's wartime administration. The ambassador had offended many liberals, Jews, and bureaucrats in the president's inner circle. He lumped them together as "a lot of bastards"—"Frankfurter, Hopkins and Cohen," along with "Perkins, Rosenman, Ickes and Morgenthau" as well as the "Palace Guard of Ickes, Frankfurter, Corcoran, and Hopkins."[222] Some of them maintained an unrelenting vendetta against him and his stand on the war; but he blamed their hostility and Hopkins's opposition in particular on Kennedy's political conservatism. Kennedy also accused the Jews of holding a deep grudge against him because of his position on refugees a few years earlier.[223] The "bastards" kept up their opposition to him and succeeded in blocking his return to Washington. Moreover, Kennedy suspected that Roosevelt had "a decidedly anti-Catholic feeling" deep down in his heart that was shared by the entire Roosevelt family. The president had not yet appointed any other notable Catholic to any important position so far, Kennedy noted in his diary.[224]

Felix Frankfurter, in his diary, offered his own explanation about why Kennedy had been offered no important post during the war. Writing in 1943, he said that Kennedy

was not only venting his gorge against the New Deal, but more particularly his personal resentment against Harry Hopkins and me, who he, in his foolish and ignorant way, blames for his exclusion from participation in the conduct of the war. I don't suppose it ever enters the head of a Joe Kennedy that one who was so hostile to the war effort as he was . . . , and so outspoken in his foulmouthed hostility to the President himself, barred his own way to a responsible share in the conduct of the war.[225]

And Hopkins and Frankfurter were not alone. When an old adversary, Joe Curran, head of the CIO's National Maritime Union, heard the news that Kennedy was being considered for a government position, he attacked him in the press. "If you want to win the war you don't put in a key spot, like shipping, a man who wants to make peace with Hitler."[226]

Nothing came of the job offers. "To hell with it," Kennedy wrote in his diary.[227] Feeling sorry for himself for being treated like a pariah and relegated to being little more than an observer of the dramatic events being played out on the great global stage upon which he so loved performing, he wrote to John Boettiger, FDR's son-in-law. "Now, if my statements and my position mean that, outside of the ever-loyal Boettigers, I am to be a social outcast by the administration, well so be it. . . . if that's the way it is, it's just too bad."[228]

But the primary reason Kennedy was not reemployed by the Roosevelt administration was the president himself. Who had more reason for distrusting and disliking Kennedy? The doors to government service stayed locked and remained so throughout the war.[229] In a letter to his son-in-law, who had forwarded Kennedy's letter to him, FDR wrote:

> It is, I think a little pathetic that he worries about being, with his family, social outcasts. As a matter of fact, he ought to realize . . . that he had only himself to blame for the country's opinion as to his testimony before the Committees. Most people and most papers got the feeling that he was blowing hot and blowing cold at the same time—trying to carry water on both shoulders.
>
> The truth of the matter is that Joe is and always has been a temperamental Irish boy, terrifically spoiled at an early age by huge financial success; thoroughly patriotic, thoroughly selfish and thoroughly obsessed with the idea that he must leave each of his nine children with a million dollars apiece when he dies (he has told me that often). He has a positive horror of any change in the present methods of life in America. To him, the future of a small capitalistic class is safer under a Hitler than under a Churchill. This is sub-conscious on his part and he does not admit it.[230]

Roosevelt had it right.

Conclusion

Joseph Kennedy had "tempt[ed] all the Gods of the World" by accepting the ambassadorship to the Court of St. James's.[1] Boake Carter had advised him not to take the job, warning him that he didn't have what it took to be an ambassador and predicting that he would be hurt as never before. Carter was right. Kennedy's performance showed that he did not have the diplomatic skills, training, judgment, expertise, and temperament. Lacking education and experience in foreign affairs, a broad vision of international relations, a capacity for the impersonal assessment of events, and a steady temperament, Kennedy failed to understand the shifting treaties and alliances dominating the international order, and the expansionist nature of Nazism. Kennedy's hubris, complete confidence in his abilities, and his ambition to protect and enhance his family's fame and fortune blinded him to his limitations. Bred to conquer, wanting "everything,"[2] loving to be at the center of the action, and thirsting for social recognition and revenge against the Boston Brahmins, Kennedy found it impossible to decline the honor of being the first Irish-Catholic ambassador to the Court of St. James's. Roosevelt thought that appointing Kennedy to the post was "a great joke, the greatest joke in the world."[3] But when Kennedy's ambassadorship was over, nobody was laughing. It ended in self-inflicted disgrace, just as Boake Carter had foretold.

Kennedy failed to realize how different World War I and World War II were, and how dissimilar Kaiser William II and Adolph Hitler were.[4] "[Joe] could never understand how anyone could really believe that all that killing and bloodshed could ever settle anything. As he saw it," Rose explained to Doris Kearns Goodwin, "the essence of war was waste and destruction—the destruction of wealth, the destruction of order, the destruction of property and the destruction of lives. And nothing, he believed, could ever be worth all that destruction." War was "certain to ruin the victors as well as the vanquished"—a statement that described his view in 1914, a statement that still described his view in 1939.[5] These views he would repeat in the late 1930s as ambassador to the Court of St. James's.

Throughout the 1920s and 1930s, Kennedy's views on foreign affairs reflected warmed-over opinions of others like William Hearst and Father Coughlin, or uninformed fears from Americans worried about overseas adventures. Kennedy lacked the ability to distinguish his country's interests from his family's, and he evaluated events on the guiding principle of their effect on his family and his fortune. He supported a policy of isolationism in American foreign policy because he believed that it would keep the United States out of war and keep his sons safe. "I have four sons and I don't want them to be killed in a foreign war," he often said.[6]

The Roosevelt administration's foreign policy reflected the overwhelming desire among the American public for a policy of isolationism and for a passive policy embedded in the neutrality legislation. It was makeshift, poorly defined, and lacked strong leadership, a policy of "pinpricks and righteous protests."[7] Early in Kennedy's ambassadorship, while Roosevelt was groping for a foreign policy appropriate to the expansionist demands of Hitler and Mussolini, Kennedy had a unique opportunity to influence the president's views; but he did not do so. His inability to accept guidance or authority from Washington undermined his close relationship with Roosevelt. So, too, did his willingness to be "taken in" by the British establishment, much to Roosevelt's surprise. A rift developed between him and Roosevelt over his insubordination to Washington, over rumors of his presidential or vice-presidential ambitions, and over his long-distance wooing of the press. It widened and deepened as Roosevelt began to question Kennedy's diplomatic judgment and impartiality, his temperament, and his motives. After Munich, as Roosevelt began to grope for a policy of "methods short of war"[8] and to develop a more active foreign policy, his suspicion and dislike of Kennedy grew. And when World War II broke out and Kennedy argued for a compromise peace, Roosevelt ignored him. Roosevelt appointed his own representatives and sent them on fact-finding trips that circumvented Kennedy. FDR did not inform Kennedy of his decisions, transferred key discussions to Washington, and disregarded Kennedy's advice. Kennedy became bitterly resentful over his isolation and lack of information. And once Winston Churchill became prime minister and Roosevelt began to work closely with him, Kennedy was even more isolated. Kennedy accused Churchill of being an unscrupulous warmonger intent on dragging the United States into war. And Churchill disliked Kennedy's attempts to keep the interests of the two countries separate, despised his gloomy dispatches describing Britain's precarious position, and detested his arguments for a negotiated peace.

Upon becoming ambassador, Kennedy received little guidance in foreign affairs from Washington and was left to his own diplomatic devices. He relied on his own wits and judgment as he represented a policyless nation confused and divided on foreign policy. He was temperamentally unable and unwilling to subordinate his views to those of his superiors in Washington or to carry out their policies. Repeatedly he initiated his own policies from

London—"shirt-sleeve diplomacy"[9] he called it—often flouting Washington's authority or failing to get Washington's consent for Chamberlain's appeasement policy. His diplomatic initiatives were meant to prevent war, but they threatened both American isolation and British appeasement.

Lacking firm direction from Washington, Kennedy fell prey to the views of his host country, or those of Neville Chamberlain and the British establishment. Kennedy's lack of experience in, or understanding of, diplomacy and Washington's non-guidance made him an eager pupil of Chamberlain. Impressed by the prime minister's realism and practicality in foreign affairs, Kennedy believed that only the prime minister and his policy of appeasement could save England from war. But Kennedy's perspective was too limited. He failed to seek out the opinions of those outside of the British government, and he dismissed Chamberlain's critics, like Winston Churchill, who argued for a Grand Alliance. Kennedy blamed Churchill for urging war on an unprepared Britain.

Kennedy and Chamberlain had similar views of international problems and their solutions. Both had limited vision of international affairs. Both failed to understand the expansive and aggressive nature of Nazism and Hitler; both failed to see that the appeasement policy served to increase Hitler's demands, and later failed to see that Hitler's demands could not be peacefully accommodated. Kennedy couldn't change because he was mired in his family and fortune; Chamberlain couldn't change because he was mired in Victorian values. Kennedy supported Chamberlain's policy so long as it could be pursued without the collaboration of the United States. He believed that it would prevent war. And when war did break out, Kennedy urged that the United States ensure that the war be contained in Europe and that the United States only provide the British with military matériel, such as destroyers. He also did and did not support Lend-Lease. Ultimately Kennedy went much further than Chamberlain in rejecting war as an instrument of statecraft and called upon Roosevelt to initiate a negotiated peace.

Kennedy interpreted most international events in economic terms. He viewed the Anschluss as an opportunity to secure markets, and he did not understand the political transformation in the balance of power or the increased threat to Czechoslovakia. He urged the United States to do nothing—exactly what Roosevelt intended to do. Although Kennedy was a shrewd negotiator for the Anglo-American Trade Agreement, far superior to Secretary of State Cordell Hull and the State Department, the negotiations nearly led to the destruction of his relationship with Hull and undermined his influence in Washington. Kennedy agreed with Hull's economic nationalism and saw the value of the agreement to world peace. But he did not understand that the importance of the agreement was national rather than international. It enhanced American exports and the U.S. balance of trade, but it disregarded the importance of political issues.

The crisis over Czechoslovakia in the summer and fall of 1938 illustrated Kennedy's naive and simplistic view of the threat that Hitler posed. Kennedy's interpretation of events and his repeated attempts to get Roosevelt's support for Chamberlain's policy revealed his ineptness as a diplomat by undercutting his intention to support British appeasement and American isolationism. Instead, his personal diplomacy, his attempts at creating an American-German rapprochement, his call for Washington's reassurance to Britain, for trips to Germany, for blank checks, for film censorship, and for Chamberlain's broadcast, could have made Hitler all the more determined to expand and get the settlement he wanted.

Kennedy's narrow diplomatic views and his near hysteria over war blinded him to the realization that without American diplomatic or military support, his sweeping promises of American aid meant nothing and violated the very policy of isolationism he so championed. His views could also lead to war, the thing he deplored. He seemed convinced that Hitler cared about American attitudes toward Europe and that Hitler could be restrained without American military support for appeasement. Like many others, Kennedy did not grasp Hitler's ambitions.

Kennedy's repeated attempts to get Roosevelt's support for Chamberlain's policy vis-à-vis Czechoslovakia in the summer and fall of 1938 made the president believe that Kennedy had become a pawn of the prime minister, who wanted to shift the blame for Britain's decision about going to war onto the United States. But Kennedy, either blinded by or indifferent to events, thought along other lines. Repeatedly he involved himself in the foreign affairs of the allied nation to which he was posted and acted contrary to his own country's foreign policy. Kennedy conferred with British officials and other dignitaries and spoke nearly daily to Washington, earning high praise for his reports and for keeping officials well informed. He was deliberately creating the impression of continuous consultations between the British and American governments, contrary to Washington's wishes, as well as pursuing his own private foreign policy with a London-Paris-Washington peace axis.

But Roosevelt would have none of it: no personal diplomacy, no rapprochement with Germany, no reassurances to Britain, no trips to Germany, no blank checks, no Chamberlain broadcasts. Nevertheless, Washington did little to correct Kennedy or to offer him another policy. It had none. Washington would not compromise American neutrality and continued its twin strategies: avoid war for which the United States was not prepared and oppose Hitler's aggression with outrage and finger-wagging. The United States and Britain had complementary policies: the American policy of isolation underlay Britain's appeasement policy but gave Britain no aid, and Chamberlain's policy permitted the United States to ignore the need for a more aggressive foreign policy. Roosevelt encouraged Chamberlain to stand up to Hitler without giving him the means to do so, and Chamberlain allowed the United States to continue its policy of no commitments, no alliances.

The Munich Agreement thrilled Kennedy, who provided a credible argument in favor of it. It had bought Britain time to rearm and to strengthen its military. But it gave the Germans time, too, and they used it more wisely. When war broke out in September 1939, the British were weaker than they had been a year earlier, but the Germans were not. Kennedy also concluded that the German people did not want war, that Chamberlain's persistence prevented collapse of the negotiations, that Mussolini exercised a restraining influence on Hitler, and that Roosevelt's messages to Hitler had been decisive. But Kennedy overestimated Roosevelt's influence on Hitler. Kennedy also failed to urge the adoption of friendlier relations with the Soviet Union, which had not been invited to Munich, or to follow Churchill's advice and adopt a policy of firmness or to pursue a Grand Alliance. Kennedy's policy for the United States was to continue to follow a neutral policy in Europe—odd advice from someone who seldom followed it himself.

Kennedy understood that in the fall of 1938 Britain lacked the diplomatic alliances, the military strength, and the public support for a war over Czechoslovakia. Britain also lacked support from her dominions, or from the Soviet Union, or from the United States. Kennedy loyally continued to regard Chamberlain as a realist in the pursuit of appeasement at Munich and in his distrust of Hitler, and continued to reject Churchill's anti-fascist league, which would divide Europe into two armed camps and could lead to war. But Kennedy concluded that there was no valid peaceful response to Germany's demand for the Sudetenland; ironically, it would have to be answered by war. This was hugely contradictory: he argued for no war and yet that war was the only way to solve the problem.

In the aftermath of Munich, Kennedy advocated a policy of coexistence with the dictators—a policy that led to his embarrassment and greater estrangement from Washington, especially after Kristallnacht, Hitler's pogrom against the Jews. Perhaps Kennedy's embarrassment and Washington's reaction led him to argue for "The Kennedy Plan" to resettle Germany's Jews. It was a proposal that he once again made on his own initiative and without the administration's approval. It received much fanfare in the press but led to accusations of anti-Semitism, a lifelong charge that Kennedy always resented. The publicity surrounding it led to criticism that Kennedy was acting in his interests, not the country's, and deepened the rift between him and Roosevelt, who was by now no longer laughing at his "greatest joke."[10]

After Munich, Roosevelt began to look for ways to aid the victims of aggression. He developed a policy of "methods short of war" and suggested revising the Neutrality Act. His ambassador in London, by contrast, advised him in two memos to pursue a passive foreign policy and to adopt a "live and let live" approach to the dictators.[11] The military defeat of the democracies would require the United States to survive alone in a totalitarian world, Kennedy predicted. It would have to adopt an American form of fascism, a policy of isolation and of virtual pacifism. Despite Kennedy's fatalistic conclusions, he continued to urge a policy of no entangling alliances, even though alliances might prevent the war he so dreaded. Although Kennedy desperately wanted peace, he failed to see how the United States could help sustain it—that was a problem for others. To guarantee peace and safeguard the Kennedy family, any people must be sacrificed—the Czechs, the Jews, and later the Poles—and any price must be paid, including democracy itself. But Roosevelt, who had a deeper understanding of Hitler and never doubted the strength of democratic institutions, ignored his ambassador's advice.

Chamberlain, too, was searching for a way to deal with Hitler in the aftermath of Munich. He reversed Britain's foreign policy and provided guarantees to Poland, Greece, and Rumania after Hitler's absorption of the rest of Czechoslovakia in March 1939, a reversal that Kennedy unaccountably loyally supported. But Chamberlain's new system of commitments from the Baltic Sea to the Black Sea and the Aegean, intended to protect the independence of the countries, could actually bring on what Kennedy most feared—war.

Chamberlain and Kennedy began to diverge on foreign policy: the British appeaser would stop Hitler's aggression by war; the American appeaser would advocate isolationism and pacifism regardless of what Hitler did. But Kennedy also supported the repeal of the Neutrality Act and the buildup of the American military, which he believed would deter Hitler from going to war. Kennedy seemed unable to decide what policy would best prevent war and safeguard the security of his family and the country.

Throughout the summer of 1939, Chamberlain's government had been debating its stance toward the Soviet Union. But Chamberlain was not able to overcome his aversion to the Soviet Union, which was excluded from Britain's system of commitments and left isolated, just as it had been at Munich. Kennedy shared Chamberlain's distrust of the Soviet Union and had predicted that short of military action, either the Soviets would be dominated by Germany or they would retire into splendid isolation to watch the Western powers devour themselves. Thus the opportunity for an Anglo-Russian alliance melted away because no agreement could be achieved about three small countries—Estonia, Latvia, and Lithuania.

Kennedy was utterly shocked and in complete despair when the Germans and the Soviets announced the Nazi-Soviet Nonaggression Pact on August 23, 1939. He urged Roosevelt, at the request of the Chamberlain government, to put pressure on the Poles to accept Hitler's demands and work for a Polish Munich to preserve peace. Buy time; Kennedy wanted more time. He desired time to buy peace; peace was familial and financial, not theoretical or national. Peace was more important than stopping Hitler. Roosevelt refused to buy time and Chamberlain refused to violate his new agreement with Poland.

With the outbreak of war, Roosevelt continued to oppose playing any part in any arrangement that would allow Hitler to remain in power or to dominate central Europe. Kennedy, by contrast, saw Nazism as a source of stability in central Europe. If Hitler were defeated, Kennedy predicted there would be a rise of a new social order in central Europe, and Nazism could give way to socialism or worse—communism. Why not just give Hitler what he wanted? Give him central Europe, Kennedy advised. Britain didn't need it. Surely a different government would come to power in Germany in the future. Even Hitler's behavior, "God-awful" as it was,[12] was still better than war, he argued. Anything was better than war; he would prevent war "single-handedly, if necessary."[13]

Kennedy's shortsighted view of Nazism blinded him to the obvious—that Britain had no choice but to fight. If Britain abandoned the Poles, especially after signing the Anglo-Polish Agreement, it would lose its moral authority and international prestige, a consequence that Kennedy either didn't understand or didn't care about. But Roosevelt did. Unlike Roosevelt, Kennedy doubted the strength and vitality of democratic institutions; he was skeptical of the ability of leaders of democratic countries to throw off restraints after wartime and to restore civil liberties and freedom to their peoples. Kennedy's fatalism kept him from taking account of Britain's strengths: its united empire, its strong morale, Churchill's excellent wartime leadership, its international experience and prestige, and enough military resources to hold on until, "in God's good time, the New World, with all its power and might, steps forth to the rescue and the liberation of the Old.[14]

To be pessimistic about Britain's chances for victory with the outbreak of war in 1939 was to be well informed. Kennedy had been shown the balance sheets about Britain's finances, diplomacy, and military might. Most British officials and military experts agreed with him. He became an unrelenting prophet of doom, blinded by fear and fatalism, certain of Britain's destruction and scared about America's entry into war.

With war, Kennedy found London chilly. Chamberlain became chilly; the cabinet closed ranks as Kennedy lost status and influence. Once immensely popular with the public and on very friendly terms with the royal family and the British establishment, Kennedy had been seen as a defender of their interests. He had been treated with respect and confidences by Chamberlain, Halifax, and the Foreign Office. But war changed everything. Kennedy continued making the rounds of officials' offices and giving unsolicited advice to Chamberlain and Roosevelt, but he refused to see that neither was paying much attention to him. He no longer represented the views of his own government, nor did he have the confidence of his host government. He was now seen as duplicitous and treacherous as word of his defeatism and pessimism leaked back to British officials.

Kennedy's swan song to Washington was that British eyes will constantly be on the United States. Britain will want aid as it tries to drag the U.S. into war. We must safeguard our own interests and tell the British that we don't want any part of this mess. "This is not our war," he said again and again.[15] And yet he did want to help Britain and France by revising the neutrality laws and giving as much aid as possible, the germ of Lend-Lease. And he did urge that Roosevelt become "the savior of the world"[16] by being "a combination of the Holy Ghost and Jack Dempsey"[17] and offering a proposal for peace. Washington quickly rejected the proposal, told Kennedy to mind his own business, and stated that there were no circumstances in which the president would sponsor a peace initiative. FDR continued to ignore Kennedy's advice.

During the "phony war," Kennedy continued to be kept informed of Britain's plans, to attend sessions at the House of Commons, and to pass on insightful and shrewd opinions to Washington. His dispatches reflected admiration for the British and advice on protecting American self-interest. His constant refrain became: If we have to fight, let us do so in our own backyard. Let's help Britain and France stand on their own two feet.

With the Nazi onslaught on the West, Kennedy repeatedly urged Roosevelt to negotiate a peace settlement. He believed that Britain's cause was lost—the British simply lacked the resources for survival—and the United States should look to its own defenses. The Allied cause was very nearly lost as Britain's troops stood with their backs to the sea. Only a miracle could save the British, Kennedy told Washington. A miracle did save them: the Dunkirk evacuation. Roosevelt turned a deaf ear to Kennedy's advice and ignored his predictions of doom. By 1940 Roosevelt decided that peace was not possible but aid to the Allies was. He began to believe that Britain's cause was not lost and that American aid would make all the difference between victory and defeat.

Roosevelt sent his representatives—Sumner Welles, William Donovan, Admiral Robert Ghormley, and General George Strong—to see how much and in what form that aid might be. All could speak directly to heads of government on behalf of the president; all could circumvent Kennedy. All returned with more favorable reports about Britain's morale and resources and ability to hold out than Kennedy gave, and all contributed to the decline of his influence.

The decline of Kennedy's influence and prestige was hastened by Churchill's rise to power and his confidential relationship with Roosevelt. Kennedy played messenger boy between the two most powerful political figures in the English-speaking world, a role he resented deeply despite his willingness to protect it in the Tyler Kent case. Communication between Churchill and Roosevelt came to be centered in Washington, and Kennedy was even more isolated. Kennedy profoundly misjudged and disliked Churchill. The antipathy was mutual, and for good reason. Churchill was a bitter foe of Hitler and Hitlerism and argued for the total destruction of Nazism. Defeat was unthinkable. He opposed anyone like Kennedy who argued for a negotiated peace. Churchill, like Roosevelt, simply ignored Kennedy's advice and went behind his back to get what he wanted.

Churchill asked Roosevelt for forty or fifty old destroyers, and for airplanes, anti-aircraft equipment, and ammunition, and hoped that Britain would be *given* the equipment when the British could no longer afford to pay. Roosevelt agreed to a swap of destroyers for naval bases. Initially Kennedy supported the destroyer deal and the sale of military equipment to Britain. They would be a tremendous psychological boost to the British. But his enthusiasm for the destroyer deal waned and he said in the fall of 1940 that it was the worst thing ever. His attitude toward the destroyer deal, just as with Lend-Lease, was vacillating, muddled, and equivocal, reflecting his desire to help the British and to protect American interests. Kennedy seems not to have realized that with military aid to Britain the United States was now on a limited-war footing and had slid from neutrality to non-belligerency. Churchill had gotten the better of Kennedy; he had dragged the United States halfway into war, as Churchill had predicted to Randolph.

Throughout the summer and fall of 1940, Kennedy had been looking for a graceful exit, one that would not bring criticism or embarrassment on the family. But Roosevelt thought that Kennedy was safer in London and less likely, from Washington's point of view, to get into trouble. The president worried that Kennedy might sabotage his foreign policy; or undercut the aid to Britain; or undermine his reelection; or turn the Irish Americans and Catholics, essential to a Democratic victory, against Roosevelt's running for a third term; or sit out the election or, worse yet, endorse Wendell Willkie, the Republican candidate. Finally Kennedy was authorized to return to the United States for consultations. His resignation was not accepted until February 1941.

The old Roosevelt magic worked. Kennedy was charmed into campaigning for the president. It was also good politics to support the president, whose blessing would be essential for any other job that Kennedy or his children might want in politics. In a persuasive radio address, Kennedy argued that Roosevelt was indispensable and would not get the United States into war.

But the relationship between Roosevelt and Kennedy further deteriorated after Roosevelt's reelection and after Kennedy's *Boston Globe* interview, which set off a firestorm. It offended everyone on both sides of the Atlantic and cost Kennedy Britain's affection. Kennedy's remarks were nothing that he had not already said in private, but they were not what a discreet diplomat would say in public. He predicted Britain's defeat, the death of democracy in Britain, and the rise of national socialism. Kennedy destroyed himself; his ambassadorship was coming to an inglorious close.

Still the president did not dismiss Kennedy. Roosevelt wanted his support for Lend-Lease, and Kennedy wanted another job and Roosevelt's endorsement for his sons' political careers. Roosevelt played a cat-and-mouse game with him to gain his support in his radio address and in his congressional testimony on Lend-Lease. The magic worked again. The radio address and the Lend-Lease testimony were Mr. Kennedy vs. Mr. Kennedy. The effect was confusing and muddled and designed to give the impression that he and Roosevelt were in complete agreement.

In his radio address, Kennedy argued for giving the utmost aid to Britain because it was in America's self-interest. His congressional testimony reflected his confusion about isolation and intervention and between support and rejection of the Lend-Lease bill's broad presidential powers. Although he stated that the United States would be worse off if Britain were defeated, he still argued that Britain's present danger was not an emergency for the U.S. The only way the United States could help Britain was through military aid and Lend-Lease, maybe, but not through an allied coalition against Hitler. Kennedy's response, "I don't know what I'm talking about," was apt.[18] He seemed not to grasp that Lend-Lease, like the destroyer deal, was an irrevocable "unwritten alliance"[19] by the United States to aid Britain. The bill passed both houses of Congress, and the American people slid from neutrality to non-belligerency to intervention through an "unwritten alliance."

Kennedy's last two addresses as ambassador were as confusing as his radio address and Lend-Lease testimony. In an address at Oglethorpe University he argued for isolation, the view he really held. The United States should rearm and aid Britain, he said, but stay out of war. But in his Notre Dame address he urged cooperation with Roosevelt's policy of increased aid to Britain, to show that he and the president were in agreement on foreign policy. The two speeches canceled each other out, leaving Kennedy marginalized in the debate on American foreign policy.

With America's entry into World War II, Kennedy became an unrestrained critic of Roosevelt's wartime leadership and of the Allied concepts of total war and unconditional surrender. Kennedy thought that they would prolong the war needlessly by prohibiting a negotiated peace. And yet he did not lose all heart. He told John Boettiger: "I do not look forward with any great hope for our future but I am convinced that a country as great as ours can do lots better than anybody thinks we can do if we unite and put our shoulders to the wheel and boy, we are going to have to do it to come out of this mess with anything but grief."[20] Kennedy was right. And the American people did put their shoulders to the wheel and did come out of the mess.

After his resignation as ambassador, Kennedy never held another position in government. Roosevelt was through with him, and when Roosevelt was through, he was through. Kennedy had destroyed himself. He had been unable or unwilling to distinguish his family's fortunes from the country's, to resist equating the death of unfettered capitalism with the death of democracy, to interpret events in terms of principles not personalities, to look at situations calmly and rationally, to accept his own limitations, to realize that he was not an expert in international affairs—all this contributed to his diplomatic destruction. He was brought down by his own fatal flaws, just as Boake Carter had foretold.

Roosevelt thought that appointing Kennedy to that post was "a great joke, the greatest joke in the world."[21] But was the joke on Roosevelt?

In the years after his resignation, Kennedy turned his attention to his family and his fortune. His Midas touch was never more apparent than when in 1945, for $12,956,516, he bought Chicago's twenty-four-story Merchandise Mart, making him the owner of the largest commercial building in the world, with ninety-three acres of floor space.[22] It was his largest single investment.

But Kennedy was envied more for his success as a father than as a businessman and for siring a dynasty to immortalize his name and attain the political power he could barely grasp at and never reach. His children and their careers became the most important things in his life. "His idea of life," his old friend Richard Cardinal Cushing said, "was the success of his children."[23] In 1943, Kennedy told Lord Beaverbrook that "the political career of my two sons, if that is what they want to follow, is the only concern of mine now. I can honestly say that I have no further desire for public office. . . . I could get all the thrills and excitement watching the careers of my children. I do not have to have it centered on me any more, I have had mine."[24]

Richard Whalen, one of Kennedy's biographers, wrote that by 1962 when Teddy was elected to Jack's old Senate seat, "Joe Kennedy's triumph was complete. The Kennedys, all of them, had won all that was worth winning," and then saw it slowly slip away.[25]

The family also continued its tradition of elected political service through the grandchildren and great-grandchildren of Joe and Rose. Kathleen Kennedy Townsend, the eldest child of Robert Kennedy and the namesake of her aunt, was from 1995 to 2003 lieutenant governor of Maryland. From 1987 to 1999, her eldest brother, Joseph P. Kennedy II, was a member of the House of Representatives from the Eighth Congressional District in Massachusetts; and since 2013 his son, Joseph P. Kennedy III, has represented the Massachusetts Fourth Congressional District. Edward's eldest son, Edward M. Kennedy Jr., was a member of the Connecticut Senate from 2015 to 2019. His brother, Patrick Joseph Kennedy, was a member of the Rhode Island House of Representatives from 1989 to 1993, and from 1995 to 2011 a representative from Rhode Island's First Congressional District. Two of the children of Eunice Kennedy Shriver and Robert Sargent Shriver have held elective office. Robert S. Shriver III, the eldest of their five children, served on the Santa Monica City Council from 2004 to 2012, as mayor pro tem in 2006, and as mayor for part of 2010. His brother, Mark Shriver, the fourth child of their parents, sat in the Maryland House of Delegates from 1995 to 2003. Seldom has there not been a Kennedy in politics since John Kennedy's election to the House of Representatives in 1946.

Two other members of the Kennedy political dynasty also became ambassadors: In 1993 Jean Kennedy Smith was appointed ambassador to Ireland by President Clinton and served until 1998; and in 2013 Caroline Bouvier Kennedy, the daughter of John Kennedy and Jacqueline Bouvier Kennedy, was appointed ambassador to Japan by President Obama. She was briefly a candidate in 2008 for her uncle Robert's old Senate seat, but in 2009 withdrew her name.

And yet even with his family, happiness and success slipped away. In 1941 Kennedy agreed to an operation to lobotomize Rosemary, his eldest daughter. It failed horribly and left her mind severely impaired. Rose wrote that "Rosemary's was the first of the tragedies that were to befall us."[26] Then in August 1944 came the death of the beloved eldest son, Joe Jr., killed in action, that baby sleeping in his crib whose adoring father had looked down on him and said, "This is the only happiness that lasts."[27] But it didn't last. After the death of Joe Jr., his father was never the same. The pain never went away. He was permanently scarred, openly weeping, unable to speak, unable to control himself at the mention of his son's name, unsustained by his religion.[28] Two weeks after Joe Jr.'s death, Kick received the news that her husband had been killed in action. Then in 1948 Kick was killed in a plane crash and Kennedy had to identify her mangled body. On November 22, 1963, President John Kennedy was assassinated. And on June 5, 1968, Senator Robert Kennedy. Joe Kennedy "had outlived four of his nine children."[29] More tragedy was to come.

On December 19, 1961, at the age of seventy-four, Kennedy himself had a stroke that left him "a gnarled, crippled, drooling, speechless, wheelchair-bound, utterly dependent shell of a man. His right arm and leg were paralyzed, his right hand had frozen into a clawlike appendage curled up at the wrist; the right side of his face drooped." "No!" was all he could say.[30]

On November 18, 1969, he died at Hyannis Port as Rose and the family recited the Lord's Prayer.[31] He was eighty-one.

Notes

Preface

1. Amanda Smith, ed., *Hostage to Fortune: The Letters of Joseph P. Kennedy* (New York: Viking Press, 2001), viii.

2. Mary Bailey Gimbel, interview by Arthur M. Schlesinger Jr., February 19, 1975, as quoted in Arthur M. Schlesinger Jr., *Robert Kennedy and His Times* (Boston: Houghton Mifflin, 1978), 12.

3. JPK to Rose Kennedy, April 5, 1940, as cited in Smith, *Hostage to Fortune*, 415.

4. Joe Kennedy Jr. to his parents, August 4, 1944, Joseph P. Kennedy Collection, box 2, John Fitzgerald Kennedy Library, Boston [hereafter referred to as JPK and JFKL].

5. Anthony Cave Brown, *Bodyguard of Lies: The Extraordinary True Story behind D-Day*, vol. 2 (New York: Harper & Row, 1975), 810.

6. "Joseph P. Kennedy, Jr.," The Kennedy Family, The John F. Kennedy Family, John F. Kennedy Museum, https://jfkhyannismuseum.org.

7. Schlesinger Jr., *Robert Kennedy and His Times*, 60.

8. Richard J. Whalen, *The Founding Father: The Story of Joseph P. Kennedy* (1964; repr. Washington, DC: Regnery Gateway, 1993), 373–74.

9. Schlesinger Jr., *Robert Kennedy and His Times*, 56.

10. David E. Koskoff, *Joseph P. Kennedy: A Life and Times* (Englewood Cliffs, NJ: Prentice Hall, 1974), 375.

11. Whalen, *The Founding Father*, 375; Doris Kearns Goodwin, *The Fitzgeralds and the Kennedys: An American Saga* (New York: Simon and Schuster, 1987), 738–40.

12. Whalen, *The Founding Father*, 375; Goodwin, *The Fitzgeralds and the Kennedys*, 741.

13. Whalen, *The Founding Father*, 494.

Chapter 1. The Irish Prince

1. Goodwin, *The Fitzgeralds and the Kennedys*, 227–28.

2. David Nasaw, *The Patriarch: The Remarkable Life and Turbulent Times of Joseph P. Kennedy* (New

York: Penguin Press, 2012), 22; Whalen, *The Founding Father.*

3. Whalen, *The Founding Father*, 4.

4. Goodwin, *The Fitzgeralds and the Kennedys*, 213.

5. Goodwin, *The Fitzgeralds and the Kennedys*, 213–14. Nasaw discusses the "several Harvards" and their significance in the lives of their members. He writes that Kennedy "had to have been disappointed not to get into Fly or Porcellian or A.D., though not as much as when he failed to make the starting baseball team. Joe Kennedy was, even at the age of twenty-one, too sure of himself to suffer for long because a group of Republican Episcopalians preferred not to live and dine with him. . . . In his senior year, . . . he was tapped for Delta Upsilon, a worthy (if not top-rank) Harvard club." Nasaw, *The Patriarch*, 22–26.

6. Goodwin, *The Fitzgeralds and the Kennedys*, 213–14.

7. Goodwin, *The Fitzgeralds and the Kennedys*, 216.

8. James MacGregor Burns, *Roosevelt: The Lion and the Fox, 1882–1940* (New York: Harper and Row, 1956), 18.

9. Goodwin, *The Fitzgeralds and the Kennedys*, 235.

10. Rose Kennedy, *Times to Remember* (Garden City, NY: Doubleday, 1974), 49–50.

11. Rose Kennedy, *Times to Remember*, 51.

12. Rose Kennedy, *Times to Remember*, 65.

13. Goodwin, *The Fitzgeralds and the Kennedys*, 235.

14. Rose Kennedy, *Times to Remember*, 66; Barbara A. Perry, *Rose Kennedy: The Life and Times of a Political Matriarch* (New York: W.W. Norton, 2013), 41.

15. Jerome Beatty, "Nine Kennedys and How They Grew," *Reader's Digest*, April 1939, 83; Smith, ed. *Hostage to Fortune*, 14.

16. Rose Kennedy, *Times to Remember*, 71.

17. Peter Collier and David Horowitz, *The Kennedys: An American Drama* (New York: Summit Books, 1984), 45.

18. Schlesinger, *Robert Kennedy and His Times*, 12.

19. Schlesinger, *Robert Kennedy and His Times*, 12.

20. Goodwin, *The Fitzgeralds and the Kennedys*, 223, 226, 269.

21. Goodwin, *The Fitzgeralds and the Kennedys*, 223, 226.

22. Goodwin, *The Fitzgeralds and the Kennedys*, 232, 269.

23. Goodwin, *The Fitzgeralds and the Kennedys*, 331.

24. Goodwin, *The Fitzgeralds and the Kennedys*, 269.

25. Goodwin, *The Fitzgeralds and the Kennedys*, 268.

26. Goodwin, *The Fitzgeralds and the Kennedys*, 272.

27. Goodwin, *The Fitzgeralds and the Kennedys*, 272.

28. Martin Gilbert, *The First World War: A Complete History* (New York: Henry Holt, 1994), 258.

29. John Keegan, *The First World War* (New York: Alfred A. Knopf, 1999), 299; Goodwin, *The Fitzgeralds and the Kennedys*, 272.

30. M. Gilbert, *The First World War*, 258.

31. Edmund Blunden, a well-known soldier/poet, wrote about July 1, 1916: "By the end of the day both sides had seen, in a sad scrawl of broken earth and murdered men, the answer to that question. No road. No thoroughfare. Neither race had won, nor could win, the War. The War had won, and would go on winning"; *The Mind's Eye* (London: Jonathan Cape, 1934), 38. Paul Fussell, *The Great War and Modern Memory* (New York: Oxford University Press, 1975), 13.

32. Keegan, *The First World War*, 298.

33. Keegan, *The First World War*, 299; David M. Kennedy, *Freedom from Fear: The American People in Depression and War, 1929–1945* (New York: Oxford University Press, 1999), 382.

34. John Keegan, *The Face of Battle: A Study of Agincourt, Waterloo, and the Somme* (New York: Viking Press, 1976), 270.

35. Goodwin, *The Fitzgeralds and the Kennedys*, 270.

36. Goodwin, *The Fitzgeralds and the Kennedys*, 275.

37. Goodwin, *The Fitzgeralds and the Kennedys*, 268.

38. Goodwin, *The Fitzgeralds and the Kennedys*, 276.

39. Ronald Kessler, *The Sins of the Father: Joseph P. Kennedy and the Dynasty He Founded* (New York: Warner Books, 1996), 32.

40. Goodwin, *The Fitzgeralds and the Kennedys*, 277.

41. Smith, *Hostage to Fortune*, 18. Smith has a revealing letter that Kennedy wrote to his draft board on February 18, 1918, requesting a deferral; JPK to District Draft Board, no. 5, February 18, 1918, as cited in Smith, *Hostage to Fortune*, 15–18.

42. JPK to District Draft Board, no. 5, February 18, 1918, as cited in Smith, *Hostage to Fortune*, 18.

43. Goodwin, *The Fitzgeralds and the Kennedys*, 281, 283; Nasaw, *The Patriarch*, 50–54.

44. Burns, *Roosevelt: The Lion and the Fox*, 51–52, 55.

45. *Daily Boston Globe*, September 25, 1932, 3; Smith, *Hostage to Fortune*, 5; Michael R. Beschloss, *Kennedy and Roosevelt: The Uneasy Alliance* (New York: W.W. Norton, 1980), 45.

46. *Daily Boston Globe*, September 25, 1932, 3; Beschloss, *Kennedy and Roosevelt*, 45–46; Smith, *Hostage to Fortune*, 5; Goodwin, *The Fitzgeralds and the Kennedys*, 428. Nasaw writes that Kennedy "would later boast loudly and often of having negotiated a deal with Assistant Secretary of the Navy Franklin Delano Roosevelt on a matter involving Argentine dreadnoughts that had been built at Fore River and returned for repairs. There is, however, no evidence and little likelihood that he ever dealt directly with Roosevelt or any decision makers in Washington, Boston, or Bethlehem headquarters in Pennsylvania"; *The Patriarch*, 55.

47. Ernest K. Lindley, "Will Kennedy Run for President?," *Liberty Magazine*, May 21, 1938, 27, repr. ed., Fall 1971; Smith, *Hostage to Fortune*, 6; Whalen, *The Founding Father*, 49; Beschloss, *Kennedy and Roosevelt*, 46. Goodwin mentions only that *Kennedy and Roosevelt* had had an "adversarial" relationship marked by "Frustration and anger"; *The Fitzgeralds and the Kennedys*, 428. Not all of Kennedy's biographers mention or accept the legitimacy of this story.

48. *Daily Boston Globe*, September 25, 1932, 3.

49. Whalen, *The Founding Father*, 207.

50. Beschloss, *Kennedy and Roosevelt*, 63. Rose Kennedy, *Times to Remember*, 195, also mentions Kennedy's numerous contacts.

51. Koskoff, *Joseph P. Kennedy*, 33.

52. "Many of Boston's old families passed the summer in Cohasset and were resentful of newcomers, particularly Irish newcomers. When Kennedy sought membership in the Cohasset Country Club, he was blackballed"; Whalen, *The Founding Father*, 59. Nasaw treats the incident of being blackballed by Cohasset more lightly. He writes, "The committee would never formally turn down Kennedy's application, but by not acting on it before the summer was over, they made their wishes known. Kennedy biographers and family historians would later make much of the fact that he had been denied admission to the Cohasset Golf Club. Kennedy never did. Neither did Rose, who told her ghostwriter that she had taken it in stride." She had learned that there were certain places where Catholics could not go, and she accepted that. The golf club was one of them. Nasaw also says that the Kennedys returned to Cohasset the next summer, "further evidence that the rejection had not meant much to Joe or his family"; *The Patriarch*, 81–82.

53. Collier and Horowitz, *The Kennedys*, 37, 44.

54. Herbert S. Parmet, *Jack: The Struggles of John F. Kennedy* (New York: Dial Press, 1980), 25.

55. Nasaw writes that Rose "denied emphatically" to her ghostwriter, Robert Coughlin, "that Kennedy had moved the family" because of the Boston freeze or that "he felt that he had been socially snubbed in Boston and because it was difficult for the children." Rose said that the family moved because Kennedy's business was in New York; *The Patriarch*, 105.

56. Joe McCarthy, *The Remarkable Kennedys* (New York: Dial Press, 1960), 53; Perry, *Rose Kennedy*, 65.

57. Jerome Beatty, "Nine Kennedys and How They Grew," *Reader's Digest*, April 1939, 83.

58. "Rose Kennedy: Recollection," cited in Smith, *Hostage to Fortune*, 161.

59. Arthur Schlesinger Jr., *The Crisis of the Old Order, 1919–1933* (Boston: Houghton Mifflin, 1964), 366.

60. Schlesinger, *Crisis of the Old Order*, 366–67; Robert Dallek, *Franklin D. Roosevelt and American Foreign Policy, 1932–1945* (New York: Oxford University Press, 1979), 18.

61. Jane Vieth, "Joseph P. Kennedy and British Appeasement: The Diplomacy of a Boston Irishman," in *U.S. Diplomats in Europe, 1919–1941*, ed. Kenneth Paul Jones (Santa Barbara, CA: ABC-Clio, 1981), 166. Portions of this general discussion on American foreign policy can be found in the article by Jane Vieth, "The Diplomacy of the Depression: The Foreign Policy of Franklin D. Roosevelt, 1938–1940," in *Modern American Diplomacy*, ed. John M. Carroll and George C. Herring (Wilmington, DE: Scholarly Resources, 1986), 71–88; Dallek, *Franklin D. Roosevelt and American Foreign Policy*, 16–19; David Kennedy, *Freedom from Fear*, 385–88.

62. Joseph P. Kennedy, *I'm for Roosevelt* (New York: Reynal and Hitchcock, 1936), 3; *New York Post Daily Magazine*, January 11, 1961, 37; Nasaw, *The Patriarch*, 70.

63. Rose Kennedy, *Times to Remember*, 194.

64. Rose Kennedy, *Times to Remember*, 195; Beschloss, *Kennedy and Roosevelt*, 290.

65. *New York Times Magazine*, August 12, 1934, 3; *Literary Digest*, December 25, 1937, 6; *Newsweek*,

September 12, 1960, 28.

66. *New York Times*, August 12, 1934, 4.

67. Lindley, "Will Kennedy Run for President?" 27; Nasaw, *The Patriarch*, 174.

68. McCarthy, *The Remarkable Kennedys*, 58; Smith, *Hostage to Fortune*, 66; Nasaw, *The Patriarch*, 171.

69. Victor Lasky, *JFK: The Man and the Myth: A Critical Portrait* (New Rochelle, NY: Arlington House, 1966), 25–27, 43. Lasky's extremely critical account emphasizes Kennedy's opportunism and cites several examples of the family stress on winning. He also suggests a further motive—money. He argues that one reason Kennedy supported FDR in 1932 was Roosevelt's opposition to Prohibition. Anticipating the repeal of the Volstead Act, Kennedy set up a major liquor-importing company, Somerset Importers, Ltd.

70. Goodwin, *The Fitzgeralds and the Kennedys*, 427–28. Goodwin cites Joseph P. Kennedy, *I'm for Roosevelt*, 3, and her own interview with Morton Downey.

71. *New York Post Daily Magazine*, January 11, 1961, 37; Rose Kennedy, *Times to Remember*, 196; Alfred B. Rollins Jr., *Roosevelt and Howe* (New York: Alfred A. Knopf, 1962), 312; Raymond Moley, *The First New Deal* (New York: Harcourt, Brace and World, 1966), 381.

72. Kennedy knew a great deal about financial affairs and Wall Street and realized that there would be a widespread demand for reform. "It was therefore good politics to be on the side of the angels." Moley further believed "that Kennedy's contempt for the stupidity and reaction of those financial interests was the major source of his indignation"; *The First New Deal*, 380–81.

73. *Fortune* 16, no. 3 (September 1937): 57; *Newsweek*, September 12, 1960, 29, the sum lent was $10,000. Kessler claims Kennedy contributed $50,0000 directly and raised another $150,000 for the campaign—about $2.2 million in today's values; *The Sins of the Father*, 94. Joe Kane, Kennedy's cousin, estimated that his support came to $3.8 million; Nasaw, *The Patriarch*, 182–83. Kennedy had not been a success as a fundraiser and "he had outlived his usefulness" in that role. Although he had given $10,000 on September 9, 1932, several other Democrats had given significantly more. Kennedy did give an additional $5,000 in October after he was invited to rejoin Roosevelt's campaign train for its final leg in the South. He had also lent the campaign $50,000, which was repaid. Whalen, *The Founding Father*, 119; Koskoff, *Joseph P. Kennedy*, 47; Moley, *The First New Deal*, 380; Perry, *Rose Kennedy*, 85.

74. *New York American*, April 24, 1932, 1; Charles A. Beard, *American Foreign Policy in the Making, 1932–1940: A Study in Responsibilities* (New Haven, CT: Yale University Press, 1946), 97–99; Whalen, *The Founding Father*, 123–26.

75. *New York Times*, May 9, 1932, 8; W. A. Swanberg, *Citizen Hearst* (New York: Bantam, 1961), 516; Nasaw, *The Patriarch*, 173–74; David Nasaw, *The Chief: The Life of William Randolph Hearst* (Boston: Houghton Mifflin, 2000), 455.

76. Moley, *The First New Deal*, 379; Nasaw, *The Patriarch*, 175.

77. *New York American*, February 25, 1932, 12. See also Nasaw, *The Chief*, 454, for similar views from Hearst.

78. JPK to William Randolph Hearst, October 19, 1932, JPK Collection, JFKL. For Kennedy's thank-you

note to Hearst, see Smith, *Hostage to Fortune*, 66, 100. Arthur Krock, *Memoirs: Sixty Years on the Firing Line* (New York: Funk and Wagnalls, 1968), 330. Cordell Hull writes that he and Daniel C. Roper went to McAdoo to see whether he would "cast California's vote for Roosevelt in exchange for an arrangement to nominate Garner for Vice President. I do not know what other persons, save Farley and Howe, undertook to figure in this arrangement. . . . We were vain enough to feel satisfied that this conference with him . . . played its full part in the favorable understanding reached"; *The Memoirs of Cordell Hull* (New York: Macmillan, 1948), 153–54. Although Hull's account does not mention Kennedy's playing any significant role in Roosevelt's nomination, James Farley gives Kennedy credit for influencing Hearst's decision: "Joseph P. Kennedy, who was closely associated with Hearst, called the publisher to warn him of the blossoming Baker movement and to urge him to use his influence to get the California delegation to switch to Roosevelt"; *Jim Farley's Story: The Roosevelt Years* (New York: Whittlesey House, 1948), 24. This accounting is also supported by *The Reminiscences of Arthur Krock*, Oral History Research Office, Columbia University, n.d., 8. Rose Kennedy in *Times to Remember* loyally attributed the publisher's change of heart to her husband's "successful intervention," which "clinched Roosevelt's victory on the fourth ballot" (195–96).

See Goodwin, *The Fitzgeralds and the Kennedys*, 429; Koskoff, *Joseph P. Kennedy*, 45. Nasaw has an excellent detailed description of the relationship between Kennedy and Hearst and of Kennedy's successful attempts to get Hearst to support Roosevelt. It earned Kennedy his reputation as "an important member of the Roosevelt campaign team." Hearst claimed the credit for Roosevelt's nomination and Kennedy insisted that he had delivered Hearst's vote. "Both men exaggerated their roles"; *The Patriarch*, 176–77. He also states that the delegates would have moved to Roosevelt on the fourth or fifth ballot even without Hearst's intervention. That would have guaranteed him the nomination.

In *The Chief*, Nasaw writes that there is considerable debate over Kennedy's influence on Hearst and its consequences for Roosevelt's nomination (455–56). Raymond Moley in *After Seven Years* states that two people "who deserve more credit for the negotiations than anyone else were Sam Rayburn of Texas and Tom Storke of Santa Barbara, California. Arthur F. Mullen also materially helped win over Garner through Congressman Howard in Washington" (New York: Harper and Bros., 1939), 31. Charles A. Beard also writes in *American Foreign Policy in the Making*, "Although Governor Roosevelt's supporters were far from sure of victory when the Democratic convention assembled in 1932, they managed, with the aid of 'Garner and McAdoo and Hearst and Joe Kennedy and Jim Farley,' to nominate the Governor after a brief season of 'agonizing' uncertainty" (101). According to The Unofficial Observer [pen name of John Franklin Carter], Kennedy "was on the inside track with Roosevelt . . . and he helped swing Hearst to Roosevelt's side"; *The New Dealers* (New York: Simon and Schuster, 1934), 355. Whalen, in *The Founding Father*, writes that "many men had a hand in the decisive switch of the Hearst-controlled votes, but Kennedy later claimed full credit. He boasted long afterward that his telephone call had brought Hearst around, "but you don't find any mention of it in the history books." It seems probable that Kennedy did have considerable clout with the volatile publisher but that he was only one of a number of people trying to influence the decision of "W. R." (124–25).

79. Moley, *After Seven Years*, 32; Moley, *The First New Deal*, 380; Whalen, *The Founding Father*, 125.

80. Farley, *Jim Farley's Story*, 26; Samuel Irving Rosenman, *Working with Roosevelt* (New York: Harper & Bros., 1952), 68–79.

81. *East Boston Leader*, 1932–1933, box 43, Democratic Convention, JPK Collection, JFKL.

82. Rosenman, in *Working with Roosevelt*, refers to Kennedy as a member of Roosevelt's "Brain Trust" (88).

83. Lorena Hickok, September 26, 1932, box 43, Democratic Convention, JPK Collection, JFKL.

84. James Kieran, [unknown newspaper], November 20, 1932, box 43, Democratic Convention, JPK Collection, JFKL.

85. JPK, memorandum, as cited in Smith, *Hostage to Fortune*, 128; Rose Kennedy, *Times to Remember*, 196; Rollins, *Roosevelt and Howe*, 350.

86. Koskoff, *Joseph P. Kennedy*, 46–47; Beschloss, *Kennedy and Roosevelt*, 75.

87. Rose Kennedy, in *Times to Remember*, recalled that when Hearst made his contribution to Roosevelt's campaign, "it was through Joe he channeled it." "I'm the one who got the Hearst check and gave it directly to Roosevelt," Joe said to her, "and in politics that meant I was the one who had 'delivered Hearst' to the Convention. W. R. meant it that way and FDR understood it" (196).

88. JPK to Hearst, October 19, 1932, box 44, William Hearst, JPK Collection, JFKL; Nasaw, *The Patriarch*, 183; Nasaw, *The Chief*, 458.

89. Franklin D. Roosevelt, *The Public Papers and Addresses of Franklin D. Roosevelt*, vol. 1, *The Genesis of the New Deal, 1928–1932*, comp. Samuel I. Rosenman (New York: Random House, 1938), 672–82.

90. Rose Kennedy, *Times to Remember*, 196; Moley, *After Seven Years*, 53; Moley, *The First New Deal*, 380.

91. Hickok, September 26, 1932, Democratic Convention; Nasaw, *The Patriarch*, 179; Perry, *Rose Kennedy*, 85.

92. Hickok, September 26, 1932, Democratic Convention; Nasaw, *The Patriarch*, 180.

93. *Boston Globe*, November 3, 1932, 10; Goodwin has a charming description of Kennedy riding "the Roosevelt Special" during the campaign, spreading charm and goodwill among them. She also notes that it was the first time he had experienced a group's comradery similar to that of soldiers in war; *The Fitzgeralds and the Kennedys*, 430–35. Nasaw also writes about "the friendly intimacy of the campaign train" and that Kennedy "became one of the inner circle"; *The Patriarch*, 180.

94. *Fortune*, September 1937, 142; Arthur Schlesinger Jr., *The Politics of Upheaval* (Boston: Houghton Mifflin, 1960), 24–26, 250; Whalen, *The Founding Father*, 128.

95. David B. Woolner and Richard G. Kurial, eds., *FDR, The Vatican, and the Roman Catholic Church in America, 1933–1945* (New York: Palgrave Macmillan, 2003), 269; Mary A. Dempsey, "The Many Faces of Father Coughlin," *Michigan History Magazine* (July/August 1999): 36; Nasaw, *The Patriarch*, 230.

96. Dempsey, "The Many Faces of Father Coughlin," 31–34.

97. Summary of Facts in the Father Coughlin Incident, October 5, 1937, to January 9, 1938, Archives, Archdiocese of Detroit, Michigan.

98. Michael Grupa to Archbishop Edward Mooney, September 24, 1937, Archives, Archdiocese of Detroit, Michigan; Joseph C. Linck and Raymond J. Kupke, eds., *Building the Church in America: Studies in Honor of Monsignor Robert F. Trisco on the Occasion of His Seventieth Birthday* (Washington, DC: Catholic University of America Press, 1999), 201.

99. JPK to Felix Frankfurter, December 5, 1933, in Smith, *Hostage to Fortune*, 122.

100. Dempsey, "The Many Faces of Father Coughlin," 31–34.

101. Drew Pearson, *Washington Post*, October 1, 1960, D15; Whalen, *The Founding Father*, 129.

102. *East Boston Leader*, 1932–1933, box 43, Democratic Convention, JPK Collection, JFKL; Nasaw, *The Patriarch*, 186; Perry, *Rose Kennedy*, 85.

103. JPK, memorandum, n.d., in Smith, *Hostage to Fortune*, 128–29.

104. JPK, memorandum, n.d., in Smith, *Hostage to Fortune*, 127; Nasaw, *The Patriarch*, 207.

105. JPK, memorandum, n.d., in Smith, *Hostage to Fortune*, 129; JPK to Joseph P. Kennedy, Jr., May 4, 1934, in Smith, *Hostage to Fortune*, 134.

106. Smith, *Hostage to Fortune*, 108; JPK to James Roosevelt, January 8, 1937, in Smith, *Hostage to Fortune*, 190.

107. Goodwin, *The Fitzgeralds and the Kennedys*, 431; Nasaw, *The Patriarch*, 180.

108. JPK to Joseph P. Kennedy, Jr., February 27, 1936, in Smith, *Hostage to Fortune*, 176.

109. Whalen, *The Founding Father*, 135–36; Nasaw, *The Patriarch*, 193.

110. JPK, memorandum, n.d., in Smith, *Hostage to Fortune*, 129, describes Roosevelt's attempts to woo Kennedy to this post. Perry, *Rose Kennedy*, 87.

111. Moley, *The First New Deal*, 518–19; Goodwin, *The Fitzgeralds and the Kennedys*, 447–48.

112. *Newsweek*, November 12, 1960, 29; Nasaw, *The Patriarch*, 205–9, 213.

113. JPK, memorandum, n.d., in Smith, *Hostage to Fortune*, 137.

114. Moley, *The First New Deal*, 519.

115. JPK, memorandum, in Smith, *Hostage to Fortune*, 136–39, presents an interesting account from Kennedy's point of view of his negotiations with Roosevelt and the decision regarding the chairmanship. See also Goodwin, *The Fitzgeralds and the Kennedys*, for a compelling account of Kennedy's maneuvering to be chairman (447–50).

116. Moley, *The First New Deal*, 519.

117. Beschloss, *Kennedy and Roosevelt*, 86.

118. JPK, memorandum, n.d., in Smith, *Hostage to Fortune*, 138; Moley, *After Seven Years*, 288; Nasaw, *The Patriarch*, 209.

119. JPK, memorandum, n.d., in Smith, *Hostage to Fortune*, 138.

120. Moley, *After Seven Years*, 288.

121. Smith, *Hostage to Fortune*, 111. See JPK, memorandum, n.d., in Smith, *Hostage to Fortune*, 136–39, for an example of the criticism he received. See also Rose Kennedy, *Times to Remember*, 199–200, for an excellent general discussion. Moley, *The First New Deal*, 519–20; Goodwin, *The Fitzgeralds and the Kennedys*, 447–50; Nasaw, *The Patriarch*, 210.

122. JPK, memorandum, n.d., in Smith, *Hostage to Fortune*, 138.

123. *Philadelphia Record*, November 1934, JPK Collection, JFKL, quoted in Goodwin, *The Fitzgeralds and the Kennedys*, 450.

124. Joseph F. Dinneen, *The Kennedy Family* (Boston: Little, Brown and Co., 1959), 49.

125. JPK to FDR, September 6, 1935, JPK Collection, JFKL; Nasaw, *The Patriarch*, 235.

126. *New York Times*, September 21, 1935, 4.

127. Moley, *The First New Deal*, 520; Goodwin, *The Fitzgeralds and the Kennedys*, 454–55; Nasaw, *The Patriarch*, 213–20, 226–37.

128. Goodwin, *The Fitzgeralds and the Kennedys*, 454.

129. *New York Times*, September 21, 1935, 1.

130. *New York Times*, April 28, 1935, sec. 4, p. 3; Nasaw, *The Patriarch*, 229.

131. *Washington Herald*, September 18, 1937, 8.

132. See Beschloss, *Kennedy and Roosevelt*, 96–98, for a delightful rendition of an evening at the Kennedys', and p. 105 for a description of an evening at the White House. Nasaw, *The Patriarch*, 213–15.

133. John Morton Blum, *From the Morgenthau Diaries*, vol. 1, *Years of Crisis, 1928–1938* (Boston: Houghton Mifflin, 1959), 241.

134. Beschloss, *Kennedy and Roosevelt*, 112–13; Ralph F. de Bedts, *Ambassador Joseph Kennedy, 1938–1940: An Anatomy of Appeasement* (New York: Peter Lang, 1983).

135. See Krock, *Memoirs*, 328–30, for his description of his affection, respect, and intimacy with Kennedy and his family. Nasaw writes about the unusual relationship between Kennedy and Krock. Krock became an "intimate of the family" shortly after Kennedy became the chair of the SEC. For the next twenty-five years, Krock served as Kennedy's "unofficial, clandestine press agent, speechwriter, political adviser, informant, and all-purpose consultant." Krock wrote that he "was as scrupulous as [Kennedy] in excluding material considerations from this relationship," a statement that Nasaw disputes. Nasaw found evidence in Kennedy's letters that he offered to pay Krock "generous weekly salaries" for his editorial help, and no evidence that Krock refused. Nasaw concludes that "on the whole, the correspondence reveals something quite disturbing, if not corrupt, about Krock's willingness to do Kennedy's bidding, to advise him or write a speech for him, then praise it in his column, to take money for ghostwriting Kennedy's *I'm for Roosevelt* campaign book in 1936, to assist Jack in turning his college thesis into a book, *Why England Slept*, to allow Kennedy to pay for vacations in Palm Beach and travel to London, all without any acknowledgment to his superiors at the *Times* or his readers"; *The Patriarch*, 211–13, 262–63.

136. JPK to Russell Davenport, May 17, 1937, box 7, U.S. Maritime Commission, JPK Collection, JFKL; Nasaw, *The Patriarch*, 262–63.

137. JPK to Russell Davenport, draft, May 24, 1937, in Smith, *Hostage to Fortune*, 199–210, contains a paragraph-by-paragraph set of corrections of statements that Kennedy disliked or disagreed with in the *Fortune* article.

138. Collier and Horowitz, *The Kennedys*, 77.

139. Editorial, *Chicago Tribune*, January 18, 1936, 12.

140. JPK to Robert Rutherford McCormick, January 31, 1936, in Smith, *Hostage to Fortune*, 171–72; Editorial, *Chicago Tribune*, January 18, 1936, 12.

141. JPK to Missy LeHand, telegram, February 17, 1937, in Smith, *Hostage to Fortune*, 194, has a reference from Kennedy to Missy LeHand about sending her stone crabs. Roosevelt thanked Kennedy for a fishing rod, in FDR to JPK, January 3, 1940, FDRL. Whalen, *The Founding Father*, 145–46, 156–57, 180, 199, refers to a "glowing" article written by Arthur Krock that helped Kennedy land the SEC chairmanship. Kennedy never forgot the favor and frequently expressed his gratitude to Krock, who became a family friend. Whalen wrote that it showed Kennedy's ability to "befriend the 'right' people in any environment." Whalen also refers to a thank-you note written by FDR: "How much I am enjoying the contents of the two trunks. I am saving some for you." The trunks were bottles of scotch from Somerset Importers. Kennedy's generous hospitality in sunny Florida at his estate on North Ocean Boulevard in Palm Beach or at his twenty-five-room rented retreat at Marwood in the Maryland countryside was another source of his influence. His hospitality embraced anyone he wanted to cultivate. Harry Hopkins convalesced in Palm Beach after cancer surgery in 1937–38. Other recipients of Kennedy's "midwinter hospitality" included "Missy" LeHand, Mrs. Jimmy Roosevelt, Bishop Spellman, as well as Krock. Roosevelt enjoyed Kennedy's double martinis and movies at Marwood, where he was often joined by other members of his political family. See also Nasaw, *The Patriarch*, for additional examples of lavish gift-giving that included sending lobsters, and for a description of Palm Beach and of Marwood and Kennedy's life there (187–88, 190, 213–15, 240–41).

142. Kessler, *Sins of the Father*, 127.

143. Franklin D. Roosevelt, *F.D.R.: His Personal Letters, 1928–1945*, 2 vols., ed. Elliott Roosevelt (New York: Duell, Sloan and Pearce, 1950), 1:450.

144. FDR to JPK in Kennedy's "Diplomatic Memoirs" unpublished manuscript, chap. 1, p. 1, JPK Collection, JFKL [hereafter cited as "DM"]. During his tenure as ambassador, Kennedy kept a record of his activities for his Diplomatic Memoir. It was supplemented with his diaries, as well as official documents, dispatches, and correspondence and was intended to be published after he retired as ambassador. In the 1940s James Landis wrote a first draft of the memoir. It is housed in the Library of Congress Manuscript Division under the James M. Landis Papers. From 1949 to 1955, under Kennedy's watchful eye, Landis wrote and rewrote several more drafts of the memoir. Copies of these versions are in the John F. Kennedy Library in the Joseph P. Kennedy Papers. What began as a "breezy chronicle of the new ambassador's first forays into international politics and society" as Europe lurched toward war became a detailed description of the ways Roosevelt and his administration mistreated their ambassador, ignoring his advice and circumventing and publicly humiliating him. It also documented the careful steps Roosevelt took as he quietly moved from isolationism and neutrality into greater non-neutrality and more intervention in opposition to Kennedy's steadfast support of appeasement, isolationism, and "peace above all," leaving the American public ignorant of the president's actions and motives. The memoir was never published. Smith, *Hostages to Fortune*, 225–26. Per Koskoff, *Joseph P. Kennedy*, James Landis told David E.

Koskoff that Kennedy feared it might prove embarrassing to John Kennedy's political career (514). Goodwin, *The Fitzgeralds and the Kennedys*, 515; Beschloss, *Kennedy and Roosevelt*, 283.

145. Bernard Baruch to Winston Churchill, telegram, September 25, 1935, Baruch Papers, quoted in Beschloss, *Kennedy and Roosevelt*, 122; Nasaw, *The Patriarch*, 238–39.

146. Rose Kennedy, "Visit to Churchill," in Smith, *Hostage to Fortune*, 162. Smith surmises the date as October 7, 1935.

147. Rose Kennedy, "Visit to Churchill," in Smith, *Hostage to Fortune*, 162–63; Schlesinger, *Robert Kennedy and His Times*, 10; Beschloss, *Kennedy and Roosevelt*, 122.

148. JPK to FDR, cable, February 10, 1935, box 71, Roosevelt and Related Correspondence 1935, JPK Collection, JFKL; Rose Kennedy, "Visit to Churchill," in Smith, *Hostage to Fortune*, 162.

149. JPK to FDR, cable, February 10, 1935, box 71, Roosevelt and Related Correspondence 1935, JPK Collection, JFKL.

150. JPK to FDR, cable, February 10, 1935, box 71, Roosevelt and Related Correspondence 1935, JPK Collection, JFKL; JPK to FDR, cablegram draft, February 10, 1935, in Smith, *Hostage to Fortune*, 161–62.

151. "DM," chap. 1, p. 1, JPK Collection, JFKL; Beschloss, *Kennedy and Roosevelt*, 122.

152. Beschloss, *Kennedy and Roosevelt*, 122.

153. "DM," chap. 1, p. 3, JPK Collection, JFKL.

154. JPK to Missy LeHand, June 15, 1936, PPF 207, FDRL; JPK to LeHand, June 15, 1936, in Smith, *Hostage to Fortune*, 185.

155. JPK to LeHand, June 15, 1936, in Smith, *Hostage to Fortune*, 185; JPK to Arthur Krock, June 24, 1936, in Smith, *Hostage to Fortune*, 186; Nasaw, *The Patriarch*, 247.

156. JPK to Robert S. Allen, August 8, 1936, in Smith, *Hostage to Fortune*, 186.

157. *Christian Century*, October 14, 1936, 1361; *New Republic*, September 23, 1936, 189; *New York Times*, August 23, 1936, sec. 3, p. 1.

158. Kennedy, *I'm for Roosevelt*, 3.

159. *Saturday Review of Literature*, September 5, 1936, 189; *The Nation*, September 12, 1936, 314.

160. Kennedy, *I'm for Roosevelt*, 8, 14–15.

161. *Saturday Review of Literature*, September 5, 1936, 12.

162. *Review of Reviews*, September 1936, 24.

163. This was reported to Whalen by "a visitor to the Kennedy home"; *The Founding Father*, 186.

164. FDR to JPK, letter, n.d., box 71, Roosevelt and Politics, 1936, JPK Collection, JFKL.

165. Whalen, *The Founding Father*, 185; Nasaw, *The Patriarch*, 249–50.

166. *Boston Globe*, July 27, 1936, 28; *New York Times*, July 26, 1936, 1; Whalen, *The Founding Father*, 184.

167. *Boston Sunday Post*, August 16, 1936, 14; *New York Times*, October 6, 1936, 14; November 1, 1936, 49.

168. *Review of Reviews*, September 1936, 24.

169. *New York Times Magazine*, September 6, 1936, 1–2, 21.

170. James Roosevelt, interview by Michael Beschloss, May 17, 1978, quoted in *Kennedy and Roosevelt*, 125–26.

171. *New York Times*, October 22, 1936, 13.

172. JPK to FDR, January 20, 1936, in Smith, *Hostage to Fortune*, 169–70; Roosevelt, *F.D.R.: His Personal Letters, 1928–1945*, 1:547; Beschloss, *Kennedy and Roosevelt*, 114, 123; Nasaw, *The Patriarch*, 245.

173. Presidential Press Conferences of Franklin D. Roosevelt, September 11, 1935, 150–51, FDRL, and personal interviews, in Beschloss, *Kennedy and Roosevelt*, 119–20; Sheldon Marcus, *Father Coughlin: The Tumultuous Life of the Priest of the Little Flower* (Boston: Little, Brown and Co., 1973), 99–100; Schlesinger, *The Politics of Upheaval*, 341; Charles J. Tull, *Father Coughlin and the New Deal* (Syracuse, NY: Syracuse University Press, 1965), 101; Whalen, *The Founding Father*, 187; Nasaw, *The Patriarch*, 235–36; Dempsey, "The Many Faces of Father Coughlin," 31–37.

174. Beschloss, *Kennedy and Roosevelt*, 123.

175. James Roosevelt interview, quoted in Beschloss, *Kennedy and Roosevelt*, 117–18.

176. *Detroit News*, July 17, 1936, 6; *Detroit Free Press*, July 17, 1936, 1; Grace Tully, *FDR, My Boss* (New York: Charles Scribner's Sons, 1949), 156; Whalen, *The Founding Father*, 184; Beschloss, *Kennedy and Roosevelt*, 126–27.

177. *New York Times*, November 1, 1936, 48; *Boston Sunday Post*, August 16, 1936, 14; JPK to Father Coughlin, August 18, 1936, in Smith, *Hostage to Fortune*, 187; Whalen, *The Founding Father*, 187.

178. JPK to Robert Worth Bingham, October 6, 1936, as cited in Smith, *Hostage to Fortune*, 188.

179. *New York Times*, October 25, 1936, 33; *New York Times*, November 6, 1936, 1; Whalen, *The Founding Father*, 187; Nasaw, *The Patriarch*, 252–53; Perry, *Rose Kennedy*, 93–94.

180. Clare Boothe Luce, interview by Michael Beschloss, quoted in *Kennedy and Roosevelt*, 127.

181. JPK to G. A. Richards, November 9, 1936, as cited in Smith, *Hostage to Fortune*, 189.

182. Smith, *Hostage to Fortune*, 189n171; Dempsey, "The Many Faces of Father Coughlin," 39.

183. Michael Grupa to Archbishop Edward Mooney, September 24, 1937, Archives, Archdiocese of Detroit, Michigan; Dempsey, "The Many Faces of Father Coughlin," 39; Linck and Kupke, *Building the Church in America*, 201, 209–10; Earl Boyea, "The Reverend Charles Coughlin and the Church: The Gallagher Years, 1930–1937," *Catholic Historical Review* 81 (April 1997): 211–25.

184. Woolner and Kurial, *FDR, the Vatican, and the Roman Catholic Church*, 272.

185. Farley, *Jim Farley's Story*, 115.

186. *New York Times*, March 10, 1937, 22.

187. FDR to JPK, February 26, 1937, box 7, misc., JPK Collection, JFKL; Goodwin, *The Fitzgeralds and the Kennedys*, 498–99; Nasaw, *The Patriarch*, 255. See Whalen, *The Founding Father*, for a particularly good description of Kennedy as head of the Maritime Commission (187–94).

188. "DM," chap. 1, p. 4, JPK Collection, JFKL; JPK to FDR, March 2, 1937, in Smith, *Hostage to Fortune*, 194.

189. Rose Kennedy, *Times to Remember*, 211.

190. *Time* magazine, March 22, 1937, 64.

191. JPK to John Boettiger, March 22, 1937, Boettiger Papers, FDRL; Smith, *Hostage to Fortune*, 197; Beschloss, *Kennedy and Roosevelt*, 128; Nasaw, *The Patriarch*, 255–56.

192. "DM," chap. 1, p. 4, JPK Collection, JFKL.

193. *Daily Mirror*, May 27, 1937, n.p., box 10, Boake Carter, JPK Collection, JFKL.

194. *Time*, November 22, 1937, 20.

195. *New Republic*, August 11, 1937, 7.

196. *Time*, November 22, 1937, 20.

197. JPK to Joseph Curran, November 4, 1937, in Smith, *Hostage to Fortune*, 215; Nasaw, *The Patriarch*, 268.

198. Krock, *Memoirs*, 332; Koskoff, *Joseph P. Kennedy*, 97.

199. Smith, *Hostage to Fortune*, 215n214.

200. *New York Times*, January 8, 1938, 3.

201. JPK to FDR, box 7, Personal Chronology, 1937–1938, JPK Collection, JFKL.

202. Emory Scott Land, *Winning the War with Ships: Land, Sea and Air—Mostly Land* (New York: R. M. McBride, 1958), 6.

203. "DM," chap. 1, p. 4, JPK Collection, JFKL.

204. FDR to JPK, February 18, 1938, 1705 Official File, FDRL; Nasaw, *The Patriarch*, 279.

205. *Boston Herald*, October 3, 1937, JPK Collection, JFKL.

206. *Time*, March 22, 1937, 64.

207. *New York Journal*, July 24, 1937, box 8, JPK Collection, JFKL.

208. Rose Kennedy, *Times to Remember*, 211–12; Nasaw, *The Patriarch*, 272.

209. JPK to James F. Byrnes, December 23, 1937; Smith, *Hostage to Fortune*, 219–20.

210. James Roosevelt interview, quoted in Beschloss, *Kennedy and Roosevelt*, 151.

211. *New York Times*, December 8, 1937, 22; December 9, 1937, 6; October 16, 1937, 1.

212. Baruch Papers, December 8, 1937, quoted in Beschloss, *Kennedy and Roosevelt*, 152; Koskoff, *Joseph P. Kennedy*, 114.

213. Rose Kennedy, *Times to Remember*, 211–12.

214. "DM," chap. 1, p. 5, JPK Collection, JFKL; Goodwin, *The Fitzgeralds and the Kennedys*, 513.

215. "DM," chap. 1, p. 5, JPK Collection, JFKL.

216. Beschloss, *Kennedy and Roosevelt*, 155.

217. Frank Kent to Bernard Baruch, June 14, 1937, Baruch Papers, quoted in Beschloss, *Kennedy and Roosevelt*, 153.

218. James Roosevelt, *My Parents: A Differing View* (Chicago: Playboy Press, 1976), 208; Kent to Baruch, June 14, 1937, Baruch Papers, quoted in Beschloss, *Kennedy and Roosevelt*, 153; Nasaw, *The Patriarch*, 272.

219. J. Roosevelt, *My Parents*, 208–9; Beschloss, *Kennedy and Roosevelt*, 153; Nasaw, *The Patriarch*, 272–73.

220. Beschloss, *Kennedy and Roosevelt*, 157; Kennedy's description in his "Diplomatic Memoirs" of who initiated the appointment and why is markedly different from that cited in the text. He wrote that it was Roosevelt who offered him the ambassadorship after he declined appointment to be the secretary of commerce. He refused that post because of the chronic difference of opinion between him and Secretary of State Henry Morgenthau and between him and Secretary of Labor

Frances Perkins, people with whom he would have to work closely at Commerce. He feared that "the potential disharmony that I would necessarily bring into his [Roosevelt's] cabinet seemed a sufficient ground for me to decline his offer. . . . It was then that he turned . . . , and offered me the Ambassadorship to the Court of St. James [*sic*]. . . . The President's suggestion was a complete surprise," Kennedy wrote, and added that he did not know whether the suggestion originated with Roosevelt or with one of his advisers, but the deft FDR asked to speak with Rose about her husband's taking the position. Kennedy explained that the importance of writing about these events lay in their "personal nature" and in the "informal circumstances" with which he came to accept that post; "DM," chap. 1, p. 3, JPK Collection, JFKL; *Liberty* (Fall 1971): 27; *New York Post Daily Magazine*, January 11, 1961, 37; and Dorothy Schiff, interview by Michael Beschloss, January 11, 1978, quoted in *Kennedy and Roosevelt*, 157. Schiff was publisher of the *New York Post* and a Roosevelt friend, who was present at the dinner along with FDR, Mrs. Roosevelt, and the president's mother.

221. Jane Vieth, "The Donkey and the Lion: The Ambassadorship of Joseph P. Kennedy at the Court of St. James's, 1938–1940," *Michigan Academician* 10 (Winter 1978): 273–81; Vieth, "Joseph P. Kennedy and British Appeasement," 165–82.

222. *Liberty*, May 21, 1938, rpt. ed. (Fall 1971): 26–27; *Daily News*, December 10, 1937, 22; *Washington Post*, March 15, 1938, 15. "The Look Years," *Look* magazine (1972): 5, ran a story about Kennedy's presidency. This rumor was repeated in William J. Duncliffe's biography, *The Life and Times of Joseph P. Kennedy* (New York: MacFadden-Bartell, 1965), 94; and C. L. Sulzburger's *A Long Row of Candles: Memoirs and Diaries, 1934–1954* (New York: Macmillan, 1969), 23.

223. Morgenthau Diary, book 8, July 1, 1935, 16, FDRL.

224. J. Roosevelt, *My Parents*, 209–10; Beschloss, *Kennedy and Roosevelt*, 154; Tully, *FDR, My Boss*, 157.

225. FDR to JPK, January 17, 1938, Dept. of State.

226. FDR to Owen D. Young, January 28, 1938, box 71, Roosevelt and Politics, JPK Collection, JFKL.

227. JPK to James F. Byrnes, December 23, 1937, in Smith, *Hostage to Fortune*, 219; Beschloss, *Kennedy and Roosevelt*, 155–56.

228. Beschloss, *Kennedy and Roosevelt*, 154. Beschloss primarily uses J. Roosevelt's *My Parents* (208–10), but that source does not mention the concern about JPK's Catholicism in Britain.

229. *New York Times*, December 9, 1937, 1; Krock, *Memoirs*, 333; Nasaw, *The Patriarch*, 273.

230. Morgenthau Diary, December 8, 1937, 69–70, FDRL.

231. Morgenthau Diary, December 8, 1937, 69–70, FDRL; Nasaw, *The Patriarch*, 274.

232. J. Roosevelt interview, quoted in Beschloss, *Kennedy and Roosevelt*, 154; Sulzberger, *A Long Row of Candles*, 22–23.

233. Krock to JPK, December 8, 1937, box 10, Boake Carter-Arthur Krock, JPK Collection, JFKL; *Boston Globe*, February 7, 1938; Beschloss, *Kennedy and Roosevelt*, 155. Nasaw claims Krock intimated that the story had come from the State Department; *The Patriarch*, 273.

234. "The Krock story came directly from the White House, but without the President's knowledge, then or afterward"; Farley, *Jim Farley's Story*, 126–27. Apparently Jimmy Roosevelt authorized its release without checking with the president.

235. Farley, *Jim Farley's Story*, 126; Morgenthau Diary, December 8, 1937, 69–70, FDRL.

236. Senator Key Pittman to JPK, January 13, 1938, box 16, Appointments as Ambassador, JPK Collection, JFKL.

237. Byrnes to Krock, December 13, 1937, box 10, Arthur Krock, JPK Collection, JFKL.

238. Krock to Byrnes, December 14, 1937, box 93, U.S. Maritime Commission Correspondence, JPK Collection, JFKL.

239. William Phillips to Arthur Murray, December 27, 1939, M.S. 8805–24, 1937–1944, Elibank Papers, National Library of Scotland [NLS].

240. Eleanor Roosevelt to JPK, January 17, 1938, FDRL; Eleanor Roosevelt to JPK, January 17, 1938, box 71, Roosevelt and Politics, JPK Collection, JFKL.

241. JPK to Eleanor Roosevelt, n.d., box 71, Roosevelt and Politics, JPK Collection, JFKL.

242. *Boston Globe*, February 7, 1938, 2.

243. *New York Times*, December 12, 1937, sec. 4, p. 3.

244. Drew Pearson to JPK, *Washington Times*, January 5, 1938, box 114, Drew Pearson and Robert Allen Pearson, JPK Collection, JKFL.

245. Harold Ickes, *The Secret Diary of Harold Ickes*, vol. 2, *The Inside Struggle, 1936–1939* (New York: Simon and Schuster, 1954), April 17, 1938, 370.

246. Sir Ronald Lindsay to British Foreign Office, March 8, 1938, F.O. 371/21526, A1971/64/45, dispatch no. 222, Public Records Office (PRO), London. The *Times*, on February 28, 1938, 15–16, described Kennedy as "one of the few restraining influences on the President."

247. The *Times* (London), February 28, 1938, 15–16. The *Times* also emphasized Kennedy's "humble" parentage and birth in its biographical essay, but Patrick Jr., Joe's father, was fairly prosperous and something of a power in Boston politics. *Newsweek*, September 12, 1960, 276, makes the same point.

248. *Economist*, January 15, 1938, 106.

249. *Daily News*, December 10, 1937, 22.

250. Boake Carter to JPK, December 28, 1937, box 10, JPK Collection, JFKL; Nasaw, *The Patriarch*, 276–77; Goodwin, *The Fitzgeralds and the Kennedys*, 510–11.

251. Goodwin, *The Fitzgeralds and the Kennedys*, 511; Nasaw, *The Patriarch*, 277.

252. *St. Louis Star Times*, January 22, 1938, stated that "an authoritative source" said that Kennedy and Morgenthau would swap jobs sometime in March 1939. "This plan, evolved by President Roosevelt himself, not only has the entire approval of both men but was agreed upon long before the announcement of Kennedy's appointment to the London post." Morgenthau himself in a phone conversation with Kennedy discussed the article, which claimed that "a deal has been made that you're not to go to England and I am." Kennedy said he had heard the charge that "Morgenthau had got rid of Kennedy—by sending him to England." "It's 'God-damned' embarrassing [to Morgenthau]," Kennedy said, and "it's 'God-damned' embarrassing to me." Morgenthau Diary, February 2, 1938, FDRL. See also Morgenthau Diary, January 28, 1938, 184–87, FDRL. Both *Fortune* 16, no. 3 (September 1937): 142, and Rose Kennedy, *Times to Remember*, 197, state that Kennedy's interest in the Treasury was of long standing and went back at least to 1932. Koskoff, *Joseph P.*

Kennedy, 114–19, emphasizes how much he wanted the position. Koskoff argues that Kennedy was motivated primarily by social reasons, a "show them" attitude; Nasaw, *The Patriarch*, 277.

253. "DM," chap. 1, pp. 5–6, JPK Collection, JFKL.

254. JPK to FDR, telegram, January 13, 1938, Presidential Secretary File, FDRL.

255. Rose Kennedy to FDR, letter, n.d., President's Private File, Joseph P. Kennedy 207, FDRL.

256. *Literary Digest*, December 25, 1937, 6.

257. Beschloss, *Kennedy and Roosevelt*, 154.

258. McCarthy, *The Remarkable Kennedys*, 68–69.

259. "DM," chap. 1, p. 8, JPK Collection, JFKL; JPK Diary, February 18, 1938, JPK Collection, JFKL; Smith, *Hostage to Fortune*, 237; Perry, *Rose Kennedy*, 96–97.

260. Dallek, *Franklin D. Roosevelt and American Foreign Policy*, 156; David Kennedy, *Freedom from Fear*, 401–4.

261. "DM," chap. 1, pp. 4–5, 8–11, JPK Collection, JFKL.

262. "DM," chap. 1, p. 9, JPK Collection, JFKL; David Kennedy, *Freedom from Fear*, 406–9.

263. Moley, *After Seven Years*, 379.

264. Robert Self, ed., *The Neville Chamberlain Diary Letters*, vol. 4, *The Downing Street Years, 1934–1940* (Burlington, VT: Ashgate Publishing, 2005), 297–98. Chamberlain wrote in his diary that Roosevelt's secret proposal on January 12, 1938, for a worldwide conference on arms limitation from the dictators in exchange for equal access to raw materials and agreement on international conduct landed like a "bombshell" in his lap. Chamberlain's "blunt" rejection of Roosevelt's overture provoked a crisis with Eden, who believed that "Anglo-American cooperation was so important that it demanded a warmly supportive response to the President's appeal"; Robert Self, *Neville Chamberlain: A Biography* (Burlington, VT: Ashgate Publishing, 2006), 281. Eden's account of this tumultuous period is described in his memoirs, *The Eden Memoirs: Facing the Dictators* (London: Cassell, 1962), 547–71. Eden argued for Anglo-American cooperation and stressed the significance of encouraging Roosevelt's plan. Chamberlain said that he feared that Roosevelt's "naive and woolly" proposal would undermine his own initiatives to the dictators, particularly his intention to grant de jure recognition of Italy's conquest of Abyssinia, something that Roosevelt opposed strongly. Doing so, the prime minister believed, would provide an opportunity to enhance Britain's position in the Mediterranean. Eden greatly distrusted Mussolini and opposed granting formal recognition of the Italian conquest of Abyssinia unless and until it was part of a general settlement with Italy, fully supported by France, and accompanied by the withdrawal of Italian volunteers from the Spanish Civil War. De jure recognition of the Italian conquest of Abyssinia had been a smoldering issue between Chamberlain and Eden throughout the summer and fall of 1937.

William Rock's book, *Chamberlain and Roosevelt: British Foreign Policy and the United States, 1937–1940* (Columbus: Ohio State University Press, 1988), 55–77, includes analysis of Roosevelt's initiative, Chamberlain's rejection of it, and Eden's subsequent reaction. Rock wrote that Roosevelt's initiative in 1937 was greater than historians usually suggest. He also argues that although it is "impossible to know 'what might have been,'" what "we do know is that Chamberlain proceeded vigorously with his efforts at appeasement . . . and Roosevelt stood aside. . . . It seems likely that Roosevelt, feeling rebuffed, inclined further toward the isolationism already characteristic of so many Americans and the possibility of Anglo-American cooperation in the interest of peace, however limited already, dwindled. Roosevelt was content thereafter to stand by and watch while Chamberlain tried to handle things. And Chamberlain liked it that way."

Larry William Fuchser, *Neville Chamberlain and Appeasement: A Study in the Politics of History* (New York: W.W. Norton, 1982), 97–102, describes Chamberlain's response to Roosevelt's initiative as "immediate, curt, and negative." Fuchser added that "the United States was simply not a power whose actions could be dismissed with such cavalier disdain." Also see Donald Watt, "Roosevelt and Neville Chamberlain: Two Appeasers," *International Journal* 28 (Spring 1973): 185–204, for an intriguing assessment of FDR's motives and action over his note to Chamberlain proposing a conference. Also R. A. C. Parker, *Chamberlain and Appeasement: British Policy and the Coming of the Second World War* (New York: St. Martin's Press, 1993), 115–16, 118, has an excellent discussion of Roosevelt's motives and Chamberlain's actions regarding the president's proposal.

265. "DM," chap. 1, pp. 11–12, JPK Collection, JFKL.
266. "DM," chap. 1, p. 12, JPK Collection, JFKL; Smith, *Hostage to Fortune*, 225–26; Beschloss, *Kennedy and Roosevelt*, 162.
267. *Boston Globe*, February 23, 1938, 1, 7.
268. "DM," chap. 1, p. 12, JPK Collection, JFKL.

Chapter 2. The Lion's Mouth

1. Joseph P. Kennedy, Diary, unpublished, February 23, 1938, JPK Collection, JFKL [hereafter cited as JPK Diary]; JPK Diary, February 18, 1938, in Smith, *Hostage to Fortune*, 237; Collier and Horowitz, *The Kennedys*, 81.
2. *New York Times*, February 24, 1938, 8.
3. *Boston Globe*, February 7, 1938, 2.
4. David Kennedy discusses Roosevelt's proposal, Chamberlain's reaction to it, and David Kennedy's appraisal as "fanciful"; *Freedom from Fear*, 406–9.
5. David Kennedy, *Freedom from Fear*, 393–95, 397, 399–401, gives background information on American foreign policy in the mid-1930s and the neutrality legislation.
6. The question as to what Kennedy's instructions from the president were varies according to which version of Kennedy's diplomatic memoirs one reads. His earliest version of his farewell meeting with Roosevelt on February 22, 1938, indicated that Roosevelt and Kennedy had "discussed the foreign situation in general." The president affirmed his intention of keeping the United States out of all foreign commitments, that the situation was too uncertain for the United States to do anything. Further he showed no resentment of Chamberlain's appeasement position. Kennedy's second version of the memoirs, apparently ghostwritten by Harold Hinton, implies that FDR's mandate to Kennedy was to maintain neutrality, but then adds: "The president had given me no instructions" and "I was on my own." From 1949 to 1955 under Kennedy's supervision, his friend

and former SEC colleague James Landis rewrote the memoir from diplomatic diaries, dispatches, and correspondence. This version gives a much more detailed account of Roosevelt's instructions in their farewell meeting; Smith, *Hostage to Fortune*, 224–26.

7. "DM," chap. 1, p. 4, JPK Collection, JFKL.

8. John H. Davis, *The Kennedys: Dynasty and Disaster, 1848–1983* (New York: McGraw-Hill, 1984), 78; Goodwin, *The Fitzgeralds and the Kennedys*, 514; Nasaw, *The Patriarch*, 291.

9. Collier and Horowitz, *The Kennedys*, 82.

10. Smith, *Hostage to Fortune*, 231.

11. JPK Diary, March 1, 1938, JPK Collection, JFKL.

12. *New York Times*, March 2, 1938, 14.

13. Davis, *The Kennedys*, 78.

14. *New York Times*, March 2, 1938, 14.

15. *New York Times*, March 2, 1938, 14; see *Boston Globe*, March 21, 1938, 1, for additional reaction; Whalen: "This off-the-record gathering was recalled by a former London correspondent, whose notes were made available to the author"; *The Founding Father*, 214–15.

16. JPK to James Roosevelt, London, March 3, 1938, in Smith, *Hostage to Fortune*, 238; Nasaw, *The Patriarch*, 287.

17. Rose Kennedy, *Times to Remember*, 218.

18. McCarthy, *The Remarkable Kennedys*, 70.

19. JPK to James Roosevelt, London, March 3, 1938, in Smith, *Hostage to Fortune*, 238; Nasaw, *The Patriarch*, 285.

20. Howard Fyfe to Harry Havens, Esq., February 28, 1938, JPK Collection, JFKL.

21. JPK Diary, March 8, 1938, JPK Collection, JFKL.

22. "DM," chap. 5, p. 6, JPK Collection, JFKL.

23. Krock, *Memoirs*, 334.

24. JPK to James Roosevelt, March 3, 1938, box 107, Hull Papers, Library of Congress.

25. "DM," chap. 2, p. 3, JPK Collection, JFKL.

26. Andrew Roberts, *The Holy Fox: A Biography of Lord Halifax* (London: Weidenfeld and Nicolson, 1991), 2.

27. "DM," chap. 2, p. 3, JPK Collection, JFKL; Goodwin, *The Fitzgeralds and the Kennedys*, 528.

28. Roberts, *The Holy Fox*, 140.

29. Robert Self, *Neville Chamberlain: A Biography* (Burlington, VT: Ashgate Publishing, 2006), 291.

30. David Reynolds, *The Creation of the Anglo-American Alliance, 1937–41: A Study in Competitive Co-operation* (London: Europa Publications, 1981), 40.

31. "DM," chap. 2, p. 3A, JPK Collection, JFKL; Self, *Neville Chamberlain*, 280–89; Peter T. Marsh, *The Chamberlain Litany: Letters within a Governing Family from Empire to Appeasement* (London: Haus Publishing, 2010), 290–96; Nick Smart, *Neville Chamberlain* (London: Routledge, 2010), 230–32.

32. "DM," chap. 2, p. 4, JPK Collection, JFKL; Nasaw, *The Patriarch*, 291.

33. "DM," chap. 2, pp. 4, 6, JPK Collection, JFKL.

34. Robert Self, *The Neville Chamberlain Diary Letters*, vol. 4, *The Downing Street Years, 1934–1940* (Burlington, VT: Ashgate Publishing, 2005), 16, 294.

35. Self, *Chamberlain Diary Letters*, 4:267.

36. Self, *Chamberlain Diary Letters*, 4:273.

37. Self, *Chamberlain Diary Letters*, 4:284.

38. "DM," chap. 2, pp. 5–6, JPK Collection, JFKL; Nasaw, *The Patriarch*, 289.

39. JPK to Cordell Hull, March 2, 1938, 800 General, Dept. of State; JPK to Hull, March 4, 1938, 800 General, Dept. of State; Johnson to Hull, March 4, 1938, 711.41/389, Dept. of State.

40. JPK Diary, March 11, 1938, JPK Collection, JFKL.

41. JPK to FDR, March 11, 1938, London, box 10, FDRL; "DM," chap. 2, pp. 10–11, JPK Collection, JFKL; JPK Diary, March 11, 1938, JPK Collection, JFKL; Smith, *Hostage to Fortune*, 240.

42. "DM," chap. 2, p. 9, JPK Collection, JFKL.

43. "DM," chap. 2, pp. 8–10, JPK Collection, JFKL.

44. JPK Diary, March 11, 1938, JPK Collection, JFKL.

45. "DM," chap. 2, p. 7, JPK Collection, JFKL.

46. JPK Diary, March 4, 1938, JPK Collection, JFKL; JPK to FDR, London, March 11, 1938, box 10, Roosevelt Papers, FDRL; "DM," chap. 2, p. 7, JPK Collection, JFKL; Goodwin, *The Fitzgeralds and the Kennedys*, 514. Kennedy's title, "Ambassador to the Court of St. James's," harkened back to the reign of Henry VIII, when the Court was housed at St. James's Palace. Ever since 1850 the royal family has lived at Buckingham Palace, but the ambassador has retained the traditional title; Smith, *Hostage to Fortune*, 240–43.

47. "DM," chap. 2, p. 7, JPK Collection, JFKL; JPK to Krock, March 8, 1938, as cited in Goodwin, *The Fitzgeralds and the Kennedys*, 515.

48. JPK to Krock, March 8, 1938, quoted in Goodwin, *The Fitzgeralds and the Kennedys*, 515; Beschloss, *Kennedy and Roosevelt*, 160.

49. *Boston Globe*, March 2, 1938, 1.

50. "DM," chap. 2, p. 7, JPK Collection, JFKL.

51. Tully, *FDR, My Boss*, 157; McCarthy, *The Remarkable Kennedys*, 72.

52. *New York Times*, March 9, 1938, 1.

53. "DM," chap. 1, p. 6, JPK Collection, JFKL.

54. "DM," chap. 1, pp. 6–7, JPK Collection, JFKL; Nasaw, *The Patriarch*, 285.

55. *Saturday Evening Post*, February 4, 1938, 66; Whalen, *The Founding Father*, 212.

56. Whalen, *The Founding Father*, 212.

57. JPK to James Roosevelt, March 3, 1938, Hull Papers, FDRL; JPK to James Smith, *Hostage to Fortune*, 238; *Boston Globe*, February 7, 1938, 2.

58. "DM," chap. 5, p. 4, JPK Collection, JFKL.

59. *Saturday Evening Post*, February 4, 1938, 66; Whalen, *The Founding Father*, 212.

60. Whalen, *The Founding Father*, 212.

61. "DM," chap. 5, p. 4, JPK Collection, JFKL; JPK Diary, May 12, 1938, JPK Collection, JFKL.

62. *New York Times*, April 10, 1938, 36; JPK to James Roosevelt, March 3, 1938, Hull Papers, Library of Congress.

63. "DM," chap. 5, p. 2, JPK Collection, JFKL; JPK to Hull, March 18, 1938, as cited in Smith, *Hostage to Fortune*, 245; McCarthy, *The Remarkable Kennedys*, 72.

64. *New York Times*, April 10, 1938, 1, 36; JPK to Hull, April 8, 1938, Court Presentations, Dept. of State.

65. "DM," chap. 5, p. 3, JPK Collection, JFKL.

66. *Washington Herald*, April 13, 1938, 1, box 131, JPK Collection, JFKL.

67. JPK Diary, April 2, 1938, JPK Collection, JFKL.

68. Henry Cabot Lodge to JPK, April 9, 1938, box 131, JPK Collection, JFKL; unknown newspaper, April 19, 1938, 1, box 131, JPK Collection, JFKL.

69. "DM," chap. 5, p. 3, JPK Collection, JFKL.

70. FDR to Hull, March 21, 1938, FDRL; Hull to JPK, March 22, 1938, Dept. of State; Rose Kennedy, *Times to Remember*, 225–29.

71. "DM," chap. 2, p. 7, JPK Collection, JFKL.

72. Boake Carter, *Daily Mirror*, March 10, 1938, box 129, JPK Collection, JFKL.

73. *Boston Globe*, March 21, 1938, 1.

74. *Time* magazine, March 14, 1938, 19. "DM," chap. 2, p. 7, JPK Collection, JFKL, gives Kennedy as "less interested in foreign affairs than in how and whether he was going to eat and the chances of the Boston Braves [then the Bees] to snatch the pennant"; Nasaw, *The Patriarch*, 289.

75. *Time*, March 14, 1938, 19.

76. *Time*, September 18, 1939, 14; Rabbi Stephen Wise to FDR, March 4, 1938, PSF: Great Britain, box 29, FDRL, as cited in Rock, *Chamberlain and Roosevelt*, 87; Koskoff, *Joseph P. Kennedy*, 122; McCarthy, *The Remarkable Kennedys*, 71.

77. Speech by Lord Halifax, March 22, 1938, FO 371/21692/A2144, 291–92, PRO; *Times* (London), March 19, 1938, 17.

78. Lord Riverdale to Thomas J. Watson, Esq., March 24, 1938, FDRL.

79. Arthur Murray to William Phillips, June 21, 1938, Elibank Papers, National Library of Scotland, Edinburgh [hereafter NLS].

80. William Phillips to Arthur Murray, June 25, 1938, Elibank Papers, NLS.

81. *Boston Globe*, March 25, 1938, 9.

82. Dick B (illegible) to JPK, letter, May 11, 1938, box 16, JPK Collection, JFKL; Smith, *Hostage to Fortune*, 254n69.

83. Anecdote from Balderston correspondence, MS at Library of Congress Manuscript Division, Washington, DC, as cited in Koskoff, *Joseph P. Kennedy*, 123.

84. Andrew Boyle, *Montagu Norman: A Biography* (London: Cassell, 1967), 315, cites an interview with Norman's widow; as cited in Koskoff, *Joseph P. Kennedy*, 123.

85. Lord Francis-Williams, *Nothing So Strange* (New York: American Heritage Press, 1970), 155; as cited in Koskoff, *Joseph P. Kennedy*, 123.

86. Leonard Mosley, *Backs to the Wall: London under Fire, 1939–1945* (London: Weidenfeld and Nicolson,

1971), 36n; as cited in Koskoff, *Joseph P. Kennedy*, 123.

87. C. L. Sulzberger, *A Long Row of Candles*, 22.

88. Boake Carter, April 10, 1938, box 129, JPK Collection, JFKL.

89. McCarthy, *The Remarkable Kennedys*, 70.

90. McCarthy, *The Remarkable Kennedys*, 70–71.

91. *Time*, March 14, 1938, 28.

92. William Duncliffe, *Record-American*, January 21, 1964, box 6, JPK Papers, JFKL; McCarthy, *The Remarkable Kennedys*, 71.

93. Cablegram from Rosa (Rose Kennedy) to JPK, March 7, 1938, box 1, JPK Papers, JFKL; Nasaw, *The Patriarch*, 286.

94. Lester David, *Ted Kennedy: Triumphs and Tragedies* (New York: Grosset and Dunlap, 1971), 39.

95. McCarthy, *The Remarkable Kennedys*, 70–71.

96. David, *Ted Kennedy*, 40.

97. Duncliffe, *Record-American*, January 21, 1964, box 6, JPK Papers, JFKL; McCarthy, *The Remarkable Kennedys*, 70; Gail Cameron, *Rose: A Biography of Rose Fitzgerald Kennedy* (New York: G.P. Putnam's Sons, 1971), 126.

98. "DM," chap. 5, p. 6, JPK Collection, JFKL; Rose Kennedy, *Times to Remember*, 221.

99. JPK Diary, April 10, 1938, JPK Collection, JFKL; Smith, *Hostage to Fortune*, 250–54.

100. "DM," chap. 5, p. 6A, JPK Collection, JFKL; Goodwin, *The Fitzgeralds and the Kennedys*, 525.

101. Rose Kennedy, *Times to Remember*, 221; Goodwin, *The Fitzgeralds and the Kennedys*, 526.

102. "DM," chap. 5, p. 6A and B, JPK Collection, JFKL; Goodwin, *The Fitzgeralds and the Kennedys*, 526.

103. "DM," chap. 5, p. 6C, JPK Collection, JFKL; Goodwin, *The Fitzgeralds and the Kennedys*, 526.

104. "DM," chap. 5, pp. 6C, 6D, JPK Collection, JFKL; Goodwin, *The Fitzgeralds and the Kennedys*, 526–27.

105. "DM," chap. 5, p. 6D, JPK Collection, JFKL.

106. Goodwin, *The Fitzgeralds and the Kennedys*, 527, interview with Rose Kennedy.

107. "DM," chap. 5, p. 6D, JPK Collection, JFKL.

108. "DM," chap. 5, p. 6D, JPK Collection, JFKL; JPK Diary, April 9, 1938 (written evening of April 10, 1938), JPK Collection, JFKL; Smith, *Hostage to Fortune*, 250–51.

109. Rose Kennedy to Patricia Kennedy, April 10, 1938, as cited in Smith, *Hostage to Fortune*, 252.

110. Rose Kennedy, *Times to Remember*, 223.

111. JPK Diary, April 10, 1938, JPK Collection, JFKL.

112. "DM," chap. 5, pp. 6E–6G, JPK Collection, JFKL.

113. "DM," chap. 5, pp. 6G and 6H, JPK Collection, JFKL; Goodwin, *The Fitzgeralds and the Kennedys*, 529.

114. "DM," chap. 5, p. 6H, JPK Collection, JFKL.

115. "DM," chap. 5, pp. 6H and 6J, JPK Collection, JFKL; Smith, *Hostage to Fortune*, 253–54.

116. Rose Kennedy, *Times to Remember*, 221.

117. Beschloss, *Kennedy and Roosevelt*, 160, interview with James Roosevelt.

118. JPK to FDR, March 11, 1938, box 10, FDRL; Smith, *Hostage to Fortune*, 242.

119. Goodwin, *The Fitzgeralds and the Kennedys*, 529.

120. Morgenthau Diaries, May 2, 1938, 43, FDRL.

121. "DM," chap. 1, p. 7, JPK Collection, JFKL; Roosevelt, *F.D.R.: His Personal Letters, 1928–1945*, 2 vols., ed. Elliott Roosevelt (New York: Duell, Sloan and Pearce, 1950), 2:769.

122. Speech by Lord Halifax, March 22, 1938, 293–94, Dept. of State.

123. Whalen, *The Founding Father*, 214; Koskoff, *Joseph P. Kennedy*, 126, 277–78, for an engaging description of the ambassador's social life in England.

124. Goodwin, *The Fitzgeralds and the Kennedys*, 517; Whalen, *The Founding Father*, 214.

125. *New York Times*, February 24, 1938, 8; Whalen, *The Founding Father*, 216–19.

126. *New York Times*, February 24, 1938, 8; *Boston Globe*, March 21, 1938, 1; Nasaw, *The Patriarch*, has a very interesting interpretation, 292–94.

127. Ernest K. Lindley, "Will Kennedy Run for President?" *Liberty* magazine, May 21, 1938, rpt. ed. (Fall 1971): 26; Telford Taylor, *Munich: The Price of Peace* (Garden City, NY: Doubleday, 1979), 766; Whalen, *The Founding Father*, 214; Nasaw, *The Patriarch*, 301.

128. JPK to Anthony Biddle, April 5, 1938, box 103, JPK Collection, JFKL.

129. "The Reminiscences of Alan Goodrich Kirk," part 1 (Columbia University: Oral History Research Office, 1962), 212.

130. "DM," chap. 9, p. 8, JPK Collection, JFKL; Smith, *Hostage to Fortune*, 266; Whalen, *The Founding Father*, 232.

131. JPK to FDR, March 11, 1938, box 10, FDRL; Smith, *Hostage to Fortune*, 243.

132. William W. Kaufmann, "Two American Ambassadors: Bullitt and Kennedy," in *The Diplomats, 1919–39: The Thirties*, ed. Gordon Craig and Felix Gilbert (New York: Princeton University Press, 1953), 660.

133. Lindley, "Will Kennedy Run for President?," 26; Taylor, *Munich*, 766; Craig and Gilbert, eds., *The Diplomats, 1919–39*, 660.

134. Craig and Gilbert, eds., *The Diplomats, 1919–39*, 660, 667–68.

135. JPK Diary, June 13, 1938, JPK Collection, JFKL; Smith, *Hostage to Fortune*, 266; Whalen, *The Founding Father*, 232.

136. Memorandum of transatlantic telephone conversation between the ambassador in the United Kingdom (Kennedy) and the Under Secretary of State (Welles), September 26, 1938, U.S. Department of State, *Foreign Relations of the United States: Diplomatic Papers* [hereafter *FRUS*], 1:660–61; Taylor, *Munich*, 767.

137. *New York Times*, July 23, 1938, sec. 4, p. 5.

138. Koskoff, *Joseph P. Kennedy*, 275, interview with James Roosevelt, 563n9.

139. Taylor, *Munich*, 767.

140. Ickes Diary, October 26, 1939, reel 3, 3840, Library of Congress; Beschloss, *Kennedy and Roosevelt*, 186.

141. Freda Kirchwey, "Watch Joe Kennedy!" *The Nation*, December 14, 1940, 593.

142. Taylor, *Munich*, 767.

143. Self, *Chamberlain Diary Letters*, 4:16–17.

144. Nasaw, *The Patriarch*, 291.

145. George Bilainkin, *Diary of a Diplomatic Correspondent* (London: George Allen & Unwin, 1942), 195; Koskoff, *Joseph P. Kennedy*, 275.

146. Craig and Gilbert, eds., *The Diplomats, 1919–39*, 678.

147. Charles Lock Mowat, *Britain between the Wars* (Chicago: University of Chicago Press, 1955), 414.

148. *Fortune* magazine, December 1938, 116; Self, *Neville Chamberlain*, 4.

149. Keith Grahame Feiling, *The Life of Neville Chamberlain* (London: Macmillan, 1970), 124.

150. Marsh, *The Chamberlain Litany*, 288.

151. Self, *Chamberlain Diary Letters*, 4:4.

152. Self, *Chamberlain Diary Letters*, 4:392.

153. Self, *Neville Chamberlain*, 364.

154. R. A. C. Parker, *Chamberlain and Appeasement: British Policy and the Coming of the Second World War* (New York: St. Martin's Press, 1993), 6, 8–11. Historians differ in their interpretations of Chamberlain's personal qualities and their significance for his political decisions. For additional views on Chamberlain's personality and his conduct of foreign policy, see Self, *Chamberlain Diary Letters*, 4:5–33. Self also has an excellent discussion of the recent historiography on Chamberlain. Marsh, *The Chamberlain Litany*, 284–85; Smart, *Neville Chamberlain*, 228–29; Self, *Neville Chamberlain*, 278–80; Andrew David Stedman, *Alternatives to Appeasement: Neville Chamberlain and Hitler's Germany* (London: I.B. Tauris, 2011), 12; David Dutton, *Neville Chamberlain* (London: Arnold, 2001), 140–43, 203.

155. Whalen, *The Founding Father*, 234–35.

156. Peake memo dated October 12, 1939, of visit with Hillman on October 11, 1939, 164, as cited in Koskoff, *Joseph P. Kennedy*, 286; Rose Kennedy, *Times to Remember*, 241: "Joe despised everything about Hitler and Nazism."

157. Self, *Chamberlain Diary Letters*, 4:18, 307; Feiling, *The Life of Neville Chamberlain*, 347; Dutton, Neville Chamberlain, 168.

158. "DM," chap. 40, p. 13, JPK Collection, JFKL; Joseph P. Kennedy, *The Landis Papers*, chap. 40, p. 549, MS Division, Library of Congress [hereafter referred to as *The Landis Papers*].

159. Memo to FDR, March 3, 1939, PSF: box 10, Gt. Britain, FDRL.

160. Self, *Chamberlain Diary Letters*, 4:396.

161. Self, *Neville Chamberlain*, 3–4, 237, 267, 272–73, 295–97; Marsh, *The Chamberlain Litany*, 298; Stedman, *Alternatives to Appeasement*, 9–11; Smart, *Neville Chamberlain*, 229.

162. Feiling, *The Life of Neville Chamberlain*, 320; Larry William Fuchser, *Neville Chamberlain and Appeasement: A Study in the Politics of History* (New York: W.W. Norton, 1982), 21–23; Dutton, Neville Chamberlain, 11, 169, 192.

163. Herschel Johnson to Hull, July 6, 1938, 2, 741, Dept. of State.

164. Fuchser, *Chamberlain and Appeasement*, xi.

165. Whalen, *The Founding Father*, 234, interview in New York on October 24, 1962.

166. Irwin Ross, "The True Story of Joseph P. Kennedy," *New York Post Daily Magazine*, January 11, 1961, 37; Beschloss, *Kennedy and Roosevelt*, 162.

167. Walter Millis, ed., *The Forrestal Diaries* (New York: Viking Press, 1951), 121–22.

168. Martin Gilbert, *The Roots of Appeasement* (London: Weidenfeld and Nicolson, 1966), 157.

169. JPK to James Roosevelt, March 3, 1938, as cited in Smith, *Hostage to Fortune*, 238.

170. Taylor, *Munich*, 767.

171. René Kraus, *The Men around Churchill* (New York: J.B. Lippincott, 1941), 15.

172. Roberts, *The Holy Fox*, 6.

173. Nasaw, *The Patriarch*, 291.

174. Roberts, *The Holy Fox*, 145.

175. JPK to Krock, March 21, 1938, as cited in Smith, *Hostage to Fortune*, 247.

176. JPK to Krock, March 21, 1938, as cited in Smith, *Hostage to Fortune*, 247; Goodwin, *The Fitzgeralds and the Kennedys*, 528; Parker, *Chamberlain and Appeasement*, 123; Alan Campbell Johnson, *Viscount Halifax: A Biography* (New York: Ives Washburn, 1941), 16; Nasaw, *The Patriarch*, 291; Roberts, *The Holy Fox*, 6.

177. Goodwin, *The Fitzgeralds and the Kennedys*, 529.

178. *The Nation*, December 14, 1940, 593.

179. David Dilks, ed., *The Diaries of Sir Alexander Cadogan, 1938–1945* (New York: G.P. Putnam's Sons, 1972), 62.

180. "The Reminiscences of Alan Goodrich Kirk," pt. 1, p. 215.

181. JPK to Lord Beaverbrook, April 20, 1960, May 27, 1960, as cited in Smith, *Hostage to Fortune*, 687–88. In Smith's book of her grandfather's correspondence there are several letters from Kennedy addressed to "Dear Max" and signed "Your devoted friend" or "My best to you always." They discuss current political events, especially Jack Kennedy's presidential campaign. They reveal a good friendship between them, and Beaverbrook's support of Jack's candidacy.

182. Morgenthau Diaries, March 16, 1938, 186, FDRL.

183. JPK to Hull, March 30, 1938, Dept. of State.

184. "DM," chap. 4, pp. 13–14, JPK Collection, JFKL; Whalen, *The Founding Father*, 220.

185. Whalen, *The Founding Father*, 221.

186. *Boston Sunday Globe*, editorial, April 3, 1938, 1.

187. "DM," chap. 5, p. 5, JPK Collection, JFKL; Smith, *Hostage to Fortune*, 255n74.

188. JPK to Lady Astor, May 10, 1938, as cited in Smith, *Hostage to Fortune*, 256.

189. Nasaw, *The Patriarch*, 305–6.

190. Ickes, *The Secret Diary of Harold L. Ickes*, vol. 3, *The Lowering Clouds, 1939–1941* (New York: Simon and Schuster, 1954), December 1, 1940, 377.

191. Pearson and Allen, "The Washington Merry-Go-Round," April 22, 1938, box 114, JPK Collection, JFKL; Smith, *Hostage to Fortune*, 255.

192. JPK to Drew Pearson, telegram, May 3, 1938, JPK Collection, JFKL; Smith, *Hostage to Fortune*, 255.

193. Pearson to JPK, May 4, 1938, box 114, JPK Collection, JFKL; "DM," chap. 5, p. 6, JPK Collection, JFKL;

Nasaw, *The Patriarch*, 304–5.

194. "DM," chap. 3, p. 2, JPK Collection, JFKL; Nasaw, *The Patriarch*, 305.

195. *Annual Report* 1938, FO 371/22832/2099, 33, London, Public Records Office [hereafter PRO].

196. Morgenthau Diaries, September 1, 1938, 34, FDRL.

197. March 15, 1938, journal entry of Joseph Davies, chronological file 11–15 March 1938, Library of Congress.

198. Samuel John Gurney Hoare Templewood, *Nine Troubled Years* (London: Collins, 1954), 282. See Parker, *Chamberlain and Appeasement*, 132–36, for a discussion of Chamberlain's and Halifax's reaction.

199. JPK to Krock, March 21, 1938, as cited in Smith, *Hostage to Fortune*, 246–47.

200. JPK to FDR, March 11, 1938, box 10, FDRL; "DM," chap. 3, p. 6, JPK Collection, JFKL; JPK to FDR, March 11, 1938, as cited in Smith, *Hostage to Fortune*, 240–43.

201. JPK to Krock, March 21, 1938, as cited in Smith, *Hostage to Fortune*, 246; Whalen, *The Founding Father*, 220.

202. JPK to FDR, March 11, 1938, box 10, FDRL; "DM," chap. 3, p. 6, JPK Collection, JFKL; JPK to FDR, March 11, 1938, as cited in Smith, *Hostage to Fortune*, 240–43.

203. Telephone conversation between JPK and Henry Morgenthau, Jr., March 16, 1938, Morgenthau Diaries, 182–89, FDRL.

204. JPK to FDR, March 11, 1938, box 10, FDRL; "DM," chap. 3, p. 6, JPK Collection, JFKL; Smith, *Hostage to Fortune*, 242.

205. Beatrice Bishop Berle and Travis Beal Jacobs, eds., *Navigating the Rapids, 1918–1971: From the Papers of Adolf A. Berle* (New York: Harcourt Brace Jovanovich, 1973), 169; Dallek, *Franklin D. Roosevelt and American Foreign Policy*, 158; William R. Rock, *Chamberlain and Roosevelt: British Foreign Policy and the United States, 1937–1940* (Columbus: Ohio State University Press, 1988), 92.

206. Nancy Harvison Hooker, ed., *The Moffat Papers: Selections from the Diplomatic Journals of Jay Pierrepont Moffat, 1919–1943* (Cambridge, MA: Harvard University Press, 1956), 189.

207. JPK to Hull, March 22, 1938, box 109, JPK Collection, JFKL; Cordell Hull, *The Memoirs of Cordell Hull*, vol. 2 (New York: Whittlesey House, 1948), 575.

208. JPK to Hull, March 12, 1938, 841.5151/831, Dept. of State; Smart, *Neville Chamberlain*, 232–34; Self, *Neville Chamberlain*, 293–94.

209. JPK to Hull, March 22, 1938, file 104, Hull Papers, Library of Congress.

210. JPK to Hull, March 14, 1938, 800 Austria, Dept. of State; JPK to Hull, March 12, 1938, 800 Austria, Dept. of State; Hull, *Memoirs*, 2:581; Arnold A. Offner, *American Appeasement: United States Foreign Policy and Germany, 1933–1938* (New York: W.W. Norton, 1969), 233.

211. C. P. Snow, "Winston Churchill," in *The Look Years: A View of our 35 Tumultuous Years, the Heroes, the Villains, the Violence and the Glory, Fun, Fads, Victories, Defeats, Told with the Great Photographs of Our Time, and Words by Hemingway, Shirer, Gunther, Lord, Manchester, Snow, Rosten, Commager*, comp. by the editors of Look (Cowles Communications, 1972), 38.

212. Winston Churchill, March 14, 1938, *House of Commons Debates, 1937–1938*, vol. 333, March 14–April

1, p. 99.

213. Self, *Chamberlain Diary Letters*, 4:307; Self, *Neville Chamberlain*, 295; Feiling, *The Life of Neville Chamberlain*, 347; Marsh, *The Chamberlain Litany*, 297; Stedman, *Alternatives to Appeasement*, 235.

214. Self, *Chamberlain Diary Letters*, 4:305; Feiling, *The Life of Neville Chamberlain*, 341–42.

215. JPK to Hull, April 11, 1938, Britain-Italy, 800 Germany, Dept. of State; Self, *Neville Chamberlain*, 303.

216. JPK to Hull, March 25, 1938, 741.00/178, Dept. of State.

217. JPK to Hull, March 23, 1938, Austria Diplomatic Missions, Dept. of State.

218. "DM," chap. 4, pp. 2–3, JPK Collection, JFKL; JPK to Hull, memorandum, March 23, 1938, Dept. of State; John Harvey, ed., *The Diplomatic Diaries of Oliver Harvey, 1937–1940* (London: Collins, 1970), 123; JPK to Krock, March 28, 1938, as cited in Smith, *Hostage to Fortune*, 248; Nasaw, *The Patriarch*, 302.

219. Neville Chamberlain, March 24, 1938, *House of Commons Debates, 1937–1938*, vol. 333, March 14–April 1, 1938, 1405–6; "DM," chap. 4, pp. 5–6, JPK Collection, JFKL; Self, *Chamberlain Diary Letters*, 4:309; Self, *Neville Chamberlain*, 296: "Chamberlain and Halifax concluded the best method of exerting British influence and maintaining peace was to revive the 'guessing Position' . . . under which Germany could never be sure that H.M.G. would not intervene in Central Europe and the French could never be sure we *would*—thereby discouraging both from forward policies."

220. JPK to Krock, London, March 28, 1938, as cited in Smith, *Hostage to Fortune*, 248.

221. JPK to Krock, London, March 28, 1938, as cited in Smith, *Hostage to Fortune*, 248–49; Nasaw, *The Patriarch*, 302–3.

222. JPK to Krock, London, March 28, 1938, as cited in Smith, *Hostage to Fortune*, 249.

223. Parker, *Chamberlain and Appeasement*, 133.

224. JPK to Krock, London, March 28, 1938, as cited in Smith, *Hostage to Fortune*, 248–49.

225. "DM," chap. 3, p. 8, JPK Collection, JFKL.

226. London to JPK, January 26, 1938, 123 Kennedy, Dept. of State; JPK Diary, March 18, 1938, JPK Collection, JFKL.

227. "DM," chap. 3, p. 8, JPK Collection, JFKL.

228. JPK Diary, March 12, 1938, JPK Collection, JFKL; Nasaw, *The Patriarch*, 291–92.

229. Hull to JPK, March 11, 1938, 123 Kennedy, Dept. of State; Hull to JPK, March 14, 1938, as cited in Smith, *Hostage to Fortune*, 243–44; Koskoff, *Joseph P. Kennedy*, 127.

230. Hull to JPK, March 14, 1938, 123 Kennedy, Joseph P./45, Dept. of State; Hull to FDR, March 14, 1938, FDRL; "DM," chap. 3, pp. 8–9, JPK Collection, JFKL.

231. Hull to JPK, March 14, 1938, 123 Kennedy, Joseph P./45, Dept. of State; Hull to FDF, March 14, 1938, FDRL; "DM," chap. 3, pp. 8–9, JPK Collection, JFKL.

232. JPK to Hull, March 17, 1938, 123 Kennedy, Joseph P./48, Dept. of State; "DM," chap. 3, pp. 8–9, JPK Collection, JFKL.

233. Koskoff, *Joseph P. Kennedy*, 127.

234. JPK Diary, March 15, 1938, JPK Collection, JFKL; Nasaw, *The Patriarch*, 292–93.

235. "DM," chap. 3, p. 9, JPK Collection, JFKL; Koskoff, *Joseph P. Kennedy*, 127; Nasaw, *The Patriarch*, 294.

236. Hull, *Memoirs*, 2:576.

237. Hull, *Memoirs*, 2:576–77; Radio Bulletin #62, Washington, DC, March 17, 1938, 304–5 PRO FO371 21692; Sir Ronald Lindsay to Viscount Halifax, March 1, 1938; Sir Ronald Lindsay to Viscount Halifax, March 21, 1938, 130, PRO.

238. Johnson to Hull, text of Ambassador's address, Pilgrim's Dinner, March 19, 1938, 123 Kennedy, Joseph P./58, Dept. of State; the entire text was also reprinted in the *New York Times*, March 19, 1938, 1 and 6; *Times*, March 19, 1938, 17; *Boston Globe*, March 19, 1938, 1, 20; "DM," chap. 3, pp. 9–13, JPK Collection, JFKL.

239. Johnson to Hull, text of Ambassador's address, Pilgrim's Dinner, March 19, 1938, 6, Dept. of State; Nasaw, *The Patriarch*, 294–95.

240. JPK to Krock, March 21, 1938, as cited in Smith, *Hostage to Fortune*, 246–47.

241. "DM," chap. 3, p. 13, JPK Collection, JFKL.

242. *Times*, March 19, 1938, 17; Goodwin, *The Fitzgeralds and the Kennedys*, 521–22.

243. *Economist*, March 26, 1938, 17.

244. "DM," chap. 3, p. 13, JPK Collection, JFKL.

245. *Boston Globe*, March 23, 1938, 17.

246. JPK to Hull, March 22, 1938, F104, Hull Papers, FDRL.

247. Johnson to Hull, April 1, 1938, Dept. of State; JPK Diary, March 24, 1938, JPK Collection, JFKL.

248. Douglas Jenkins to Cordell Hull, April 7, 1938, Dept. of State.

249. JPK to Hull, March 22, 1938, JPK Collection, JFKL.

250. JPK to Hull, March 25, 1938, Dept. of State; memorandum of conversation, by the Under Secretary of State (Welles), March 8, 1938, *FRUS*, 1:128; Rock, *Chamberlain and Roosevelt*, 93–94; memorandum of conversation with Lord Halifax from JPK, April 6, 1938, Dept. of State.

251. JPK to FDR, March 11, 1938, 3, box 10, JPK Collection, JFKL.

252. JPK to Hull, March 22, 1938, JPK Collection, JFKL.

253. JPK to Senator William Borah, reprinted in Marian C. McKenna, *Borah* (Ann Arbor: University of Michigan Press, 1961), 354.

254. JPK to Hull, March 22, 1938, Hull Papers, Library of Congress.

255. Memorandum of conversation, by the Under Secretary of State (Welles), March 8, 1938, *FRUS*, 1:128; Rock, *Chamberlain and Roosevelt*, 93–94.

256. JPK to Hull, March 28, 1938, Dept. of State; Beschloss, *Kennedy and Roosevelt*, 164–65.

257. Memorandum of conversation, by the Under Secretary of State (Welles), March 8, 1938, *FRUS*, 1:128; Memorandum of conversation with Halifax from JPK, April 6, 1938, Dept. of State; "DM," chap. 6, p. 4, JPK Collection, JFKL; Rock, *Chamberlain and Roosevelt*, 93–94; William L. Langer and S. Everett Gleason, *The Challenge to Isolation: The World Crisis of 1937–1940 and American Foreign Policy*, vol. 1 (New York: Harper Torchbooks, 1952), 28–29. A serious misunderstanding arose, caused by Lindsay, the British ambassador to the United States. He informed his government that Welles had said that "the President regarded recognition [of the Italian conquest of Ethiopia] as an unpleasant

pill which we should both have to swallow and he wished that we should both swallow it together." This was certainly a compromising statement and probably it was inaccurately reported, perhaps intentionally. Despite this misunderstanding, the British were not deterred from their efforts; Offner, *American Appeasement*, 223, argues that "Welles said very nearly, if not exactly, the words Lindsay attributed to him. Americans generally might have looked unfavorably upon abandoning non-recognition, but Welles did write Roosevelt's message to Chamberlain (which Hull approved) that recognition of Mussolini's conquest of Ethiopia 'at some appropriate time may have to be regarded as an accomplished fact.'" "Apparently," wrote Offner, "the prospect of the British independently giving immediate recognition, without making it an 'integral part of measures for world appeasement,' distressed American diplomats. Unfortunately, they did not make their distress as clear as they should have to the British, for Roosevelt expressed 'deep gratification' at Chamberlain's second message, and Lindsay reported that the proposed British course, including support of Roosevelt's conference, 'entirely met the President's views.' The English thus could assume that the Americans had reached similar conclusions about measures to preserve peace and now had only to await their next move"; Nasaw, *The Patriarch*, 303–4.

258. JPK to Krock, April 14, 1938, box 110, JPK Collection, JFKL; "The quotations from Kennedy's 'Private and Confidential' letters are common to letters from Kennedy in the Baruch, Byrnes, Kent, Krock, Lippmann, and Pearson papers," as cited in Beschloss, *Kennedy and Roosevelt*, 165–66n297.

259. "DM," chap. 6, p. 5, JPK Collection, JFKL; JPK to Hull, telegram, April 15, 1938, *FRUS*, 1:143–45; JPK to Halifax, April 6, 1938, Dept. of State.

260. JPK to Bernard Baruch, April 14, 1938, MS in Baruch Papers, as cited in Koskoff, *Joseph P. Kennedy*, 131.

261. FDR to Hull, April 18, 1938, *FRUS*, 1:147; FDR to Hull, memorandum, April 18, 1938, FDRL; Ritchie Ovendale, *"Appeasement" and the English Speaking World* (Cardiff: University of Wales Press, 1975), 115.

262. Hull, *Memoirs*, 2:581.

263. Johnson to Hull, May 3, 1938, 710 Brit-Italy, Dept. of State; Ovendale, *"Appeasement" and the English Speaking World*, 115; Smart, *Neville Chamberlain*, 227–28, 234–35; Marsh, *The Chamberlain Litany*, 300; Self, *Neville Chamberlain*, 283–84, 297–98.

264. "DM," chap. 6, p. 6, JPK Collection, JFKL; Presidential Statement on Accord Reached between Great Britain and Italy, April 19, 1938, in *The Public Papers and Addresses of Franklin D. Roosevelt*, 1938 vol., *The Continuing Struggle for Liberalism* (New York: Macmillan, 1941), 248–49; Rock, *Chamberlain and Roosevelt*, 95.

265. Welles to Halifax, April 20, 1938, 710 Brit-Italy, Dept. of State; JPK to Halifax, April 23, 1938, 710 Brit.-Italy, Dept. of State; "DM," chap. 6, p. 10, JPK Collection, JFKL; Hull, *Memoirs*, 2:582; Rock, *Chamberlain and Roosevelt*, 95; Nasaw, *The Patriarch*, 303–4.

266. JPK to FDR, April 18, 1938, FDRL: "With reference to our telephone conversation of this morning, I am enclosing herewith for your consideration a suggestion of what you might wish to say at your press conference tomorrow with regard to the British-Italian Agreement"; "DM," chap. 6, p. 7, JPK

Collection, JFKL: "As this Government has on frequent occasions made it clear, the United States is advocating the maintenance of international law and order, believes in the promotion of world peace through the friendly solution by peaceful negotiation between nations of controversies which may arise between them as well as in the promotion of peace through the finding of means for economic appeasement. Without attempting to pass upon the political features of the accord recently reached between Great Britain and Italy, this Government has seen the conclusion of the agreement with sympathetic interest."

267. Dallek, *Franklin D. Roosevelt and American Foreign Policy*, 158.

268. "DM," chap. 6, pp. 6–7, 9–10, JPK Collection, JFKL.

269. Halifax to JPK, April 23, 1938, Dept. of State.

270. Ickes, *The Secret Diary of Harold L. Ickes*, vol. 2, *The Inside Struggle, 1936–1939* (New York: Simon and Schuster, 1954), April 23, 1938, 377.

271. Ickes, *The Secret Diary of Harold Ickes*, vol. 2, May 1, 1938, 380.

272. Smart, *Neville Chamberlain*, 227–28, 234, 252; Self, *Neville Chamberlain*, 275, 343–44.

273. Dallek, *Franklin D. Roosevelt and American Foreign Policy*, 126–27.

274. Ickes, *The Secret Diary of Harold Ickes*, vol. 2, April 23, 1938, 377–78.

275. Burns, *Roosevelt: The Lion and the Fox*, 356.

276. Hull, *Memoirs*, 2:517.

277. Ickes, *The Secret Diary of Harold Ickes*, vol. 2, May 12, 1938, 390; J. David Valack, "Catholics, Neutrality, and the Spanish Embargo, 1937, 1938," *Journal of American History* 54, no. 1 (June 1967): 83.

278. Ickes, *The Secret Diary of Harold Ickes*, vol. 2, May 12, 1938, 390.

279. Valack, "Catholics, Neutrality, and the Spanish Embargo," 83n41; Hugh Thomas, *The Spanish Civil War* (New York: Harper Colophon Books, 1963), 536: when Kennedy learned that the embargo might be lifted, he responded with alarm and argued that it could extend the Civil War. Kingsley Martin, ed., *"New Statesman" Years, 1931–1945* (Chicago: Henry Regnery, 1968), 213–14, argues that Kennedy's pressure on Roosevelt, along with that of other Catholics, caused the president to renew the embargo on Spain and described Kennedy as playing a "pusillanimous part in influencing U.S. policy."

280. Pearson to JPK, May 14, 1938, box 114, JPK Collection, JFKL.

281. Martin, *"New Statesman" Years*, 213–14; Koskoff, *Joseph P. Kennedy*, 134.

282. "Josiah C. Wedgewood attributes the suggestion to Zionist leader Rabbi Stephen Wise in letter to Lord Halifax, October 3, 1938, FO371/22453/R1177/153/37," as cited in Koskoff, *Joseph P. Kennedy*, 134, 519n109.

283. JPK to Hull, telegram, May 9, 1938, *FRUS*, 1:191–92; JPK to Hull, May 9, 1938, 800 Spain, Dept. of State.

284. Ickes, *The Secret Diary of Harold Ickes*, vol. 2, May 1, 1938, 380; JPK to FDR, March 11, 1938, Roosevelt Papers, FDRL, as cited in Beschloss, *Kennedy and Roosevelt*, 164; Valack, "Catholics, Neutrality, and the Spanish Embargo," 83.

285. "The Morgenthau Diaries," *Collier's*, October 11, 1947, 79; Ickes, *The Secret Diary of Harold Ickes*, vol.

2, June 26, 1938, 405.

286. Morgenthau Diaries, June 14, 1938, 350, FDRL.

287. Morgenthau Diaries, June 14, 1938, 350, FDRL.

288. Ickes, *The Secret Diary of Harold Ickes*, vol. 2, June 26, 1938, 405.

289. *Time*, September 18, 1939, 14.

290. Ickes, *The Secret Diary of Harold Ickes*, vol. 2, July 9, 1938, 420.

291. *Chicago Tribune*, June 23, 1938, 2; "DM," chap. 9, p. 3, JPK Collection, JFKL.

292. JPK to T. J. White, April 27, 1938, as cited in Smith, *Hostage to Fortune*, 254–55.

293. Sulzberger, *A Long Row of Candles*, 22; Goodwin, *The Fitzgeralds and the Kennedys*, 532.

294. "DM," chap. 9, pp. 3–4, JPK Collection, JFKL.

295. Boake Carter, April 10, 1938, box 129, Ambassador Correspondence, JPK Collection, JFKL.

296. *Chicago Tribune*, June 23, 1938, 1; Lasky, *JFK: The Man and the Myth*, 52–53.

297. Whalen, *The Founding Father*, 222: "interviews in New York and Washington with newspapermen with whom Kennedy corresponded," 517.

298. Whalen, *The Founding Father*, 222.

299. JPK to Hull, May 5, 1938, Dept. of State.

300. Ickes, *The Secret Diary of Harold Ickes*, vol. 2, June 26, 1938, 405; "DM," chap. 9, p. 5, JPK Collection, JFKL; *Kansas City Star*, July 2, 1938, box 129, JPK Collection, JFKL.

301. *Times*, June 14, 1938, 16; *Kansas City Star*, June 20, 1938; *New York Times*, June 21, 1938, 6.

302. *New York Daily News*, June 20, 1938, as cited in Whalen, *The Founding Father*, 225.

303. "DM," chap. 9, p. 5, JPK Collection, JFKL; Nasaw, *The Patriarch*, 314–15.

304. *New York Times*, Arthur Krock column, "In the Nation," June 23, 1938, 20.

305. *New York Times*, May 18, 1938, 19; Goodwin, *The Fitzgeralds and the Kennedys*, 535; Nasaw, *The Patriarch*, 312–13.

306. Goodwin, *The Fitzgeralds and the Kennedys*, 532; Whalen, *The Founding Father*, 228.

307. *New Yorker*, June 24–July 7, 2019, 44, refers to Kennedy as a "reputed former bootlegger." "Despite the stories, there is no evidence, no mention, not even a report of any rumors of bootlegging in any of Kennedy's FBI files or those that refer to him. No allegations surfaced during his three confirmation hearings for SEC chairman, Maritime Commission chairman, and ambassador to Great Britain in the 1930s or in the four investigations conducted in the 1950s after he was recommended for presidential commissions," writes Nasaw, *The Patriarch*, 80.

308. Goodwin, *The Fitzgeralds and the Kennedys*, 534–35. Nasaw, *The Patriarch*, 312, writes that Kennedy's resentment about the rejection led to a lifelong anger against Harvard. He refused to attend any further reunions or to give any more money to the university.

309. *Boston Evening Globe*, June 22, 1938, 1.

310. "DM," chap. 9, p. 4, JPK Collection, JFKL; Koskoff, *Joseph P. Kennedy*, 138–39.

311. Ickes, *The Secret Diary of Harold Ickes*, vol. 2, July 3, 1938, 415–16; Whalen, *The Founding Father*, 229.

312. "DM," chap. 9, p. 6, JPK Collection, JFKL.

313. *Boston Evening Globe*, June 22, 1938, 5: Joe Kennedy watched his son John participate in an intercollegiate race; Goodwin, *The Fitzgeralds and the Kennedys*, 535; Nasaw, *The Patriarch*, 317.

314. *New York Times*, Arthur Krock column, "In the Nation," June 23, 1938, 20.

315. "DM," chap. 9, p. 6, JPK Collection, JFKL; Smith, *Hostage to Fortune*, 265–66.

316. Beschloss, *Kennedy and Roosevelt*, 171: In an interview with Walter Trohan, Beschloss was told that Early offered the story to him. Ironically, Early's informant was Arthur Krock, who told the White House about the existence of the correspondence, no doubt intending to bolster Kennedy in Roosevelt's eyes; Whalen, *The Founding Father*, 517n43.

317. *Chicago Tribune*, June 23, 1938, 1; "DM," chap. 7, JPK Collection, JFKL; JPK to Malcolm Bingay, July 22, 1938, as cited in Smith, *Hostage to Fortune*, 268–69; Koskoff, *Kennedy and Roosevelt*, 141.

318. Whalen, *The Founding Father*, 230.

319. *New York Times*, June 22, 1938, 4.

320. Krock to JPK, memorandum, June 23, 1938, box 110, ambassador correspondent file, JPK Collection, JFKL; Nasaw, *The Patriarch*, 317–18.

321. "DM," chap. 9, pp. 6–9, JPK Collection, JFKL; Nasaw, *The Patriarch*, 318–19.

322. Ickes, *The Secret Diary of Harold Ickes*, vol. 2, July 3, 1938, 415.

323. Moley, *After Seven Years*, 192.

324. Unofficial Observer, *The New Dealers*, 355; Whalen, *The Founding Father*, 230; Goodwin, *The Fitzgeralds and the Kennedys*, 429–30.

325. "DM," chap. 9, p. 9, JPK Collection, JFKL; *New York Times*, January 22, 1938, 4; Kennedy also wrote a letter to the *Boston Herald* on July 11, 1938, denying the story, JPK Collection, JFKL; Nasaw, *The Patriarch*, 320–21.

Chapter 3. Shirt-Sleeve Diplomacy: Trade, Treaties, Troubles

1. John Cudahy to Cordell Hull, July 11, 1938, 123 Kennedy, Joseph P. /97, Dept. of State; *New York Times*, July 8, 1938, 10; Goodwin, *The Fitzgeralds and the Kennedys*, 538.

2. *New York Times*, July 8, 1938, 10; Cudahy to Hull, July 11, 1938, 123 Kennedy, Joseph P. /97, Dept. of State.

3. Whalen, *The Founding Father*, 231.

4. "DM," chap. 10, p. 16, JPK Collection, JFKL.

5. Associated Press, *Triumph and Tragedy: The Story of the Kennedys*, ed. Sidney C. Moody (New York: Morrow, 1968), 11; Whalen, *The Founding Father*, 231.

6. Goodwin, *The Fitzgeralds and the Kennedys*, 538.

7. *New York Times*, July 8, 1938, 10.

8. Ickes, *The Secret Diary of Harold L. Ickes*, 2:416.

9. Foreign Office Minutes, June 28, 1938, FO 371/21548/A5134/45, PRO; Koskoff, *Joseph P. Kennedy*, 142.

10. *Irish Press*, July 9, 1938, n.p.; Cudahy to Hull, July 11, 1938, Dept. of State.

11. *New York Times*, July 8, 1938, 10; "DM," chap. 10, p. 16, JPK Collection, JFKL.

12. "DM," chap. 6, p. 10, JPK Collection, JFKL.

13. The Prime Minister, April 26, 1938, *House of Commons Debates, 1937–1938*, vol. 335, April 26–May 13, 31; Winston S. Churchill, *The Second World War*, vol. 1, *The Gathering Storm* (Boston: Houghton Mifflin, 1948), 248.

14. "DM," chap. 6, p. 11, JPK Collection, JFKL; The Earl of Longford and Thomas P. O'Neill, *Eamon DeValera* (London: Hutchinson, 1970), 318, as cited in Koskoff, *Joseph P. Kennedy*, 132, 518n89.

15. Interview with an official in the Colonial Office, July 1972, as cited in Koskoff, *Joseph P. Kennedy*, 131–32; Halifax to Lindsay, April 6, 1938, FO 371/21494/A2707, 1/45, PRO; Halifax to Malcolm MacDonald, FO800/310, XI, 187, 206; Halifax to Lindsay, April 6, 1938, FO371/21494/6544, as cited in Koskoff, *Joseph P. Kennedy*, 131–32.

16. "DM," chap. 6, p. 12, JPK Collection, JFKL.

17. David Reynolds, *The Creation of the Anglo-American Alliance, 1937–41: A Study in Competitive Co-operation* (London: Europa Publications, 1981), 188.

18. Self, *Chamberlain Diary Letters*, 306, 317–18; Self, *Neville Chamberlain*, 298; Feiling, *The Life of Neville Chamberlain*, 310.

19. Churchill, *The Second World War*, 1:248–49.

20. Winston Churchill, May 5, 1938, *House of Commons Debates, 1937–1938*, vol. 335, April 26–May 13, 1101.

21. "DM," chap. 6, p. 13, JPK Collection, JFKL; Self, *Neville Chamberlain*, 299.

22. MacDonald to Halifax, April 29, 1938, FO 371/21495/A3356, PRO.

23. JPK to Baruch, May 3, 1938, MS in Baruch Papers, as cited in Koskoff, *Joseph P. Kennedy*, 133.

24. "DM," chap. 10, p. 16, JPK Collection, JFKL; Malcolm MacDonald to Halifax, April 29, 1938, FO 371/21495/A3356/1/45, PRO.

25. *Chicago Tribune*, June 23, 1938, 2; Koskoff, *Joseph P. Kennedy*, 133.

26. JPK to Krock, May 2, 1938, box 110, JPK Papers, JFKL.

27. MacDonald to Halifax, April 29, 1938, FO 371/21495/A3356, PRO.

28. "DM," chap. 6, pp. 10–11, JPK Collection, JFKL.

29. Lindsay to Halifax, May 9, 1938, January–June, 414/275, A3884/1/45, no. 36, PRO; Lindsay to Halifax, May 17, 1938, FO 371/21496/A3834, PRO; Koskoff, *Joseph P. Kennedy*, 132.

30. Koskoff, *Joseph P. Kennedy*, 132.

31. MacDonald to Halifax, April 29, 1938, FO 371/21495/A3356/1/45, PRO; JPK Diary, April 22, 1938, JPK Collection, JFKL; Koskoff, *Joseph P. Kennedy*, 133.

32. MacDonald to Halifax, April 29, 1938, FO 371/21495/A3356, PRO; Lindsay to Halifax, April 29, 1938, FO 371/21495/A3356, PRO; Koskoff, *Joseph P. Kennedy*, 133.

33. JPK Diary, April 22, 1938, JPK Collection, JFKL; Koskoff, *Joseph P. Kennedy*, 133.

34. Morgenthau Diary, September 14, 1938, 0042, FDRL.

35. Ickes, *The Secret Diary of Harold Ickes*, 2:416; Ickes Diary, July 3, 1938, 2830, Library of Congress; "DM," chap. 6, p. 12, JPK Collection, JFKL.

36. Morgenthau Diary, September 14, 1938, 0042, FDRL; "DM," chap. 6, p. 12, JPK Collection, JFKL.

37. Morgenthau Diary, September 14, 1938, 0042, FDRL.

38. Ickes, *The Secret Diary of Harold Ickes*, 2:405.

39. Dallek, *Franklin D. Roosevelt and American Foreign Policy*, 84.

40. Hull, *Memoirs*, 518–19; Dallek, *Franklin D. Roosevelt and American Foreign Policy*, 84, 92–93; William Leuchtenburg, *Franklin D. Roosevelt and the New Deal* (New York: Harcourt, Brace and World, 1963), 204–5; Burns, *Roosevelt: The Lion and the Fox*, 252.

41. Burns, *Roosevelt: The Lion and the Fox*, 252.

42. Hull, *Memoirs*, 518–19.

43. "DM," chap. 9, p. 1, JPK Collection, JFKL.

44. Foreign Office Minutes, March 1, 1938, FO 371/21492/A1525/1/45, PRO.

45. Foreign Office Minutes, March 10, 1938, FO 371/21492/1850/1/45, PRO; March 1, 1938, FO 371/21492/A1525/1/45, 8–9, PRO; Self, *Chamberlain Diary Letters*, 284: Chamberlain also saw the Anglo-American Trade Agreement as a way "to educate American opinion to act more and more with us"; Self, *Neville Chamberlain*, 277.

46. Foreign Office Minutes, March 10, 1938, FO 371/21492/A1850/1/45, 99, PRO.

47. Hull to American Embassy, January 31, 1938, 841.4061 Motion Pictures/96, Dept. of State.

48. See Hull to Johnson, January 12, 1938, *FRUS*, 2:3–5, for a list of "what the Industry considers would approximate the minimum needs of the Industry in so far as the pending British legislation is concerned." "Mr. Will Hays has, at our request, submitted a list of what the Industry considers would approximate the minimum needs of the Industry in so far as the pending British legislation is concerned. The list does not however represent the treatment which the Industry feels it is justified in expecting." The list is as follows:

  (1) The requirement of the quota of British films to be limited to a percentage of the number, not total footage, of foreign feature (long) films for both renters and exhibitors. Such percentage for the first year of the new Quota Act (April 1, 1938) should be 10 percent and under no circumstances exceed 12½ percent, and to be rateably decreased each year thereafter until completely eliminated.

  (2) The quota requirement for renters not to exceed the quota requirement for exhibitors.

  (3) Each quota film to be available for use by both renter and exhibitor for quota requirements.

  (4) The cost test for all quota films to be determined upon a cost-per-foot basis; and there is to be no Viewing Test or other quality test except that based on cost-per-foot basis.

  (5) The following credits for renters' and for exhibitors' quotas to be given:

    1. Credit for labor costs when the amount expended is £1 per foot.

    2. Credits for labor costs when the amount expended is £3 per foot.

    3. Credits for labor costs when the amount expended is £4 or more.

  (6) One quota credit to be given for each British nonquota film acquired for distribution in any one country foreign to the British Empire, for not less than £10,000.

  (7) One quota credit in addition to the renters' multiple credit provided for in above to be given the renter for each quota film produced or acquired for world distribution and costing not less than £4 per foot in labor costs.

(8) Quota credits to be freely transferable.

(9) A restatement of the definition of a British film to be made to permit the employment of a larger percentage of non-British technical employees until such time as there are readily available for employment in the production of quota films a sufficient number of trained and experienced technicians of British citizenship. Accordingly, the cost of at least four non-British technicians in accepted categories to be deducted from the total cost of a quota film before computing the 75 percent British and 25 percent other foreign categories, this being an extension of the present terms of subsection 1, clause 25 of the Quota Bill.

(10) The quota reduction granted exhibitors under the present Act until expiration thereof to be granted renters, or the current Act to be extended for a year from the date now provided for its expiration.

(11) There is to be no "Control Commission." The new Quota Act to provide that no revisions may be made by any board, commission, or committee which will result in any increase in the number of quota films required, or in any increase in the prescribed amount of labor costs, or in the minimum sum payable for foreign rights of any quota film.

(12) There should be no quota for short films, but if there be one, it should be equal for exhibitors and renters without any quality tests.

(13) For offenses under the new Quota Act for which an exhibitor is equally at fault with a renter, both the exhibitor and the renter to be responsible.

(14) The definition of British films to include the statement that if the films are photographed, excepting background shots, in His Majesty's dominions, such films to be treated as British films.

Johnson to Hull, January 18, 1938, *FRUS*, 2:6–9, for further discussion between the American and British representatives to each of the fourteen points from the Hays memo and the British concessions on multiple credit and reciprocity.

49. Foreign Office Minutes, January 11, 1938, FO 371/21530/A1791, PRO.

50. Hull to Halifax, February 15, 1938, 841.4061 Motion Pictures, 106B, Dept. of State; Hull to Johnson, February 15, 1938, Washington, *FRUS*, 2:19.

51. Lindsay to Halifax, February 2, 1938, FO 371/21530/A1791, 39, PRO.

52. Koskoff, *Joseph P. Kennedy*, 171–72.

53. JPK to Hull, March 16, 1938, 841.4061 Motion Pictures/117, Dept. of State.

54. JPK to Hull, March 14, Dept. of State; JPK to Hull, March 14, 1938, *FRUS*, 2:23. Kennedy made the same points about the futility of altering existing legislation in an April dispatch to Cordell Hull; JPK to Hull, April 26, 1938, 841.4061 Motion Pictures/139, Dept. of State; JPK to Hull, June 2, 1938, 841.4061 Motion Pictures/143, Dept. of State: the technical problems included the reciprocity agreement and the triple credit.

55. Will H. Hays to Cordell Hull, May 27, 1938, 841.4061 Motion Pictures/142, Dept. of State.

56. "DM," chap. 18, p. 6, JPK Collection, JFKL; Koskoff, *Joseph P. Kennedy*, 173.

57. "Chamberlain report of discussion with Kennedy at cabinet meeting of July 28, 1938. MS. at Public

Record Office, London, cab. 23, vol. 94, 264. It is unclear from the minutes whether the quotation is supposed to be Kennedy's words or the Prime Minister's paraphrase of the gist of his argument," as cited in Koskoff, *Joseph P. Kennedy*, 530n11.

58. Burns, *Roosevelt: The Lion and the Fox*, 274.

59. Franklin D. Roosevelt, Samuel I. Rosenman, and William D. Hassett, eds., *The Public Papers and Addresses of Franklin D. Roosevelt* Vol. 1, *The Genesis of the New Deal, 1928–1932* (New York: Random House, 1938), 166–68.

60. Transatlantic telephone conversation, Hull to JPK, March 30, 1938, box 66, Hull Papers, Library of Congress.

61. "DM," chap. 18, p. 8, JPK Collection, JFKL; Koskoff, *Joseph P. Kennedy*, 173.

62. JPK to Hull, July 26, 1938, 631 Britain-U.S., Dept. of State.

63. "DM," chap. 11, p. 10, JPK Collection, JFKL.

64. Hull to JPK, July 25, 1938, *FRUS*, 2:41.

65. "DM," chap. 18, p. 6, JPK Collection, JFKL.

66. "DM," chap. 11, p. 10, JPK Collection, JFKL.

67. "DM," chap. 18, p. 6, JPK Collection, JFKL.

68. CAB [cabinet minutes] 23/96, October 19, November 7, 1938, 20–21 PRO; Rock, *Chamberlain and Roosevelt*, 138.

69. Lindsay to Halifax, October 8, 1938, FO414/275, PRO.

70. JPK to Hull, October 18, 1938, London, *FRUS*, 2:65–66; "DM," chap. 18, p. 7, JPK Collection, JFKL.

71. "DM," chap. 18, p. 7, JPK Collection, JFKL.

72. JPK to Hull, October 7, 1938, *FRUS*, 2:59–60; JPK to Hull, October 7, 1938, 631 Britain-U.S., Dept. of State.

73. "DM," chap. 8, JPK Collection, JFKL.

74. JPK to Hull, October 18, 1938, *FRUS*, 2:65–66; JPK to Hull, October 18, 1938, 631 Britain-U.S., Dept. of State; Telephone conversation between Hull and JPK, October 14, 1938, JPK Collection, JFKL.

75. Hull to JPK, October 18, 1938, *FRUS*, 2:66; JPK to Hull, October 19, 1938, 631 Britain-U.S., Dept. of State.

76. JPK to Hull, October 21, 1938, 631 Britain-U.S., Dept. of State; Nasaw, *The Patriarch*, 352–53.

77. Hull to JPK, October 22, 1938, 631 Britain-U.S., Dept. of State.

78. Hull to JPK, November 3, 1938, 631 Britain-U.S., Dept. of State.

79. JPK Diary, November 4, 1938, JPK Collection, JFKL.

80. "DM," chap. 18, p. 8, JPK Collection, JFKL; Koskoff, *Joseph P. Kennedy*, 174.

81. Hull to JPK, November 4, 1938, 631 Britain-U.S., Dept. of State; "DM," chap. 18, p. 9, JPK Collection, JFKL.

82. "DM," chap. 18, p. 9, JPK Collection, JFKL; Koskoff, *Joseph P. Kennedy*, 174.

83. Halifax to Lindsay, November 17, 1938, FO 414/275/A886/1/45, 62, PRO.

84. Annual Report 1938, FO 371/22832/2099, 8–38, PRO.

85. Hull to JPK, November 3, 1938, *FRUS*, 2:69–70; Hull to JPK, November 3, 1938, 631 Britain-U.S., Dept.

of State.

86. "DM," chap. 18, p. 9, JPK Collection, JFKL.

87. "DM," chap. 18, p. 10, JPK Collection, JFKL.

88. *Times* (London), November 30, 1938, 9.

89. Rudolf E. Schoenfeld (for the Ambassador, Kennedy) to Hull, London, November 29, 1938, 123 Joseph P. Kennedy/154, Dept. of State; *Times*, November 29, 1938, 9; November 30, 1938, 9.

90. Dallek, *Franklin D. Roosevelt and American Foreign Policy*, 92–93.

91. Hull, *Memoirs*, 530.

92. Hull, *Memoirs*, 530.

93. Koskoff, *Joseph P. Kennedy*, 174–75.

94. "DM," chap. 11, pp. 10–11, JPK Collection, JFKL.

95. "DM," chap. 11, pp. 8–9, JPK Collection, JFKL; JPK Diary, April 8, 1938, JPK Collection, JFKL.

96. "DM," chap. 11, p. 9, JPK Collection, JFKL.

97. JPK Diary, April 8, 1938, JPK Collection, JFKL.

98. "DM," chap. 11, p. 10, JPK Collection, JFKL.

99. "DM," chap. 12, pp. 1–6, JPK Collection, JFKL.

100. Johnson to Hull, April 7, 1938, 811.0141 Phoenix Group/76, Dept. of State; Annual Report 1938, FO 371/22832/2099, 8–38; IAC 494 (Committee on International Air Communications), FO 371/21518/1863, PRO. It gives Kennedy credit for being Roosevelt's mouthpiece for proposing the president's scheme.

101. Johnson to Hull, May 24, 1938, 811.0141 Phoenix Group/87, Dept. of State; Annual Report 1938, FO 371/22832/2099, 8–38, PRO.

102. IAC, FO 371/21518/1863, 494, PRO.

103. Foreign Office Minutes, May 23, 1938, no. 434, FO 414/275/A2707/1/45, 156–57 PRO; "DM," chap. 12, pp. 3–4, JPK Collection, JFKL.

104. *Daily Express*, August 12, 1938, 1; FW 811.0141 Phoenix Group/97, Dept. of State.

105. *Washington Star*, September 2, 1938, n.p., 811.0141 Phoenix Group/103, Dept. of State; "DM," chap. 12, pp. 4–5, JPK Collection, JFKL.

106. "DM," chap. 12, p. 4, JPK Collection, JFKL; *Washington Star*, September 2, 1938, 811.0141, Phoenix Group/103, Dept. of State.

107. *New York Times*, September 3, 1938, 3.

108. JPK to Hull, March 23, 1938, *FRUS*, 1:40.

109. JPK to Hull, March 23, 1938, *FRUS*, 1:40.

110. Reynolds, *The Creation of the Anglo-American Alliance*, 33.

111. "DM," chap. 6, p. 17, JPK Collection, JFKL.

112. Feiling, *The Life of Neville Chamberlain*, 343.

113. "DM," chap. 6, p. 17, JPK Collection, JFKL.

114. "DM," chap. 6, p. 17, JPK Collection, JFKL.

115. Ian Colvin, *The Chamberlain Cabinet: How the Meetings in 10 Downing Street, 1937–1939, Led to the*

Second World War (London: Victor Gollancz, 1971), 102–15, details the cabinet discussions; Parker, *Chamberlain and Appeasement*, 134–35, for background information.

116. JPK to Hull, March 9, 1938, 800 General, Dept. of State; JPK to Hull, March 9, 1938, 741.00/169, Dept. of State.

117. JPK to Krock, March 28, 1938 (second in JPK's series of "political letters"), as cited in Smith, *Hostage to Fortune*, 247–49.

118. JPK to Hull, May 5, 1938, *FRUS*, 1:50–51; JPK to Hull, May 5, 1938, 710 Britain-France, Dept. of State; Parker, *Chamberlain and Appeasement*, 148–49; Taylor, *Munich*, 390–95.

119. "DM," chap. 7, p. 7, JPK Collection, JFKL.

120. JPK to Hull, May 14, 1938, *FRUS*, 1:499–500; JPK to Hull, May 14, 1938, 800 Czechoslovakia, Dept. of State.

121. "DM," chap. 7, p. 8, JPK Collection, JFKL; JPK to Hull, May 14, 1938, 800 Czechoslovakia, Dept. of State.

122. JPK to Hull, May 14, 1938, 800 Czechoslovakia, Dept. of State; "DM," chap. 9, p. 8, JPK Collection, JFKL; Smith, *Hostage to Fortune*, 266.

123. "DM," chap. 7, p. 12, JPK Collection, JFKL.

124. "DM," chap. 7, p. 10, JPK Collection, JFKL; JPK to Hull, May 22, 1938, 800 Czechoslovakia, Dept. of State; The Ambassador in Germany (Wilson) to the Secretary of State (Hull), May 21, 1938, Berlin, *FRUS*, 1:506; Dilks, *Cadogan Diaries*, 78–80; Offner, *American Appeasement*, 249–50.

125. "DM," chap. 7, p. 11, JPK Collection, JFKL.

126. "DM," chap. 7, p. 15, JPK Collection, JFKL.

127. JPK to Hull, May 22, 1938, 800 Czechoslovakia, Dept. of State; Rock, *Chamberlain and Roosevelt*, 102.

128. "DM," chap. 7, p. 16, JPK Collection, JFKL.

129. "DM," chap. 8, p. 1, JPK Collection, JFKL; JPK Diary, May 23, 1938, JPK Collection, JFKL.

130. Self, *Chamberlain Diary Letters*, 325; Feiling, *The Life of Neville Chamberlain*, 354; Rock, *Chamberlain and Roosevelt*, 102; Self, *Neville Chamberlain*, 304: "In reality, the 'May crisis' was a chimera. There was no German plan for the invasion of Czechoslovakia and thus no retreat before British firmness. But this is not how it was perceived at the time. On the contrary, Chamberlain now appeared 'really . . . a strong man' whose 'masterly' handling of the crisis was proclaimed as a success 'in doing the very thing [Sir Edward] Grey [Britain's foreign secretary on the eve of World War I] failed to do in 1914, namely make Germany realize the dangers of precipitate action.' This was certainly how Chamberlain saw it."

131. "DM," chap. 10, p. 2, JPK Collection, JFKL.

132. "DM," chap. 10, p. 8, JPK Collection, JFKL.

133. JPK to James Roosevelt, May 31, 1938, as cited in Smith, *Hostage to Fortune*, 258–59.

134. "DM," chap. 7, p. 11, JPK Collection, JFKL.

135. Hull, *Memoirs*, 583.

136. Hull, *Memoirs*, 583.

137. Burns, *Roosevelt: The Lion and the Fox*, 385.

138. The German Ambassador in Great Britain (Herbert von Dirksen) to the State Secretary (Ernst Baron von Weizsäcker), May 31, 1938, *Documents on German Foreign Policy*, ser. D, 2:368–69 [hereafter *DGFP*]; Offner, *American Appeasement*, 251–54.

139. von Dirksen to von Weizsäcker, June 13, 1938, *DGFP*, ser. D, 1:714–18.

140. von Dirksen to von Weizsäcker, June 13, 1938, *DGFP*, ser. D, 1:714–18.

141. von Dirksen to von Weizsäcker, June 13, 1938, *DGFP*, ser. D, 1:714–18.

142. von Dirksen to von Weizsäcker, June 13, 1938, *DGFP*, ser. D, 1:714–18.

143. von Dirksen to von Weizsäcker, June 13, 1938, *DGFP*, ser. D, 1:718; Koskoff, *Joseph P. Kennedy*, 136–38.

144. *New York Times*, July 27, 1938, 7; *Newsweek*, September 12, 1960, 29; The German Ambassador in the United States (Hans-Heinrich Dieckhoff) to the German Foreign Ministry, June 25, 1938, *DGFP*, ser. D, 1:719; von Dirksen to Baron von Weizsäcker, June 13, 1938, *DGFP*, ser. D, 1:714–18; Hull, *Memoirs*, 584–85; Vieth, "Munich Revisited through Joseph P. Kennedy's Eyes," *Michigan Academician* 18 (Winter 1986): 73–85; Hooker, ed., *The Moffat Papers*, 196. Offner, *American Appeasement*, 251–53, also describes Kennedy's negotiations with von Dirksen. Although von Dirksen's dispatches are the only known historical source for their conversations, a comparison of them to Kennedy's views documented elsewhere leads to the conclusion that they are a substantially correct summary of Kennedy's real views.

145. Ickes, *The Secret Diary of Harold L. Ickes*, 2:405; Taylor, *Munich*, 769.

146. Memorandum by the Foreign Minister (Joachim von Ribbentrop), June 10, 1938, *DGFP*, ser. D, 1:713; Beschloss, *Kennedy and Roosevelt*, 164; Koskoff, *Joseph P. Kennedy*, 279: "One of Kennedy's friends attributed the content of the von Dirksen dispatches to the fact that everyone always had the feeling that Kennedy agreed with them. Why? There was always the need for current approval."

147. "DM," chap. 11, p. 1, JPK Collection, JFKL; JPK Diary, July 12, 1938, JPK Collection, JFKL.

148. JPK Diary, July 18, 1938, JPK Collection, JFKL.

149. "DM," chap. 11, p. 2, JPK Collection, JFKL; *Times*, July 13, 1938, 13; JPK to Hull, July 5, 1938, 123 Kennedy, Joseph P./90, Dept. of State; JPK to Hull, July 12, 1938, 123 Kennedy, Joseph P./95, Dept. of State; Johnson to Hull, July 16, 1938, 123 Kennedy, Joseph P./99, Dept. of State.

150. Johnson to Hull, July 3, 1938, 123 Kennedy, Joseph P./90, Dept. of State.

151. Johnson to Hull, July 16, 1938, 123 Kennedy, Joseph P./99, Dept. of State.

152. Self, *Chamberlain Diary Letters*, 335.

153. John Harvey, ed., *The Diplomatic Diaries of Oliver Harvey, 1937–1940* (London: Collins, 1970), 160.

154. JPK to Hull, July 6, 1938, London, *FRUS*, 1:56–57; JPK to Hull, July 6, 1938, 800 General, Dept. of State; Rock, *Chamberlain and Roosevelt*, 108.

155. Rock, *Chamberlain and Roosevelt*, points out how Kennedy undermined his own credibility with his attempts to visit Germany to win some sort of personal triumph in diplomacy (108); Robert Keith Middlemas, *The Strategy of Appeasement: The British Government and Germany, 1937–39* (Chicago: Quadrangle Books, 1972), 284.

156. JPK to Hull, July 6, 1938, 800 General, Dept. of State.

157. JPK to Hull, July 6, 1938, 800 General, Dept. of State; JPK to Hull, July 6, 1938, *FRUS*, 1:56–57.

158. Ickes, *The Secret Diary of Harold L. Ickes*, 2:420.

159. von Dirksen to von Weizsäcker, July 20, 1938, *DGFP*, ser. D, 1:721–23.

160. von Dirksen to von Weizsäcker, July 20, 1938, *DGFP*, ser. D, 1:721–23.

161. von Dirksen to von Weizsäcker, July 20, 1938, *DGFP*, ser. D, 1:721–23.

162. von Dirksen to von Weizsäcker, July 20, 1938, *DGFP*, ser. D, 1:721–23.

163. The Under State Secretary in the German Foreign Ministry (Ernst Wörmann) to the German Chargé d'Affaires in Great Britain (Theodor Kordt), August 16, 1938, *DGFP*, ser. D, 1:725.

164. Taylor, *Munich*, 769.

165. JPK to Hull, July 20, 1938, 710 Britain-Germany, Dept. of State; Koskoff, *Joseph P. Kennedy*, 143–44.

166. Smith, *Hostage to Fortune*, 232; Whalen, *The Founding Father*, 253; Nasaw, *The Patriarch*, 311. After Kennedy's remarks were published, he said they had been grossly distorted. Regardless, Nasaw argues that they were a true reflection of Kennedy's belief, a position with which I agree.

167. JPK to Hull, July 20, 1938, ser. 8.6, JPK Papers, JFKL; JPK to Hull, July 20, 1938, 710 Britain-Germany, Dept. of State; JPK to Hull, July 21, 1938, 710 Britain-Germany, Dept. of State; Smith, *Hostage to Fortune*, 267; Koskoff, *Joseph P. Kennedy*, 144.

168. "DM," chap. 10, p. 11, JPK Collection, JFKL; Annual Report 1938, FO 371/22832/2099, PRO.

169. JPK to Hull, July 20, 1938, ser. 8.6, JPK Papers, JFKL; JPK to Hull, July 20, 1938, 710 Britain-Germany, Dept. of State; Koskoff, *Joseph P. Kennedy*, 144.

170. JPK to Hull, July 20, 1938, 710 Britain-Germany, Dept. of State; Koskoff, *Joseph P. Kennedy*, 144.

171. Dilks, *Cadogan Diaries*, 87.

172. JPK to Hull, July 21, 1938, 710 Britain-Germany, Dept. of State.

173. JPK to Hull, July 21, 1938, 710 Britain-Germany, Dept. of State; "DM," chap. 10, p. 11, JPK Collection, JFKL; Dilks, *Cadogan Diaries*, 87–88; Frederick Winston Furneaux Smith Birkenhead, *Halifax: The Life of Lord Halifax* (London: Hamish Hamilton, 1965), 389.

174. Birkenhead, *Halifax*, 389; Fuchser, *Neville Chamberlain and Appeasement*, 134.

175. Smith, *Hostage to Fortune*, 232.

176. "DM," chap. 10, p. 15, JPK Collection, JFKL.

177. Hull to JPK, July 26, 1938, 800 General, Dept. of State; Johnson to Hull, July 28, 1938, 741.00/198, Dept. of State; *House of Commons Debates*, July 26, 1938, 2959; JPK to Hull, July 26, 1938, 800 Britain, Dept. of State. According to Birkenhead, "the introduction of this mild and conventional Liberal into the European snake pit was a striking example of the Prime Minister's lack of insight into the realities of foreign affairs"; *Halifax*, 389–90. Birkenhead also notes that Chamberlain announced Runciman's appointment to Parliament in such a way as to make a "grave departure from the truth in saying that it had been made in response to a request from the Government of Czechoslovakia."

178. "DM," chap. 10, p. 15, JPK Collection, JFKL.

179. "DM," chap. 10, p. 14, JPK Collection, JFKL.

180. Walter Runciman to FDR, July 28, 1938, PSF: Great Britain, FDRL; Rock, *Chamberlain and Roosevelt*, 107.

181. JPK to Hull, July 26, 1938, 800 General, Dept. of State.

182. "DM," chap. 10, p. 15, JPK Collection, JFKL; JPK to Hull, July 29, 1938, London, *FRUS*, 1:537–39; JPK to Hull, July 29, 1938, 800 Czechoslovakia, Dept. of State; Foreign Office Minutes, FO 371/22832/2099; Watt, *Roosevelt and Neville Chamberlain*, 109: Chamberlain was unconcerned about the absence of American support and advised Kennedy that any statement by FDR could be more harmful than beneficial.

183. Rock, *Chamberlain and Roosevelt*, 107.

184. "DM," chap. 13, p. 2, JPK Collection, JFKL; JPK to Hull, August 31, 1938, 800 Czechoslovakia, Dept. of State; JPK to Hull, August 31, 1938, ser. 8.6, 267, JPK Papers, JFKL; Smith, *Hostage to Fortune*, 270–71.

185. Lord Runciman's Mission Extracts from White Paper, September 21, 1938, FO 800, vol. 304–8, 296, PRO.

186. Cari Beauchamp, "It Happened at the Hôtel du Cap," *Vanity Fair*, March 2009, 210.

187. Koskoff, *Joseph P. Kennedy*, 144.

188. "DM," chap. 13, p. 1, JPK Collection, JFKL.

189. Prem 1/265 XC/A/2682, August 30, 1938, 184, PRO; JPK to Hull, August 30, 1938, 800 Czechoslovakia, Dept. of State; JPK to Hull, August 30, 1938, ser. 8.6, 267, JPK Papers, JFKL; Smith, *Hostage to Fortune*, 269–70; Self, *Chamberlain Diary Letters*, 308.

190. Prem 1/265 XC/A/2682, August 30, 1938, 184, PRO; Halifax to Lindsay, September 2, 1938, ser. 3, vol. 2, in *Documents on British Foreign Policy, 1919–1939*, ed. E. L. Woodward and Rohan d'Olier Butler (London: H.M. Stationery Office, 1947), 212–13 [hereafter cited as *DBFP*.]

191. JPK to Hull, August 30, 1938, 800 Czechoslovakia, Dept. of State; JPK to Hull, August 30, 1938, ser. 8.6, 267, JPK Papers, JFKL; Smith, *Hostage to Fortune*, 269–70.

192. JPK to Hull, August 30, 1938, 800 Czechoslovakia, Dept. of State; JPK to Hull, August 30, 1938, ser. 8.6, 267, JPK Papers, JFKL; "DM," chap. 13, p. 1, JPK Collection, JFKL; Smith, *Hostage to Fortune*, 269–70.

193. JPK to Hull, August 30, 1938, 800 Czechoslovakia, Dept. of State; JPK to Hull, August 30, 1938, ser. 8.6, 267, JPK Papers, JFKL; "DM," chap. 13, p. 2, JPK Collection, JFKL; Smith, *Hostage to Fortune*, 269–70.

194. Prem 1/265 XC/A/3482, August 30, 1938, 183–85, PRO; Annual Report 1938, FO 371/22832/2099/ 1938, 176, PRO; Halifax to Lindsay, September 2, 1938, *DBFP*, ser. 3, 2:212–13.

195. Prem 1/265 XC/A/3482, August 30, 1938, 183–85, PRO.

196. JPK to Hull, August 31, 1938, 800 Czechoslovakia, Dept. of State; JPK to Hull, August 31, 1938, ser. 8.6, 267, JPK Papers, JFKL; Smith, *Hostage to Fortune*, 270–71.

197. Halifax to Lindsay, September 2, 1938, *DBFP*, ser. 3, 2:212–13.

198. Halifax to Lindsay, September 2, 1938, *DBFP*, ser. 3, 2:212–13.

199. JPK to Hull, August 31, 1938, 800 Czechoslovakia, Dept. of State; JPK to Hull, August 31, 1938, ser. 8.6, 267, JPK Papers, JFKL; Smith, *Hostage to Fortune*, 270–71.

200. Halifax to Lindsay, September 2, 1938, *DBFP*, ser. 3, 2:212–13; Middlemas, *Strategy of Appeasement*, 285.

201. JPK to Hull, August 31, 1938, 800 Czechoslovakia, Dept. of State; JPK to Hull, August 31, 1938, ser. 8.6,

267, JPK Papers, JFKL; Smith, *Hostage to Fortune*, 270–71.

202. Hull to JPK, September 1, 1938, 123 Kennedy, Joseph P./109, Dept. of State.

203. Lindsay to Halifax, August 16, 1938, FO 414/275/A6602/64/45, PRO.

204. Hull, *Memoirs*, 587–88; *The Economist*, August 27, 1938, 404; Burns, *Roosevelt: The Lion and the Fox*, 386.

205. Hooker, *Moffat Papers*, 194.

206. Annual Report 1938, FO 371/22832/2099, 8–38, PRO; Hull, *Memoirs*, 588.

207. Hull, *Memoirs*, 588; Lindsay to Halifax, August 16, 1938, FO 414/275/A6602/64/45, PRO.

208. Beschloss, *Kennedy and Roosevelt*, 174.

209. *Boston Evening American*, August 31, 1938, 1, 5; "DM," chap. 13, pp. 15–16, JPK Collection, JFKL.

210. *Time*, September 12, 1938, 29.

211. "DM," chap. 13, p. 16, JPK Collection, JFKL; Hull to JPK, September 1, 1938, 123 Kennedy, Joseph P./109, Dept. of State.

212. JPK to Hull, September 3, 1938, 123/110, Dept. of State.

213. FDR to JPK, September 7, 1938, PSF: Kennedy, FDRL; FDR to JPK, September 7, 1938, as cited in Smith, *Hostage to Fortune*, 273.

214. "DM," chap. 13, pp. 16, 18, JPK Collection, JFKL.

215. Smith, *Hostage to Fortune*, 281n139; Beschloss, *Kennedy and Roosevelt*, 175.

216. Joseph Alsop and Robert Kintner, "Clues to the News," *National Issues* (February 1939): 22; Beschloss, *Kennedy and Roosevelt*, 175.

217. "DM," chap. 13, pp. 5–6, 159, JPK Collection, JFKL; JPK to Hull, August 31, 1938, PSF: Kennedy, FDRL; JPK to Hull, August 31, 1938, 123 Kennedy, Joseph P./106, Dept. of State.

218. John Morton Blum, *From the Morgenthau Diaries*, vol. 1, *Years of Crisis, 1928–1938* (Boston: Houghton Mifflin, 1959), 518; Whalen, *The Founding Father*, 237.

219. Neville Chamberlain, "Radio Speech to the British People," September 27, 1938, as cited in Neville Chamberlain, *The Struggle for Peace* (London: Hutchinson Publishing Group, 1939), 274–76; Walter L. Arnstein, ed., *The Past Speaks: Sources and Problems in British History*, vol. 2, *Since 1688* (Lexington, MA: D.C. Heath, 1993), 368–70; Whalen, *The Founding Father*, 238.

220. Johnson to Hull, September 3, 1938, 123 Kennedy, Joseph P./113, Dept. of State; *New York Times*, September 3, 1938, 2; *Times*, September 3, 1938, 6, 10.

221. Ickes, *The Secret Diary of Harold L. Ickes*, 2:415.

222. Ickes, *The Secret Diary of Harold L. Ickes*, 2:420.

223. Koskoff, *Joseph P. Kennedy*, 120–21.

224. Morgenthau Diaries, 138:34, FDRL; Blum, *From the Morgenthau Diaries*, 1:518.

225. Morgenthau Diaries, 138:35, FDRL.

226. Berle and Jacobs, eds., *Navigating the Rapids*, 184n23; Hooker, *Moffat Papers*, 203; Joseph Alsop and Robert Kintner, *American White Paper: The Story of American Diplomacy and the Second World War* (New York: Simon and Schuster, 1940), 7.

227. *Moffat Diary*, September 9, 1938, as cited in Koskoff, *Joseph P. Kennedy*, 148.

228. Koskoff: "found no evidence that the State Department ever attempted to make this clear to Kennedy. Either Kennedy did not understand this, did not wish to understand it, or did not care"; *Joseph P. Kennedy*, 148. Goodwin, *The Fitzgeralds and the Kennedys*, 551, makes essentially the same point as Koskoff does.

229. Morgenthau Diaries, 138:34, FDRL.

230. Hooker, *The Moffat Papers*, 203.

231. Koskoff, *Joseph P. Kennedy*, 148.

232. Morgenthau Diaries, 138:20–21, FDRL.

233. Morgenthau Diaries, 138:34–35, FDRL.

234. Middlemas, Strategy for Appeasement, 285.

Chapter 4. Peace for Our Time

1. "DM," chap. 14, p. 2, JPK Collection, JFKL.

2. Whalen, *The Founding Father*, 238. Whalen's description is particularly colorful but does not mention who Kennedy's friend was.

3. *New York Times*, September 13, 1938, 1.

4. JPK to Hull, September 12, 1938, *FRUS*, 1:591; "DM," chap. 14, pp. 3–4, JPK Collection, JFKL.

5. "DM," chap. 14, p. 3, JPK Collection, JFKL.

6. JPK to Hull, September 13, 1938, *FRUS*, 1:592; JPK to Hull, September 10, 1938, 267, public forum, JPK Collection, JFKL; Smith, *Hostage to Fortune*, 274.

7. "DM," chap. 14, p. 7, JPK Collection, JFKL.

8. "DM," chap. 14, p. 7, JPK Collection, JFKL.

9. The British cabinet was divided over whether it should unequivocally warn Hitler against the use of force. A few days earlier, on September 9, Kennedy had learned from Halifax and Cadogan that it had agreed to send a strongly worded message to Berlin declaring that Britain would stand by France if war broke out. Kennedy reported that Henderson, however, opposed the message and asked that it not be delivered. His view prevailed. Chamberlain never really seemed convinced that such a message would persuade Hitler. JPK to Hull, September 10, 1938, 267, public forum, JPK Collection, JFKL; JPK to Hull, September 10, 1938, 800 Czechoslovakia, Dept. of State; Smith, *Hostage to Fortune*, 274.

10. Hooker, *Moffat Papers*, 200.

11. JPK to Hull, September 17, 1938, *FRUS*, 1:608; *New York Times*, September 13, 1938, 1; Whalen, *The Founding Father*, 238.

12. Memorandum, September 12, 1938, *DGFP*, ser. D, 2:743–44.

13. JPK Diary, September 27, 1938, JPK Collection, JFKL; Smith, *Hostage to Fortune*, 287; Nasaw, *The Patriarch*, 334.

14. *Life*, November 28, 1938, 24; Charles A. Lindbergh, *The Wartime Journals of Charles A. Lindbergh* (New York: Harcourt Brace Jovanovich, 1970), 79.

15. JPK Diary, September 27, 1938, JPK Collection, JFKL; Smith, *Hostage to Fortune*, 287.

16. "DM," chap. 14, pp. 3–6, JPK Collection, JFKL.

17. Memorandum of trans-Atlantic telephone conversation between Kennedy and the Under Secretary of State (Welles), September 26, 1938, *FRUS*, 1:661.

18. JPK to Hull, September 10, 1938, *FRUS*, 1:586; JPK to Hull, September 10, 1938, 800 Czechoslovakia, Dept. of State; JPK to Hull, September 10, 1938, 267, JPK Collection, JFKL; Smith, *Hostage to Fortune*, 274.

19. The German Chargé d'Affaires in Great Britain (Theodor Kordt) to the German Foreign Ministry, September 12, 1938, *DGFP*, ser. D, 2:744; Nasaw, *The Patriarch*, 334–35.

20. Harvey, *The Diplomatic Diaries of Oliver Harvey*, 176; Lindbergh, *Wartime Journals*, 79.

21. Lindsay to Halifax, September 11, 1938, *DBFP*, ser. 3, 2:296; Koskoff, *Joseph P. Kennedy*, 149.

22. Sir Thomas Inskip Diaries, Churchill College, Cambridge (private papers) 8–9, Churchill College, Archive Ctr., Cambridge, as cited in Rock, *Chamberlain and Roosevelt*, 114.

23. Lindsay to Halifax, September 12, 1938, *DBFP*, ser. 3, 2:301.

24. Rock, *Chamberlain and Roosevelt*, 114.

25. Hooker, *Moffat Papers*, 202.

26. Blum, *From the Morgenthau Diaries*, 1:518.

27. "DM," chap. 14, p. 10, JPK Collection, JFKL; JPK Diary, September 14, 1938, JPK Collection, JFKL, as cited in Smith, *Hostage to Fortune*, 275; Hooker, *Moffat Papers*, 202.

28. JPK to Hull, September 14, 1938, Great Britain, FDRL; JPK to Hull, September 14, 1938, 800 Czechoslovakia, Dept. of State; *Times* (London), September 15, 1938, 10; Smith, *Hostage to Fortune*, 275–76; Self, *Chamberlain Diary Letters*, 342; Self, *Neville Chamberlain*, 308, 310–11; Parker, *Chamberlain and Appeasement*, 160–61, 345–46; Fuchser, *Neville Chamberlain and Appeasement*, 138; Colvin, *The Chamberlain Cabinet*, 150–54; Roger Parkinson, *Peace for Our Time: Munich to Dunkirk—The Inside Story* (New York: David McKay, 1971), 23: "the plan had been in his mind at least as early as 25 August."

29. "DM," chap. 14, p. 9; JPK to Hull, September 14, 1938, JPK Collection, JFKL; Smith, *Hostage to Fortune*, 276.

30. JPK to Hull, September 14, 1938, JPK Collection, JFKL; JPK to Hull, September 14, 1938, 800 Czechoslovakia, Dept. of State; "DM," chap. 14, pp. 9–10; Smith, *Hostage to Fortune*, 276.

31. Hull, *Memoirs*, 589.

32. Ickes, *The Secret Diary of Harold Ickes*, 2:468.

33. Hooker, *Moffat Papers*, 203.

34. Hull, *Memoirs*, 589; statement issued by the Dept. of State, September 15, 1938, *FRUS*, 1:605.

35. "DM," chap. 14, p. 10, JPK Collection, JFKL.

36. William L. Shirer, *Berlin Diary: The Journal of a Foreign Correspondent, 1934–1941* (New York: Alfred A. Knopf, 1941), 131; Parkinson, *Peace for Our Time*, 24.

37. Ovendale, *"Appeasement" and the English Speaking World*, 152.

38. Parkinson, *Peace for Our Time*, 24; Martin Gilbert and Richard Gott, *The Appeasers* (London: Wiedenfeld and Nicolson, 1963), 144.

39. "DM," chap. 14, p. 12, JPK Collection, JFKL; JPK to Hull, diplomatic dispatch, 950, 1:00 P.M., September 17, 1938, ser. 8.6, JPK Collection, JFKL; Smith, *Hostage to Fortune*, 277.

40. JPK to Hull, diplomatic dispatch, 1:00 P.M., 800 Czechoslovakia, Dept. of State; JPK to Hull, diplomatic dispatch, 950, 1:00 P.M., September 17, 1938, ser. 8.6, JPK Collection, JFKL; JPK to Hull, diplomatic dispatch, 2:00 P.M., 800 Czechoslovakia, Dept. of State; JPK to Hull, diplomatic dispatch, 10:00 P.M., 800 Czechoslovakia, Dept. of State; JPK to Hull, September 17, 1938, FDRL; Smith, *Hostage to Fortune*, 277; Koskoff, *Joseph P. Kennedy*, 275.

41. Moffat to JPK, September 20, 1938, MS in Moffat Papers, Houghton Library, Harvard, Cambridge, MA, as cited in Koskoff, *Joseph P. Kennedy*, 275.

42. JPK to Hull, diplomatic dispatch, September 17, 1938, ser. 8.6, 267, JPK Collection, JFKL; JPK to Hull, 1:00 P.M., September 17, 1938, 800 Czechoslovakia, Dept. of State; JPK to Hull, September 17, 1938, *FRUS*, 1:607; JPK to Hull, 1:00 P.M., September 17, 1938, file: Personal & Confidential, FDRL; Smith, *Hostage to Fortune*, 277; Parker, *Chamberlain and Appeasement*, 162–63.

43. JPK to Hull, diplomatic dispatch, September 17, 1938, ser. 8.6, 267, JPK Collection, JFKL; JPK to Hull, 1:00 P.M., September 17, 1938, 800 Czechoslovakia, Dept. of State; JPK to Hull, September 17, 1938, *FRUS*, 1:607; JPK to Hull, 1:00 P.M., September 17, 1938, file: Personal & Confidential, FDRL; Smith, *Hostage to Fortune*, 277; Parkinson, *Peace for Our Time*, 25.

44. JPK to Hull, 10:00 P.M., September 17, 1938, 800 Czechoslovakia, Dept. of State; Kennedy to Hull, September 17, 1938, *FRUS*, 1:610.

45. Parkinson, *Peace for Our Time*, 25.

46. JPK to Hull, September 17, 1938, *FRUS*, 1:608; Kennedy to Hull, 1:00 P.M., September 17, 1938, file: Personal & Confidential, FDRL; JPK to Hull, diplomatic dispatch, September 17, 1938, ser. 8.6, 267, JPK Collection, JFKL; JPK to Hull, 1:00 P.M., September 17, 1938, 800 Czechoslovakia, Dept. of State; Smith, *Hostage to Fortune*, 277.

47. Self, *Chamberlain Diary Letters*, 346–48; Self, *Neville Chamberlain*, 314.

48. JPK to Hull, 10:00 P.M., September 17, 1938, Dept. of State; JPK to Hull, September 17, 1938, *FRUS*, 1:610–12.

49. "DM," chap. 14, p. 21, JPK Collection, JFKL; JPK to Hull, diplomatic dispatch, September 19, 1938, ser. 8.6, 267, JPK Collection, JFKL; JPK to Hull, September 19, 1938, *FRUS*, 1:621–22; JPK to Hull, September 19, 1938, 800 Czechoslovakia, Dept. of State; Smith, *Hostage to Fortune*, 278; Self, *Neville Chamberlain*, 315.

50. JPK to Hull, September 19, 1938, *FRUS*, 1:618–19; Birkenhead, *Halifax*, 395–96; Colvin, *The Chamberlain Cabinet*, 159–60; Parkinson, *Peace for Our Time*, 32; Fuchser, *Neville Chamberlain and Appeasement*, 145–46.

51. JPK to Hull, September 19, 1938, *FRUS*, 1:622; JPK to Hull, September 19, 1938, 800 Czechoslovakia, Dept. of State; JPK to Hull, diplomatic dispatch, September 19, 1938, ser. 8.6, 267, JPK Collection, JFKL; Smith, *Hostage to Fortune*, 278–79; Self, *Neville Chamberlain*, 315.

52. "DM," chap. 14, p. 24, JPK Collection, JFKL; Goodwin, *The Fitzgeralds and the Kennedys*, 555.

53. Hooker, *The Moffat Papers*, 205–6; Berle and Jacobs, eds., *Navigating the Rapids*, 186; Rock,

Chamberlain and Roosevelt, 117–18.

54. Lindsay from Halifax, September 19, 1938, FO 371/21527; Lindsay to Halifax, September 20, 1938, *DBFP*, ser. 3, 7:627–29; Foreign Office Minutes, September 19, 1938, FO 371/21527/A7504, No. 349, PSF: Gr. Britain, FDRL; Joseph P. Lash, *Roosevelt and Churchill, 1939–1941* (New York: W.W. Norton, 1976), 25–28; Dallek, *Franklin D. Roosevelt and American Foreign Policy*, 164–65; Rock, *Chamberlain and Roosevelt*, 118: FDR was also convinced that Japan was Germany's ally and bound by treaty to come to her aid. The president's outline reminded Lindsay of Roosevelt's speech a year earlier in Chicago, in which he called on peace-loving nations to "quarantine" an aggressor; Nasaw, *The Patriarch*, 338: when Roosevelt summoned Lindsay to discuss his plan for blockading Germany, the president did not inform Kennedy about it. Only six months into his ambassadorship Kennedy was already outside "the diplomatic loop," although he did not realize it yet.

55. Lindsay to Halifax, September 12, 1938, *DBFP*, ser. 3, 2:301; Rock, *Chamberlain and Roosevelt*, 113: "In the first two weeks of September certain moves by Roosevelt showed his preference for a strong stand against Germany. But the crucial difference between making a stand oneself and urging it upon others must always be borne in mind."

56. Lindsay to Halifax, September 23, 1938, *DBFP*, ser. 3, vol. 7, appendix, 630, PSF: Great Britain, FDRL.

57. Reynolds, *The Creation of the Anglo-American Alliance*, 36.

58. Dallek, *Franklin D. Roosevelt and American Foreign Policy*, 164–65.

59. JPK to Hull, September 21, 1938, *FRUS*, 1:631–32; JPK to Hull, September 21, 1938, 800 Czechoslovakia, Dept. of State; Smith, *Hostage to Fortune*, 279–80; Parker, *Chamberlain and Appeasement*, 167–68.

60. "DM," chap. 14, p. 29, JPK Collection, JFKL.

61. *Chicago Daily Tribune*, November 24, 1938, 1; "DM," chap. 15, p. 8, JPK Collection, JFKL.

62. "DM," chap. 15, p. 9, JPK Collection, JFKL.

63. "DM," chap. 15, pp. 8–9, JPK Collection, JFKL; *Chicago Daily Tribune*, November 24, 1938, 1; Koskoff, *Joseph P. Kennedy*, 161–62.

64. "DM," chap. 15, p. 9, JPK Collection, JFKL; *Chicago Daily Tribune*, November 24, 1938, 1; Whalen, *The Founding Father*, 244.

65. *Chicago Daily Tribune*, November 24, 1938, 1.

66. *New York Times*, December 8, 1938, 23; *New York Times*, November 24, 1938, 1; *Chicago Daily Tribune*, November 24, 1938, 1; *House of Commons Debates*, November 23, 1938, 1938–1939, vol. 341, November 8–November 25, 1727–28; JPK to Hull, September 17, 1938, *FRUS*, 1:611; Koskoff, *Joseph P. Kennedy*, 161–62. Apparently there was some truth in the charge that the government was exercising if not a kind of censorship, then certainly a very close scrutiny. Kennedy reported that Hoare visited the editor of the *Daily Herald* and the editor of the *News Chronicle*, among others, and spent two and a half hours trying to persuade them to support Chamberlain's policy. Richard Cockett describes Chamberlain's censorship of the press in *Twilight of Truth: Chamberlain, Appeasement, and the Manipulation of the Press* (New York: St. Martin's, 1989), 75.

67. JPK Diary, September 22, 1938, JPK Collection, JFKL; JPK quote from Joseph F. Dinneen, *Boston Globe*

(morning edition), December 16, 1938, 9; Koskoff, *Joseph P. Kennedy*, 162.

68. JPK Diary, September 22, 1938, JPK Collection, JFKL; *Chicago Daily Tribune*, November 24, 1938, 2.

69. Lindbergh, *Wartime Journals*, 159.

70. Lindbergh, *Wartime Journals*, 79.

71. Lindbergh, *Wartime Journals*, 26.

72. Lindbergh, *Wartime Journals*, 159.

73. Lindbergh, *Wartime Journals*, 26.

74. Anne Morrow Lindbergh, *The Flower and the Nettle: Diaries and Letters of Anne Morrow Lindbergh, 1936–1939* (New York: Harcourt, Brace, Jovanovich, 1976), 529, 262, 260, 270; Rose Kennedy, Diary, September 21, 1938, as cited in Smith, *Hostage to Fortune*, 280–81, for a charming description of Lindbergh by Rose Kennedy.

75. "DM," chap. 15, p. 3, JPK Collection, JFKL; Lindbergh, *The Flower and the Nettle*, 407–9.

76. JPK to Hull, September 22, 1938, 824.8, Lindbergh report on European air strength, Dept. of State; Smith, *Hostage to Fortune*, 281–82, 290–91.

77. Lindbergh, *Wartime Journals*, 72.

78. Koskoff, *Joseph P. Kennedy*, 151.

79. JPK to Hull, September 22, 1938, *FRUS*, 1:72; *Life*, January 16, 1939, 18; Whalen, *The Founding Father*, 241.

80. *Life*, January 16, 1939, 18; Hull, *Memoirs*, 590; Koskoff, *Joseph P. Kennedy*, 153; Nasaw, *The Patriarch*, 339.

81. Taylor, *Munich*, 852.

82. Kennedy's deletions are significant. He eliminated phrases like "it seems to me essential to avoid a general European war in the near future at almost any cost" and "I am convinced that it is wiser to permit Germany's eastward expansion than to throw England and France, unprepared, into war at this time." Kennedy's cable included Lindbergh's strategic estimates and evaluations. They pointed to the same conclusion. The ambassador also bragged to Walter Winchell that he had shown Lindbergh's letter to Chamberlain and that Chamberlain had been impressed by it. It had confirmed his decision not to go to war. *Life*, January 16, 1939, 18; JPK to Hull, September 22, 1938, *FRUS*, 1:72–73; Hull, *Memoirs*, 590; Taylor, *Munich*, 849–52. Today's historians believe that Lindbergh's evaluations were "unrealistically bleak" and that he had greatly overestimated the volume of Germany's airplane production. Koskoff, *Joseph P. Kennedy*, 151–52. What Lindbergh brought to England at that moment was sincerity, "misinformation and misjudgment, the product of his lack of military expertise, gullibility, susceptibility to certain aspects of German lifestyle, a distaste for British casualness and Russian sloppiness. . . . Lindbergh came carrying doom and destruction and counseled only the hopelessness of anything other than surrender to the German juggernaut"; Taylor, *Munich*, 852.

83. Joseph Alsop and Robert Kintner, *American White Paper: The Story of American Diplomacy and the Second World War* (New York: Simon and Schuster, 1940), 12; Whalen, *The Founding Father*, 231, 241. (Note that it was difficult to estimate Germany's capacity and output, so various sources had

widely different estimates.)

84. Margaret L. Coit, *Mr. Baruch* (Boston: Houghton Mifflin, 1957), 466.

85. Coit, *Mr. Baruch*, 469.

86. Notes on a conversation between Chamberlain and Hitler at Godesberg, September 22, 1938, *DBFP*, ser. 3, 2:463–73; Self, *Neville Chamberlain*, 316–17; Feiling, *The Life of Neville Chamberlain*, 370; F. S. Northedge, *The Troubled Giant: Britain among the Great Powers, 1916–1939* (London: G. Bell & Sons, 1966), 531–32; Colvin, *The Chamberlain Cabinet*, 162; Parkinson, *Peace for Our Time*, has a detailed discussion of events, 35–40; Fuchser, *Neville Chamberlain and Appeasement*, 147, 152; Taylor, *Munich*, 815–17; Parker, *Chamberlain and Appeasement*, 167–68.

87. Whalen, *The Founding Father*, 240; Parkinson, *Peace for Our Time*, 40.

88. "DM," chap. 15, pp. 1, 11, JPK Collection, JFKL; "DM," chap. 16, pp. 7, 13, JPK Collection, JFKL.

89. JPK Diary, September 24, 1938, JPK Collection, JFKL.

90. JPK to Hull, September 23, 1938, 800 Czechoslovakia, Dept. of State.

91. JPK to Hull, September 23, 1938, 800 Czechoslovakia, Dept. of State; Hull, *Memoirs*, 590; Hooker, *The Moffat Papers*, 212; Colvin, *The Chamberlain Cabinet*, 162–63; Self, *Neville Chamberlain*, 318–19; Fuchser, *Neville Chamberlain and Appeasement*, 152.

92. Smart, Neville Chamberlain, 244.

93. JPK to Hull, September 23, 1938, 800 Czechoslovakia, Dept. of State.

94. JPK Diary, October 6, 1938, JPK Collection, JFKL.

95. JPK to Hull, 4:00 P.M., September 26, 1938, 800 Czechoslovakia, Dept. of State; JPK to Hull, September 26, 1938, *FRUS*, 1:662; JPK Diary, September 26, 1938, JPK Collection, JFKL; Smith, *Hostage to Fortune*, 284; Hull, *Memoirs*, 592.

96. JPK to Hull, 11:00 P.M., September 26, 1938, Czechoslovakia, Dept. of State.

97. JPK to Hull, September 26, 1938, *FRUS*, 1:662.

98. JPK Diary, September 26, 1938, JPK Collection, JFKL; Smith, *Hostage to Fortune*, 284; Hull, *Memoirs*, 592–93.

99. Self, *Neville Chamberlain*, 320–22; Birkenhead, *Halifax*, 403; Parkinson, *Peace for Our Time*, 50–52; Taylor, *Munich*, 872.

100. Birkenhead, *Halifax*, 403; Taylor, *Munich*, 872; Feiling, *The Life of Neville Chamberlain*, 371–72; Colvin, *The Chamberlain Cabinet*, 165.

101. "DM," chap. 16, p. 7, JPK Collection, JFKL; JPK to Hull, September 27, 1938, *FRUS*, 1:673; Birkenhead, *Halifax*, 403–4; Colvin, *The Chamberlain Cabinet*, 165–66; Fuchser, *Neville Chamberlain and Appeasement*, 153–55: British foreign policy was proceeding along two divergent lines: Wilson had requested that Hitler accept a revision of the Godesberg demands, and Halifax had issued a press statement promising that Britain "would certainly stand by France" should she and Russia assist their Czech ally if war erupted.

102. "DM," chap. 15, pp. 13–14, JPK Collection, JFKL; Rock, *Chamberlain and Roosevelt*, 120.

103. Rock, *Chamberlain and Roosevelt*, 120.

104. FDR to Hitler, September 26, 1938, *FRUS*, 1:658; Hull, *Memoirs*, 591–92.

105. FDR to Hitler, September 26, 1938, *FRUS*, 1:658; Hull to FDR, September 28, 1938, PSF: Great Britain, FDRL.

106. Hull, *Memoirs*, 592–93; Rock, *Chamberlain and Roosevelt*, 121.

107. JPK to Hull, September 27, 1938, *FRUS*, 1:673.

108. Hull, Memoirs, 592–93; Berle and Jacobs, eds., *Navigating the Rapids*, 186–88; Dallek, *Franklin D. Roosevelt and American Foreign Policy*, 166.

109. JPK to Hull, September 24, 1938, *FRUS*, 1:643; Offner, *American Appeasement*, 263; Rock, *Chamberlain and Roosevelt*, 122; Nasaw, *The Patriarch*, 342.

110. Hull, *Memoirs*, 593; *Times*, September 28, 1938, 10; Goodwin, *The Fitzgeralds and Kennedys*, 558; Rock, *Chamberlain and Roosevelt*, 122.

111. Memorandum of trans-Atlantic telephone conversation between Kennedy and the Under Secretary of State (Welles), September 26, 1938, *FRUS*, 1:661, states that at 1:30 P.M. Kennedy discussed broadcasting Chamberlain's speech to the American people. Welles told him that "the President wants to let you know that he does not want [it] done." Kennedy countered: "Supposing it isn't just a broadcast to America but that American companies pick up this broadcast to England." Welles said, "That would be all to the good." "I'll fix that up—just broadcast to England and American companies pick it up." Welles warned Kennedy that "a direct broadcast would be interpreted as an appeal to the United States and would be undesirable at this moment." Kennedy promised: "I will take care of it." On that same day at 4:00 P.M. Kennedy told Hull that Chamberlain intended to broadcast the next evening and was considering including the United States in his address. The *Times* on September 28, 1938, 10, said that the prime minister's broadcast to the nation and the Empire "was broadcast on all the B.B.C. transmitters and was heard in America on the short wave." The American correspondent in Washington for the *Times* wrote on September 27: "The speech of the Prime Minister to the British Empire and to the world was heard here with deep interest and—by all with whom immediate contact was possible—with the fullest sympathy. President Roosevelt and the members of the Cabinet he had called into special session met at the very hour the address opened, and it served as a prelude to their discussion." Offner, *American Appeasement*, 263: when Chamberlain hinted that the address could be broadcast to Americans, Welles told Kennedy that the president nixed the suggestion because it "might be misconstrued." But American stations could pick up the address anyhow. Offner cites the Welles-Kennedy Conversation in *FRUS* on September 26, 1938, 1:660–61; Rock, *Chamberlain and Roosevelt*, 122: through Kennedy, Chamberlain appealed that he address the American people on September 27, 1938. Middlemas, *The Strategy of Appeasement*, 383, states that Roosevelt refused Chamberlain's request to broadcast, but that "American radio networks were left free to transmit it if they chose." Although the evidence is circumstantial, it does lead this writer to believe that indeed Kennedy did in fact "take care of it" and arranged for Chamberlain's address to be heard by the American public. If Kennedy did make the arrangement, it certainly would have been in keeping with his practice of operating on his own and without regard to diplomatic niceties. It is also possible that Roosevelt was not entirely displeased by his ambassador's independence.

112. *Times*, September 28, 1938, 10, for complete text; Smith, *Hostage to Fortune*, 286; Feiling, *The Life of Neville Chamberlain*, 372; Self, *Neville Chamberlain*, 321.

113. Memorandum of trans-Atlantic telephone conversation between Kennedy and Welles, September 27, 1938, *FRUS*, 1:679.

114. Whalen, *The Founding Father*, 242; Parkinson, *Peace for Our Time*, 56; Coit, *Mr. Baruch*, 467; Self, *Neville Chamberlain*, 322; William L. Shirer, The *Rise and Fall of the Third Reich: A History of Nazi Germany* (New York: Simon and Schuster, 1960), 402; Robert Graves and Alan Hodge, *The Long Week-End: A Social History of Great Britain, 1918–1939* (New York: W.W. Norton, 1963), 444.

115. JPK to Hull, September 12, 1938, *FRUS*, 1:673.

116. Rose Kennedy, Diary, September 27, 1938, ser. 1, Rose Kennedy Papers, JFKL; Smith, *Hostage to Fortune*, 288.

117. Rose Kennedy, Diary, September 28, 1938, ser. 1, Rose Kennedy Papers, JFKL; Smith, *Hostage to Fortune*, 287; Rose Kennedy, *Times to Remember*, 238.

118. Coit, *Mr. Baruch*, 467.

119. Whalen, *The Founding Father*, 246.

120. Shirer, The *Rise and Fall of the Third Reich*, 555.

121. JPK to Hull, September 27, 1938, 800 Czechoslovakia, Dept. of State; JPK Diary, September 27, 1938, JPK Collection, JFKL; "DM," chap. 16, p. 10, JPK Collection, JFKL; Smith, *Hostage to Fortune*, 287.

122. Chamberlain to Hitler, September 28, 1938, PSF: Great Britain, FDRL; Self, *Neville Chamberlain*, 322; Feiling, *The Life of Neville Chamberlain*, 372; Parkinson, *Peace for Our Time*, 57.

123. "DM," chap. 16, p. 13, JPK Collection, JFKL; Goodwin, *The Fitzgeralds and the Kennedys*, 559, 869; Nasaw, *The Patriarch*, 345.

124. Nasaw, *The Patriarch*, 345.

125. "DM," chap. 16, pp. 13–14.

126. JPK, Diary, June 1938, JPK Collection, JFKL; Smith, *Hostage to Fortune*, 260. Smith notes that Lord Stanley Baldwin's full title is Lord Stanley Baldwin, Earl Baldwin of Bewdley and Viscount Corvedale.

127. JPK to Hull, September 28, 1938, *FRUS*, 1:692–93; JPK to Hull, diplomatic dispatch, September 28, 1938, ser. 8.6, JPK Collection, JFKL; "DM," chap. 16, p. 14, JPK Collection, JFKL; *The Landis Papers*, chap. 17, p. 171, box 51, Manuscript Division, Library of Congress; Smith, *Hostage to Fortune*, 288–89; Goodwin, *The Fitzgeralds and the Kennedys*, 559–61; Fuchser, *Neville Chamberlain and Appeasement*, 159–60; Gilbert and Gott, *The Appeasers*, 173.

128. *Daily Mail*, September 29, 1938, 7, 10; Goodwin, *The Fitzgeralds and the Kennedys*, 559–60; Whalen, *The Founding Father*, 243; Fuchser, *Neville Chamberlain and Appeasement*, 159–60. Fuchser gives a description of the event, "atmosphere laden with apprehension and emotional intensity," but no applause or description of Chamberlain's appearance.

129. *Daily Mail*, September 23, 1938, 11; Goodwin, *The Fitzgeralds and the Kennedys*, 560; Birkenhead, *Halifax*, 405. Fuchser, *Neville Chamberlain and Appeasement*, 160n8, makes the astonishing remark that Chamberlain staged the Munich invitation. He offers no hard evidence to prove it was

choreographed but believes it to be at least somewhat staged. "It is therefore possible to speculate that Chamberlain suspected or at least hoped that events would happen as they did and that he deliberately prolonged his speech in the hope that a positive reply from Hitler would arrive. Still, the author was unable to uncover any hard evidence that the event was consciously contrived." In the absence of any evidence, this author rejects Fuchser's speculation. Self, *Neville Chamberlain*: "Contrary to unfounded allegations that it was 'a pre-arranged drama' in which Chamberlain cynically cast himself as 'director, producer and leading actor,' this climax was all the more remarkable because Chamberlain had no idea that his speech would end in this manner" (323); Self, *Chamberlain Diary Letters*: Hitler's message coming just as he was closing his speech was "a piece of drama that no work of fiction ever surpassed," Chamberlain wrote in a letter (349); Roberts, *The Holy Fox*: Chamberlain's announcement was such good theatre that it has created unfounded rumors of stage-management (12).

130. *Daily Mail*, September 29, 1938, 7, 10; "DM," chap. 16, p. 14, JPK Collection, JFKL; Goodwin, *The Fitzgeralds and the Kennedys*, 559–60; Nasaw, *The Patriarch*, 345–46: Hoare gave Chamberlain the note, not Simon. Self, *Neville Chamberlain*, 323, said it was Simon, as does Roberts, *The Holy Fox*, 121.

131. Nigel Nicolson, ed., *Harold Nicolson Diaries and Letters, 1930–39* (Bungay, Suffolk, GB: William Collins Sons, 1966), 364; *Daily Mail*, September 29, 1938, 7, 10; Self, *Neville Chamberlain*, 323.

132. Self, *Neville Chamberlain*, 324.

133. *Daily Mail*, September 29, 1938, 7, 10; Goodwin, *The Fitzgeralds and the Kennedys*, 560; Parker, *Chamberlain and Appeasement*, 178–79; Fuchser, *Neville Chamberlain and Appeasement*, 150; Whalen, *The Founding Father*, 243.

134. "DM," chap. 16, p. 15, JPK Collection, JFKL; JPK to Hull, September 28, 1938, JPK Collection, JFKL; JPK to Hull, September 28, 1938, *FRUS*, 1:692–93; Smith, *Hostage to Fortune*, 288; Roberts, *The Holy Fox*, 121; Fuchser, *Neville Chamberlain and Appeasement*, 160; Whalen, *The Founding Father*, 243.

135. *Daily Mail*, September 29, 1938, 7, 10; "DM," chap. 16, pp. 15–16, JPK Collection, JFKL; Shirer, *The Rise and Fall of the Third Reich*, 411; Goodwin, *The Fitzgeralds and the Kennedys*, 561.

136. Self, *Neville Chamberlain*, 323.

137. Rose Kennedy, Diary, September 27, 1938, ser. 1, Rose Kennedy Papers, JFKL; Rose Kennedy, *Times to Remember*, 239; Smith, *Hostage to Fortune*, 288.

138. Shirer, *Rise and Fall of the Third Reich*, 411; Goodwin, *The Fitzgeralds and the Kennedys*, 561.

139. Nicolson, ed., *Harold Nicolson Diaries and Letters*, 366, 364.

140. Martin Gilbert, *Winston S. Churchill*, vol. 5, *The Prophet of Truth, 1922–1939* (Boston: Houghton Mifflin, 1977), 987.

141. Nicolson, ed., *Harold Nicolson Diaries and Letters*, 365.

142. JPK Diary, September 28, 1938, JPK Collection, JFKL.

143. JPK to Hull, September 28, 1938, *FRUS*, 1:693; JPK to Hull, September 28, 1938, ser. 8.6, JPK Collection, JFKL; Smith, *Hostage to Fortune*, 289.

144. "DM," chap. 16, p. 16, JPK Collection, JFKL; Hull to JPK, September 28, 1938, *FRUS*, 1:688. Without

getting directly involved or making any commitments, Roosevelt had attempted to exert some influence by appealing to all participants to keep negotiations going. Although he lacked confidence in Chamberlain and was deeply concerned about Hitler's behavior, Roosevelt's worry over the "terrible sacrifices" demanded of the Czechs did not include "vain resistance." He did not offer detailed advice or personal services. Such influence as he did employ no doubt helped create the settlement that was eventually agreed to. His "Good man" message probably connoted nothing more than relief; Offner, *American Appeasement*, 268–69. Rock, *Chamberlain and Roosevelt*, asks: "What two words could better show his full approval of Chamberlain's efforts?" (124–25).

145. JPK Diary, October 3, 1938, JPK Collection, JFKL; Smith, *Hostage to Fortune*, 291–92.

146. JPK to Hull, September 28, 1938, *FRUS*, 1:693; JPK to Hull, diplomatic dispatch, September 28, 1938, ser. 8.6, JPK Collection, JFKL; Smith, *Hostage to Fortune*, 288.

147. JPK to Hull, September 29, 1938, *FRUS*, 1:700.

148. Hull, Memoirs, 595; Ickes, *The Secret Diary of Harold Ickes*, 2:479; Hooker, Moffat Papers, 217.

149. JPK to Hull, September 28, 1938, *FRUS*, 1:693; JPK to Hull, diplomatic dispatch, September 28, 1938, ser. 8.6, JPK Collection, JFKL; Smith, *Hostage to Fortune*, 289.

150. Halifax to Lindsay, September 29, 1938, *DBFP*, ser. 3, 2:625.

151. JPK to Hull, October 5, 1938, as cited in Smith, *Hostage to Fortune*, 293.

152. JPK to Hull, diplomatic dispatch draft, October 5, 1938, as cited in Smith, *Hostage to Fortune*, 292–93; Dallek, *Franklin D. Roosevelt and American Foreign Policy*, 166; Gerhard L. Weinberg, *A World at Arms: A Global History of World War II* (Cambridge: Cambridge University Press, 1994), 27–28; Ovendale, *"Appeasement" and the English Speaking World*, 175; Rock, *Chamberlain and Roosevelt*, 123–25.

153. "DM," chap. 16, p. 16, JPK Collection, JFKL.

154. JPK to Hull, September 28, 1938, *FRUS*, 1:693; JPK to Hull, diplomatic dispatch, September 28, 1938, ser. 8.6, JPK Collection, JFKL; Smith, *Hostage to Fortune*, 288.

155. Lindbergh, *Wartime Journals*, 78.

156. "DM," chap. 16, pp. 14–15, JPK Collection, JFKL; JPK to Hull, diplomatic dispatch, September 28, 1938, ser. 8.6, JPK Collection, JFKL; JPK to Hull, September 28, 1938, *FRUS*, 1:693; Smith, *Hostage to Fortune*, 289; Goodwin, *The Fitzgeralds and the Kennedys*, 565.

157. "DM," chap. 16, p. 16, JPK Collection, JFKL.

158. Duff Cooper, *Old Men Forget: The Autobiography of Duff Cooper* (Viscount Norwich) (London: Hart-Davis, 1953), 241; Self, *Neville Chamberlain*, 324.

159. Halifax to Lindsay, September 29, 1938, *DBFP*, ser. 3, 2:625.

160. Roberts, *The Holy Fox*, 102.

161. Birkenhead, *Halifax*, 407.

162. Parkinson, *Peace for Our Time*, 60; Birkenhead, *Halifax*, 406–7; Parker, *Chamberlain and Appeasement*, 179–80.

163. Gilbert and Gott, *The Appeasers*, 178; Parkinson, *Peace for Our Time*, gives a detailed description of the conference, 60–66; Fuchser, *Neville Chamberlain and Appeasement*, 161–62.

164. Feiling, *The Life of Neville Chamberlain*, 381; Gilbert and Gott, *The Appeasers*, 179; Fuchser, *Neville Chamberlain and Appeasement*, 162–64; Parkinson, *Peace for Our Time*, 60.

165. Self, *Chamberlain Diary Letters*, 350; Self, *Neville Chamberlain*, 324–25; Feiling, *The Life of Neville Chamberlain*, 377; Parkinson, *Peace for Our Time*, 60.

166. Alec Douglas-Home, *The Way the Wind Blows: An Autobiography* (London: Collins, 1976); Rock, *Chamberlain and Roosevelt*, 124.

167. Feiling, *The Life of Neville Chamberlain*, 380.

168. Whalen, *The Founding Father*, 244.

169. Self, *Neville Chamberlain*, 325; Parkinson, *Peace for Our Time*, 61.

170. Roberts, *The Holy Fox*, 123.

171. Cooper, *Old Men Forget*, 247.

172. Self, *Chamberlain Diary Letters*, 351; Self, *Neville Chamberlain*, 325–26; Feiling, *The Life of Neville Chamberlain*, 381; Parkinson, *Peace for Our Time*, 61–62; Fuchser, *Neville Chamberlain and Appeasement*, 164–67.

173. Roberts, *The Holy Fox*, 122.

174. Parker, *Chamberlain and Appeasement*, 180.

175. Graves and Hodge, *The Long Week-End*, 445.

176. "DM," chap. 17, p. 1, JPK Collection, JFKL.

177. Feiling, *The Life of Neville Chamberlain*, 378–79.

178. "DM," chap. 17, p. 1, JPK Collection, JFKL; Self, *Neville Chamberlain*, 329.

179. Roberts, *The Holy Fox*, 123.

180. Goodwin, *The Fitzgeralds and the Kennedys*, 562.

181. Beschloss, *Kennedy and Roosevelt*, 177.

182. Gilbert and Gott, *The Appeasers*, 181.

183. "DM," chap. 17, p. 1, JPK Collection, JFKL.

184. "DM," chap. 17, p. 2, JPK Collection, JFKL; Self, *Chamberlain Diary Letters*, 351–54, has Chamberlain's description of the debate; Self, *Neville Chamberlain*, 330–32.

185. JPK Diary, October 3, 1938, JPK Collection, JFKL; Smith, *Hostage to Fortune*, 291.

186. "DM," chap. 17, pp. 2–3, JPK Collection, JFKL.

187. *New York World-Telegram*, April 11, 1960, 3; Whalen, *The Founding Father*, 244. Lasky, *JFK: The Man and the Myth: A Critical Portrait*, 54, assumed that Kennedy meant "to use it against FDR," but Rose Kennedy, *Times to Remember*, 242, wrote that her husband wanted to protect the president. Goodwin, *The Fitzgeralds and the Kennedys*, 563, said that Roosevelt had ordered Kennedy to give the message orally.

188. "DM," chap. 17, p. 9, JPK Collection, JFKL; Langer and Gleason, *The Challenge to Isolation*, 35; Goodwin, *The Fitzgeralds and the Kennedys*, 563.

189. Churchill, *The Second World War*, 1:292.

190. "DM," chap. 17, p. 3, JPK Collection, JFKL; Goodwin, *The Fitzgeralds and the Kennedys*, 563.

191. T. D. Burridge, *Clement Attlee: A Political Biography* (London: J. Cape, 1985), 134; Rock, *Appeasement*

on Trial, 143.

192. Churchill, *House of Commons Debates*, October 5, 1938, 1937–1938, vol. 339, September 26–October 6, 366; Churchill, *The Second World War*, 1:293; M. Gilbert, *Winston S. Churchill*, 5:998.

193. Churchill, *House of Commons Debates*, October 5, 1938, 1937–1938, vol. 339, September 26–October 6, 373; M. Gilbert, *Winston S. Churchill*, 5:1001; Churchill, *The Second World War*, 1:293; John Allsebrook Simon, *Retrospect: The Memoirs of the Rt. Hon. Viscount Simon* (London: Hutchinson, 1952), 249.

194. JPK to Hull, diplomatic dispatch, October 5, 1938, as cited in Smith, *Hostage to Fortune*, 292–93.

195. Gerhard Weinberg, *Germany, Hitler and World War II: Essays in Modern German and World History* (Cambridge: Cambridge University Press, 1995), 116.

196. Weinberg, *A World at Arms*, 45, 27–28.

197. Weinberg, *A World at Arms*, 86.

198. JPK to Hull, October 5, 1938, as cited in Smith, *Hostage to Fortune*, 292–93.

199. Koskoff, *Joseph P. Kennedy*, 164; Goodwin, *The Fitzgeralds and the Kennedys*, 564–65.

200. Whalen, *The Founding Father*, 245.

201. Whalen, *The Founding Father*, 246; Goodwin, *The Fitzgeralds and the Kennedys*, 573.

202. Burns, *Roosevelt: The Lion and the Fox*, 385.

203. Hull, *Memoirs*, 596.

204. "DM," chap. 17, p. 9, JPK Collection, JFKL.

205. "DM," chap. 17, p. 9, JPK Collection, JFKL; Dutton, *Neville Chamberlain*, 207–11; Bentley Brinkerhoff Gilbert, *Britain, 1914–1945: The Aftermath of Power* (Wheeling, IL: Harlan Davidson, 1996), 100; Koskoff, *Joseph P. Kennedy*, 156–57; Whalen, *The Founding Father*, 247.

206. Koskoff, *Joseph P. Kennedy*, 159.

207. B. Gilbert, *Britain, 1914–1945*, 103; Middlemas, *The Strategy of Appeasement*, 421.

208. B. Gilbert, *Britain, 1914–1945*, 100, 103.

209. Middlemas, *The Strategy of Appeasement*, 421; Koskoff, *Joseph P. Kennedy*, 157; B. Gilbert, *Britain, 1914–1945*, 100.

210. "DM," chap. 17, pp. 5–7, JPK Collection, JFKL; B. Gilbert, *Britain, 1914–1945*, 100, 107; Shirer, *Rise and Fall*, 424; Koskoff, *Joseph P. Kennedy*, 156. Middlemas, *The Strategy of Appeasement*, 419–20, offers an opposing hypothesis for consideration. Not only was Britain militarily stronger in 1938 than in 1939, he wrote, but it is also possible that Russia might have fought alongside France in September 1938; with Czechoslovakia's boundaries and armament factories still in place, the Nazis would have had to fight for the Czech territory that Chamberlain had bargained away at Munich, and the stronger Czech forces could have resisted longer and more vigorously than the Poles did in 1939. Because Germany's greater military weakness in 1938 than in 1939 could have delayed its victory in the east, the Nazis might not have been poised to devour the West in 1940. Furthermore, French morale was higher in 1938 than in 1939, and possibly the French could have taken Germany's still unfinished West Wall (or the Siegfried Line, as Americans called it) and the Ruhr and maintained a blockade of the North Sea and the Mediterranean against German imports. Perhaps Belgium would

not have been overrun and the Battle of Britain would have been postponed or put off indefinitely. Italy, as it did in World War I, might have changed sides, and Japan might have stayed out. The majority of the dominions would have provided assistance, Middlemas argued, making American aid unnecessary. No less a figure than Major-General Hastings Ismay of the Committee of Imperial Defense thought that Britain could have successfully fought Germany in 1938. Thus it is possible that a war in Europe in 1938 would have been a short, localized war ending in a victory for the Allies. In that case, Munich, not Warsaw, could have been a better place to force a showdown with Hitler, something Kennedy would have found abhorrent. If the myth of Munich was a dubious proposition that Kennedy helped to propagate, so too was his opinion that Munich was not the place to force a showdown with Germany.

211. "DM," chap. 17, pp. 3–5, 7, JPK Collection, JFKL.
212. JPK to Hull, October 12, 1938, 800 Britain, PRO; "DM," chap. 20, p. 2, JPK Collection, JFKL.
213. "DM," chap. 17, pp. 4–7, 9, JPK Collection, JFKL.
214. "DM," chap. 14, p. 11, JPK Collection, JFKL.
215. "DM," chap. 17, pp. 6, 8, JPK Collection, JFKL.
216. Dutton, *Neville Chamberlain*, 208, 219: "that Munich was in all the circumstances of September 1938, the best outcome that Chamberlain or anyone else could have hoped for." Had Chamberlain not placated Hitler then and had war broken out, Britain would probably have lacked the unity at the home front and throughout the Empire from end to end and lacked the determination that were characteristic of 1939. Even with the failure of appeasement to prevent war, and with hindsight it was bound to be a failure, Dutton argues, there was no dishonor in having tried it. Chamberlain "was right to be wrong," wrote Dutton. But if Chamberlain failed to understand the nature of the man with whom he was dealing and the movement he spawned, if he saw Nazism as nothing more than the ranting of "mad men" about vague and superficial ideas, so too did most of Britain's elite, to say nothing of several million citizens in Germany. If Chamberlain's greatest error was to believe in peace longer than it was reasonable to do so, it was an error shared by so many others, including Kennedy.
217. "DM," chap. 17, pp. 5–7, JPK Collection, JFKL; Parker, *Chamberlain and Appeasement*, 346–47. The opening of British archives in the late 1960s provided an opportunity for a review of Chamberlain's decisions about the policy of appeasement. Parker argued that the public documents show that the prime minister had options; there were viable alternatives to the choices he made and were known to him at that time, but he did not pursue them. Chamberlain made two crucial errors, according to Parker: He chose not to develop a closer association either with the USSR or with France, something Kennedy applauded him for. Parker wrote that the historical record is unclear about whether the Soviet Union could have been wooed to join in the Allies' attempt to oppose Hitler's expansion in eastern Europe. But Chamberlain did not try. He snubbed the Soviet Union, not inviting it to Munich; it was "undesirable and unnecessary," he thought, and it would antagonize Hitler. Both Chamberlain and Kennedy—wrongly as events proved—assumed that an alliance between the Soviet Union and Nazi Germany was unthinkable and impossible. In addition, after Munich,

Chamberlain could have negotiated a closer relationship with France and created a Franco-British alliance to encircle Germany. Other countries who opposed Hitler's ambitions might well have joined such an alliance. But after March 1939 Britain's attempts to erect a barrier to prevent Hitler's expansion were "either half-hearted or too late." Chamberlain's intractability, his lack of skill in political maneuvering, and his unwillingness to recognize his political errors and correct them prevented any serious chance of averting World War II or of forestalling the very destruction and chaos that he and Kennedy so desperately wanted to forestall. But it did not have to be that way. Was that choice the only hope for peace? Stedman, *Alternatives to Appeasement*, 2, 3: "What could Chamberlain do, other than what Chamberlain did? We are still waiting for a definitive answer." There is still no consensus on appeasement among contemporary historians who examine the same evidence and draw widely different conclusions from it.

Chapter 5. Into an Abyss

1. Whalen, *The Founding Father*, 247.
2. JPK to FDR, December 19, 1938, PSF: Gt. Britain, FDRL; JPK to FDR, December 19, 1938, file 1938–1940, box 91, JPK Collection, JFKL.
3. Memorandum to FDR, March 28, 1939, PSF: box 10, Great Britain, FDRL; JPK Personal Papers, file 1938–1940, JPK Collection, JFKL; Beschloss, *Kennedy and Roosevelt*, 184–85.
4. "DM," chap. 18, pp. 1–2, JPK Collection, JFKL; *New York Times*, October 20, 1938, 10; *Times* (London), October 20, 1938, 6; *Newsweek*, October 31, 1938, 10–11; JPK to Hull, October 17, 1938, JPK Papers, JFKL; Smith, *Hostage to Fortune*, 294.
5. "DM," chap. 18, p. 4, JPK Collection, JFKL; JPK to Hull, October 17, 1938, JPK Papers, JFKL; Smith, *Hostage to Fortune*, 295–97; Nasaw, *The Patriarch*, 353.
6. "DM," chap. 18, pp. 2–3, JPK Collection, JFKL; JPK to Hull, October 17, 1938, JPK Papers, JFKL; *New York Times*, October 20, 1938, 16; Smith, *Hostage to Fortune*, 295–96.
7. *Times*, October 20, 1938, 16; JPK to Hull, October 17, 1938, JPK Papers, JFKL; Smith, *Hostage to Fortune*, 297.
8. *New York Times*, October 20, 1938, 10; Nasaw, *The Patriarch*, 354.
9. *Times*, October 20, 1938, 16; *Times*, October 21, 1938, 15.
10. *Times*, October 20, 1938, 16.
11. *Times*, October 21, 1938, 15; JPK to Hull, October 17, 1938, JPK Papers, JFKL; Smith, *Hostage to Fortune*, 297.
12. *Times*, October 21, 1938, 15; Koskoff, *Joseph P. Kennedy*, 159.
13. *Newsweek*, October 31, 1938, 10–11.
14. Frank R. Kent, "Strained Relations: The Great Game of Politics," *Wall Street Journal*, October 28, 1938, 4; JPK to Doris Fleeson, November 9, 1938, as cited in Smith, *Hostage to Fortune*, 298; Beschloss, *Kennedy and Roosevelt*, 178.
15. Marcelle Schubert and Janet Dinkelspiel, October 28, 1938, OF 3060, FDRL.
16. *Newsweek*, October 31, 1938, 11.

17. Walter Lippmann, "Today and Tomorrow," *Washington Post*, October 22, 1938, 9; JPK to Fleeson, November 9, 1938, as cited in Smith, *Hostage to Fortune*, 298.

18. Lippmann, "Today and Tomorrow," *Washington Post*, October 22, 1938, 9; JPK to Fleeson, November 9, 1938, as cited in Smith, *Hostage to Fortune*, 298; Joseph P. Kennedy Jr., *"Answer to Lippmann Editorial against Dad,"* as cited in Smith, *Hostage to Fortune*, 301; Nasaw, *The Patriarch*, 357.

19. Joseph P. Kennedy Jr., *"Answer to Lippmann Editorial against Dad,"* as cited in Smith, *Hostage to Fortune*, 301–2; Nasaw, *The Patriarch*, 357, believes that this letter was never sent.

20. James M. Burns, *John F. Kennedy* (New York: Harcourt, 1960), 37; Whalen, *The Founding Father*, 249; Lasky, *JFK: The Man and the Myth*, 53.

21. "DM," chap. 18, p. 4, JPK Collection, JFKL; *Newsweek*, October 31, 1938, 10–11.

22. *New York Times*, October 21, 1938, 8; October 23, 1938, E3; Memo from the Department of State on October 20, 1938, #204, 123 Kennedy, Joseph P./134, Dept. of State; Nasaw, *The Patriarch*, 354.

23. Arthur Krock, *New York Times*, October 23, 1938, 69, E3.

24. Arthur Krock, *New York Times*, October 23, 1938, 69, E3; "DM," chap. 18, p. 1, JPK Collection, JFKL; Hooker, *Moffat Papers*, 220–21.

25. "DM," chap. 18, p. 1, JPK Collection, JFKL; Hull to JPK, October 18, 1938, 123/131, Dept. of State. The dispatch contains Hull's criticisms of Kennedy's speech and his suggested revisions. There was not a word about Kennedy's "pet theory."

26. Hooker, *Moffat Papers*, 220–21.

27. Franklin D. Roosevelt, *The Public Papers and Addresses of Franklin D. Roosevelt*, 1939 vol., *War and Neutrality*, comp. Samuel I. Rosenman (New York: Macmillan, 1941), 563–64; Hull, *Memoirs*, 597.

28. "DM," chap. 18, p. 6, JPK Collection, JFKL; *Times*, October 27, 1938, 16.

29. Beschloss, *Kennedy and Roosevelt*, 179.

30. JPK to Fleeson, November 9, 1938, as cited in Smith, *Hostage to Fortune*, 298.

31. Joseph P. Kennedy Jr., *"November 21,"* as cited in Smith, *Hostage to Fortune*, 303–4.

32. John Boettiger to JPK, October 28, 1938, Boettiger Papers, FDRL; Beschloss, *Kennedy and Roosevelt*, 179.

33. JPK to Boettiger, November 25, 1938, Boettiger Papers, FDRL; Smith, *Hostage to Fortune*, 304; Beschloss, *Kennedy and Roosevelt*, 179.

34. Boake Carter, "But . . . by Boake Carter," *New York Daily Mirror*, November 12, 1938, 13; Whalen, *The Founding Father*, 251.

35. *Wall Street Journal*, October 28, 1938, 4.

36. Krock to JPK, October 28, 1938, JPK Papers, ser. 8.2.1, Ambassador: Correspondence File, London, 1938, box 110, JPK Collection, JFKL.

37. "DM," chap. 18, pp. 4–5, JPK Collection, JFKL.

38. JPK to White, November 12, 1938, as cited in Smith, *Hostage to Fortune*, 299.

39. Beschloss, *Kennedy and Roosevelt*, 157.

40. JPK to Fleeson, November 9, 1938, as cited in Smith, *Hostage to Fortune*, 298.

41. JPK to Hull, April 9, 1938, JPK Files, 8.2.2, Ambassador: Correspondence, Nuns, box 129, JPK

Collection, JFKL.

42. JPK files, 8.2.2, Ambassador: Correspondence, Nuns, box 129, JPK Collection, JFKL; *New York Times*, July 22, 1938, 1; Whalen, *The Founding Father*, 253.

43. JPK files, 8.2.2, Ambassador: Correspondence, Nuns, box 129, JPK Collection, JFKL; cable to Secretary of State, April 9, 1938, Dept. of State.

44. Halifax to Lindsay, April 6, 1938, FO 414/275/A2707/1/45, 135, PRO.

45. "DM," chap. 8, p. 6, JPK Collection, JFKL.

46. *New York Times*, July 22, 1938, 1; Whalen, *The Founding Father*, 253.

47. JPK Diary, July 20, 1938, JPK Collection, JFKL; Smith, *Hostage to Fortune*, 233.

48. JPK to Hull, April 9, 1938, JPK Files, 8.2.2, Ambassador: Correspondence, Nuns, box 129, JPK Collection, JFKL.

49. Joan Caron to JPK, September 23, 1938, JPK Papers, 8.2.2, Ambassador: Correspondence, Nuns, box 129, JPK Collection, JFKL.

50. Shirer, *The Rise and Fall of the Third Reich*, 580; Ian Kershaw, *Hitler: 1936–1945 Nemesis* (New York: W.W. Norton, 2000), 136.

51. Whalen, *The Founding Father*, 251; Goodwin, *The Fitzgeralds and the Kennedys*, 568; Shirer, *The Rise and Fall of the Third Reich*, 580; Kershaw, Hitler, 136–43.

52. "DM," chap. 19, p. 6, JPK Collection, JFKL.

53. *New York Times*, November 15, 1938, 1.

54. Self, *Chamberlain Diary Letters*, 363.

55. Self, *Neville Chamberlain*, 344–45.

56. JPK to Lindbergh, December 8, 1938, as cited in Smith, *Hostage to Fortune*, 305.

57. "DM," chap. 20, p. 11, JPK Collection, JFKL; JPK to Lindbergh, November 12, 1938, as cited in Smith, *Hostage to Fortune*, 300–301.

58. Joseph P. Kennedy Jr., December 10, 1938, as cited in Smith, *Hostage to Fortune*, 306.

59. "DM," chap. 20, p. 12, JPK Collection, JFKL; JPK to Lindbergh, November 12, 1938, as cited in Smith, *Hostage to Fortune*, 300–301.

60. Hull, *Memoirs*, 599; "DM," chap. 19, p. 6, JPK Collection, JFKL; *New York Times*, November 16, 1938, 1.

61. *New York Times*, December 17, 1938, 8, 18; Dinneen, *The Kennedy Family*, 65.

62. *Life*, November 28, 1938, 24; *New York Times*, November 16, 1938, 1; *New York Times*, November 27, 1938, 75; Beschloss, *Kennedy and Roosevelt*, 180.

63. *New York Times*, November 15, 1938, 6; *Times*, November 15, 1938, 6, JPKL ser. 8.5, Ambassador: Subject File 1938, box 163, JPK Collection, JFKL.

64. Roberts, *The Holy Fox*, 128, records Halifax's admission of anti-Semitism; Fuchser, *Neville Chamberlain and Appeasement*, 172, has a discussion of Chamberlain's anti-Semitism; Goodwin, *The Fitzgeralds and the Kennedys*, 472–74, has an excellent analysis of Kennedy's anti-Semitism.

65. Fuchser, *Neville Chamberlain and Appeasement*, 172; Goodwin, *The Fitzgeralds and the Kennedys*, 568–69.

66. Self, *Chamberlain Diary Letters*, 433.

67. Roberts, *The Holy Fox*, 128–29.

68. "DM," chap. 21, p. 13, JPK Collection, JFKL; Smith, *Hostage to Fortune*, 308.

69. "DM," chap. 19, pp. 1, 3, JPK Collection, JFKL; Acting Secretary of State (Welles) to the Minister in Rumania (Gunther), April 21, 1938, *FRUS*, 1:743.

70. Sir Ronald Lindsay to Foreign Office, November 18, 1938, FO371/21637/C14092, PRO; Koskoff, *Joseph P. Kennedy*, 175.

71. JPK to Hull, October 12, 1938, *FRUS*, 1:796–98; JPK to Hull, October 12, 1938, 800 Political Refugees, Dept. of State; Visit of May 28, 1938, FO371/21749/C5319/2289/18, as cited in Koskoff, *Joseph P. Kennedy*, 176.

72. "DM," chap. 8, p. 7, JPK Collection, JFKL.

73. Hull to JPK, March 23, 1938, *FRUS*, 1:740; Hull to Certain American Diplomatic Representatives, May 7, 1938, *FRUS*, 1:743–44; JPK to Hull, June 1, 1938, *FRUS*, 1:745; Welles to FDR, October 10, 1938, Memorandum of trans-Atlantic telephone conversation, *FRUS*, 1:795–96; Koskoff, *Joseph P. Kennedy*, 175, has an interesting description of Kennedy's role.

74. "DM," chap. 19, p. 1, JPK Collection, JFKL.

75. Joseph P. Kennedy Jr., December 10, 1938, as cited in Smith, *Hostage to Fortune*, 306.

76. "DM," chap. 8, p. 7, JPK Collection, JFKL.

77. Hugh Wilson to Cordell Hull, November 15, 1938, *FRUS*, 1:824; "The Reminiscences of George Rublee" (Columbia University: Oral History Research Office, 1950–1951), 283–84; Whalen, *The Founding Father*, 253.

78. Rublee, "Reminiscences," 284; Whalen, *The Founding Father*, 253–54.

79. Rublee, "Reminiscences," 283–85; Koskoff, *Joseph P. Kennedy*, 175–81.

80. Johnson to Hull, August 12, 1938, *FRUS*, 1:764.

81. Memorandum of trans-Atlantic telephone conversation, October 10, 1938, *FRUS*, 1:796; a cable from *The Nation*'s London correspondent reported that Kennedy "politely ignored Rublee's efforts" to gain his support, but that Kennedy did say he would give him "moral support"; JPK Papers, ser. 8.5, Ambassador: Subject File 1938, box 163, JPK Collection, JFKL; Nasaw, *The Patriarch*, 350, 359.

82. Rublee, "Reminiscences," 283–85.

83. von Dirkson to Weizsäcker, July 20, 1938, *DGFP*, ser. D, 1:723; June 13, 1938, *DGFP*, ser. D, 1:715; May 31, 1938, *DGFP*, ser. D, 2: 368–69; Rublee, "Reminiscences," 283–87.

84. *New York Times*, November 15, 1938, 6; *Times*, November 15, 1938, 6; JPK Papers, ser. 8.5, Ambassador: Subject File 1938, box 163, JPK Collection, JFKL; Whalen, *The Founding Father*, 253.

85. Nasaw, *The Patriarch*, 351.

86. Welles to JPK, October 5, 1938, *FRUS*, 1:791–92; Nasaw, *The Patriarch*, 349.

87. "DM," chap. 19, p. 1, JPK Collection, JFKL; Nasaw, *The Patriarch*, 349.

88. Welles to JPK, October 5, 1938, *FRUS*, 1:791–92; President to the Prime Minister, JPK Papers, ser. 8.5, Ambassador: Subject File undated, box 163, JFKL; Nasaw, *The Patriarch*, 349.

89. Lindsay to Hull, October 7, 1938, *FRUS*, 1:794–95; Nasaw, *The Patriarch*, 349.

90. "DM," chap. 19, p. 5, JPK Collection, JFKL.

91. JPK to Hull, November 18, 1938, diplomatic dispatch, JPK Papers, JFKL; "DM," chap. 19, p. 5, JPK Collection, JFKL; JPK Personal Papers, 8.6, Ambassador: Dispatch 267, 000 File, box 1, JPK Collection, JFKL; Smith, *Hostage to Fortune*, 302.

92. "DM," chap. 19, pp. 4–5, JPK Collection, JFKL.

93. "DM," chap. 19, p. 5, JPK Collection, JFKL; Rublee, "Reminiscences," 283–84.

94. John Mendelsohn, ed., *The Holocaust* (18 vols.), vol. 6, *Jewish Emigration, 1938–1940: Rublee Negotiations and the Intergovernmental Committee* (New York: Garland Publishing, 1982), 3.

95. "DM," chap. 19, p. 5, JPK Collection, JFKL.

96. *New York Times*, November 15, 1938, 1, 9; *New York Times*, November 16, 1938, 9.

97. *New York Times*, November 15, 1938, 6; *Evening Post*, November 15, 1938, JPK Papers, ser. 8.5, Ambassador: Subject File, 1938, box 163, JPK Collection, JFKL; diplomatic dispatch, November 18, 1938, JPK Papers, ser. 8.6, Ambassador: Subject File, 1938, box 163, JPK Collection, JFKL; Memorandum of Conversation, by the Under Secretary of State (Welles), November 17, 1938, *FRUS*, 1:830; Smith, *Hostage to Fortune*, 302.

98. JPK to Hull, November 25, 1938, 800 Political Refugees, Dept. of State; JPK to Hull, November 18, 1938, JPK Papers, JFKL; Smith, *Hostage to Fortune*, 303. Nasaw, *The Patriarch*, 361, has an interesting analysis of Kennedy as a "terrier" clinging to his "magic panacea for Europe's ills," resettling German and Austrian Jews somewhere within the British Empire.

99. JPK to Hull, November 14, 1938, *FRUS*, 1:82.

100. *New York Times*, November 15, 1938, 6; *Times*, November 15, 1938, 6, JPK Papers, ser. 8.5, Ambassador: Subject File, 1938, box 163, JPK Collection, JFKL; Diplomatic Dispatch, November 18, 1938, JPK Papers, ser. 8.6, Ambassador: Subject File, 1938, box 163, JPK Collection, JFKL; Smith, *Hostage to Fortune*, 302; Nasaw, *The Patriarch*, 361.

101. JPK to Hull, November 18, 1938, JPK Papers, JFKL; JPK Personal Papers, 8.6, Ambassador: Dispatch 267, 000 File, box 1; Smith, *Hostage to Fortune*, 302. Nasaw, *The Patriarch*, 361, wrote that "the Kennedy plan was not nearly as fanciful—or as original—as it might have appeared." Washington had already been trying to find territories outside Palestine and the United States, of course, for the Jewish refugees.

102. *New York Times*, November 15, 1938, 6; *Times*, November 15, 1938, n.p., JPK Papers, ser. 8.5, Ambassador: Subject File, 1938, box 163, JPK collection, JFKL.

103. *J.T.A. News*, November 16, 1938, JPK Papers, ser. 8.5, Ambassador: Subject File, 1938, box 163, JPK Collection, JFKL.

104. JPK Papers, ser. 8.6, Ambassador: Dispatch 267, JPK Collection, JFKL; JPK Diary, "Just Notes," November 15, 1938, box 91, JPK Personal Papers, 000 File, JPK Collection, JFKL; Smith, *Hostage to Fortune*, 303; Nasaw, *The Patriarch*, 362.

105. Halifax to Lindsay, November 15, 1938, FO 414/C113900/1667/62, PRO; Nasaw, *The Patriarch*, 363.

106. Halifax to Lindsay, November 15, 1938, FO 414/C113900/1667/62, PRO; Lindsay to Halifax, November 17, 1938, FO 414/275, PRO; Halifax to Lindsay, November 16, 1938, FO 371/21637/NAUK, PRO. Memorandum of conversation, by Welles, November 17, 1938, *FRUS*, 1:830–31, discusses the

pressure—"blackmail" it was called—that Kennedy brought to bear on the British government "by insinuating that American revulsion against the 'treatment accorded Jews and Catholics in Germany' was provoking vehement and widespread criticism in America against the policy of appeasement pursued by Mr. Chamberlain"; Nasaw, *The Patriarch*, 363–64.

107. JPK Papers, ser. 8.6, Ambassador: Dispatch 26, JPK Collection, JFKL; JPK Personal Papers, 8.6, Ambassador Dispatch: 267, 000 File, box 1, JPK Collection, JFKL; Smith, *Hostage to Fortune*, 302–3; Nasaw, *The Patriarch*, 363.

108. "DM," chap. 19, p. 6, JPK Collection, JFKL; Halifax to Lindsay, November 15, 1938, FO 414/ C113900/1667/62, PRO.

109. *New York Times*, November 16, 1938, 9.

110. *New York Times*, December 11, 1938, 49.

111. *J.T.A. News*, November 16, 1938, JPK Papers, ser. 8.5, Ambassador: Subject File, 1938, box 163, JPK Collection, JFKL; Goodwin, *The Fitzgeralds and the Kennedys*, 569–70, argues that Kennedy missed the point entirely—that it was madness for Hitler to confiscate the Jews' property and throw them out of Germany; Nasaw, *The Patriarch*, 361.

112. Joseph P. Kennedy Jr., "*November 21*," as cited in Smith, *Hostage to Fortune*, 303.

113. Joseph P. Kennedy Jr., December 10, 1938, as cited in Smith, *Hostage to Fortune*, 306.

114. Joseph P. Kennedy Jr., "*November 21*," as cited in Smith, *Hostage to Fortune*, 303.

115. *New York Times*, November 22, 1938, 9.

116. *New York Times*, November 15, 1938, 1, 6; *New York Times*, November 27, 1938, 73; *Evening Post*, November 15, 1938, n.p., November 10, 1939, 11, JPK Papers, ser. 8.5, Ambassador: Subject File, 1938, box 163, JPK Collection, JFKL.

117. Joseph P. Kennedy Jr., "*November 21*," as cited in Smith, *Hostage to Fortune*, 303.

118. *New York Times*, November 27, 1938, 75.

119. "DM," chap. 19, p. 7, JPK Collection, JFKL; *New York Times*, November 27, 1938, 75; *New York Times*, November 22, 1938, 9.

120. *New York Times*, November 27, 1938, 75.

121. *Life*, November 28, 1938, 24, as cited in McCarthy, *The Remarkable Kennedys*, 79–80. Koskoff, *Joseph P. Kennedy*, 178–81, has a detailed review of Kennedy's activities; see also Whalen, *The Founding Father*, 255.

122. *New York Times*, November 27, 1938, 75; Whalen, *The Founding Father*, 255.

123. Tony Biddle to JPK, November 19, 1938, JPK Papers, ser. 8.2.1, Ambassador: Correspondence File, London, 1938, box 103, JPK Collection, JFKL.

124. Memorandum of Conversation, by Welles, November 17, 1938, *FRUS*, 1:831.

125. Moffat Diary MS, November 16, 1938, 4, as cited in Koskoff, *Joseph P. Kennedy*, 177; Whalen, *The Founding Father*, 255.

126. Moffat Diary MS, November 17, 1938, 2, as cited in Koskoff, *Joseph P. Kennedy*, 178.

127. Joseph P. Kennedy Jr., "*November 21*," as cited in Smith, *Hostage to Fortune*, 303.

128. Hull to JPK, November 18, 1938, *FRUS*, 1:832.

129. Memorandum of Conversation, by Welles, November 17, 1938, *FRUS*, 1:831.

130. Moffat Diary MS, November 22, 1938, as cited in Koskoff, *Joseph P. Kennedy*, 179.

131. "DM," chap. 19, p. 1, JPK Collection, JFKL.

132. Memorandum of conversation, by Welles, November 17, 1938, *FRUS*, 1:829–30.

133. "DM," chap. 19, pp. 3–4, JPK Collection, JFKL; Goodwin, *The Fitzgeralds and the Kennedys*, 570–71.

134. "DM," chap. 19, p. 4, JPK Collection, JFKL; JPK to Hull, November 18, 1938, JPK Papers, JFKL; Smith, *Hostage to Fortune*, 302.

135. "DM," chap. 11, p. 4, JPK Collection, JFKL.

136. "DM," chap. 19, p. 14; Nasaw, *The Patriarch*, 351.

137. JPK to Hull, November 22, 1938, 800 General, Dept. of State; JPK to Hull, Telegram 3/1347, 8:00 P.M., November 22, 1938. Nasaw, *The Patriarch*, 385–93, discusses Kennedy's peripheral role in Britain's continued and mostly half-hearted efforts to hold an international conference in London on the future of Palestine. "There was not the slightest hope that anything would emerge from the deliberations." That was correct; nothing did emerge except the British White Paper on Palestine published in May 1939, even more disappointing than the Zionists expected. It said that within ten years the British would establish an independent state of Palestine with a majority of Arabs. To safeguard the Arab majority, the British were restricting Jewish immigration to ten thousand a year for the next five years with special consideration given to children and dependents. It was "an unworkable plan with no timetable for execution and only the vaguest commitment from the president [Roosevelt]." Like Roosevelt, Kennedy always believed that the issues of rescuing the Jews and emigration to Palestine were two separate issues. No archangel was forthcoming.

138. "DM," chap. 19, pp. 8–10, JPK Collection, JFKL; Memorandum by the Director of the Political Department (Ernst Woermann), November 12, 1938, *DGFP*, ser. D, 5:904; Koskoff, *Joseph P. Kennedy*, 181; Kershaw, *Hitler*, 42, 147–48: for Göring's policy and Hitler's attitude toward it.

139. Rublee, "Reminiscences," 304; Whalen, *The Founding Father*, 256; Koskoff, *Joseph P. Kennedy*, 181.

140. JPK to Hull, October 12, 1938, *FRUS*, 1:796–98; JPK to Hull, October 12, 1938, 800 Political Refugees, Dept. of State.

141. Rublee to Welles, Memorandum of trans-Atlantic telephone conversation, October 10, 1938, *FRUS*, 1:796; Rublee to Hull and Welles, October 12, 1938, 800 Political Refugees, Dept. of State.

142. Rublee, "Reminiscences," 285.

143. Koskoff, *Joseph P. Kennedy*, 181, cites an interview of a British negotiator in London, July 17, 1972.

144. Rose Kennedy, *Times to Remember*, 243; Smith, *Hostage to Fortune*, 232; Whalen, *The Founding Father*, 253.

145. JPK to White, November 12, 1938, as cited in Smith, *Hostage to Fortune*, 299.

146. Joseph P. Kennedy Jr., December 10, 1938, as cited in Smith, *Hostage to Fortune*, 305–6.

147. Nasaw, *The Patriarch*, 366.

148. Smith, *Hostage to Fortune*, 233: Kennedy's granddaughter wrote that "accusations of anti-Semitism would follow [Kennedy] throughout his life. His experience in film, business and government had brought him into contact to a far greater degree than many of his contemporaries, Irish Catholic or

otherwise, with people of differing recent-immigrant backgrounds, particularly Eastern European Jews. Although rumors persist of dismissive cracks that he made in the 1920s . . . , typically these survive as secondhand or overheard comments recollected by others years later and are for that reason difficult to trace or substantiate." Smith notes Kennedy's affection and cordial relations with many Jews such as Bernard Baruch and Louis Brandeis, as well as those Kennedy later developed hostile feelings for such as Henry Morgenthau, Felix Frankfurter, and Walter Lippmann; Goodwin, *The Fitzgeralds and the Kennedys*, 569: "while we may never know the true nature of Joe Kennedy's feelings toward the Jews, one thing is clear. In the late thirties, his passion for peace—and with it his perception that peace provided the only protection for himself and his family—was so overriding that he was willing to sacrifice almost anything to achieve it."

149. *Newsweek*, September 12, 1960, 29.

150. Whalen, *The Founding Father*, 388n53, 529: "Dinneen recalled the 1944 interview in an interview with William J. Gill on November 8, 1962, and furnished him with his original typescript of Kennedy's unpublished remarks."

151. *Newsweek*, September 12, 1969, 29.

152. Whalen, *The Founding Father*, 389.

153. Goodwin, *The Fitzgeralds and the Kennedys*, 473.

154. "DM," chap. 20, p. 15, JPK Collection, JFKL.

155. Whalen, *The Founding Father*, 256.

156. Joseph P. Kennedy Jr., "*Visit to Plymouth*," December 6, 1938, as cited in Smith, *Hostage to Fortune*, 304.

157. Ickes, *The Secret Diary of Harold Ickes*, vol. 2, 377, 528, 571, 676, has examples of his attitude toward fascists.

158. Whalen, *The Founding Father*, 221.

159. Louis Fischer, *Men and Politics: An Autobiography* (New York: Duell, Sloan and Pearce, 1941), 568; Whalen, *The Founding Father*, 260–61.

160. Morgenthau Diaries, 367, FDRL; Beschloss, *Kennedy and Roosevelt*, 180, cites the document as dated December 5, 1938; FDRL cites it as December 16–December 19, 1939.

161. Johnson to Morgenthau, December 28, 1938, 800 .2 U.S., Dept. of State.

162. "DM," chap. 20, p. 15, JPK Collection, JFKL.

163. Whalen, *The Founding Father*, 256.

164. JPK to Lindbergh, December 8, 1938, as cited in Smith, *Hostage to Fortune*, 305.

165. *New York Times*, December 11, 1938, sec. L, p. 49.

166. *New York Times*, December 13, 1938, 24.

167. "DM," chap. 21, p. 3, JPK Collection, JFKL.

168. Morgenthau Diaries, 0106–07, FDRL; Beschloss, *Kennedy and Roosevelt*, 182.

169. "DM," chap. 21, p. 1, JPK Collection, JFKL.

170. *New York Times*, December 16, 1938, 13; *Times*, December 19, 1938, 21; "DM," chap. 21, p. 1, JPK Collection, JFKL.

171. *Boston Globe*, April 20, 1939, 12.

172. "DM," chap. 21, p. 3, JPK Collection, JFKL.

173. "DM," chap. 21, pp. 1–2, JPK Collection, JFKL; *New York Times*, December 17, 1938, 8.

174. "DM," chap. 21, pp. 2–3, JPK Collection, JFKL.

175. *New York Times*, December 17, 1938, 8.

176. *New York Times*, December 19, 1938, 13; Whalen, *The Founding Father*, 257.

177. *Life*, January 16, 1939, 18; "DM," chap. 21, pp. 4–5, JPK Collection, JFKL; Whalen, *The Founding Father*, 257.

178. Whalen, *The Founding Father*, 257.

179. JPK Diary, March 28, 1940, JPK Collection, JFKL; Smith, *Hostage to Fortune*, 412; Beschloss, *Kennedy and Roosevelt*, 182–83.

180. Langer and Gleason, *The Challenge to Isolation*, 48; FDR, The Public Papers and Addresses of Franklin D. Roosevelt, 1939 vol., comp. Rosenman, 3–4, 36–53, 70–74.

181. Beschloss, *Kennedy and Roosevelt*, 182.

182. "DM," chap. 21, p. 2, JPK Collection, JFKL; William W. Kaufmann, "Two American Ambassadors: Bullitt and Kennedy," in *The Diplomats, 1919–39*, ed. Gordon A. Craig and Felix Gilbert (New York: Princeton University Press, 1953), 666.

183. Craig and Gilbert, eds., *The Diplomats, 1919–39*, 662–63, 665.

184. JPK to FDR, December 19, 1938, PSF: Gt. Britain, FDRL; JPK to FDR, December 19, 1938, File 1938–1940, box 91, JPK Collection, JFKL.

185. Joseph P. Kennedy Jr., December 10, 1938, as cited in Smith, *Hostage to Fortune*, 306.

186. JPK to FDR, December 19, 1938, PSF: Gt. Britain, FDRL; JPK to FDR, December 19, 1938, File 1938–1940, box 91, JPK Collection, JFKL; Craig and Gilbert, eds., *The Diplomats, 1919–39*, 663, 665; Nasaw, *The Patriarch*, 368.

187. Lord Lothian Papers, December 8, 1938, HNKY 8/41, as cited in Rock, *Chamberlain and Roosevelt*, 143; Lothian to Hankey, December 8, 1938, HNKY 4/30, as cited in Rock, *Chamberlain and Roosevelt*, 143; Hankey to Phipps, February 13, 1939, HNKY 4/31, as cited in Rock, *Chamberlain and Roosevelt*, 143; Lothian Papers, GD 40/17/444, as cited in Rock, *Chamberlain and Roosevelt*, 143.

188. JPK to FDR, December 19, 1938, PSF: Gt. Britain, FDRL; JPK to FDR, December 19, 1938, File 1938–1940, box 91, JPK Collection, JFKL; Nasaw, *The Patriarch*, 368; Beschloss, *Kennedy and Roosevelt*, 181–82.

189. "DM," chap. 20, p. 16, JPK Collection, JFKL.

190. "DM," chap. 20, p. 16, JPK Collection, JFKL.

191. Craig and Gilbert, eds., *The Diplomats, 1919–39*, 665.

192. Craig and Gilbert, eds., *The Diplomats, 1919–39*, 667.

193. *New York Times*, January 11, 1939, 1, 13; *New York Times*, January 11, 1939, 9.

194. "DM," chap. 21, pp. 3–5, JPK Collection, JFKL.

195. *Times*, January 12, 1939, 10.

196. *New York Times*, January 11, 1939, sec. E1, p. 13.

197. "DM," chap. 21, pp. 3–4, JPK Collection, JFKL.

198. *New York Times*, January 11, 1939, 1, 13; *Times*, January 11, 1939, 9; January 12, 1939, 10; "DM," chap. 21, p. 3, JPK Collection, JFKL.

199. *New York Times*, January 11, 1939, 1, 13; *Times*, January 12, 1939, 10; "DM," chap. 21, pp. 3–4, JPK Collection, JFKL.

200. "DM," chap. 21, pp. 3–4, JPK Collection, JFKL; *New York Times*, January 11, 1939, 1.

201. "DM," chap. 21, pp. 4–5, JPK Collection, JFKL; Goodwin, *No Ordinary Time*, 48: Roosevelt definitely believed that Lindbergh was a Nazi; Ted Morgan, *FDR: A Biography* (New York: Simon and Schuster, 1985), 523.

202. "DM," chap. 21, pp. 4–5, JPK Collection, JFKL.

203. Koskoff, *Joseph P. Kennedy*, 533n98, writes: "Among the reports was one that Kennedy had prophesized [*sic*] that the next move in the appeasement policy was to grant Germany military bases in Canada or the West Indies." For a denial, see *New York Times*, January 14, 1939, 3; Johnson to Hull, January 12, 1939, 800 General, Dept. of State; "DM," chap. 21, p. 4, JPK Collection, JFKL.

204. *Times*, January 11, 1939, 9; Koskoff, *Joseph P. Kennedy*, 183.

205. "DM," chap. 21, p. 12, JPK Collection, JFKL.

206. JPK Diary, February 9, 1939, JPK Collection, JFKL; Smith, *Hostage to Fortune*, 306–7.

207. "DM," chap. 21, pp. 12–13; JPK Diary, as cited in Smith, *Hostage to Fortune*, 308.

208. *Boston Globe*, April 20, 1939, 1, 2.

209. Edward T. Folliard, *Washington Post*, February 22, 1939, 9; Koskoff, *Joseph P. Kennedy*, 185–86.

210. Ickes, *The Secret Diary of Harold Ickes*, 2:420; Koskoff, *Joseph P. Kennedy*, 185.

211. Interview with James Roosevelt about the president's decision to leave Kennedy in London, as cited in Beschloss, *Kennedy and Roosevelt*, 184.

212. Craig and Gilbert, eds., *The Diplomats, 1919–39*, 667.

213. Halifax to Lindsay, February 17, 1939, FO 371/22829/A1385/1292/45, PRO, as cited in Koskoff, *Joseph P. Kennedy*, 187.

214. "DM," chap. 22, pp. 1, 4, JPK Collection, JFKL; JPK to Hull, February 17, 1939, 800 General, Dept. of State; JPK to Hull, February 17, 1939, *FRUS*, 2:14–17.

215. JPK to Hull, February 17, 1939, 800 General, Dept. of State; JPK to Hull, February 17, 1939, *FRUS*, 2:14–17.

216. "DM," chap. 22, pp. 1, 4, JPK Collection, JFKL; JPK to Hull, February 17, 1939, 800 General, Dept. of State; JPK to Hull, February 17, 1939, *FRUS*, 2:14–17.

217. "DM," chap. 22, p. 7, JPK Collection, JFKL; JPK to Hull, March 3, 1939, 800 General, Dept. of State.

218. Hull to FDR, February 21, 1939, PSF: Kennedy, FDRL.

219. JPK to Hull, February 17, 1939, 800 General, Dept. of State; JPK to Hull, February 17, 1939, *FRUS*, 2:14–17.

220. "DM," chap. 22, p. 7, JPK Collection, JFKL; JPK to Hull, February 27, 1939, 800 General, Dept. of State.

221. Sumner Welles memorandum, February 20, 1939, *FRUS*, 1:18–19; Nasaw, *The Patriarch*, 372.

222. Self, *Neville Chamberlain*, 348, 351, writes of Chamberlain's "absolute immunity from worrying

or brooding. He makes up his mind what is the best *immediate* thing to do, and does it with all his might, to the exclusions of doubts and alternatives." His optimism in the face of facts to the contrary in early 1939 was an illustration of Chamberlain's decision-making process and raised major questions about his judgment.

223. Memorandum by Sumner Welles, February 20, 1939, *FRUS*, 1:18–19; Nasaw, *The Patriarch*, 372.

224. "DM," chap. 22, pp. 5–6; JPK to Hull, JPK Collection, JFKL, February 23, 1939, *FRUS*, 1:21–22; JPK to Hull, February 23, 1939, 800 General, Dept. of State.

225. Nasaw, *The Patriarch*, 373.

226. Memo to FDR, March 3, 1939, PSF: box 10, Gt. Britain, FDRL; Beschloss, *Kennedy and Roosevelt*, 184–85; Nasaw, *The Patriarch*, 373.

227. Memo to FDR, March 3, 1939, PSF: box 10, Gt. Britain, FDRL; Beschloss, *Kennedy and Roosevelt*, 184–85; Nasaw, *The Patriarch*, 315: Kennedy was advocating a fascist form of government for the United States as early as July 3, 1938, according to a conversation that Roosevelt had with Ickes. Ickes supposedly wrote in his diary on that date that Roosevelt told Ickes that he was angry with Kennedy because he presumed to lecture him (Roosevelt) on foreign policy and because Kennedy candidly told him that the United States would have to adopt some form of fascism. "The President thinks," Ickes wrote, "that Joe Kennedy, if he were in power, would give us a Fascist form of government. He would organize a small powerful committee under himself as chairman and this committee would run the country without much reference to Congress." Nasaw cited Ickes's diary of July 3, 1938, 415, but this passage does not appear there.

228. Beschloss, *Kennedy and Roosevelt*, 185.

Chapter 6. Peace at Any Price

1. "DM," chap. 23, pp. 9–10, JPK Collection, JFKL.

2. JPK Diary, March 18, 1938, JPK Collection, JFKL; "DM," chap. 24, p. 15, JPK Collection, JFKL.

3. Craig and Gilbert, eds., *The Diplomats, 1919–39*, 666–67.

4. Memo to FDR, March 3, 1939, PSF: box 10, Gt. Britain, FDRL; Beschloss, *Kennedy and Roosevelt*, 184–85.

5. Beschloss, *Kennedy and Roosevelt*, 188.

6. Goodwin, *The Fitzgeralds and the Kennedys*, 569.

7. Koskoff, *Joseph P. Kennedy*, 193.

8. *Time*, March 20, 1939, 50–51; *New York Times*, March 12, 1939, 1.

9. Moffat to JPK, March 2, 1930, Moffat Papers at Houghton Library, Harvard University, Cambridge, MA, as cited in Koskoff, *Joseph P. Kennedy*, 189.

10. JPK to Moffat, March 17, 1939, JPK Files: ser. 8.2.1, Moffat, J. Pierrepont, box 112, JPK Collection, JFKL; Kennedy to Moffat, March 17, 1939, Moffat Papers, as cited in Koskoff, *Joseph P. Kennedy*, 189.

11. *New York Times*, March 8, 1939, 9.

12. Koskoff, *Joseph P. Kennedy*, 189.

13. "DM," chap. 22, p. 8, JPK Collection, JFKL; JPK Diary, March 5, 1939, JPK Collection, JFKL.

14. "DM," chap. 39, pp. 1–2, JPK Collection, JFKL: Kennedy writes that it was Welles who initially "had the happy thought of having the President appoint me as his personal representative to the Pope's Coronation in 1938." It was also Welles who thought it advisable to put U.S. relations on a more permanent basis with the Vatican by sending a representative to it and thereby gaining an ally with the pope. Doing so would undermine Fr. Coughlin, who was trying to imply that the Church supported his views. When Kennedy was in Washington, he discussed the matter again with Welles and urged him to nudge Roosevelt to appoint a representative to the Vatican. Kennedy said that he was "pleasantly surprised" when the president announced Myron Taylor to be his representative to the Vatican; Hull to JPK, March 7, 1939, box 172, JPK Collection, JFKL, as cited in Nasaw, *The Patriarch*, 374–75; Koskoff, *Joseph P. Kennedy*, 189.

15. "DM," chap. 22, pp. 8–9; Hull to JPK, March 7, 1939, box 172, JPK Collection, JFKL, as cited in Nasaw, *The Patriarch*, 374–75.

16. *New York Times*, March 11, 1939, 40; "DM," chap. 23, pp. 1–2, JPK Collection, JFKL.

17. *Times* (London), March 14, 1939, 14; JPK Papers, March 9, 1939, Alphabet: Correspondence, London, box 97, JPK Personal Papers, JPK Collection, JKFL. It may well be that Joe Jr. remained in Spain with his father's blessing and his mother's ignorance. The Kennedy papers contain a telegram from Joe senior saying: "Wire received. We are attending popes coronation Rome Sunday representing president Stay Madrid if you think safe Nothing here Good Luck and Love, Dad."

18. *New York Times*, March 12, 1939, 40; "DM," chap. 23, p. 3, JPK Collection, JFKL; JPK Diary, March 12, 1939, JPK Collection, JFKL; Rose Kennedy Diary, March 11, 1939, Rose F. Kennedy Papers, ser. 1, Diaries, 1939, box 2, JPK Collection, JFKL; Perry, *Rose Kennedy*, 134.

19. *New York Times*, March 11, 1939, 4; "DM," chap. 23, p. 2, JPK Collection, JFKL.

20. "DM," chap. 23, pp. 2–3, JPK Collection, JFKL.

21. *New York Times*, March 12, 1939, 1; "DM," chap. 23, p. 4, JPK Collection, JFKL; JPK Papers, ser. 8.2.2, Ambassador: Correspondence Subject File 1939, box 130, JPK Collection, JFKL; Whalen, *The Founding Father*, 261–62. In his memoirs, Kennedy says that his car was decked with American and Papal flags, though the *New York Times* and Whalen say to the contrary.

22. *New York Times*, March 12, 1939, 1; JPK Diary, March 12, 1939, JPK Collection, JFKL; "DM," chap. 23, pp. 4–5, JPK Collection, JFKL. Arthur Houghton also kept a diary of the events, JPK Papers, ser. 8.2.2., Ambassador: Correspondence Subject File, 1939, box 130, JPK Collection, JFKL [hereafter cited as Houghton's Diary with the date of the entry]; Smith, *Hostage to Fortune*, 316–20.

23. JPK Diary, March 12, 1939, JPK Collection, JFKL; "DM," chap. 23, p. 5, JPK Collection, JFKL; Smith, *Hostage to Fortune*, 317, 322.

24. JPK Diary, March 12, 1939, JPK Collection, JFKL; JPK Papers, ser. 8.2.2, Ambassador: Correspondence Subject File 1939, box 130, JPK Collection, JFKL; "DM," chap. 23, p. 5, JPK Collection, JFKL; Smith, *Hostage to Fortune*, 317, 322.

25. JPK Diary, March 12, 1939, JPK Collection, JFKL; "DM," chap. 23, p. 6, JPK Collection, JFKL; Smith, *Hostage to Fortune*, 317.

26. Koskoff, *Joseph P. Kennedy*, 189, 535n24, states that it was "eight children plus two nurses and the

Eddie Moores"; Nasaw, *The Patriarch*, 374–75, mentions that for the ceremony, accommodations for *twelve more* had to be made.

27. Koskoff, *Joseph P. Kennedy*, 189.

28. *New York Times*, March 12, 1939, 40; *Time*, March 20, 1939, 50: Rumor had it that the seating was so tight that not even His Holiness Himself could get the fifty tickets he had personally requested; Koskoff, *Joseph P. Kennedy*, 190.

29. New York Herald Tribune, March 14, 1939, 20; Whalen, *The Founding Father*, 262.

30. "DM," chap. 23, p. 6, JPK Collection, JFKL; JPK Papers, ser. 8.2.2, Ambassador: Correspondence Subject File 1939, box 130, JPK Collection, JFKL.

31. Houghton's Diary, March 13, 1939, JPK Papers, ser. 8.2.2, Ambassador: Correspondence Subject File 1939, box 130, JPK Collection, JFKL.

32. *New York Times*, March 14, 1939, 7; *Times*, March 14, 1939, 14; *Time*, March 27, 1939, 45; "DM," chap. 23, p. 7, JPK Collection, JFKL; Rose Kennedy Diary, March 13, 1939, Rose F. Kennedy Papers, ser. 1, Diaries, 1939, box 2, JPK Collection, JFKL.

33. *New York Times*, March 14, 1939, 7; JPK Diary, March 12, 1939, JPK Collection, JFKL; Smith, *Hostage to Fortune*, 317–18. Kennedy too "broke custom"—by crossing his knees, something a European would not do, except for Lord Halifax, who despite his crossed knees had "acted most reverently" toward the pope. Kennedy "listened most attentively."

34. *New York Times*, March 14, 1939, 7; *New York Herald Tribune*, March 14, 1939, 1; JPK Diary, March 12, 1939, JPK Collection, JFKL; "DM," chap. 23, p. 7, JPK Collection, JFKL; Smith, *Hostage to Fortune*, 317–18.

35. "DM," chap. 23, pp. 7–8, JPK Collection, JFKL.

36. JPK Diary, March 13, 1939, JPK Collection, JFKL; Smith, *Hostage to Fortune*, 317–18.

37. *New York Times*, March 14, 1939, 7; "DM," chap. 23, p. 1, JPK Collection, JFKL; Smith, *Hostage to Fortune*, 317–19.

38. *New York Herald Tribune*, March 14, 1939, 1; JPK Diary, March 13, 1939, JPK Collection, JFKL; "DM," chap. 23, p. 8; Houghton's Diary, March 13, 1939, JPK Papers, ser. 8.2.2, Ambassador: Correspondence Subject File 1939, box 130, JPK Collection, JFKL; Smith, *Hostage to Fortune*, 318.

39. Perry, *Rose Kennedy*, 134.

40. Rose Kennedy Diary, March 13, 1939, 25, Rose F. Kennedy Papers, ser. 1, Diaries, 1939, box 2, JPK Collection, JFKL.

41. *New York Times*, March 14, 1939, 7; *Time*, March 27, 1939, 45; JPK Diary, March 13, 1939, JPK Collection, JFKL.

42. JPK Diary, March 15, 1939, JPK Collection, JFKL; Smith, *Hostage to Fortune*, 320; Edward M. Kennedy, *True Compass: A Memoir* (New York: Twelve, 2009), 56.

43. JPK Diary, March 13, 1939, JPK Collection, JFKL; "DM," chap. 23, p. 8, JPK Collection, JFKL; Smith, *Hostage to Fortune*, 318.

44. Koskoff, *Joseph P. Kennedy*, 189.

45. JPK Diary, March 15, 1939, JPK Collection, JFKL; Smith, *Hostage to Fortune*, 320.

46. JPK Papers, March 13, 1939, ser. 8.2.2, Ambassador's Correspondence: Subject File 1939, box 130, JPK Collection, JFKL.

47. JPK Diary, March 13, 1939, JPK Collection, JFKL; "DM," chap. 23, p. 9, JPK Collection, JFKL; Smith, *Hostage to Fortune*, 319.

48. JPK to Hull, March 17, 1939, ser. 8.6, JPK Collection, JFKL; "DM," chap. 23, pp. 9–10, JPK Collection, JFKL; JPK to Hull, March 17, 1939, 800 Italy, Dept. of State; Smith, *Hostage to Fortune*, 322.

49. "DM," chap. 23, p. 10, JPK Collection, JFKL; JPK Diary, March 13, 1939, JPK Collection, JFKL; JPK to Hull, March 17, 1939, ser. 8.6, JPK Collection, JFKL; JPK to Hull, March 17, 1939, 800 Italy, Dept. of State; Smith, *Hostage to Fortune*, 322.

50. JPK Diary, March 13, 1939, JPK Collection, JFKL; Smith, *Hostage to Fortune*, 319. Kennedy, never known for fidelity to his marriage vows, kept his own numerous affairs private. He was "very sophisticated about that," said one official close to him; interview, September 20, 1973, as cited in Koskoff, *Joseph P. Kennedy*, 191. In *The Patriarch*, Nasaw notes that Kennedy seemed to have well deserved his reputation as a "ladies' man" and singles out Kennedy's affairs with Gloria Swanson and Clare Boothe Luce as being especially significant, 47–48, 76–77, 146–47, 241, 379–80, 610–11, 680.

51. JPK Diary, March 13, 1939, JPK Collection, JFKL; Smith, *Hostage to Fortune*, 319.

52. JPK to Hull, diplomatic dispatch, 354, March 17, 1939, ser. 8.6, JPK Collection, JFKL; JPK to Hull, March 17, 1939, 800 Italy, Dept. of State; JPK Diary, March 13, 1939, JPK Collection, JFKL; "DM," chap. 23, p. 10, JPK Collection, JFKL; Smith, *Hostage to Fortune*, 321–22.

53. JPK to Hull, diplomatic dispatch, 354, March 17, 1939, ser. 8.6, JPK Collection, JFKL; JPK Diary, April 14, 1939, JPK Collection, JFKL; Smith, *Hostage to Fortune*, 321–22.

54. JPK to Hull, diplomatic dispatch, 354, March 17, 1939, ser. 8.6, JPK Collection, JFKL; JPK to Hull, March 17, 1939, 800 Italy, Dept. of State; Houghton Diary, March 14, 1939; JPK Papers, ser. 8.2.1, Ambassador: Correspondence File, London, 1939, box 117, JPK Collection, JFKL; Smith, *Hostage to Fortune*, 322.

55. JPK to Welles, April 5, 1939, JPK Papers, ser. 8.2.1, Ambassador: Correspondence File, London, 1939, box 117, JPK Collection, JFKL.

56. JPK Diary, March 17, 1939, JPK Collection, JFKL; JPK to Hull, March 20, 1939, 800 General, Dept. of State; Smith, *Hostage to Fortune*, 321; Nasaw, *The Patriarch*, 372.

57. JPK to Hull, diplomatic dispatch, 354, March 17, 1939, ser. 8.6, JPK Collection, JFKL; JPK to Hull, March 17, 1939, 800 Italy, Dept. of State; Smith, *Hostage to Fortune*, 322.

58. "DM," chap. 23, p. 11, JPK Collection, JFKL.

59. "DM," chap. 24, p. 1, JPK Collection, JFKL.

60. "DM," chap. 24, p. 1, JPK Collection, JFKL; Hooker, *Moffat Papers*, 230–31; Hitler's proclamation to the German people, March 15, 1939, as cited in John W. Wheeler-Bennett, *Munich: Prologue to Tragedy* (New York: Duell, Sloan and Pearce, 1962), 346.

61. JPK Diary, March 17, 1939, JPK Papers, ser. 8.2.2, Ambassador: Correspondence Subject File 139, box 130, JPK Collection, JFKL; Smith, *Hostage to Fortune*, 321.

62. Roberts, *The Holy Fox*, 142.

63. *Parliamentary Debates*, Commons, 5th series (1938–39), March 15, 1939, 345:438–39; Feiling, *The Life of Neville Chamberlain*, 399.

64. "DM," chap. 24, p. 1, JPK Collection, JFKL; JPK Diary, March 17, 1939, JPK Collection, JFKL; Smith, *Hostage to Fortune*, 321; Self, *Neville Chamberlain*, 351–52; Roberts, *The Holy Fox*, 142.

65. Viscount Halifax to Sir Ronald Lindsay, March 17, 1939, *DBFP*, ser. 3, 4:364–66.

66. "DM," chap. 24, p. 2, JPK Collection, JFKL.

67. Self, *Neville Chamberlain*, 352–53.

68. "DM," chap. 24, p. 3, JPK Collection, JFKL.

69. Self, *Chamberlain Diary Letters*, 394; Halifax to Lindsay, March 17, 1939, *DBFP*, ser. 3, 4:364.

70. Times, March 18, 1939, 12, 14; Self, *Chamberlain Diary Letters*, 393; Self, *Neville Chamberlain*, 353; Parker, *Chamberlain and Appeasement*, 202.

71. "DM," chap. 24, p. 2, JPK Collection, JFKL.

72. "DM," chap. 24, p. 2, JPK Collection, JFKL. The historical debate continues about what the guarantee to Poland was and what it did. Examples of recent scholarship on the subject include Dutton, *Neville Chamberlain*, 213, who writes that Prague, though significant, was not a reversal of Chamberlain's appeasement policy. Chamberlain had not abandoned appeasement, because he was willing to consider further negotiations over Poland's territorial integrity, such as the Polish Corridor, though not Poland's independence. Parker, *Chamberlain and Appeasement*, 214–15, argues that the guarantee to Poland was intended to prevent a Polish-German agreement, not a war between the two. It was a political, not a military arrangement designed to convince the Germans not to risk war between Germany and the British Empire and France. Stedman, *Alternatives to Appeasement*, 224, is similar to Parker and writes that the value of the Polish guarantee, although criticized for making little military sense since it lacked Soviet support, lay in the deterrence it could give Hitler for going to war. Chamberlain's biographer, Self, *Neville Chamberlain*, 361, believes that Chamberlain regarded the Polish guarantee to be an "epoch-making step" for Britain. It was considered to be a complete reversal of the appeasement policy at the time. But Self also writes that if Prague was a watershed in Chamberlain's thought, as Halifax argues, it was "one of method and approach" rather than of policy. Gilbert, *Britain 1914–1945*, 102–3, says that Chamberlain announced the end of appeasement on March 17 and two weeks later gave a unilateral guarantee to Poland. He moved from the belief that peace was possible to war was inevitable. The only question was when. Roberts states that the guarantee to Poland would not have been given had not Halifax been foreign secretary. Any other foreign secretary would have allowed Chamberlain to see Prague "as a setback," nothing more, and certainly not a "major reversal"; *The Holy Fox*, 143, 147–48. It was Halifax's "pet scheme"; he was the godfather of it. It ended Britain's "guessing position."

73. Self, *Neville Chamberlain*, 353.

74. JPK to Chamberlain: telegram draft, March 18, 1939, as cited in Smith, *Hostage to Fortune*, 322.

75. JPK Diary, April 14, 1939, JPK Collection, JFKL; Smith, *Hostage to Fortune*, 328.

76. Self, *Chamberlain Diary Letters*, 394.

77. Halifax to Lindsay, March 18, 1939, *DBFP*, ser. 3, 4:380.

78. JPK Diary, March 18, 1939, JPK Collection, JFKL.

79. Halifax to Lindsay, March 18, 1939, *DBFP*, ser. 3, 4:380; Rock, *Chamberlain and Roosevelt*, 166–67; Koskoff, *Joseph P. Kennedy*, 193.

80. Halifax to Lindsay, March 18, 1939, *DBFP*, ser. 3, 4:380; Dallek, *FDR and American Foreign Policy*, 183; Koskoff, *Joseph P. Kennedy*, 193.

81. Roberts, *The Holy Fox*, 147.

82. "DM," chap. 24, pp. 6–8, 10–11, JPK Collection, JFKL; JPK to Hull, March 20, 1939, 800 General, Dept. of State; JPK to Hull, March 22, 1939, *FRUS*, 1:92–93; Self, *Chamberlain Diary Letters*, 396; Self, *Neville Chamberlain*, 354.

83. Self, *Neville Chamberlain*, 354–55; Northedge, *The Troubled Giant*, 570–72.

84. "DM," chap. 24, pp. 6–7, 10–11, JPK Collection, JFKL.

85. JPK to Hull, March 22, 1939, London, *FRUS*, 1:92–93.

86. "DM," chap. 24, p. 10, JPK Collection, JFKL; JPK to Hull, March 24, 1939, London, *FRUS*, 1:98; JPK to Hull, March 24, 1939, 800 General, Dept. of State; Self, *Chamberlain Diary Letters*, 404; Hooker, *Moffat Papers*, 234; Gilbert and Gott, *The Appeasers*, 239–46, 248–60; Northedge, *The Troubled Giant*, 570–77, has a further discussion of Poland's attitude.

87. Self, *Neville Chamberlain*, 355; Self, *Chamberlain Diary Letters*, 404.

88. Self, *Chamberlain Diary Letters*, 396.

89. Halifax to Lindsay, March 24, 1939, *DBFP*, ser. 3, 4:499; "DM," chap. 24, pp. 24, 8, 10–14, JPK Collection, JFKL.

90. Self, *Chamberlain Diary Letters*, 396; Self, *Neville Chamberlain*, 355–56; Roberts, *The Holy Fox*, 144.

91. Northedge, *The Troubled Giant*, 570.

92. Self, *Chamberlain Diary Letters*, 396. Chamberlain wrote to Ida on March 26 that he thought this scheme was more practical than the earlier four-power declaration, but he also worried about whether the smaller nations might stand up to Germany's penetration and leave Britain no option but to give Germany an ultimatum, an option that Britain lacked sufficient military strength to enforce. The ultimatum would mean war, an option that Chamberlain would "never be responsible for presenting." That left the only other option, rearming and gathering any help from any quarter that Britain could get it from. Perhaps Hitler's death or his realization that the British military force was too strong to go up against would break the spell, Chamberlain hoped.

93. Roberts, *The Holy Fox*, 150.

94. "DM," chap. 24, pp. 8, 12, JPK Collection, JFKL; JPK to Hull, March 24, 1939, 8:00 P.M., 800 General, Dept. of State; JPK to Hull, March 24, 1939, *FRUS*, 1:98–99; Hooker, *Moffat Papers*, 234.

95. JPK to Hull, March 28, 1939, 4:00 P.M., 800 General, Dept. of State.

96. "DM," chap. 24, p. 14, JPK Collection, JFKL; JPK to Hull, March 28, 1939, 800 General, Dept. of State; Self, *Neville Chamberlain*, 356; Roberts, *The Holy Fox*, 146.

97. "DM," chap. 24, pp. 10–11, JPK Collection, JFKL; JPK to Hull, March 31, 1939, 800 General, Dept. of State; JPK to Hull, March 31, 1939, *FRUS*, 1:105–6.

98. Dilks, *Diaries of Sir Alexander Cadigan*, 167.

99. JPK to Hull, March 31, 1939, London, *FRUS*, 1:105–6; JPK to Hull, March 31, 1939, 800 General, Dept. of State.

100. *New York Times*, July 18, 1943, 7; Self, *Neville Chamberlain*, 355–56; Roberts, *Holy Fox*, 144, 146–47.

101. *New York Times*, July 18, 1943, 7; Colvin, *The Chamberlain Cabinet*, 192–98; "DM," chap. 24, p. 14, JPK Collection, JFKL; "DM," chap. 25, p. 2, JPK Collection, JFKL; JPK to Hull, March 24, 1939, 800 General, Dept. of State; JPK to Hull, March 24, 1939, *FRUS*, 1:98–99.

102. JPK to Hull, March 28, 1939, 800 General, Dept. of State; Weinberg, *A World at Arms*, 40; Stalin's repeated requests for a rapprochement with Germany led to the Nazi-Soviet Non-Aggression Pact.

103. *New York Times*, July 18, 1943, 7; JPK to Hull, March 24, 1939, 8:00 P.M., 800 General, Dept. of State; JPK to Hull, March 24, 1939, *FRUS*, 1:98–99.

104. *Times*, March 25, 1939, 14; *New York Herald Tribune*, March 25, 1939, 6.

105. "DM," chap. 24, p. 8, JPK Collection, JFKL; Cabinet Minutes, 11:00 A.M., March 30, 1939, CAB, 23:156–67, NAUK; *Times*, March 28, 1939, 14, March 29, 1939, 16; Self, *Chamberlain Diary Letters*, 400; Self, *Neville Chamberlain*, 356; Roberts, *The Holy Fox*, 148, writes that there were only fourteen extra German divisions on Poland's border, making it unlikely that Colvin was correct; Colvin, *The Chamberlain Cabinet*, 194–95; Parker, *Chamberlain and Appeasement*, 212.

106. Self, *Chamberlain Diary Letters*, 400–401, writes that Chamberlain said that some of the information that Colvin related was so "fantastic'" that he almost doubted the man's reliability. Chamberlain had gotten the same information from a second source, the British military attaché in Berlin; Self, *Neville Chamberlain*, 356; Parker, *Chamberlain and Appeasement*, 213–14.

107. Halifax to Lindsay, March 31, 1939, *DBFP*, ser. 3, 4:555; Self, *Chamberlain Diary Letters*, 400–401. Self, *Neville Chamberlain*, 356–57, writes that Chamberlain did not see the Polish guarantee as a major step to an inevitable war but an attempt to prevent one by bringing Hitler to his senses. It was essentially a "diplomatic bluff" to show Britain's intention to resist aggression.

108. "DM," chap. 24, p. 14, JPK Collection, JFKL.

109. Chamberlain and Greenwood, March 31, 1939, *House of Commons Debates, 1938–1939*, vol. 345, March 13–April 6, 2415–17; JPK to Hull, March 31, 1939, 800 General, Dept. of State; JPK to Hull, March 31, 1939, *FRUS*, 1:105–6; Hooker, *Moffat Papers*, 237; Parker, *Chamberlain and Appeasement*, 215.

110. "DM," chap. 24, p. 15, JPK Collection, JFKL.

111. JPK to Hull, March 31, 1939, *FRUS*, 1:105–6.

112. JPK to Hull, April 5, 1939, *FRUS*, 1:113.

113. Roberts, *The Holy Fox*, 149.

114. JPK Diary, March 17, 1939, JPK Collection, JFKL; Smith, *Hostage to Fortune*, 321.

115. Ickes, *The Secret Diary of Harold Ickes*, vol. 2, March 18, 1939, 597.

116. JPK Diary, March 30, 1939, JPK Collection, JFKL; "DM," chap. 24, p. 15, JPK Collection, JFKL.

117. Halifax to Lindsay, March 31, 1939, *DBFP*, ser. 3, 4:555.

118. Dilks, *Diaries of Sir Alexander Cadigan*, 167; Self, *Chamberlain Diary Letters*, 401; Halifax to Lindsay, March 31, 1939, *DBFP*, ser. 3, 4:555; Langer and Gleason, *The Challenge to Isolationism*, 75.

119. "DM," chap. 25, p. 4, JPK Collection, JFKL; JPK to Hull, April 18, 1939, London, *FRUS*, 1:142; Roberts, *The Holy Fox*, 142–48.

120. "DM," chap. 24, p. 2, JPK Collection, JFKL.

121. JPK to Hull, April 21, 1939, *FRUS*, 1:171–72; JPK to Hull, April 20, 1939, PSF: Great Britain, FDRL; Gilbert, *Britain, 1914–1945*, 103; Keith Eubank, *The Origins of World War II* (Wheeling, IL: Harlan Davidson, 2004), 137; Self, *Neville Chamberlain*, 362, referring to the creation of the Ministry of Supply on April 20; Smart, *Neville Chamberlain*, 255.

122. "DM," chap. 25, p. 1, JPK Collection, JFKL. Several historians also discuss and dispute Kennedy's conclusion; Stedman, *Alternatives to Appeasement*, 244–45; Dutton, *Neville Chamberlain*, 218–20; Smart, *Neville Chamberlain*, 257; Parker, *Chamberlain and Appeasement*, 346–47.

123. "DM," chap. 25, p. 1, JPK Collection, JFKL.

124. Roberts, *The Holy Fox*, 145.

125. Roberts, *The Holy Fox*, 158.

126. Roberts, *The Holy Fox*, 145.

127. "DM," chap. 25, p. 2, JPK Collection, JFKL.

128. Roberts, *The Holy Fox*, 149.

129. Self, *Neville Chamberlain*, 369.

130. Joseph Edward Davies, *Mission to Moscow: A Record of Confidential Dispatches to the State Department, Official and Personal Correspondence, Current Diary and Journal Entries, Including Notes and Comment up to October, 1941* (New York: Simon and Schuster, 1941), 440; "DM," chap. 25, pp. 3–4, JPK Collection, JFKL.

131. "DM," chap. 25, p. 4, JPK Collection, JFKL.

132. Roberts, *The Holy Fox*, 157.

133. Millis, ed., *The Forrestal Diaries*, 122.

134. *New York Times*, April 15, 1939, 1; "DM," chap. 25, pp. 2–3, JPK Collection, JFKL; JPK to Hull, March 28, 1939, 800 General, Dept. of State.

135. "DM," chap. 26, p. 3, JPK Collection, JFKL; Northedge, *The Troubled Giant*, 570.

136. "DM," chap. 25, p. 2, JPK Collection, JFKL; JPK Diary, August 25, 1939, JPK Collection, JFKL; Smith, *Hostage to Fortune*, 362; Self, *Chamberlain Diary Letters*, 404.

137. "DM," chap. 25, p. 3, JPK Collection, JFKL.

138. *New York Times*, July 18, 1943, 14.

139. JPK to FDR, March 3, 1939, memo, FDRL.

140. *New York Times*, July 18, 1943, 7.

141. Millis, ed., *The Forrestal Diaries*, 122–23.

142. "DM," chap. 26, p. 5, JPK Collection, JFKL.

143. JPK Diary, April 15, 1939, JPK Collection, JFKL; JPK to Hull, April 17, 1939, *FRUS*, 1:139–40; Smith, *Hostage to Fortune*, 328; Millis, ed. *The Forrestal Diaries*, 122–23.

144. Millis, ed., *The Forrestal Diaries*, 122–23.

145. Whalen, *The Founding Father*, 265.

146. "DM," chap. 25, pp. 2–4, JPK Collection, JFKL; Self, *Neville Chamberlain*, 375.

147. "DM," chap. 25, p. 13, chap. 26, pp. 1–3, JPK Collection, JFKL.

148. Rose Kennedy Diary, April 7, 1939, ser. 1, box 2, JPK Collection, JFKL; Smith, *Hostage to Fortune*, 326.

149. JPK to Hull, April 11, 1939, *FRUS*, 1:125–26.

150. "DM," chap. 26, pp. 2–4, JPK Collection, JFKL, says that August 13 was the date upon which Chamberlain informed the House of Commons.

151. "DM," chap. 26, p. 2, JPK Collection, JFKL; Halifax to Lindsay, April 11, 1939, *DBFP*, ser. 3, 5:169; Self, *Neville Chamberlain*, 359; Feiling, *The Life of Neville Chamberlain*, 404; Parker, *Chamberlain and Appeasement*, 220–22.

152. Parker, *Chamberlain and Appeasement*, 220.

153. Halifax to Lindsay, April 11, 1939, *DBFP*, ser. 3, 5:169.

154. *New York Times*, April 15, 1939, 3; "DM," chap. 26, p. 3, JPK Collection, JFKL.

155. "DM," chap. 26, p. 6, JPK Collection, JFKL; Nasaw, *The Patriarch*, 381; David Kennedy, *Freedom from Fear*, 423; Hull, *Memoirs*, 620–22; Dallek, *FDR and American Foreign Policy*, 185–86; Burns, *Roosevelt: The Lion and the Fox*, 391; Langer and Gleason, *The Challenge to Isolationism*, 84.

156. S. Shepard Jones and Denys P. Myers, eds., *Documents on American Foreign Relations*, vol. 1 (Boston: World Peace Foundation, 1939), 326; Langer and Gleason, *The Challenge to Isolationism*, 87.

157. Norman H. Baynes, ed., *The Speeches of Adolf Hitler, April 1922–August 1939*, vol. 2 (New York: Howard Fertig, 1969), 1605–56, 1647; Burns, *Roosevelt: The Lion and the Fox*, 391; Langer and Gleason, *The Challenge to Isolationism*, 87–90.

158. Burns, *Roosevelt: The Lion and the Fox*, 391–92; Hooker, *Moffat Papers*, 239–41; Berle and Jacobs, eds., *Navigating the Rapids*, 214; Langer and Gleason, *The Challenge to Isolationism*, 87–90.

159. "DM," chap. 26, pp. 8, 10, JPK Collection, JFKL.

160. "DM," chap. 25, p. 7, JPK Collection, JFKL.

161. JPK to Hull, March 22, 1939, *FRUS*, 1:88; Hooker, *Moffat Papers*, 240; Halifax to Lindsay, April 11, 1939, no. 130, Great Britain Foreign Office, DBFP.

162. "DM," chap. 25, p. 8, JPK Collection, JFKL; JPK to Hull, March 22, 1939, *FRUS*, 1:88; Hull, *Memoirs*, 630; Foreign Office Minutes FO371/23560/F2963, March 24, 1939, PRO.

163. Halifax to Lindsay, April 11, 1939, *DBFP*, ser. 3, 5:169.

164. JPK to Hull, March 22, 1939, *FRUS*, 1:88; Dilks, *Cadogan Diaries*, 172; Hooker, *Moffat Papers*, 240; Berle and Jacobs, eds., *Navigating the Rapids*, 212; Langer and Gleason, *The Challenge to Isolationism*, 104–5.

165. JPK Diary, April 14, 1939, JPK Collection, JFKL; Smith, *Hostage to Fortune*, 326–27.

166. JPK Diary, April 14, 1939, JPK Collection, JFKL; Smith, *Hostage to Fortune*, 326–27.

167. "DM," chap. 26, p. 8, JPK Collection, JFKL.

168. "DM," chap. 25, p. 11, JPK Collection, JFKL.

169. "DM," chap. 26, pp. 8–9, JPK Collection, JFKL; JPK to Hull, April 17, 1939, *FRUS*, 1:139–40; JPK to Hull, April 17, 1939, 800 General, Dept. of State.

170. "DM," chap. 30, p. 6, JPK Collection, JFKL.

171. Charles Higham, Trading with the Enemy: An Exposé of the Nazi-American Money Plot, 1933–1949 (London: Hale, 1983), 166; Goodwin, *The Fitzgeralds and the Kennedys*, 572; Nasaw, *The Patriarch*, 382–85.

172. JPK to Welles, May 4, 1939, ser. 8.6, JPK Collection, JFKL; Smith, *Hostage to Fortune*, 331–32; Nasaw, *The Patriarch*, 384–85.

173. Higham, Trading with the Enemy, 170; Goodwin, *The Fitzgeralds and the Kennedys*, 572.

174. JPK to Hull, July 20, 1939, ser. 8.6, JPK Collection, JFKL; Smith, *Hostage to Fortune*, 348–49.

175. Higham, Trading with the Enemy, 170.

176. JPK to Morton Downey, August 23, 1954, as cited in Goodwin, *The Fitzgeralds and the Kennedys*, 573; Halifax to Lindsay, April 4, 1939, FO414/296, 37–38. Nasaw says that Wohlthat was Hitler's chief economic adviser; *The Patriarch*, 385. Goodwin describes Kennedy as referring to him as Hitler's minister of economics; *The Fitzgeralds and the Kennedys*, 572–73. Hjalma Schacht was the minister of economics and at one time head of the Reichsbank. Both Nasaw and Goodwin spell *Wohltat* as *Wohlthat*.

177. *Times*, April 22, 1939, 9; "DM," chap. 26, pp. 10–11, JPK Collection, JFKL; JPK to FDR and Hull, April 20, 1939, ser. 8.6, JPK Collection, JFKL; Smith, *Hostage to Fortune*, 330.

178. *Times*, April 22, 1939, 9; JPK to Hull, April 17, 1939, 123/190, Dept. of State; Koskoff, *Joseph P. Kennedy*, 198.

179. *Times*, May 18, 1939, 18; May 19, 1939, 17; *Manchester Guardian*, May 18, 1939, 123 Kennedy, Joseph P./204, Dept. of State.

180. *Evening Chronicle*, May 17, 1939, 123 Kennedy, Joseph P./204, Dept. of State.

181. *Manchester Guardian*, May 18, 1939, 123 Kennedy, Joseph P./204, Dept. of State.

182. *Times*, May 19, 1939, 17; Koskoff, *Joseph P. Kennedy*, 198–99.

183. *Times*, May 19, 1939, 17; *Times*, May 26, 1939, 16; *Bristol Western Daily Press*, May 26, 1939, 7, 123 Kennedy, Joseph P./213, Dept. of State; Koskoff, *Joseph P. Kennedy*, 198–99.

184. *Times*, May 26, 1939, 16; *Bristol Western Daily Press*, May 26, 1939, 10, 123 Kennedy, Joseph P./213, Dept. of State.

185. *Bristol Western Daily Press*, May 26, 1939, 1.

186. Koskoff, *Joseph P. Kennedy*, 198–99.

187. JPK Diary, April 15, 1939, JPK Collection, JFKL; "DM," chap. 26, pp. 7–9, JPK Collection, JFKL; Smith, *Hostage to Fortune*, 328–29.

188. JPK Diary, April 16, 1939, JPK Collection, JFKL; Smith, *Hostage to Fortune*, 329.

189. JPK Diary, July 21, 1939, JPK Collection, JFKL; Smith, *Hostage to Fortune*, 351.

190. "DM," chap. 30, pp. 6–7, JPK Collection, JFKL.

191. JPK Diary, August 27, 1939, JPK Collection, JFKL; Smith, *Hostage to Fortune*, 363–64.

192. Foreign Office Minutes, April 14, 1939, FO 371/22827/A2667/1090/45, 151–52, PRO.

193. "DM," chap. 30, p. 15, JPK Collection, JFKL; JPK to Hull, June 27, 1939, 800 General, Dept. of State.

194. Smith, *Hostage to Fortune*, 230; FDR to JPK, July 22, 1939, as cited in Smith, *Hostage to Fortune*, 354; David Kennedy, *Freedom from Fear*, 400–401, 420–23, has background on the neutrality laws.

195. Burns, *Roosevelt: The Lion and the Fox*, 392; Dallek, *Franklin D. Roosevelt and American Foreign Policy*, 190–91.

196. Dallek, *Franklin D. Roosevelt and American Foreign Policy*, 189–91.

197. Foreign Office Minutes, July 20, 1939, FO 371/22815 A 4991, PRO.

198. "DM," chap. 31, pp. 2–3, JPK Collection, JFKL.

199. "DM," chap. 32, p. 6, JPK Collection, JFKL; FDR to JPK, July 22, 1939, Subject File "K," FDRL; Smith, *Hostage to Fortune*, 354.

200. Lindsay to Halifax, Foreign Office Minutes, June 19, 1939, FO 371/22814, 246, PRO; Lindsay to Halifax, Foreign Office Minutes, July 20, 1939, FO 371/22815/A5008, PRO.

201. JPK to Hull, July 5, 1939, 800 General, Dept. of State.

202. Dallek, *Franklin D. Roosevelt and American Foreign Policy*, 192.

203. *Times*, June 10, 1939, 17.

204. "DM," chap. 18, pp. 11–12, JPK Collection, JFKL; "DM," chap. 5, p. 6C, JPK Collection, JFKL; Goodwin, *The Fitzgeralds and the Kennedys*, 526; Beschloss, *Kennedy and Roosevelt*, 187.

205. Arthur Krock, *New York Times*, July 18, 1939, 18; "DM," chap. 5, pp. 6B & E, chap. 18, pp. 11–12, chap. 30, p. 1, JPK Collection, JFKL.

206. JPK Diary, July 21, 1939, JPK Collection, JFKL; JPK Diary, September 27, 1938, JPK Collection, JFKL; Smith, *Hostage to Fortune*, 351.

207. "DM," chap. 18, pp. 11–12, JPK Collection, JFKL; FDR to King George VI, September 17, 1938, FO 371/21548, PRO; JPK to Hull, November 5, 1938, #1288, Safe: FDRL; David Reynolds, "F.D.R.'s Foreign Policy and the British Royal Visit to the U.S.A., 1939," *The Historian* (August 1939): 461–72.

208. "DM," chap. 30, p. 13, chap. 30, p. 1, JPK Collection, JFKL.

209. "DM," chap. 30, pp. 2–3, JPK Collection, JFKL; Rose Kennedy Diary, May 4, 1939, JPK, JFKL; Smith, *Hostage to Fortune*, 332.

210. Lord Chamberlain's Office, April 14, 1939, JPK Papers, ser. 8.2.2, Ambassador: Correspondence, Royal Visit to U.S., 1939, box 131, JFKL.

211. FDR to King George VI, September 17, 1938, FO 371/21548, PRO; JPK to Hull, November 5, 1938, #1288, Safe: FDRL; Reynolds, "F.D.R.'s Foreign Policy and the British Royal Visit to the U.S.A., 1939," 461–72.

212. Reynolds, "F.D.R.'s Foreign Policy and the British Royal Visit to the U.S.A., 1939," 461–72; Rock, *Chamberlain and Roosevelt*, 188–91.

213. JPK to Hull, diplomatic dispatch, 1259, October 28, 1938, ser. 8.6, JPK Collection, JFKL; Smith, *Hostage to Fortune*, 297.

214. "DM," chap. 18, p. 13, JPK Collection, JFKL.

215. Interview with Thomas Corcoran, as cited in Beschloss, *Kennedy and Roosevelt*, 188.

216. "DM," chap. 30, p. 5, JPK Collection, JFKL.

217. *New York Post*, n.d. and n.p., JPK Papers, ser. 8.2.2, Ambassador: Correspondence, Royal Visit to U.S., June 1937 [*sic*], box 131, JPK Collection, JFKL.

218. *New York Times*, July 5, 1939, 8; Butler to Lindsay, June 12, 1939; Lindsay to Halifax, June 27, 1939, FO

414/276/4335, PRO, for further American press comments.

219. "DM," chap. 30, p. 3, JPK Collection, JFKL.

220. *New York Times*, July 18, 1939, 18. In a letter to Boake Carter on June 13, 1939, Kennedy specified his reasons for retiring; JPK Papers, ser. 8.21, Ambassador: Correspondence File: London 1940, box 104, JFKL.

221. *Washington Sunday Star*, June 25, 1939, as cited in Whalen, *The Founding Father*, 266–67.

222. Koskoff, *Joseph P. Kennedy*, 201–2.

223. Whalen, *The Founding Father*, 267.

224. Ickes, *The Secret Diary of Harold Ickes*, 2:685; Ickes Diary, August 29, 1939, reel 3, 3669, Library of Congress.

225. Whalen, *The Founding Father*, 267.

226. Ickes, *The Secret Diary of Harold Ickes*, 2:707; Whalen, *The Founding Father*, 267.

227. Ickes, *The Secret Diary of Harold Ickes*, 2:712.

228. JPK to Pearson, Telegram, Grosvenor Square, May 3, 1938, JPK Collection, JFKL; Smith, *Hostage to Fortune*, 255n73.

229. W. N. Colze to O'Connor, June 14, 1939, PSF: box 10, FDRL; Colze spells Count Sforza's name "Count Sporja"; Edwin Trent to Cordell Hull, *Dépêche de Toulouse*, June 26, 1939, 123 Kennedy, Joseph P., 217, Dept. of State; Koskoff, *Joseph P. Kennedy*, 202; Nasaw, *The Patriarch*, 393–94.

230. Ickes, *The Secret Diary of Harold Ickes*, 2:676; Ickes Diaries, July 2, 1939, reel 3, 3564, September 27, 1939, reel 3, 3765, Library of Congress; Whalen, *The Founding Father*, 267.

231. Claud Cockburn column, "The Crisis," *The Week*, no. 315 (May 17–June 3, 1939): 6; JPK to Pearson, telegram, Grosvenor Square, May 3, 1938, JPK Collection, JFKL; Smith, *Hostage to Fortune*, 255; Beschloss, *Kennedy and Roosevelt*, 187; Koskoff, *Joseph P. Kennedy*, 202.

232. Cockburn, "The Crisis," 6; Nasaw, *The Patriarch*, 393.

233. JPK to Stout, London, May 10, 1939, as cited in Smith, *Hostage to Fortune*, 334–35.

234. JPK to Stout, London, May 10, 1939, as cited in Smith, *Hostage to Fortune*, 334–35; the rumor that Kennedy was speculating in the stock market was also mentioned in Ickes Diary, July 24, 1939, reel 3, 3609, Library of Congress.

235. "DM," chap. 26, p. 10, JPK Collection, JFKL.

236. *New York Times*, April 21, 1939, 8, 15.

237. *New York Times*, April 25, 1939, 12; Foreign Office Minutes, April 28, 1939, FO 371/22814/A3264/98/45, PRO; "Neutrality, Peace Legislation, and Our Foreign Policy," Hearings before the Committee on Foreign Relations of the US Senate, 76th Congress, 1st Session, part 10, April 24, 1939, 227; Koskoff, *Joseph P. Kennedy*, 201.

238. *New York Times*, April 27, 1939, 24.

239. JPK to Stout, London, May 10, 1939, as cited in Smith, *Hostage to Fortune*, 335.

240. Berle and Jacobs, eds., *Navigating the Rapids*, 214.

241. *New York Times*, April 21, 1939, 8.

242. *New York Times*, April 21, 1939, 8; Press Statement, April 20, 1939, 123/196, Dept. of State; *Times*,

April 21, 1939, 15.

243. JPK to Stout, May 10, 1939, as cited in Smith, *Hostage to Fortune*, 334–35.

244. John M. Coffee to FDR, February 13, 1939, 3060, FDRL.

245. "DM," chap. 32, p. 6, JPK Collection, JFKL; FDR to JPK, July 22, 1939, PSF: Subject File "K," FDRL; Ickes Diary, August 12, 1939, reel 3, 3630, Library of Congress; Ickes Diary, April 29, 1939, reel 3, 3406, Library of Congress; reported Tom Corcoran's belief that Krock was on Kennedy's payroll; Smith, *Hostage to Fortune*, 353–54; Nasaw, *The Patriarch*, 812.

246. *New York Times*, July 18, 1939, 18; FDR to JPK, Hyde Park, NY, July 22, 1939, as cited in Smith, *Hostage to Fortune*, 353.

247. Morgenthau Diaries, April 15, 1935, 207, FDRL. See Morgenthau for a conversation on Kennedy as Roosevelt's choice to head up the Allotment Board, which would include Harold Ickes. Kennedy declined because he did not want to work with Ickes; Morgenthau Diaries, April 15, 1935, 205, 252, FDRL.

248. "DM," chap. 32, p. 6, JPK Collection, JFKL; FDR to JPK, July 22, 1939, JPK Collection, JFKL; FDR to JPK, July 22, 1939, PSF: Subject File "K," FDRL; Smith, *Hostage to Fortune*, 353–54; Whalen, *The Founding Father*, 267–68.

249. *New York Times*, July 18, 1939, 8.

250. JPK to Hull, July 12, 1939, 123/226, Dept. of State.

251. JPK Diary, July 20, 1939, JPK Collection, JFKL; Smith, *Hostage to Fortune*, 349.

252. *New York Times*, July 18, 1943, 35.

253. JPK to Hull, July 20, 1939, 800 General, Dept. of State.

254. *New York Times*, July 21, 1939, 8, July 22, 1939, 2; JPK to Hull, July 20, 1939, 800 General, Dept. of State; JPK to Hull, July 20, 1939, ser. 8.6, JPK Collection, JFKL; Smith, *Hostage to Fortune*, 348–49.

255. Whalen, *The Founding Father*, 268.

256. "DM," chap. 32, p. 1, JPK Collection, JFKL.

257. "DM," chap. 32, p. 1, JPK Collection, JFKL.

258. "DM," chap. 32, pp. 6–7; JPK to FDR, August 9, 1939, PSF: Kennedy, FDRL; JPK to FDR, Cannes, August 9, 1939, as cited in Smith, *Hostage to Fortune*, 354–55.

259. Self, *Neville Chamberlain*, 374; Self, *Chamberlain Diary Letters*, 442.

260. Roberts, *The Holy Fox*, 166–67.

261. "DM," chap. 32, pp. 8–9, JPK Collection, JFKL.

262. "DM," chap. 22, p. 3, JPK Collection, JFKL; Roberts, *The Holy Fox*, 166–67.

263. "DM," chap. 32, p. 9, JPK Collection, JFKL.

264. H. V. Kaltenborn, *Fifty Fabulous Years, 1900–1950* (New York: G.P. Putnam's Sons, 1950), 215; Lasky, *JFK: The Man and the Myth*, 55; Whalen, *The Founding Father*, 268; Koskoff, *Joseph P. Kennedy*, 206–7.

265. Smith, *Hostage to Fortune*, 231.

266. *New York Times*, July 18, 1943, 37; JPK to Hull, August 23, 1938, 7:00 P.M., 800 General, Dept. of State; JPK to Hull, August 23, 1939, *FRUS*, 1:342; *A Record of Events before the War, 1939*, FO 800/217/216,

82–84, PRO.

267. JPK Diary, August 25, 1939, JPK Collection, JFKL; Smith, *Hostage to Fortune*, 362.

268. JPK to Hull, August 23, 1939, *FRUS*, 1:355–56; JPK to Hull, August 23, 1939, 8:00 P.M., 800 General, Dept. of State.

269. JPK Diary, August 25, 1939, JPK Collection, JFKL; Smith, *Hostage to Fortune*, 362.

270. JPK Diary, August 31, 1939, JPK Collection, JFKL; Nasaw, *The Patriarch*, 404. The nickname was given to him by Sir Horace Wilson and was an appropriate image for Kennedy.

271. JPK to Hull, August 23, 1939, *FRUS*, 1:355–56; JPK to Hull, August 23, 1939, 8:00 P.M., 800 General, Dept. of State.

272. Kaltenborn, *Fifty Fabulous Years*, 215; Koskoff, *Joseph P. Kennedy*, 206.

273. JPK to Hull, August 24, 1939, written August 23, 10:00 P.M., 800 General, Dept. of State; Berle and Jacobs, eds., *Navigating the Rapids*, 242.

274. Berle and Jacobs, eds., *Navigating the Rapids*, 242.

275. *New York Times*, Krock's column, July 18, 1943, 37; JPK to Hull, August 24, 1939, 800 General, Dept. of State; Koskoff, *Joseph P. Kennedy*, 206–7.

276. Charles Peake, October 11–2, 1939, FO 371/22827/A7195/1090/45, 164, PRO; Koskoff, *Joseph P. Kennedy*, 206; Beschloss, *Kennedy and Roosevelt*, 195–97; Nasaw, *The Patriarch*, 418–19.

277. JPK to Welles, August 24, 1939, 800 General, Dept. of State; JPK to Welles, 11 A.M., August 24, 1939; Smith, *Hostage to Fortune*, 361; Koskoff, *Joseph P. Kennedy*, 207; Whalen, *The Founding Father*, 268.

278. JPK to Welles, August 24, 1939, 800 General, Dept. of State; Koskoff, *Joseph P. Kennedy*, 207; Whalen, *The Founding Father*, 268.

279. Hooker, *Moffat Papers*, 253; Hull, *Memoirs*, 662; Koskoff, *Joseph P. Kennedy*, 207.

280. Hooker, *Moffat Papers*, 253.

281. Berle and Jacobs, eds., *Navigating the Rapids*, 243.

282. JPK Diary, August 24, 1939, JPK Collection, JFKL; Smith, *Hostage to Fortune*, 357; Hooker, *Moffat Papers*, 253; Berle and Jacobs, eds., *Navigating the Rapids*, 243; Beschloss, *Kennedy and Roosevelt*, 189.

283. Berle and Jacobs, eds., *Navigating the Rapids*, 243.

284. Hooker, *Moffat Papers*, 253–54; Hull, *Memoirs*, 662; Berle and Jacobs, eds., *Navigating the Rapids*, 243.

285. Berle and Jacobs, eds., *Navigating the Rapids*, 243.

286. Hull, *Memoirs*, 663.

287. Berle and Jacobs, eds., *Navigating the Rapids*, 244.

288. JPK to Hull, August 25, 1939, *FRUS*, 1:369–70.

289. JPK to Hull, August 25, 1939, *FRUS*, 1:369–70; JPK to FDR, August 25, 1939, Safe: Kennedy, FDRL; JPK to Hull, August 25, 1939, 800 General, Dept. of State; JPK to Welles, Received Diplomatic Dispatch, August 24, midnight, as cited in Smith, *Hostage to Fortune*, 361.

290. Ickes, *The Secret Diary of Harold Ickes*, 2:707.

291. JPK Diary, August 24, 1939, JPK Collection, JFKL; Smith, *Hostage to Fortune*, 359–60.

292. JPK Diary, August 24, 1939, JPK Collection, JFKL; Smith, *Hostage to Fortune*, 359–60.

293. Nasaw, *The Patriarch*, 402.

294. JPK Diary, August 24, 1939, JPK Collection, JFKL; Smith, *Hostage to Fortune*, 359–60.

295. *New York Times*, July 18, 1943, 37.

296. JPK Diary, June 13, 1938, JPK Collection, JFKL; Smith, *Hostage to Fortune*, 362–63.

297. JPK to Hull, August 30, 1939, London, *FRUS*, 1:386–87; JPK to Hull, August 30, 1939, *FRUS*, 1:390–92; JPK to Hull, August 30, 1939, *FRUS*, 1:392, Dept. of State; Hull, *Memoirs*, 663.

298. Hooker, *Moffat Papers*, 256; Whalen, *The Founding Father*, 269.

299. JPK to Hull, August 30, 1939, *FRUS*, 1:392; JPK to Hull, August 30, 1939, 800 General, Dept. of State.

300. Rock, *Chamberlain and Roosevelt*, 117; Berle and Jacobs, eds., *Navigating the Rapids*, 186.

301. Hooker, *Moffat Papers*, 255.

302. JPK to Missy LeHand, August 31, 1939, JPK Papers, ser. 8.2.2., Ambassadorial Correspondence: Royal Visit to U.S. 1939, box 131, JPK Collection, JFKL.

303. JPK to Eleanor Roosevelt, August 31, 1939, FDRL; JPK to Eleanor Roosevelt, August 31, 1939, JPK Papers, ser. 5.1, Roosevelt and Politics: Correspondence 1939, box 71, JPK Collection, JFKL.

304. Eleanor Roosevelt to JPK, September 12, 1939, 100, FDRL; Eleanor Roosevelt to JPK, September 12, 1939, JPK Papers, ser. 5.1, Roosevelt and Politics: Correspondence 1939, box 71, JPK Collection, JFKL.

305. JPK to Stout, London, May 10, 1939, as cited in Smith, *Hostage to Fortune*, 335.

Chapter 7. It's the End of the World . . . The End of Everything . . .

1. "DM," chap. 33, pp. 16–17, JPK Collection, JFKL.

2. Hull, *Memoirs*, 671–72.

3. JPK Diary, September 3, 1939, JPK Collection, JFKL; Smith, *Hostage to Fortune*, 367; Whalen, *The Founding Father*, 269.

4. JPK to Hull, September 1, 1939, 4:00 P.M., *FRUS*, 1:405.

5. JPK to Hull, September 1, 1939, 4:00 P.M., *FRUS*, 1:405; JPK to Hull, September 1, 1939, 5:00 P.M., *FRUS*, 1:406; Kennedy to Hull, September 1, 1939, 8:00 P.M., *FRUS*, 1:406; JPK to Hull, September 1, 1939, 12:00 A.M., *FRUS*, 1:408; Statement by the Secretary of State for Foreign Affairs in the House of Lords, September 1, 1939, FO 800/317/1316, 87–88, PRO; JPK to Hull, September 1, 1939, 800 General, Dept. of State; JPK to Hull, September 1, 1939, Safe: Kennedy, FDRL; Lothian to Hull, September 1, 1939, PSF: Great Britain, FDRL.

6. "DM," chap. 34, p. 3, JPK Collection, JFKL.

7. Self, *Chamberlain Diary Letters*, 443–44; Self, *Neville Chamberlain*, 378–79; Roberts, *The Holy Fox*, 172–75; R. J. Overy and Andrew Wheatcroft, *Road to War* (London: Penguin, 1999), 118.

8. "DM," chap. 33, p. 18, JPK Collection, JFKL.

9. JPK to Hull, September 1, 1939, 4:00 P.M., *FRUS*, 1:405. Another explanation for France's delay was General Gamelin's desire to gain more time to complete mobilization and evacuate children since French officials believed Paris would be bombed immediately; *Sunday Times*, September 6, 1964, 1, 3; Dilks, *Cadogan Diaries*, 212; John Allsebrook Simon, *Retrospect: The Memoirs of the Rt. Hon.*

Viscount Simon (London: Hutchinson, 1952), 252; Birkenhead, *Halifax*, 447.

10. JPK to Hull, September 1, 1939, 4:00 P.M., *FRUS*, 1:405.

11. Bullitt to Hull, September 2, 1939, *FRUS*, 1:409; Overy and Wheatcroft, *The Road to War*, 118; Self, *Neville Chamberlain*, 379–80.

12. Hull, *Memoirs*, 675; see Statement by Secretary of State for Foreign Affairs in the House of Lords, September 1, 1939, FO 800/317/1316, 87–90, for a summary of the events; *A Record of Events before the War, 1939*, FO 800/317/1314, 83 (n.d.).

13. Self, *Neville Chamberlain*, 378–79; Roberts, *The Holy Fox*, 173–74.

14. Nicolson, *Diaries and Letters*, 412–13.

15. Nicolson, *Diaries and Letters*, 412–13; Birkenhead, *Halifax*, 446; Robert Rhodes James, *Churchill: A Study in Failure, 1900–1939* (New York: World Publishing, 1970), 379; Roberts, *The Holy Fox*, 173; Self, *Neville Chamberlain*, 380.

16. *New York Times*, September 3, 1939, 13; Arthur Greenwood, *House of Commons Debates, 1938–1939*, September 2, 1939, vol. 351, August 24–October 5, 282–83; "DM," chap. 33, p. 18, JPK Collection, JFKL; Smith, *Hostage to Fortune*, 365.

17. JPK Diary, September 3, 1939, JPK Collection, JFKL; Smith, *Hostage to Fortune*, 365.

18. Dilks, *Cadogan Diary*, 212; Self, *Neville Chamberlain*, 380–81; Roberts, *The Holy Fox*, 173–74; Birkenhead, *Halifax*, 446–47.

19. *Sunday Times*, September 6, 1964, 1, 3; *New York Times*, September 3, 1939, 3.

20. "DM," chap. 33, p. 19, JPK Collection, JFKL; Dilks, *Cadogan Diaries*, 212.

21. *Sunday Times*, September 6, 1939, 1, 3.

22. *Sunday Times*, September 6, 1939, 1, 3.

23. "DM," chap. 33, p. 19, JPK Collection, JFKL; *Time*, September 18, 1939, 13; Whalen, *The Founding Father*, 269.

24. Alsop and Kintner, *American White Paper*, 68; Beschloss, *Kennedy and Roosevelt*, 190; Whalen, *The Founding Father*, 270.

25. Self, *Neville Chamberlain*, 381; Nevile Henderson, *Failure of a Mission: Berlin, 1937–1939* (New York: G.P. Putnam's Sons, 1940), 298–99.

26. JPK Diary, September 3, 1939, JPK Collection, JFKL; "DM," chap. 34, p. 1, JPK Collection, JFKL; JPK Papers, ser. 8.6, Ambassador Dispatches: Outgoing 1939: September 16–20, JPK Collection, JFKL; Smith, *Hostage to Fortune*, 366; Goodwin, *The Fitzgeralds and the Kennedys*, 587.

27. *New York Times*, September 4, 1939, 8; JPK Diary, September 3, 1939, JPK Collection, JFKL; "DM," chap. 34, p. 3, JPK Collection, JFKL; Rose Kennedy, *Times to Remember*, 252; Feiling, *The Life of Neville Chamberlain*, 416; Smith, *Hostage to Fortune*, 366.

28. JPK Diary, September 3, 1939, JPK Collection, JFKL; "DM," chap. 34, pp. 1, 3, JPK Collection, JFKL; Smith, *Hostage to Fortune*, 366.

29. Self, *Neville Chamberlain*, 381.

30. JPK Diary, September 3, 1939, JPK Collection, JFKL; "DM," chap. 34, pp. 1–2, JPK Collection, JFKL; Self, *Neville Chamberlain*, 445: Chamberlain recorded in his diary: "While war was still averted, I

felt I was indispensable for no one else could carry out my policy. Today the position has changed. Half a dozen people could take my place while war is in progress and I do not see that I have any particular part to play until it comes to discussing peace terms—and that may be a long way off"; Smith, *Hostage to Fortune*, 366.

31. JPK to Hull, September 3, 1939, ser. 8.6, JPK Collection, JFKL; Smith, *Hostage to Fortune*, 367.

32. JPK Diary, September 3, 1939, JPK Collection, JFKL; Smith, *Hostage to Fortune*, 366–67; Rose F. Kennedy, ser. 1, Diaries, Undated Notes, box 7, JFKL; Self, *Neville Chamberlain*, 382.

33. JPK Diary, September 3, 1939, JPK Collection, JFKL; Smith, *Hostage to Fortune*, 366–67.

34. Draft of Press Statement by various officials connected with the investigation, September 22, 1939, October 25–26, 1939, FO 371/22841/2030, 48–55, PRO; JPK to Hull, September 4, 1939, 9:00 P.M., 848 *Athenia*, Dept. of State; "DM," chap. 34, pp. 4–7, JPK Collection, JFKL; JPK Papers, ser. 8.5, Ambassador: Subject File 1939, box 164, S.S. *Athenia*, September 5, JFKL; *New York Times*, September 4, 1939, 1; Whalen, *The Founding Father*, 272–73.

35. *New York Times*, September 4, 1939, 5.

36. JPK Papers, ser. 8.5, Ambassador: Subject File 1939, box 164, September 4, 1939, JFKL; JPK to Hull, September 4, 1939, 11:00 A.M., 848 *Athenia*, Dept. of State; Joseph P. Kennedy Jr., "September 4, 1939," as cited in Smith, *Hostage to Fortune*, 369.

37. Associated Press, *Triumph and Tragedy: The Story of the Kennedys*, 67; Whalen, *The Founding Father*, 273.

38. JPK to Hull, September 4, 1939, 11:00 A.M., #1417, 848 *Athenia*, Dept. of State.

39. JPK to Hull, September 8, 1939, ser. 8.6, JPK Collection, JFKL; Smith, *Hostage to Fortune*, 370–71.

40. Collier and Horowitz, *The Kennedys*, 102.

41. *New York Times*, September 7, 1939, 16.

42. *Time*, September 18, 1939, 15; *New York Times*, September 4, 1939, 1, 5; Churchill, *The Second War*, 1:423.

43. JPK Papers, ser. 8.5, Ambassador: Subject File 1939, box 164, JPK Collection, JFKL; Press Release, American Embassy, October 16, 1939, 848 *Athenia*, Dept. of State; Churchill, *The Second War*, 1:423; Whalen, *The Founding Father*, 273; Nasaw, *The Patriarch*, 409; "DM," chap. 34, pp. 6–7. Writing his diplomatic memoir years later, Kennedy said that the State Department had insisted upon an investigation into the matter for the purposes of insurance—a matter of damages, who is going to pay?—contrary to the wishes of Winston Churchill, the First Lord of the Admiralty, who had not ordered an investigation and presumably did not intend to do so since he already knew who was responsible for the attack: Germany. Lord Lothian, the British ambassador in Washington, said that the "evidence" showed that "the Athenia had been the victim of a German submarine," a conclusion reached despite the fact that "no 'legal' evidence existed" to support the ambassador's claim and no investigation had taken place, Kennedy pointed out. Despite Churchill's refusal to cooperate, the American authorities further pressed the British for evidence. On December 11, 1939, the Foreign Office did transmit the relevant documents to the American embassy but told officials that the Admiralty would do nothing further. Kennedy learned that Churchill "refused to issue an official

report which had been prepared by the officers of the Admiralty"; to do so would "play into the hands of the enemy." Worldwide opinion had already agreed that Germany had sunk the *Athenia*, Churchill argued. On April 6, 1940, the State Department did receive the sworn statements of eyewitnesses: "the six officers, seven crew members and three passengers," all of whom supported the Admiralty's position that the ship had been attacked "by a submarine of nationality unknown" and offered "very strong presumptive evidence" that it was German.

It was not until after the war when the Nuremburg trials were held, Kennedy wrote in his memoir, that "the mystery of the Athenia was, indeed, cleared up. . . . Admiral Raeder testified to the fact that it had been sunk by a German submarine commanded by an inexperienced officer who had acted upon his own initiative and whose action at the time had not been reported back to naval headquarters." Kennedy received a check for $5,325 ($21,513) from the owners of the *Athenia*, which he gratefully acknowledged in a public statement as "a splendid gesture" toward the cost of returning the survivors to the United States and praised "the splendid cooperation" of the British Board of Trade, with whom Kennedy negotiated the sum. Upon the recommendation of his son, the ambassador also thanked the people of Galway and Glasgow who "did everything within their power," John Kennedy said, to aid the survivors who were taken there; JPK Papers, ser. 8.5, Ambassador: Subject File 1939, box 164, JPK Collection, JFKL; Press Release, American Embassy, October 16, 1939, 848 *Athenia*, Dept. of State.

44. JPK to Hull, September 8, 1939, #1519, ser. 8.6, Ambassador Dispatches: Outgoing 1939: May 6–18, September 16–20, box 73, JPK Collection, JFKL; Smith, *Hostage to Fortune*, 370.

45. Associated Press, *Triumph and Tragedy: The Story of the Kennedys*, 67–68; *Time*, September 18, 1939, 15.

46. *Time*, September 18, 1939, 15; McCarthy, *The Remarkable Kennedys*, 82; Whalen, *The Founding Father*, 273.

47. JPK Papers, ser. 8.5, Ambassador: Subject File, 1939, box 164, JFKL; JPK to Hull, September 16, 1939, 848 *Athenia*, Dept. of State; McCarthy, *The Remarkable Kennedys*, 82; Whalen, *The Founding Father*, 273.

48. Associated Press, *Triumph and Tragedy: The Story of the Kennedys*, 65.

49. JPK Papers, ser. 8.6, Ambassador Dispatches: Outgoing: September 16–20, 1939, box 173, JPK Collection, JFKL; JPK to Hull, diplomatic dispatch #1519, September 8, 1939; Smith, *Hostage to Fortune*, 371.

50. *Time*, September 18, 1939, 13; Whalen, *The Founding Father*, 273–74; Collier and Horowitz, *The Kennedys*, 102.

51. *Time*, September 18, 1939, 13; Whalen, *The Founding Father*, 272, 274–75; Nasaw, *The Patriarch*, 409–10.

52. Whalen, *The Founding Father*, 274.

53. *Time*, September 18, 1939, 13–14; Whalen, *The Founding Father*, 274–75.

54. *Time*, September 18, 1939, 13; Whalen, *The Founding Father*, 272; Nasaw, *The Patriarch*, 409.

55. Whalen, *The Founding Father*, 272.

56. *Time*, September 18, 1939, 13; Whalen, *The Founding Father*, 272; Nasaw, *The Patriarch*, 409–10.

57. *Time*, September 18, 1939, 13; Whalen, *The Founding Father*, 274.

58. Whalen, *The Founding Father*, 272.

59. Nasaw, *The Patriarch*, 403.

60. Collier and Horowitz, *The Kennedys*, 102.

61. Smith, *Hostage to Fortune*, 379n373.

62. *Time*, September 18, 1939, 13; Goodwin, *The Fitzgeralds and the Kennedys*, 590; Collier and Horowitz, *The Kennedys*, 102; Nasaw, *The Patriarch*, 410.

63. JPK to Rose Kennedy, Wall Hall, Watford, September 18, 1939, as cited in Smith, *Hostage to Fortune*, 379–80.

64. "DM," chap. 34, p. 8, JPK Collection, JFKL; Whalen, *The Founding Father*, 274.

65. *New York Herald Tribune*, September 7, 1939, 16; "DM," chap. 34, p. 3, JPK Collection, JFKL; Associated Press, *Triumph and Tragedy: The Story of the Kennedys*, 67; Nasaw, *The Patriarch*, 409; Whalen, *The Founding Father*, 272, 274.

66. *New York Herald Tribune*, September 7, 1939, 16; JPK to Hull, September 15, 1939, 300 Evacuation, Dept. of State; "DM," chap. 34, p. 8, JPK Collection, JFKL; Smith, *Hostage to Fortune*, 370; Whalen, *The Founding Father*, 274; Nasaw, *The Patriarch*, 409.

67. "DM," chap. 34, p. 8, JPK Collection, JFKL.

68. *New York Herald Tribune*, September 7, 1939, 1, 16; Hull to JPK, September 8, 1939, 300 Evacuation, Dept. of State; Nasaw, *The Patriarch*, 410.

69. JPK to Hull, September 8, 1939, ser. 8.6, JPK Collection, JFKL; Smith, *Hostage to Fortune*, 370.

70. JPK to Morgenthau, September 7, 1939, 851 British US, Dept. of State; "DM," chap. 34, pp. 8–9, JPK Collection, JFKL; Nasaw, *The Patriarch*, 411–12.

71. JPK to Morgenthau, September 7, 1939, 851 British US, Dept. of State; Koskoff, *Joseph P. Kennedy*, 228.

72. Koskoff, *Joseph P. Kennedy*, 228: Hull suggested that he deliberately ignore Kennedy during a Cabinet meeting.

73. "DM," chap. 34, p. 9, JPK Collection, JFKL.

74. Nasaw, *The Patriarch*, 412.

75. "DM," chap. 37, pp. 1–2, JPK Collection, JFKL; Langer and Gleason, *The Challenge to Isolation*, 285.

76. Whalen, *The Founding Father*, 274.

77. Morgenthau Diary, October 18, 1939, 15, FDRL.

78. JPK to Hull, October 18, 1939, 857 Britain, Dept. of State; Morgenthau Diary, October 18, 1939, 112, FDRL.

79. JPK to FDR, September 10, 1939, box 10, PSF: Great Britain, Kennedy, FDRL; JPK to FDR, September 10, 1939, JPK Collection, JFKL; Smith, *Hostage to Fortune*, 373.

80. Nasaw, *The Patriarch*, 412.

81. "DM," chap. 39, p. 9, JPK Collection, JFKL.

82. JPK to Hull, Diplomatic Dispatch #1443, September 4, 1939, JPK Collection, JFKL; "DM," chap. 34, pp. 9–10, JPK Collection, JFKL; Smith, *Hostage to Fortune*, 368.

83. "DM," chap. 34, pp. 10–11, JPK Collection, JFKL.

84. JPK Papers, ser. 8.6, Ambassador Dispatches: Outgoing 1939: September 16–20, box 173, JPK Collection, JFKL; Smith, *Hostage to Fortune*, 375; B. Gilbert, *Britain, 1914–1945: The Aftermath of Power*, 110: Chamberlain told his sister that war would be over in the spring of 1940.

85. "DM," chap. 34, pp. 11–12, JPK Collection, JFKL.

86. JPK to Hull, September 4, 1939, Diplomatic Dispatch #1443, JPK Collection, JFKL; "DM," chap. 34, p. 10; Smith, *Hostage to Fortune*, 368.

87. JPK to Hull, September 4, 1939, Diplomatic Dispatch #1443, JPK Collection, JFKL; Smith, *Hostage to Fortune*, 368.

88. JPK to FDR, September 10, 1939, box 10, PSF: Great Britain, Kennedy, FDRL; "DM," chap. 35, pp. 3–4, JPK Collection, JFKL; JPK to FDR, September 10, 1939, as cited in Smith, *Hostage to Fortune*, 372–73.

89. JPK to FDR, September 10, 1939, box 10, PSF: Great Britain, Kennedy, FDRL; JPK to FDR, September 10, 1939, as cited in Smith, *Hostage to Fortune*, 372–74; Nasaw, *The Patriarch*, 412.

90. JPK to Hull, September 11, 1939, *FRUS*, 1:423; JPK to Hull and FDR, September 11, 1939, Diplomatic Dispatch, ser. 8.6, JPK Collection, JFKL; "DM," chap. 34, pp. 12–13, JPK Collection, JFKL; Smith, *Hostage to Fortune*, 374; Nasaw, *The Patriarch*, 412.

91. JPK to Hull and FDR, September 11, 1939, ser. 8.6, JPK Collection, JFKL; JPK to George VI, September 14, 1939, as cited in Smith, *Hostage to Fortune*, 376–77; John W. Wheeler-Bennett, *King George VI: His Life and Reign* (New York: St. Martin's Press, 1965), 420.

92. Smith, *Hostage to Fortune*, 376n361.

93. Wheeler-Bennett, *King George VI*, 420.

94. JPK to His Majesty The King, Buckingham Palace, September 14, 1939, Northwestern University Archives, Evanston, IL; Kennedy to George VI, September 14, 1939, as cited in Smith, *Hostage to Fortune*, 376–77.

95. JPK to Hull and FDR, September 11, 1939, Diplomatic Dispatch #1578, ser. 8.6, Ambassador's Dispatches: Outgoing 1939: May 8–16, September 16–20, box 173, JPK Collection, JFKL; JPK to Hull, September 11, 1939, *FRUS*, 1:421–24; JPK to FDR, September 11, 1939, FDRL; "DM," chap. 34, pp. 12–14, JPK Collection, JFKL; Smith, *Hostage to Fortune*, 374–76; Nasaw, *The Patriarch*, 413: "Kennedy's recommendation was recklessly bizarre. Roosevelt could not make peace in Europe because he had nothing of substance to offer Hitler, other than perhaps Poland, which was already within his grasp. To even get Hitler to the bargaining table, Roosevelt would have had to recognize his seizure of Austria and Czechoslovakia, which he could not possibly do without making a mockery of American pronouncements and principles. The attempt to appease Hitler would surely fail, and failure this time would be catastrophic. It would weaken Roosevelt internationally, cripple him politically a year before a presidential election, embolden Hitler to continue his aggression, offer Italy and Japan tacit assurance that the 'democracies' would eventually recognize their conquests, and represent one of the grandest double crosses in world history." Another interpretation of Kennedy's proposal, offered by Langer and Gleason, *The Challenge to Isolation*, 250, may have been that the British intended to "smoke out" Roosevelt and they succeeded.

96. Hull to JPK, September 11, 1939, #905, FDRL; "DM," chap. 34, p. 14, JPK Collection, JFKL; JPK to FDR, September 30, 1939, as cited in Smith, *Hostage to Fortune*, 382n383.

97. "DM," chap. 34, p. 15, JPK Collection, JFKL.

98. Nasaw, *The Patriarch*, 413.

99. Berle and Jacobs, eds., *Navigating the Rapids*, 256–57; Dallek, *Franklin D. Roosevelt and American Foreign Policy*, 207; Langer and Gleason, *The Challenge to Isolation*, 247; Koskoff, *Joseph P. Kennedy*, 212.

100. Berle and Jacobs, eds., *Navigating the Rapids*, 256–57; Smith, *Hostage to Fortune*, 393–94n402.

101. Langer and Gleason, *The Challenge to Isolation*, 247–48; Dallek, *Franklin D. Roosevelt and American Foreign Policy*, 207.

102. Berle and Jacobs, eds., *Navigating the Rapids*, 256–57.

103. Dallek, *Franklin D. Roosevelt and American Foreign Policy*, 207; Langer and Gleason, *The Challenge to Isolation*, 247–49.

104. Whalen, *The Founding Father*, 276; Nasaw, *The Patriarch*, 413.

105. October 30, 1939, in Franklin D. Roosevelt, *F.D.R.: His Personal Letters, 1928–1945*, 2 vols., ed. Elliott Roosevelt (New York: Duell, Sloan and Pearce, 1950), 2:949.

106. Farley, Jim Farley's Story: The Roosevelt Years, 198–99; Smith, *Hostage to Fortune*, 376n360.

107. Farley, Jim Farley's Story: The Roosevelt Years, 198–99.

108. Morgenthau Diaries, October 3, 1939, O317, FDRL; Dallek, *Franklin D. Roosevelt and American Foreign Policy*, 207.

109. FDR to Chamberlain, September 11, 1939, PSF: Great Britain, King and Queen, FDRL; JPK Diary, October 5, 1939, JPK Collection, JFKL; "DM," chap. 36, pp. 2–3, JPK Collection, JFKL; Smith, *Hostage to Fortune*, 392. According to Franklin D. Roosevelt in Francis L. Loewenheim, Harold D. Langley, and Manfred Jonas, eds., *Roosevelt and Churchill: Their Secret Wartime Correspondence* (New York: Saturday Review Press, 1975), 5, Roosevelt and Chamberlain had met once. As Woodrow Wilson's assistant secretary of the Navy, Roosevelt had been sent to London on a mission. On the evening of July 29, 1918, at Gray's Inn in London, Roosevelt attended a dinner for the War Cabinet. Churchill, as the minister of state for War and as Air minister for Prime Minister Lloyd George, also attended. Neither man was particularly impressed by the other nor made any mention of the other or of the occasion, although they diplomatically said that they "recalled" the event years later. They had no contact with each other for twenty years, but in the 1930s they began to admire each other: Churchill applauded Roosevelt's New Deal reforms; Roosevelt appreciated Churchill's role as Britain's gadfly.

110. Nasaw, *The Patriarch*, 414–15.

111. Whalen, *The Founding Father*, 281.

112. Roosevelt, Churchill, et al., *Roosevelt and Churchill: Their Secret Wartime Correspondence*, xv; Nasaw, *The Patriarch*, 414–15; Whalen, *The Founding Father*, 280–81.

113. JPK Diary, October 5, 1939, JPK Collection, JFKL; "DM," chap. 36, pp. 2–3, JPK Collection, JFKL; Smith, *Hostage to Fortune*, 392–93; Nasaw, *The Patriarch*, 415.

114. JPK Diary, September 17, 1939, JPK Collection, JFKL; "DM," chap. 35, pp. 7–8, JPK Collection, JFKL; Smith, *Hostage to Fortune*, 378.

115. JPK to Rose Kennedy, September 18, 1939, as cited in Smith, *Hostage to Fortune*, 380.

116. JPK to FDR, September 30, 1939, box 10, PSF: Kennedy, FDRL; JPK to FDR, September 30, 1939, as cited in Smith, *Hostage to Fortune*, 386; Goodwin, *The Fitzgeralds and the Kennedys*, 593.

117. Overy and Wheatcroft, *The Road to War*, 365.

118. "DM," chap. 35, p. 12, JPK Collection, JFKL.

119. "DM," chap. 35, p. 22, JPK Collection, JFKL.

120. JPK to Hull and FDR, September 11, 1939, ser. 8.6, Ambassador Dispatches: Outgoing 1939: May 8–16, September 16–20, box 173, JPK Collection, JFKL; JPK to Hull, September 11, 1939, #1578, FDRL; JPK to Hull, September 11, 1939, *FRUS*, 1:423; Smith, *Hostage to Fortune*, 375.

121. JPK to FDR, September 30, 1939, box 10, PSF: Kennedy, FDRL; JPK to FDR, September 30, 1939, as cited in Smith, *Hostage to Fortune*, 383–84.

122. Chamberlain to FDR, October 4, 1939, PSF: Great Britain, King and Queen, FDRL.

123. Overy and Wheatcroft, *The Road to War*, 362; Gilbert, *Britain, 1914–1945*, 109.

124. JPK to FDR, September 30, 1939, box 10, PSF: Kennedy, FDRL; JPK to FDR, September 30, 1939, as cited in Smith, *Hostage to Fortune*, 383.

125. JPK to FDR, September 30, 1939, box 10, PSF: Kennedy, FDRL; JPK to FDR, September 30, 1939, as cited in Smith, *Hostage to Fortune*, 383.

126. Johnson to Hull, September 22, 1939, 711 Dept. of State.

127. JPK to Hull and FDR, September 11, 1939, ser. 8.6, JPK Collection, JFKL; Smith, *Hostage to Fortune*, 376n361. See Johnson to Hull, September 22, 1939, 711, Dept. of State, for a summary of Britain's war aims.

128. JPK to FDR, September 30, 1939, box 10, PSF: Kennedy, FDRL; JPK to FDR, September 30, 1939, as cited in Smith, *Hostage to Fortune*, 383.

129. JPK to FDR, September 30, 1939, box 10, PSF: Kennedy, FDRL; JPK to FDR, September 30, 1939, as cited in Smith, *Hostage to Fortune*, 383; Rock, *Chamberlain and Roosevelt*, 219, 236.

130. Hooker, *The Moffat Papers*, 298; Koskoff, *Joseph P. Kennedy*, 243.

131. JPK to FDR, September 30, 1939, box 10, PSF: Kennedy, FDRL; JPK to FDR, September 30, 1939, as cited in Smith, *Hostage to Fortune*, 385.

132. JPK to FDR, September 30, 1939, box 10, PSF: Kennedy, FDRL; JPK to FDR, September 30, 1939, as cited in Smith, *Hostage to Fortune*, 385–86.

133. Overy and Wheatcroft, *The Road to War*, 365.

134. Cadogan to Peake, October 12, 1939, FO 371/22827/A7195, 164, PRO; Wheeler-Bennett, *King George VI*, 419–20; Rock, *Chamberlain and Roosevelt*, 236.

135. JPK to FDR, September 30, 1939, box 10, PSF: Kennedy, FDRL; JPK to FDR, September 30, 1939, as cited in Smith, *Hostage to Fortune*, 383.

136. JPK to FDR, September 30, 1939, box 10, PSF: Kennedy, FDRL; JPK to FDR, September 30, 1939, as cited in Smith, *Hostage to Fortune*, 385.

137. Wheeler-Bennett, *King George VI*, 419–20.

138. Overy and Wheatcroft, *The Road to War*, 362–63.

139. JPK to FDR, September 30, 1939, box 10, PSF: Kennedy, FDRL; JPK to FDR, September 30, 1939, as cited in Smith, *Hostage to Fortune*, 383.

140. JPK to Joseph P. Kennedy Jr. and John F. Kennedy, October 13, 1939, ser. 1.1, JPK Collection, JFKL; Smith, *Hostage to Fortune*, 395.

141. JPK to FDR, September 30, 1939, box 10, PSF: FDRL; JPK to FDR, September 30, 1939, as cited in Smith, *Hostage to Fortune*, 383–84.

142. JPK to FDR, September 30, 1939, box 10, PSF: Kennedy, FDRL; JPK to FDR, September 30, 1939, as cited in Smith, *Hostage to Fortune*, 385.

143. JPK to Hull, September 30, 1939, 851 Britain, Dept. of State; JPK to FDR, September 30, 1939, as cited in Smith, *Hostage to Fortune*, 382.

144. JPK to Hull, September 30, 1939, #1873, 851 Britain, Dept. of State; JPK Diary, September 27, 1939, JPK Collection, JFKL; Morgenthau Diaries, Telegram #1873, September 30, 1939, FDRL; "DM," chap. 35, p. 14, JPK Collection, JFKL; "DM," chap. 37, p. 6, JPK Collection, JFKL; JPK to FDR, September 30, 1939, as cited in Smith, *Hostage to Fortune*, 382.

145. Overy and Wheatcroft, *The Road to War*, 334.

146. JPK to FDR, September 30, 1939, box 10, PSF: Kennedy, FDRL; JPK to Hull, September 30, 1939, Telegram #1873, 851 Britain, Dept. of State; Morgenthau Diaries, Telegram #1873, September 30, 1939, FDRL; "DM," chap. 35, p. 14, JPK Collection, JFKL; JPK Diary, September 27, 1939, JPK Collection, JFKL; JPK to FDR, September 30, 1939, as cited in Smith, *Hostage to Fortune*, 382.

147. JPK to FDR, September 30, 1939, box 10, PSF: Kennedy, FDRL; JPK to FDR, September 30, 1939, as cited in Smith, *Hostage to Fortune*, 386.

148. Overy and Wheatcroft, *The Road to War*, 358.

149. JPK to FDR, September 30, 1939, box 10, PSF: Kennedy, FDRL; JPK to FDR, September 30, 1939, as cited in Smith, *Hostage to Fortune*, 385–86.

150. FDR to JPK, October 30, 1939, box 10, PSF: Kennedy, FDRL; Roosevelt, *F.D.R.: His Personal Letters, 1928–1945*, 2:949.

151. FDR to JPK, October 30, 1939, box 10, PSF: Kennedy, FDRL; Roosevelt, *F.D.R.: His Personal Letters, 1928–1945*, 2:949–50.

152. JPK to FDR, September 30, 1939, box 10, PSF: Kennedy, FDRL; JPK to FDR, September 30, 1939, as cited in Smith, *Hostage to Fortune*, 386.

153. JPK to FDR, September 30, 1939, box 10, PSF: Kennedy, FDRL; JPK Diary, September 27, 1939, JPK Collection, JFKL; JPK to FDR, September 30, 1939, as cited in Smith, *Hostage to Fortune*, 384.

154. JPK Diary, November 8, 1939, JPK Collection, JFKL; Smith, *Hostage to Fortune*, 399; Dallek, *Franklin D. Roosevelt and American Foreign Policy*, 201.

155. JPK to FDR, September 30, 1939, box 10, PSF: Kennedy, FDRL; JPK to FDR, September 30, 1939, as cited in Smith, *Hostage to Fortune*, 386.

156. JPK to FDR, September 30, 1939, box 10, PSF: Kennedy, FDRL; JPK Diary, September 27, 1939, JPK

Collection, JFKL; "DM," chap. 35, p. 19, JPK Collection, JFKL; JPK to FDR, September 30, 1939, as cited in Smith, *Hostage to Fortune*, 384.

157. JPK to FDR, November 3, 1939, box 44, PSF: Kennedy, FDRL; JPK to FDR, November 3, 1939, as cited in Smith, *Hostage to Fortune*, 398.

158. Wheeler-Bennett, *King George VI*, 419–20, Whalen, *The Founding Father*, 277; Gilbert and Craig, eds., *The Diplomats: 1919–1939*, 665.

159. JPK to FDR, September 30, 1939, box 10, PSF: Kennedy, FDRL; JPK to FDR, September 30, 1939, as cited in Smith, *Hostage to Fortune*, 384; Gilbert and Craig, eds., *The Diplomats: 1919–1939*, 670.

160. Illegible author of memo to Cadogan, September 19, 1939, FO 371/22835/A6531, 192, PRO; J. V. Perowne, September 20, 1939, FO 371/228/6561/1090/45, 157, PRO; Unsigned memo, October 19, 1940, FO 371/24251/A4483/605/45, PRO; Gilbert and Craig, eds., *The Diplomats: 1919–1939*, 666–67; Rock, *Chamberlain and Roosevelt*, 217.

161. Gilbert and Craig, eds., *The Diplomats: 1919–1939*, 670.

162. JPK to Rose Kennedy, October 11, 1939, as cited in Smith, *Hostage to Fortune*, 393–94n402.

163. "DM," chap. 37, p. 8, JPK Collection, JFKL; Nasaw, *The Patriarch*, 420.

164. JPK to Rose Kennedy, October 11, 1939, as cited in Smith, *Hostage to Fortune*, 393–94.

165. Roosevelt, *F.D.R.: His Personal Letters, 1928–1945*, 2:950.

166. Dallek, *Franklin D. Roosevelt and American Foreign Policy*, 199, 201–2.

167. JPK to FDR, September 10, 1939, box 10, PSF: Great Britain, Kennedy, FDRL; "DM," chap. 35, pp. 3–4, JPK Collection, JFKL; JPK to FDR, September 10, 1939, as cited in Smith, *Hostage to Fortune*, 372.

168. Hull, *Memoirs*, 693; "DM," chap. 35, pp. 5–6, JPK Collection, JFKL.

169. JPK Diary, September 15, 1939, JPK Collection, JFKL; "DM," chap. 35, p. 6, JPK Collection, JFKL; Smith, *Hostage to Fortune*, 378.

170. JPK to Rose Kennedy, September 18, 1939, as cited in Smith, *Hostage to Fortune*, 380.

171. Kennedy to George VI, September 14, 1939, as cited in Smith, *Hostage to Fortune*, 377.

172. Gage, September 20, 1939, FO 371/22827/A6561/1090/45, 156, PRO.

173. JPK to Hull, October 2, 1939, Diplomatic Dispatch #1893, as cited in Smith, *Hostage to Fortune*, 390.

174. Roosevelt, *F.D.R.: His Personal Letters, 1928–1945*, 2:919; Dallek, *Franklin D. Roosevelt and American Foreign Policy*, 202.

175. Dallek, *Franklin D. Roosevelt and American Foreign Policy*, 202; Michael J. Lyons, *World War II: A Short History*, 2nd ed. (Englewood Cliffs, NJ: Prentice Hall, 1994), 139.

176. Dallek, *Franklin D. Roosevelt and American Foreign Policy*, 202.

177. JPK Diary, November 8, 1939, JPK Collection, JFKL; "DM," chap. 37, p. 9, JPK Collection, JFKL; Smith, *Hostage to Fortune*, 399.

178. Gage, September 20, 1939, FO 371/22827/A6561/1090/45, 157, 160, PRO; Rock, *Chamberlain and Roosevelt*, 217, 236; Dilks, *Cadogan Diary*, 215.

179. Peake to Cadogan, October 12, 1939, FO 371/22827/A7195, 164, PRO; Beschloss, *Kennedy and Roosevelt*, 195–97; Nasaw, *The Patriarch*, 418–19.

180. Gage, September 20, 1939, FO 371/22827/A6561/1090/45, 154–55, PRO; Beschloss, *Kennedy and*

Roosevelt, 195–97.

181. Gage, September 20, 1939, FO 371/22827/A6561/1090/45, 154–55, PRO; Beschloss, *Kennedy and Roosevelt*, 195–97; Rock, *Chamberlain and Roosevelt*, 218.

182. Gage, September 20, 1939, FO 371/22827/A6561/1090/45, 153–58, PRO; Beschloss, *Kennedy and Roosevelt*, 195–97; Rock, *Chamberlain and Roosevelt*, 218; Nasaw, *The Patriarch*, 417–19.

183. Lothian, October 3, 1939, FO 371/22827/A6561/1090/45, 162, PRO; Nasaw, *The Patriarch*, 417–19.

184. Gage, September 20, 1939, FO 371/22827/A6561/1090/45, 153–58, PRO.

185. Foreign Office Minutes, September 20, 1939, FO 371/22827/A6561/1090/45, 154–61, PRO; Beschloss, *Kennedy and Roosevelt*, 195–97; Rock, *Chamberlain and Roosevelt*, 218; Nasaw, *The Patriarch*, 418.

186. Whalen, *The Founding Father*, 279.

187. Whalen, *The Founding Father*, 279.

188. Nigel Nicolson, ed., *Harold Nicolson Diaries and Letters*, 396; Whalen, *The Founding Father*, 279–80.

189. Whalen, *The Founding Father*, 280.

190. Nigel Nicolson, *Harold Nicolson Diaries and Letters*, 396.

191. M. Gilbert, *Churchill*, 425–28; Whalen, *The Founding Father*, 231.

192. JPK Diary, October 5, 1939, JPK Collection, JFKL; Smith, *Hostage to Fortune*, 393.

193. JPK to FDR, November 3, 1939, box 10, PSF: box 44, JPK to FDR, FDRL; JPK to FDR, November 3, 1939, as cited in Smith, *Hostage to Fortune*, 398. Although he does not say who the "close friends" were, they may well have been Walter Lippmann and Bernard Baruch.

194. JPK to Rose Kennedy, October 2, 1939, as cited in Smith, *Hostage to Fortune*, 391.

195. JPK Diary, November 8, 1939, JPK Collection, JFKL; "DM," chap. 37, p. 10, JPK Collection, JFKL; Smith, *Hostage to Fortune*, 399.

196. Smith, *Hostage to Fortune*, 394n402.

197. "DM," chap. 37, pp. 8–9, JPK Collection, JFKL.

198. JPK to Hull, October 2, 1939, Diplomatic Dispatch #1893, as cited in Smith, *Hostage to Fortune*, 390; Whalen, *The Founding Father*, 280.

199. Whalen, *The Founding Father*, 275.

200. JPK to Will Hays, telegram, November 12, 1939, JPK Personal Papers, ser. 8.2.2, Ambassador: Correspondence Subject File, "Mr. Smith Goes to Washington," box 128, JPK Collection, JFKL; Smith, *Hostage to Fortune*, 400, 412–14n.

201. JPK to Will Hays, telegram, November 12, 1939, JPK Personal Papers, ser. 8.2.2, Ambassador: Correspondence Subject File, "Mr. Smith Goes to Washington," box 128, JPK Collection, JFKL; JPK to Harry Cohn, November 17, 1939, box 10, PSF: FDRL; JPK to Cohn, London, November 17, 1939, as cited in Smith, *Hostage to Fortune*, 400–401.

202. Frank Capra and Cohn to JPK, November 13, 1939, JPK Papers, ser. 8.2.2, Ambassador: Correspondence Subject File, "Mr. Smith Goes to Washington," box 128, JPK Collection, JFKL; JPK to Cohn, November 17, 1939, box 10, PSF: FDRL; JPK to Cohn, November 17, 1939, as cited in Smith, *Hostage to Fortune*, 400–401; Whalen, *The Founding Father*, 281.

203. Whalen, *The Founding Father*, 281.

204. Awardsdatabase.oscars.org.

205. JPK to Rose Kennedy, October 2, 1939, as cited in Smith, *Hostage to Fortune*, 391–92; Rose Kennedy, *Times to Remember*, 258.

206. JPK to Rose Kennedy, October 11, 1939, as cited in Smith, *Hostage to Fortune*, 394.

207. Kennedy to Rose Kennedy, October 2, 1939, as cited in Smith, *Hostage to Fortune*, 391–92.

208. JPK to Rose Kennedy, October 11, 1939, as cited in Smith, *Hostage to Fortune*, 393.

209. Rose Kennedy, *Times to Remember*, 255; Nasaw, *The Patriarch*, 422–23.

210. "DM," chap. 37, p. 6, JPK Collection, JFKL.

211. Gordon Jackson, "Early Modern European Seaport Studies: Highlights and Guidelines," in *European Seaport Systems in the Early Modern Age: A Comparative Approach: International Workshop Proceedings*, ed. Amélia Polónia and Helena Osswald, 8–26 (Porto: IHM-UP, 2007).

212. "DM," chap. 37, p. 1, JPK Collection, JFKL.

213. "DM," chap. 37, pp. 3–5, JPK Collection, JFKL.

214. JPK to Fisher, October 23, 1939, as cited in Smith, *Hostage to Fortune*, 396.

215. JPK Diary, December 10, 1939, JPK Collection, JFKL; "DM," chap. 37, p. 13, JPK Collection, JFKL; Smith, *Hostage to Fortune*, 404n424.

216. *New York Times*, November 24, 1939, 3; Whalen, *The Founding Father*, 282.

217. Whalen, *The Founding Father*, 282.

218. *New York Times*, May 18, 1947, sec. 3, p. 1; Whalen, *The Founding Father*, 282.

219. Whalen, *The Founding Father*, 282.

220. JPK to FDR, September 30, 1939, FDRL; JPK to FDR, September 30, 1939, as cited in Smith, *Hostage to Fortune*, 387–89.

221. *New York Times*, November 23, 1939, 7; *New York Times*, November 24, 1938, 3.

222. Whalen, *The Founding Father*, 282.

223. *New York Times*, November 24, 1939, 3; Hull to JPK, November 18, 1939, 123 Kennedy, Joseph P./ 255, Dept. of State.

224. *New York Times*, November 24, 1939, 3; *New York Times*, November 25, 1939, 2; JPK Diary, n.d., November 1939, JPK Collection, JFKL.

225. Whalen, *The Founding Father*, 282. Whalen does not say who the caller was.

226. "DM," chap. 37, pp. 15–16, JPK Collection, JFKL; JPK Diary, November 28, 1939, JPK Collection, JFKL; Smith, *Hostage to Fortune*, 402–3.

227. JPK Diary, November 28, 1939, JPK Collection, JFKL; Smith, *Hostage to Fortune*, 403–5. However, "DM," chap. 37, pp. 17–18; Nasaw, *The Patriarch*, 428; Beschloss, *Kennedy and Roosevelt*, 199, all say that the message was, if Roosevelt agreed, "MY WIFE CANNOT EXPRESS AN OPINION."

228. "DM," chap. 37, pp. 17–18, 22, 37, JPK Collection, JFKL; JPK Diary, November 28, 1939, JPK Collection, JFKL; Smith, *Hostage to Fortune*, 403. Churchill predicted that the future lay with England, the United States, Russia, and Japan. Kennedy remarked: "He may be right but that is certainly not the line-up today."

229. "DM," chap. 37, p. 21, JPK Collection, JFKL; JPK Diary, September 27, 1939, JPK Collection, JFKL.

230. "DM," chap. 37, pp. 18–20, JPK Collection, JFKL; JPK Diary, November 30, 1939, JPK Collection, JFKL.

231. Bilainkin, *Diary of a Diplomatic Correspondent*, 61.

232. *New York Times*, December 7, 1939, 3.

Chapter 8. This Is Not Our Fight

1. Burns, *Roosevelt: The Lion and the Fox*, 408.

2. Whalen, *The Founding Father*, 281.

3. *Philadelphia Inquirer*, December 7, 1939, 3, as cited in Koskoff, *Joseph P. Kennedy*, 230.

4. "DM," chap. 38, p. 4, JPK Collection, JFKL.

5. *Daily Telegraph and Morning Post*, December 7, 1939; *Times* (London), December 10, 1939, FO 371/22827, 168, PRO.

6. Interview in New York on October 24, 1962, as cited in Whalen, *The Founding Father*, 283. The Irishman Kennedy spoke to is not named.

7. *New York Times*, December 9, 1939, 1, 3; "DM," chap. 38, pp. 3–4, JPK Collection, JFKL; Whalen, *The Founding Father*, 284.

8. *New York Times*, December 12, 1939, 26; Ickes Diary, December 10, 1939, reel 3992, Library of Congress. Harold Ickes was quite surprised at Kennedy's endorsement of Roosevelt for a third term.

9. *New York Times*, December 13, 1938, 24.

10. *New York Times*, December 9, 1939, 3; "DM," chap. 38, p. 5, JPK Collection, JFKL; Nasaw, *The Patriarch*, 429.

11. JPK Diary, December 10, 1939, JPK Collection, JFKL; "DM," chap. 38, pp. 4–5, JPK Collection, JFKL; Smith, *Hostage to Fortune*, 404.

12. JPK Diary, November 28, 1939, JPK Collection, JFKL; JPK Diary, December 10, 1939, JPK Collection, JFKL; "DM," chap. 38, pp. 4–5, JPK Collection, JFKL; Smith, *Hostage to Fortune*, 403–5. However, Nasaw, *The Patriarch*, 428, and Beschloss, *Kennedy and Roosevelt*, 199, say that the message was "MY WIFE CANNOT EXPRESS AN OPINION."

13. JPK Diary, December 10, 1939, JPK Collection, JFKL; "DM," chap. 38, p. 5, JPK Collection, JFKL; Smith, *Hostage to Fortune*, 404–5.

14. JPK Diary, December 10, 1939, JPK Collection, JFKL; "DM," chap. 38, p. 6, JPK Collection, JFKL; Smith, *Hostage to Fortune*, 405.

15. Nasaw, *The Patriarch*, 429.

16. JPK Diary, December 10, 1939, JPK Collection, JFKL; "DM," chap. 38, p. 7, JPK Collection, JFKL; Smith, *Hostage to Fortune*, 405.

17. JPK Diary, March 28, 1940, JPK Collection, JFKL; "DM," chap. 38, p. 10, JPK Collection, JFKL; Smith, *Hostage to Fortune*, 411.

18. JPK Diary, December 10, 1939, JPK Collection, JFKL; "DM," chap. 38, pp. 7–9, and chap. 39, p. 9, JPK Collection, JFKL; Smith, *Hostage to Fortune*, 405–6; Beschloss, *Kennedy and Roosevelt*, 199–200.

19. JPK Diary, December 10, 1939, March 28, 1940, JPK Collection, JFKL; "DM," chap. 38, pp. 9–10, JPK Collection, JFKL; Smith, *Hostage to Fortune*, 404–6, 411; Beschloss, *Kennedy and Roosevelt*, 200.

20. "DM," chap. 38, p. 10, JPK Collection, JFKL.

21. Ickes, *The Secret Diary of Harold Ickes*, 3:85.

22. *New York Times*, December 9, 1939, 1, 3.

23. *New York Times*, December 12, 1939, 2, 8; *Times*, December 11, 1939, 8, 12, and December 12, 1939, 8; *Daily Telegraph*, December 7, 1939; *Morning Post*, December 7, 1939; Foreign Office Minutes, December 13–15, 1939, FO 371/22827/A8763, PRO; "DM," chap. 38, p. 10, JPK Collection, JFKL; Whalen, *The Founding Father*, 285.

24. Whalen, *The Founding Father*, 285.

25. *New York Herald Tribune*, December 16, 1938, 8; "DM," chap. 38, p. 11, JPK Collection, JFKL.

26. "DM," chap. 38, pp. 11–12, JPK Collection, JFKL.

27. Foreign Office Minutes, December 13–15, 1939, FO 371/22827/A8763/1091/45, PRO.

28. Report of Ambassador Kennedy to a group of Army and Navy officers, December 15, 1939, *Morgenthau Diaries*, vol. 230: 3 ff.; *Moffat Diary*, December 8, 15, 1939, as cited in Langer and Gleason, *The Challenge to Isolation*, 1:345.

29. JPK to FDR, January 18, 1940, PSF: box 10, FDRL; JPK Diary, December 10, 1939, JPK Collection, JFKL; "DM," chap. 38, p. 12, JPK Collection, JFKL; Smith, *Hostage to Fortune*, 404; Beschloss, *Kennedy and Roosevelt*, 201; Nasaw, *The Patriarch*, 431: "the doctors could find nothing organically the matter with his stomach but wanted him to have another set of tests." Dr. Sara Jordan, Kennedy's gastroenterologist, told the president that Kennedy had "an acute phase" of "chronic gastritis."

30. "DM," chap. 38, pp. 15–16, JPK Collection, JFKL.

31. "DM," chap. 39, p. 14, JPK Collection, JFKL.

32. *New York Times*, February 14, 1940, 13; "DM," chap. 39, p. 17, JPK Collection, JFKL. According to his memoir, Kennedy actually sailed on the *Manhattan* in February. The *Boston Daily Globe*, February 13, 1940, 1, confirms that.

33. *Boston Evening Globe*, February 13, 1940, 1, disputes the issue of Kennedy's consent. "The Ambassador to Great Britain, it is understood, gave his consent to the filing of a state pledged to his candidacy from Washington."

34. *Boston Evening Globe*, February 13, 1940, 1; Koskoff, *Joseph P. Kennedy*, 236.

35. "DM," chap. 39, pp. 9–10, JPK Collection, JFKL; *Boston Daily Globe*, February 14, 1940, 1.

36. *New York Times*, February 14, 1940, 13; *Times*, February 14, 1940, 7; *Boston Daily Globe*, February 14, 1940, 10.

37. Koskoff, *Joseph P. Kennedy*, 236.

38. *New York Times*, February 14, 1940, 13; *Boston Daily Globe*, February 14, 1940, 10; Koskoff, *Joseph P. Kennedy*, 237.

39. "DM," chap. 39, p. 10; Jim Farley, *Jim Farley's Story*, 264; Whalen, *The Founding Father*, 285–86.

40. The Destroyer Deal, concluded in September 1940 between the United States and Great Britain, traded destroyers to the Royal Navy with ninety-nine-year leases on bases in the Caribbean. These included islands such as the East Bahamas, South Jamaica, West St. Lucia, West Trinidad, Bermuda, and British Guiana. Could these bases have been a consideration in the Destroyer Deal?

41. "DM," chap. 39, pp. 14–16, JPK Collection, JFKL.

42. *Boston Daily Globe*, February 13, 1940, 1, and February 14, 1940, 10.

43. Breckinridge Long and Fred L. Israel, *The War Diary of Breckinridge Long: Selections from the Years 1939–1944* (Lincoln: University of Nebraska Press, 1966), 59.

44. FDR to Churchill, February 1, 1940, PSF: Great Britain, FDRL.

45. Bilainkin, *Diary of a Diplomatic Correspondent*, 61.

46. "DM," chap. 39, pp. 10–11, JPK Collection, JFKL.

47. *New York Times*, February 13, 1940, 10; Craig and Gilbert, eds., *The Diplomats, 1919–39*, 670–74.

48. "DM," chap. 39, pp. 10–11, JPK Collection, JFKL.

49. Langer and Gleason, *The Challenge to Isolation*, 1:345.

50. "DM," chap. 39, pp. 11–12, JPK Collection, JFKL.

51. JPK to Rose Kennedy, September 18, 1939, as cited in Smith, *Hostage to Fortune*, 380; Beschloss, *Kennedy and Roosevelt*, 204.

52. Ickes, *The Secret Diary of Harold Ickes*, 3:147.

53. Whalen, *The Founding Father*, 286.

54. Ickes, *The Secret Diary of Harold Ickes*, 3:147; Whalen, *The Founding Father*, 286.

55. Whalen, *The Founding Father*, 286.

56. Morgenthau Diaries, 218:17–18, FDRL; Blum, *From the Morgenthau Diaries*, 2:104.

57. Blum, *From the Morgenthau Diaries*, 2:106.

58. Morgenthau Diaries, 0390, FDRL; Blum, *From the Morgenthau Diaries*, 2:106–7.

59. Morgenthau Diaries, 123, FDRL; Nasaw, *The Patriarch*, 437.

60. Morgenthau Diaries, 129, FDRL; Nasaw, *The Patriarch*, 437–38: "The reality that no one in London or Washington would have believed was that Kennedy had virtually stopped trading stocks when he'd entered government service, first, because the rules he had written at the SEC made selling short much more difficult, and second, because he knew that there were spies everywhere looking to brand him as an unscrupulous, unpatriotic stock swindler. He wasn't going to give them the chance to do so."

61. Blum, *From the Morgenthau Diaries*, 2:107.

62. Blum, *From the Morgenthau Diaries*, 2:109.

63. Foreign Office Minutes, January 18, 1940, FO 371/24251/A605/604/45, PRO; Rock, *Chamberlain and Roosevelt*, 276; Koskoff, *Joseph P. Kennedy*, 233.

64. Foreign Office Minutes, January 25, 1940, FO 371/24251/A605/604/45, 54–57, PRO; Rock, *Chamberlain and Roosevelt*, 276; Koskoff, *Joseph P. Kennedy*, 233.

65. Foreign Office Minutes, March 2, 1940, FO 371/24251/A1945/86, PRO; Koskoff, *Joseph P. Kennedy*, 239; Rock, *Chamberlain and Roosevelt*, 276–77.

66. Foreign Office Minutes, March 3–4, 1940, FO 371/24251, 85–86, PRO; Warner to Balfour, March 3, 1940, FO 371/24251, PRO; Foreign Office Minutes, March 6–9, 1940, FO 371/24251, 65–66, PRO, as cited in Rock, *Chamberlain and Roosevelt*, 277; William Shakespeare, *The Complete Works*, ed. Alfred Harbage (New York: Viking, 1969), *Hamlet, Prince of Denmark*, ed. William Farnham, act 4,

scene 4, 961, this edition.

67. Nigel Nicolson, ed., *Harold Nicolson Diaries and Letters*, 1930–39, 2:60; Nasaw, *The Patriarch*, 431.

68. Vansittart, Foreign Office Minutes, January 18, 1940, FO 371/24251/A605/604/45, PRO; Nasaw, *The Patriarch*, 431; Koskoff, *Joseph P. Kennedy*, 239; Rock, *Chamberlain and Roosevelt*, 276.

69. Vansittart, Foreign Office Minutes, January 25, 1940, FO 371/24251/A605/604/45, PRO; Rock, *Chamberlain and Roosevelt*, 276.

70. Whitehead, Foreign Office Minutes, January 25, 1940, FO 371/24251/A605/604/45, PRO; Rock, *Chamberlain and Roosevelt*, 277; Nasaw, *The Patriarch*, 431.

71. Foreign Office Minutes, March 6, 1940, FO 371/24251/A1723/605/45, 62, PRO, as cited in Rock, *Chamberlain and Roosevelt*, 277; as cited in Koskoff, *Joseph P. Kennedy*, 239.

72. Foreign Office Minutes, March 3, 1940, FO 371/24251/A1723/605/45, as cited in Koskoff, *Joseph P. Kennedy*, 239.

73. Foreign Office Minutes, March 18, 1940, FO 371/24251/A1945/605/45, as cited in Koskoff, *Joseph P. Kennedy*, 239n10. Koskoff wrote that Cadogan's message was so secret as to have been omitted from the minutes, but copies of responses have been received from other responses and are contained in the Foreign Office files.

74. Foreign Office Minutes, February 14, 1940, FO 371/24251/A1384/605/45, 6, PRO; Foreign Office Minutes, January 18, 1940, FO 371/24251/A605/604/45; Rock, *Chamberlain and Roosevelt*, 276.

75. *The Spectator*, March 8, 1940, 327.

76. JPK Diary, March 28, 1940, JPK Collection, JFKL; Smith, *Hostage to Fortune*, 411.

77. Sumner Welles, *The Time for Decision* (New York: Harper and Bros., 1944), 73.

78. JPK to Hull and FDR, September 11, 1939, #1578, *Joseph P. Kennedy*, ser. 8.6, Ambassador Dispatches: Outgoing 1939: September 1939, September 16–20, 1939, box 173, JPK Collection, JFKL; JPK to Hull, #1578, September 11, 1939, FDRL; JPK to FDR, September 30, 1939, as cited in Smith, *Hostage to Fortune*, 382n383.

79. "DM," chap. 34, pp. 12–14, JPK Collection, JFKL; JPK to FDR, November 3, 1939, PSF: box 44, FDRL; JPK to FDR, November 3, 1939, as cited in Smith, *Hostage to Fortune*, 398.

80. Dallek, *Franklin D. Roosevelt and American Foreign Policy, 1932–1945*, 216–17.

81. *The Economist* 138, no. 5034 (February 17, 1940): 281–82.

82. Welles, *The Time for Decision*, 77.

83. "DM," chap. 39, p. 13, JPK Collection, JFKL.

84. "DM," chap. 39, pp. 12–13, JPK Collection, JFKL.

85. "DM," chap. 40, pp. 2–3, JPK Collection, JFKL.

86. Robert Murphy, *Diplomat among Warriors* (New York: Doubleday, 1964), 38.

87. "DM," chap. 40, p. 5, JPK Collection, JFKL; JPK to Rose Kennedy, March 14, 1940, JPK Collection, JFKL; Smith, *Hostage to Fortune*, 406–8; Nasaw, *The Patriarch*, 432–33.

88. *New York Times*, March 8, 1940, 8; JPK to FDR, March 14, 1940, ser. 1.1, Family: Correspondence, 1940, box 2, JPK Collection, JFKL; Press Release, JPK Papers, ser. 8.2.2, Ambassador: Correspondence, Newspaper and Miscellaneous Publications 1940, box 129, JPK Collection, JFKL; Smith, *Hostage to*

Fortune, 408n445.

89. JPK to FDR, March 14, 1940, ser. 1.1, Family: Correspondence, 1940, box 2, JPK Collection, JFKL; Smith, *Hostage to Fortune*, 408.

90. *Sunday Graphic*, Foreign Office Minutes, March 13, 1940, FO 371/24238/A1940/151/45, PRO; Whalen, *The Founding Father*, 287.

91. "DM," chap. 40, pp. 6–7, JPK Collection, JFKL.

92. Dilks, *The Diaries of Sir Alexander Cadogan, 1938–1945*, 250.

93. J. V. Perowne, Foreign Office Minutes, January 18, 1940, FO 371/24251/A605/604/45, PRO; Scott, Foreign Office Minutes, February 7, 1940, FO 371/24238/A1309/131/45, PRO, as cited in Koskoff, *Joseph P. Kennedy*, 243n35, 549; Foreign Office Minutes, March 3, 1940, FO 71/24251, NAUK.

94. Scott minute, Foreign Office Minutes, February 5, 1940, FO 371/24238/A1309/131/45, PRO; Koskoff, *Joseph P. Kennedy*, 243n36, 549, has it cited as a Vansittart minute.

95. Vansittart, Foreign Office Minutes, February 9, 1940, FO 371/24238/A1309/131/45, PRO; Koskoff, *Joseph P. Kennedy*, 243; Rock, *Chamberlain and Roosevelt*, 266.

96. Hooker, *Moffat Papers*, 298.

97. "DM," chap. 40, pp. 12–13, JPK Collection, JFKL.

98. Sir Samuel Hoare to Lord Lothian, February 13, 1940, *Templewood Papers*, Cambridge University Library, Cambridge, England.

99. JPK Diary, March 11, 1940, JPK Collection, JFKL; "DM," chap. 40, p. 22, JPK Collection, JFKL. Nasaw, *The Patriarch*, 434, writes that Kennedy did not tell Rose about the snub. In his diary Kennedy wrote that he believed it was intentional. Halifax's secretary said that Kennedy was deliberately left out.

100. Hooker, *The Moffat Papers*, 297.

101. "DM," chap. 40, p. 16, JPK Collection, JFKL.

102. JPK Diary, March 10, 1940, JPK Collection, JFKL; "DM," chap. 40, p. 15, JPK Collection, JFKL.

103. Welles, *The Time for Decision*, 130–34, describes his trip to London and his reactions to the people he met.

104. JPK to Rose Kennedy, March 14, 1940, ser. 1.1, Family: Correspondence, 1940, box 2, JPK Collection, JFKL; Smith, *Hostage to Fortune*, 408.

105. JPK Diary, March 11, 1940, 3, JPK Collection, JFKL; "DM," chap. 40, pp. 25–27, JPK Collection, JFKL.

106. Welles, *The Time for Decision*, 130–31.

107. JPK Diary, March 11, 1940, 4, JPK Collection JFKL; "DM," chap. 40, pp. 25–27, JPK Collection, JFKL.

108. Welles, *The Time for Decision*, 131.

109. "DM," chap. 40, pp. 27–28, JPK Collection, JFKL; JPK Diary, March 11, 1940, 4, JPK Collection, JFKL, has a copy of the note.

110. JPK Diary, March 11, 1940, 4–5, JPK Collection, JFKL; Welles, *The Time for Decision*, 131.

111. JPK Diary, March 11, 1940, 4–5, JPK Collection, JFKL; "DM," chap. 40, p. 28, JPK Collection, JFKL.

112. Welles, *The Time for Decision*, 132.

113. JPK Diary, March 11, 1940, 6, JPK Collection, JFKL; "DM," chap. 40, pp. 28–31, JPK Collection, JFKL.

114. Welles, *The Time for Decision*, 131.

115. JPK Diary, March 12, 1940, JPK Collection, JFKL; "DM," chap. 40, p. 32, JPK Collection, JFKL.

116. JPK Diary, March 14, 1940, 3–4, JPK Collection, JFKL.

117. JPK Diary, March 14, 1940, 4, JPK Collection, JFKL; "DM," chap. 40, p. 36, JPK Collection, JFKL.

118. JPK Diary, March 13, 1940, 1–8, JPK Collection, JFKL; "DM," chap. 40, pp. 37–42, JPK Collection, JFKL; Viscount Halifax Private Papers, 1938–1940, March 13, 1940, FO 800/326, 18, General, PRO.

119. JPK Diary, March 14, 1940, 2, JPK Collection, JFKL; "DM," chap. 40, pp. 42–43, JPK Collection, JFKL.

120. Hooker, *Moffat Papers*, 303.

121. Welles, *The Time for Decision*, 133–47.

122. "DM," chap. 40, p. 43, JPK Collection, JFKL.

123. Hull, *Memoirs*, 740.

124. JPK to Rose Kennedy, March 14, 1940, ser. 1.1, JPK Collection, JFKL; "DM," chap. 40, p. 14, JPK Collection, JFKL; Smith, *Hostage to Fortune*, 408.

125. JPK to Rose Kennedy, March 20, 1940, as cited in Smith, *Hostage to Fortune*, 410.

126. JPK to Rose Kennedy, March 14, 1940, as cited in Smith, *Hostage to Fortune*, 409.

127. "DM," chap. 41, p. 6, JPK Collection, JFKL.

128. Bilainkin, *Diary of a Diplomatic Correspondent*, 60–61.

129. McCarthy, *The Remarkable Kennedys*, 83.

130. Jebb, Foreign Office Minutes, February 14, 1940, FO 371/24418/C2461/1285, 13, as cited in Koskoff, *Joseph P. Kennedy*, 240, 548n13.

131. Gage, Foreign Office Minutes, March 2, 1940, FO 371/24251/A1945, 193, PRO, as cited in Koskoff, *Joseph P. Kennedy*, 240, 548n14.

132. Foreign Office Minutes, February 3, 1940, FO 371/24251/A1945/605/45, 86, PRO, as cited in Koskoff, *Joseph P. Kennedy*, 240, 548n16, "those to whom [he] spoke certainly did."

133. "DM," chap. 41, pp. 4–6, JPK Collection, JFKL; JPK to Rose Kennedy, April 5, 1940, as cited in Smith, *Hostage to Fortune*, 413; Nasaw, *The Patriarch*, 433.

134. JPK to Rose Kennedy, March 20, 1940, as cited in Smith, *Hostage to Fortune*, 410–11; Nasaw, *The Patriarch*, 433–34.

135. Foreign Office Minutes, March 17, 1940, FO 371/24238/A1904/131/45, 275, PRO; *Times*, and *Sunday Dispatch*, March 17, 1940, 8; *Times*, March 18, 1940, 8; *Daily Telegraph*, March 18, 1940, n.p., as cited in Koskoff, *Joseph P. Kennedy*, 242; Cable News, March 16, 1940, James Seymour from Wallace Carroll, United Press Associations, March 23, 1940, JPK Papers, ser. 8.2.2, Ambassador: Correspondence, Newspaper and Miscellaneous Publications, 1940, box 129, JPK Collection, JFKL.

136. "DM," chap. 41, p. 7, JPK Collection, JFKL; *A German White Book*, March 30, 1940, JPK Papers, ser. 8.2.2, Ambassador: Correspondence, Newspapers & Miscellaneous Publications, 1940, box 129, JFKL; JPK to Rose Kennedy, April 5, 1940, as cited in Smith, *Hostage to Fortune*, 414. The document is sometimes referred to as the *German White Book* in *The Landis Papers*, chap. 41, n.p.

137. "DM," chap. 41, p. 7, JPK Collection, JFKL.

138. Jane Karoline Vieth, "Joseph P. Kennedy: Ambassador to the Court of St. James's, 1938–1940,"

2:384–85 (PhD diss., The Ohio State University, 1975); *Landis Papers*, chap. 41, n.p. The *Landis Papers* do not contain the information about the dispatch from Jan Wszelaki or Kennedy's response to it, or a reference to Joe Jr.'s visit to Poland or of his father's bragging to Roosevelt about his son's views; JPK to Rose Kennedy, April 5, 1940, Smith, *Hostage to Fortune*, 415; Smith, *Hostage to Fortune*, 414n458.

139. "DM," chap. 41, p. 7, JPK Collection, JFKL; Long and Israel, *The War Diary of Breckinridge Long*, 73–74.

140. Long and Israel, *The War Diary of Breckinridge Long*, 73–74.

141. "DM," chap. 41, pp. 7–8, JPK Collection, JFKL; JPK to Rose Kennedy, April 5, 1940, as cited in Smith, *Hostage to Fortune*, 414.

142. "DM," chap. 41, p. 8, JPK Collection, JFKL; JPK Diary, March 10, 1940, 2, JPK Collection, JFKL.

143. "DM," chap. 40, p. 17, JPK Collection, JFKL; JPK Diary, March 10, 1940, 2, JPK Collection, JFKL.

144. Millis, *Forrestal Diaries*, 121–22. Years later, Kennedy told James Forrestal "that Hitler would have fought Russia without any later conflict with England if it had not been for Bullitt's urging on Roosevelt in the summer of 1939 that the Germans must be faced down about Poland; neither the French nor the British would have made Poland a cause of war if it had not been for the constant needling from Washington."

145. JPK Diary, March 10, 1940, 2, JPK Collection JFKL; "DM," chap. 40, p. 17, JPK Collection, JFKL.

146. Bilainkin, *Diary of a Diplomatic Correspondent*, 54–55, 59.

Chapter 9. England at Bay

1. Whalen, *The Founding Father*, 281.

2. Churchill, *The Second World War*, 1:376.

3. Weinberg, *A World at Arms*, 102, argued that Stalin may in fact not have been sure what he wanted, and his intentions are not yet known to historians because not much documentation has been released from the Soviet period. Weinberg published his book in 1994, when some of the Soviet documents were being released. He said that we do not know Stalin's views because so few of the documents have been published.

4. "DM," chap. 41, p. 8, JPK Collection, JFKL.

5. Michael J. Lyons, *World War II: A Short History*, 2nd ed. (Englewood Cliffs, NJ: Prentice Hall, 1994), 78–80; Weinberg, *A World at Arms*, 104–6.

6. "DM," chap. 41, p. 1, JPK Collection, JFKL.

7. "DM," chap. 40, p. 14, JPK Collection, JFKL.

8. JPK Diary, March 10, 1940, 4, JPK Collection, JFKL.

9. "DM," chap. 40, p. 14, JPK Collection, JFKL; Self, *Chamberlain Diary Letters*, 4:505–9.

10. "DM," chap. 41, pp. 9–11, JPK Collection, JFKL.

11. "DM," chap. 41, pp. 1, 8–9, JPK Collection, JFKL; Churchill, *The Second World War*, 1:543–44; Lyons, *World War II: A Short History*, 79.

12. "DM," chap. 41, p. 1, JPK Collection, JFKL.

13. "DM," chap. 41, pp. 1–2, JPK Collection, JFKL.

14. "DM," chap. 41, pp. 8–11, JPK Collection, JFKL.

15. "DM," chap. 41, p. 11, JPK Collection, JFKL; Self, *Neville Chamberlain*, 415.

16. "DM," chap. 41, p. 11, JPK Collection, JFKL.

17. "DM," chap. 42, pp. 1–3, JPK Collection, JFKL; Self, *Neville Chamberlain*, 415–16.

18. Weinberg, *A World at Arms*, 116; Lyons, *World War II: A Short History*, 81; Burns, *Roosevelt: The Lion and the Fox*, 418; B. Gilbert, *Britain, 1914–1945*, 113; Nasaw, *The Patriarch*, 437.

19. "DM," chap. 42, p. 4, JPK Collection, JFKL; JPK Papers, ser. 8.2.2, Ambassador Correspondence: Newspaper and Misc. Publications, 1940, box 129, JFKL; Weinberg, *A World at Arms*, 116.

20. Weinberg, *A World at Arms*, 116–18; Lyons, *World War II: A Short History*, 81–84; B. Gilbert, *Britain, 1914–1945*, 114–15.

21. "DM," chap. 42, p. 7, JPK Collection, JFKL.

22. "DM," chap. 42, p. 11, JPK Collection, JFKL.

23. Weinberg, *A World at Arms*, 113–21.

24. Churchill, *The Second World War*, 1:542; Self, *Neville Chamberlain*, 416; Lyons, *World War II: A Short History*, 84.

25. Martin Gilbert, *Winston S. Churchill*, vol. 6, *Finest Hour, 1939–1941* (Boston: Houghton Mifflin, 1983), 213.

26. Self, *Neville Chamberlain*, 417.

27. Weinberg, *A World at Arms*, 113–21; Ian Kershaw, *Fateful Choices*, 23.

28. "DM," chap. 42, p. 1, JPK Collection, JFKL.

29. JPK to Rose Kennedy, April 26, 1940, as cited in Smith, *Hostage to Fortune*, 418.

30. "DM," chap. 42, p. 11, JPK Collection, JFKL; B. Gilbert, *Britain, 1914–1944*, 109.

31. JPK to Rose Kennedy, April 26, 1940, as cited in Smith, *Hostage to Fortune*, 418–19.

32. JPK to Hull, April 26, 1940, 711 Dept. of State; "DM," chap. 43, p. 2, JPK Collection, JFKL.

33. "DM," chap. 43, p. 2, JPK Collection, JFKL.

34. JPK to Hull, April 26, 1940, 711 Dept. of State.

35. Franklin D. Roosevelt, *F.D.R.: His Personal Letters, 1928–1945*, 2 vols., ed. Elliot Roosevelt (New York: Duell, Sloan and Pearce), 2:1020.

36. JPK to Rose Kennedy, April 5, 1940, as cited in Smith, *Hostage to Fortune*, 413; Leslie Hore-Belisha, a Jew and the secretary of state for War, had been replaced by Oliver Stanley, and Sir Kingsley Wood was replaced by Sir Samuel Hoare as secretary of state for Air; Smith, *Hostage to Fortune*, 413n455.

37. JPK to Rose Kennedy, April 5, 1940, as cited in Smith, *Hostage to Fortune*, 413.

38. JPK to Rose Kennedy, April 5, 1940, as cited in Smith, *Hostage to Fortune*, 415.

39. JPK to Rose Kennedy, April 5, 1940, as cited in Smith, *Hostage to Fortune*, 414; Nasaw, *The Patriarch*, 436.

40. Nasaw, *The Patriarch*, 436.

41. JPK to Rose Kennedy, April 5, 1940, as cited in Smith, *Hostage to Fortune*, 415; Nasaw, *The Patriarch*, 436.

42. Self, *Neville Chamberlain*, 417.

43. Self, *Chamberlain Diary Letters*, 4:513, 527–28. In a letter to Hilda, Chamberlain disputes his own belief that Churchill was "absolutely loyal" and describes some of the mischief he created; Self, *Neville Chamberlain*, 417.

44. "DM," chap. 43, p. 8, JPK Collection, JFKL; JPK Diary, May 9, 1940, JPK Collection, JFKL; Smith, *Hostage to Fortune*, 422–23; B. Gilbert, *Britain, 1914–1945*, 117.

45. Kershaw, *Fateful Choices*, 23.

46. Self, *Neville Chamberlain Diary Letters*, 4:528.

47. Carlo D'Este, *Warlord: A Life of Winston Churchill at War, 1874–1945* (New York: HarperCollins, 2009), 369.

48. Self, *Neville Chamberlain*, 423; D'Este, *Warlord*, 369.

49. "DM," chap. 43, p. 7, JPK Collection, JFKL.

50. Churchill, *The Second World War*, 1:589–90; Birkenhead, *Halifax*, 452; Self, *Neville Chamberlain*, 425.

51. JPK Diary, May 9, 1940, JPK Collection, JFKL; Smith, *Hostage to Fortune*, 422n474; B. Gilbert, *Britain, 1914–1945*, 116; Nasaw, *The Patriarch*, 439, gives slightly different figures; D'Este, *Warlord*, 370.

52. Self, *Neville Chamberlain*, 425–28.

53. "DM," chap. 43, p. 8, JPK Collection, JFKL; JPK Diary, May 9, 1940, JPK Collection, JFKL; Smith, *Hostage to Fortune*, 422; JPK to Hull, May 9, 1940, #1148, 800 Britain, Dept. of State.

54. JPK to Hull, May 9, 1940, #1148, 800 Britain, Dept. of State; JPK to Hull, May 9, 1940, #1154, 800 Britain, Dept. of State.

55. "DM," chap. 43, p. 9, JPK Collection, JFKL; JPK Diary, May 9, 1940, JPK Collection, JFKL; Smith, *Hostage to Fortune*, 423; Nasaw, *The Patriarch*, 439.

56. JPK to Hull, May 9, 1940, 800 Britain, Dept. of State; "DM," chap. 43, p. 10, JPK Collection, JFKL.

57. Self, *Neville Chamberlain*, 428.

58. JPK to Hull, May 9, 1940, #1148, 800 Britain, Dept. of State; Self, *Neville Chamberlain Diary Letters*, 4:529.

59. Self, *Neville Chamberlain*, 429.

60. "DM," chap. 50, p. 10, JPK Collection, JFKL; JPK Diary, October 19, 1940, JPK Collection, JFKL; Smith, *Hostage to Fortune*, 476. The biographers of the major candidates offer interesting perspectives on the motives of the candidates. Self, *Neville Chamberlain*, 430, writes that Chamberlain believed correctly that Labour preferred Halifax over Churchill and Chamberlain attempted to maneuver the meeting to that result. But his efforts at manipulation failed because Churchill was more effective in exploiting the crisis to his benefit and Halifax was reluctant to press his claim. Attlee was primarily concerned about getting rid of Chamberlain. Self, *Neville Chamberlain Diary Letters*, 4:529, confirms that Halifax was Chamberlain's first choice. Roberts, *The Holy Fox*, 308, writes that Halifax's natural modesty and shrewdness and his "inability to say the stirring thing" led him to believe that he had to decline the premiership. "If guilt and innocence are a question of dates, Halifax . . . before the bar of History, can cite in his defence his noble self-denial during the fateful

interview on the afternoon of Thursday, 9 May 1940." His refusal of the premiership, the summit of his career, was something of a "modern miracle," an assessment this author agrees with, and an example of the "finger of God in contemporary history." By declining the premiership, Halifax was a real hero of WWII. Birkenhead, *Halifax*, 453, 536, states that Halifax, though flattered to be considered, was so concerned about the prospect of becoming prime minister and so averse to it that he felt sick in his stomach when it was discussed. He had no illusions about his suitability for the role and was quite aware that his gifts were exactly the opposite of those required at that moment. As the military leader of a forlorn cause, he lacked the determination and ruthlessness demanded by the situation. But Churchill had them. Halifax believed Churchill to be "an authentic genius" and unsurpassed in determination and ruthlessness. All of Churchill's turbulent life seemed to have been a preparation for this moment in history, Halifax believed—a view Churchill held too. Bentley Gilbert, *Britain, 1914–1945*, 117, writes that Churchill seemed to regard his succession to the premiership as inevitable; but that was certainly not the case. Many of his own party who admired him were distrustful of his judgment and mental stability and his arrogance and bullheadedness about having his own way. Gilbert argues that Churchill was able to serve as prime minister only because Chamberlain remained in his cabinet and, as the leader of the Conservative Party, kept the rank and file in line in support of Churchill and his policies. Few people so unceremoniously swept from office could have brought themselves to do this, Gilbert states. D'Este, *Warlord*, 370–72, offers another interpretation. Citing Halifax's biographer Roberts, D'Este writes that Halifax might have believed that Churchill would fail. "Then perhaps, Halifax could step in to clean up the mess and rally the sensible for a sensible peace."

61. JPK to Hull, #1158, May 10, 1940, 800 Britain, Dept. of State; "DM," chap. 43, p. 10, JPK Collection, JFKL; Self, *Neville Chamberlain Diary Letters*, 4:529–30; Self, *Neville Chamberlain*, 429–30.
62. JPK to Hull, May 10, 1940, #1168, 800 Britain, Dept. of State.
63. Self, *Neville Chamberlain Diary Letters*, 4:530n85; Self, *Neville Chamberlain*, 430.
64. Churchill, *The Second World War*, 1:594; M. Gilbert, *Winston S. Churchill*, 6:313.
65. M. Gilbert, *Winston S. Churchill*, 6:305, 315–17.
66. Kershaw, *Fateful Choices*, 23.
67. M. Gilbert, *Winston S. Churchill*, 6:314; John Lukacs, *Five Days in London, May 1940* (New Haven, CT: Yale University Press, 1999), 6; D'Este, *Warlord*, 373.
68. Churchill, *The Second World War*, 1:596
69. "DM," chap. 43, p. 12, JPK Collection, JFKL; JPK Diary, August 1, 1940, JPK Collection, JFKL.
70. JPK Diary, May 10, 1940, JPK Collection, JFKL.
71. Koskoff, *Joseph P. Kennedy*, 248.
72. JPK Diary, May 16, 1940, JPK Collection, JFKL; Smith, *Hostage to Fortune*, 427.
73. JPK to Chamberlain: *Draft*, May 18, 1940, as cited in Smith, *Hostage to Fortune*, 429.
74. JPK Diary, May 10, 1940, JPK Collection, JFKL.
75. *Spectator*, February 16, 1940, 200; D'Este, *Warlord*, 362.
76. Kirk, "Reminiscences," 47; Koskoff, *Joseph P. Kennedy*, 251.

77. JPK to Hull, May 10, 1940, #1158, 800 Britain, Dept. of State; Churchill, *The Second World War*, 1:595. Despite what Kennedy said, Churchill wrote that he told the king at 10:00 P.M. that night, not 6:00, who would serve in his cabinet.

78. JPK Diary, May 10, 1940, JPK Collection, JFKL; "DM," chap. 44, p. 5, JPK Collection, JFKL; Smith, *Hostage to Fortune*, 423–24.

79. Kershaw, *Fateful Choices*, 24; B. Gilbert, *Britain, 1914–1945*, 121.

80. "DM," chap. 44, p. 1, JPK Collection, JFKL; Churchill, *The Second World War*, 2:22.

81. Burns, *Roosevelt: The Lion and the Fox*, 418–19; Shirer, *Berlin Diary*, 332; Langer and Gleason, *The Challenge to Isolation, 1937–1940*, 2:447.

82. "DM," chap. 44, pp. 4–5, JPK Collection, JFKL; Burns, *Roosevelt: The Lion and the Fox*, 418–19; Langer and Gleason, *The Challenge to Isolation, 1937–1940*, 2:446.

83. Weinberg, *A World at Arms*, 124–27.

84. JPK (Churchill) to FDR, May 15, 1940, 711 Dept. of State; Burns, *Roosevelt: The Lion and the Fox*, 419; Weinberg, *A World at Arms*, 124–27.

85. Shirer, The *Rise and Fall of the Third Reich*, 952.

86. "DM," chap. 44, p. 7, JPK Collection, JFKL; Langer and Gleason, *The Challenge to Isolation, 1937–1940*, 2:448–49; Shirer, *The Rise and Fall of the Third Reich*, 952–55.

87. Halifax to Lothian, May 13, 1940, FO 371/24239/A3242/131/45, PRO.

88. "DM," chap. 45, pp. 1–2, 10, JPK Collection, JFKL; JPK Diary, May 22, 1940, 8, JPK Collection, JFKL. Roosevelt had also offered to help arrange for the safe transportation of Crown Princess Martha of Norway and her three children by inviting them to the White House as his guests. The princess accepted the president's invitation and arrived there in the fall of 1940 to the utter delight of the president, always a ladies' man. So began a long and important friendship between Roosevelt and the Crown Princess; "DM," chap. 46, pp. 112–13, JPK Collection, JFKL. Doris Kearns Goodwin, *No Ordinary Time—Franklin and Eleanor Roosevelt: The Home Front in World War II* (New York: Simon and Schuster, 1995), 149–54, writes extensively about their relationship.

89. B. Gilbert, *Britain, 1914–1945*, 119.

90. Langer and Gleason, *The Challenge to Isolationism, 1937–1940*, 2:448; Weinberg, *A World at Arms*, 127–29.

91. Churchill (via JPK) to FDR (via Hull), May 15, 1940, #1216, 711 Dept. of State.

92. Burns, *Roosevelt: The Lion and the Fox*, 419.

93. Halifax to Lothian, May 13, 1940, FO371/24239/A3242/131/45, PRO; "DM," chap. 44, pp. 6–7, JPK Collection, JFKL; JPK Diary, May 13, 1940, JPK Collection, JFKL.

94. Halifax to Lothian, May 13, 1940, FO371/24239/A3242/131/45, PRO.

95. JPK to Rose Kennedy, London, April 26, 1940, as cited in Smith, *Hostage to Fortune*, 418–19.

96. "DM," chap. 44, p. 8, JPK Collection, JFKL; Kershaw, *Fateful Choices*, 26.

97. JPK Diary, May 15, 1940, JPK Collection, JFKL; Smith, *Hostage to Fortune*, 425–26; Nasaw, *The Patriarch*, 441.

98. JPK Dairy, May 16, 1940, JPK Collection, JFKL.

99. "DM," chap. 44, pp. 8–9, JPK Collection, JFKL.

100. "DM," chap. 44, p. 10, JPK Collection, JFKL; JPK to Hull, May 15, 1940, #1211, 711 Dept. of State.

101. Churchill (via JPK) to FDR (via Hull), May 15, 1940, #1216, 711 Dept. of State; "DM," chap. 44, pp. 10–11, JPK Collection, JFKL; Churchill, *The Second World War*, 2:21.

102. Nasaw, *The Patriarch*, 442.

103. "DM," chap. 44, p. 10, JPK Collection, JFKL; JPK to FDR and Hull, May 15, 1940, #1211, 711 Dept. of State; JPK to Hull, May 15, 1940, Safe: Kennedy, FDRL; Smith, *Hostage to Fortune*, 424–25; Langer and Gleason, *The Challenge to Isolation, 1937–1940*, vol. 2; Nasaw, *The Patriarch*, 441; Whalen, *The Founding Father*, 291–92.

104. JPK Diary, May 16, 1940, JPK Collection, JFKL; JPK Diary, May 15, 1940, JPK Collection, JFKL; Smith, *Hostage to Fortune*, 427.

105. FDR to JPK (Churchill), May 16, 1940, 711, Dept. of State; "DM," chap. 44, p. 12, JPK Collection, JFKL; Churchill, *The Second World War*, 2:22; Smith, *Hostage to Fortune*, 427n489.

106. "DM," chap. 44, p. 13, JPK Collection, JFKL.

107. Burns, *Roosevelt: The Lion and the Fox*, 420.

108. Goodwin, *No Ordinary Time*, 44.

109. Rosenman, *The Public Papers and Addresses of Franklin D. Roosevelt, 1940*, 9:198–212; U.S. Department of State, *Peace and War: United States Foreign Relations, 1931–1941* (Washington, DC: Government Printing Office, 1943), 528–31; *New York Times*, May 17, 1940, 1, 10; Joseph Kennedy Jr. to JPK, May 18, 1940, orig. ser. 1:1, Family Correspondence 1940, box 2, 429, JPK Collection, JFKL; Smith, *Hostage to Fortune*, 429n494; Goodwin, *No Ordinary Time*, 44; Burns, *Roosevelt: The Lion and the Fox*, 419–20.

110. Hull, *Memoirs*, 766; Nasaw, *The Patriarch*, 442–43.

111. "DM," chap. 44, p. 13, JPK Collection, JFKL; JPK to FDR and Hull, May 17, 1940, 711 Dept. of State.

112. Churchill, *The Second World War*, 2:37.

113. Churchill, *The Second World War*, 2:41; Shirer, The *Rise and Fall of the Third Reich*, 949.

114. JPK to FDR and Hull, diplomatic dispatch, May 16, 1940, #1237, as cited in Smith, *Hostage to Fortune*, 428.

115. Churchill (via JPK) to FDR and Hull, May 18, 1940, # 1267, 711 Dept. of State; Churchill, *The Second World War*, 2:49–50.

116. Loewenheim et al., eds., *Roosevelt and Churchill: Their Secret Wartime Correspondence*, Churchill to FDR, May 20, 1940, 97; Churchill, *The Second World War*, 2:49–50.

117. "DM," chap. 45, p. 3, JPK Collection, JFKL.

118. JPK to Rose Kennedy, May 20, 1940, as cited in Smith, *Hostage to Fortune*, 432–33; Nasaw, *The Patriarch*, 447.

119. Bilainkin, *Diary of a Diplomatic Correspondent*, 94, 190; Koskoff, *Joseph P. Kennedy*, 252n107; "DM," chap. 45, pp. 8–10, JPK Collection, JFKL.

120. JPK to Hull, May 24, 1940, 711 Dept. of State; "DM," chap. 45, p. 4, JPK Collection, JFKL.

121. Roberts, *The Holy Fox*, 211–12; Nasaw, *The Patriarch*, 448; Kershaw, *Fateful Choices*, 30–31, 37–53;

Weinberg, *A World at Arms*, 152, writes that although Churchill was willing to use the threat of a successor government surrendering the fleet to the Germans to press the United States to extend more aid, the record shows that the government had no intention of exploring any negotiated peace offer.

122. M. Gilbert, *Winston S. Churchill*, 6:420.

123. "DM," chap. 45, pp. 6–7, JPK Collection, JFKL; JPK Diary, May 22, 1940, 3, JPK Collection, JFKL; Nasaw, *The Patriarch*, 448–49.

124. "DM," chap. 45, pp. 7–8, JPK Collection, JFKL; Whalen, *The Founding Father*, 292–93; JPK to Cordell Hull, May 27, 1940, 711 Dept. of State.

125. Churchill, *The Second World War*, 2:87; "DM," chap. 45, p. 15, JPK Collection, JFKL.

126. Burns, *Roosevelt: The Lion and the Fox*, 419.

127. Churchill, *The Second World War*, 2:87–88, 91; "DM," chap. 45, pp. 15–16, JPK Collection, JFKL; JPK to Hull, May 27, 1940, 711 Dept. of State.

128. Churchill, *The Second World War*, 2:100; B. Gilbert, *Britain, 1914–1945*, 118.

129. Martin Gilbert, *Churchill: A Life* (New York: Henry Holt, 1991), 650.

130. Churchill, *The Second World War*, 2:100–102; "DM," chap. 45, p. 18, JPK Collection, JFKL; JPK to Hull, May 28, 1940, 711 Dept. of State; Erik Larson, *The Splendid and the Vile: A Saga of Churchill, Family, and Defiance During the Blitz* (New York: Crown Publishers, 2020), 58; Thomas Maier, *When Lions Roar: The Churchills and the Kennedys* (New York: Crown Publishers, 2014), 256.

131. Koskoff, *Joseph P. Kennedy*, 252.

132. Bilainkin, *Diary of a Diplomatic Correspondent*, 102; M. Gilbert, Winston S. Churchill, 6:467.

133. Shirer, The *Rise and Fall of the Third Reich*, 972; Bilainkin, *Diary of a Diplomatic Correspondent*, 100, 102.

134. Bilainkin, *Diary of a Diplomatic Correspondent*, 106.

135. Bilainkin, *Diary of a Diplomatic Correspondent*, 103–6.

136. Shirer, *The Rise and Fall of the Third Reich*, 972; Weinberg, *A World at Arms*, 131.

137. Shirer, *The Rise and Fall of the Third Reich*, 973.

138. Craig and Gilbert, *The Diplomats, 1919–39*, 675; Langer and Gleason, *The Challenge to Isolation, 1937–1940*, 2:462; Leuchtenburg, *Franklin D. Roosevelt and the New Deal, 1932–1940*, 302.

139. Leuchtenburg, *Franklin D. Roosevelt and the New Deal, 1932–1940*, 302.

140. Kershaw, *Fateful Choices*, 129, 156.

141. "DM," chap. 46, p. 7, JPK Collection, JFKL: Kennedy writes that Reynaud has used the phrase several times in his cables with Bullitt. It was included in the draft of Roosevelt's speech from the State Department, but Welles wanted it removed. He was afraid that it might anger Mussolini and make him uncooperative at the peace table. Roosevelt reinserted it when he learned that Mussolini had declared war, according to Kennedy; Craig and Gilbert, *The Diplomats, 1919–39*, 675–76.

142. Foreign Office Minutes, June 10, 1940, FO 371/24239, 294, PRO; "DM," chap. 46, p. 6, JPK Collection, JFKL; FDR, *The Public Papers and Addresses of Franklin D. Roosevelt*, 1940 vol., *War and Aid to Democracy*, comp. Samuel I. Rosenman (New York: Macmillan, 1941), 263–64; *Time*, June 17, 1940,

13; Whalen, *The Founding Father*, 298; Burns, *Roosevelt: The Lion and the Fox*, 421; Leuchtenburg, *Franklin D. Roosevelt and the New Deal, 1932–1940*, 302; Goodwin, *No Ordinary Time*, 67–68; Weinberg, *A World at Arms*, 132.

143. *Time*, June 17, 1940, 13; Goodwin, *No Ordinary Time*, 68.

144. FDR, *The Public Papers and Addresses of Franklin D. Roosevelt*, 1940 vol., comp. Rosenman, 263–64.

145. "DM," chap. 46, p. 7, JPK Collection, JFKL; Churchill, *The Second World War*, 2:114; M. Gilbert, *Winston S. Churchill*, 6:492; Whalen, *The Founding Father*, 299.

146. JPK to Hull, June 10, 1940, 711 Dept. of State.

147. "DM," chap. 46, p. 5, JPK Collection, JFKL; JPK Diary, June 11, 1940, JPK Collection, JFKL; Smith, *Hostage to Fortune*, 438.

148. JPK to Hull, June 10, 1940, June 12, 1940, 711 Dept. of State; JPK Diary, June 11, June 12, 1940, JPK Collection, JFKL; "DM," chap. 46, pp. 6, 8, JPK Collection, JFKL; JPK to Hull, June 12, 1940, Safe: Kennedy, FDRL; Smith, *Hostage to Fortune*, 438–39; Whalen, *The Founding Father*, 299.

149. "DM," chap. 46, p. 8, JPK Collection, JFKL; Loewenheim et al., eds., *Roosevelt and Churchill: Their Secret Wartime Correspondence*, 98–99; Whalen, *The Founding Father*, 299.

150. JPK to Hull, June 12, 1940, 711 Dept. of State; "DM," chap. 46, pp. 8–9, JPK Collection, JFKL; JPK Diary, June 12, 1940, JPK Collection, JFKL; JPK to Hull, June 12, 1940, Safe: Kennedy, FDRL; Smith, *Hostage to Fortune*, 438–39; Koskoff, *Joseph P. Kennedy*, 253–55.

151. JPK Diary, June 12, 1940, JPK Collection, JFKL; Smith, *Hostage to Fortune*, 439; JPK to Hull, June 12, 1940, 711 Dept. of State.

152. Kershaw, *Fateful Choices*, 184.

153. Goodwin, *The Fitzgeralds and the Kennedys*, 599; Ray Bearse and Anthony Read, *Conspirator: The Untold Story of Tyler Kent* (New York: Doubleday, 1991), 198.

154. JPK to Hull, June 12, 1940, Safe: Kennedy, FDRL; JPK Diary, June 12, 1940, JPK Collection, JFKL; "DM," chap. 46, p. 9, JPK Collection, JFKL; JPK to Hull, June 12, 1940, 711 Dept. of State; JPK to Hull, June 6, 1940, 711 Dept. of State; JPK to Hull, June 10, 1940, 711 Dept. of State; Smith, *Hostage to Fortune*, 439.

155. JPK to Hull, June 10, 1940, #1571, 711 Dept. of State; Hull to JPK, June 10, 1940, *FRUS*, 3:34–35; Whalen, *The Founding Father*, 297–98.

156. Whalen, *The Founding Father*, 297–98.

157. "DM," chap. 46, pp. 2–3, JPK Collection, JFKL; JPK to Hull, June 6, 1940, #1524, 711 Dept. of State; Hull to JPK, June 6, 1940, *FRUS*, 3:33.

158. "DM," chap. 46, pp. 2–3, JPK Collection, JFKL; Hull to JPK, June 7, 1940, *FRUS*, 3:33–34; Whalen, *The Founding Father*, 297.

159. JPK to Hull, June 10, 1940, *FRUS*, 3:34; Whalen, *The Founding Father*, 297.

160. Whalen, *The Founding Father*, 296; Koskoff, *Joseph P. Kennedy*, 253.

161. *Times* (London), June 7, 1940, 6; Craig and Gilbert, *The Diplomats, 1919–39*, 672–74.

162. Telegram from JPK, May 31, 1940, as cited in Langer and Gleason, *The Challenge to Isolation*, 2:493; Whalen, *The Founding Father*, 296.

163. D. Kennedy, *Freedom from Fear*, 453.

164. Craig and Gilbert, *The Diplomats, 1919–39*, 670.

165. "DM," chap. 46, p. 26, JPK Collection, JFKL; JPK Diary, June 14, 1940, JPK Collection, JFKL; Smith, *Hostage to Fortune*, 442; JPK to Hull, 1:00 A.M., June 14, 1940, #1643, 711 Dept. of State; JPK (former Naval Person) to Hull, June 14, 1940, 3 A.M., 711 Dept. of State.

166. "DM," chap. 46, p. 18, JPK Collection, JFKL; JPK Diary, June 14, 1940, JPK Collection, JFKL; Smith, *Hostage to Fortune*, 440n518–19; M. Gilbert, *Winston S. Churchill*, 6:539.

167. "DM," chap. 46, pp. 19–20, JPK Collection, JFKL; JPK Diary, June 14, 1940, JPK Collection, JFKL; Smith, *Hostage to Fortune*, 441.

168. JPK to Hull (former Naval Person), June 14, 1940, 711 Dept. of State.

169. "DM," chap. 46, pp. 19–20, JPK Collection, JFKL; JPK Diary, June 14, 1940, JPK Collection, JFKL; Smith, *Hostage to Fortune*, 441; Nasaw, *The Patriarch*, 452–53.

170. JPK to Hull, June 14, 1940, #1643, 711 Dept. of State.

171. JPK Diary, June 14, 1940, JPK Collection, JFKL; Smith, *Hostage to Fortune*, 441.

172. M. Gilbert, *Winston S. Churchill*, 6:539.

173. "DM," chap. 46, pp. 21–22, JPK Collection, JFKL. Beschloss, *Kennedy and Roosevelt*, 208, writes that Herbert Hoover, with whom Kennedy discussed the phone call, said that when the call came through, Kennedy, who opposed publication, was with Churchill. Kennedy convinced the president not to publish the message. "Said Churchill hated him from then on."

174. "DM," chap. 46, pp. 22–23, JPK Collection, JFKL; JPK Diary, June 14, 1940, JPK Collection, JFKL; Smith, *Hostage to Fortune*, 442n523; Nasaw, *The Patriarch*, 453–53.

175. JPK (former Naval Person) to Hull, 3:00 A.M., June 14, 1940, 711 Dept. of State; "DM," chap. 46, p. 26, JPK Collection, JFKL; M. Gilbert, *Winston S. Churchill*, 6:541.

176. "DM," chap. 46, pp. 27–29, JPK Collection, JFKL; JPK Diary, June 14, 1940, JPK Collection, JFKL; JPK to Hull, June 14, 1940, Safe: Kennedy, FDRL; Smith, *Hostage to Fortune*, 441–43n526; Nasaw, *The Patriarch*, 453–55.

177. M. Gilbert, *Winston S. Churchill*, 6:542, 546.

178. "DM," chap. 46, p. 34, JPK Collection, JFKL; JPK to Hull, June 16, 1940, #1680, 711 Dept. of State; JPK to Hull, June 16, 1940, Safe: Kennedy, FDRL; Smith, *Hostage to Fortune*, 445.

179. JPK to Hull, June 10, 1940, 711 Dept. of State; Whalen, *The Founding Father*, 297.

180. M. Gilbert, *Winston S. Churchill*, 6:548.

181. Nasaw, *The Patriarch*, 453–55, details Kennedy's diary notes and his self-pity and rage against Roosevelt for speaking out of "both sides of his mouth" and not following Kennedy's advice to explain emphatically why the United States could not come to France's aid. It compromised our relationship with Britain too. Kennedy felt lonely, tired, and scared.

182. M. Gilbert, *Winston S. Churchill*, 6:543.

183. JPK to Hull, June 14, 1940, 711 Dept. of State.

184. B. Gilbert, *Britain, 1914–1945*, 120.

185. JPK to Hull, June 17, 1940, 711 Dept. of State.

186. JPK to Hull, June 16, 1940, June 17, 1940, 711 Dept. of State; "DM," chap. 46, p. 37, JPK Collection, JFKL.

187. JPK to Hull, June 14, 1940, #1650, 711 Dept. of State.

188. Bilainkin, *Diary of a Diplomatic Correspondent*, 114.

189. Shirer, *The Rise and Fall of the Third Reich*, 975–81: an American journalist gives an eyewitness account of the events of the Franco-German armistice.

190. M. Gilbert, *Winston S. Churchill*, 6:543n3.

191. Bilainkin, *Diary of a Diplomatic Correspondent*, 112, 114.

192. Churchill, *The Second World War*, 2:193; M. Gilbert, *Winston S. Churchill*, 6:570–71; B. Gilbert, *Britain, 1914–1945*, 121; Hansard Parliamentary Debate Compendium, June 18, 1940, vol. 362, *cc.* 51–61.

193. M. Gilbert, *Winston S. Churchill*, 6:469.

194. B. Gilbert, *Britain, 1914–1945*, 120.

195. B. Gilbert, *Britain, 1914–1945*, 121.

196. "DM," chap. 46, p. 40, JPK Collection, JFKL.

197. Kershaw, *Fateful Choices*, 213.

198. B. Gilbert, *Britain, 1914–1945*, 121.

Chapter 10. Very Well, Alone

1. Shirer, The *Rise and Fall of the Third Reich*, 982.

2. D'Este, *Warlord*, xvi, 16, 383; Kershaw, *Fateful Choices*, 441; Keith Robbins, *Churchill* (London: Longman, 1992), 28.

3. Robert E. Sherwood, *Roosevelt and Hopkins: An Intimate History* (New York: Harper & Bros., 1948), 238; D'Este, *Warlord*, 335, 383; Goodwin, *The Fitzgeralds and the Kennedys*, 598; Goodwin, *No Ordinary Time*, 33.

4. Virginia Cowles, *Winston Churchill: The Era and the Man* (New York: Harper & Bros., 1956), 4–9.

5. Ralph G. Martin, *Jennie: The Life of Lady Randolph Churchill*, vol. 1, *The Romantic Years, 1854–1895* (New York: Signet Book, 1970), 110–11; D'Este, *Warlord*, 5.

6. Martin, *Jennie*, 1:63–64, 114; D'Este, *Warlord*, 36–37; Maxwell P. Schoenfeld, *Sir Winston Churchill: His Life and Times* (Malabar, FL: Robert E. Krieger, 1973), 1–5.

7. Martin, *Jennie*, 1:14; D'Este, *Warlord*, 6; Whalen, *The Founding Father*, 279.

8. D'Este, *Warlord*, 11–12, 378; Martin, *Jennie*, 1:247.

9. D'Este, *Warlord*, xiv–xv; Goodwin, *The Fitzgeralds and the Kennedys*, 598; William Manchester and Paul Reid, *The Last Lion—Winston Spencer Churchill: Defender of the Realm, 1940–1965* (Boston: Little, Brown and Co., 2012), 8.

10. D'Este, *Warlord*, xiii, xv.

11. D'Este, *Warlord*, 378.

12. Goodwin, *No Ordinary Time*, 302.

13. JPK to FDR, July 20, 1939, File: Personal, FDRL; JPK Papers, ser. 8.2.1, Hull, Cordell, July 20, 1939, box 109, JPK Collection, JFKL; Self, *Neville Chamberlain*, 386; D'Este, *Warlord*, 376.

14. D'Este, *Warlord*, 376, 384.

15. D'Este, *Warlord*, xv.

16. D'Este, *Warlord*, 48–49, 378; Manchester and Reid, *The Last Lion*, 5.

17. D'Este, *Warlord*, 343, 384.

18. Manchester and Reid, *The Last Lion*, 5.

19. Manchester and Reid, *The Last Lion*, 25.

20. D'Este, *Warlord*, 383–86; Cowles, *Winston Churchill*, 325.

21. D'Este, *Warlord*, 383.

22. JPK Diary, August 23, 1940, 5, JPK Collection, JFKL; D'Este, *Warlord*, 342–43.

23. Kershaw, *Fateful Choices*, 21.

24. D'Este, *Warlord*, 379.

25. B. Gilbert, *Britain, 1914–1945*, 119.

26. M. Gilbert, *Churchill*, 6:358.

27. D'Este, *Warlord*, xv, 375.

28. JPK Diary, August 14, 1940, JPK Collection, JFKL; Smith, *Hostage to Fortune*, 460–61.

29. Goodwin, *No Ordinary Time*, 33.

30. Churchill to FDR, #1216, May 15, 1940, 711 Dept. of State; Loewenheim et al., eds., *Roosevelt and Churchill*, 94–95.

31. Loewenheim et al., eds., *Roosevelt and Churchill*, 95.

32. Bilainkin, *Diary of a Diplomatic Correspondent*, 106.

33. JPK Diary, June 24, 1940, JPK Collection, JFKL; Smith, *Hostage to Fortune*, 446.

34. JPK Diary, June 12, 1940, JPK Collection, JFKL; JPK to Hull, #1603, June 12, 1940, Safe: Kennedy, FDRL; Smith, *Hostage to Fortune*, 439; Whalen, *The Founding Father*, 279.

35. JPK Diary, June 24, 1940, JPK Collection, JFKL; Smith, *Hostage to Fortune*, 446; Koskoff, *Joseph P. Kennedy*, 250; Whalen, *The Founding Father*, 280.

36. Moffat Diary MS, entry of December 8, 1939, as cited in Koskoff, *Joseph P. Kennedy*, 250, 553n95, a reference to Bernard Baruch, a friend of Churchill's; Joseph E. Persico, *Roosevelt's Secret War: FDR and World War II Espionage* (New York: Random House, 2001), 30.

37. Sherwood, Roosevelt and Hopkins, 238; Whalen, *The Founding Father*, 279–80.

38. Koskoff, *Joseph P. Kennedy*, 552n81, states that Queenstown was correct.

39. Koskoff, *Joseph P. Kennedy*, 249.

40. JPK Diary, June 14, 1940, JPK Collection, JFKL; Smith, *Hostage to Fortune*, 440.

41. JPK Diary, June 11, 1940, JPK Collection, JFKL; Smith, *Hostage to Fortune*, 438–39.

42. "DM," chap. 48, p. 18, JPK Collection, JFKL; JPK Diary, June 14, 1940, JPK Collection, JFKL; Smith, *Hostage to Fortune*, 438, 460; Koskoff, *Joseph P. Kennedy*, 249.

43. JPK Diary, June 13, 1940, JPK Collection, JFKL; Smith, *Hostage to Fortune*, 440.

44. JPK Diary, August 15, 1940, JPK Collection, JFKL; "DM," chap. 48, p. 18, JPK Collection, JFKL; Koskoff, *Joseph P. Kennedy*, 249; Nasaw, *The Patriarch*, 468.

45. Landis MS, 402, as cited in Koskoff, *Joseph P. Kennedy*, 249; Beschloss, *Kennedy and Roosevelt*, 206.

46. JFK Diary, June 12, 1940, 3, JPK Collection, JFKL.

47. John Howland Snow, *The Case of Tyler Kent* (New York: Domestic and Foreign Affairs/Chicago: Citizens Press, 1946), 13, 35. Snow gives an interesting analysis of the Tyler Kent case and claims to be writing "in the interest of justice." He likens it to the attack on Pearl Harbor.

48. Smith, *Hostage to Fortune*, 431n502; Whalen, *The Founding Father*, 309; Bearse and Read, *Conspirator*, 6.

49. Whalen, *The Founding Father*, 281, 311.

50. "The American Tearoom Spy," *Times* (London), December 4, 1982, 6; John Costello, *Ten Days to Destiny: The Secret Story of the Hess Peace Initiative and British Efforts to Strike a Deal with Hitler* (New York: William Morrow, 1991), 109; J. H. Snow, *The Case of Tyler Kent*, 5; Bearse and Read, *Conspirator*, 9; Whalen, *The Founding Father*, 309–10, 312. According to Persico in *Roosevelt's Secret War*, James Reston, *New York Times* journalist at the London office, said of Kennedy that "he couldn't keep his mouth shut or his pants on" (21, 69); the same might have been said of Kent.

51. "The American Tearoom Spy," *Times*, December 4, 1982, 6; Anthony Cave Brown, *Bodyguard of Lies* (New York: Harper and Row, 1975), 1:74.

52. Bearse and Read, *Conspirator*, interview with Kent: TGK Papers, xiv, 173; Brown, *Bodyguard of Lies*, 1:75.

53. Persico, *Roosevelt's Secret War*, 21; Bearse and Read, *Conspirator*, 9–10; Whalen, *The Founding Father*, 311–12; Costello, *Ten Days to Destiny*, 108–10.

54. "The American Tearoom Spy," *Times*, December 4, 1982, 6.

55. Bearse and Read, *Conspirator*, 140; M. Gilbert, *Churchill*, 6:359–60.

56. "DM," chap. 44, p. 14, JPK Collection, JFKL; Smith, *Hostage to Fortune*, 430; Nasaw, *The Patriarch*, 444–46; Bearse and Read, *Conspirator*, 139; Costello, *Ten Days to Destiny*, 17–18, 100–107; Peter Rand, *Conspiracy of One: Tyler Kent's Secret Plot against FDR, Churchill, and the Allied War Effort* (Guilford, CT: Lyons Press, 2013), 106.

57. "The American Tearoom Spy," *Times*, December 4, 1982, 6.

58. "DM," chap. 44, p. 17, JPK Collection, JFKL; Smith, *Hostage to Fortune*, 431–32; J. H. Snow, *The Case of Tyler Kent*, 10–13.

59. "The American Tearoom Spy," *Times*, December 4, 1982, 6.

60. "The American Tearoom Spy," *Times*, December 4, 1982, 6; Smith, *Hostage to Fortune*, 232; Persico, *Roosevelt's Secret War*, 30; Costello, *Ten Days to Destiny*, 104.

61. JPK Diary, September 11, 1940, JPK Collection, JFKL; "DM," chap. 44, p. 14, JPK Collection, JFKL; Smith, *Hostage to Fortune*, 430; Whalen, *The Founding Father*, 316.

62. "The American Tearoom Spy," *Times*, December 4, 1982, 6; J. H. Snow, *The Case of Tyler Kent*, 36–37.

63. Anna de Wolkoff is also referred to as Anna Wolkoff; Smith, *Hostage to Fortune*, 430n501. J. H. Snow, *The Case of Tyler Kent*, 11–13, gives a good description of Anna Wolkoff's relationship to Kent and her involvement in his case.

64. "The American Tearoom Spy," *Times*, December 4, 1982, 6; Bearse and Read, *Conspirator*, 88.

65. "DM," chap. 44, p. 14, JPK Collection, JFKL; Smith, *Hostage to Fortune*, 430; Persico, *Roosevelt's Secret War*, 23; Brown, *Bodyguard of Lies*, 1:75.

66. "The American Tearoom Spy," *Times*, December 4, 1982, 6; "DM," chap. 44, p. 15, JPK Collection, JFKL; Smith, *Hostage to Fortune*, 431.

67. "DM," chap. 44, p. 15, JPK Collection, JFKL; Smith, *Hostage to Fortune*, 430.

68. Weinberg, *A World at Arms*, 156; Persico, *Roosevelt's Secret War*, 27.

69. "DM," chap. 44, p. 15, JPK Collection, JFKL; Smith, *Hostage to Fortune*, 431; Bearse and Read, *Conspirator*, 140; Brown, *Bodyguard of Lies*, 1:75; J. H. Snow, *The Case of Tyler Kent*, 11; Rand, *Conspiracy of One*, 109, 127: Kennedy had authority to revoke Kent's diplomatic immunity under "an executive order signed by President Roosevelt in September 1939 that permitted the executive branch of the U.S. government to revoke the diplomatic immunity of Foreign Service employees, who had previously inhabited a special realm immune to legal consequences. Kent had occupied that realm for all but several years of his entire life." There is no document that shows that Kennedy had authority at that time from the State Department or from the police to hand Kent over to the British authorities, but he did it anyway. "Kennedy had distinguished himself as having a mind so fast that no principle could flag it down when roaring forward at full speed."

70. Whalen, *The Founding Father*, 313; Bearse and Read, *Conspirator*, 162, 173; J. H. Snow, *The Case of Tyler Kent*, 9, 11, 12, 14, 15, 44.

71. Smith, *Hostage to Fortune*, 431n503.

72. *New York Times*, June 2, 1940, 35; Bearse and Read, *Conspirator*, 173–74.

73. Bearse and Read, *Conspirator*, 172; Whalen, *The Founding Father*, 313.

74. Smith, *Hostage to Fortune*, 431n502; Rand, *Conspiracy of One*, 117.

75. "DM," chap. 44, p. 16, JPK Collection, JFKL; Smith, *Hostage to Fortune*, 431; Brown, *Bodyguard of Lies*, 1:75; Rand, *Conspiracy of One*, jacket cover, xii; Costello, *Ten Days to Destiny*, 106, 120; Lukacs, *Five Days in London, May 1940*, 74.

76. "The American Tearoom Spy," *Times*, December 4, 1982, 6; Whalen, *The Founding Father*, 320; Bearse and Read, *Conspirator*, 147; Costello, *Ten Days to Destiny*, 106–7, 120–23.

77. "DM," chap. 44, p. 16, JPK Collection, JFKL; Smith, *Hostage to Fortune*, 431; Brown, *Bodyguard of Lies*, 1:75.

78. Persico, *Roosevelt's Secret War*, 27; Brown, *Bodyguard of Lies*, 1:75.

79. Long and Israel, *The War Diary of Breckinridge Long*, 113.

80. Long and Israel, *The War Diary of Breckinridge Long*, 100–101; Bearse and Read, *Conspirator*, 163.

81. Long and Israel, *The War Diary of Breckinridge Long*, 113; Nasaw, *The Patriarch*, 446–47; Bearse and Read, *Conspirator*, 164.

82. Bearse and Read, *Conspirator*, 174–75; Whalen, *The Founding Father*, 313.

83. *Washington Daily News*, September 5, 1944, 2, 28; *Newsweek*, September 18, 1944, 47; "DM," chap. 44, p. 18, JPK Collection, JFKL; Smith, *Hostage to Fortune*, 432; Brown, *Bodyguard of Lies*, 1:76. Whalen, *The Founding Father*, 320, writes that if it were true that there was a blackout throughout the American diplomatic service, Kennedy could not have communicated confidentially with Washington on May 24 and 27, 1940, six and nine days respectively after he knew about the allegations against his employee. But he did send confidential cables on those days and in one of

them discussed the possibility of England's capitulation—information of tremendous strategic and propaganda value to Germany—if, of course, the code had been broken. Whalen disputes Kennedy's account and charges that he "had improved on the case"; Bearse and Read, *Conspirator*, 251, agree with Whalen.

84. "DM," chap. 44, pp. 16–17, JPK Collection, JFKL; Smith, *Hostage to Fortune*, 431.

85. Bearse and Read, *Conspirator*, 148–49; Rand, *Conspiracy of One*, 119–25.

86. Bearse and Read, *Conspirator*, 149, 154.

87. Letter from Tyler Kent to Whalen, February 5, 1964, as cited in Whalen, *The Founding Father*, 310–11; Persico, *Roosevelt's Secret War*, 28.

88. "DM," chap. 44, p. 17, JPK Collection, JFKL; Smith, *Hostage to Fortune*, 432; Bearse and Read, *Conspirator*, 149; Costello, *Ten Days to Destiny*, 123.

89. "DM," chap. 44, pp. 17–18, JPK Collection, JFKL; Smith, *Hostage to Fortune*, 432; Bearse and Read, *Conspirator*, 148; Costello, *Ten Days to Destiny*, 110–11.

90. "DM," chap. 44, p. 17, JPK Collection, JFKL; Smith, *Hostage to Fortune*, 432.

91. "The American Tearoom Spy," *Times*, December 4, 1982, 6; "DM," chap. 44, p. 18, JPK Collection, JFKL; Smith, *Hostage to Fortune*, 432; JPK Diary, August 15, 1940, JPK Collection, JFKL, states that Churchill wanted the Tyler Kent case postponed until after the 1940 election not because of any fear of embarrassment to Roosevelt or Churchill, but because it would be difficult to keep Ramsay imprisoned without producing the evidence; M. Gilbert, *Churchill*, 6:485–86; Nasaw, *The Patriarch*, 468.

92. Department of State, 123 National Archives, Washington, DC, as cited in Bearse and Read, *Conspirator*, 175n314; J. H. Snow, *The Case of Tyler Kent*, 13.

93. *Chicago Daily Tribune*, June 2, 1940; Whalen, *The Founding Father*, 313; Bearse and Read, *Conspirator*, 178.

94. "The American Tearoom Spy," *Times*, December 4, 1982, 6; Persico, *Roosevelt's Secret War*, 31; Whalen, *The Founding Father*, 313.

95. *New York Times*, November 8, 1940, n.p.; Whalen, *The Founding Father*, 314n85; J. H. Snow, *The Case of Tyler Kent*, 10, 12, 54; Bearse and Read, *Conspirator*, 172, 177–78, 205, 207. The U.S. government had no objection to the charges, leaving open the possibility that Kent could still be charged under the Yardley Act.

96. Tyler Gatewood Kent papers, "Central Criminal Court, no. 334, *Rex v. Tyler Gatewood Kent*," Charles B. Parsons Collection, Manuscript and Archives, Yale University Library, as cited in Whalen, *The Founding Father*, 314; Bearse and Read, *Conspirator*, 204.

97. Bearse and Read, *Conspirator*, 203–5; Rand, *Conspiracy of One*, 117–18; J. H. Snow, *The Case of Tyler Kent*, 11–12, 15.

98. Bearse and Read, *Conspirator*, 205.

99. M. Gilbert, *Churchill*, 6:485.

100. Long and Israel, *The War Diary of Breckinridge Long*, 114.

101. Bearse and Read, *Conspirator*, 220; Persico, *Roosevelt's Secret War*, 31; J. H. Snow, *The Case of Tyler*

Kent, 13–16; Whalen, *The Founding Father*, 318.

102. *New York Times*, November 8, 1940, n.p.; Whalen, *The Founding Father*, 318–19.

103. Bearse and Read, *Conspiracy*, 5–6.

104. *Washington Daily News*, September 5, 1944, 2, 28; *Newsweek*, September 18, 1944, 47–48; Whalen, *The Founding Father*, 319; Bearse and Read, *Conspiracy*, 251; J. H. Snow, *The Case of Tyler Kent*, 26.

105. "The American Tearoom Spy," *Times*, December 4, 1982, 6; M. Gilbert, *Churchill*, 6:486n1.

106. *New York Post*, December 4, 1945, n.p.; Whalen, *The Founding Father*, 320; Persico, *Roosevelt's Secret War*, 444; J. H. Snow, *The Case of Tyler Kent*, 27.

107. FO file 371/38704/44628, as cited in Bearse and Read, 251n316; *Washington Times Herald*, November 12, 1941, n.p.; Whalen, *The Founding Father*, 318–19; Rand, *Conspiracy of One*, 180; J. H. Snow, *The Case of Tyler Kent*, 8.

108. *Chicago Daily Tribune*, October 17, 1944, 15; Costello, *Ten Days to Destiny*, 125; Rand, *Conspiracy of One*, 116.

109. *New York Times*, September 3, 1944, 19; *New York Times*, Press Release No. 405, September 2, 1944, as cited in Snow, *The Case of Tyler Kent*, 10–13; U.S. Department of State, Press Release No. 405, September 2, 1944, as cited in Bearse and Read, *Conspirator*, 250–51; Whalen, *The Founding Father*, 318–19.

110. Washington Daily News, September 5, 1944, 2, 28; Snow, *The Case of Tyler Kent*, 26; Whalen, *The Founding Father*, 319–20; Costello, *Ten Days to Destiny*, 125.

111. Bearse and Read, *Conspirator*, 252; Costello, *Ten Days to Destiny*, 125, 542n50, writes that Roosevelt asked Kennedy to defuse the political situation by telling the press that Kent had been spying for the Germans.

112. *Washington Daily News*, September 5, 1944, 2, 28; Whalen, *The Founding Father*, 319–20; Bearse and Read, *Conspirator*, 251.

113. *Newsweek*, September 18, 1944, 47; *Chicago Daily Tribune*, October 17, 1944, 15; J. H. Snow, *The Case of Tyler Kent*, 27.

114. Whalen, *The Founding Father*, 313, 320.

115. Report of a talk by Mrs. Kent at the Friends Meeting House, Washington, DC, on July 20, 1944, styled "Mrs. Anne H. P. Kent on Tyler Kent Case," Charles B. Parsons Collection, Manuscript and Archives, Yale University Library, as cited in Whalen, *The Founding Father*, 320.

116. JPK to Bartholomew Brickley, October 12, 1945, as cited in Smith, *Hostage to Fortune*, 621; Costello, *Ten Days to Destiny*, 126–27.

117. JPK to Lord Beaverbrook, November 28, 1950, as cited in Smith, *Hostage to Fortune*, 645.

118. Costello, *Ten Days to Destiny*, 108; Rand, *Conspiracy of One*, 220; Bearse and Read, *Conspirator*, 269, 271, 274: In 1946 Kent married Clara Hyatt Hodgson after she divorced her first husband, a diplomatic colleague of Kent's at the State Department. She was some ten years older than he. They lived a lavish life—eighty-acre estate, yachts, cruises on British luxury liners, expensive clothes tailored in London—from her inheritance of the "Carter's Little Liver Pills" fortune. But her fortune was largely lost in unwise Mexican investments and the collapse of the peso in the 1970s. By 1982

they were living in a mobile home in a trailer park in Kerrville, Texas. Even so, Kent continued to order Champagne with his meals, to drink with his little finger extended, and to maintain his array of suits and jackets, all memorials to his hubris. On November 11, 1988, Kent was admitted to the hospital in Kerrville, Texas: he died there nine days later from colon cancer. He was seventy-seven.

119. Nasaw, *The Patriarch*, 444–47; Bearse and Read, *Conspirator*, xiv.

120. Bearse and Read, *Conspirator*, xiv.

121. Rand, *Conspiracy of One*, jacket cover.

122. Costello, *Ten Days to Destiny*, 149.

123. Whalen, *The Founding Father*, 311.

124. Persico, *Roosevelt's Secret War*, 30.

125. Beschloss, *Kennedy and Roosevelt*, 207.

126. Bearse and Read, *Conspirator*, 199: a bonus to Churchill was the fact that Kennedy would not be able to use information against Roosevelt to charge him with warmongering or collusion with Churchill.

127. Lukas, *Five Days in London, May 1940*, 74.

128. The debate over whether or not all the relevant materials have been released by the federal archives perpetuates the mystery and increases the speculation surrounding the Tyler Kent case. Whalen, *The Founding Father*, 311, 320: Richard Whalen wrote in the 1993 edition of his biography that "the whole truth about Tyler Kent is inseparable from the documents he took, the most revealing of which, after almost a quarter of a century, still are hidden from public view in the Roosevelt Library at Hyde Park, New York—a claim that the director vigorously denied when asked about the charge. Thomas Maier, *When Lions Roar: The Churchills and the Kennedys* (New York: Crown Publishers, 2014), 249, writes that because key testimony has been withheld from the public, it is difficult to assess Churchill's influence on the investigation; Weinberg, *A World at Arms*, 156–57, published in 1994, argues that "all the details and implications of this security disaster have not yet been clarified."

129. "DM," chap. 48, p. 5, JPK Collection, JFKL; JPK to Rose Kennedy, August 2, 1940, as cited in Smith, *Hostage to Fortune*, 455.

130. JPK to Rose Kennedy, March 14, 1940, as cited in Smith, *Hostage to Fortune*, 409.

131. Goodwin, *The Fitzgeralds and the Kennedys*, 599–600.

132. JPK to Rose Kennedy, August 2, 1940, as cited in Smith, *Hostage to Fortune*, 455; JPK Diary, August 2, 1940, JPK Collection, JFKL.

133. JPK to Rose Kennedy, April 26, 1940, as cited in Smith, *Hostage to Fortune*, 418–19.

134. JPK to Rose Kennedy, March 14, 1940, as cited in Smith, *Hostage to Fortune*, 409; JPK to Rose Kennedy, March 20, 1940, as cited in Smith, *Hostage to Fortune*, 410–11.

135. Foreign Office Minutes, April 30, 1940, FO371/24251, PRO: Herschel Johnson from the American embassy notified the Foreign Office that Rose Kennedy would be returning to England. She planned to arrive in Lisbon on May 7. Kennedy asked the Foreign Office "if it could be arranged without inconvenience" that she continue to London by Imperial Airways, a company making experimental flights between the cities throughout the summer. British officials in the Air Ministry were "very

reluctant" to accommodate Mrs. Kennedy and had promised the Portuguese officials that no passengers would be allowed on the experimental flights. The British suggested that if she delayed for ten days, they would try to accommodate her on the first regular plane leaving Lisbon on May 23. Rose resigned herself to not returning to Britain.

136. JPK to Rose Kennedy, May 20, 1940, as cited in Smith, *Hostage to Fortune*, 432–33.
137. JPK to Rose Kennedy, April 26, 1940, as cited in Smith, *Hostage to Fortune*, 419.
138. JPK to Rose Kennedy, April 5, 1940, as cited in Smith, *Hostage to Fortune*, 415.
139. JPK to Rose Kennedy, March 20, 1940, as cited in Smith, *Hostage to Fortune*, 411.
140. Rose Kennedy to JPK, June 24, 1940, as cited in Smith, *Hostage to Fortune*, 447.
141. Rose Kennedy to JPK, June 1, 1940, as cited in Smith, *Hostage to Fortune*, 436.
142. Rose Kennedy to JPK, May 8, 1940, June 1, 1940, June 24, 1940, as cited in Smith, *Hostage to Fortune*, 421, 436, 447.
143. JPK to Rosemary Kennedy, undated telegram, as cited in Smith, *Hostage to Fortune*, 433.
144. Rosemary Kennedy to JPK, April 4 (?), 1940, as cited in Smith, *Hostage to Fortune*, 412, 458.
145. Joe Kennedy Jr. to JPK, April 5, 1940, ser. 1.1, JPK Collection, JFKL; Smith, *Hostage to Fortune*, 416.
146. Edward Kennedy to JPK, April 8, 1940, as cited in Smith, *Hostage to Fortune*, 416.
147. John F. Kennedy to JPK, ser. 1.1, JPK Collection, JFKL; Smith, *Hostage to Fortune*, 417.
148. Rose Kennedy to JPK, May 8, 1940, as cited in Smith, *Hostage to Fortune*, 421.
149. Robert Kennedy to JPK, as cited in Smith, *Hostage to Fortune*, 448.
150. John F. Kennedy to JPK, ser. 1.1, JPK Collection, JFKL; Smith, *Hostage to Fortune*, 417.
151. Robert Kennedy to JPK, as cited in Smith, *Hostage to Fortune*, 448.
152. Rose Kennedy to JPK, May 8, 1940, as cited in Smith, *Hostage to Fortune*, 421.
153. Rose Kennedy to JPK, June 24, 1940, as cited in Smith, *Hostage to Fortune*, 447.
154. John F. Kennedy, 22, to Kennedy, ser. 1.1, JPK Collection, JFKL; Smith, *Hostage to Fortune*, 417.
155. Rose F. Kennedy, ser. l, Diaries, undated notes, box 7, JPK Collection, JFKL.
156. JPK to John F. Kennedy, May 22, 1940, ser. 1.1, JPK Collection, JFKL; Smith, *Hostage to Fortune*, 435; James MacGregor Burns, *John Kennedy: A Political Profile* (New York: Harcourt, Brace & World, 1961), 40; Whalen, *The Founding Father*, 294; Goodwin, *The Fitzgeralds and the Kennedys*, 582, 604–5.
157. Joe Kennedy Jr. to JPK, March 17, 1940, ser. 1.1, JPK Collection, JFKL; Smith, *Hostage to Fortune*, 410.
158. Burns, *John Kennedy*, 42; Whalen, *The Founding Father*, 295.
159. Whalen, *The Founding Father*, 295; Burns, *John Kennedy*, 42–43.
160. John F. Kennedy to JPK, ser. 1.1, JPK Collection, JFKL; Smith, *Hostage to Fortune*, 417.
161. John F. Kennedy to JPK, as cited in Smith, *Hostage to Fortune*, 444; Nasaw, *The Patriarch*, 435.
162. Gene Schoor, *Young John Kennedy* (New York: Harcourt, Brace & World, 1963), 129, as cited in Whalen, *The Founding Father*, 294.
163. Goodwin, *The Fitzgeralds and the Kennedys*, 604; Whalen, *The Founding Father*, 295; Burns, *John Kennedy*, 40–41.
164. JPK to John F. Kennedy, May 20, 1940, ser. 1.1, JPK Collection, JFKL; Smith, *Hostage to Fortune*, 433–35.

165. Whalen, *The Founding Father*, 295; Burns, *John Kennedy*, 43.

166. John Kennedy, *Why England Slept* (New York: Wilfred Funk, 1940), 230–31; Goodwin, *The Fitzgeralds and the Kennedys*, 605.

167. JPK to John F. Kennedy, May 20, 1940, ser. 1.1, JPK Collection, JFKL; Smith, *Hostage to Fortune*, 433–35; Whalen, *The Founding Father*, 296.

168. JPK to Joe Kennedy Jr., June 6, 1940, ser. 1.1, JPK Collection, JFKL; Smith, *Hostage to Fortune*, 437n510.

169. Associated Press [A.P.] and Moody, eds., *Triumph and Tragedy: The Story of the Kennedys*, 70; Whalen, *The Founding Father*, 296.

170. Rose Kennedy, ser. 1, Diaries, undated notes, box 7, JFKL.

171. JPK to Joe Kennedy Jr., June 6, 1940, ser. 1.1, JPK Collection, JFKL; Smith, *Hostage to Fortune*, 437.

172. JPK to John F. Kennedy, May 22, 1940, ser. 1.1, JPK Collection, JFKL; Smith, *Hostage to Fortune*, 453–54.

173. John F. Kennedy, ed., *As We Remember Joe* (Cambridge, MA: University Press, 1945), 52, as cited in Whalen, *The Founding Father*, 227, 359.

174. Joe Kennedy Jr., *Notes*, June 10, 1939, as cited in Smith, *Hostage to Fortune*, 339.

175. JPK to Joe Kennedy Jr., June 6, 1940, ser. 1.1, JPK Collection, JFKL; Smith, *Hostage to Fortune*, 436.

176. JPK to Joe Kennedy Jr., July 23, 1940, ser. 1.1, JPK Collection, JFKL; Smith, *Hostage to Fortune*, 452.

177. Rose Kennedy, ser. 1, Diaries, undated notes, box 7, JFKL.

178. J. F. Kennedy, ed., *As We Remember Joe*, 43, Whalen, *The Founding Father*, 172.

179. A.P. and Moody, eds., *Triumph and Tragedy*, 70.

180. Goodwin, *The Fitzgeralds and the Kennedys*, 600–601; Whalen, *The Founding Father*, 303.

181. Joe Kennedy Jr. to JPK, May 4, 1940, ser. 1.1, JPK Collection, JFKL; Smith, *Hostage to Fortune*, 419; Goodwin, *The Fitzgeralds and the Kennedys*, 601.

182. Krock, *Memoirs*, 340.

183. JPK to Joseph Medill Patterson, August 22, 1940, as cited in Smith, *Hostage to Fortune*, 461–62; Farley, *Jim Farley's Story*, 264; A.P. and Moody, ed., *Triumph and Tragedy*, 71; Whalen, *The Founding Father*, 305.

184. Farley, *Jim Farley's Story*, 264; Krock, *Memoirs*, 340; Whalen, *The Founding Father*, 305.

185. Joe Kennedy Jr. to JPK, July 22, 1940, JPK Papers, ser. 1:1, Family Correspondence 1940, box 2, JPK Collection, JFKL; Smith, *Hostage to Fortune*, 450; Goodwin, *The Fitzgeralds and the Kennedys*, 604.

186. JPK to James Farley, telegram, July 19, 1940, ser. 8.21, JPK Collection, JFKL; Smith, *Hostage to Fortune*, 448.

187. Joe Kennedy Jr. to JPK, July 22, 1940, ser. 1.1., Family Correspondence 1940, box 2, JPK Collection, JFKL; Smith, *Hostage to Fortune*, 449–51.

188. JPK to Joe Kennedy Jr., July 23, 1940, ser. 1.1, JPK Collection, JFKL; Smith, *Hostage to Fortune*, 452.

189. "DM," chap. 41, pp. 3–4, JPK Collection, JFKL; Beschloss, *Kennedy and Roosevelt*, 209.

190. Langer and Gleason, *The Challenge to Isolation*, 2:569–75; Dallek, *FDR and American Foreign Policy*, 231.

191. James F. Byrnes, *All in One Lifetime* (New York: Harper & Bros., 1958), 125.

192. Interview with Arthur Krock, March 19, 1963, Washington, DC, as cited in Whalen, *The Founding Father*, 289; Beschloss, *Kennedy and Roosevelt*, 210.

193. Joe Kennedy Jr. to JPK, July 22, 1940, JPK Papers, ser. 1:1, Family Correspondence 1940, box 2, JPK Collection, JFKL; Smith, *Hostage to Fortune*, 451.

194. *Time*, November 4, 1940, 19; *New York Times*, October 8, 1940, 24; *New York Times*, September 23, 1940, 1; *New York Times*, December 2, 1940, 16.

195. JPK to Joe Kennedy Jr., July 23, 1940, JPK Papers, ser. 1:1, Family Correspondence 1940, box 2, JPK Collection, JFKL; Smith, *Hostage to Fortune*, 452.

196. Nasaw, *The Patriarch*, 464.

197. "DM," chap. 48, pp. 2–6, JPK Collection, JFKL; JPK Diary, August 1, 1940, JPK Collection, JFKL; Smith, *Hostage to Fortune*, 452–53; Nasaw, *The Patriarch*, 462.

198. "DM," chap. 48, pp. 4–6, JPK Collection, JFKL; JPK Diary, August 2, 1940, JPK Collection, JFKL; JPK to Rose Kennedy, August 2, 1940, as cited in Smith, *Hostage to Fortune*, 455; Nasaw, *The Patriarch*, 464.

199. Nasaw, *The Patriarch*, 459, 462.

200. JPK to Hull, July 5, 1940, Dept. of State; Lord Halifax's Diary, July 9, 1940, Papers of the First Earl of Halifax, Borthwick Institute for Archives, University of York, York, UK, 194; "DM," chap. 47, p. 3, JPK Collection, JFKL.

201. "DM," chap. 48, p. 5, JPK Collection, JFKL; JPK to John F. Kennedy, August 2, 1940, ser. 1.1, JPK Collection, JFKL; Smith, *Hostage to Fortune*, 454.

202. JPK to Joseph Medill Patterson, August 22, 1940, as cited in Smith, *Hostage to Fortune*, 462.

203. JPK to Rose Kennedy, August 2, 1940, as cited in Smith, *Hostage to Fortune*, 456–57.

204. JPK to John F. Kennedy, August 2, 1940, ser. 1.1, JPK Collection, JFKL; Smith, *Hostage to Fortune*, 454.

205. JPK to Robert Kennedy, July 23, 1940, ser. 1.1, JPK Collection, JFKL; Smith, *Hostage to Fortune*, 451–52.

206. JPK to John F. Kennedy, August 2, 1940, JPK Papers, ser. 1:1, Family Correspondence, 1940, box 2, JPK Collection, JFKL; Smith, *Hostage to Fortune*, 454.

207. JPK to Rose Kennedy, August 2, 1940, as cited in Smith, *Hostage to Fortune*, 456–57.

208. JPK to Robert Kennedy, July 23, 1940, ser. 1.1, JPK Collection, JFKL; Smith, *Hostage to Fortune*, 451–52.

209. "DM," chap. 48, p. 5, JPK Collection, JFKL; JPK to Rose Kennedy, August 2, 1940, as cited in Smith, *Hostage to Fortune*, 457; JPK Diary, August 14, 1940, JPK Collection, JFKL.

210. JPK to Hull, July 31, 1940, 711 Dept. of State; "DM," chap. 47, p. 6, JPK Collection, JFKL; Whalen, *The Founding Father*, 303.

211. Whalen, *The Founding Father*, 323; Goodwin, *The Fitzgeralds and the Kennedys*, 599.

212. Goodwin, No Ordinary Time, 64–65; Dallek, *FDR and American Foreign Policy*, 231.

213. FDR, *The Public Papers and Addresses of Franklin D. Roosevelt*, 1940 vol., comp. Rosenman, 264; Kershaw, Fateful Choices, 187.

214. Timothy P. Mulligan, "According to Colonel Donovan: A Document from the Records of German

Military Intelligence," *The Historian* 46, no. 1 (November 1983): 78–86; Forrest Davis and Ernest K. Lindley, *How War Came: An American White Paper: From the Fall of France to Pearl Harbor* (New York: Simon & Schuster, 1942), 96; Persico, *Roosevelt's Secret War*, 65–69; Nasaw, *The Patriarch*, 459; Whalen, *The Founding Father*, 302–3.

215. JPK Diary, July 17, 1940, JPK Collection, JFKL; JPK to Hull, diplomatic dispatch, August 7, 1940, ser. 8.6, JPK Collection, JFKL; Smith, *Hostage to Fortune*, 458–59; Persico, *Roosevelt's Secret War*, 69.

216. J. V. Perowne, September 3, 1940, FO 371/24251/A1945/605/45, PRO.

217. Whalen, *The Founding Father*, 303.

218. JPK to FDR, diplomatic dispatch, August 27, 1940, ser. 8.6, JPK Collection, JFKL; JPK to Hull, diplomatic dispatch, August 7, 1940, ser. 8.6, JPK Collection, JFKL, 459; Smith, *Hostage to Fortune*, 459, 463.

219. JPK Diary, August 8, 1940, JPK Collection, JFKL; "DM," chap. 48, pp. 7–8, JPK Collection, JFKL; JPK to Hull, diplomatic dispatch, August 7, 1940, ser. 8.6, JPK Collection, JFKL; Smith, *Hostage to Fortune*, 459; JPK Diary, August 15, 1940, 2, August 16, 1940, 1, 2, 3, JPK Collection, JFKL; Kennedy's diary of August 8, 1940, says that "it was Roosevelt pure and simple" who set up the Ghormley staff talks with the British; Nasaw, *The Patriarch*, 467.

220. JPK to Hull, diplomatic dispatch, August 7, 1940, ser. 8.6, JPK Collection, JFKL; Smith, *Hostage to Fortune*, 459.

221. *The Tatler* (London), October 30, 1940, PSF: Great Britain, FDRL; "DM," chap. 48, p. 4, JPK Collection, JFKL. JPK Diary, August 16, 1940, JPK Collection, JFKL, mentions Kennedy's resentment about the British knowing about Admiral Robert Ghormley's visit before he did too.

222. JPK to Rose Kennedy, August 2, 1940, as cited in Smith, *Hostage to Fortune*, 455.

223. *The Tatler*, October 30, 1940, PSF: Great Britain, FDRL.

224. *New York Times*, October 28, 1940, 5; Davis and Lindley, *How War Came: An American White Paper*, 96; Whalen, *The Founding Father*, 301, 303; Nasaw, *The Patriarch*, 460.

225. *The Spectator* 165 (December 13, 1940): 629; Nasaw, *The Patriarch*, 461.

226. Foreign Office Minutes, November 28, 1940, FO 371/24251/A4955/605/45, PRO; Whalen, *The Founding Father*, 301.

227. JPK Diary, August 16, 1940, JPK Collection, JFKL; Nasaw, *The Patriarch*, 467.

228. B. Gilbert, *Britain, 1914–1945*, 122.

229. Shirer, The *Rise and Fall of the Third Reich*, 1016–17.

230. Goodwin, *No Ordinary Time*, 138, 146.

231. Goodwin, *No Ordinary Time*, 138; Whalen, *The Founding Father*, 306.

232. JPK to Patterson, August 22, 1940, as cited in Smith, *Hostage to Fortune*, 462.

233. Churchill to FDR, July 31, 1940, FO 371/24240/A3582/131/45, PRO; Loewenheim et al., eds., *Roosevelt-Churchill Correspondence*, 107–8; "DM," chap. 47, p. 7, JPK Collection, JFKL; JPK to Hull, July 31, 1940, *FRUS*, 3:57–58. Kershaw, *Fateful Choices*, 214–20, gives an excellent analysis of the political pressures and lobbying that influenced Roosevelt, along with a description of Churchill's concerns about the deal.

234. King George VI to FDR, June 26, 1940, PSF: Great Britain, FDRL.

235. FDR to George VI, July 15, 1940, PSF, box 6, FDRL; Wheeler-Bennett, *King George VI*, 511.

236. Halifax to Churchill, July 31, 1940, FO 371/24240/A3582/131/45, 513–15, PRO; Koskoff, *Joseph P. Kennedy*, 205n, 206, 558–59.

237. JPK to Hull, July 31, 1940, *FRUS*, 3:57–58; Churchill to FDR, July 31, 1940, FO 371/24240/131/45, 513–15, PRO; "DM," chap. 47, p. 7, JPK Collection, JFKL; Nasaw, *The Patriarch*, 466.

238. "DM," chap. 47, p. 3, JPK Collection, JFKL.

239. JPK to Hull, July 5, 1940, 711 Dept. of State.

240. Memorandum by President Roosevelt, August 2, 1940, *FRUS*, 3:58–59; Lothian to Churchill, August 2, 1940, FO 371/24240/A3582/131/45, PRO; Foreign Office Minutes, August 3, 1940, FO 371/24241/3670/1313/45, 197, PRO; "DM," chap. 48, pp. 10–11, JPK Collection, JFKL; Loewenheim et al., eds., *Roosevelt and Churchill*, 108; Nasaw, *The Patriarch*, 466; Kershaw, *Fateful Choices*, 216.

241. *New York Times*, August 11, 1940, sec. 4, p. 8; Whalen, *The Founding Father*, 306; Nasaw, *The Patriarch*, 471; Langer and Gleason, *The Challenge to Isolation*, 2:757; Kershaw, *Fateful Choices*, 215–18.

242. Persico, *Roosevelt's Secret War*, 69.

243. Lothian to Halifax, August 3, 1940, FO 371/24241/A3640, PRO; J. Balfour, August 6, 1940, FO 371/24241, 198; Foreign Office Minutes, August 13, 1940, FO 371/24241, 203, PRO.

244. "DM," chap. 48, pp. 11–12, JPK Collection, JFKL; Loewenheim et al., eds., *Roosevelt and Churchill*, 107–8; Langer and Gleason, *The Challenge to Isolation*, 2:758–59.

245. JPK Diary, August 23, 1940, box 100, JPK Collection, JFKL; JPK Diary, August 14, 1940, JPK Collection, JFKL; Smith, *Hostage to Fortune*, 460–61; Whalen, *The Founding Father*, 307; Nasaw, *The Patriarch*, 470.

246. Loewenheim et al., eds., *Roosevelt and Churchill*, 110; JPK (Churchill) to Hull, August 15, 1940, *FRUS*, 3:66–67.

247. JPK to Hull, August 15, 1940, *FRUS*, 3:68.

248. JPK to Patterson, August 22, 1940, as cited in Smith, *Hostage to Fortune*, 462.

249. JPK Diary, October 3, 1940, JPK Collection, JFKL; FDR to JPK, August 28, 1940, PSF: Kennedy, FDRL; Roosevelt, *F.D.R.: His Personal Letters, 1928–1945*, 2:1061; Nasaw, *The Patriarch*, 471.

250. JPK to Hull, August 14, 1940, *FRUS*, 3:66; Whalen, *The Founding Father*, 307.

251. JPK to FDR, diplomatic dispatch, August 27, 1940, ser. 8.6, JPK Collection, JFKL: Smith, *Hostage to Fortune*, 463; Nasaw, *The Patriarch*, 470–71; Beschloss, *Kennedy and Roosevelt*, 211.

252. FDR to Hull, August 28, 1940, in Roosevelt, *F.D.R.: His Personal Letters, 1928–1945*, 2:1061; Whalen, *The Founding Father*, 307; Nasaw, *The Patriarch*, 471; Beschloss, *Kennedy and Roosevelt*, 212.

253. JPK to Hull, August 29, 1940, *FRUS*, 3:71–72.

254. JPK Diary, September 2, 1940, box 100, JPK Collection, JFKL, as cited in Nasaw, *The Patriarch*, 471–72.

255. JPK Diary, October 3, 1940, 2, JPK Collection, JFKL; Beschloss, *Kennedy and Roosevelt*, 211.

256. "DM," chap. 48, pp. 7–8, JPK Collection, JFKL; "DM," chap. 49, p. 1, JPK Collection, JFKL; JPK Diary,

September 2, 1940, JPK Collection, JFKL; Smith, *Hostage to Fortune*, 463.

257. "DM," chap. 48, p. 15, JPK Collection, JFKL; JPK Diary, August 23, 1940, JPK Collection, JFKL.

258. "DM," chap. 48, p. 11, JPK Collection, JFKL; JPK Diary, August 14, 1940, JPK Collection, JFKL; Smith, *Hostage to Fortune*, 460–61n556; Nasaw, *The Patriarch*, 466–67.

259. JPK Diary, September 2, 1940, JPK Collection, JFKL; Smith, *Hostage to Fortune*, 464–65.

260. "DM," chap. 49, p. 1, JPK Collection, JFKL; JPK Diary, September 2, 1940, JPK Collection, JFKL; Smith, *Hostage to Fortune*, 464.

261. "DM," chap. 49, pp. 1–2, JPK Collection, JFKL; JPK Diary, September 2, 1940, JPK Collection, JFKL; Smith, *Hostage to Fortune*, 464–65.

262. "DM," chap. 48, p. 16, JPK Collection, JFKL; JPK Diary, August 30, 1940, JPK Collection, JFKL.

263. "DM," chap. 49, pp. 1–2, JPK Collection, JFKL; JPK Diary, September 2, September 5, 1940, JPK Collection, JFKL; Smith, *Hostage to Fortune*, 464–65.

264. JPK to Hull, August 29, 1940, *FRUS*, 3:73.

265. King George VI to FDR, September 5, 1940, PSF: Great Britain, FDRL.

266. Goodwin, No Ordinary Time, 148–49; Burns, *Roosevelt: The Lion and the Fox*, 441–42.

267. JPK to Hull, August 29, 1940, *FRUS*, 3:73; Whalen, *The Founding Father*, 308.

268. Kershaw, Fateful Choices, 219–20; Whalen, *The Founding Father*, 308; Burns, *Roosevelt: The Lion and the Fox*, 441.

269. M. Gilbert, *Churchill*, 6:347; Whalen, *The Founding Father*, 308.

270. Kershaw, Fateful Choices, 218–19; Burns, *Roosevelt: The Lion and the Fox*, 440–41.

271. Krock, *Memoirs*, 336.

272. *New York Times*, September 4, 1940, 1; "DM," chap. 49, pp. 3–4, JPK Collection, JFKL; JPK Diary, September 4, 1940, 2, JPK Collection, JFKL; Whalen, *The Founding Father*, 309; B. Gilbert, *Britain, 1914–1945*, 125.

273. JPK to FDR and Hull, diplomatic dispatch, September 6, 1940, ser. 8.6, JPK Collection, JFKL; Smith, *Hostage to Fortune*, 465; JPK Diary, September 6, 1940, box 100, JPK Collection, JFKL; Nasaw, *The Patriarch*, 473.

274. B. Gilbert, *Britain, 1914–1945*, 125–26.

275. Winston Churchill, "'Some Chicken—Some Neck!' Mr. Churchill at Ottawa," *British Pathé*, December 30, 1941, video 3:10, https://www.britishpathe.com/video/some-chicken-some-neck-mr-churchill-at-ottawa/query/some+chicken.

276. B. Gilbert, *Britain, 1914–1945*, 124–26.

277. JPK to Hull, September 11, 1940, 711 Dept. of State.

278. JPK to Robert Kennedy, September 11, 1940, ser. 1.1, JPK Collection, JFKL; Smith, *Hostage to Fortune*, 469–70.

279. JPK to Hull, September 11, 1940, 711 Dept. of State.

280. JPK to Hull, September 20, 1940, 711 War, Dept. of State.

281. JPK to Rose Kennedy, August 2, 1940, as cited in Smith, *Hostage to Fortune*, 433, 455.

282. JPK to John F. Kennedy, September 10, 1940, as cited in Smith, *Hostage to Fortune*, 468–69.

283. JPK to Rose Kennedy, September 10, 1940, as cited in Smith, *Hostage to Fortune*, 466–67.

284. JPK to Hull, September 11, 1940, 711 Dept. of State.

285. JPK to Rose Kennedy, September 10, 1940, as cited in Smith, *Hostage to Fortune*, 466.

286. JPK to Hull, September 11, 1940, 711 Dept. of State; JPK to John F. Kennedy, September 10, 1940, as cited in Smith, *Hostage to Fortune*, 469.

287. Whalen, *The Founding Father*, 322; Dinneen, *The Kennedy Family*, 80.

288. JPK to Hull, September 11, 1940, 711 Dept. of State; "DM," chap. 49, pp. 6–7, JPK Collection, JFKL, contains interesting descriptions of life at the embassy during the Blitz.

289. Foreign Office Minutes, October 11, 1940, FO 371/24251/A4485/605/45, PRO; Whalen, *The Founding Father*, 322.

290. D'Este, *Warlord*, 407.

291. Lord Halifax's Diary, August 29, 1940, 260; Nasaw, *The Patriarch*, 469.

292. Rose Kennedy, *Times to Remember*, 273.

293. *New York Times*, August 26, 1940, 1.

294. *New York Times*, October 2, 1940, 4.

295. *New York Times*, October 12, 1940, 4.

296. *New York Times*, September 24, 1940, 3.

297. *New York Times*, November 7, 1940, 15; Whalen, *The Founding Father*, 322.

298. *New York Times*, October 2, 1940, 4; October 6, 1940, 72; October 8, 1940, 24.

299. JPK to Rose Kennedy, September 10, 1940, as cited in Smith, *Hostage to Fortune*, 467.

300. Kennedy envisioned traditional roles for his daughters, who, unlike the boys, were educated in convent and Catholic schools.

301. JPK to John F. Kennedy, September 10, 1940, as cited in Smith, *Hostage to Fortune*, 468.

302. JPK to Rose Kennedy, August 2, 1940, ser. 1.1, JPK Collection, JFKL; Smith, *Hostage to Fortune*, 454.

303. JPK to John F. Kennedy, September 10, 1940, as cited in Smith, *Hostage to Fortune*, 468.

304. JPK to Robert Kennedy, September 11, 1940, ser. 1.1, JPK Collection, JFKL; Smith, *Hostage to Fortune*, 470.

305. JPK to Edward Kennedy, September 11, 1940, as cited in Smith, *Hostage to Fortune*, 471.

306. JPK to Rose Kennedy, September 10, 1940, as cited in Smith, *Hostage to Fortune*, 466.

307. JPK to Rose Kennedy, September 11, 1940, as cited in Smith, *Hostage to Fortune*, 471.

308. JPK to Rose Kennedy, August 2, 1940, as cited in Smith, *Hostage to Fortune*, 455–56.

309. JPK to Rose Kennedy, September 10, 1940, as cited in Smith, *Hostage to Fortune*, 466.

310. JPK to Rose Kennedy, August 2, 1940, as cited in Smith, *Hostage to Fortune*, 456; "DM," chap. 48, p. 4, JPK Collection, JFKL.

311. JPK to Rose Kennedy, August 2, 1940, as cited in Smith, *Hostage to Fortune*, 455–56.

312. JPK to Brendan Bracken, August 8, 1940, ser. 8.2.1, JPK Collection, JFKL; Smith, *Hostage to Fortune*, 460.

313. JPK to Rose Kennedy, September 10, 1940, as cited in Smith, *Hostage to Fortune*, 467.

314. JPK to Rose Kennedy, September 10, 1940, as cited in Smith, *Hostage to Fortune*, 466.

315. JPK to Rose Kennedy, September 10, 1940, as cited in Smith, *Hostage to Fortune*, 467.

316. JPK Diary, August 16, 1940, JPK Collection, JFKL; Nasaw, *The Patriarch*, 467.

317. Krock, *Memoirs*, 334.

318. *The Economist*, May 25, 1940, 925.

319. Foreign Office Minutes, August 22, 1940, FO 371/24251/A1945/605/45, 77, PRO.

320. *New York Times*, October 6, 1940, sec. 4, p. 72.

321. Bilainkin, *Diary of a Diplomatic Correspondent*, 239.

322. *Boston Globe*, November 10, 1940, 21; Whalen, *The Founding Father*, 327.

323. Nasaw, *The Patriarch*, 478.

324. Foreign Office Minutes, August 22, 1940, FO 371/24251/A1945/605/45, 77, PRO.

325. Foreign Office Minutes, October 11, 1940, FO 371/24251/A4485/605/45, 94, PRO.

326. Foreign Office Minutes, August 22, 1940, FO 371/24251/A1945/605/45, 77, PRO.

327. Foreign Office Minutes, October 11, 1940, FO 371/24251/A4485/605/45, 95, PRO.

328. Foreign Office Minutes, August 22, 1940, September 3, 1940, FO 371/24251/A4485/605/45, 95, PRO.

329. Bilainkin, *Diary of a Diplomatic Correspondent*, 244.

330. Memo by Graham Hatton, October 18, 1940, FO 371/24251/A4485/605/45, PRO.

331. Foreign Office Minutes, October 10, 1940, FO 371/24251/A4485/605/45, PRO; Nasaw, *The Patriarch*, 483.

332. Foreign Office Minutes, October 10, 1940, FO 371/24251/A4485/605/45, PRO.

333. Unsigned memo, October 19, 1940, FO 371/24251/A4483/605/45, PRO.

334. *New York Times*, October 15, 1940, 4.

335. Krock, *Memoirs*, 335.

336. *New York Times*, October 8, 1940, 24.

337. Krock, *Memoirs*, 335; Whalen, *The Founding Father*, 329; Nasaw, *The Patriarch*, 481–82.

338. *New York Times*, October 16, 1940, 6.

339. FDR to JPK, October 17, 1940, as cited in Smith, *Hostage to Fortune*, 475; Nasaw, *The Patriarch*, 482–83.

340. *New York Times*, October 16, 1940, 6.

341. Alsop and Kintner, *Atlanta Constitution*, October 8, 1940, 6; Nasaw, *The Patriarch*, 481.

342. Alsop and Kintner, *Atlanta Constitution*, October 8, 1940, 6; Nasaw, *The Patriarch*, 481.

343. Bilainkin, *Diary of a Diplomatic Correspondent*, 244.

344. International News Service, New York Survey, October 15, 1940, FO 371/24251/A4485/605/45, 98, PRO.

345. Alsop and Kintner, *Atlanta Constitution*, October 8, 1940, 6; Nasaw, *The Patriarch*, 481.

346. *New York Times*, October 8, 1940, 24.

347. Rose Kennedy to JPK, October 7, 1940, as cited in Smith, *Hostage to Fortune*, 474–75.

348. Whalen, *The Founding Father*, 328.

349. JPK Diary, October 11, 1940, 2–4, JPK Collection, JFKL.

350. *Time*, November 4, 1940, 19.

351. Lord Halifax's Diary, October 17, 1940, 309; JPK Diary, October 18, 1940, 2, JPK Collection, JFKL; Nasaw, *The Patriarch*, 483; Koskoff, *Joseph P. Kennedy*, 296, writes that Joe Jr. was publicly urging the reelection of Roosevelt. Ever loyal to his father, he may have known that his father would not embarrass Roosevelt.

352. JPK Diary, October 15, 1940, 1–5, JPK Collection, JFKL; Nasaw, *The Patriarch*, 483–84.

353. JPK Diary, October 16, 1940, 5, JPK Collection, JFKL.

354. JPK Diary, October 16, 1940, 2–3, JPK Collection, JFKL.

355. JPK Diary, October 16, 1940, 6, JPK Collection, JFKL; Nasaw, *The Patriarch*, 484.

356. Nasaw, *The Patriarch*, 484–85.

357. JPK to Hull, July 31, 1940, 711 Dept. of State.

358. "DM," chap. 50, p. 10, JPK Collection, JFKL; Smith, *Hostage to Fortune*, 477.

359. "DM," chap. 50, pp. 10–11, JPK Collection, JFKL; JPK Diary, October 19, 1940, JPK Collection, JFKL; Smith, *Hostage to Fortune*, 476–77; JPK Diary, November 9, 1940, JPK Collection, JFKL; Smith, *Hostage to Fortune*, 493.

360. *Time*, November 4, 1940, 19.

361. *Liverpool Post*, August 6, 1940, JPK Papers, ser. 8.2.2, Ambassador Correspondence, Newspapers and Misc. Publications, 1940, box 129, JPK Collection, JFKL.

362. *New York Times*, October 23, 1940, 4; *Times*, October 22, 1940, 5.

363. *Time*, November 4, 1940, 19.

364. Bilainkin, *Diary of a Diplomatic Correspondent*, 241–42: Kennedy writes in his diary that he left on October 21; Diary, October 22, 1940, JPK Collection, JFKL; Smith, *Hostage to Fortune*, 478–79.

365. JPK to Hull, September 27, 1940, 711 Dept. of State.

366. JPK Diary, September 24, 1940, JPK Collection, JFKL; Smith, *Hostage to Fortune*, 472–73.

Chapter 11. To Be *and* Not to Be

1. *New York Times*, October 27, 1940, 24; *Business Insider*, August 23, 2013, n.p.; Pan American Historical Foundation has extensive information and photos of this plane.

2. "DM," chap. 51, p. 1, JPK Collection, JFKL; JPK Diary, October 22, 1940, JPK Collection, JFKL; Smith, *Hostage to Fortune*, 478; *Times* (London), October 23, 1940, 4; *New York Times*, October 24, 1940, 4, 5; October 25, 1940, 3; October 26, 1940, 3; October 27, 1940, 24.

3. Chamberlain to JPK, October 19, 1940, JPK Papers, ser. 8.2.1, Ambassador Correspondence file, 1040, box 104, JPK Collection, JFKL; JPK Diary, October 27, 1940, JPK Collection, JFKL; Smith, *Hostage to Fortune*, 481n591.

4. "DM," chap. 51, pp. 1–2, JPK Collection, JFKL; JPK to Chamberlain, October 22, 1940, ser. 8.2.1, JPK Collection, JFKL; Smith, *Hostage to Fortune*, 477.

5. Taylor, *Munich*, 767.

6. *New York Times*, November 11, 1940, 4; "DM," chap. 52, p. 3, JPK Collection, JFKL; JPK Diary, November 9, 1940, JPK Collection, JFKL; Smith, *Hostage to Fortune*, 493; Nasaw, *The Patriarch*, 485.

7. Craig and Gilbert, *The Diplomats, 1919–39*, 669; Whalen, *The Founding Father*, 265.

8. JPK Diary, October 22, 1940, JPK Collection, JFKL; Smith, *Hostage to Fortune*, 479.

9. "DM," chap. 51, p. 1, JPK Collection, JFKL; JPK Diary, October 22, 1940, JPK Collection, JFKL; Smith, *Hostage to Fortune*, 478.

10. *New York Times*, October 24, 1940, 5; Whalen, *The Founding Father*, 330.

11. *New York Times*, October 25, 1940, 3.

12. Memo to FDR from E.M.W. Col. Watson, October 25, 1940, PSF: Great Britain, Kennedy, FDRL.

13. Memo to Missy LeHand from Lauchlin Currie, October 25, 1940, PSF: Great Britain, Kennedy, box 37, FDRL; Krock, *Memoirs*, 335; Nasaw, *The Patriarch*, 490.

14. "DM," chap. 51, pp. 1–2, JPK Collection, JFKL; JPK Diary, October 25, 1940, JPK Collection, JFKL; FDR to JPK, telegram, October 25, 1940, JPK Collection, JFKL; Smith, *Hostage to Fortune*, 479. Krock in his *Memoirs*, 399, describes a conversation he had with Lyndon B. Johnson, who said he was present and overheard a phone call between Kennedy and Roosevelt when Kennedy arrived in the United States. FDR said, "'Ah, Joe, old friend, it is so good to hear your voice. Please come to the White House tonight for a little family dinner. I'm dying to talk to you.' As Johnson told Krock, Roosevelt putting down the telephone, drew his forefinger, razor-fashion, across his throat." Koskoff in *Joseph P. Kennedy: His Life and Times* (569n16) gives different interpretations as to what the cut-throat gesture meant; Beschloss, *Kennedy and Roosevelt*, 215, refers to the same incident.

15. James F. Byrnes, *All in One Lifetime* (New York: Harper & Bros., 1958), 125–26.

16. *New York Times*, October 28, 1940, 1, 7.

17. FDR to JPK, October 27, 1940, as cited in Smith, *Hostage to Fortune*, 480.

18. *New York Times*, October 28, 1940, 7; *Time*, November 4, 1940, 19; Nasaw, *The Patriarch*, 490; Beschloss, *Kennedy and Roosevelt*, 215.

19. *New York Times*, October 28, 1940, 1, 7; Whalen, *The Founding Father*, 331; Koskoff, *Joseph P. Kennedy*, 296: Joseph P. Kennedy Jr. was publicly campaigning for Roosevelt's reelection, evidence that the ambassador would do so, too. "The Ambassador's son, ever loyal to his father, must have known something that few others—not even Roosevelt—knew. Kennedy had determined that at the end he was not going to embarrass the President."

20. "DM," chap. 51, p. 4, JPK Collection, JFKL; JPK Diary, October 27, 1940, JPK Collection, JFKL; Smith, *Hostage to Fortune*, 481; Gail Cameron, *Rose: A Biography of Rose Fitzgerald Kennedy* (New York: G.P. Putnam's Sons, 1971), 145.

21. Interview with Arthur Krock, March 19, 1963, in Washington, DC, as cited in Whalen, *The Founding Father*, 333; Beschloss, *Kennedy and Roosevelt*, 216.

22. Schlesinger Jr., *Robert Kennedy and His Times*, 35.

23. Rose F. Kennedy Papers, ser. 1, Diaries 1939–1940, box 3, JFKL; *New York Times*, October 28, 1940, 1; Schlesinger Jr., *Robert Kennedy and His Times*, 35.

24. Krock, *Memoirs*, 335; interview with Arthur Krock, March 19, 1963, in Washington, DC, as cited in Whalen, *The Founding Father*, 333.

25. "DM," chap. 51, p. 3, JPK Collection, JFKL; JPK Diary, October 27, 1940, JPK Collection, JFKL; Smith, *Hostage to Fortune*, 481.

26. Krock, *Memoirs*, 336; "DM," chap. 51, pp. 3–4, JPK Collection, JFKL; JPK Diary, October 27, 1940, JPK Collection, JFKL; Smith, *Hostage to Fortune*, 481; Rose F. Kennedy Papers, ser. 1, Diaries 1939–1940, box 3, JFKL. Rose wrote in her diary that she was asked to go on the radio and speak as a mother assuring other American mothers that Roosevelt would not get the country into war.

27. JPK Diary, October 27, 1940, JPK Collection, JFKL; Smith, *Hostage to Fortune*, 481.

28. "DM," chap. 51, p. 4, JPK Collection, JFKL; Krock, *Memoirs*, 336.

29. JPK Diary, October 27, 1940, JPK Collection, JFKL; Smith, *Hostage to Fortune*, 481.

30. Rose Kennedy, *Times to Remember*, 275.

31. Krock, *Memoirs*, 336; "DM," chap. 51, p. 4, JPK Collection, JFKL; JPK Diary, October 27, 1940, JPK Collection, JFKL; Smith, *Hostage to Fortune*, 481; Beschloss, *Kennedy and Roosevelt*, 217; Goodwin, *The Fitzgeralds and the Kennedys*, 612.

32. Rose Kennedy, *Times to Remember*, 274.

33. "DM," chap. 51, p. 4, JPK Collection, JFKL; JPK Diary, October 27, 1940, JPK Collection, JFKL; Smith, *Hostage to Fortune*, 481.

34. Krock, *Memoirs*, 336.

35. "DM," chap. 51, p. 4, JPK Collection, JFKL; JPK Diary, October 27, 1940, JPK Collection, JFKL; Smith, *Hostage to Fortune*, 481.

36. Byrnes, *All in One Lifetime*, 126; Whalen, *The Founding Father*, 331.

37. "DM," chap. 51, p. 5, JPK Collection, JFKL; JPK Diary, October 27, 1940, JPK Collection, JFKL; Smith, *Hostage to Fortune*, 481.

38. JPK Diary, October 27, 1940, JPK Collection, JFKL; Smith, *Hostage to Fortune*, 482; Goodwin, *The Fitzgeralds and the Kennedys*, 612.

39. Byrnes, *All in One Lifetime*, 126; Goodwin, *The Fitzgeralds and the Kennedys*, 612; Whalen, *The Founding Father*, 332.

40. Rose Kennedy, *Times to Remember*, 274. Bearse and Read, *Conspirator*, 222, write that there is another version of those events from President Lyndon B. Johnson. He said that at the meeting between Roosevelt and Kennedy, Roosevelt had "thrown the red meat on the floor" and told Kennedy that "confirmed intelligence reports that the ambassador had been associating with a German propagandist, a Dr. Westphal, and with pro-German industrialists such as James Mooney of General Motors. In essence, according to Johnson, Roosevelt was saying, 'Give me public support or I'll throw you to the public as a pro-German bastard.' The blackmail worked, and Kennedy stepped into line with his Tuesday night radio speech."

41. "DM," chap. 51, p. 5, JPK Collection, JFKL; JPK Diary, October 27, 1940, JPK Collection, JFKL; Smith, *Hostage to Fortune*, 482.

42. Byrnes, *All in One Lifetime*, 126.

43. Interview with Rose Kennedy as cited in Goodwin, *The Fitzgeralds and the Kennedys*, 612.

44. Beschloss, *Kennedy and Roosevelt*, 218.

45. JPK Diary, October 27, 1940, JPK Collection, JFKL; Smith, *Hostage to Fortune*, 480–82; Nasaw, *The Patriarch*, 493.

46. "DM," chap. 51, p. 6, JPK Collection, JFKL; JPK Diary, October 27, 1940, JPK Collection, JFKL; Smith, *Hostage to Fortune*, 482.

47. Byrnes, *All in One Lifetime*, 126; "DM," chap. 51, p. 6, JPK Collection, JFKL.

48. "DM," chap. 52, pp. 1–2, JPK Collection, JFKL; Kennedy, *Notes Dictated by Ambassador for His Diary*, November 4, 1940, as cited in Smith, *Hostage to Fortune*, 491; Whalen, *The Founding Father*, 332; Nasaw, *The Patriarch*, 491–92. Kennedy writes in his memoir that in the week before the election, Supreme Court Justice Frank Murphy told Kennedy that about ten days prior to the election, Justice Frankfurter asked him what could be done to save the shrinking Catholic vote. Murphy said that the only remedy would be to have Kennedy make a speech for the president. "He's the only one who can do it"; Kennedy "was a 'must,'" the president's advisers agreed, and decided to leave it to Roosevelt to approach him.

49. *New York Herald Tribune*, October 28, 1940, 4; JPK Diary, October 27, 1940; Smith, *Hostage to Fortune*, 482; Beschloss, *Kennedy and Roosevelt*, 219.

50. Rose F. Kennedy Papers, ser. 1, Diaries 1939–1940, box 3, JFKL. Rose Kennedy wrote in her diary that she and Kennedy spent the night at the White House. She seems to have been confused. Only she spent the night there. *New York Times*, October 28, 1940, 1; Beschloss, *Kennedy and Roosevelt*, 219; Whalen, *The Founding Father*, 334; Nasaw, *The Patriarch*, 494.

51. *New York Herald Tribune*, October 28, 1940, 1, 4; Whalen, *The Founding Father*, 334–35.

52. *New York Times*, October 29, 1940, 19.

53. Byrnes, *All in One Lifetime*, 126; Whalen, *The Founding Father*, 335.

54. *New York Times*, October 29, 1940, 3.

55. *New York Times*, October 29, 1940, 19; Whalen, *The Founding Father*, 335.

56. Clare Luce to JPK, October 28, 1940, box 100, JPK Collection, JFKL.

57. Bilainkin, *Diary of a Diplomatic Correspondent*, 252.

58. Koskoff, *Joseph P. Kennedy*, 298.

59. *New York Times*, October 30, 1940, 1, 8; Kennedy, Radio Address, October 29, 1940, as cited in Smith, *Hostage to Fortune*, 482–89.

60. FDR to JPK, telegram, October 29, 1940, as cited in Smith, *Hostage to Fortune*, 489.

61. Byrnes, *All in One Lifetime*, 126.

62. John F. Kennedy to JPK, telegram, October 30, 1940, as cited in Smith, *Hostage to Fortune*, 489.

63. Kathleen Kennedy to JPK, October 30, 1940, as cited in Smith, *Hostage to Fortune*, 489.

64. F. A. Williamson, Los Angeles, CA, to White House, October 29, 1940, Kennedy: 1938–1940, box 1, FDRL.

65. W. H. Nichols, Cincinnati, OH, to White House, October 29, 1940, Kennedy: 1938–1942, box 1, FDRL.

66. Egerton Shore, Los Angeles, CA, to White House, October 29, 1940, Kennedy: 1938–1942, box 1, FDRL.

67. *Life*, January 27, 1941, 27.

68. *New York Times*, October 31, 1940, 19.

69. Krock, *Memoirs*, 334–37.

70. Whalen, *The Founding Father*, 332.

71. *New York Times*, October 28, 1940, 7.

72. Rose Kennedy, *Times to Remember*, 275.

73. *New York Times*, December 2, 1940, 16.

74. Stewart Alsop's column, *Saturday Evening Post*, August 13, 1960, 59; Koskoff, *Joseph P. Kennedy*, 297: John Kennedy was asked whether Roosevelt offered Joe Kennedy the presidential nomination in 1944 and John laughed it off as if to dismiss it. He said: "I don't know—my father certainly thought he had"; Beschloss, *Kennedy and Roosevelt*, 218: it was vintage Roosevelt to "offer" the presidential nod to various people whom he needed; Whalen, *The Founding Father*, 332–33.

75. Interview with Clare Boothe Luce as cited in Beschloss, *Kennedy and Roosevelt*, 221; Smith, *Hostage to Fortune*, 482n593.

76. Whalen, *The Founding Father*, 333.

77. Cameron, *Rose Kennedy*, 145–46; Whalen, *The Founding Father*, 333–34.

78. *New York Times*, October 31, 1940, 1, 14.

79. *Chicago Herald American*, October 30, 1940, 1, as cited in Beschloss, *Kennedy and Roosevelt*, 221.

80. *New York Times*, October 31, 1940, 1, 14; Smith, *Hostage to Fortune*, 489n594; Sherwood, *Roosevelt and Hopkins*, 191–92.

81. Beschloss, *Kennedy and Roosevelt*, 259.

82. *New York Times*, October 31, 1940, 14; Sherwood, *Roosevelt and Hopkins*, 191–92.

83. Sherwood, *Roosevelt and Hopkins*, 191–92.

84. *New York Times*, November 1, 1940, 1.

85. *New York Times*, November 2, 1940, 7.

86. Dallek, *FDR and American Foreign Policy*, 250; Burns, *Roosevelt: The Lion and the Fox*, 454.

87. JPK Papers, ser. 5.1, Roosevelt and Politics: Correspondence 1940, box 71, JPK Collection, JFKL.

88. "DM," chap. 52, pp. 2–3, JPK Collection, JFKL; Kennedy, *Notes Dictated by Ambassador for His Diary*, November 4, 1940, as cited in Smith, *Hostage to Fortune*, 491–92; Koskoff, *Joseph P. Kennedy*, 299; Whalen, *The Founding Father*, 338.

89. "DM," chap. 52, p. 4, JPK Collection, JFKL; JPK Diary, November 30, 1940, JPK Collection, JFKL; Smith, *Hostage to Fortune*, 495; Koskoff, *Joseph P. Kennedy*, 299.

90. Goodwin, *No Ordinary Time*, 100.

91. Nasaw, *The Patriarch*, 496–97.

92. Long and Israel, *The War Diary of Breckinridge Long*, 146–48.

93. *Times*, November 9, 1940, 3; *Boston Sunday Globe*, November 10, 1940, 1, 21.

94. JPK Diary, November 30, 1940, JPK Collection, JFKL; Smith, *Hostage to Fortune*, 494; *New York Post*, January 9, 1961, 85; Louis M. Lyons, *Newspaper Story: One Hundred Years of the Boston Globe* (Cambridge, MA: Belknap Press of Harvard University Press, 1971), 290; Joseph F. Dinneen, *The Kennedy Family* (Boston: Little, Brown and Co., 1959), 81.

95. Cong. Rec. A6624 (November 12, 1940) (*Boston Evening Transcript*).

96. Cong. Rec. A6624 (November 10, 1940) (*Boston Sunday Globe*, 21); Lyons, *Newspaper Story*, 291;

Goodwin, *The Fitzgeralds and the Kennedys*, 614.

97. Lyons, *Newspaper Story*, 291.

98. Dinneen, *The Kennedy Family*, 81–82; Goodwin, *The Fitzgeralds and the Kennedys*, 614.

99. JPK Diary, November 30, 1940, JPK Collection, JFKL; Smith, *Hostage to Fortune*, 494; Goodwin, *The Fitzgeralds and the Kennedys*, 614; Whalen, *The Founding Father*, 339.

100. Lyons, *Newspaper Story*, 291; Nasaw, *The Patriarch*, 498.

101. Cong. Rec. A6623 (November 10, 1940) (*Boston Sunday Globe*, 21).

102. Cong. Rec. A6622 (November 10, 1940) (*Boston Sunday Globe*, 1); Dinneen, *The Kennedy Family*, 85–86.

103. Cong Rec. A6624 (November 12, 1940) (*Boston Evening Transcript*); Lyons, *Newspaper Story*, 292.

104. Cong. Rec. A6623 (November 10, 1940) (*Boston Sunday Globe*, 21); Dinneen, *The Kennedy Family*, 85–86; Goodwin, *The Fitzgeralds and the Kennedys*, 615; Whalen, *The Founding Father*, 339–42.

105. Cong. Rec. A6623 (November 10, 1940) (*Boston Sunday Globe*, 21); Lyons, *Newspaper Story*, 292; Whalen, *The Founding Father*, 342.

106. *New York Post*, January 9, 1961, 85–86; Dinneen, *The Kennedy Family*, 83–86; Lyons, *Newspaper Story*, 292; Whalen, *The Founding Father*, 343; Nasaw, *The Patriarch*, 499–500.

107. Cong. Rec. A6624 (November 12, 1940) (*Boston Evening Transcript*).

108. Cong. Rec. A6622–23 (November 10, 1940) (*Boston Sunday Globe*, 1, 21); (November 19, 1940) (*Saint Louis Post-Dispatch*, 1); Lyons, *Newspaper Story*, 291–92; Dinneen, *The Kennedy Family*, 84; Whalen, *The Founding Father*, 340–42.

109. Cong. Rec. A6622–24 (November 10, 1940) (*Boston Sunday Globe*, 1, 21); (November 19, 1940) (*Saint Louis Post-Dispatch*, 1); *New York Herald Tribune*, December 5, 1940, 4; Dinneen, *The Kennedy Family*, 86; Lyons, *Newspaper Story*, 292; Whalen, *The Founding Father*, 340–42; Nasaw, *The Patriarch*, 498–99.

110. Dinneen, *The Kennedy Family*, 86; *New York Times*, November 12, 1940, 5.

111. Dinneen, *The Kennedy Family*, 86; Whalen, *The Founding Father*, 343, 345.

112. Ickes, *The Secret Diary of Harold Ickes*, vol. 3, December 1, 1940, 386.

113. Cong. Rec. A6624 (November 12, 1940) (*New York Times*, 5); *Times*, November 13, 1940, 3, 99, FO 371/24251A4485/605/45.

114. Cong. Rec. A6624 (November 11, 1940).

115. *New York Times*, November 12, 1940, 5; Whalen, *The Founding Father*, 344.

116. *New York Post*, January 9, 1961, 85–86; Edward Linn, "The Truth about Joe Kennedy," *Saga*, July 1961, 86; Whalen, *The Founding Father*, 344.

117. Lyons, *Newspaper Story*, 293; Whalen, *The Founding Father*, 344. George Tinkham, a Republican congressman, included a copy of the *Globe* article and follow-up articles in the *New York Times* and the *Boston Evening Transcript* as appendices in the *Congressional Record* on November 19, 1940. Cong. Rec. A6624 (November 19, 1940) (*Boston Globe, New York Times, Boston Evening Transcript*) (ent. Cong. Pinkham); Nasaw, *The Patriarch*, 500.

118. Dinneen, *The Kennedy Family*, 87.

119. Koskoff, *Joseph P. Kennedy*, 570n45.

120. Lyons, *Newspaper Story*, 290–94; Edward Linn's article in the *New York Post*, January 9, 1961, 85, says Lyons made "meticulously careful notes. Nothing was said about any of the conversation being off-the-record."

121. Interview with James M. Landis in New York on September 21, 1962, as cited in Whalen, *The Founding Father*, 344.

122. Interview with Arthur Krock in Washington, DC, on March 19, 1963, as cited in Whalen, *The Founding Father*, 344.

123. Krock, *Memoirs*, 337.

124. *News Chronicle*, November 13, 1940, FO 371/24251/A1945/605/45, PRO.

125. J. V. Perowne, November 25, 1940, FO 371/24251/A1945/605/45, 72, PRO.

126. Lord Lothian, Dispatch #2659, November 13, 1940, FO 371/24251/A4485/605/45, 99, PRO.

127. *New York Times*, November 26, 1940, 4; *Times*, November 26, 1940, 4.

128. *New York Times*, December 7, 1940, 6; Koskoff, *Joseph P. Kennedy*, 305–6.

129. *Daily Mail*, November 29, 1940, 2; Whalen, *The Founding Father*, 347.

130. *The Economist*, November 30, 1940, 664.

131. *Times*, November 26, 1940, 4.

132. Bilainkin, *Diary of a Diplomatic Correspondent*, 262.

133. JPK Papers ser. 8.2.1, Ambassador Correspondence File, London 1940, box 104, JPK Collection, JFKL.

134. *New York Times*, November 30, 1940, 6; Foreign Office Minutes, December 1940, FO 371/24251/A1945/605/45, 71.

135. Bilainkin, *Diary of a Diplomatic Correspondent*, 262.

136. JPK to James Seymour, December 9, 1940, FO 371/24251/A1945/604/45, n.p., PRO, as cited in Goodwin, *The Fitzgeralds and the Kennedys*, 874n617.

137. Interview with Wheeler by Whalen, October 19, 1962, in Washington, DC, as cited in Whalen, *The Founding Father*, 356, 518n13.

138. JPK to James Seymour, December 9, 1940, FO 371/24251/A1945/605/45 1941, PRO, as cited in Goodwin, *The Fitzgeralds and the Kennedys*, 617, 874; "The Washington Merry-Go-Round," *Boston Transcript*, November 26, 1940, OF 3060, FDRL; Ickes, *The Secret Diary of Harold Ickes*, vol. 3, December 1, 1940, 386, says that there were two hundred people in attendance; Beschloss, *Kennedy and Roosevelt*, 226; Koskoff, *Joseph P. Kennedy*, 304.

139. Douglas Fairbanks Jr. to FDR, November 19, 1940, Kennedy: 1938–1942, box 1, FDRL; Beschloss, *Kennedy and Roosevelt*, 226; Nasaw, *The Patriarch*, 501–2.

140. "The Washington Merry-Go-Round," *Boston Transcript*, November 26, 1940, OF 3060, FDRL; Whalen, *The Founding Father*, 346.

141. JPK Diary, July 7, 1941, 530–31, JPK Collection, JFKL; Nasaw, *The Patriarch*, 501–2, 507–9, for an interesting discussion of his view of Kennedy's anti-Semitism, which Nasaw described as "paranoia about Jewish influence." Kennedy blamed the Jews for his having become an outsider.

142. JPK to Hearst, November 26, 1940, as cited in Smith, *Hostage to Fortune*, 494.

143. Marion Davies, *The Times We Had: Life with William Randolph Hearst* (New York: Bobbs-Merrill Co., 1975), 222; Beschloss, *Kennedy and Roosevelt*, 227–28.

144. John Boettiger to FDR, February 19, 1941, Anna Roosevelt Halsted Papers, FDRL; Beschloss, *Kennedy and Roosevelt*, 228.

145. Ickes, *The Secret Diary of Harold Ickes*, vol. 3, December 1, 1940, 386; Beschloss, *Kennedy and Roosevelt*, 226; Nasaw, *The Patriarch*, 505; Whalen, *The Founding Father*, 347; Koskoff, *Joseph P. Kennedy*, 304. Beschloss, *Kennedy and Roosevelt*, 231, wrote that Roosevelt uncovered a campaign for businessmen and financiers to negotiate a peace and discussed it during a Cabinet meeting. The movement was apparently led by Bernard E. Smith, who traveled to Vichy in December to discuss the issue with members of the Pétain government. The *Chicago Daily News* published the story on December 4 and named Kennedy as the person behind Smith's mission. Kennedy told the newspaper that he barely knew Smith and hadn't seen him for two years. When asked whether he had anything to do with Smith's meeting with the Pétain government, Kennedy said, "I think my first statement answers all questions." But Carroll Binder of the *Daily News* reported to a British diplomat that Kennedy had been trying to bring about a peace settlement and confirmed that he had sent Smith to Pétain and Hitler to try to establish a negotiated peace. Binder then said that Roosevelt discovered Kennedy's plan and asked Ambassador William Leahy to persuade Pétain not to meet with Smith. Ickes, *The Secret Diary of Harold L. Ickes*, 395, said that Roosevelt specifically mentioned Kennedy and Smith among others as "our appeasers" in a Cabinet meeting.

146. Ickes, *The Secret Diary of Harold Ickes*, vol. 3, December 1, 1940, 386.

147. *New York Daily News*, June 20, 1938, 2; Whalen, *The Founding Father*, 225.

148. *New York Review of Books*, November 18, 1971, Gore Vidal, *Eleanor and Franklin: The Story of Their Relationship Based on Eleanor Roosevelt's Private Papers by Joseph P. Lash*; Joseph P. Lash, *Eleanor: The Years Alone* (New York: W.W. Norton, 1972), 287; Beschloss, *Kennedy and Roosevelt*, 229.

149. *New York Times*, December 3, 1940, 14; Nasaw, *The Patriarch*, 503–4.

150. JPK Diary, December 1, 1940, JPK Collection, JFKL; Smith, *Hostage to Fortune*, 496–97; "DM," chap. 52, pp. 5–6, JPK Collection, JFKL; Dallek, *FDR and American Foreign Policy*, 253.

151. *New York Times*, December 2, 1940, 1; JPK to FDR, JPK Papers, ser. 5.1, Roosevelt and Politics: Correspondence 1940, box 71, JPK Collection, JFKL; JPK Papers, ser. 8.2.1, Ambassador Correspondence File, London 1940, box 104; JPK, Press Release, December 1, 1940, as cited in Smith, *Hostage to Fortune*, 497; Foreign Office Minutes, FO 371/24251/A1945/6054/45, PRO.

152. JPK Diary, December 1, 1940, JPK Collection, JFKL; Smith, *Hostage to Fortune*, 496.

153. Whalen, *The Founding Father*, 345.

154. *New York Times*, December 3, 1940, 11; Whalen, *The Founding Father*, 345.

155. *New York Herald Tribune*, December 5, 1940, 4.

156. *New York Times*, December 2, 1940, 6.

157. *New York Times*, December 3, 1940, 11.

158. Ickes, *The Secret Diary of Harold Ickes*, vol. 3, December 1, 1940, 370.

159. *New York Times*, November 24, 1940, 42; *Washington Times-Herald*, January 10, 1940; *New York*

Daily News, January 14, 1941, all as cited in Cong. Rec. (January 10, 1940), 77th Cong., 1st Sess., May 2, 1941–June 2, 1941, Cong. Rec., vol. 87, pt. 1, 92–93.

160. *New York Herald Tribune*, December 5, 1940, 4; Nasaw, *The Patriarch*, 505.

161. *New York Times*, December 20, 1940, 7; Koskoff, *Joseph P. Kennedy*, 306.

162. JPK to Hearst, November 26, 1940, as cited in Smith, *Hostage to Fortune*, 494.

163. *Washington Times Herald*, January 10, 1940, as cited in Cong. Rec. (January 10, 1940), 77th Cong., 1st Sess., May 2, 1941–June 2, 1941, Cong. Rec., vol. 87, pt. 1, 92–93. Boake Carter of the *Boston Globe* and an unnamed national director of the antiwar America First Committee wrote to Kennedy urging him to work on its behalf: "I believe that you can do one of the finest jobs for America that has befallen any citizen. I think your real worth to your fellow countrymen is just beginning." Kennedy declined the offer and preferred to maintain his own independence; JPK Papers, ser. 8.2.1, Ambassador Correspondence File, London 1940, box 104, JPK Collection, JFKL; Beschloss, *Kennedy and Roosevelt*, 232.

164. *New York Times*, December 8, 1940, sec. 4, p. 3.

165. *New York Times*, December 3, 1940, 24.

166. Sherwood, *Roosevelt and Hopkins*, 230; Nasaw, *The Patriarch*, 507.

167. FDR, *The Public Papers and Addresses*, 1940 vol., comp. Rosenman, 643; Goodwin, *No Ordinary Time*, 194–95.

168. FDR, *The Public Papers and Addresses*, 1940 vol., comp. Rosenman, 630–44; *Times*, December 30, 1940, 4; Dallek, *FDR and American Foreign Policy*, 255–57.

169. *Times*, December 30, 1940, 2, 4; December 31, 1940, 1, 2, 4; Goodwin, *No Ordinary Time*, 195–96.

170. *Times*, December 31, 1940, 4; Churchill, *The Second World War*, 2:489; Goodwin, *No Ordinary Time*, 195–96.

171. Goodwin, *No Ordinary Time*, 195.

172. Dallek, *FDR and American Foreign Policy*, 255.

173. Goodwin, *No Ordinary Time*, 210.

174. JPK, *Diary Notes*, January 21, 1941, JPK Collection, JFKL; Smith, *Hostage to Fortune*, 524n2.

175. JPK, *Diary Notes*, January 21, 1941, JPK Collection, JFKL; Smith, *Hostage to Fortune*, 524.

176. JPK, *Diary Notes*, January 21, 1941, JPK Collection, JFKL; Smith, *Hostage to Fortune*, 524–25n7. Elliott Roosevelt had often been the subject of adverse newspaper commentary ever since his father became president. He was criticized because he had been the manager of some of Hearst's business enterprises and because of his divorce and quick remarriage in 1933. The press was even more critical because he became a captain in the Air Corps Reserve despite having poor vision and lacking aviation experience.

177. JPK, *Diary Notes*, January 21, 1941, JPK Collection, JFKL; Smith, *Hostage to Fortune*, 528.

178. JPK to Boettiger, Palm Beach, February 10, 1941, as cited in Smith, *Hostage to Fortune*, 529.

179. JPK, *Diary Notes*, January 21, 1941, JPK Collection, JFKL; Smith, *Hostage to Fortune*, 525–29; "DM," chap. 52, pp. 6–9, JPK Collection, JFKL.

180. Koskoff, *Joseph P. Kennedy*, 316.

181. *Life*, January 27, 1941, 27–28; Whalen, *The Founding Father*, 352.

182. *New York Herald Tribune*, January 22, 1941, 1.

183. *Christian Century*, January 29, 1941, 142–43; Whalen, *The Founding Father*, 352–53.

184. John F. Kennedy: Memorandum, December 6, 1940, JPK Papers, ser. 1:1, Family Correspondence, 1940, box 2, JPK Collection, JFKL; Smith, *Hostage to Fortune*, 498–505; Nasaw, *The Patriarch*, 514–15.

185. Cong. Rec. A196-A198 (January 27, 1941) (*Life*, 27–28); (January 19, 1941) (*New York Times*, 35); Cong. Rec. January 3, 1941–March 1941, vol. 87; *New York Times*, January 20, 1941, 16; Nasaw, *The Patriarch*, 515.

186. Cong. Rec. (January 28, 1941) (January 27, 1941) (*Life*, 27–28); (January 19, 1941) (*New York Times*, 35).

187. *New York Times*, January 19, 1941, 1; Nasaw, *The Patriarch*, 517.

188. Cong. Rec. A196-A198 (January 27, 1941) (*Life*, 27–28); (January 19, 1941) (*New York Times*, 35); Cong. Rec. January 3, 1941–March 1941, vol. 87.

189. *New York Herald Tribune*, January 22, 1941, 17; Koskoff, *Joseph P. Kennedy*, 309.

190. Ickes, Diary, January 19, 1941, as cited in Nasaw, *The Patriarch*, 516.

191. *Life*, February 3, 1941, 17–21; *New York Times*, January 22, 1941, 1, 4.

192. *New York Times*, January 22, 1941, sec. 4, p. 1; January 26, 1941, 4.

193. *Life*, February 3, 1941, 17–21.

194. *New York Times*, January 22, 1941, sec. 4, p. 1.

195. *Life*, February 3, 1941, 18.

196. *New York Times*, January 22, 1941, 1, 4; *Wall Street Journal*, January 22, 1941, 1; Beschloss, *Kennedy and Roosevelt*, 239.

197. *Life*, February 3, 1941, 19; Whalen, *The Founding Father*, 355.

198. *New York Times*, January 22, 1941, 1, 4; *New York Times*, January 26, 1941, E1.

199. *Life*, February 3, 1941, 20.

200. "DM," chap. 52, p. 10, JPK Collection, JFKL; Beschloss, *Kennedy and Roosevelt*, 239.

201. Dallek, *FDR and American Foreign Policy*, 260.

202. *Life*, February 3, 1941, 17; Whalen, *The Founding Father*, 357.

203. Whalen, *The Founding Father*, 357.

204. Dallek, *FDR and American Foreign Policy*, 267.

205. Cong. Rec. (May 2, 1941–June 2, 1941), vol. 87, A2510-A2512, 77th Cong., 1st Sess., May 2, 1941–June 2, 1941, Cong. Rec. vol. 87, pt. 4, 3525–4650; Koskoff, *Joseph P. Kennedy*, 311–13; *New York Times*, May 23, 1941, 2; Nasaw, *The Patriarch*, 530.

206. *New York Times*, June 2, 1941, 20; Beschloss, *Kennedy and Roosevelt*, 242; Koskoff, *Joseph P. Kennedy*, 313; Nasaw, *The Patriarch*, 530–31.

207. JPK Diary, January 17, 1942, JPK Collection, JFKL; Smith, *Hostage to Fortune*, 537.

208. JPK to FDR, telegram, December 7, 1941, ser. 5.1, JPK Collection, JFKL; Smith, *Hostage to Fortune*, 512, 533, 542; March 7, 1941, in Roosevelt, *F.D.R.: His Personal Letters, 1928–1945*, 2:1290.

209. JPK Personal Papers, ser. 5.1, Roosevelt and Politics: White House, 1934–1942; JPK Diary, January 7, 1942, JPK Collection, JFKL; Smith, *Hostage to Fortune*, 534; Whalen, *The Founding Father*, 362; Early

to JPK, December 9, 1941, PPF to 207, FDRL, as cited in Nasaw, *The Patriarch*, 539.

210. FDR to JFK, January 12, 1942, Roosevelt Papers, P.P.F. 207, FDRL; Whalen, *The Founding Father*, 362.

211. JPK Diary, January 7, 1942, JPK Collection, JFKL; Smith, *Hostage to Fortune*, 534.

212. JPK to FDR, March 4, 1942, Roosevelt Papers, P.P.F. 207, FDRL; Whalen, *The Founding Father*, 362.

213. JPK to FDR, Palm Beach, March 4, 1942, as cited in Smith, *Hostage to Fortune*, 541–42; March 7, 1941, in Roosevelt, *F.D.R.: His Personal Letters, 1928–1945*, 2:1290.

214. FDR to JPK, March 7, 1940, JPK Papers, ser. 5.1, Roosevelt and Politics: Correspondence 1942, box 71, JPK Collection, JFKL; JPK to FDR, March 7, 1942, as cited in Smith, *Hostage to Fortune*, 542n50; March 7, 1941, in Roosevelt, *F.D.R.: His Personal Letters, 1928–1945*, 2:1290.

215. March 7, 1941, in Roosevelt, *F.D.R.: His Personal Letters, 1928–1945*, 2:1290.

216. JPK to FDR, Palm Beach, March 12, 1942, ser. 5.1, Roosevelt and Politics, box 71, JPK Collection, JFKL; Smith, *Hostage to Fortune*, 543–44; March 7, 1941, in Roosevelt, *F.D.R.: His Personal Letters, 1928–1945*, 2:1290; Whalen, *The Founding Father*, 363.

217. JPK Diary, April 10, 1942, JPK Collection, JFKL; Smith, *Hostage to Fortune*, 544.

218. JPK Diary, April 10, 1942, JPK Collection, JFKL; Smith, *Hostage to Fortune*, 545–46; JPK to FDR, March 12, 1942, 3060, FDRL.

219. March 7, 1942, in Roosevelt, *F.D.R.: His Personal Letters, 1928–1945*, 2:1290.

220. President's Press Conference, 820, April 21, 1942, Press Conferences, 19:290–91, FDRL; Koskoff, *Joseph P. Kennedy*, 318.

221. Nasaw, *The Patriarch*, 543–44.

222. Smith, *Hostage to Fortune*, 513; JPK Diary, July 7, 1941, as cited in Smith, *Hostage to Fortune*, 530; JPK, Diary Notes on the 1944 Political Campaign, JPK Collection, JFKL; JPK Diary, 1942–51, JPK Collection, JFKL; Whalen, *The Founding Father*, 364.

223. Smith, *Hostage to Fortune*, 513; JPK Diary, July 7, 1941, as cited in Smith, *Hostage to Fortune*, 530–31.

224. JPK Diary, January 17, 1942, JPK Collection, JFKL; Smith, *Hostage to Fortune*, 537n42: Kennedy had been told by a friend that Alice Roosevelt Longworth, a daughter of Theodore Roosevelt, uncle of Eleanor, distant relative of FDR, and widow of the speaker of the House, Nicholas Longworth, had told him that the Roosevelt family had a "firmly imbedded" anti-Catholic prejudice; Nasaw, *The Patriarch*, 539, 549.

225. Smith, *Hostage to Fortune*, 513.

226. *Time*, May 4, 1942, 15.

227. JPK Diary, April 10, 1942, JPK Collection, JFKL; Smith, *Hostage to Fortune*, 546.

228. JPK to Boettiger, February 10, 1941, as cited in Smith, *Hostage to Fortune*, 529.

229. See the letters on Kennedy in the FDRL under "OF 48," box 2, written by many "ordinary" Americans. They are unrestrained in their virulence and hatred.

230. FDR to Boettiger, February 10, 1941, Boettiger Papers, FDRL, as cited in Goodwin, *No Ordinary Time*, 211–12.

Conclusion

1. Boake Carter to JPK, December 28, 1937, box 10, JPK Collection, JFKL.

2. Collier and Horowitz, *The Kennedys: An American Drama*, 45.

3. Beschloss, *Kennedy and Roosevelt*, 157.

4. Weinberg, *A World at Arms*, 1–5.

5. Goodwin, *The Fitzgeralds and the Kennedys*, 268, 272.

6. Irwin Ross, "The True Story of Joseph P. Kennedy," *New York Post Daily Magazine*, January 11, 1961, 37; Beschloss, *Kennedy and Roosevelt*, 162.

7. Burns, *Roosevelt: The Lion and the Fox*, 381.

8. Langer and Gleason, *The Challenge to Isolation*, 48; Samuel I. Rosenman, ed., *The Public Papers and Addresses of Franklin D. Roosevelt*, 1939 vol., *War and Neutrality* (New York: Macmillan Co., 1941), 3–4, 36–53, 70–74.

9. "DM," chap. 9, p. 8, JPK Collection, JFKL; Smith, *Hostage to Fortune*, 266.

10. Beschloss, *Kennedy and Roosevelt*, 679.

11. "DM," chap. 20, p. 16, JPK Collection, JFKL.

12. JPK to FDR, September 30, 1939, box 10, PSF: Kennedy, FDRL; JPK to FDR, September 30, 1939, as cited in Smith, *Hostage to Fortune*, 385.

13. Nasaw, *The Patriarch*, xxii.

14. Churchill, *The Second World War*, vol. 2, *Their Finest Hour*, 102.

15. *New York Times*, December 12, 1939, 2, 8; *Times* (London), December 11, 1939, 8, 12, and December 12, 1939, 8; *Daily Telegraph*, December 7, 1939; *Morning Post*, December 7, 1939; Foreign Office Minutes, December 13–14, 1939, FO 371/22827/A8763, PRO; "DM," chap. 38, p. 10, JPK Collection, JFKL; Whalen, *The Founding Father*, 285.

16. JPK 8.6 Ambassadorial, Dispatches Outgoing, 12939, May 8–16, 1939, box 173, FDRL; Smith, *Hostage to Fortune*, 376.

17. JPK to FDR, November 3, 1939, box 44, PSF: Kennedy, FDRL; JPK to FDR, November 3, 1939, as cited in Smith, *Hostage to Fortune*, 398.

18. *Life*, February 3, 1941, 19; Whalen, *The Founding Father*, 355.

19. *Life*, February 3, 1941, 20.

20. Smith, *Hostage to Fortune*, 529.

21. Beschloss, Michael R. *Kennedy and Roosevelt: The Uneasy Alliance*. New York: W.W. Norton, 1980, 157.

22. Whalen, *The Founding Father*, 379, writes: "Four years later he had increased his equity by almost $4,000,000."

23. Whalen, *The Founding Father*, 486.

24. JPK Diary, June 17, 1943, JPK Collection, JFKL; Smith, *Hostage to Fortune*, 557; Nasaw, *The Patriarch*, 550.

25. Whalen, *The Founding Father*, 482.

26. Rose Kennedy, *Times to Remember*, 286; Nasaw, *The Patriarch*, 535–37.

27. Goodwin, *The Fitzgeralds and the Kennedys*, 272.

28. Koskoff, *Joseph P. Kennedy*, 375; Goodwin, *The Fitzgeralds and the Kennedys*, 693.

29. Nasaw, *The Patriarch*, 787.

30. Nasaw, *The Patriarch*, 777.

31. Whalen, *The Founding Father*, 495.

Bibliography

Archives and Private Collections

Arthur Houghton Diary, Joseph Patrick Kennedy Papers, John Fitzgerald Kennedy Library (JFKL).

David Margesson Correspondence, Churchill College, Cambridge University (CU).

Elibank Papers, National Library of Scotland, Edinburgh, Scotland (NLS).

Father Charles Coughlin Papers, Archdiocese of Detroit, Archives.

George Rublee Reminiscences, Oral History Research Office, Columbia University.

Great Britain, Public Records Office, Kew, Prime Minister's Papers (PREM1).

Harold Ickes Papers, Library of Congress (LC).

Henry Morgenthau, Jr., Papers. Franklin D. Roosevelt Library, Hyde Park, New York (FDRL).

Henry Morgenthau, Jr., Diaries, LC.

Hull Papers, LC.

James M. Landis Papers, LC.

John Boettiger Papers, FDRL.

Joseph P. Kennedy Collection (JPK), John Fitzgerald Kennedy Library, Columbia Point, Boston (JKFL).

Lady Nancy Astor Papers, University of Reading Library.

Lord Chatfield Papers, National Maritime Museum, Greenwich.

Lord Halifax Papers, Borthwick Institute, York.

Lord Lothian Papers, Scottish Record Office, Edinburgh (formerly National Archives of Scotland).

Lord Templewood Papers (CU).

Maurice Hankey Diaries and Correspondence, Churchill College (CU).

National Archives, Washington, DC

Neville Chamberlain Papers, Birmingham University Library.

National Archives, UK (formerly the Public Record Office, London) (PRO).

President's Official Files (FDRL).

President's Personal Files (FDRL).

President's Secretary Files (FDRL).

Rose Fitzgerald Kennedy Personal Papers (JFKL).

Sir John Simon Diaries, Bodleian Library, Oxford.

Sir Thomas Inskip Diaries, Churchill College, (CU).

Walter Runciman Papers, University of Newcastle Library.

Publications

Alsop, Joseph, and Robert Kintner. *American White Paper: The Story of American Diplomacy and the Second World War*. New York: Simon and Schuster, 1940.

———. "Capital Canada." *Atlanta Constitution*, October 8, 1940.

———. "Clues to the News." *National Issues*, February 1939.

Arnstein, Walter L., ed. *The Past Speaks: Sources and Problems in British History*. Vol. 2, *Since 1688*. Lexington, MA: D.C. Heath, 1993.

Associated Press and Sidney C. Moody, Jr., eds. *Triumph and Tragedy: The Story of the Kennedys*. New York: Morrow, 1968.

Attlee, C. R. *As It Happened*. New York: Viking, 1954.

Baynes, Norman H., ed. *The Speeches of Adolf Hitler, April 1922–August 1939*. Vol. 2. New York: Howard Fertig, 1969.

Beard, Charles A. *American Foreign Policy in the Making, 1932–1940: A Study in Responsibilities*. New Haven, CT: Yale University Press, 1946.

Bearse, Ray, and Anthony Read. *Conspirator: The Untold Story of Tyler Kent*. New York: Doubleday, 1991.

Beatty, Jerome. "Nine Kennedys and How They Grew." *Reader's Digest*, April 1939, 83.

Bell, P. M. H. *The Origins of the Second World War in Europe*. London: Longman, 1986.

Berle, Beatrice Bishop, and Travis Beal Jacobs, eds. *Navigating the Rapids, 1918–1971: From the Papers of Adolf A. Berle*. New York: Harcourt Brace Jovanovich, 1973.

Beschloss, Michael R. *Kennedy and Roosevelt: The Uneasy Alliance*. New York: W.W. Norton, 1980.

Bethell, Nicholas. *The War Hitler Won: The Fall of Poland, September 1939*. New York: Holt, Rinehart and Winston, 1972.

Bilainkin, George. *Diary of a Diplomatic Correspondent*. London: George Allen & Unwin Ltd., 1942.

Birkenhead, Frederick Winston Furneaux Smith. *Halifax: The Life of Lord Halifax*. London: Hamish Hamilton, 1965.

Blum, John Morton. *From the Morgenthau Diaries*. Vol. 1, *Years of Crisis, 1928–1938*. Boston: Houghton Mifflin, 1959.

———. *From the Morgenthau Diaries*. Vol. 2, *Years of Urgency, 1938–1941*. Boston: Houghton Mifflin Co., 1964.

Blunden, Edmund. *The Mind's Eye*. London: Jonathan Cape, 1934.

Bohlen, Charles E. *Witness to History, 1929–1969*. New York: W.W. Norton and Co., 1973.

Boyle, Andrew. *Montagu Norman: A Biography*. London: Cassell and Co., 1967.

Brinkley, Alan. *Franklin Delano Roosevelt*. Oxford: Oxford University Press, 2010.

Brown, Anthony Cave. *Bodyguard of Lies: The Extraordinary True Story behind D-Day*. New York: Harper and Row, 1975.

Bullock, Alan. *Hitler: A Study in Tyranny*. New York: Harper and Row, 1962.

Burns, James MacGregor. *John Kennedy: A Political Profile*. New York: Harcourt, Brace & World, 1960.

———. *Roosevelt: The Lion and the Fox, 1882–1940*. New York: Harper and Row, 1956.

———. *Roosevelt: The Soldier of Freedom*. New York: Harcourt Brace Jovanovich, 1970.

Burridge, T. D. *Clement Attlee: A Political Biography*. London: J. Cape, 1985.

Byrnes, James F. *All in One Lifetime*. New York: Harper and Brothers, 1958.

Cameron, Gail. *Rose: A Biography of Rose Fitzgerald Kennedy*. New York: G.P. Putnam's Sons, 1971.

Carter, Boake. "But . . . by Boake Carter." *New York Daily Mirror*, November 12, 1938, 13.

Chamberlain, Neville. *The Struggle for Peace*. London: Hutchinson Publishing Group, Ltd., 1939.

Charmley, John. *Chamberlain and the Lost Peace*. Chicago: Ivan R. Dee, 1999.

Churchill, Winston S. *Memoirs of the Second World War*. Boston: Houghton Mifflin, 1959.

———. *The Second World War*. Vol. 1, *The Gathering Storm*. Boston: Houghton Mifflin, 1948.

———. *The Second World War*. Vol. 2, *Their Finest Hour*. Boston: Houghton Mifflin, 1949.

Cockburn, Claude. "The Crisis." *The Week*, no. 315 (May 17–June 3, 1939): 6.

Cockett, Richard. *Twilight of Truth: Chamberlain, Appeasement, and the Manipulation of the Press*. New York: St. Martin's, 1989.

Coit, Margaret L. *Mr. Baruch*. Boston: Houghton Mifflin, 1957.

Collier, Peter, and David Horowitz. *The Kennedys: An American Drama*. New York: Summit Books, 1984.

Colvin, Ian. *The Chamberlain Cabinet: How the Meetings in 10 Downing Street, 1937–1939, Led to the Second World War*. London: Victor Gollancz Ltd., 1971.

Cooper, Duff. *Old Men Forget: The Autobiography of Duff Cooper* (Viscount Norwich). London: Hart-Davis, 1953.

Costello, John. *Ten Days to Destiny: The Secret Story of the Hess Peace Initiative and British Efforts to Strike a Deal with Hitler*. New York: William Morrow and Co., 1991.

Cowles, Virginia. *Winston Churchill: The Era and the Man*. New York: Universal Library, 1956.

Craig, Gordon Alexander, and Felix Gilbert, eds. *The Diplomats, 1919–39*. New York: Princeton University Press, 1953.

Dallek, Robert. *The American Style of Foreign Policy: Cultural Politics and Foreign Affairs*. New York: Alfred A. Knopf, 1983.

———. *Franklin D. Roosevelt and American Foreign Policy, 1932–1945*. New York: Oxford University Press, 1979.

Damore, Leo. *The Cape Cod Years of John Fitzgerald Kennedy*. Englewood Cliffs, NJ: Prentice-Hall, 1967.

David, Lester. *Ted Kennedy: Triumphs and Tragedies*. New York: Grosset and Dunlap, 1971.

Davies, Joseph Edward. *Mission to Moscow: A Record of Confidential Dispatches to the State Department, Official and Personal Correspondence, Current Diary and Journal Entries, Including Notes and Comment up to October, 1941*. New York: Simon and Schuster, 1941.

Davies, Marion. *The Times We Had: Life with William Randolph Hearst*. New York: Bobbs-Merrill, 1975.

Davis, Forrest, and Ernest K. Lindley. *How War Came: An American White Paper: From the Fall of France to Pearl Harbor*. New York: Simon & Schuster, 1942.

Davis, John H. *The Kennedys: Dynasty and Disaster, 1848–1983*. New York: McGraw-Hill, 1984.

de Bedts, Ralph F. *Ambassador Joseph Kennedy 1938–1940: An Anatomy of Appeasement*. New York: Peter Lang, 1983.

Dempsey, Mary A. "The Many Faces of Father Coughlin." *Michigan History Magazine* (July/August 1999).

D'Este, Carlo. *Warlord: A Life of Winston Churchill at War, 1874–1945*. New York: HarperCollins, 2009.

Dilks, David. *Churchill and Company: Allies and Rivals in War and Peace*. London: I. B. Tauris and Co., 2012.

Dilks, David, ed. *The Diaries of Sir Alexander Cadogan, 1938–1945*. New York: G.P. Putnam's Sons, 1972.

Dinneen, Joseph F. *The Kennedy Family*. Boston: Little, Brown and Co., 1959.

Divine, Robert A. *The Illusion of Neutrality*. Chicago: University of Chicago Press, 1962.

Divine, Robert A., ed. *Causes and Consequences of World War II*. Chicago: Quadrangle Books, 1969.

Documents of German Foreign Policy, 1918–1945. Series D. Washington, D.C., 1949–54 (*DGFP*).

Documents on British Foreign Policy, 1919–1939. Edited by E. L. Woodward and Rohan Butler. Third Series. London, 1949–55 (*DBFP*).

Douglas-Home, Alec. *The Way the Wind Blows: An Autobiography*. London: Collins, 1976.

Duncliffe, William J. *The Life and Times of Joseph P. Kennedy*. New York: MacFadden-Bartell, 1965.

Dutton, David. *Neville Chamberlain*. London: Arnold, 2001.

Eden, Anthony. *The Eden Memoirs: Facing the Dictators*. London: Cassell, 1962.

———. *Full Circle: The Memoirs of Sir Anthony Eden*. London: Cassell and Co., 1960.

Eubank, Keith. *The Origins of World War II*. Wheeling, IL: Harlan Davidson, 2004.

Farley, James A. *Jim Farley's Story: The Roosevelt Years*. New York: Whittlesey House, 1948.

Feiling, Keith Grahame. *The Life of Neville Chamberlain*. London: Macmillan and Co., 1970.

Fischer, Louis. *Men and Politics: An Autobiography*. New York: Duell, Sloan and Pearce, 1941.

Flynn, George Q. *American Catholics and the Roosevelt Presidency, 1932–36*. Lexington: University Press of Kentucky, 1968.

Francis-Williams, Lord. *Nothing So Strange*. New York: American Heritage Press, 1970.

Freidel, Frank. *Franklin D. Roosevelt: A Rendezvous with Destiny*. New York: Little, Brown and Co., 1990.

Fuchser, Larry William. *Neville Chamberlain and Appeasement: A Study in the Politics of History*. New York: W.W. Norton & Co., 1982.

Fussell, Paul. *The Great War and Modern Memory*. New York: Oxford University Press, 1975.

Gardner, Lloyd C. *Spheres of Influence: The Great Powers Partition Europe from Munich to Yalta*. Chicago: Ivan R. Dee, 1993.

Gelb, Norman. Dunkirk: *The Complete Story of the First Step in the Defeat of Hitler*. New York: William Morrow and Co., 1989.

George, Margaret. *The Warped Vision: British Foreign Policy, 1933–1939*. Pittsburgh, PA: University of Pittsburgh Press, 1965.

Gilbert, Bentley Brinkerhoff. *Britain, 1914–1945: The Aftermath of Power*. Wheeling, IL: Harlan Davidson,

Inc., 1996.

———. *Britain since 1918*. New York: St. Martin's, 1980.

Gilbert, Martin. *Churchill: A Life*. New York: Henry Holt and Co., 1991.

———. *The First World War: A Complete History*. New York: Henry Holt and Co., 1994.

———. *The Roots of Appeasement*. London: Weidenfeld and Nicolson, 1966.

———. *The Second World War*. New York: Henry Holt and Co., 1991.

———. *Winston S. Churchill*. Vol. 5, *The Prophet of Truth, 1922–1939*. Boston: Houghton Mifflin, 1977.

———. *Winston S. Churchill*. Vol. 6, *Finest Hour, 1939–1941*. Boston: Houghton Mifflin, 1983.

Gilbert, Martin, and Richard Gott. *The Appeasers*. London: Weidenfeld and Nicolson, 1963.

Goldman, Eric F. *Rendezvous with Destiny*. New York: Vintage Books, 1956.

Goodwin, Doris Kearns. *The Fitzgeralds and the Kennedys: An American Saga*. New York: Simon and Schuster, 1987.

———. *No Ordinary Time—Franklin and Eleanor Roosevelt: The Home Front in World War II*. New York: Simon and Schuster, 1995.

Graves, Robert, and Alan Hodge. *The Long Week-End: A Social History of Great Britain, 1918–1939*. New York: W.W. Norton, 1963.

Grigg, John. *Nancy Astor: Portrait of a Pioneer*. London: Sidgwick and Jackson, 1980.

Harvey, John, ed. *The Diplomatic Diaries of Oliver Harvey, 1937–1940*. London: Collins, 1970.

Hathaway, Robert. *Ambiguous Partnership: Britain and America, 1944–1947*. New York: Columbia University Press, 1982.

Heinrichs, Waldo. *Threshold of War: Franklin D. Roosevelt and American Entry into World War II*. Oxford: Oxford University Press, 1988.

Henderson, Nevile. *Failure of a Mission: Berlin, 1937–1939*. New York: G.P. Putnam's Sons, 1940.

Higham, Charles. *Trading with the Enemy: An Exposé of the Nazi-American Money Plot, 1933–1949*. London: Hale, 1983.

Hooker, Nancy Harvison, ed. The Moffat Papers: Selections from the Diplomatic Journals of Jay Pierrepont Moffat, 1919–1943. Cambridge, MA: Harvard University Press, 1956.

Hull, Cordell. *The Memoirs of Cordell Hull*, 2 vols. New York: Whittlesey House, 1948.

Ickes, Harold L. *The Secret Diary of Harold L. Ickes*. Vol. 2, *The Inside Struggle, 1936–1939*. New York: Simon and Schuster, 1954.

———. *The Secret Diary of Harold L. Ickes*. Vol. 3, *The Lowering Clouds, 1939–1941*. New York: Simon and Schuster, 1954.

James, Robert Rhodes. *Churchill: A Study in Failure, 1900–1939*. New York: World Publishing Co., 1970.

Johnson, Alan Campbell. *Viscount Halifax: A Biography*. New York: Ives Washburn, Inc., 1941.

Jonas, Manfred. *Isolationism in America, 1935–1941*. Ithaca, NY: Cornell University Press, 1966.

Jones, S. Shepard, and Denys P. Myers, ed. *Documents on American Foreign Relations*. Vol. 1. Boston: World Peace Foundation, 1939.

Kaltenborn, H. V. *Fifty Fabulous Years, 1900–1950*. New York: G.P. Putnam's Sons, 1950.

Kaufmann, William W. "Two American Ambassadors: Bullitt and Kennedy." In *The Diplomats, 1919–39*, edited by Gordon Craig and Felix Gilbert. New York: Princeton University Press, 1953.

Keegan, John. The Face of Battle: A Study of Agincourt, Waterloo, and the Somme. New York: Viking Press, 1976.

———. *The First World War*. New York: Alfred A. Knopf, 1999.

———. *The Second World War*. New York: Viking, 1989.

Kennan, George F. *From Prague after Munich: Diplomatic Papers, 1938–1940*. Princeton, NJ: Princeton University Press, 1968.

Kennedy, David M. *Freedom from Fear: The American People in Depression and War, 1929–1945*. New York: Oxford University Press, 1999.

Kennedy, Edward M. *True Compass: A Memoir*. New York: Twelve, 2009.

Kennedy, John F. *Why England Slept*. New York: Wilfred Funk, 1940.

Kennedy, John F., ed. *As We Remember Joe*. Cambridge, MA: University Press, 1945.

Kennedy, Joseph P. *I'm for Roosevelt*. New York: Reynal and Hitchcock, 1936.

Kennedy, Rose. *Times to Remember*. Garden City, NY: Doubleday and Co., 1974.

Kershaw, Ian. *Fateful Choices: Ten Decisions That Changed the World, 1940 1941*. New York: Penguin, 2007.

———. *Hitler: 1936–1945 Nemesis*. New York: W.W. Norton, 2000.

Kessler, Ronald. *The Sins of the Father: Joseph P. Kennedy and the Dynasty He Founded*. New York: Warner Books, 1996.

Kinsella, William E., Jr. *Leadership in Isolation: FDR and the Origins of the Second World War*. Boston: G. K. Hall and Co., 1978.

Kirchwey, Freda. "Watch Joe Kennedy!" *The Nation*, December 14, 1940, 593.

Koskoff, David E. *Joseph P. Kennedy: A Life and Times*. Englewood Cliffs, NJ: Prentice Hall, Inc., 1974.

Kraus, René. *The Men around Churchill*. New York: J.B. Lippincott Co., 1941.

Krock, Arthur. *Memoirs: Sixty Years on the Firing Line*. New York: Funk and Wagnalls, 1968.

Lafore, Laurence. *The End of Glory: An Interpretation of the Origins of World War II*. Philadelphia: J.B. Lippincott Co., 1970.

Land, Emory Scott. *Winning the War with Ships: Land, Sea and Air—Mostly Land*. New York: R. M. McBride Co., 1958.

Langer, William L., and S. Everett Gleason. *The Challenge to Isolation: The World Crisis of 1937–1940 and American Foreign Policy*. Vols. 1 and 2. New York: Harper Torchbooks, 1952.

Larson, Erik. *The Splendid and the Vile: A Saga of Churchill, Family, and Defiance During the Blitz*. New York: Crown Publishers, 2020.

Lash, Joseph P. *Eleanor: The Years Alone*. New York: W.W. Norton, 1972.

———. *Roosevelt and Churchill, 1939–1941*. New York: W.W. Norton, 1976.

Lasky, Victor. *JFK: The Man and the Myth: A Critical Portrait*. New York: Arlington House, 1966.

Leuchtenburg, William. *Franklin D. Roosevelt and the New Deal*. New York: Harcourt, Brace & World, 1963.

Leutze, James R. *Bargaining for Supremacy: Anglo-American Naval Collaboration, 1937–1941*. Chapel Hill: University of North Carolina Press, 1977.

Linck, Joseph C., and Raymond J. Kupke, eds. *Building the Church in America: Studies in Honor of*

Monsignor Robert F. Trisco on the Occasion of His Seventieth Birthday. Washington, DC: Catholic University of America Press, 1999.

Lindbergh, Anne Morrow. *The Flower and the Nettle: Diaries and Letters of Anne Morrow Lindbergh, 1936–1939.* New York: Harcourt, Brace, Jovanovich, 1976.

Lindbergh, Charles A. *The Wartime Journals of Charles A. Lindbergh.* New York: Harcourt, Brace, Jovanovich, 1970.

Lindley, Ernest K. "Will Kennedy Run for President?" *Liberty Magazine,* May 21, 1938, 27.

———. "Will Kennedy Run for President?" *Liberty: The Nostalgia Magazine,* Fall 1971, 26.

Lippmann, Walter. "Today and Tomorrow." *Washington Post,* October 22, 1938.

Loewenheim, Francis L., Harold D. Langley, and Manfred Jonas, eds. *Roosevelt and Churchill: Their Secret Wartime Correspondence.* New York: Saturday Review Press, 1975.

Long, Breckinridge, and Fred L. Israel. *The War Diary of Breckinridge Long: Selections from the Years 1939–1944.* Lincoln: University of Nebraska Press, 1966.

Longford, The Earl of, and Thomas P. O'Neill. *Eamon DeValera.* London: Hutchinson & Co., 1970.

Lukacs, John. *Five Days in London, May 1940.* New Haven, CT: Yale University Press, 1999.

Lyons, Lewis M. *Newspaper Story: One Hundred Years of the Boston Globe.* Cambridge, MA: Belknap Press of Harvard University Press, 1971.

Lyons, Michael J. *World War II: A Short History.* 2nd ed. Englewood Cliffs, NJ: Prentice Hall, 1994.

Maier, Thomas. *When Lions Roar: The Churchills and the Kennedys.* New York: Crown Publishers, 2014.

Manchester, William, and Paul Reid. *The Last Lion—Winston Spencer Churchill: Defender of the Realm, 1940–1965.* Boston: Little, Brown and Co., 2012.

Marcus, Sheldon. Father Coughlin: *The Tumultuous Life of the Priest of the Little Flower.* Boston: Little, Brown and Co., 1973.

Marsh, Peter T. *The Chamberlain Litany: Letters within a Governing Family from Empire to Appeasement.* London: Haus Publishing, 2010.

Martin, Kingsley, ed. *"New Statesman" Years, 1931–1945.* Chicago: Henry Regnery, 1968.

Martin, Ralph G. *Jennie: The Life of Lady Randolph Churchill.* Vol. 1, *The Romantic Years, 1854 1895.* New York: Signet, 1970.

———. *Jennie: The Life of Lady Randolph Churchill.* Vol. 2, *The Dramatic Years, 1895 1921.* New York: Signet, 1971.

McCarthy, Joe. *The Remarkable Kennedys.* New York: Dial Press, 1960.

McKenna, Marian C. *Borah.* Ann Arbor: University of Michigan Press, 1961.

Medlicott, W. N. *British Foreign Policy since Versailles, 1919–63.* London: Methuen and Co., Ltd., 1968.

Mendelsohn, John, ed. *The Holocaust.* (18 vols.) Vol. 6, *Jewish Emigration, 1938–1940: Rublee Negotiations and the Intergovernmental Committee.* New York: Garland Publishing, 1982.

Middlemas, Robert Keith. *The Strategy of Appeasement: The British Government and Germany, 1937–39.* Chicago: Quadrangle Books, 1972.

Millis, Walter, ed. *The Forrestal Diaries.* New York: Viking Press, 1951.

Minnex, R. J. *The Private Papers of Hore-Belisha.* London: Collins, 1960.

Moley, Raymond. *After Seven Years*. New York: Harper and Bros., 1939.

———. *The First New Deal*. New York: Harcourt, Brace & World, 1966.

Morgan, Ted. *FDR: A Biography*. Simon and Schuster: New York, 1985.

Mosley, Leonard. *Backs to the Wall: London under Fire, 1939–1945*. London: Weidenfeld and Nicolson, 1971.

Mowat, Charles Lock. *Britain between the Wars*. Chicago: University of Chicago Press, 1955.

Mulligan, Timothy P. "According to Colonel Donovan: A Document from the Records of German Military Intelligence." *The Historian* 46, no. 1 (November 1983): 78–86.

Murphy, Robert. *Diplomat among Warriors*. New York: Doubleday, 1964.

Murray, Williamson. *The Change in the European Balance of Power, 1938–1939: The Path to Ruin*. Princeton, NJ: Princeton University Press, 1984.

Nasaw, David. *The Chief: The Life of William Randolph Hearst*. Boston: Houghton Mifflin, 2000.

———. *The Patriarch: The Remarkable Life and Turbulent Times of Joseph P. Kennedy*. New York: Penguin Press, 2012.

Nicolson, Nigel, ed. *Harold Nicolson Diaries and Letters, 1930–39*. Bungay, Suffolk, UK: William Collins Sons, 1966.

Northedge, F. S. *The Troubled Giant: Britain among the Great Powers, 1916–1939*. London: G. Bell & Sons, 1966.

Offner, Arnold A. *American Appeasement: United States Foreign Policy and Germany, 1933–1938*. New York: W.W. Norton, 1969.

Ovendale, Ritchie. *"Appeasement" and the English Speaking World*. Cardiff: University of Wales Press, 1975.

Overy, R. J., and Andrew Wheatcroft. *Road to War*. London: Penguin, 1999.

Parker, R. A. C. *Chamberlain and Appeasement: British Policy and the Coming of the Second World War*. New York: St. Martin's Press, 1993.

Parkinson, Roger. *Peace for Our Time: Munich to Dunkirk—The Inside Story*. New York: David McKay Co., 1971.

Parliamentary Debates, vol. 360. House of Commons, vol. 6 of Session 1939–40. London: His Majesty's Stationery Office, 1940.

Parliamentary Debates (Great Britain) *House of Lords*. Fifth Series.

Parliamentary Debates (Great Britain), *House of Commons*. Fifth Series.

Parmet, Herbert S. *Jack: The Struggles of John F. Kennedy*. New York: Dial Press, 1980.

Perry, Barbara A. *Rose Kennedy: The Life and Times of a Political Matriarch*. New York: W.W. Norton, 2013.

Persico, Joseph E. *Roosevelt's Secret War: FDR and World War II Espionage*. New York: Random House, 2001.

Post, Gaines, Jr. *Dilemmas of Appeasement: British Deterrence and Defense, 1934–1937*. Ithaca, NY: Cornell University Press, 1993.

Rand, Peter. *Conspiracy of One: Tyler Kent's Secret Plot against FDR, Churchill, and the Allied War Effort*. Guilford, CT: Lyons Press, 2013.

Rauch, Basil. *Roosevelt: From Munich to Pearl Harbor*. New York: Barnes and Noble, 1967.

"The Reminiscences of Alan Goodrich Kirk." Part 1. New York: Columbia University: Oral History Research Office, 1962.

"The Reminiscences of George Rublee." New York: Columbia University: Oral History Research Office, 1950–1951.

Reynolds, David. *The Creation of the Anglo-American Alliance, 1937–41: A Study in Competitive Co-operation.* London: Europa Publications, 1981.

———. "F.D.R.'s Foreign Policy and the British Royal Visit to the U.S.A., 1939." *The Historian* (August 1938): 461–72.

Robbins, Keith. *Churchill.* London: Longman, 1992.

Roberts, Andrew. *The Holy Fox: A Biography of Lord Halifax.* London: Weidenfeld and Nicolson, 1991.

Rock, William R. *Chamberlain and Roosevelt: British Foreign Policy and the United States, 1937–1940.* Columbus: Ohio State University Press, 1988.

Rollins, Alfred B., Jr. *Roosevelt and Howe.* New York: Knopf, 1962.

Roosevelt, Eleanor. *This I Remember.* Westport, CT: Greenwood Press, 1949.

Roosevelt, Elliott, and James Brough. *An Untold Story: The Roosevelts of Hyde Park.* New York: G.P. Putman's Sons, 1973.

Roosevelt, Franklin D. *F.D.R.: His Personal Letters.* Vol. 1, *Early Years, 1905–1927.* Edited by Elliott Roosevelt. New York: Duell, Sloan and Pearce, 1950.

———. *F.D.R.: His Personal Letters.* Vol. 2, *1928–1945.* Edited by Elliott Roosevelt. New York: Duell, Sloan and Pearce, 1950.

———. *The Public Papers and Addresses of Franklin D. Roosevelt, 1928–1932* vol. 1, *The Genesis of the New Deal.* Compiled by Samuel I. Rosenman. New York: Random House, 1938.

———. *The Public Papers and Addresses of Franklin D. Roosevelt.* 1938 vol., *The Continuing Struggle for Liberalism.* Compiled by Samuel I. Rosenman. New York: Macmillan, 1941.

———. *The Public Papers and Addresses of Franklin D. Roosevelt.* 1939 vol., *War—and Neutrality.* Compiled by Samuel I. Rosenman. New York: Macmillan, 1941.

———. *The Public Papers and Addresses of Franklin D. Roosevelt.* 1940 vol., *War and Aid to Democracy.* Compiled by Samuel I. Rosenman. New York: Macmillan, 1941.

Roosevelt, Franklin D., Samuel I. Rosenman, and William D. Hassett. *The Public Papers and Addresses of Franklin D. Roosevelt.* New York: Random House, 1938.

Roosevelt, James. *My Parents: A Differing View.* Chicago: Playboy Press, 1976.

Rosenman, Samuel Irving. *Working with Roosevelt.* New York: Harper and Bros., 1952.

Ross, Irwin. "The True Story of Joseph P. Kennedy." *New York Post Daily Magazine,* January 11, 1961, 37.

Schlesinger, Arthur M., Jr. *Robert Kennedy and His Times.* Boston: Houghton Mifflin, 1978.

Schlesinger, Arthur, Jr. *The Coming of the New Deal: The War on Poverty of the Thirties.* Boston: Houghton Mifflin, 1965.

———. *The Crisis of the Old Order, 1919–1933.* Boston: Houghton Mifflin, 1964.

———. *The Politics of Upheaval, 1935–1936.* Boston: Houghton Mifflin, 1960.

Schmidt, Gustav. *The Politics and Economics of Appeasement: British Foreign Policy in the 1930s.*

Translated by Jackie Bennette-Ruete. New York: St. Martin's Press, 1986.

Schoenfeld, Maxwell Philip. *Sir Winston Churchill: His Life and Times*. Malabar, FL: Krieger, 1986.

Schoor, Gene. *Young John Kennedy*. New York: Harcourt, Brace & World, Inc., 1963.

Self, Robert. *Neville Chamberlain: A Biography*. Burlington, VT: Ashgate Publishing, 2006.

Self, Robert, ed. *The Neville Chamberlain Diary Letters*. Vol. 4, *The Downing Street Years, 1934–1940*. Burlington, VT: Ashgate Publishing, 2005.

Shakespeare, William. *The Complete Works*. Edited by Alfred Harbage. New York: Viking, 1969.

Sherwood, Robert E. *Roosevelt and Hopkins: An Intimate History*. New York: Harper & Brothers, 1948.

Shirer, William L. *Berlin Diary: The Journal of a Foreign Correspondent, 1934–1941*. New York: Alfred A. Knopf, 1941.

———. *The Rise and Fall of the Third Reich: A History of Nazi Germany*. New York: Simon and Schuster, 1960.

Simon, John Allsebrook. *Retrospect: The Memoirs of the Rt. Hon. Viscount Simon*. London: Hutchinson, 1952.

Smart, Nick. *Neville Chamberlain*. London: Routledge, 2010.

Smith, Amanda, ed. *Hostage to Fortune: The Letters of Joseph P. Kennedy*. New York: Viking Press, 2001.

Snow, C. P. "Winston Churchill." In *The Look Years: A View of our 35 Tumultuous Years, the Heroes, the Villains, the Violence and the Glory, Fun, Fads, Victories, Defeats, Told with the Great Photographs of Our Time, and Words by Hemingway, Shirer, Gunther, Lord, Manchester, Snow, Rosten, Commager*. Compiled by the editors of *Look*. Cowles Communications, 1972.

Snow, John Howland. *The Case of Tyler Kent*. New York: Domestic and Foreign Affairs, 1946.

Sorensen, Theodore. *Kennedy*. New York: Harper and Row, 1965.

Stedman, Andrew David. *Alternatives to Appeasement: Neville Chamberlain and Hitler's Germany*. London: I. B. Tauris, 2011.

Sulzberger, C. L. *A Long Row of Candles: Memoirs and Diaries, 1934–1954*. New York: Macmillan, 1969.

Swanberg, W. A. *Citizen Hearst*. New York: Bantam, 1961.

Swift, Will. *The Kennedys amidst the Gathering Storm: A Thousand Days in London, 1938–1940*. New York: Smithsonian Books, 2008.

Sykes, Christopher. *Nancy: The Life of Lady Astor*. New York: Harper and Row, 1972.

Talese, Gay. *The Kingdom and the Power*. Cleveland, OH: World Publishing, 1969.

Tansill, Charles Callan. *Back Door to War: The Roosevelt Foreign Policy, 1933–1941*. Chicago: Henry Regnery Co., 1952.

Taylor, A. J. P. *English History, 1914–1945*. Oxford: Oxford University Press,

Taylor, Telford. *Munich: The Price of Peace*. Garden City, NY: Doubled.

Templewood, Samuel John Gurney Hoare. *Nine Troubled Years*. Londo

The Unofficial Observer [John Franklin Carter]. *The New Dealers*. New

Thomas, Evan. *Robert Kennedy: His Life*. New York: Simon and Schuster,

Thomas, Hugh. *The Spanish Civil War*. New York: Harper Colophon Book

Thorne, Christopher. *The Approach of War, 1938–1939*. London: Macmillar.

Tull, Charles J. *Father Coughlin and the New Deal*. Syracuse, NY: Syracuse University Press, 1965.

Tully, Grace. *FDR, My Boss*. New York: Charles Scribner's Sons, 1949.

U.S. Department of State. *Foreign Relations of the United States (FRUS): Diplomatic Papers, 1938*. Vols. 1 & 2. Washington, DC: U.S. Government Printing Office, 1939.

———. *Foreign Relations of the United States (FRUS): Diplomatic Papers, 1939*. Vols. 1 & 2. Washington, DC: U.S. Government Printing Office, 1940.

———. *Foreign Relations of the United States (FRUS): Diplomatic Papers, 1940*. Vols. 1–5. Washington, DC: U.S. Government Printing Office, 1955–56.

———. *Peace and War: United States Foreign Relations, 1931–1941*. Washington, DC: Government Printing Office, 1943.

Valack, J. David. "Catholics, Neutrality, and the Spanish Embargo, 1937, 1938." *Journal of American History* 54, no. 1 (June 1967).

Vieth, Jane. "The Diplomacy of the Depression: The Foreign Policy of Franklin D. Roosevelt, 1938–1940." In *Modern American Diplomacy*, ed. John Martin Carroll and George C. Herring. Wilmington, DE: Scholarly Resources, 1986.

———. "The Donkey and the Lion: The Ambassadorship of Joseph P. Kennedy at the Court of St. James's, 1938–1940." *Michigan Academician* 10 (Winter 1978): 273–81.

———. "Joseph P. Kennedy: Ambassador to the Court of St. James's, 1938 1940." Unpublished dissertation, Ohio State University, 1975.

———. "Joseph P. Kennedy and British Appeasement: The Diplomacy of a Boston Irishman." In *U.S. Diplomats in Europe, 1919–1941*, ed. Kenneth Paul Jones. Santa Barbara, CA: ABC-Clio, 1981.

———. "Munich Revisited through Joseph P. Kennedy's Eyes." *Michigan Academician* 18 (Winter 1986): 73–85.

Watt, D. C. *Britain Looks to Germany: A Study of British Opinion and Policy since 1945*. London: Oswald Wolff, 1965.

———. *How War Came: The Immediate Origins of the Second World War*. New York: Pantheon, 1989.

———. "Roosevelt and Neville Chamberlain: Two Appeasers." *International Journal* 28 (Spring 1973): 185–204.

Weinberg, Gerhard L. *A World at Arms: A Global History of World War II*. Cambridge: Cambridge University Press, 1994.

———. *Germany, Hitler and World War II: Essays in Modern German and World History*. Cambridge: Cambridge University Press, 1995.

Welles, Sumner. *Seven Decisions That Shaped History*. New York: Harper and Bros., 1951.

———. *The Time for Decision*. New York: Harper and Bros., 1944.

Whalen, Richard J. *The Founding Father: The Story of Joseph P. Kennedy*. 1964; reprint, Washington, DC: Regnery Gateway, 1993.

-Bennett, John W. *King George VI: His Life and Reign*. New York: St. Martin's Press, 1965.

nich: Prologue to Tragedy. New York: Duell, Sloan and Pearce, 1962.

e Kennedy Imprisonment: A Meditation on Power. Boston: Atlantic Monthly Press/Little,

Brown and Co., 1981.

Wiltz, John E. *From Isolation to War, 1931–1941.* New York: Thomas Y. Crowell Co., 1968.

Wofford, Harris. *Of Kennedys and Kings.* New York: Farrar, Straus, Giroux, 1980.

Woodward, E. L., and Rohan d'Olier Butler, eds. *Documents on British Foreign Policy 1919–1939.* London: H.M. Stationery Office, 1947.

Woolner, David B., and Richard G. Kurial, eds. *FDR, The Vatican, and the Roman Catholic Church in America, 1933–1945.* New York: Palgrave Macmillan, 2003.

Index

Agreement of Mutual Assistance (1939), 211

Albania, Italian invasion of, 187–88

Allen, Robert S., 21, 59, 371

Allied powers: Finnish campaign and, 268; formation of, 293; stance of, 229; war preparations of, 269. *See also* France; United Kingdom; United States of America

Alsop, Joseph, 110, 341–42, 353, 375

Alsop, Stewart, 359

Amery, Leo, 212, 273

Anglo-American Trade Agreement (1938), 39, 41, 43, 81, 90–92, 154; JPK and, 80–89, 90–92

Anglo-German Naval Agreement (1938), 133; Hitler destruction of, 188

Anglo-German rapprochement, 105

Anglo-Irish Treaty (1938), 82–85

Anglo-Italian Agreement (1938), 69–71, 72

Anglo-Polish Alliance (1939), 228, 397

Anglo-Russian Alliance (1939), 187, 396

Anschluss, vii, viii, 60, 62–64; JPK and, 393

anti-Semitism, 99, 152–53, 160; Joseph P. Kennedy Jr. and, 146; JPK and, 100, 143, 371–72, 395, 463–64 (n. 148); Poland and, 158; Tyler Kent affair and, 303, 304–5, 307; United Kingdom and, 371. *See also* Anschluss; Kristallnacht

Appeasement at Munich (JFK), 314–17

appeasement, ix, x, 70–71, 161; Chamberlain policy of, vii–viii, 56, 57, 69, 83, 456–57 (n. 217); Churchill opposition to, 235–36; Cliveden Set and, 59; Halifax and, 58; JPK and, 99, 163, 164, 314–16, 334, 361–62, 381; Munich Agreement and, 134; United Kingdom policy of, 113, 144

Astor, Lady Nancy Witcher Langhorne, 161, 262, 268, 273; JPK and, 337. *See also* Cliveden Set

Astor, Lord Waldorf, 59. *See also* Cliveden Set

Athenia, 214–15, 483–84 (n. 43)

Atherton, Ray, 52

Attlee, Clement, 64, 122, 131, 185, 259, 275, 300, 343, 366; Munich Agreement and, 135

Axis powers, 166, 171–72, 187, 188, 229, 261; JPK on, 61; war preparations of, 269–70. *See also* Germany; Italy; Japan

Baker, Newton D., 13, 408 (n. 78)

Baldwin, Lord Stanley, 91, 130, 316, 451 (n. 126); Churchill and, 299, 300

Balfour, Sir John, 235, 252–53

Barkley, Senator Alben, 387

Baruch, Bernard M., 16, 17, 20, 87, 156; European reports of, 124, 125; JPK relationship with,

198–99, 464 (n. 148)

Baxter, A. Beverly, "My Dear Ambassador—Why Didn't You Tell Them?" 255–56

Bearse, Ray, *Conspirator*, 311, 312

Beatrice, Princess, 192

Beaverbrook, Lord William Maxwell Aitken "Max," 58, 224–25, 291, 329, 330, 338, 401

Beck, Józef, 181, 184

Belgium, 226, 237; German invasion of, 277, 279, 455 (n. 210)

Beneš, Eduard, 106, 121, 128; and Czechoslovakian crisis, 96–97, 115, 118; resignation of, 134–35. *See also* Czechoslovakia

Berle, Adolf, 199–200, 206, 222

Bernhard, Prince, 279

Beschloss, Michael, 359; *Kennedy and Roosevelt*, 312

Bevin, Ernest, 54, 120, 343

Biddle, Anthony J. Drexel, Jr., 37, 52, 157–58. *See also* European refugees

Bilainkin, George, 262, 312, 339, 370; *German White Paper* and, 265; meeting with JPK, 287

Bingham, Robert Worth, 24; illness of, 28, 31

Black, Hugo, 35

Boettinger, John, 372, 389, 400; JPK relationship with, 148

Bonnet, Georges, 213; and Czechoslovakian crisis, 121. *See also* Czechoslovakia

Boothby, Robert John "Bob," 212

Borah, William F., 68, 72

Boston Globe: Lyons's interview with JPK in, 347, 362–68, 370–71; JPK and, 369, 399

Bracken, Brendan, 275

Breckinridge, Long, 353; *German White Paper* and, 264; JPK meetings with, 250; JPK resignation and, 361, 362; Tyler Kent affair and, 307

Broun, Heywood, 145

Bruce, S. M., Welles Mission and, 259. *See also* Welles Mission

Bullitt, William, 264, 265, 287, 288, 290, 303; before

Congress, 167, 168; *German White Paper* and, 263; on JPK, x; JPK meetings with, 93, 179; JPK relationship with, 250–51

Byrnes, James F. "Jimmy," 30, 32, 147, 319, 350, 351, 352, 353, 357

Cadogan, Alexander, 54, 58, 63, 82, 97, 130, 132, 182, 212, 234–35, 247, 270; Welles Mission and, 256

Capra, Frank, *Mr. Smith Goes to Washington* and, 238

Carol II, King, 156

Carter, Boake, 26, 47, 67, 75–76, 163, 148, 391; JPK correspondence with, 33–34, 531 (n. 163)

Case, Margaret, 255

Cavendish, Kathleen Kennedy "Kick," xiii, 10, 216, 314; death of, xiii, 401–2

Cavendish, William, xiii, 234; death of, 401–2

Chamberlain, Lady Austen, 59

Chamberlain, Neville, vii; on Americans, 43; Chequers Estate and, 192, 193; on Churchill, 127; four-party proposal of, 181, 182; on Hitler, 133–34; Hitler meetings with, 118–20, 122, 123, 126, 133; Hitler negotiations with, 127, 129, 130; Hitler relationship with, 180; JPK last meeting with, 344; JPK meeting with, 42–43, 135, 213; JPK relationship with, 53–54, 55, 69, 92–93, 237, 348–49, 393; as party leader, 277; physical description of, 5; as prime minister, vii, viii, 36, 55–56; resignation of, 271, 273–74, 275; speeches of, 180, 181, 213, 269, 450 (n. 111); war preparations of, 206–7, 208, 211–13; Windsor Castle visit (1938), 48–50

Chamberlain, Norman, 56

Channon, Henry, on JPK, 47

Chatfield, Lord Ernie, 170, 189

Churchill, Lord Randolph, 298

Churchill, Randolph, 43, 45, 300; JPK relationship with, 301; and Tyler Kent affair, 304

Churchill, Winston, 54, 136; becomes prime minister, 275, 276, 501–2 (n. 60); birth of, 297–98; on Chamberlain, 44, 55; Chartwell and, 20, 304; childhood of, 298; drinking habits of, 299, 301; as First Lord of the Admiralty, 211, 223–24, 235–36, 273; *The Gathering Storm*, 276; inaugural speech as prime minister, 278–79; JPK meetings with, 20, 43–44, 241, 280–81, 288, 292, 342; JPK relationship with, 236, 237, 300–302, 330, 392, 507 (n. 173); physical description of, 297; as secretary of state for War and Air, 236; speeches of, 192, 386, 291, 294

Ciano, Countess Edda, 173, 193; meeting JPK, 178–79

Ciano, Galeazzo, Count, 176, 178, 241

Citrine, Walter, 120

Cliveden Set, 58, 59, 198, 242–43; and fascism, 161; JPK and, 162, 163

Cockburn, Claud, 59, 198

Coglan, Ralph, 363, 365, 366, 368–69. See also *Boston Globe*

Cohen, Harry, 238

Colvin, Ian, 183, 473 (n. 105–6)

communism, 24, 186, 223, 227; Jews and, 303

Congress of Industrial Organizations (CIO), 222

Conspiracy of One (Rand), 311

Conspirator (Bearse and Read), 311, 312

containment: Churchill and, 139, 150; JPK and, 171–72

Cook, Captain James, 214

Cooper, Duff, 54, 126, 134, 135; resignation of, 136

Corbin, Charles, 43, 120, 212–13, 273, 337

Corcoran, Thomas "Tom," 29, 162, 196

Costello, John, *Ten Days to Destiny*, 311–12. See also *Ten Days to Destiny* (Costello)

Coughlin, Father Charles E., 14–15, 19, 24–25, 392, 468 (n. 14); relationship with JPK, 200

Cox, James, 10

Crowley, Robert, 311. See also *Conspirator* (Bearse and Read)

Cudahy, John, 82, 85, 197–98, 274, 277

Cummings, A. J., 123, 369

Curran, Joseph, 26, 389

Cushing, Richard Cardinal, 401

Czechoslovakia: crisis of, 81, 95–99, 105–6, 115–18, 121–22, 127–28, 140, 395, 439 (n. 130); German annexation of, 173, 179, 180; German invasion of, viii, 138; Hitler and, 179, 180; JPK and, 394; League of Nations and, 139; Munich Agreement and, 133

Daladier, Édouard, vii–viii, 133, 213; Czechoslovakian crisis and, 121, 128; removal from office, 268

Dalton, Hugh, 120, 185

Davies, Joseph E., 185–86

Davis, William R., as negotiator, 222

de Valera, Eamon, 82, 83, 176

Democratic National Convention: Joesph P. Kennedy Jr. and, 249, 318–19; in 1932, 12

Denmark, German invasion of, 269–70, 271

destroyer deal, 326–29, 330, 331–32, 398, 494 (n. 40); JPK and, 245

Dieckhoff, Hans, 104

Dinneen, Joseph, 160; Lyons's *Boston Globe* interview and, 364. See also *Boston Globe*

Dirksen, Herbert von, 105; meetings with JPK, 99–102, 103–4, 104–5, 440 (n. 144)

Disraeli, Benjamin, 134

Donovan, Colonel William "Wild Bill" J., 327, 341; reporting mission of, 323, 324–25, 398

Dorman-Smith, Sir Reginald, 213

Douglas, Bill, 246, 248

Douglas-Home, Sir Alex, 54, 130

Downey, Morton, 190

Dunn, Elizabeth, 176, 177

Dunn, Jimmy, 65

Early, Stephen, 78, 373–74, 375, 387, 388, 433 (n. 316)

Eastman, Joe, 388

Economist, 370

Eden, Anthony, 43, 54, 131, 136, 211, 273, 332; Anglo-American cooperation and, 418 (n. 264); anti-American sentiment and, 268; resignation as foreign secretary, viii, ix, 36, 42; Welles Mission and, 256, 257, 259. *See also* Welles Mission

Edison, Charles, 323

Edmondson, Charles K., 363, 364, 366. See also *Boston Globe*

Edward VIII, King, 100

Elizabeth, Princess, 192, 263, 275

Elizabeth, Queen (Consort of King George VI), 45, 46, 130; JPK and, 220, 337; visit to the United States, 195, 196

Elizabeth II, Queen. *See* Elizabeth, Princess

Emmanuel, Victor, 205

Emmons, Major General Delos Carleton, 325

Emory, Scott Land, 27, 388

Ethiopia: Italian invasion of, 20, 21; United States and, 71, 429–30 (n. 257)

European refugees, 151–60, 463 (n. 137); FDR and, 503 (n. 88). *See also* Kennedy Plan; Jews

Fairbanks, Douglas, Jr., 370–71

Farley, James "Jim," 29, 85, 161, 223, 250, 319, 408 (n. 78); as presidential candidate, 74, 79, 249

Finland, Soviet invasion of, 246, 267–68

Fischer, Louis, 161

Fish, Hamilton, 378, 383, 384

Fisher, Lawrence, 10

Fisher, Robert, 239

Fisher, Sir Darien, 98

Fleeson, Doris, 251; JPK and, 147

Follette, Philip F. La, 199, 200

France, 481 (n. 9); alliance with United Kingdom, 63, 64, 95, 107, 119, 293, 444 (n. 9), 449 (n. 101), 456–57 (n. 217); Axis power armistices with, 294; declaration of war, 214; German crossing of Maginot Line, 286–87; German invasion of, 278, 283

Francis-Williams, Lord, 47

Franco, Francisco, 72

Frankfurter, Felix, 162, 389, 526 (n. 48)

Gage, Berkeley, 234, 247

Galbraith, John Kenneth, 289

Gardner, George Peabody, Jr., on JPK, 46

Garner, John Nance, 12, 74, 408 (n. 78)

Gathering Storm, The (Churchill), 276

George VI, King, 45, 276, 326; correspondence to JPK, 220–21; JPK meetings with, 44, 241; visit to the United States, 195, 196

German White Paper, 263–65

Germany: Aryanization of, 159; Hiterlism and, 223; Jewish persecution and, 152–53, 154, 155; Munich Agreement and, 395; occupation of Paris, 293; occupation of Sudetenland, 133; rearmament of, vii, viii, 138; rise of Nazi Party, viii

Ghormley, Robert, Welles Mission and, 324, 325, 329, 330, 331. *See also* Welles Mission

Gilbert, Bentley, 295, 502 (n. 60)

Goebbels, Joseph, 136–37, 199, 200

Goldsmith, Arthur, 349

Gordon, George, 277

Göring, Hermann, 136–37, 222; Battle of Britain and, 325; European refugees and, 159; on JPK, xii

Gowen, Franklin C., 177

Grandi, Count Dino, 36, 69

Greenwood, Arthur, 212, 275

Grynszpan, Herschel, Kristallnacht and, 152. *See also* Kristallnacht

Halifax, Lord, 51, 182, 183, 185, 189, 219, 268, 269,

277, 333, 469 (n. 33); as candidate for prime minister, 275, 501–2 (n. 60); career of, 58; on JPK, 46; JPK last meeting with, 342; JPK meetings with, 42, 117, 180–81, 187, 204, 241, 279, 340; JPK relationship with, 58, 71, 95, 123, 193, 397. *See also* destroyer deal; European refugees; Welles Mission

Hankey, Maurice, memo of, 165–67

Harding, Warren G., 10

Harris, Robert, 303

Harvey, Oliver, 103

Hatton, Graham, memorandum of, 339–40

Hays, Will, 87, 88, 123, 124, 371, 435–36 (n. 48)

Head, Alice, on JPK, 46

Healy, Maurice, 308

Hearst, William Randolph, 11, 12–13, 14, 150, 392; FDR's 1932 presidential campaign and, 408 (n. 78), 409 (n. 87); JPK meetings with, 372, 373; JPK relationship with, 75

Henderson, Sir Nevile, 50, 130, 206, 208, 444 (n. 9); declaration of war and, 213

Henlein, Konrad, 95, 96, 97, 105, 118. *See also* Czechoslovakia

Hennessy, Luella, 176, 177

Henning, Arthur Sears, 310

Hickey, Mary Augusta, 1

Hillman, William, 233, 234, 348

Hinsley, Arthur Cardinal, 43

Hinton, Harold, 419 (n. 6); JPK relationship with, 40

Hitler, Adolf, 396; background of, viii; Battle of Britain and, 325, 326; Blitz and, 333, 334; JPK critique of, 150; and *Mein Kampf*, 50; Nuremberg radio broadcast of, 115; opinion of United States, 194–95; rise to power, 36; self-determination argument of, 50; speeches of, 278; threat to Europe, 181, 182, 183, 184, 186

Hoare, Sir Samuel Hoare, first Viscount Templewood, "Sam," 58, 116, 123, 130, 221, 274, 447 (n. 66)

Holland, German invasion of, 239, 277

Hoover, Herbert, 11, 323, 375

Hoover, J. Edgar, 198

Hopkins, Harry, 246, 376, 389, 412 (n. 131)

Houghton, Arthur, 177

Howard, Roy, 17, 372

Howe, Louis, 11, 13, 15

Hull, Cordell, 74, 88, 89, 126, 132, 188, 246, 277, 285, 408 (n. 78); economic nationalism and, 393; JPK's ambassadorial resignation and, 361; JPK meetings with, 35; JPK relationship with, 79, 90, 92, 112, 149; JPK's speeches and, 65, 91, 146–47, 191; press statements of, 99, 119, 146, 263, 305, 340; radio address of, 108–9; speeches of, 66; support for JPK, 86, 87, 200

I'm for Roosevelt (JPK), 21–22

Ickes, Harold L., 29, 33, 79–80, 161, 198; on JPK, 59, 71, 74–75, 76, 197, 372, 383

Immigration Act (1924), 8

Inskip, Sir Thomas, 118

Intergovernmental Committee on Political Refugees, 153, 158, 159. *See also* European refugees

internationalism: FDR and, 10, 12, 322–23; Hearst and, 11; Hull and, 65, 66, 67, 68; Trade Agreement Act (1934) and, 86; United States and, 72

Ireland, World War II and, 84. *See also* Anglo-Irish Treaty

Irish Catholics, 29–30, 34, 82; prejudice of, xi, 2, 3, 9, 47, 77

Ironside, General, 241–42, 269

isolationism, vii; destroyer deal and, 327; Father Charles E. Coughlin and, 19; FDR and, 10, 39, 128; Hearst and, 19; Hull and, 109; JPK and, ix, 65–67, 109–11, 112, 144, 171–72, 243, 246, 247, 248, 255, 317, 356; U.S. policy of, 72,

107–8, 109, 113, 122, 127, 138, 144, 193, 194, 289, 392; after World War I, 8

Italy, entrance into World War II, 287–88. *See also* Ethiopia; Mussolini, Benito

Jackson, Gordon, 239

Jackson, Robert, 246

Japan, attack on Pearl Harbor, 387

Jerome, Jennie, 298

Jews, 463 (n. 137); German policy toward, 99; Palestine and, 155, 158, 159; persecution of, 111, 152–53, 154, 155; relocation of, 153, 156, 159, 461 (n. 98). *See also* anti-Semitism; European refugees; Kennedy Plan; Kristallnacht

Johnson, Alva, 80

Johnson, Herschel, 52, 57, 168, 235, 304, 335

Johnson, Hugh S., 199, 322

Jowitt, William, 308–9

Juliana, Princess, 279

Kaltenborn, H. V., 203

Kaufmann, William W., 167

Kelly, Frank, 217

Kennedy and Roosevelt (Beschloss), 312

Kennedy family: Cannes vacation of (1939), 202; correspondence of, 313–14, 336–38; at Court of St. James, 45–46, 195; departure from United Kingdom (1939), 216–17; European tour of (1935), 20–21; first arrival in United Kingdom, 47; at JFK's Harvard graduation, 314; JPK weekly calls with, 239; move to Wall Hall, 216; papal coronation and, 175, 176, 177; at Parliament, 214; political service tradition of, 401

Kennedy Plan, 143, 151, 157, 158, 159, 395. *See also* European refugees; Jews

Kennedy, Caroline Bouvier (granddaughter), 401

Kennedy, Edward M., Jr. (grandson), 401

Kennedy, Edward Moore "Ted" (son), 217, 314, 336, 401; and Chappaquiddick Incident, xiii–xiv; Senate election of, xii

Kennedy, Eunice (daughter), 216, 314

Kennedy, Francis (brother), 1

Kennedy, Jack, 348

Kennedy, John B., 81

Kennedy, John F. "Jack" (son), 314, 336, 372, 401; assassination of, xiii, 402; as consultant to JPK, 380–81; political support for JPK, 146; war preparations and, 129

Kennedy, Joseph P., II (grandson), 401

Kennedy, Joseph P., III (great-grandson), 401

Kennedy, Joseph P., Jr. (son), 314, 317–19; "Answer to Lippmann Editorial Against Dad," 145–46; birth of, 4; death of, xii, 401; and Democratic National Convention, 249; on JPK as ambassador, 148; legacy of, xii–xiii; trip to Germany, 208

Kennedy, Joseph P., Sr.: ambassadorial appointment of, ix, 30–32, 415–16 (n. 220); ambassadorial inauguration of, 35; ambassadorial residence of, 262; as banker, 3–4; before Congress, 167–68; and Bethlehem Steel, 6; birth of, 1; Blitz and, 334–35; as broker, 9; as business emissary for FDR, 23–4; "A Businessman's Estimate of the New Deal," 23; at Court (1938), 44–45; critiques of, 47, 110, 145, 160, 161, 168, 198, 199–200, 263, 269–72, 375; diplomatic style of, 53, 87–88; economic internationalism and, 62, 68, 393; education of, 1–2; and FDR presidential campaigns, xi, 11, 12, 13, 14, 21–22, 407 (n. 69), 407 (n. 73), 409 (n. 93); fortune made by, 9, 10–11; Hollywood career of, 9; homes of, 4, 15, 41, 164, 217, 239, 248; honorary degrees of, 82, 191, 192; liquor importing business of, 16, 80, 92, 432 (n. 307); as Maritime Commission chairman, xi, 25–26, 27; papal coronation and, 175, 176, 467–68 (n. 14), 469 (n. 33); personal diplomacy of, 97, 99, 101, 112, 116–17, 123, 124, 143, 158, 190, 392–93, 394; public image of, 18–19, 27; as outsider, 9, 15–16, 76, 77, 82, 389, 404 (n. 5), 406 (n. 52), 406 (n. 55); radio addresses of, 355–57, 399, 380, 381–82; report on Europe by (1935), 20–21; relationship with the press, 32–3, 40–1, 45, 46, 47, 76–77, 78–79, 112, 148; relationship with UK officials, ix–x, 58, 82, 206–7, 218, 219, 227, 233–35, 252–53, 338–39, 340, 369, 397; resignation as ambassador, 340–41, 342, 344–45, 360, 361, 374–75, 400; resignation as SEC chairman, 17–18; as SEC chairman, 16, 17; speeches of, 92, 102, 110–11, 143, 144–45, 145–46, 148–49, 151, 160, 190–91, 197, 201, 247, 347, 385–86, 400; stomach problems of, 248, 272–73, 494 (n. 29); stroke of, 402; trip to Italy (1940), 255; war preparations of, 126, 262, 402

Kennedy, Loretta (sister), 1, 39

Kennedy, Margaret (sister), 1

Kennedy, Patricia (daughter), 216, 314, 381

Kennedy, Patrick Joseph (father), 1, 401

Kennedy, Robert F. "Bobby" (son), 216, 314, 336; assassination of, 402; career of, xiii

Kennedy, Rose Fitzgerald (wife), 20, 195, 313, 317, 336, 337, 338, 342, 350, 359, 381, 514 (n. 135); on Boston society, 3; dinner at the White House, 351–52, 354; family life of, 4, 10–11, 41, 239, 314; on JPK, 2, 5, 391; as outsider, 406 (n. 52); war preparations and, 129

Kennedy, Rosemary (daughter), 217, 239, 314; lobotomy of, 401

Kent, Ann H. P., 310–11. *See also* Kent, Tyler

Kent, Frank, 28, 29, 87, 148

Kent, Tyler, 513–14 (n. 118); affair of, 302–4, 304–8, 308–13, 511 (n. 69), 511–12 (n. 83), 514 (n. 128)

King, MacKenzie, 196

Kintner, Robert, 110, 341–42, 375

Kirk, Alan G., 52

Kleffens, M. Van, 279

Klemmer, Harvey, 40

Knight, Maxwell, 304, 306, 309. *See also* Kent, Tyler

Knox, Colonel Frank, 323

Koskoff, David, 84, 85, 276, 368

Kristallnacht, 151–52, 395

Krock, Arthur, 22, 32, 35, 45, 78, 79, 146, 162, 200–201, 319, 332, 342; and JFK, 315, 316, 317, 411 (n. 135), 412 (n. 141); and Joseph P. Kennedy Jr., 318; and JPK, 18–19, 21, 31, 149, 375–76

Lamont, Thomas, 164

Landis, James M., 16, 365, 368; "Diplomatic Memoirs" (JPK) and, 412 (n. 144), 419–20 (n. 6). See also *Boston Globe*

Laski, Harold, 163, 317, 318

League of Nations, vii, viii, 20, 21, 139; Finland invasion and, 268. *See also* Czechoslovakia; Ethiopia; Treaty of Versailles

LeHand, Marguerite Alice "Missy," 21, 148, 246, 351, 354, 358, 412 (n. 141)

Lend-Lease, 290; Bill of (1941), 289, 378, 379; JPK and, ix, 380, 382, 383–84, 399–400; policy development of, 231, 279–80, 281, 288, 324–25

Lerner, Max, on Nazi Germany, 149–50

Lewis, John L., 222

Lindbergh, Anne Morrow, 124

Lindbergh, Charles, 116, 322; German air force report of, 100, 124–25, 167, 168, 448 (n. 82); JPK meeting with, 124

Lindsay, Ronald, 33, 69, 84, 87, 122, 158, 170, 429–30 (n. 257)

Lippmann, Walter, 69, 145, 236, 263

Lloyd, George, 136, 185, 259, 273

Locarno Agreement (1925), 20, 96

Lodge, Henry Cabot, JPK correspondence plot with, 45

Lothian, Lord, 161, 218, 290, 324, 369

Low, David, 294

Low, Sidney, 45

Luce, Clare Boothe, 255, 272, 304, 355, 359

Luce, Henry R., 19, 216, 317

Ludlow, Louis, 375

Lusitania, sinking of, 214

Lyons, Louis M., 362; JPK *Boston Globe* interview by, 363, 365, 367–68, 529 (n. 120); *Newspaper Story: One Hundred Years of the Boston Globe*, 368. See also *Boston Globe*

MacDonald, Malcolm, 155, 156, 157; JPK meeting with, 83. *See also* European refugees

MacLeish, Archibald, JPK *Boston Globe* interview and, 368. See also *Boston Globe*

Macmillan, Harold, 136

Maglione, Luigi Cardinal, 174–75, 178

Maisky, Ivan, 273

Mander, Geoffrey, JPK's personal diplomacy and, 123

Margaret, Princess, 263

Marshall, George, 322

Mary, the Queen Mother, 45, 130

Masaryk, Jan, 131, 132; JPK meeting with, 97

Maxton, James, 259

McCarthy, Joe, 9, 11

McCarthy, John F., Jr., 249

McCormack, John W., 387

McCormick, Colonel Robert, 19, 164

McNutt, Paul, 246

Meyer, Eugene, 19

Moffat, Jay Pierrepont, 62, 65, 66, 71, 109, 120, 146; on JPK, 158; Welles Mission and, 254, 257. *See also* Welles Mission

Moley, Raymond, 14, 16, 17, 408 (n. 78)

Molotov, Vyacheslav, 203

Molyneux, Edward, 214

Montini, Giovanni Battista Cardinal (later Pope Paul VI), 177

Mooney, Archbishop Edward, 25

Mooney, James, 189–90

Moore, Edward "Eddie," 14, 176, 177, 272, 341, 355

Moore, Mary, 176, 177

Morgenthau, Henry J., Jr., 11, 15, 18, 31, 74, 417 (n. 252); on JPK, 85, 112, 201; relationship with JPK, 251–52; war debts and, 217–18

Morrison, Herbert, 120, 343

Mościcki, Ignacy, 206

Mosley, Oswald, 308

Mowrer, Edgar, 323

Mr. Smith Goes to Washington (Capra), 238

Munich Agreement (Munich Pact) (1938), 95, 116, 118, 130–37, 394–95; Chamberlain and, 451–52 (n. 129); Churchill and, 121; FDR and, 138; Hitler and, 188; JPK and, 239, 163. *See also* Czechoslovakia

Murphy, Frank, 246, 526 (n. 48)

Murphy, Paul, 208

Murphy, Robert, 255

Murphy, William, 78

Murray, Arthur, on JPK, 46

Murray, George, 369

Mussolini, Benito: entering World War II, 287–88; Five-Power Conference of, 212; support for Hitler, 60. *See also* Ethiopia; Italy

Nasaw, David, 344; on JPK's relationship with British political officials, 54

Nazi-Soviet Nonaggression Pact (1939), 174, 185, 203–4, 396

Nelson, Lord Horatio, 144

Netherlands, German invasion of, 278–79

Neutrality Act (1937), 218, 231–33; FDR and, 103, 164, 165, 223; JPK and, 193, 243

New Deal, 21, 22; JPK on, 23, 244

Newspaper Story: One Hundred Years of the Boston Globe (Lyons), 368. See also *Boston Globe*; Lyons, Louis M.

Nicolson, Harold, 130, 131, 136, 253

Niles, David, 162

nonintervention, 72, 73; JPK and, 365, 366, 382

Norman, Montagu, 58, 338; meeting with JPK, 229, 240; relationship with JPK, 47

Norway: German invasion of, 269–71, 273; Soviet Union and, 268

Nye, Gerald, 322, 327

Pacelli, Eugenio Cardinal (later Pope Pius XII), 175; meeting with FDR and JPK, 25; papal election of, 174; summer residence of, 178. See also Pius XII

Page, Walter Hines, 53, 111–12, 247

Parker, R. A. C., 134, 456 (n. 217), 472 (n. 72)

Patterson, Joseph M., 251, 321, 372

Peake, Charles, 233, 234

Pearson, Drew, 19, 59, 73, 371

Pecora, Ferdinand, 16

Perowne, J. V., 234, 235, 247, 252, 256, 369

Perry, Barbara, 177

Pétain, Marshal, 294, 530 (n. 145)

Phillips, William, 32, 46, 175, 178, 225, 280

Phipps, Eric, 213

Phoenix Islands, Anglo-American dispute over, 93–94

Pittman, Key, 31, 194

Pius XI (pope), death of, 174

Pius XII (pope), private audience with Kennedy family, 175, 176, 177. See also Pacelli, Eugenio Cardinal

Poland: crisis of, 20, 204, 205, 206–7, 208, 211, 212–13, 471 (n. 72), 499 (n. 144); German aggression toward, 183, 203; German attacks on, viii; Soviet invasion of, 224

Powell, Joseph, 7

Puhl, Emil, 190

Raczyński, Edward, 126, 205

Ramsay, Captain Archibald, 304, 306, 308, 309, 310. See also Kent, Tyler

Rand, Peter, *Conspiracy of One*, 311

Rath, Baron Ernst vom, death of, 152. See also Kristallnacht

Read, Anthony, *Conspirator*, 311, 312

Reed, Edward, 277

Reed, Stanley, 35

Reston, James B., 332

Reynaud, Paul, 268, 269, 283, 291; resignation of, 294

Rhineland: German invasion of, 20; remilitarization of, vii, viii, 60

Ribbentrop, Joachim von, 60, 183, 203, 213, 258

Riverdale, Lord Arthur, on JPK, 46

Robinson, Dr. Paschal, 82

Roosevelt, Anna, 372

Roosevelt, Eleanor, 29, 282, 288, 373; on FDR, 2; JPK and, 32, 365

Roosevelt, Franklin D. (FDR): Axis powers, appeals to, 128, 132, 188, 206, 418–19 (n. 264), 452–53 (n. 144); before Congress, 382–83; campaign contributions to, 12; Chamberlain opinion of, 112–13; Churchill relationship with, 223–24, 246, 300, 302, 398, 487 (n. 109); on JPK, x; JPK appointed ambassador by, 30–32; JPK appointed Maritime Commission chairman by, 25–26; JPK appointed SEC Chairman by, 16–17; JPK relationship with, xi, 7–8, 18, 79, 80, 110, 111, 112, 144, 147, 148–49, 163, 169, 196, 198, 200–201, 202, 223, 254–55, 272, 328–29, 339, 341, 342, 347–48, 352, 353, 354, 373, 387, 392, 399, 524 (n. 14), 525 (n. 40); JPK's 1935 report on Europe and, 20–22; and JPK's resignation as ambassador, 340, 341, 342, 360–61, 373; and JPK's resignation from SEC,

18; meetings with JPK, 7–8, 24, 36, 245–46, 360, 267, 373, 374, 378–80, 388, 419–20 (n. 6); presidential victory celebration (1932), 15; presidential victory (1940), 360; radio addresses of, 147, 376–78, 386; speeches of, 89, 165, 322, 359–60, 526 (n. 48); vice-presidential campaign of (1920), 10

Roosevelt, Franklin, Jr., 288

Roosevelt, James, 29, 30, 31, 35, 39, 76, 80, 169, 416 (n. 234); relationship with JPK, 15–16

Roper, Daniel, 24

Rosenman, Sam, 376

Rothschild, Anthony de, 156

Rublee, George, 153, 154, 155, 159–60. *See also* Czechoslovakia; European refugees

Runciman, Lord Walter: mission of, 105–6; Trade Agreement Act (1934) and, 86

Schlesinger, Arthur, Jr., xiii, 4

Schuschnigg, Kurt von, 36; resignation of, 60, 61

Schwab, Charles M., 8

Scott, David, 234–35

Seymour, James, 370

Sforza, Count Carlo, 198

Sherwood, Robert, 376

Shriver, Eunice Kennedy (daughter), 314, 401

Shriver, Mark (grandson), 401

Shriver, Robert S., III (grandson), 401

Shriver, Robert Sargent, 401

Simon, Sir John, 58, 123, 130, 227

Sinclair, Archibald, 185, 259

Smith, Al, 12

Smith, Jean Kennedy (daughter), 217, 335, 350, 401

Soviet Union (USSR): Chamberlain distrust of, 56; invasion of Finland, 267–68; negotiations with United Kingdom, 185, 186; Red Army of, 140, 267. *See also* Finland; Poland

Spain, Civil War of, 72, 73

Stalin, Joseph, 185, 203, 267, 473 (n. 102), 499 (n. 3)

Stanley, Edward Villiers, 65

Stanley, Oliver, 88, 89, 126

Steed, Wickham, 123

Stevens, Frederick, 348

Stewart, Robert, 350

Stimson, Henry L., 323

Stokes, Richard R., 310

Stout, Wesley Winans, 199

Strong, General George, 324, 325. *See also* Welles Mission

Sulzberger, Cyrus L., 47

Sunday Dispatch (London), 370

Taylor, Henry J., 310

Taylor, Myron C., 25, 153, 158, 254–55

Ten Days to Destiny (Costello), 311–12

Thomas, Norman, 72

Thompson, Dorothy, 149, 380, 382–83

Thompson, W. H., 276

Times (London), 370

Townsend, Kathleen Kennedy (granddaughter), 401

Trade Agreement Act (1934), 85–86; and Hull, 220

Treaty of Versailles (1920), vii, viii, 20, 181, 229; Hitler's violations of, 60. *See also* Locarno Agreement

Trohan, Walter D., 78

Truitt, Max, 350

Truman, Harry, 360

Tully, Grace, 387, 388

United Kingdom: air raids of, 214, 325–26, 333–35, 377; attack on French fleet, 295; declaration of war (1939), 213; military draft of, 184; Norwegian invasion and, 270–71, 273; Operation Dynamo and, 285–86; rearmament of, 63, 64, 135, 138–39, 169; Spanish policy of, 73; war preparations and, 128–29

United States of America: arms embargo of, 72, 73,

233; film negotiations with United Kingdom, 86–87, 88; foreign policy of, 39, 71–2, 146, 147; Japanese attack on Pearl Harbor, 387; neutrality policy of, 231–32; rearmament of, 164, 165, 169, 282–83

Vansittart, Robert, 82, 253, 256; on JPK, x
Victoria, Princess Helena, 192
von Selzam, Edward, meeting with JPK, 116, 117

Walsh, David, 322, 327
Wedgwood, Josiah, 33, 136
Welles Mission, 243, 253–61, 398
Welles, Sumner, 53, 62, 65, 72, 146, 170, 218, 349, 353, 361, 378, 429–30 (n. 257); *German White Paper* and, 265; JPK and, 117, 450 (n. 111), 467–68 (n. 14); JPK resignation and, 361; Tyler Kent affair and, 305. *See also* Welles Mission
Weygand, Maxime, 333
Whalen, Richard, 187, 236, 311, 312, 358, 401, 511–12 (n. 83)
Wheeler, Burton, 363
White, Harry, 252
Whitehead, T. North, 253
Why England Slept (JFK), 138, 315, 317, 344, 357, 411 (n. 135). See also *Appeasement at Munich*

(JFK)
Wiedemann, Captain Fritz, 105
Wilhelmina, Queen, 278–79
Willkie, Wendell, as presidential candidate, 321, 340, 357, 359, 360
Wilson, Hugh, 152
Wilson, Sir Horace, 58, 205; meeting with Hitler, 127; meeting with JPK, 206–7
Wilson, Warden, 349
Winchell, Walter, 164, 199
Winship, Laurence, 362, 364, 367–68. See also *Boston Globe*
Wohlthat, Helmuth, 190, 476 (n. 176)
Wolkoff, Anna de, 305, 306, 308, 309, 310. *See also* Kent, Tyler
Wood, Kingsley, 130, 285
Woodin, William H., 15
Woodring, Harry, 323
World Court, U.S. Senate rejection of, 8, 19
World War I, vii; armistice of, 8; Battle of the Somme, 6; JPK and, 5, 6. *See also* Treaty of Versailles
World War II: Battle of Britain, 325–26, 333; Battle of the Atlantic, 321; potential strategies of, 455–56 (n. 210)
Wszelaki, Jan, 263